Data
Management

An Organizational Perspective

Data Management

An Organizational Perspective

Richard T. Watson

John Wiley & Sons, Inc.
New York • Chichester • Brisbane • Toronto • Singapore

Acquisitions Editor	Beth L. Golub
Assistant Marketing Manager	Leslie Hines
Senior Production Editor	John Rouselle
Senior Designer	Kevin Murphy
Assistant Manufacturing Manager	Mark Cirillo
Photo Researcher	Hilary Newman
Illustration Freelance Coordinator	Jaime Perea
Illustrators	Wellington Studios

This book was set in 10/12 Minion by Digitype and printed and bound by Donnelley/Crawfordsville. The cover was printed by Phoenix Color.

Recognizing the importance of preserving what has been written, it is a policy of John Wiley & Sons, Inc. to have books of enduring value published in the United States printed on acid-free paper, and we exert our best efforts to that end.

ISBN: 0-471-30534-0

Printed in the United States of America

10 9 8 7 6 5 4 3

To Clare

Preface

Information is a key resource for modern organizations. It is a critical input to managerial tasks. Because managers need high quality information to manage change in a turbulent, global environment, many organizations have established systems for storing and retrieving data, the raw material of information. These storage and retrieval systems are an organization's memory. The organization relies on them, just as individuals rely on their personal memory, to continue as a going concern.

The central concern of information systems management is to design, build, and maintain information delivery systems. Information systems management needs to discover its organization's information requirements so that it can design systems to serve these needs. It must merge a system's design and information technology to build an application that provides the organization with data in a timely manner, appropriate format, and at a convenient location. Furthermore, it must manage applications so they evolve to meet changing needs, continue to operate under adverse conditions, and are protected from unauthorized access.

An information delivery system has two components: organizational memory and processes. This book focuses on organizational memory, which is customarily thought of as a database. I deliberately set out to extend this horizon, however, by including all forms of organizational memory, because I believe students need to understand the role of data management that is aligned with current practice. In my view, data management is the design and maintenance of computer-based organizational memory. Thus, you will find a complete section devoted to organizational memory technologies such as hypertext, groupware, and imaging systems.

This book is written for students learning to design and manage organizational memory. Typically, these students are majoring in information systems and taking a required database course. Although this book covers the material found in a typical database text, it is broader in a number of ways. First, it takes the viewpoint that databases are one component of an expansive organizational memory. Information systems professionals need to develop this wider perspective if they are to comprehend the organizational role of information technology. Second, because managers use organizational memory to initiate change, there is considerable discussion of how, why, and when managers use organizational memory.

The decision to start the book with a managerial perspective arises from the belief that successful information systems practice is based on matching managerial needs, social system constraints, and technical opportunities. I want readers to appreciate the "big picture" before they become immersed in the intricacies of data modeling and SQL. In line with this perspective, business stories are used to support and enhance the text. Many of these vignettes serve double duty because they also alert students to current economic trends such as the globalization of business and the growth of the service sector. To provide an international flavor, I selected organizational stories from a variety of nations. The broad, international, managerial approach is one of several innovative pedagogical features.

The first chapter introduces the case study, *The Expeditioner*, which is used in most subsequent chapters to introduce the key themes discussed. Often it sets the scene for the ensuing material by presenting a common business problem. I hope the case study also injects a little humor.

The second section of the book provides depth in data modeling and SQL. Data modeling is the foundation of database quality. A solid grounding in data modeling principles and extensive practice are necessary for successful database design. In addition, this book exposes students to the full power of SQL.

The book intertwines the treatment of data modeling and SQL because my database teaching experience indicates that students more readily understand the intent of data modeling when they grasp the long-term goal—querying a well-designed relational database. The double helix, upward, intertwined, spiraling of data modeling and SQL is another unique pedagogical feature. Classroom testing indicates it is a superior method of teaching compared to handling data modeling and SQL separately. Students quickly understand the reason for data modeling and appreciate why it is a valuable skill. Also, rapid exposure to SQL means students gain hands-on experience that much sooner.

I intend this book to be a long-term investment for students. There are useful reference sections for data modeling and SQL. The data modeling section details the standard structures and their relational mappings. The SQL section contains an extensive list of queries that serves as a basis for developing other SQL queries. The purpose of these sections is to facilitate "pattern matching." For example, a student with an SQL query that is similar to a previous problem can rapidly search the SQL reference section to find the closest match. The student can then use the model answer as a guide to formulating the SQL query for the problem at hand. These reference sections are another unique teaching feature that will serve students well during the course and in their subsequent careers.

While I set out to cast data management in a new light, I have not ignored the traditional core of a database course. Section 3 presents database architectures and their implementation. Coverage includes data storage technologies, data and file structures, and the relational, hierarchical, network, and object-oriented models. Naturally, this section reflects a managerial perspective and discusses the trade-offs for the various options facing the data manager.

In keeping with the organizational memory theme introduced in Chapter 1, Section 4 covers other information technologies including the Internet, information services, hypertext, groupware, and imaging systems.

The final section examines the management of organizational memory. The outstanding features of this section are the rigorous treatment of data integrity and data administration.

A student completing this text will:

- have a broad, managerial perspective of an organization's need for a memory;
- be able to design and create a relational database;
- be able to formulate complex SQL queries;
- have a sound understanding of database architectures and their managerial implications;
- be familiar with the full range of information technologies available for organizational memory;
- understand the fundamentals of data administration;
- know about data management developments and their organizational implications.

My purpose is to create a data management text that is innovative, relevant, and lively. I trust that you will enjoy reading this book and learn a great deal about managing organizational memory in today's organization.

SUPPLEMENTS

Accompanying this book are several aids for the instructor:

- an instructor's manual;
- overhead slides in Power Point 4.0 format;
- all relational tables in the book in electronic format;
- a World Wide Web site to provide additional tracking material.

Instructors should contact their Wiley representative to gain access to these aids.

ACKNOWLEDGMENTS

The support of Beth Golub and David Kear at John Wiley & Sons was much appreciated. They were always cooperative, supportive, and willing to try something new.

I wish to recognize the important contribution of my copyeditor Lorena Akioka. As well as assuring me that someone appreciated my sense of humor, she made the text cleaner and more consistent. I thank John Rouselle, production editor, for his friendly advice and willingness to consider changes to the format of the final work.

I would like to thank my reviewers for their many excellent suggestions and ideas for improving the quality of the content and presentation of this book:

Mohammad Dadashzadeh	Wichita State University
George Federman	Santa Barbara City College
Thomas Lucy-Bouler	Auburn University
Scott McIntyre	University of Colorado
Anthony F. Norcio	University of Maryland
Thomas E. Sandman	California State University—Sacramento
Avanti Sethi	Wichita State University
Linda Volonino	Canisius College

I thank Tore Ørvik of Agder College, Norway for his major contribution to the chapter on object-oriented database. His experience and knowledge of the object-oriented approach were most valuable.

My mate and colleague, Bob Bostrom of The University of Georgia, provided many insights and suggestions, as well as writing two chapters. His extremely thorough review of the manuscript added considerable value. I am very grateful for his many contributions to this project.

Richard T. Watson

Brief Table of Contents

Preface   vii

Section 1   **The Managerial Perspective**   1

Chapter 1   Organizational Memory   5
Chapter 2   Information   35

Section 2   **Data Modeling and SQL**   59

Chapter 3   The Single Entity   61
Chapter 4   The One-to-Many Relationship   89
Chapter 5   The Many-to-Many Relationship   108
Chapter 6   One-to-One and Recursive Relationships   124
Chapter 7   Data Modeling   142
Chapter 8   Basic Structures and the Relational Model   185
Chapter 9   SQL   198
Chapter 10   The SQL Playbook   235

Section 3   **Database Architectures and Implementations**   271

Chapter 11   Data Structure and Storage   275
Chapter 12   Data Storage and Data Processing Architectures   307
Chapter 13   The Relational Model   327
Chapter 14   Hierarchical and Network Models   344
Chapter 15   Object-Oriented Database Management Systems   365

Section 4   **Organizational Memory Technologies**   399

Chapter 16   Groupware, Hypertext, and Imaging   401
Chapter 17   Internet and Information Services   435

Section 5	Managing Organizational Memory	469
Chapter 18	Data Integrity	470
Chapter 19	Data Administration	503

Glossary	539

Photo Credits	554

Index	555

Contents

Preface   vii

Section 1   The Managerial Perspective   1

Chapter 1   Organizational Memory   5

Learning objectives   5
Introduction   5
Individual memory systems   6
Organizational memory   9
Components of organizational memory   15
Problems with organizational memory systems   26
Data, information, and knowledge   28
The challenge   30
Summary   31
Key terms and concepts   32
References and additional readings   32
Exercises   32

Chapter 2   Information   35

Learning objectives   35
Introduction   35
A historical perspective   36
Information characteristics   37
Information and organizational change   40
Information and managerial work   47
Information delivery systems   49
Summary   55
Key terms and concepts   56
References and additional readings   56
Exercises   57
Case questions   58

Section 2   Data Modeling and SQL   59

Chapter 3   The Single Entity   61

Learning objectives   61
The Expeditioner   *61*
Introduction   61
Modeling a single entity database   62

Creating a single table database   63
Querying a single table database   68
Summary   85
Key terms and concepts   85
Exercises   85

Chapter 4   The One-to-Many Relationship   89

Learning objectives   89
The Expeditioner   89
Relations   89
Creating a database with a one-to-many relationship   91
Querying a two-table database   95
Summary   104
Key terms and concepts   105
Exercises   105

Chapter 5   The Many-to-Many Relationship   108

Learning objectives   108
The Expeditioner   108
The many-to-many relationship   109
Creating a relational database with a many-to-many relationship   111
Querying a many-to-many relationship   113
Summary   121
Key terms and concepts   121
Exercises   121

Chapter 6   One-to-One and Recursive Relationships   124

Learning objectives   124
The Expeditioner   124
Modeling the one-to-one relationship   125
Mapping a one-to-one relationship   126
Mapping a recursive relationship   126
Querying a one-to-one relationship   128
Querying a recursive relationship   128
The Expeditioner   132
Modeling a one-to-one recursive relationship   132
Mapping a one-to-one recursive relationship   133
Querying a one-to-one recursive relationship   133
The Expeditioner   135
Modeling a many-to-many recursive relationship   135
Mapping a many-to-many recursive relationship   136
Querying a many-to-many recursive relationship   137
Summary   139
Key terms and concepts   139
Exercises   139

Chapter 7   Data Modeling   **142**

Introduction   142
The building blocks   142
Data model quality   146
Quality improvement   147
Entity types   159
Data modeling hints   162
Normalization   168
Other data modeling methods   179
Summary   180
Key terms and concepts   181
References and additional readings   181
Exercises   181

Chapter 8   Basic Structures and the Relational Model   **185**

One entity   185
Two entities   189
Relationship descriptors as identifiers   191
Exercises   196

Chapter 9   SQL   **198**

Learning objectives   198
Introduction   198
Data definition   199
Data manipulation   211
Nulls—much ado about missing information   223
Security   223
Synonyms   226
The catalog   226
Embedded SQL   227
Summary   231
Key terms and concepts   232
References and additional readings   233
Exercises   233

Chapter 10   The SQL Playbook   **235**

1.   A slow full toss   236
2.   Skinning a cat   236
3.   Another full toss   238
4.   Subtracting from all   238
5.   Dividing   239
6.   At least some number   240
7.   A friendly IN for an SQL traveler   240

8. Joining a table with itself   240
9. A combination of subtract from all and a self-join   241
10. Self-join with GROUP BY   241
11. A self-join with two matching conditions   241
12. Averaging with grouping   242
13. Self-join with a GROUP BY and HAVING   242
14. An IN with GROUP BY and COUNT   242
15. A self-join with some conditions   243
16. Making comparisons   243
17. An IN with GROUP BY and SUM   243
18. A double divide!   244
19. A slam dunk   245
20. A 6-inch putt for a birdie   245
21. Making the count   245
22. Minus and divide   245
23. Division with copies   246
24. A difficult pairing   247
25. Two divides and an intersection   247
26. A divide with a matching condition   248
27. Restricted divide   248
28. A NOT IN variation on divide   249
29. All and only   249
30. Divide with an extra condition   250
31. At least some count   250
32. Double divide with a restriction   250
33. Triple divide with an intersection   251
34. An easy one count   252
35. The only one   252
36. At least some number   253
37. A three-table join   253
38. Using NOT IN like NOT EXISTS   253
39. Minus after grouping   254
40. Something to all   254
41. Intersection (AND)   254
42. Union (OR)   255
43. Intersection/union   255
44. Averaging with a condition   256
45. Averaging with grouping   256
46. Averaging with a join, condition, and grouping   256
47. Averaging with multiple joins   256
48. Complex counting   257
49. Summing with joins and conditions   257
50. Summing with joins, conditions, and grouping   257
51. Advanced summing   258
52. Comparing to the average with a join   258

53. Comparing to the average with a product   259
54. Averaging with multiple grouping   259
55. More than the average with grouping   259
56. The simplest average   260
57. Difference from the average   260
58. Averaging with multiple joins, multiple grouping, and a condition   260
59. Detailed averaging   261
60. Counting pairs   261
61. No Booleans   261
Summary   262
Key terms and concepts   262
Exercises   262
Appendix—Data for Tables   265

Section 3   Database Architectures and Implementations   271

Chapter 11   Data Structure and Storage   275
Learning objectives   275
The Expeditioner   275
Introduction   276
Data structures   276
Data storage devices   290
Conclusion   302
Summary   303
Key terms and concepts   304
Exercises   305

Chapter 12   Data Storage and Data Processing Architectures   307
Learning objectives   307
The Expeditioner   307
Introduction   307
Client/server   315
Distributed database   319
A hybrid architecture   320
Summary   324
Key terms and concepts   325
References and additional readings   325
Exercises   325

Chapter 13   The Relational Model   327
Learning objectives   327
Background   327
Data structures   328

Integrity rules   331
Manipulation—relational algebra   331
A primitive set of relational operations   337
A fully relational database   337
Summary   341
Key terms and concepts   342
References and additional readings   343
Exercises   343

Chapter 14   Hierarchical and Network Models   **344**

Learning objectives   344
The Expeditioner   344
Introduction   345
The hierarchical model   346
The network data model and CODASYL/DBTG   355
Data extraction   361
Summary   361
Key terms and concepts   362
Exercises   362

Chapter 15   Object-Oriented Database Management Systems   **365**

Learning objectives   365
Introduction   365
Historical development   366
Key OO concepts   367
Why OO?   370
Objects and information system modeling   373
The Expeditioner   376
Persistent objects   390
Object-oriented database management systems   390
The future of ODBMS   394
Summary   394
Key terms and concepts   395
References and additional readings   396
Exercises   396

Section 4   Organizational Memory Technologies   **399**

Chapter 16   Groupware, Hypertext, and Imaging   **401**

Learning objectives   401
Introduction   401
The Expeditioner   401
Groupware   402
The Expeditioner   418

Hypertext   418
The Expeditioner   *424*
Imaging   425
Summary   431
Key terms and concepts   432
References and additional readings   433
Exercises   433

Chapter 17   Internet and Information Services   **435**

Learning objectives   435
Introduction   435
The Internet   436
Information services   455
Summary   466
Key terms and concepts   466
References and additional readings   467
Exercises   467

Section 5   Managing Organizational Memory   **469**

Chapter 18   Data Integrity   **470**

Learning objectives   470
The Expeditioner   *470*
Introduction   470
Single-user and multi-user database systems   474
Protecting existence   475
Maintaining quality   483
Ensuring confidentiality   490
Summary   499
Key terms and concepts   500
References and additional readings   501
Exercises   501

Chapter 19   Data Administration   **503**

Learning objectives   503
The Expeditioner   *503*
Introduction   504
Management of the database environment   505
Data administration   508
Database Management System (DBMS)   527
Organizing data administration   530
Summary   536
Key terms and concepts   536

References and additional readings   536

Exercises   537

Glossary   **539**

Photo Credits   **554**

Index   **555**

The Managerial Perspective

The first section prepares you to see the role of data and information in an organization. The managerial perspective on data management concentrates on why organizations design and maintain memories. Chapter 1 examines this topic by detailing the components of organizational memory and then discussing some of its common problems. The intention is to make you aware of the scope of organizational memory and its many facets.

The second chapter discusses the use of memory in supporting organizational goals. Again, a very broad outlook is adopted in order to provide a sweeping perspective on the relationship of organizational memory to organizational change.

At this point, we want to give you some "maps" for understanding the terrain you will explore. Since the territory is possibly very new, these maps initially may be hard to read and so you may need to read them several times before you understand the terrain you are about to enter.

The first map (see Figure S1–1) is based on the Newell-Simon model[1] of the human information processing system, which shows that humans receive input, process it, and produce output. The processing is done by a processor, which is linked to a memory divided into data and processes. The processor retrieves both data and processes from memory.

To understand this model, consider a person receiving a message to telephone a close friend. The message is input to the human information processing system. The person retrieves the friend's telephone number from the data portion of his memory. He or she also retrieves the process, or instructions, for making a telephone call (e.g., pick up hand piece, press numbers, and so on). The person then makes the phone call, the processing of the input message. The phone call is the output. Sometimes these processes are so well

---

[1] A. Newell and H. A. Simon, *Human Problem Solving* (Englewood Cliffs, NJ: Prentice-Hall, 1972).

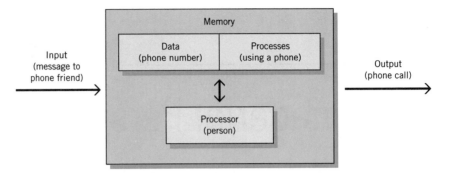

Figure S1–1   The Simon-Newell model of human information processing

ingrained in our memory we never think about retrieving them, we just do it automatically.

Human information processing systems can get overloaded easily. Our memory is limited, and our ability to process data is restricted; thus we use a variety of external tools to extend and augment our capacities. A telephone book is an example of external data memory. A recipe, a description of the process for preparing food, is an example of external process memory. Calculators and computer pro-

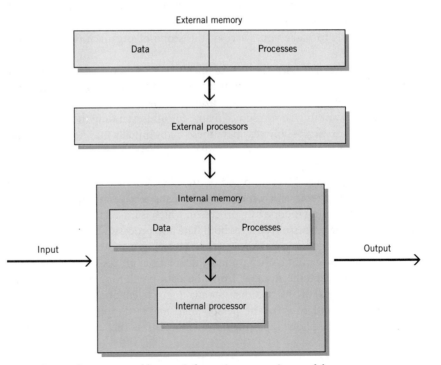

Figure S1–2   An augmented human information processing model grams are examples of external processors we use to augment our limited processing capacity.

The original model of human information processing can be extended to include external memory, for storing data and processes, and external processors, for executing processes (see Figure S1–2).

This model of augmented human information processing translates directly to an organizational setting. Organizations collect inputs from the environment—market research, customer complaints, competitor actions, and so forth. They process this data and produce outputs—sales campaigns, new products, price changes, and so on. Figure S1–3 gives an example of how an organization might process data. As a result of some market research (input) a marketing analyst (an internal processor) retrieves sales data (data) and does a sale forecast (process). The analyst also requests a marketing consultant (an external processor) to analyze (process) some demographic data (data) before deciding to launch a new promotion (output).

Organizational memory comes in a variety of forms, as you will see in Chapter 1. This memory also can be divided into data and processes. The data part may contain information about customers. The process portion may store details of how to process a customer order. Organizations use a variety of processors to handle data, including people and computers. Organizations also rely on external sources to extend their information-processing capacity. For example, a business may use a specialist credit agency to check a customer's credit wor-

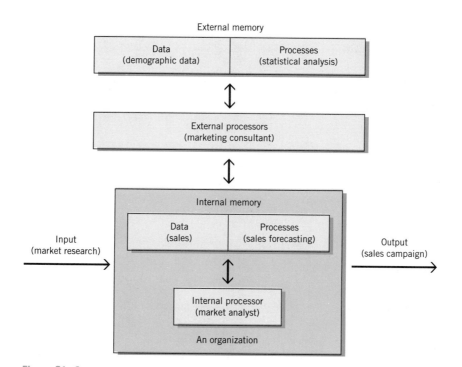

Figure S1–3   An organizational information processing model thiness, or an engineering firm may buy time on a university's supercomputer for structural analysis of a bridge. Viewed this way, the augmented human information processing model becomes an organizational information processing system.

This book focuses on the data side of organizational memory. While it is primarily concerned with data stored within the organization, there is also coverage of data in external memory. The process side of organizational memory is typically covered in a systems analysis and design course.

Chapter 1

Organizational Memory

All the value of this company is in its people. If you burned down all our plants, and we just kept our people and our information files, we should soon be as strong as ever.

Thomas Watson, Jr., former chairman of IBM[1]

Learning Objectives

Students completing this chapter will:

- understand the concept of organizational memory;
- recognize that there are many components of organizational memory;
- understand the problems with existing organizational memory systems;
- realize that successful data management requires an integrated understanding of organizational behavior and information technology.

INTRODUCTION

The organization that loses its memory, loses its life. Imagine what would happen to the bank that forgot who owed it money or the software company that lost all its source code. Both would soon be in serious difficulty, if not out of business. Organizations have memories to record the myriad of details necessary for transacting business and making informed decisions. Societies and organizations have always maintained memories. In some cases, the memory system is as simple as carving a notch in a stick to keep a tally, or as intricate as modern database technology. A memory system can be as personal as a "to do" list or as public as a library.

The management of organizational memory, generally known as **data management**, requires skills in designing, using, and managing the memory systems of modern organizations. It requires multiple perspectives. Data managers need to see the organization as a social system and to understand data management technology. The integration of these views, the socio-technical perspective, is a prerequisite for successful data management.

Individuals also need to manage data. You undoubtedly are more familiar with individual memory management systems. They provide a convenient way of introducing some of the key concepts of organizational memory.

---

[1]As reported in B. J. Quinn, *Intelligent Enterprise: A Knowledge and Service based Paradigm for Industry* (New York: Free Press, 1992), 244.

INDIVIDUAL MEMORY SYSTEMS

As humans, we are well aware of our limited capacity to remember many things. The brain, our **internal memory**, can get overloaded with too much detail and its memory decays with time. We store a few things internally: home and work telephone numbers, where we last parked our car, and faces of people we have met recently. We use **external memory** to keep track of those many things we know we should remember. External memories come in a variety of forms.

We carry diaries to remind us of meetings and project deadlines. We have address books to record the addresses and phone numbers of those we contact frequently. We use to-do lists to remind us of the things we must do today or this week. The interesting thing about these aides-mémoire is that each has a unique way of storing data and supporting its rapid retrieval.

Diaries come in many shapes and forms, but they are all based on the same organizing principle. A set amount of space is allocated for each day of the year, and the spaces are organized in date order, which supports rapid retrieval of any date. Some diaries have added features to speed up access. A bookmark can be used to mark the current date. Perforated tear-offs on the bottom right corner of the righthand pages are often used to assist rapid location of current data.

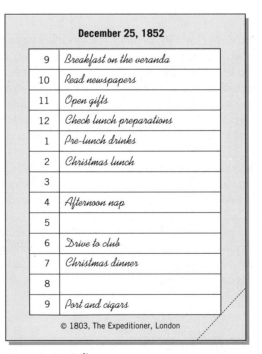

Figure 1–1   A diary

```
                                                    K–L

    Name        Rudyard Kipling
    Address     PO Kyhber Pass
                Northwest Frontier
                India


    Name        Jack London
    Address     PO Klondike
                Alaska
                                                         K
                                                         L
    Name
    Address



    Name
    Address




            © 1815, The Expeditioner, London
```

Figure 1–2   An address book

Address books also have a standard format. They typically contain preprinted spaces for storing address details (e.g., name, street, city, zip, and phone). Another common feature is the use of alphabetic tabs to separate the sections. For example, if we are searching for Jack London, we first locate the L tab to find the appropriate set of pages on which to check more closely.

The structure of to-do lists tends to be fairly standard. They are often pads with ruled lines and a small lefthand margin. The idea is to write each item to be done on the right side of the page. The left side is used to check (✔) or mark those tasks that have been completed. The beauty of the check method is that you can quickly scan the left side to identify tasks yet uncompleted.

Many people use some form of the individual memory system just described. They are frequently marketed as time management systems in leading business magazines. Stationery stores devote considerable space to them. Some of these systems are conveniently packaged into wallets containing a diary, address book, to-do list pad, and other forms for individual memory support. Packaging features prominently in the buyer's decision making because the buyer has to make a trade-off between the portability of pocket size and the spaciousness of desk size. Portability means reduced space for storing data. A spacious desk edition allows detailed record keeping, but lacks the convenience of being easily portable.

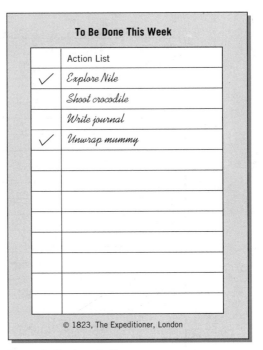

Figure 1–3   A to-do list

These three examples of individual memory systems illustrate some features common to all memory systems:

- There is a storage medium. Data are written on paper in each of these examples.
- There is a structure for storing data. For instance, the address directory has labeled spaces for entering pertinent data.
- The storage device is organized for rapid data entry and retrieval. A diary is in date sequence so that the data space for any date can be found quickly.
- The selection of a memory system frequently requires a trade-off decision. In this example, the trade-off is portability versus spaciousness.

There are differences between internal and external memories. Our internal memory is small, fast, and convenient (our brain is always with us—well, most of the time). External memory is large, slow, and not as convenient. The two systems are interconnected. We rely on our internal memory to access the external memory. We need to remember that appointments are stored in a diary. Our internal memory and our brain's processing skills manage the use of external memories.

Again, we see some trade-offs. Ideally, we would like to store everything in our fast and convenient internal memory, but its limited capacity means that we are forced to use larger capacity, slower external memory for many items.

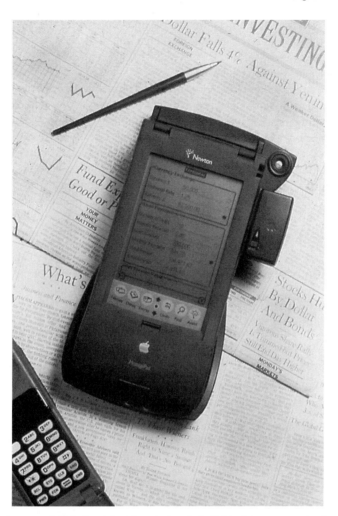

A personal digital assistant (an electronic individual memory system).

ORGANIZATIONAL MEMORY

When people work together they need to keep an organizational memory, data from the organization's past that can be used in current decisions. If you look around any office, you will see examples of the apparatus of organizational memory: people, filing cabinets, policy manuals, planning boards, and computers. The same principles found in individual memory systems apply to organizational memory systems.

There is a storage medium. In the case of computers, the storage medium varies. Small files might be stored on a floppy disk and large, archival files on optical disk. In Chapter 11, we discuss electronic storage media in more detail.

There is a structure for storing data; a common one is the table. For example, if we want to store details of customers, we can set up a table with each row containing individual details of a customer and each column containing data on a particular feature (e.g., customer identification code).

Storage devices are organized for rapid data entry and retrieval. Time is the manager's enemy: too many things to be done in too little time. Because customers expect rapid responses to their questions and quick processing of their transactions, rapid data access is a key goal of nearly all organizational memory systems. Rapid access always comes at a price, however. Fast access memories cost more, so there is nearly always a trade-off between access speed and cost.

As you will see, selecting *how* and *where* to store organizational memories frequently involves a trade-off. Data managers need to know and understand what the trade-offs entail. They must know the key questions to ask when evaluating trade-offs.

When we move from individual to organizational memory, some other factors come into play. To understand these factors, we need to know why organizations maintain organizational memories. There are two principal reasons: transaction processing and decision making.

Transaction Processing

Organizations need to process the routine transactions of day-to-day business. Typical transactions include:

- A customer buying an item.
- Receipt of an order from a supplier.
- An inquiry regarding hotel room availability and price.
- Processing a medical claim form.

To understand the importance of transactions, let's examine the sale of an item by a department store. Assume a customer buys a television set for $250 and pays with a credit card. Associated with this transaction are some data recording actions:

- The store's revenue is increased by $250.
- The store's liability for sales tax is increased by $12.50 (assuming a 5% sales tax).
- The sales count of that particular television set is increased by 1.
- The inventory of that particular television set is decreased by 1.
- The salesperson's total sales are increased by $250.
- The store records a receivable of $262.50 from the credit card company.

Each one of these events results in changing some aspect of organizational memory. Without a memory the store would not know whether it was profitable, how much it owed in sales tax, how many TV sets it has sold or had in stock, and so forth. The data from a sale are usually captured by an accounting system, one form of organizational memory that has been in use for many years. Organizations need memories to record data about business transactions.

Decision Making

Besides handling everyday business, organizations need to plan for future business. The department store must decide which items to stock, quantities to order, how many people to employ, and so on. Decisions can be as short-term as deciding how to handle a salesperson's one-day absence or as long-term as deciding whether to expand into Europe or Asia. Although decisions come in a variety of flavors, all require data. You can't decide how to handle the absent salesperson if you don't know the present allocation of staff within the store. The decision to expand abroad will require extensive analysis of location costs, demographic trends, consumer behavior, disposable income, and economic growth. The quality of decisions is determined by the quality of the data on which they are based.

POS sells flowers

Marks & Spencer has sold clothes and household goods to British consumers for more than a century. In 1993, 14 million people spent $11 billion at more than 600 stores in the United Kingdom and overseas. As part of its routine business, Marks & Spencer uses point-of-sale (POS) terminals to capture data on the 3.5 million customers who charge their purchases to the company's credit card.

Marketing analysts use this data to determine who is likely to buy a particular product. For instance, in March 1992, recent purchasers of cut flowers received a direct-mail offer for a home-delivery flower service. The offer received an overwhelming response, and Marks & Spencer has now captured 10% of the home-delivery flower market.

This strategy of targeting selected customers based on their past buying habits has enabled Marks & Spencer to increase its mail-order business from $15 million in 1990 to $75 million in 1993. Smart marketing analyzes organizational memory to pinpoint the most likely customers, and does not waste promotional offers on poor prospects.[2]

Decision making is the central activity of modern organizations.[3] Today's organizations are busy turning out goods, services, and decisions. It is estimated that there are 62 million managers, information workers, and knowledge workers in the United States.[4] These people are decision makers. Their success, and their organization's success, depends on the quality of their decisions.

Industrial society was a producer of goods, and the hallmark of success was product quality. Japanese manufacturers convincingly demonstrated that focusing on product quality was the key to market leadership and profitability. The methods and the philosophy of quality gurus, such as Deming,[5] have been internationally recognized and adopted by many providers of goods and services.

---

[2]Adapted from J. DeJong, "Smart Marketing," *Computerworld*, 7 February 1994, 113, 117–118.

[3]G. P. Huber and R. R. McDaniel, "The Decision-making Paradigm of Organizational Design," *Management Science* 32 (5): 572–589 (1986).

[4]K. C. Laudon and J. P. Laudon, *Management Information Systems: A Contemporary Perspective*, 2nd ed. (New York: Macmillan, 1991), 427.

[5]W. E. Deming, "Improvement of Quality and Productivity Through Action by Management," *National Productivity Review*, December 1981, 12–22.

Figure 1–4 The linkage between organizational memory and organizational success

As we make the transition from an industrial society to one based on knowledge and services, the key determinant of success is likely to shift from product quality to decision quality. In the turbulent environment of global business, successful organizations will be those able to make high quality decisions quickly. Even in an industrial society, decision quality is critical because it precedes product quality. Organizations must first decide which products meet consumers' needs. High quality products that no one will buy are worthless. Decision quality always has been important, it just becomes more so in a post-industrial society.

Now that we have established the importance of decision making and decision quality, we need to explore their relationship to organizational memories. Figure 1–4 helps us to see the linkages. Organizational memory is a source of data. For example, it contains sales data that can be analyzed to determine market trends and consumer preferences. Decision makers need convenient methods of extracting data from organizational memory. They want quick and convenient access to data that will help them formulate a high quality decision. As a result, the organization can deliver highly reliable products and services that meet customers' needs. And the organization is successful.

An example illustrates the sequence of events shown in Figure 1–4. A manufacturer of a luxury car maintains, among other things, records of all customer correspondence, service claims, dealer reports, and competitors' offerings (organizational memory). A senior manager has analyzed these records to determine products or services that could enhance the value of the car to the customer (data). She has found that, above all else, customers seek reliability. As a result, she recommends (quality decision) to senior management that the warranty should be extended to five years or 50,000 miles (quality product) and free emergency road service supplied with purchase of a car (quality service).

Now, let's review the foregoing discussion. We set out to establish why organizations need memories. We have shown that organizational memories are required to support transaction processing and decision making, which we have learned is the central activity of modern organizations. Thus we see that memory is an essential component of modern organizations because it supports critical business processes.

Attributes of Organizational Memory

Once we realize the critical importance of organizational memory, we can recognize some desirable attributes (see Table 1–1) of an organizational memory system.

Table 1–1   Desirable Attributes of Organizational Memory

Shareable	Readily accessed by more than one person at a time
Transportable	Easily moved to a decision maker
Secure	Protected from destruction and unauthorized use
Accurate	Reliable, precise records
Timely	Current and up-to-date
Relevant	Appropriate to the decision

Shareable

Organizations contain many decision makers. There are occasions when more than one person will require access to the same data at the same time. For example, in a large bank it would not be uncommon for two customer representatives simultaneously to want data on the latest rate for a three–year certificate of deposit.

Organizations use a wide variety of approaches to handle the need for shareability. The success of these methods depends very much on the volatility of the data—the rate at which they change. Low volatility data are often printed, bound, and distributed as a book. This way, each potential user has a copy. Telephone books and policy manuals are examples of low volatility organizational memories. As data become more volatile, shareability becomes more of a problem. For instance, consider a restaurant. The permanent menu is printed, today's special might be displayed on a blackboard, and the waiter tells you what is no longer available.

Stock and commodity markets are classic examples of the need for shareability and a highly volatile environment. Because brokers are at a major disadvantage if they don't know the very latest price, they traditionally have gathered at a common location. Current buying and selling data are displayed on a board visible to all brokers on the floor of the market.

The Deserted Trading Floor

In 1986, the London International Stock Exchange introduced screen-based trading as an alternative to the trading floor. Brokers no longer needed to be on the trading floor to know the latest buying and selling data. They could work from their offices, where they also could consult economic reports and colleagues. The office was data rich compared to the trading floor. More data were available to support trading decisions. Information technology overcame the need for physical assembly at one point, and the trading floor was rapidly abandoned.[6]

---

[6]Adapted from E. K. Clemons and B. W. Weber, "London's Big Bang: A Case Study of Information Technology, Competitive Impact, and Organizational Change," *Journal of Management Information Systems* 6 (4): 41–60 (1990).

Transportable

Data should be transportable from its storage location to the decision maker. Technologies that transport data have a long history. Homing pigeons were used to relay messages by the Egyptians and Persians 3000 years ago. The telephone revolutionized business and social life because it rapidly transmitted voice data. Fax machines have accelerated organizational correspondence because they transport both text and visual data. Computers have changed the nature of many aspects of business because they enable the transport of text, visual, and voice data.

Today, transportability is more than just getting data to a decision maker's desk. It means getting product availability data to a salesperson in a client's office, or advising a delivery driver, en route, of address details for an urgent parcel pickup. The general notion is that decision makers should have access to relevant data whenever and wherever required, although most organizations are a long way from reaching this target.

Secure

In a post-industrial society, data are a highly valuable resource. As we have already learned, data support day-to-day business transactions and decision making. Because the forgetful organization will soon be out of business, organizations are very vigilant in protecting their data. There are a number of actions that organizations take to protect data against loss, sabotage, and theft. A common approach is to duplicate data and store the copy, or copies, at other locations. This technique is popular for data stored in computer systems. Access to data is often restricted through the use of physical barriers (e.g., a vault) or electronic barriers (e.g., a password). Another approach, which is becoming popular with knowledge workers, is a non-competitive contract. For example, some software companies legally restrain computer programmers from working for a competitor for two years after they leave, hoping to prevent the transfer of valuable data, in the form of the programmer's knowledge of software, to competitors.

Accurate

You probably remember students who excelled in exams because of their good memory. Similarly, organizations with an accurate memory will do better than their less precise competitors. Organizations need to remember many details accurately. For example, an airline needs to recall exact seat assignments for a particular flight. Imagine the chaos and disgruntled customers if seating gets confused. The quality of decision making will drop dramatically if managers use inaccurate data.

Polluted data threatens a firm's profitability. One recent study[7] suggests missing, wrong, and otherwise bad data cost U.S. firms billions of dollars annually. The consequences of bad data include improper billing, cost overruns, delivery delays, and product recalls. In 1990, a major New York securities firm lost more than $200 million because of a data entry error in a risk management system. Because data accuracy is so critical, organizations need to be watchful when capturing data—the point at which data accuracy is most vulnerable.

---

[7]B. Knight, "The Data Pollution Problem," *Computerworld*, 28 September 1992, 81, 83.

Timely

The value of data are often determined by its age and can decay rapidly with time. You can fantasize about how rich you would be if you knew tomorrow's stock prices today. Although decision makers are most interested in current data, the required currency of data can vary with the task. Operational managers often want real time data. They want to tap the pulse of the production line so that they can react quickly to machine breakdowns or quality slippages. In contrast, strategic planners might be content with data that are months old because they are more concerned with detecting long-term trends.

Relevant

The purpose of organizational memories is to maintain data that are relevant to transaction processing and decision making. When processing a credit card application, the most relevant data might be the customer's credit history, current employment status, and income level. Hair color would be irrelevant. When assessing the success of a new product line, a marketing manager probably would want an aggregate report of sales by marketing region. A voluminous report detailing every sale would be irrelevant. Data are relevant when they pertain directly to the decision and are aggregated appropriately.

Relevance is a key concern in designing organizational memories. Users have to decide what should be stored because it is pertinent now or could have future relevance. Of course, identifying data that might be relevant in the future is difficult, and there is a tendency to accumulate too much—most noticeably with government forms.

Relevance also is a key concern in extracting and processing data from organizational memories. Provided the pertinent data are available, then query languages can be used to aggregate data appropriately.

In summary, an organizational memory system supports transaction processing and decision making. Its contents must be shareable, secure and accurate. Ideally, users of organizational memory must be able to get timely and relevant data when and where required. A major challenge for data management professionals is to create organizational memory systems that meet these criteria. Unfortunately, many existing systems fail in this regard, though we can understand some of the reasons why by reviewing the components of existing organizational memory systems.

COMPONENTS OF ORGANIZATIONAL MEMORY

Organizational memory[8] is stored on a variety of media in a variety of ways. It resides in people, standard operating procedures, roles, organizational culture, physical storage equipment, and electronic devices. It is scattered around the organization—a jigsaw designed by Sal-

---

[8]For an advanced treatment of organizational memories, see J. P. Walsh and G. R. Ungson, "Organizational Memory," *Academy of Management Review* 16 (1): 57–91 (1991).

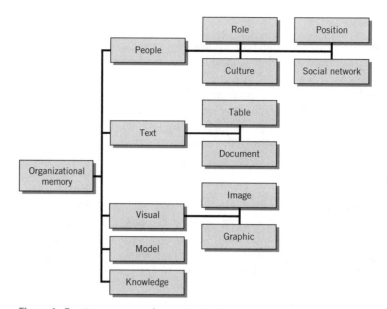

Figure 1–5   Components of organizational memory

vador Dali.[9] The pieces don't fit together, they sometimes overlap, there are gaps, and there are no edge pieces to define the boundaries. Organizations struggle to design structures and use information technology to link some of the pieces. To understand the complexity of this wicked puzzle, we need to examine some of the pieces (see Figure 1–5). Data managers have a particular need to understand the different forms of organizational memory because their activities often influence a number of the components.

People

People are the linchpin of organizational memory. They recall previous decisions and business actions. They create, maintain, evolve, and use organizational memory systems. They are the major component of an organization's memory because they know how to use all the other components. People extract data from the various components of organizational memory to provide as complete a picture of a situation as possible. People play a similar role in organizational memory as internal memory plays for individuals. They both manage and use other memories.

When people join an organization they become parts of its memory system. They are taught both formally and informally how the organization works. Formal classroom instruction teaches new employees business policy and procedures. They are trained for a particular organizational role.

---

[9]The Spanish painter Salvador Dali (1904–89) was a leader of surrealism with a declared ambition to "systemize confusion."

Each person in an organization has a **role** and a **position** in the hierarchy. Role and position are both devices for remembering how the organization functions and how to process data. By labeling people (e.g., Chief Information Officer) and placing their names on an organizational chart, the organization creates another form of organizational memory.

Organizational culture is the set of shared beliefs, values, attitudes, and norms that influence the behavior and expectations of each person in an organization. It is a long-lived and very stable memory system. It determines acceptable behavior and influences decision making. Through formal training sessions, from informal discussions in corridors, at social events, and over lunch, new employees learn organizational culture. Gradually they are infused with the organization's beliefs, values, symbols, jargon, and way of doing business.

People develop skills for doing their particular job, learning what to do, how to do it, and who can help them get things done. For example, they might discover someone in employee benefits who can handle personnel problems or a contact in a computer company who can answer questions promptly. For a salesperson, it is frequently critical to know the person who can authorize a purchase. These **social networks**, which often take years to develop, are used to make things happen and learn about the business environment. Despite their high value, they are rarely documented, at least not beyond an address book or Rolodex, and are typically lost when a person leaves an organization.

The Conversational Organization

The conversation is the organization at McKinsey & Company, an internationally prominent management consulting company. At McKinsey, conversations are a way of exchanging knowledge and discovering what colleagues know. Because information exchange is so critical to its business, McKinsey has a director of knowledge management who has created a series of electronic databases and networks to facilitate conversations. There is an information system for sharing lessons learned by project leaders and a database of core documents contributed by each of the management consulting offices. The On-Call Consultant (OCC) system puts company members in contact with an appropriate senior consultant, who is available for several weeks per year to have conversations with any company member seeking guidance, advice, and ideas.[10]

Conversations are an important method for knowledge workers to create, modify, and share organizational memory in a post-industrial society, and a way to build relationships and social networks. Discussions with customers are a key device for learning how to improve an organization's products and services and learning about competitors. The conversational company can detect change faster and react more rapidly. The telephone, fax, electronic mail,

---

[10]Adapted from T. Peters, *Liberation Management: Necessary Disorganization for the Nanosecond Nineties* (New York: Alfred A. Knopf, 1992).

coffee machine, cocktail hour, and cafeteria are all devices for promoting conversation and creating networks. McKinsey recognizes the value of these conversations, and has deliberately created structures for supporting conversations and to make the people component of organizational memory more effective.

Standard operating procedures exist for many organizational tasks. Processing a credit application, selecting a marketing trainee, and preparing a departmental budget are typical procedures that are clearly defined by many organizations. They are described in procedure manuals, computer programs, and job specifications. They are the way an organization remembers to perform routine activities.

Successful people learn how to use organizational memory. They learn what data are stored where, how to retrieve them, and how to put them together. In promoting a new product, a salesperson might send the prospect a package containing some brochures, a copy of a product review in a trade journal, and supply the phone number of the firm's technical expert for that product. People's recall of how to use organizational memory is the core component of organizational memory. Academics call this metamemory; people in business call it learning the ropes. New employees spend a great deal of time building their metamemory so that they can use organizational memory effectively. Without this knowledge, organizational memory would have little value.

Tables

A table with rows and columns is a common form of storing organizational data. Table 1–2 shows a price list in tabular form. Often, the first row defines the meaning of data in subsequent rows.

A table is a general form that describes a variety of other structures used to store data, thus becoming a building block of a relational database system. Computer-based files are tables or can be transformed into tables; the same is true for general ledger and worksheets, and spreadsheets. Accounting systems make frequent use of tables. Card files can be readily transformed into tables. Each card becomes one row and each field on the card becomes a column (see Figure 1–6).

Table 1–2   A Price List

Product	Price
Pocket knife–Nile	4.50
Compass	10.00
Geo positioning system	500.00
Map measure	4.90

Item _____

Item code _____

Order point _____   Order quantity _____

Supplier _____

Supplier code _____

↓

Item	Item code	Order point	Order quantity	Supplier	Supplier code
...	...	...	...	...	...

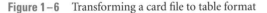

Figure 1–6   Transforming a card file to table format

Data stored in tables typically have certain characteristics:

- Data in one column are of the same type. For example, each cell of the column headed price contains a number. (Of course, the exception is the first or header column.)
- Data are limited by width of space. Usually each item is less than 20 characters and rarely more than 50.

Rapid searching is one of the prime advantages of a table. For example, if the price list is sorted by product name, you can quickly find the price of any product.

Tables are a common form of storing organizational data because their structure is readily understood. People learn to read and build tables in the early years of their schooling. Also, a great deal of the data organizations want to remember can be stored in tabular form. As you will see, tables are the building blocks of a relational database system.

Documents

The document, of which reports, manuals, brochures, and memos are examples, is a common medium for storing organizational data. A document consists of pages of text made up of alphabetic characters, digits, or symbols. Although documents may be subdivided into chapters, sections, paragraphs, and sentences, they lack the regularity and discipline of a table. Each row of a table has the same number of columns, but each paragraph of a document does not have the same number of sentences.

Many documents are now stored electronically. Because of the widespread use of word processing, text files are a quite common means of storing documents. A document prepared using a word processor can be easily converted to a text file and shared with many users. Typically, such files are read sequentially like a book. Although there is support for limited searching of the text, such as finding the next occurrence of a specified text string, text files are processed linearly.

Hypertext is a more convenient format, from the user's perspective, of document storage. A hypertext document has built-in linkages between sections of text that permit the reader to jump quickly from one part to another. As a result, readers can find data they require more rapidly. Because the first section of a hypertext document is typically the table of contents, the reader can move to any section listed by simply positioning the pointer on the relevant area and clicking the mouse button. Links can be embedded throughout the text. A common practice is to link important terms to their definitions. For example, a reader who comes across the word 'byte' and wants to find out what it means would simply point, click, and jump to the definition. Hypertext is a popular format for storing the help data associated with many computer programs.

Although hypertext is certainly more user-friendly than a flat, sequential text file, it takes time and expertise to establish the links between the various parts of the text. Someone familiar with the topic has to decide what should be linked and then establish these links. While it takes the author more time to prepare a document this way, the payoff is the speed at which readers of the document can find what they want.

Images

Images are visual data: photographs, sketches, and videos. Image banks are maintained for several reasons. First, images are widely used for identification and security. Police departments keep fingerprints and mug shots. Immigration officials keep passport photographs. Second, images are used as evidence. Highly valuable items such as paintings and jewelry often are photographed for insurance records. Third, images are used for advertising and promotional campaigns, and organizations need to maintain records of material used in these ventures. Image archiving and retrieval are essential for mail order company L. L. Bean, which produces several photo-laden catalogs every year.[11] Fourth, some organizations specialize in selling images and maintain extensive libraries of clip art and photographs.

A recent development, document imaging, has substantially increased the presence of images in organizational memory. Organizations receive an avalanche of letters, application forms, and reports every day, and it takes considerable time and effort to process and store these data. It also means that a lot of office space, often in high rent business districts, is devoted to storing paper. Imaging technology can be used to convert a paper document to a format that can be stored electronically. As a result, considerable storage space is saved and document retrieval is accelerated. Furthermore, imaged documents can be shared and distributed more easily.

---

[11]M. Waltz, "Mac Keeps L. L. Bean Catalogs in Step," *MacWeek* 7 (1): 70 (1993).

A Major Mail Problem Gets Solved

San Antonio–based United Services Automobile Association (USAA) is the world's largest mail order company. It provides a broad range of investment, security, retirement, and travel products and services to current and former U.S. military officers and their dependents. Every day, it receives over 100,000 letters and mails 250,000 items. In 1988, the firm needed 3,600 m^2 (40,000 square feet) to store active paper files. Inactive files were stored in 80,000 boxes in a warehouse. This same data on optical disks could be stored in just 9 m^2 (100 square feet). Over 160 people were required to sort, deliver, and file these documents.

The policy service and underwriting section of USAA's property and casualty insurance business is spearheading the move to image processing in USAA. Each day, this group receives 15,000 letters (about 35,000 pages) and sends 50,000 letters and policies. All of these documents are entered into the image system. Incoming mail is scanned to create an electronic image, indexed, and stored in a mainframe computer. Imaged documents can be accessed from anywhere in the firm. The imaging system supports a faster, higher quality, more timely, and efficient member service. It reduces the need for clerical staff, equipment, supplies, and space.[12]

Graphics

Maps, drawings, layouts, blueprints, and charts are types of graphics stored in organizational memory. For example, an organization might maintain a map of sales territories and customers. Manufacturers have extensive libraries of engineering drawings that define the products they produce. Graphics often contain a high level of detail. An engineering drawing will define the dimensions of all parts and may refer to other drawings for finer detail about any component of a sub–assembly.

A graphic differs from an image in that it contains explicitly embedded data. Consider the difference between an engineering plan for a widget and a photograph of the same item. An engineering plan shows dimensional data and may describe the composition of the various components. The embedded data are used to manufacture the widget. A photograph of a widget does not have embedded data and contains insufficient data to manufacture the product. An industrial spy will receive far more for an engineering plan than a photograph of a widget.

Computer-aided design systems (CAD) use powerful workstations to support design and engineering work. Designers can use a system to specify a product's shape, dimensions, materials, and other features. Most systems support three-dimensional design, and an engineer

---

[12]Adapted from D. R. Lasher, B. Ives, and S. L. Jarvenpaa, "USAA–IBM Partnerships in Information Technology," *MIS Quarterly* 15 (4): 551–565 (1991).

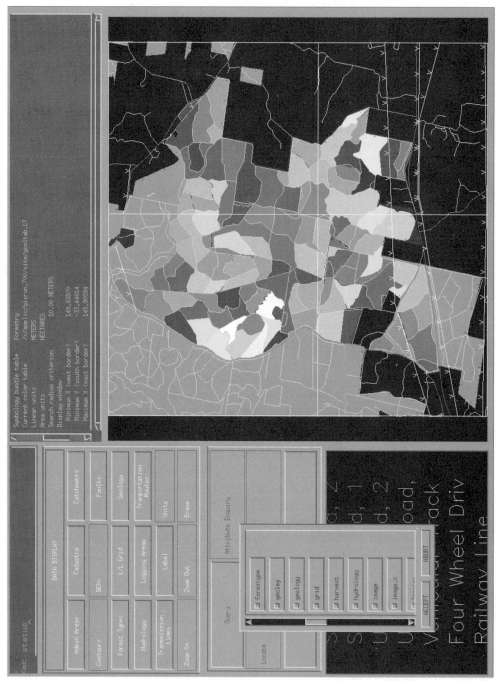

A geographic information system (GIS).

can readily define the height, width, and depth of a component and visualize it before it is manufactured.

Geographic information systems (GIS) are specialized graphical storage systems for geographic data. The underlying structure of a GIS is a map on which data are displayed. A power company can use a GIS to store and display data about its power grid and the location of transformers. Using a pointing device, such as a mouse, an engineer can click on a transformer's location to display a window of data about the transformer (e.g., type, capacity, installation date, and repair history). GISs have found widespread use in governments and organizations that have geographically dispersed resources.

Voice

Some firms conduct a great deal of their business by phone. In many cases, it is important to maintain a record of the conversation between the customer and the firm's representative.

Recording Bets in Hong Kong

The Royal Hong Kong Jockey Club, which covers horse racing gambling in Hong Kong, records all conversations between its operators and customers. The 26 million daily phone calls are stored on a highly specialized voice recorder. The unit records the time of the call and other data necessary for rapid retrieval. One day's phone calls fills about 200 tapes. In the case of a customer dispute, an operator can playback the original conversation.[13]

Models

Organizations build mathematical models to describe their business. These models, usually placed in the broader category of decision support systems (DSS), are then used to analyze existing problems and forecast future business conditions. A mathematical model can often produce substantial benefits.[14]

- A General Motors' division developed a microcomputer-based mathematical model to determine the best way to ship 300 types of components to 30 assembly plants. The system enabled GM to cut logistics costs by 26 percent and generate annual savings of $2.9 million.

---

[13]M. Johnston, "Betting on a Transaction Processing Network," *Datamation*, 1 May 1990.

[14]These examples are taken from M. Betts, "Efficiency Einsteins," *Computerworld*, 22 March 1993, 63–64.

- Weyerhaeuser, a lumber company, increased profits by $100 million by using a computer model to show lumberjacks how to cut each log to maximize profits and minimize waste. Variables in the model include log length, diameter, curvature, taper, and knots.
- American Airlines' yield management system, which contains more than 250 variables, accounts for 5 percent of the airline's revenue. The system calculates pricing and booking levels to maximize profits.

Mathematical models are a valuable organizational resource. Their construction takes a high level of skill and often takes considerable time. Organizations store these systems so that they may be easily retrieved and run by authorized users.

Knowledge

Recently, organizations have started to capture the knowledge of their experienced decision makers and problem solvers. This expertise is typically represented as a set of rules, semantic nets, and frames in a knowledge base, another form of organizational memory.

CLINT Displaces Lawyers

Metropolitan Life Insurance Co. is replacing lawyers with a software program called CLINT. When finalizing a large commercial real estate deal, paralegals use CLINT, which asks questions about the property, loan, borrower, and other important data. The software prints out a checklist of documents and required research to complete the deal.[15]

Decisions

Decision making is the central activity of modern organizations. Very few organizations, however, have a formal system for recording decisions. Most keep the minutes of meetings, but these are often very brief and record only a meeting's outcome. Because they do not record details such as the objectives, criteria, assumptions, and alternatives that were considered prior to making a decision, there is no formal audit trail for decision making. As a result, most organizations rely on humans to remember the circumstances and details of prior decisions.

---

[15]Adapted from M. Galen, "How Many Lawyers Can You Fit on a Floppy Disk? Computers Won't Replace Attorneys—But They're Making a Dent," *Business Week*, 21 December 1992, 63.

Reusable Decisions

Bell Northern Research, the research arm of Canadian communications company Northern Telecom, is investigating building a database that will record details of decisions. One of its objectives is to provide "reusable" decisions. Researchers have observed that some decisions are made repeatedly by design engineers. If prior decisions could be retrieved from a database, then some decisions would be reusable, and design engineers would save time.[16]

Specialized Memories

Because of the particular nature of their business, some organizations maintain memories rarely found elsewhere. Perfume companies, for instance, maintain a library of scents, and paint manufacturers and dye makers catalog colors.

External Memories

Organizations are not limited to their own memory stores. There are firms whose business is to store data for resale to other organizations. Such businesses have existed for many years and are growing as the importance of data in a post-industrial society expands. Lawyers, using Mead Data Central's LEXIS, can access the laws and court decisions of all fifty U.S. states and the U.S. federal government. Similar legal data services exist in many other nations. There is a range of other services that provide news, financial, business, scientific, and medical data.

Customized Marketing

Kraft USA uses data from three sources to support the work of its trade marketing team. Data from individual stores are analyzed to assess the effects of promotional activities such as displays and price reductions. Demographic and buying-habit data on the customers of 30,000 U.S. food stores is a second source of data. A third source of data, purchased from an outside vendor, contains fine-grained geo-demographic data. The trade marketing team then integrates and analyzes these data to tailor Kraft's advertising, merchandising, and operations in a single store or in several stores within a supermarket chain to the needs of those stores' customers.[17]

---

[16]Personal conversation with a Bell Northern Research engineer in March 1993.

[17]Adapted from M. Treacy and F. Wiersema, "Customer Intimacy and Other Value Disciplines," *Harvard Business Review* 71 (1): 84–93 (1992).

Table 1–3   Problems with Organizational Memory

Redundancy	Same data stored in different memories
Data control	Data is poorly managed
Interface	Difficult to access data
Delays	There are frequently long delays in responding to requests for data
Lack of reality	Organizational memories do not reflect the complexity of the real world
Lack of data integration	Data are dispersed across different systems

PROBLEMS WITH ORGANIZATIONAL MEMORY SYSTEMS

Earlier, we described organizational memory as a wicked jigsaw. Now, we look at some of the reasons why we used that label (see Table 1–3).

Redundancy

In many cases, organizational memories have grown haphazardly. As a result, it is often the case that the same pieces of data are stored in several different memories. The classic example is a customer's address, which might be stored in the sales reporting system, accounts receivable system, and the salesperson's telephone book. The danger is that when the customer changes address, the amendment is not recorded in all systems. Data redundancy causes additional work because the same item must be entered several times. Redundancy causes confusion when what is supposedly the same item has different values. This also indicates a data integrity problem, which takes time to correct.

Data Control

Allied with the redundancy problem is poor data control. Although data are an important organizational resource, they frequently do not receive the same degree of management attention as other important organizational resources such as people and money. Organizations have a personnel department to manage human resources and a treasury to handle cash. Data are often unmanaged. The MIS department looks after data captured by the computer systems they operate, but there are many other memories scattered around the organization. Data are stored everywhere in the organization (e.g., on personal computers and in departmental filing systems), but there is a general lack of data management. This is particularly surprising since many pundits claim that data are a key competitive resource.

Poor Interface

Too frequently, potential users of organizational memories have been deterred by an unfriendly interface. The computer dialogue for accessing a memory is sometimes difficult to remember for the occasional user. People become frustrated and give up because their queries are rejected and error messages are unintelligible.

Long Delays in Responding to Data Requests

The pace of business has accelerated remarkably in the last decade. Managers must make more decisions more rapidly. They cannot afford to wait for programmers to write special purpose programs to retrieve data and format reports. They expect their questions to be answered rapidly, often within a day and sometimes more quickly. Managers, or their support personnel, need query languages that provide rapid access to the data they need in a format that they want.

Unable to Answer Questions about the Real World

Organizational memories must reflect the reality and complexity of the real world. Consider a typical bank customer who might have a personal checking account, mortgage account, credit card account, and some certificates of deposit. When a customer requests an overdraft extension, the bank officer needs full details of the customer's relationship with the bank in order to make an informed decision. If customer data are scattered across unrelated organizational memories, then these data are not easily found and in some cases important data might be overlooked. The request for full customer details is reasonable and realistic, and the bank officer should expect to be able to enter a single, simple query to obtain it. Unfortunately, this is not always the case because organizational memories do not always reflect reality.

In this example, the reality is that the personal checking, mortgage, and credit card accounts, and certificates of deposit all belong to one customer. If the bank's organizational memory does not record this relationship, then it does not mimic reality. This makes it impossible to retrieve all customer data with a single, simple query of organizational memory.

Many organizations have highly fragmented organizational memories. Many systems, developed piecemeal over the last twenty years, are incompatible. One British bank estimated that it would cost more than $2 billion to overcome systems incompatibilities before its organizational memory could properly support its business needs.[18]

An organizational memory must meet the decision making needs of managers, who must be able to request both routine and ad hoc reports. In order to do so effectively, an organiza-

---

[18]T. Steiner and D. Teixeira, *Technology in Banking* (Homewood, IL: Dow Jones–Irwin, 1990).

tional memory must reflect the complexity of the real world. If it does not store required organizational data or record a real world relationship between data elements, then many managerial queries cannot be answered quickly and efficiently.

Lack of Data Integration

There is a general lack of data integration in most organizations. Data are not only dispersed in different forms of organizational memory (e.g., files and image stores), but even within the one storage format there is a lack of integration. For example, many organizations maintain file systems that are not integrated. Appropriate files in the accounting system may not be linked to the production system.

This lack will be a continuing problem for most organizations for two important reasons. First, early computer systems were not integrated because of the limitations of available technology. Organizations created simple file systems to support a particular function. Many of these systems are still in use. Second, integration is a long-term goal. As new systems are developed and old ones rewritten, and with the switch to newer database technology, organizations can evolve integrated systems. It would be too costly and disruptive to try to solve the data integration problem in one step.

Some of the problems with existing organizational memories can be solved with present methods. Data modeling and relational database technology, topics covered in Section 2, help overcome some of the problems. Nonetheless, it is clear that a new generation of technology, possibly in the form of object-oriented database systems, is needed to address these existing problems more completely. It is also apparent that organizations must develop policies and procedures for the management of organizational memories. They may need to create a data supremo who manages data as a corporate resource. The solution, as is the case with most problems, requires a harmonious interaction of managerial and technical systems.

DATA, INFORMATION, AND KNOWLEDGE

Until now, we have carefully avoided using the term *information*. Often *data* and *information* are used interchangeably, but they are distinctly different. **Data** are raw, unsummarized and unanalyzed facts. **Information** is data that has been processed into a meaningful form.

A list of a supermarket's daily receipts is data, but it is not information because it is too detailed to be very useful. Summarizing the data to give daily departmental totals is information because the store manager can use the report to monitor store performance. The same report would be data for a regional manager because again it is too detailed for meaningful decision making at the regional level. Information for a regional manager may be a weekly report of sales by department for each supermarket.

Data are always data, but one person's information can be another person's data. Information that is meaningful to one person can be too detailed for another person. A manager's notion of information can change quickly, however. If a problem is identified, a manager might request finer levels of detail to diagnose the problem's cause. Thus what was previously data suddenly becomes information because it helps solve the problem. When the problem is solved, the information reverts to data. There is a need for information systems that let man-

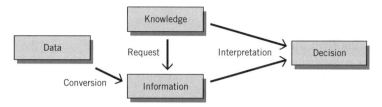

Figure 1–7   The relationship between data, information, and knowledge

agers customize the processing of data so that they always get information. As their needs change, they need to be able to adjust the detail of the reports they receive.

Knowledge is the capacity to use information. The education and experience that managers accumulate provide them with the expertise to make sense of the information they receive. Knowledge means that managers can interpret information and use it in decision making. In addition, knowledge is the capacity to recognize what information would be useful for making decisions. For example, a sales manager knows that requesting a report of profitability by product line is useful when she has to decide whether to employ a new product manager. Thus, when a new information system is delivered, managers need to be taught what information the system can deliver and what that information means.

The relationships between data, information, and knowledge are depicted in Figure 1–7. A knowledgeable person requests information to support decision making. As a result, data are converted, perhaps by a computer program, into information. Personal knowledge is then applied to interpret the requested information and reach a conclusion. Of course, the cycle could be repeated several times if more information is needed before a decision can be made. Notice how knowledge is essential for grasping what information to request and interpreting that information in terms of the required decision.

The GM Inquiry Center

General Motors Corporation's inquiry center weaves together marketplace information for effective decision making. The inquiry center uses rumors, market research, on-line news services, and sales data to build a composite picture of the business environment.

The center has three major objectives: it must integrate the logic of decision making, draw on the energy of collaboration, and stimulate the imagination of those affecting and affected by the decision. A center must sponsor and encourage information communications to foster collaborative, high quality, data supported decision making.

An information center has databases, meeting facilitation tools and software, information technology, and skilled human resources. It is used to accelerate access to data and facilitate communication within the decision-making team.[19]

---

[19]Adapted from V. P. Barabba and G. Zaltman, "Knowledge Loom of the '90s," *Computerworld*, 22 June 1992, 133, 136; and V. P. Barabba and G. Zaltman, "The Right Technical Ingredients," *Computerworld*, 22 June 1992, 137.

THE CHALLENGE

A major challenge facing organizations is to make effective use of the data stored in their diverse organizational memories and accessible in external memories. This challenge exists because these various memories are not integrated and many potential users not only lack the training to access the systems but often are unaware that they exist. But before data managers can begin to address this problem, they must understand how organizational memories are used. In particular, they need to understand the relationship between information and managerial decision making.

The Expeditioner

Alice Lindsay was enjoying the luxuries of first class travel. It was quite a change from being an undergraduate student of business. She was enjoying her filet mignon and glass of chardonnay. Good riddance to pizzas, hamburgers, and subs! Hello to fine food and gourmet restaurants. With her newly found wealth, she could travel in style and enjoy the very best restaurants. Alice, or Lady Alice to be more precise, had recently inherited a title, a valuable portfolio of stocks, and The Expeditioner. Her good fortune had coincided with the completion of her business degree. Now, instead of looking for a job, the job had found her: she was now chairman and managing director of The Expeditioner.

The Expeditioner is in a nineteenth century building in Explorer's Lane, opposite Kensington Gardens, and just a stone's throw from the Royal Geographical Society. Founded in the Middle Ages, The Expeditioner has a long history of equipping explorers, adventurers, and travelers. Its initial success was due to its development of a light, flexible chain mail armor. It did very well during the Middle Ages when highway robbery was a growth business, and travelers sought protection from the arrows and slings aimed at their fortunes. The branch office at the entrance to Sherwood Forest had done exceptionally well, thanks to passing wealthy clientele. The resident company wit, one Ned Thomas, often claims that, "The Expeditioner was the first mail order company."

The Expeditioner's customers included the famous and the legendary. Orders from Marco Polo, Columbus, Magellan, Cook, and Livingston can be found in the ledgers. The most long lived customer is a Mr. Walker,[20] who for several hundred years has had a standing yearly order of one roll of purple, premium quality, non-rip, jungle twill. The Expeditioner's hats are very popular with a Mr. I. Jones, an American.

The nineteenth century was one long boom for The Expeditioner, the supplier *de rigueur* for the guardians of the European colonies. Branch offices were opened in Bombay, Sydney, Cape Town, and Singapore. For a generous fee, cad and renown adventurer, Harry Flashman,[21] had assiduously promoted The Expeditioner's wares on his many trips. As a re-

---

[20]For Ghost Who Walks.

[21]See the *Flashman* stories by George MacDonald Fraser.

sult, orders poured in from the four corners of the globe. The Expeditioner's catalog was found in polite society and clubs throughout the British Empire.

The founder of The Expeditioner was a venturesome Scot who sought his fortune in London. Carefully guarding the family business, The Expeditioner's proprietors were inclined to be closefisted and invested their massive profits wisely. Because of their close contacts with many explorers, they made some very canny investments in mining ventures in distant lands. As a result, when business contracted during the twentieth century, the investment portfolio kept the company solvent. Traditionally, ownership of the firm was inherited by the eldest child. When the most recent owner, a bachelor, died, the firm's lawyers spent months on genealogical research to identify the legal heir.

Alice had vivid memories of the day when Mr. Mainwaring phoned her to request an appointment. Like most students, she was never home, and the message was left on her answering machine. She remembered listening to it several times because she was intrigued by both the funny accent and the message. It sounded something like, "Good afternoon Lady Alice, I am Nigel Mannering of Chumli, Crepiny, Marchbanks, and Sinjun. If you would like to hear news to your advantage, please contact me."

Two days later, Alice met with Nigel. This also had been most memorable. The opening conversation had been confusing. He started with the very same formal introduction, "Good afternoon Lady Alice, I am Nigel Mannering of Chumli, Crepiny, Marchbanks, and Sinjun. I am pleased to meet you," and handed Alice his card.

Alice quickly inspected the card, which read, "Nigel Mainwaring, LL. B., Cholmondeley, Crespigny, Majoribanks, and St. John," but he had said nothing like that. She thought, "What planet is this guy from?"

It took fifteen minutes for Alice to discover that British English was not quite the same as American English. She quickly learned, or should that be "learnt," that many proper English names have a traditional pronunciation not easily inferred from the spelling.[22]

Once this names' problem had been sorted out, Nigel (she could handle that name) told Alice of her good fortune. She was the new owner of The Expeditioner. She also inherited the title that had been conferred on a previous owner by a grateful monarch who had been equipped by The Expeditioner for traveling in the Australian outback. She was now entitled to be called "Lady Alice of Bullamakanka." Nigel was in a bit of a rush. He left Alice with a first-class ticket to London, an attaché case of folders, and with an effusive "Jolly good show," disappeared.

SUMMARY

Organizations must maintain a memory to process transactions and make decisions. Organizational memory should be shareable, transportable, secure, accurate, and provide timely, relevant data. The essential components are people (the most important component), text, visual data, models, and knowledge. A wide variety of technologies can be used to manage

---

[22]For further insights into this interesting feature of British English, see an appendix in the *Concise Oxford Dictionary*.

organizational memory. External memories enlarge the range of data available to an organization. Organizational memories often have some major shortcomings: redundancy, poor data control, poor interfaces, long lead times for query resolution, an inability to supply answers for questions posed by managers, and poor data integration. Data are raw facts; information is data processed into a meaningful form. Knowledge is the capacity to use information.

KEY TERMS AND CONCEPTS

Data	Knowledge
Data management	Organizational culture
Data security	Organizational memory
Decision making	Shareable data
Decision quality	Social networks
Documents	Standard operating procedures
External memory	Storage device
Graphics	Storage medium
Hypertext	Storage structure
Images	Tables
Information	Transaction processing
Internal memory	Voice data

REFERENCES AND ADDITIONAL READINGS

Benjamin, R. I. and J. Blunt. "Critical IT Issues: The Next Ten Years." *Sloan Management Review* 33, no. 4 (1992): 7–20.

Drucker, P. F. "The New Productivity Challenge." *Harvard Business Review* 69, no. 6 (1991): 45–53.

Wightman, K. R. "The Marriage of Retail Marketing and Information Systems: The Zellers Club Z Experience." *MIS Quarterly* 14, no. 4 (1990): 359–366.

EXERCISES

1. What are the major differences between internal and external memory?
2. What is the difference between the things you remember and the things you write down?
3. What features are common to most individual memory systems?
4. What do you think organizations did before filing cabinets were invented?
5. Discuss the memory systems you use. How do they improve your performance? What are the shortcomings of your existing systems? How can you improve them?
6. Describe the most 'organized' person you know. Why is that person so organized? Why haven't you adopted some of the same methods? Why do you think people differ in the extent to which they are organized?

7. Think about the last time you enrolled in a class. What data do you think were recorded for this transaction?

8. What roles do people play in organizational memory?

9. What do you think is the most important attribute of organizational memory? Justify your answer.

10. What is the difference between transaction processing and decision making?

11. When are data relevant?

12. Give some examples of specialized memories.

13. How can you measure the quality of a decision?

14. What is organizational culture? Can you name some organizations that have a distinctive culture?

15. What is hypertext? How does it differ from linear text? Why might hypertext be useful in an organizational memory system?

16. What is imaging? What are the characteristics of applications well-suited for imaging?

17. What is an external memory? Why do organizations use external memories instead of building internal memories?

18. What is the common name used to refer to systems that help organizations remember knowledge?

19. What is a decision support system? What's its role in organizational memory?

20. What are the major shortcomings of many organizational memories? Which do you think is the most significant shortcoming?

21. What is the relationship between data, information, and knowledge?

22. Consider the following questions about The Expeditioner.

    a. What sort of organizational memory systems would you expect to find at The Expeditioner?

    b. For each type of organizational memory that you identify, discuss it using the following themes:

        i. shareable
        ii. transportable
        iii. security
        iv. accuracy
        v. timeliness
        vi. relevance

    c. An organization's culture is the set of key values, beliefs, understandings, and norms that its members share. Discuss your ideas of the likely organizational culture of The Expeditioner

    d. How difficult do you think it will be to change the organizational culture of The Expeditioner? Do you anticipate that Alice will have problems making changes to the firm? If so, why?

23. Visit your library and find some stories about firms using organizational memory

systems. You might enter keywords such as 'database' and 'imaging' into a computer-based information retrieval system. Alternatively, you can scan business newspapers and magazines.

Identify the purpose of the system. How does the system improve organizational performance? What are the attributes of the technology that make it useful? Describe any trade-offs the organization might have made. Identify other organizations in which the same technology might be applied.

24. Make a list of the organizational memory systems identified in this chapter. Interview several people working in organizations. Ask them to indicate which organizational memory systems they use. Ask which system is most important and why. Write up your findings and your conclusion.

25. What is a personal digital assistant (PDA)? How do people use them? What do you think will happen with these products over the next few years?

Chapter 2

Information

Effective information management must begin by thinking about how people use information—not with how people use machines.

Thomas Davenport[1]

Learning Objectives

Students completing this chapter will:

* understand the importance of information to society and organizations;
* be able to describe the various roles of information in organizational change;
* be able to distinguish between soft and hard information;
* know how managers use information;
* be able to describe the characteristics of common information delivery systems.

INTRODUCTION

There are two key characteristics of the end of the twentieth century: high velocity global change and the emerging power of information organizations. Rapid changes in international relations, the globalization of business, the redrawing of political boundaries, the demise of many dictatorships, and the creation of massive trading blocs are major forces contributing to global change. Organizations are undergoing large scale restructuring as they attempt to reposition themselves to survive the threats and exploit the opportunities presented by this change.

In the last few years, some very powerful and highly profitable information-based organizations have emerged. Microsoft and Bill Gates are to the information age what Standard Oil and John Rockefeller were to the industrial era.[2] Chip maker Intel's dominance of the microprocessor market parallels General Motors' leadership of the auto industry forty years ago. CNN has become the world's news service. These examples demonstrate that information has become a foundation for organizational growth. We can obtain further insights into the value of information by considering the role of information in civilization.

---

[1]T. H. Davenport, "Saving IT's Soul: Human-Centered Information Management," *Harvard Business Review* 72 (2): 119–131 (1994).

[2]W. J. Cook, "The New Rockefeller," *U.S. News & World Report*, 15 February 1993, 64–67.

A HISTORICAL PERSPECTIVE

Three distinct phases of civilization have been identified and recently a possible fourth phase has been suggested. **Agriculture**, the first phase, arose around 3000 B.C. It prospered through the use of iron and tools. Output was recorded in units such as the bushel, a unit of volume often used for measuring the amount of grain harvested from a field. The pioneering cultures of the agricultural phase were China and Egypt. The **industrial revolution**, the second phase, commenced in the United Kingdom in the eighteenth century. Its success was based on harnessing energy, initially in the form of the steam engine and later as the internal combustion engine. The third phase, **information society**, was pioneered by the United States, where it emerged in the late twentieth century. The integrated circuit is the driving force of this society. It is the basis of computer and communication technologies that manipulate and transport data. The keyword in the information society is *data*. It is predicted that the next century will witness the development of a society based on **creation**. The key word of this civilization will be *idea*. The technology will be *idea engineering* and productivity will be measured in terms of *creative output*.[3] The form of this technology will become clearer as the new phase emerges, but groupware (see Chapter 16) and the Internet (see Chapter 17) may represent the beginnings.

A constant across all of these eras is organizational memory, or in its larger form, **social memory**. Writing and paper manufacturing developed about the same time as agricultural societies. Limited writing systems developed about 30,000 years ago. Full writing systems, which have evolved in the last 5000 years, made possible the technological transfer that enabled humanity to move from hunting and gathering to farming. Writing enables the creation of a permanent record of knowledge, and information can accumulate from one generation to the next. Before writing, knowledge was confined by the limits of human memory.

Writing is a means of encoding information. There is also a need for a technology that can store this information for extended periods and support transport of written information. The storage medium advanced from clay tablets (4000 B.C.) through papyrus (3500 B.C.) and parchment (2000 B.C.) to paper (100 A.D.). In this century, a range of new storage media has appeared (e.g., photographic, magnetic, and optical).

Organizational memories emerged with the development of large organizations such as governments, armies, churches, and trading companies. The growth of organizations during the industrial revolution saw a massive increase in the number and size of organizational memories. This growth has continued throughout the twentieth century.

This brief history shows the increasing importance of information to civilization. It demonstrates how advancement was facilitated by the discovery of means for recording and disseminating information. In our society, organizations are the predominant keepers and transmitters of information.

---

[3]T. Murakami, T. Nishiwaki, and others, *Strategy for Creation* (Cambridge, UK: Woodhead Publishing, 1991).

An early writing system.

INFORMATION CHARACTERISTICS

Two useful concepts for describing information are hardness and richness. **Information hardness** is a subjective measure of the accuracy and reliability of an item of information. **Information richness** describes the concept that information can be *rich* or *lean* depending on the information delivery medium.

Information Hardness

In 1812, the Austrian mineralogist Friedrich Mohs proposed a scale of hardness, in order of increasing relative hardness, based on ten relatively common minerals. Each mineral can scratch those with a similar or lower number, but cannot scratch higher numbered minerals.

A similar approach can be used to describe information (see Table 2–1).[4] Market infor-

---

[4]This scale is an extension of work by colleagues of the author at the University of Georgia.

Table 2–1   An Information Hardness Scale

Minerals	Scale	Data
Talc	1	Unidentified source–rumors, gossip, and hearsay
Gypsum	2	Identified non-expert source–opinions, feelings, ideas
Calcite	3	Identified expert source–predictions, speculations, forecasts, estimates
Fluorite	4	Unsworn testimony—explanations, justifications, assessments, interpretations
Apatite	5	Sworn testimony—explanations, justifications, assessments, interpretations
Orthoclass	6	Budgets, formal plans
Quartz	7	News reports, non-financial data, industry statistics, survey data
Topaz	8	Unaudited financial statements, government statistics
Corundum	9	Audited financial statements
Diamond	10	Stock exchange and commodity market data

mation, such as the current price of gold or Apple stock, is the hardest because it is measured extremely accurately. There is no ambiguity about its meaning, and its measurement is highly reliable. In contrast, the softest information, which comes from unidentified sources, is rife with uncertainty.

Audited financial statements are in the corundum zone. They are measured according to standard rules, generally accepted accounting principles which are promulgated by national accounting societies. External auditors monitor application of these standards although there is generally some leeway in their application and sometimes multiple standards for the same item. The use of different accounting principles can lead to different profit and loss statements. As a result, the information in audited financial statements has some degree of uncertainty.

There are degrees of hardness within accounting systems. The hardest data are counts, such as units sold or customers served. These are primary measures of organizational performance. Secondary measures, such as dollar sales and market share, are derived from counts. Managers vary in their preference for primary and secondary measures. Operational managers opt for counts for measuring productivity because they are uncontaminated by price changes and currency fluctuations. Senior managers, because their focus is on financial performance, select secondary measures.

The scratch test provides a convenient and reliable method of assessing the hardness of a mineral. Unfortunately, there is no scratch test for information. Managers must rely on their judgment to assess information hardness.

Although managers want hard information, there are many cases when it is not available. So they compensate by seeking information from several different sources. Although this approach introduces redundancy, this is precisely what the manager seeks. Consistent information from different sources is reassuring.

Information Richness

Information can be described as rich or lean. Information is richest when delivered face-to-face. Conversation permits immediate feedback for verification of meaning. You can always stop the other speaker and ask, "What do you mean?" Face-to-face information delivery is rich because you see the speaker's body language, hear the tone of voice, and natural language is used. A numeric document is the leanest form of information. There is no opportunity for questions, no additional information from body movements and vocal tone. The information richness of some communication media is shown in Table 2-2.

Managers seek rich information when they are trying to resolve equivocality. Equivocality means ambiguity. It means that managers cannot make sense of a situation because they arrive at multiple, conflicting interpretations of the information. An example of an equivocal situation is a class assignment where some of the instructions are missing and others are contradictory (of course, this example is an extremely rare event).

Equivocal situations cannot be resolved by collecting more information because managers are uncertain about what questions to ask and often a clear answer is not possible. Managers reduce equivocality by sharing their interpretations of the available information and reaching a collective understanding of what the information means. By exchanging opinions and recalling their experiences, they try to make sense of an ambiguous situation.

Many of the situations that managers face each day involve a high degree of equivocality. Formal organizational memories, such as databases, are not much help because the information they provide is lean. Managers rely far more on talking with colleagues and using informal organizational memories such as social networks.

Data management is almost exclusively concerned with administering the formal information systems that deliver lean information. Although this is their proper role, data man-

Table 2-2   Information Richness and Communication Media[5]

Richest				Leanest
Face-to-face	Telephone	Personal documents (letters and memos)	Impersonal written doccuments	Numeric documents

---

[5]R. L. Daft and R. H. Lengel, "Organizational Information Requirements, Media Richness, and Structural Design," *Management Science* 32 (5): 554–571 (1986).

agers must realize that they can deliver only a portion of the data required by decision makers. There are information systems, such as groupware, that can help managers to process rich information, and these will be discussed later.

INFORMATION AND ORGANIZATIONAL CHANGE

Organizations are goal-directed. They undergo continual change as they use their resources, people, technology, and financial assets to reach some future desired outcome. Goals are often clearly stated, such as to make a profit of $100 million, win a football championship, or decrease the government deficit by 25% in five years. Goals are often not easily achieved, however, and organizations continually seek information that supports goal attainment. The information they seek falls into three categories: gap, goal setting, and change (see Figure 2–1).

The emergence of an information society also means that information has dual possibilities for change. Information is used to plan change and information is a medium for change.

Goal Setting Information

Organizations set goals or levels of desired performance. Managers need information to establish goals that are challenging but realistic. A common approach is to take the previous goal and stretch it. For example, a company that had a 15 percent return on investment (ROI) might set the new goal at 17 percent ROI. This technique is known as "anchoring and adjusting." Prior performance is used as a basis for setting the new performance standards. The problem with anchoring and adjusting is that it promotes incremental improvement rather than radical change because internal information is used to set performance standards.

Planning is a common approach to goal setting for many enterprises. Recently, some organizations have turned to external information and are using benchmarking as a source of information for goal setting.

Planning

Planning is an important task for senior managers. To set the direction for the company, they need information about consumers' potential demands, and social, economic, technical, and political conditions. They use this information to determine the opportunities and threats facing the organization, thus permitting them to take advantage of opportunities and avoid threats.

Figure 2–1 Organizational information classes

Most of the information for long-term planning comes from sources external to the company. There are thinktanks that analyze trends and publish reports on future conditions. Journal articles[6] and books[7] can be important sources of information about future events. There also will be a demand for some internal information. Major planning decisions, such as building a new plant, will be based on an analysis of internal data (use of existing capacity) and external data (projected customer demand).

Merchandise Planning at Benetton

Benetton uses its customer information base to hone the merchandise offerings in each store according to the demographics of the store's immediate neighborhood. Colors, styles, and sizes are all adjusted to most closely match the needs of local customers. This is one way in which Benetton uses information for merchandise planning.[8]

Benchmarking

Benchmarking[9] establishes goals based on best industry practices. It is founded on the Japanese concept of *dantotsu*, striving to be the "best of the best." Benchmarking is externally directed. Information is sought on those companies, regardless of industry, which demonstrate outstanding performance in the areas to be benchmarked. Their methods are studied, documented, and used to set goals and redesign existing practices for superior performance.

Benchmarking at Ford

In the early 1980s, Ford Motor Company decided it could make its Accounts Payable department more efficient by rationalizing processes and installing new computer systems. Its target was to reduce the more than 500 staff in Accounts Payable in North America by 20 percent. When Ford examined best practice in the automotive industry, however, it was amazed to find that Mazda's Accounts Payable department employed five people. Using Mazda as a benchmark, Ford redefined its target head count reduction and approach to rationalizing accounts payable. It achieved a 75 percent reduction in staff and a simpler and more efficient system.[10]

---

[6]For example, see P. F. Drucker, "The New Productivity Challenge," *Harvard Business Review* 69 (6): 45–53 (1991).

[7]For example, see P. Kennedy, *Preparing for the Twenty-first Century* (New York: Random House, 1993).

[8]Adapted from B. J. Quinn, *Intelligent Enterprise: A Knowledge and Service Based Paradigm for Industry* (New York: Free Press, 1992), 108.

[9]R. C. Camp, *Benchmarking: The Search for Industry Best Practices That Lead to Superior Performance* (Milwaukee: Quality Press, 1989).

[10]Adapted from M. Hammer, "Reengineering Work: Don't Automate, Obliterate," *Harvard Business Review* 68 (4): 104–112 (1990).

Other forms of external information, such as demographic trends, economic forecasts, and competitors' actions can be used in goal setting. External information is valuable because it can force an organization to go beyond incremental goal setting.

Organizations need information to identify feasible, motivating, and challenging goals. Once these goals have been established, organizations need information on the extent to which these goals have been attained.

Gap Information

Because goals are meant to be challenging, there is often a gap between actual and desired performance. Organizations use a number of mechanisms to detect a gap and gain some idea of its size. Problem identification and scorekeeping are two principal methods of providing gap information.

Problem Identification

Business conditions are continually changing because of competitors' actions, trends in consumer demand, and government action. Often these changes are reflected in a gap between expectations and present performance. This gap is known as a problem.

To identify problems, managers use exception reports which are generated only when conditions vary from the established standard. Once a potential problem has been identified, managers collect additional information to confirm that a problem really exists. Problem identification information can also be delivered by printed report or computer screen. Once alerted, the information delivery system needs to shift into high gear. Managers will request rapid delivery of ad hoc reports from a variety of sources. The ideal organizational memory system can adapt smoothly to deliver appropriate information quickly.

Scorekeeping

Keeping track of the "score" provides gap information. Managers ask many questions: How many items did we make yesterday? What were the sales last week? Has our market share increased in the last year? They establish measurement systems to track variables that indicate whether organizational performance is on target. Keeping score is important; managers need to measure in order to manage. Also, measurement lets people know what is important. Once a manager starts to measure something, subordinates surmise that this variable must be important and pay more attention to the factors that influence it.

There are many aspects of the score that a manager can measure. The overwhelming variety of potentially available information is illustrated by the sales output information that a sales manager could track (see Table 2–3). Sales input information (e.g., number of service calls) can also be measured, and there is qualitative information to be considered. Because of time constraints, most managers are forced to limit their attention to ten or fewer key variables singled out by the critical success factors (CSF) method.[11] Scorekeeping information is usually fairly stable, and the delivery system could be a printed report or a computer screen.

Change Information

Once a gap has been detected, managers take action to close it. Change information helps them determine which actions might successfully close the gap. Accurate change information is very valuable because it enables managers to predict the outcome of various actions with some certainty. Unfortunately, change information is usually not very precise, and there are many variables that can influence the effect of any planned change. Nevertheless, organizations spend a great deal of time collecting information to support problem solving and planning.

Problem Solution

Managers collect information to support problem solution. Once a problem has been identified, a manager seeks to find its cause. A decrease in sales could be the result of competitors introducing a new product, an economic downturn, an ineffective advertising campaign,

Table 2–3 Sales Output Tracking Information[12]

Orders:	Number of current customers
	Average order size
	Batting average (orders to calls)
Sales volume:	Dollar sales volume
	Unit sales volume
	By customer type
	By product category
	Translated to market share
	Quota achieved
Margins:	Gross margin
	Net profit
	By customer type
	By product
Customers:	Number of new accounts
	Number of lost accounts
	Percentage of accounts sold
	Number of accounts overdue
	Dollar value of receivables
	Collections of receivables

---

[11]J. F. Rockart, "The Changing Role of the Information Systems Executive: A Critical Success Factors Perspective," *Sloan Management Review* 24 (1): 3–13 (1982).

[12]Adapted from R. E. Anderson et al., *Professional Sales Management* (New York: McGraw-Hill, 1988), 519.

or many other reasons. Data can be collected to test each of these possible causes. Additional data are usually required to support analysis of each alternative. For example, if the sales decrease has been caused by an economic downturn, the manager might use a decision support system to analyze the effect of a price decrease or a range of promotional activities.

Information as a Means of Change

The emergence of an information society means that information can be used as a means of changing an organization's performance. Corporations are creating information-based products and services, adding information to products, and using information to enhance existing performance or gain a competitive advantage. Further insights into the use of information as a change agent are gained by examining customer service, marketing, and empowerment.

Marketing

Marketing is a key strategy for changing organizational performance by increasing sales. Information has become an important component in marketing. Airlines and retailers have established frequent flyer and buyer programs to encourage customer loyalty and gain more information about customers. These systems are heavily dependent on database technology because of the massive volume of data that must be stored. Indeed, without database technology, some marketing strategies could never be implemented.

MCI Seeks Friends

In March 1991, MCI Communications Corp. introduced Friends & Family, an innovative marketing plan that offers a 20 percent discount to pairs of MCI customers who each belong to the plan. Naturally, if you are an MCI customer, you will be inclined to encourage friends and family members you phone frequently to join the scheme. With Friends & Family, MCI turned every one of its customers into an unpaid sales representative.

This marketing plan increased MCI's share of the long distance phone business by 3 to 17 percent—worth some $1.5 billion annually. AT&T, with about two thirds of the market, could not retaliate because its billing database lacked the flexibility to link customers all over the country.[13]

---

[13]Adapted from M. Lewyn, "MCI is Coming Through Loud and Clear. A Marketing Coup has Signaled a Rebound in the Life of the Company," *Business Week*, 25 January 1993, 84, 88.

Database technology offers the opportunity to change the very nature of communications with customers. Broadcast media have been the traditional approach to communication. Advertisements are aired on television or radio, or placed in newspapers or magazines. Database technology can be used to address customers directly. No longer just a mailing list, today's database is a memory of customer relationships—a record of every message and response between the firm and a customer. Some companies keep track of customers' preferences and customize advertisements to their needs. Leading catalog retailers now send customers only those catalogs for which they estimate there is a high probability of a purchase. For example, a customer with a history of buying jazz CDs is sent a catalog of jazz recordings instead of one featuring classical music.[14]

Customer Service

Customer service is a key competitive issue for nearly every organization. American business leaders rank customer service as their most important goal for organizational success.[15] Many of the developed economies are service economies. In the United States, services account for approximately 75 percent of the gross national product and nine out of ten new jobs.[16] Many companies now fight for customers by offering superior customer service. Information is frequently a key to this improved service, as The Valley Bank of Arizona case illustrates.

Get a Loan—Now!

In 1989 Valley Bank of Arizona introduced the fifteen minute loan. It automated the lending process to reduce service time from several days to fifteen minutes. Bankers enter customer information into their personal computers, and the automated system handles the rest. It retrieves data from the customer's file, does a credit bureau check, approves the loan, and prints documentation for the client to sign. For loans that require additional processing, the banker can transmit details to a loan center where a loan officer makes the decision and transmits the result to the banker.[17]

In services, execution is everything. The interaction with the customer has been described as the moment of truth when the customer discovers whether the organization's promises are real. Some organizations are almost obsessive in their attention to customers.

---

[14]R. C. Blattberg and J. Deighton, "Interactive Marketing: Exploiting the Age of Addressability," *Sloan Management Review* 33 (1): 5–14 (1991).

[15]R. M. Kanter, "Transcending Business Boundaries: 12,000 World Managers View Change," *Harvard Business Review* 69 (3): 151–164 (1991).

[16]V. Zeithaml, A. Parasuraman, and L. L. Berry, *Delivering Quality Service: Balancing Customer Perceptions and Expectations* (New York: Free Press, 1990).

[17]Adapted from S. Bergsman, "Valley National Streamlines Loan Processes," *American Banker*, 15 March 1989, 9–10.

Lost in Mouse Land

Disney World in Orlando, Florida makes every effort to ensure that its customers have an enjoyable experience. It even maintains a database that records which parking lots are filled at what time of the day. This information is invaluable in helping those families who cannot remember where they parked. Using a family's time of arrival, which it can almost always remember, Disney employees can locate the lost car in about twenty minutes.[18]

Empowerment

Empowerment has attracted considerable attention in the business press because many high performing businesses utilize it. In general terms, empowerment means giving employees greater freedom to make decisions. More precisely, it is sharing with frontline employees:[19]

- information about the organization's performance;
- rewards based on the organization's performance;
- knowledge and information that enables employees to understand and contribute to organizational performance;
- power to make decisions that influence organizational direction and performance.

Notice that information features prominently in the process. A critical component is giving employees access to the information they need to perform their tasks with a high degree of independence and discretion. Information is empowerment. An important task for data managers is to develop and install systems that give employees ready access to organizational memory. By linking employees to organizational memory, data managers play a pivotal role in empowering people.

Empowerment at Arthur Andersen

Arthur Andersen and Co., a leading information technology consultant, has 51,000 people in 234 offices in 54 countries. Andersen captures client history in a Customer Reference File. It stores tax, accounting, and consulting information on a CD-ROM, which field auditors can take onto a customer's site. The Chicago headquarters maintains subject files, a storehouse of information on problems and solutions encountered by auditors and consultants. An electronic bulletin board enables personal interaction between its people to discuss important problems. It also permits professionals to broadcast their problems, and anyone within Andersen with expertise to solve the problem can respond to the originator. By providing this access, Andersen is empowering its staff, giving them the information to provide high quality solutions to its clients.[20]

Organizations believe that empowerment contributes to organizational performance by increasing the quality of products and services. Together, empowerment and information are mechanisms of planned change.

INFORMATION AND MANAGERIAL WORK

Managers are a key device for implementing organizational change. Because they frequently use organizational memories in their normal activities as a source of information about change and as a means of implementing change, it is crucial for organizational memory designers to understand how managers work. Failure to take account of managerial behavior can result in a technically sound, but rarely used, system because it does not fit the social system.

Studies over several decades reveal a very consistent pattern:[21] managerial work is very fragmented. Managers spend an average of ten minutes on any task, and their day is organized into brief periods of concentrated attention to a variety of tasks. They work unrelentingly and are frequently interrupted by unexpected disturbances. Managers are action oriented and rely on intuition and judgment far more than contemplative analysis of information.

Executives strongly prefer oral communication. They spend a great deal of time conversing directly or by telephone. Managers use interpersonal communication to establish networks, which they later use as a source of information and a way to make things happen. The continual flow of verbal information helps them make sense of events and lets them feel the organizational pulse.

Managers rarely use formal reporting systems. They do not spend their time analyzing computer reports or querying databases, but resort to formal reports to confirm evidence should interpersonal communications suggest there is a problem. Even when managers are provided with a purpose built, ultra friendly executive information system (EIS), their behavior changes very little. They may access a few screens during the day, but oral communication is still their preferred method of data gathering and dissemination.

Managers' Information Requirements

Managers have certain requirements of the information they receive. These expectations shape organizational memory's content and how it is processed.

---

[18]Adapted from *Hot-Line!* (Boston: The Forum Corporation, 22 June 1987).

[19]D. E. Bowen and E. E. Lawler III, "The Empowerment of Service Workers: What, Why, How, and When," *Sloan Management Review* 33 (3): 31–39 (1992).

[20]Adapted from B. J. Quinn, *Intelligent Enterprise: A Knowledge and Service Based Paradigm for Industry* (New York: Free Press, 1992) 122.

[21]H. Mintzberg, *The Nature of Managerial Work* (New York: Harper & Row, 1973) and J. P. Kotter, *The General Managers* (New York: Free Press, 1982).

Managers expect to receive information that is useful for their current task under existing business conditions. Unfortunately, managerial tasks can change rapidly—the interlinked, global, economic environment is highly turbulent. Since managers' expectations are not stable, the information delivery system must be sufficiently flexible to meet changing requirements.

Managers' demand for information varies with their perception of its hardness; they require only one source that scores 10 on the information hardness scale. The Nikkei Index at the close of today's market is the same whether you read it in the *Asian Wall Street Journal*, *The Western Australian*, or hear it on CNN. As perceived hardness decreases, managers demand more information (see Figure 2–2), hoping that more information will resolve uncertainty and lead to an accurate assessment of a situation. When the reliability of a source is questionable, managers seek confirmation from other sources. If a number of different sources provide consistent information, a manager gains confidence in its accuracy.

It is not unusual, therefore, to have a manager seek information from a database report, a conversation with a subordinate, and a contact in another organization. If she gets essentially the same information from each source, she has the confirmation she seeks. This means each organizational memory system should be designed to minimize redundancy, but different components of organizational memory can supply overlapping information.

Managers' Needs for Information Vary Accordingly With Their Responsibilities

Operational managers need detailed, short-term information to deal with well-defined problems in areas such as sales, service, and production. This information comes almost exclusively from internal sources that report recent performance in the managers' area. A sales manager may get weekly reports of sales by each person under his supervision.

As managers move up the organizational hierarchy, their information needs both expand and contract. They become responsible for a wider range of activities and are charged with planning the future of the organization, which requires information from external sources on long-term economic, demographic, political, and social trends. Despite this long-term focus, top level managers also monitor short-term, operational performance. In this instance, they need less detail and more summary and exception reports on a small number of key indicators. To avoid information overload as new layers of information needs are added, the level of detail on the old layers naturally must decline, as illustrated in Figure 2–3.

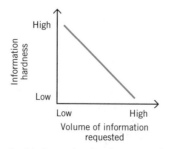

Figure 2–2   Relationship of perceived information hardness to volume of information requested

Figure 2–3   Management level and information need

Information Satisficing

Because managers face making many decisions in a short period, most do not have the time or resources to collect and interpret all the information they need to make the best decision. Consequently, they are often forced to satisfice[22]—they accept the first satisfactory decision they discover. They also satisfice in their information search, collecting only enough information to make a satisfactory decision.

Ultimately, information satisficing leads to lower quality decision making. But if information technology can be used to accelerate delivery and processing of the right information, then managers should be able to move from selecting the first satisfactory decision to selecting the best of several satisfactory decisions.

INFORMATION DELIVERY SYSTEMS

Most organizations have a variety of delivery systems to provide information to managers. Developed over many years, these systems are being integrated to give managers better access to information. There are two aspects to information delivery. First, there is a need for software that accesses an organizational memory, extracts the required data, and formats it for presentation. We can use the categories of organizational memories introduced in Chapter 1 to describe the software side of information delivery systems (see Table 2–4). The second aspect of delivery is the hardware that gets information from a computer to the manager. We will briefly discuss information delivery systems at this point and deal in depth with some more common systems in Section 4.

Software

Software is used to retrieve data from and store it in organizational memory. Unfortunately, there is usually tight coupling between software and the format of an organizational memory. For example, a relational database management system can access tables but not decision

---

[22]H. A. Simon, *Administrative Behavior: A Study of Decision-making Processes in Administrative Organization*, 3rd ed. (New York: Free Press, 1976).

Table 2–4   Information Delivery Systems Software

Organizational Memory	Delivery Systems
People	Conversation
	Electronic mail
	Meeting
	Report
	Groupware
Files	Management information system (MIS)
Documents	Office automation system (OAS)
Images	Imaging processing system (IPS)
Graphics	Computer aided design (CAD)
	Geographic information system (GIS)
Voice	Voice mail
	Voice recording system
Mathematical model	Decision support system (DSS)
Knowledge	Expert system (ES)
Decisions	Conversation
	Meeting
	Report
	Electronic mail
	Groupware

support models. Even then, not every relational database management system can access all tables. This tight coupling is particularly frustrating for managers who often need information from several organizational memories. A quick glance at Table 2–4 shows that there are many different information delivery systems. We will discuss each of these briefly to illustrate the lack of integration of organizational memories.

Verbal Exchange

Conversations, meetings, and oral reporting are commonly used methods of information delivery. Indeed, managers show a strong preference for verbal exchange as a method for gathering information.

Voice Mail

Voice mail digitizes a message and stores it for later retrieval. When the recipient is ready to listen to the message, it can be retrieved and replayed. This facility is useful for people who are frequently away from their offices because it supports asynchronous communication, the two parties to the conversation are not simultaneously connected by a communication line.

Voice mail systems also can store many prerecorded messages that can be selectively replayed using the keypad of a touch tone phone. Organizations use this feature to support standard customer queries. For example, most mutual funds have voice mail systems that enable investors to check the value of their holdings by entering a personal identification number and the code of their fund.

Electronic Mail

Electronic mail (e-mail) is increasingly becoming an important informal system of information delivery. It too supports asynchronous messaging, though it is less costly than voice mail for international communication. Chapter 17 covers e-mail in greater detail.

Written Reports

Formal, written reports have a long history in organizations. Before electronic communication, they were the main form of information delivery for vast organizations such as the British Empire. They still have a role in organizations because they are an effective method of integrating information of varying hardness and from a variety of organizational memories. For example, a report can contain text, tables, graphics, and images.

Written reports are often supplemented by a verbal presentation of the key points in the report. Such a presentation enhances the information delivered because the audience has an opportunity to ask questions and get an immediate response.

Meetings

Because managers spend between 30 and 80 percent of their time in meetings, these become a key source of information.

Groupware

Since meetings occupy so much managerial time and in many cases are poorly planned and managed, organizations are looking for improvements. Groupware is a general term applied to a range of software systems designed to improve some aspect of group work. For example, Lotus Notes is used to accelerate the exchange of information for a wide variety of business tasks (e.g., expense reporting). Other products such as GroupSystems and Resolver are used for electronic brainstorming and issue evaluation.

Groupware is becoming an important means of information delivery. Like conversations and e-mail, it is excellent at tapping soft information and the informal side of organizational memory. Groupware is discussed in depth in Chapter 16.

Management Information System

Management information systems (MIS) are a common method of delivering information from file-based organizational memory. Information can be delivered on paper or via a terminal. A preplanned query is often used to extract the data. Managers who have developed some skills in using a query language might create their own custom reports as the interface to file-based memory becomes friendlier and query languages become more powerful and easier to use.

Preplanned reports often contain too much or too detailed information because they are written in anticipation of a manager's needs. Customized reports do not have these shortcomings, but they are more expensive and time consuming for programmers to write.

MIS will remain a major vehicle for information delivery because files are widely used to store data about many business activities. Large scale transaction processing systems (TPS) are used to capture information about routine transactions that is then stored in files.

Office Automation System

Office automation systems are commonly used for document preparation, communicating, and scheduling. Word processing, desk top publishing, or hypertext software can be used for document preparation. Electronic and voice mail support communication and electronic calendars are typically used for scheduling.

Documents are the major feature of the organizational memory accessed via office automation software. Local area networks (LANs) support the easy sharing of documents. However, unless hypertext software has been used to create linkages within the document, access is often inconvenient, requiring the user to search a word-processed document sequentially.

A major problem in document retrieval is incompatibility because people within an organization can use a variety of word processors on different operating systems. Conversion programs can translate the text and maintain formatting, but embedded graphics can be lost.

Image Processing System

An image processing system (IPS) captures data using a scanner, which digitizes an image. Images in the form of letters, reports, illustrations, and graphics always have been an important type of organizational memory. An IPS permits these forms of information to be captured electronically and disseminated.

Computer–aided Design

Computer–aided design (CAD) is used extensively to prepare graphics. For example, engineers use CAD in product design and architects use it for building design. These plans are part of organizational memory. Access to this information typically requires expensive hardware and software.

Geographic Information System

A geographic information system (GIS) stores graphical data about a geographic region. Many cities use a GIS to record details of roads, utilities, and services. This graphical information is another form of organizational memory. Again, special purpose software is required to access and present the information stored in this memory.

Decision Support System

A decision support system (DSS) is frequently a computer-based mathematical model of a problem. DSS software, available in a range of packages, permits the model and data to be retrieved and executed. The user can often change the values of model parameters to investigate various solutions.

Expert System

An expert system (ES) has the captured knowledge of someone who is particularly skillful at solving a certain type of problem. It is convenient to think of an ES as a set of rules. An ES is typically used interactively as it asks the decision maker questions and uses the responses to determine the action to recommend.

Hardware

There are a number of ways to use hardware to deliver physically information. In the early days of computing, the approach was not delivery but collection. The user went to the machine to execute a program and collect the output. This approach was soon supplemented by hand delivery of computer–produced reports. Regular computer tasks were scheduled, and the output delivered using internal and external mail systems.

The next advance was to connect remote terminals, printers, and other devices to a mainframe or minicomputer; the architecture is known as host/terminal. Using this approach, data are processed on the host computer and delivered electronically to the client's terminal or printer. This method was dominant in the 1980s.

The development of personal computers, however, meant that users could do some of their processing at their desk, although they soon realized that much of the data they needed was located on mainframes or minicomputers. As a result, two new technologies were developed: local area networks and client/server.

LANs are used to connect collections of personal computers together and then to computing systems on mainframes or minicomputers. When these systems were first introduced, personal computers were frequently relegated to the role of a terminal on a mainframe network. There was minimal use of the processing capacity of the personal computer; most processing occurred on the host.

Client/server technology was introduced to take advantage of the low cost computing power of microcomputers. Client/server systems maintain organizational memory on the server—any form of fast computer with large secondary storage capacity—and deliver data to the client. Processing of data to information occurs on the client machine.

Information Integration

You can think of organizational memory as a vast, disorganized data warehouse. A fundamental problem for most organizations is that their memory is fragmented across a wide variety of formats and technologies. Too frequently, there is a one-to-one correspondence between an organizational memory for a particular functional area and the software delivery system. For example, sales information is delivered by the sales system, production information by the production system, and customer correspondence by an imaging processing system. Of course, this is not a very desirable situation because managers want all the information they need, regardless of its source or format, preferably on one screen or at least on as few screens as possible.

An executive information system (EIS).

A response to providing access to the disorganized data warehouse has been the development of software, such as an executive information system (EIS), that can integrate information from a variety of delivery systems. This situation is shown in Figure 2–4. An important task of an EIS is to integrate and present information from multiple organizational memories. At present, EIS software primarily integrates information from various independent files and databases although some systems do include access to e-mail and DSS applications.

Information integration software is really a dirty (and not necessarily very quick) fix for a very critical need. The real requirement is to integrate organizational memory so that digital data (tables, images, graphics, and voice) can be stored together. The ideal situation is shown in Figure 2–5: the entire organizational memory accessed as a single unit via one information delivery system that meets all the client's requirements.

There is a long-term trend of data integration. Early information systems were based on independent files. As these systems were rewritten, database technology was used to integrate independent files into databases. This integration dealt with files and is still an ongoing feature of many organizations. The next level of integration is to get all forms of data together. For example, the customer database might contain file data (e.g., customer name and address) and image data (e.g., correspondence from the customer, photograph of an accident scene).

Information Integration at BP

BP Australasia Ltd. has an information integrator who is responsible for:

- getting data to the people who need it;
- deploying systems to optimize business processes;
- providing access to data in several different databases;
- coordination of systems integration.

An information integrator typically reports to the CIO and consults on all projects designed to improve systems integration. This challenging role requires a person with interpersonal skills and expertise in information technology.[23]

SUMMARY

Information has become a key foundation for organizational growth. New information-based organizations are very powerful and growing rapidly. The information society is founded on computer and communications technology. The accumulation of knowledge requires a capacity to encode and share information. Hard information is very exact. Soft in-

Figure 2–4   Information integration—the present situation

---

[23]Adapted from F. M. Bruce, "The Information Integrator," *Computerworld*, 7 September 1992, 91–92.

Figure 2–5   The ideal organizational memory and information delivery system

formation is extremely imprecise. Rich information exchange occurs in face-to-face conversation. Numeric reports are an example of lean information. Organizations use information to set goals, determine the gap between goals and achievements, determine actions to reach goals, and create new products and services to enhance organizational performance. Managers depend more on informal communication systems than on formal reporting systems. They expect to receive information that meets their current, everchanging needs. Operational managers need short-term information. Senior executives require mainly long-term information but still have a need for both short- and medium-term information. When managers face time constraints, they collect only enough information to make a satisfactory decision. Most organizations have a wide variety of poorly integrated information delivery systems. Organizational memory should be integrated to provide managers with one interface to an organization's information stores.

KEY TERMS AND CONCEPTS

Benchmarking
Change information
Empowerment
Gap information
Global change
Goal setting information
Information as a means of change
Information delivery systems
Information hardness
Information integration

Information organization
Information requirements
Information richness
Information satisficing
Information society
Managerial work
Organizational change
Phases of civilization
Social memory

REFERENCES AND ADDITIONAL READINGS

Bessen, J. "Riding the Marketing Information Wave." *Harvard Business Review* 71, no. 5 (1993):150–160.

Clemons, E. K., and Row, M. C. "Information Technology at Rosenbluth Travel: Competitive

Advantage in a Rapidly Growing Global Service Company." *Journal of Management Information Systems* 8, no. 2 (1991): 53–79.

Davenport, T. H. "Savings IT's Soul: Human-Centered Information Management." *Harvard Business Review* 72, no. 2 (1994): 119–131.

Eccles, R. G. "The Performance Measurement Manifesto." *Harvard Business Review* 69, no. 1 (1991): 131–137.

Lindsey, D.; P. H. Cheney; G. M. Kasper; and B. Ives. "TELCOT: An Application of Information Technology for Competitive Advantage in the Cotton Industry." *MIS Quarterly* 14, no. 4 (1990): 347–357.

Quinn, B. J. "The Intelligent Enterprise: A New Paradigm." *Academy of Management Executive* 6, no. 4 (1992): 48–63.

Sisodia, R. S. "Singapore Invests in the Nation-Corporation." *Harvard Business Review* 70, no. 3 (1992): 40–42, 44, 45, 48–50.

EXERCISES

1. What is different about the 1990s compared to the 1980s?
2. Why are Intel and Microsoft growing so rapidly?
3. Why are paper and writing systems important?
4. What is the difference between soft and hard information?
5. What is the difference between rich and lean information exchange?
6. What are three major types of information connected with organizational change?
7. What is benchmarking? When might a business use benchmarking?
8. What is gap information?
9. Give some examples of how information is used as a means of change.
10. What sort of information do senior managers want?
11. Describe the differences between the way managers handle hard and soft information.
12. What is information satisficing?
13. Describe an incident where you used information satisficing.
14. Give some examples of common information delivery systems.
15. Who uses an EIS?
16. What is a GIS? Who might use a GIS?
17. What is groupware?
18. Why is information integration a problem?
19. Select two public companies listed on the stock exchange in your country. One of these should be an information-based organization (e.g., Microsoft) and the other an industrial era company (e.g., Ford). Compare the PE ratios, assets, revenues, and number of employees. What do you observe? What does this mean?
20. How "hard" is an exam grade?
21. Could you develop a test for the hardness of a piece of information?

22. Is it worth storing very soft information in formal organizational memory? If not, where might you draw the line?

23. If you had just failed your database exam, would you use rich or lean media to tell a parent or spouse about the result?

24. Interview a business person to determine his/her firm's critical success factors (CSFs). Remember, a CSF is something the firm must do right to be successful. Generally a firm has around seven CSFs. For the firm's top three CSFs, identify the information that will measure whether the CSF is being achieved.

25. If you were managing a fast food store, what information would you want to track store performance? Classify this information as short-, medium-, or long-term information.

26. Interview a manager. Identify the information that person uses to manage the company. Classify this information as short-, medium-, or long-term information. Comment on your findings.

27. Why is organizational memory like a data warehouse? What needs to be done to make good use of this data warehouse?

28. What information are you collecting to help determine your career or find a job? What problems are you having collecting this information? Is the information mainly hard or soft?

CASE QUESTIONS

Imagine you are the new owner of The Expeditioner (see the end of Chapter 1).

1. What information would you request to determine the present performance of the organization?

2. What information would help you to establish goals for The Expeditioner? What goals would you set?

3. What information would you want to help you assist you in changing The Expeditioner?

4. How could you use information to achieve your goals?

Data Modeling and SQL

It is a capital mistake to theorize before one has data.

Sir Arthur Conan Doyle, "Scandal in Bohemia," *The Adventures of Sherlock Holmes,* 1891.

The relational model is currently the most popular method for implementing organizational databases. This section details two key skills, data modeling and query formation, that are required to take advantage of the relational model, and concentrates on the design and use of relational databases. This very abrupt change in focus is part of our plan to give you a dual understanding of data management. Section 1 is the managerial perspective, and this section covers technical skills development. Competent data managers are able to accommodate both views and apply whichever perspective, or some blend of the two, is appropriate for particular circumstances.

In Chapter 1, many forms of organizational memory were identified, but in this section we focus on files and their components. Thus, only the file's branch of organizational memory is detailed in Figure S2–1.

A collection of related files is frequently called a database. Describing the collection of files as related means that it has a common purpose (e.g., data about students). Sometimes files are also called tables, and there are synonyms for some other terms. (Figure S2–1 shows the alternative names in parentheses.) Files contain records (or rows). Each record contains the data for one instance of the data the file stores. For example, if the file stores data about a student, each record will contain data about a single student. Records have fields (or columns) that store the fine detail of each instance (e.g., student's first name, last name, and date of birth). Fields are composed of characters (a,b,c,..., 1,2,3..., %, $, #, etc.). A byte, a unit of storage sufficient to store a single character, consists of a string of eight contiguous bits or binary digits.

The organizational memory hierarchy is useful because it identifies three database design questions that must be addressed:

Figure S2–1   Organizational memory hierarchy

- What collection of files should the database contain?
- How are these files related?
- What fields should each record in the file contain?

The first objective of this section is to describe data modeling, a technique for answering the first two questions. Data modeling helps you to understand the structure and meaning of data, which is necessary before a database can be created. Once a database has been designed, built, and loaded with data, the aim is to use it to satisfy management's requests for information. Thus the second objective of this section is to teach you how to write queries for a relational database. The learning of modeling and querying will be intertwined, making it easier to grasp the intent of database design and to understand why data modeling is so critical to making a database an effective tool for managerial decision making.

Chapter 3 covers modeling a single entity and querying a single table database. This is the simplest database that can be created and used. As you will soon discover, a **data model** is a graphical description of the components of a database. One of these components is an **entity**, some feature of the real world about which data must be stored. This section also introduces the notions of a **data definition language** (DDL), which is used to describe a database, and a **data manipulation language** (DML), which is used to maintain and query a database. Subsequent chapters in this section cover advanced data modeling concepts and querying capabilities.

Chapter 3

The Single Entity

I want to be alone.

Attributed to Greta Garbo

Learning Objectives

Students completing this chapter will be able to:
* model a single entity;
* define a single database;
* write queries for a single table database.

Alice pulled another folder out of the seemingly endless collection supplied by Mr. Mainwaring, the lawyer from Cholmondeley, Crespigny, Majoribanks, and St. John. She had certainly made one decision—to find a lawyer called Smith or Brown. It was most disconcerting to be unable to remember how to pronounce the man's name. The folder, boldly titled "Shares," contained a single sheet of paper on which was listed the names of ten companies and the number of shares held in each company. Alice thought, "This is just a mass of data. What I really need to know is how much each of these shares is worth and its annual dividend." She forcefully pressed the call button to summon the attendant for a copy of the *Financial Times*.

INTRODUCTION

Because the processing of business transactions and managerial decision making requires a database that can accurately mirror real world relationships, we will use the generally accepted relational database model. Like most construction projects, building a relational database must be preceded by a design phase. Data modeling, our design technique, is a method for creating a plan or blueprint of a database.

Rather than getting bogged down with a "theory first, application later" approach to database design and use, we will start with application. We will get back to theory when you have some experience in data modeling and database querying. After all, you did not learn to talk

Table 3–1   A Single Table

Firm's code	Firm's name	Price	Quantity	Dividend	PE ratio
FC	Freedonia Copper	27.50	10,529	1.84	16
PT	Patagonian Tea	55.25	12,635	2.50	10
AR	Abyssinian Ruby	31.82	22,010	1.32	13
SLG	Sri Lankan Gold	50.37	32,868	2.68	16
ILZ	Indian Lead & Zinc	37.75	6,390	3.00	12
BE	Burmese Elephant	.07	154,713	0.01	3
BS	Bolivian Sheep	12.75	231,678	1.78	11
NG	Nigerian Geese	35.00	12,323	1.68	10
CS	Canadian Sugar	52.78	4,716	2.50	15
ROF	Royal Ostrich Farms	33.75	1,234,923	3.00	6

by first studying sentence formation, you just started by learning and using simple words. We start with the simplest data model, a single entity, and the simplest database, a single table (see for example Table 3–1).

MODELING A SINGLE ENTITY DATABASE

The simplest database contains information about one **entity**, which is some real-world thing. Some entities are physical—CUSTOMER,[1] ORDER, and STUDENT; others are conceptual—WORK ASSIGNMENT and AUTHORSHIP. We represent an entity by a rectangle: Figure 3–1 shows a representation of the entity SHARE.[2] The name of the entity is shown in singular form in all capitals in the top part of the rectangle.

An entity has characteristics or attributes. An **attribute** is a discrete element of data; it is not usually broken down into smaller components. Attributes describe an entity and contain the entity's data we want to store. Some attributes of the entity SHARE are: identification code, firm name, price, quantity owned, dividend, and price-to-earnings ratio. Attributes are shown below the entity's name (Figure 3–2). Notice that we refer to share price, rather than price, to avoid confusion if there should be another entity with an attribute called price. Attribute names must be carefully selected so that they are self-explanatory and unique. For instance, share dividend is easily recognized as belonging to the entity SHARE.

An entity typically has multiple occurrences or instances. An **instance** is a particular occurrence of an entity (e.g., the facts for Freedonia Copper). To avoid confusion, each instance of an entity needs to be uniquely identified. Consider the case of a customer billing. In most cases, a request to bill Smith $100 cannot be accurately processed because a firm typically has

---

[1]The convention in this book is to use all uppercase for an entity's name.
[2]Share can also be known as stock, equity, or security.

Figure 3-1   The entity SHARE

Figure 3-2   The entity SHARE and its attributes

many customers called Smith. If a firm has carefully controlled procedures for ensuring that each customer has a unique means of identification, then a request to bill customer number 1789 $100 can be accurately processed. An attribute or collection of attributes that uniquely identify an instance of an entity is called an **identifier**. The identifier for the entity SHARE is share code, a unique identifier assigned by the stock exchange.

There may be several attributes, or combinations of attributes, that are feasible identifiers for an instance of an entity. Attributes that are identifiers are prefixed by an asterisk. Figure 3-3 shows an example of a representation of an entity, its attributes, and identifier.

In summary, entities are things in the environment about which we wish to store information. Attributes describe an entity. An entity must have a unique identifier.

CREATING A SINGLE TABLE DATABASE

The next stage is to translate the data model into a relational database. The translation rules are very direct:

- Each entity becomes a table;
- The entity name becomes the table name;
- Each attribute becomes a column;
- The identifier becomes the primary key.

The American National Standards Institute's (ANSI) recommended language for relational database definition and manipulation is **Structured Query Language** (SQL), which is both a **data definition language** (DDL) and a **data manipulation language** (DML). It is a

Figure 3-3   The entity SHARE is uniquely identified by its attribute share code

common standard for describing and querying databases and is available with many commercial relational database products, including DB2, SQL/DS, Oracle, R:BASE, Microsoft Access, and Microsoft FoxPro.

SQL uses the **CREATE** statement to define a table. It is not a particularly friendly command, and most products have easier methods for defining tables, but it is the standard. Because some relational databases restrict table and column names to eight characters, it is often necessary to abbreviate a data model's attribute names, as has been done in this example for the data shown in Table 3–1.

Defining a Table

The CREATE command to establish a table called SHR[3] is:

```
CREATE TABLE SHR
    (SHRCODE       CHAR(3)       NOT NULL,
    SHRFIRM        CHAR(20),
    SHRPRICE       DECIMAL(6,2),
    SHRQTY         DECIMAL(8),
    SHRDIV         DECIMAL(5,2),
    SHRPE          DECIMAL(2),
      PRIMARY KEY (SHRCODE))
```

The first line of the command names the table; subsequent lines describe each of the columns in it. The first component is the name of the column (e.g., SHRCODE). The second component is the data type (e.g., CHAR) and its length is shown in parentheses. SHRFIRM is a character field of length 20, which means it can store 20 characters, including spaces. SHRDIV stores a decimal number that can be as large as 999.99 because its total length is 5 digits and there are 2 digits to the right of the decimal point. Some examples of allowable data types are shown in Table 3–2. The third component (e.g., NOT NULL), which is optional, indicates any instance which cannot have null values. A column will have a null value when it is either unknown or not applicable. In the case of the share table, SHRCODE must be defined for each instance in the database because its purpose is to uniquely identify each row. In this example, all other attributes may be null or undefined.

The final line of the CREATE statement defines SHRCODE as the **primary key**, the unique identifier for SHR. When a primary key is defined, the relational database management system (RDBMS) will enforce the requirement that the primary key is unique. In other words, before any row is added to the table SHR, the RDBMS will first check that the value of SHRCODE for the new row does not already exist as a value for SHRCODE in an existing row of SHR. If an identical value exists, the RDBMS will not permit the new row to be inserted. The specification that SHRCODE is not null and is the primary key is known as the **entity integrity rule**. It simply means every row must have a unique, non–null pri-

---

[3]It is usual practice to give the table the same name as the entity; however, this is not always possible. In this case, SHARE is not permissible because it is a reserved word in SQL; thus we have used SHR as the table name.

Table 3–2   Some Allowable Data Types

Numeric	INTEGER	A 31-bit signed binary value
	SMALLINT	A 15-bit signed binary value
	FLOAT(p)	A scientific format number of p binary digits precision
	DECIMAL(p,q)	A packed decimal number of p digits total length; q decimal places to the right of the decimal point may be specified
String	CHAR(n)	A fixed length character string of n characters
	VARCHAR(n)	A variable length character string up to n characters
	LONG VARCHAR	A variable length character string
Date/time	DATE	Date in the form *yyyymmdd*
	TIME	Time in the form *hhmmss*
	TIMESTAMP	A combination of date and time to the nearest microsecond
Graphic	GRAPHIC(n)	A fixed length graphic string of n 16-bit bytes
	VARGRAPHIC(n)	A variable length graphic string of up to n 16-bit bytes
	LONG VARGRAPHIC	A variable length graphic string of 16-bit bytes

mary key. Allowing the primary key to take a null value implies there is a row of SHR that cannot be uniquely identified. Thus, NOT NULL should always be specified for the primary key.

Table 3–2 shows some of the data types supported by IBM's relational database, DB2. Other implementations of the relational model may support some of these data types and additional ones. For example, FoxPro supports data types of character, numeric, float, date, logical (the item can be true or false), memo (a variable length character string), general (for objects), and picture. It is a good idea to review the available data types in your relational database system before defining your first table.

Inserting Rows into a Table

The rows of a table store instances of an entity. A particular shareholding, say Freedonia Copper, is an example of an instance of the entity SHARE. The SQL statement INSERT is used to add rows to a table. Although most implementations of the relational model have an easier method of row insertion, the INSERT command is defined for completeness. The following command adds one row to the table SHR:

```
INSERT INTO SHR
    (SHRCODE,SHRFIRM,SHRPRICE,SHRQTY,SHRDIV,SHRPE)
    VALUES ('FC','Freedonia Copper',27.5,10529,1.84,16)
```

There is a one-to-one correspondence between a column name in the first set of parentheses and a value in the second set of parentheses. That is, SHRCODE has the value 'FC', SHRFIRM the value 'Freedonia Copper,' and so on.

The list of field names can be omitted when values are inserted in all fields of the table, so the above expression could be written:

```
INSERT INTO SHR
    VALUES ('FC','Freedonia Copper',27.5,10529,1.84,16)
```

The data for the SHR table shown in Table 3−3 will be used in subsequent examples. If you have ready access to a relational database, it is a good idea to create a table and enter the data. Then you will be able to use these data to practice querying the table.

Notice that SHRCODE is underlined in the relational table to show it is a primary key. In the data model it has an asterisk prefix to indicate it is an identifier. In the relational model it becomes a primary key, a column that guarantees that each row of the table can be uniquely addressed.

Query−By−Example (QBE)[4] is the other common method for working with a relational database. QBE is easier to use than SQL because you make entries in a table rather than writing commands. There is no standard for QBE. Most implementations look similar, and once you have mastered one version it is easy to use another. We will use IBM's DB2 implementation of QBE in our examples. Microcomputer-based RDBMs, such as Microsoft Access, R:BASE, and Paradox, have versions of QBE. The Microsoft Access version is particularly easy to use.

QBE can be used for data entry. The first step is to draft a skeleton for the required table:

```
SHR | SHRCODE | SHRFIRM            | SHRPRICE | SHRQTY | SHRDIV | SHRPE   |
----+---------+--------------------+----------+--------+--------+---------+
    |         |                    |          |        |        |         |
```

Table 3−3   SHR Data

SHR						
SHRCODE	**SHRFIRM**	**SHRPRICE**	**SHRQTY**	**SHRDIV**	**SHRPE**	
FC	Freedonia Copper	27.50	10,529	1.84	16	
PT	Patagonian Tea	55.25	12,635	2.50	10	
AR	Abyssinian Ruby	31.82	22,010	1.32	13	
SLG	Sri Lankan Gold	50.37	32,868	2.68	16	
ILZ	Indian Lead & Zinc	37.75	6,390	3.00	12	
BE	Burmese Elephant	.07	154,713	0.01	3	
BS	Bolivian Sheep	12.75	231,678	1.78	11	
NG	Nigerian Geese	35.00	12,323	1.68	10	
CS	Canadian Sugar	52.78	4,716	2.50	15	
ROF	Royal Ostrich Farms	33.75	1,234,923	3.00	6	

---

[4]M. M. Zloof, "Query By Example," in *Proceedings of the NCC* 44, May 1975. Zloof invented QBE.

The skeleton table has a column heading for the table name (the far left column) and each of the columns in the table. Codes that refer to the entire table are placed in the table name column. Codes or data that refer to a particular column are placed under that particular column name.

Once a skeleton table is available, data entry is straightforward. Put the code "I." under SHR to specify row insertion. Enter data for each column under the respective column headings. If a field contains embedded spaces (e.g., a firm's name) then surround it by single quotes. A sample entry is:

```
SHR | SHRCODE | SHRFIRM          | SHRPRICE | SHRQTY | SHRDIV | SHRPE  |
----+---------+------------------+----------+--------+--------+--------+
I.  | FC      | 'Freedonia Copper'| 27.50   | 10529  | 1.84   | 16     |
```

Using QBE for data input is like entering data in a spreadsheet. Indeed, most database systems have adopted a spreadsheet format for data entry, and this is typically very easy to use. We recommend that you use the spreadsheet method because the SQL INSERT command is tedious.

Data Mining

One of American Express Co.'s most cherished possessions is 500 billion bytes of data on how customers have used its 35 million charge cards to spend $350 billion since 1991. These data are stored at a secret, guarded location. American Express wants to mine the data to discover marketing opportunities. For example, it can use the database to directly market travel to Europe to all customers who have travelled there in the last three years.

Because data mining can be rather expensive when mainframe computers are used, American Express and other firms with a rich lode of data are using parallel computers, which are based on harnessing tens or hundreds of standard microchips. Whereas a mainframe computer processes data one chunk at a time, a parallel machine can break a query into multiple tasks to be performed by separate processors. The result is that queries can be processed faster and at lower cost. Parallel computers can accelerate the conversion of data into market intelligence.

Data mining is not inexpensive, however. A parallel computer can cost as much as $1 million and conversion of programs from a mainframe can be costly. Nevertheless, the rewards can be rich. Royal Caribbean Cruises Ltd. in Miami uses its system to fill berths at the last minute by offering packages to selected customers. Half of its passengers have taken cruises before, and Royal Caribbean also uses its parallel computer to identify those who may be willing to take a longer cruise or an expensive tour of Scandinavia or Russia.[5]

---

[5]Adapted from L. Hays, "Using Computers to Divine Who Might Buy a Gas Grill," *Wall Street Journal*, 16 August 1994, B1, 6.

QUERYING A SINGLE TABLE DATABASE

The objective of developing a database is to make it easier to use the stored data to solve problems. Typically, a manager raises a question (e.g., How many shares have a PE ratio greater than 12?). A question or request for information, usually called a **query**, is then translated into a specific data manipulation or query language. The most widely used query languages for relational databases are SQL and QBE. After the query has been executed, the resulting data are displayed. In the case of a relational database, the answer to a query is always a table.

For each type of query, we will present the SQL version first and then the QBE format. You probably will prefer QBE because it generally takes less time to form a query and it is less error prone. Later you will find that more complex queries require SQL.

There is also a query language called **relational algebra**, which describes a set of operations on tables. Sometimes it is useful to think of queries in terms of these operations. Also, relational algebra terms are often used for describing queries. Where appropriate we will introduce the corresponding relational algebra operation.

Generally we use a five-phase format for describing queries:

1. A brief explanation of the query's purpose;
2. The query, prefixed by ○ and in bold, as it might be phrased by a manager;
3. The SQL version of the query;
4. The results of the query;
5. The QBE version of the query.

Displaying an Entire Table

All the data in a table can be displayed using the select statement. In SQL, the "all" part is indicated by an asterisk (*).

○ **List all data in share.**

```
SELECT * FROM SHR
```

SHRCODE	SHRFIRM	SHRPRICE	SHRQTY	SHRDIV	SHRPE
FC	Freedonia Copper	27.50	10529	1.84	16
PT	Patagonian Tea	55.25	12635	2.50	10
AR	Abyssinian Ruby	31.82	22010	1.32	13
SLG	Sri Lankan Gold	50.37	32868	2.68	16
ILZ	Indian Lead & Zinc	37.75	6390	3.00	12
BE	Burmese Elephant	0.07	154713	0.01	3
BS	Bolivian Sheep	12.75	231678	1.78	11
NG	Nigerian Geese	35.00	12323	1.68	10
CS	Canadian Sugar	52.78	4716	2.50	15
ROF	Royal Ostrich Farms	33.75	1234923	3.00	6

QBE can be used to generate the same report by placing a "P." in the column headed SHR, the table name. The "P." means "present" the table. The QBE version is:

```
 SHR | SHRCODE | SHRFIRM          | SHRPRICE | SHRQTY | SHRDIV | SHRPE   |
-----+---------+------------------+----------+--------+--------+---------+
 P.  |         |                  |          |        |        |         |
```

Project — Choosing Columns

The relational algebra operation **project** creates a new table from the columns of an existing table. Project takes a vertical slice through a table by selecting all the values in specified columns. The projection of SHR on columns SHRFIRM and SHRPE produces a new table with ten rows and two columns. These columns are shaded in Table 3–4. The SQL command for project simply lists the columns to be displayed.

○   **Report a firm's name and price–earnings ratio.**

```
SELECT SHRFIRM, SHRPE FROM SHR
```

```
SHRFIRM                  SHRPE
-----------------------  -------
Freedonia Copper            16
Patagonian Tea              10
Abyssinian Ruby             13
Sri Lankan Gold             16
Indian Lead & Zinc          12
Burmese Elephant             3
Bolivian Sheep              11
Nigerian Geese              10
Canadian Sugar              15
Royal Ostrich Farms          6
```

The project operation is specified in QBE by placing "P." in the columns to be projected. In this case, "P." is placed in the columns headed SHRFIRM and SHRPE because we want to present these specified columns. The QBE version of project is:

```
 SHR | SHRCODE | SHRFIRM          | SHRPRICE | SHRQTY | SHRDIV | SHRPE   |
-----+---------+------------------+----------+--------+--------+---------+
     |         | P.               |          |        |        | P.      |
```

Table 3–4   Projection of SHRFIRM and SHRPE

SHR SHRCODE	SHRFIRM	SHRPRICE	SHRQTY	SHRDIV	SHRPE
FC	Freedonia Copper	27.50	10,529	1.84	16
PT	Patagonian Tea	55.25	12,635	2.50	10
AR	Abyssinian Ruby	31.82	22,010	1.32	13
SLG	Sri Lankan Gold	50.37	32,868	2.68	16
ILZ	Indian Lead & Zinc	37.75	6,390	3.00	12
BE	Burmese Elephant	.07	154,713	0.01	3
BS	Bolivian Sheep	12.75	231,678	1.78	11
NG	Nigerian Geese	35.00	12,323	1.68	10
CS	Canadian Sugar	52.78	4,716	2.50	15
ROF	Ruritanian Ostrich Farms	33.75	1,234,923	3.00	6

Restrict[6]—Choosing Rows

The relational algebra operation **restrict** creates a new table from the rows of an existing table. The operation restricts the new table to those rows that satisfy a specified condition. Restrict takes all columns of an existing table but only those rows that meet the specified condition. The restriction of SHR to those rows where the PE ratio is less than 12 will give a new table with five rows and six columns. These rows are indicated by shading in Table 3–5. The relational algebra restrict operation is implemented in SQL using the WHERE clause to specify the condition on which rows are restricted.

○   **Get all shares with a price-earnings ratio less than 12.**

```
SELECT * FROM SHR WHERE SHRPE < 12
```

```
SHRCODE    SHRFIRM              SHRPRICE   SHRQTY   SHRDIV   SHRPE
---------- -------------------- ---------- -------- -------- -------
PT         Patagonian Tea          55.25    12635     2.50      10
BE         Burmese Elephant         0.07   154713     0.01       3
BS         Bolivian Sheep          12.75   231678     1.78      11
NG         Nigerian Geese          35.00    12323     1.68      10
ROF        Royal Ostrich Farms     33.75  1234923     3.00       6
```

---

[6]Restrict is also known as select; however, since this could be confused with SQL's SELECT command, this book uses restrict instead.

Table 3–5   Restriction of SHR

SHR					
SHRCODE	**SHRFIRM**	**SHRPRICE**	**SHRQTY**	**SHRDIV**	**SHRPE**
FC	Freedonia Copper	27.50	10,529	1.84	16
PT	Patagonian Tea	55.25	12,635	2.50	10
AR	Abyssinian Ruby	31.82	22,010	1.32	13
SLG	Sri Lankan Gold	50.37	32,868	2.68	16
ILZ	Indian Lead & Zinc	37.75	6,390	3.00	12
BE	Burmese Elephant	.07	154,713	0.01	3
BS	Bolivian Sheep	12.75	231,678	1.78	11
NG	Nigerian Geese	35.00	12,323	1.68	10
CS	Canadian Sugar	52.78	4,716	2.50	15
ROF	Royal Ostrich Farms	33.75	1,234,923	3.00	6

The QBE form of the restrict operation has the specified condition in the appropriate column. The "P." in the table name column indicates that all columns are reported:

```
SHR | SHRCODE | SHRFIRM          | SHRPRICE | SHRQTY | SHRDIV | SHRPE |
----+---------+------------------+----------+--------+--------+-------+
 P. |         |                  |          |        |        | <12   |
```

In this example, we had a *less than* condition for the WHERE clause. Other permissible comparison operators are listed in Table 3–6.

Table 3–6   Comparison Operators

Comparison operator	Meaning
=	Equal to
<	Less than
<=	Less than or equal to
>	Greater than
>=	Greater than or equal to
< >	Not equal to

Combining Project and Restrict — Choosing Rows and Columns

Relational algebra treats project and restrict as separate operations. SQL and QBE permit these operations to be combined. A single SQL SELECT statement can specify which columns to project and which rows to restrict.

○ **List the firm's name, price, quantity, and dividend where share holding is at least 100,000.**

```
SELECT SHRFIRM, SHRPRICE, SHRQTY, SHRDIV FROM SHR
    WHERE SHRQTY >= 100000
```

SHRFIRM	SHRPRICE	SHRQTY	SHRDIV
Burmese Elephant	0.07	154713	0.01
Bolivian Sheep	12.75	231678	1.78
Royal Ostrich Farms	33.75	1234923	3.00

The QBE version is:

SHR	SHRCODE	SHRFIRM	SHRPRICE	SHRQTY	SHRDIV	SHRPE
		P.	P.	P.>=100000	P.	

More About WHERE

The WHERE clause can contain several conditions linked by AND or OR. A clause containing AND means all specified conditions must be true for a row to be selected. In the case of OR, at least one of the conditions must be true for a row to be selected.

○ **Find all shares where the PE is 12 or higher and share holding is less than 10,000.**

```
SELECT * FROM SHR
    WHERE SHRPE >= 12 AND SHRQTY < 10000
```

The QBE format is:

SHR	SHRCODE	SHRFIRM	SHRPRICE	SHRQTY	SHRDIV	SHRPE
P.				<10000		>=12

The Power of the Primary Key

The purpose of a primary key is to guarantee that any row in a table can be uniquely addressed. In this example, we can use SHRCODE to return a single row because SHRCODE is different for each instance in the SHR table.

○ **Report shares with code = 'AR'.**

```
SELECT * FROM SHR WHERE SHRCODE = 'AR'
```

SHRCODE	SHRFIRM	SHRPRICE	SHRQTY	SHRDIV	SHRPE
AR	Abyssinian Ruby	31.82	22010	1.32	13

A query based on a non-primary key column cannot guarantee that a single row is accessed, as the following query illustrates.

○ **Report shares with a dividend of 2.50.**

```
SELECT * FROM SHR WHERE SHRDIV = 2.5
```

SHRCODE	SHRFIRM	SHRPRICE	SHRQTY	SHRDIV	SHRPE
PT	Patagonian Tea	55.25	12635	2.50	10
CS	Canadian Sugar	52.78	4716	2.50	15

The IN Crowd

The keyword IN is used with a list to specify a set of values. IN is always paired with a column name. All rows for which a value in the specified column has a match in the list are selected. It is a simpler way of writing a series of OR statements.

○ **Report data on shares with codes of FC, AR, or SLG.**

```
SELECT * FROM SHR WHERE SHRCODE IN ('FC','AR','SLG')
```

The foregoing query could have also been written as:

```
SELECT * FROM SHR
    WHERE SHRCODE = 'FC' or SHRCODE = 'AR' or SHRCODE = 'SLG'
```

or specified in QBE as:

```
SHR |SHRCODE                   | SHRFIRM| SHRPRICE | SHRQTY | SHRDIV | SHRPE   |
----+--------------------------+--------+----------+--------+--------+---------+
P.  |IN ('FC', 'AR', 'SLG')|      |          |        |        |         |
```

Note: Most versions of QBE have a method of enlarging a column's entry area to allow for extended condition clauses. To add more space, use the command for extending the entry area.

to produce:

```
SHRCODE    SHRFIRM                      SHRPRICE   SHRQTY   SHRDIV   SHRPE
-------    --------------------         --------   ------   ------   -----
FC         Freedonia Copper               27.50    10529     1.84      16
AR         Abyssinian Ruby                31.82    22010     1.32      13
SLG        Sri Lankan Gold                50.37    32868     2.68      16
```

The NOT IN Crowd

A NOT IN list is used to report instances that do not match any of the values.

○   **Report all shares other than those with the code CS or PT.**

```
SELECT * FROM SHR WHERE SHRCODE NOT IN ('CS', 'PT')
```

is equivalent to:

```
SELECT * FROM SHR
    WHERE SHRCODE <> 'CS' AND SHRCODE <> 'PT'
```

and produces the report:

SHRCODE	SHRFIRM	SHRPRICE	SHRQTY	SHRDIV	SHRPE
FC	Freedonia Copper	27.50	10529	1.84	16
AR	Abyssinian Ruby	31.82	22010	1.32	13
SLG	Sri Lankan Gold	50.37	32868	2.68	16
ILZ	Indian Lead & Zinc	37.75	6390	3.00	12
BE	Burmese Elephant	0.07	154713	0.01	3
BS	Bolivian Sheep	12.75	231678	1.78	11
NG	Nigerian Geese	35.00	12323	1.68	10
ROF	Royal Ostrich Farms	33.75	1234923	3.00	6

Ordering Columns

The order of reporting columns is identical to their order in the SQL command. For instance, the query

```
SELECT SHRCODE, SHRFIRM FROM SHR WHERE SHRPE = 10
```

gives:

SHRCODE	SHRFIRM
PT	Patagonian Tea
NG	Nigerian Geese

while the query

```
SELECT SHRFIRM, SHRCODE FROM SHR WHERE SHRPE = 10
```

gives:

SHRFIRM	SHRCODE
Patagonian Tea	PT
Nigerian Geese	NG

Ordering Rows

People can process an ordered report faster than an unordered one. Imagine trying to find a name in a phone book that was not sorted by last name. That's why telephone books are ordered alphabetically by last name, and then within same last name by first name. Actually, this is not true in Iceland where the telephone book is ordered alphabetically by first name. Because of Icelandic naming traditions, it is easier to search the telephone book on the basis of first name than last name.[7]

In SQL, the ORDER BY clause specifies the row for order in a report. Rows are listed in order of significance. The default ordering sequence is ascending (A before B, 1 before 2). Descending is specified by adding DESC after the column name.

○   **List all shares where PE is at least 10, and order the report in descending PE. Where PE ratios are identical, list shares in alphabetical order.**

```
SELECT * FROM SHR WHERE SHRPE >= 10 ORDER BY SHRPE DESC, SHRFIRM
```

produces:

SHRCODE	SHRFIRM	SHRPRICE	SHRQTY	SHRDIV	SHRPE
FC	Freedonia Copper	27.50	10529	1.84	16
SLG	Sri Lankan Gold	50.37	32868	2.68	16
CS	Canadian Sugar	52.78	4716	2.50	15
AR	Abyssinian Ruby	31.82	22010	1.32	13
ILZ	Indian Lead & Zinc	37.75	6390	3.00	12

In the case of QBE, the codes AO and DO are used to specify descending and ascending order, respectively. The order of sorting is indicated by a number in parentheses after the code. The first sort key is shown as (1) and so forth.

SHR	SHRCODE	SHRFIRM	SHRPRICE	SHRQTY	SHRDIV	SHRPE
P.		AO(2).				DO(1). >11

By now, you should have a good idea of QBE principles. Because the QBE concept is implemented in different ways in RDBMSs, we will leave it to you to learn the finer details of QBE for the database you are using. We will continue to use SQL as the query language because it is the standard and is implemented to some level by nearly all RDBMSs.

---

[7]If an Icelandic man with the first name Ragnar has a daughter who is named Inga, her full name will be Inga Ragnarsdottir (literally daughter of Ragnar). If he has a son, his last name would be Ragnarsson.

Numeric Versus Character Sorting

Numeric data in character fields (e.g., a product code) do not always sort the way you initially expect. The difference arises from the way data are stored:

- numeric fields are right justified and have leading zeros.
- character fields are left justified and have trailing spaces.

For example, the value 1066 stored in a character field of four bytes would be stored as `1066` and the value 45 would be stored as `45    `. If the column containing these data is sorted in ascending order, then `1066` precedes `45    ` because `1` is less than `4`. You can avoid this problem by always storing numeric values as numeric data types (e.g., integer or decimal) or preceding numeric values with zeros when they are stored as character data.

Calculating

One of the important principles of database design is to avoid redundancy. One form of redundancy is including a column in a table when that data can be determined from other columns. For example, we do not need a column for yield because it can be calculated by dividing dividend by price and multiplying by a 100 to obtain the percentage. This means that the query language has to do the calculation when the value is required.

⭕ **Get firm name, price, quantity, and share yield.**

```
SELECT SHRFIRM, SHRPRICE, SHRQTY, SHRDIV/SHRPRICE*100 FROM SHR
```

to give:

SHRFIRM	SHRPRICE	SHRQTY	EXPRESSION 1
Freedonia Copper	27.50	10529	6.69
Patagonian Tea	55.25	12635	4.52
Abyssinian Ruby	31.82	22010	4.15
Sri Lankan Gold	50.37	32868	5.32
Indian Lead & Zinc	37.75	6390	7.95
Burmese Elephant	0.07	154713	14.29
Bolivian Sheep	12.75	231678	13.96
Nigerian Geese	35.00	12323	4.80
Canadian Sugar	52.78	4716	4.74
Royal Ostrich Farms	33.75	1234923	8.89

Note that SQL puts the results of the calculation in a column headed Expression 1. Later you will learn how to make this heading more descriptive of the data in the column.

SQL Built-in Functions

SQL has built-in functions to enhance its retrieval power and handle many common queries. Four of these functions (AVG, SUM, MIN, and MAX) work very similarly. COUNT is a little different.

Count

COUNT computes the number of rows in a table. Rows are counted even if they contain null values. Count can be used with a WHERE clause to specify a condition.

○ **How many shares are there in the portfolio?**

```
SELECT COUNT(*) FROM SHR
```

10

○ **How many shares with a holding greater than 50,000?**

```
SELECT COUNT(*) FROM SHR WHERE SHRQTY > 50000
```

3

Average

AVG computes the average of the values in a column of numeric data. Null values in the column are not included in the calculation.

○ **Find the average share dividend.**

```
SELECT AVG(SHRDIV) FROM SHR
```

2.03

○ **What is each share's average yield?**

```
SELECT AVG(SHRDIV/SHRPRICE*100) FROM SHR
```

7.53

SUM, MIN, and MAX

SUM, MIN, and MAX differ in the statistic they calculate but are used similarly to AVG. As with AVG, null values in a column are not included in the calculation. SUM computes the sum of a column of values. MIN finds the smallest value in a column; MAX finds the largest.

Subqueries

Sometimes we need the answer to another query before we can write the query of real interest. For example, to list all shares with a PE ratio greater than the portfolio average, you first must find the average PE ratio for the portfolio. You could do the query in two stages:

a.   SELECT AVG(SHRPE) FROM SHR

b.   SELECT SHRFIRM, SHRPE FROM SHR WHERE SHRPE $> x$

where x is the value returned from the first query.

Unfortunately, the two-stage method introduces the possibility of errors. You might forget the value returned by the first query or enter it incorrectly. It also takes longer to get the results of the query. We can solve these problems by using parentheses to indicate the first query is nested within the second one. As a result, the value returned by the inner or nested subquery, the one in parentheses, is used in the outer query. In the following example, the nested query returns 11.20, which is then automatically substituted in the outer query.

○   **Report all shares with a PE ratio greater than the average for the portfolio.**

```
SELECT SHRFIRM, SHRPE FROM SHR WHERE SHRPE >
   (SELECT AVG(SHRPE) FROM SHR)
```

SHRFIRM	SHRPE
Freedonia Copper	16
Abyssinian Ruby	13
Sri Lankan Gold	16
Indian Lead & Zinc	12
Canadian Sugar	15

Warning: The preceding query is often mistakenly written as

```
SELECT SHRFIRM, SHRPE FROM SHR
   WHERE SHRPE > AVG(SHRPE)
```

which may seem reasonable, but the syntax is wrong.

LIKE — Pattern Matching

Have you ever searched a major city's phone book for someone whose last name and street address you can recall but whose first name you just cannot remember? If you are looking for a Ms. Smith in Sydney, you will spend a lot of time sequentially searching through the Smiths, looking for the matching street name. LIKE solves these types of problems when you are searching a table because it searches for a specified pattern in a nominated column. LIKE uses two symbols for specifying a search pattern:

- The percentage sign (%) is the symbol for any number of characters, or none.
- The underscore (_) is the symbol for any single character.

These examples illustrate the use of LIKE.

○ **List all firms with a name starting with 'F.'**

```
SELECT SHRFIRM FROM SHR WHERE SHRFIRM LIKE 'F%'
```

```
SHRFIRM
-------------------------
Freedonia Copper
```

○ **List all firms containing 'Ruby' in their name.**

```
SELECT SHRFIRM FROM SHR WHERE SHRFIRM LIKE '%RUBY%'
```

```
SHRFIRM
-------------------------
Abyssinian Ruby
```

○ **Find firms with 't' as the third letter of their name.**

```
SELECT SHRFIRM FROM SHR WHERE SHRFIRM LIKE '__t%'
```

```
SHRFIRM
-------------------------
Patagonian Tea
```

○ **Find firms not containing an 's' in their name.**

This query is a little vague, even for academic work. Do you assume that it refers to the lower case *s*, upper case *S*, or both? In the business world, you would ask the manager who requested the data. In this world, we assume it means neither upper nor lower case.

```
SELECT SHRFIRM FROM SHR WHERE SHRFIRM NOT LIKE '%S%' AND SHRFIRM
   NOT LIKE '%s%'
```

```
SHRFIRM
------------------------
Freedonia Copper
Patagonian Tea
Indian Lead & Zinc
```

DISTINCT—Eliminating Duplicate Rows

The SQL DISTINCT clause is used to eliminate duplicate rows. It can be used with the column functions or before a column name. When used with a column function, it ignores duplicate values.

○ **Find the number of different PE ratios.**

```
SELECT COUNT(DISTINCT SHRPE) FROM SHR
```

```
COUNT(DISTINCT SHRPE)
-------------------------
                      8
```

When used before a column name, DISTINCT prevents the selection of duplicate rows.

○ **Report the different values of the PE ratio.**

```
SELECT DISTINCT SHRPE FROM SHR
```

```
SHRPE
-------
      3
      6
     10
     11
     12
     13
     15
     16
```

DELETE—Deleting Rows

Rows in a table can be deleted using the DELETE clause in an SQL statement. DELETE is typically used with a WHERE clause to specify the rows to be deleted. If there is no WHERE clause, all rows are deleted.

○ **Erase the data for Burmese Elephant. All the shares have been sold.**

```
DELETE FROM SHR WHERE SHRCODE = 'BE'
```

In this statement, SHRCODE is used to indicate the row to be deleted. We could have used WHERE SHRFIRM = 'Burmese Elephant', but using SHRCODE just takes less typing and lessens the chance of an error.

Microcomputer Database Software

There are several microcomputer implementations of a RDBMS. Unfortunately, many of these do not offer full support for SQL, but they often present a friendlier interface than standard SQL.

Microsoft FoxPro is a good example of a microcomputer RDBMS. A few sample screens illustrate the style of interface you can expect with such a system. First, let's look at table definition (see Figure 3–4). Observe that a pop-up menu ❶ is used for defining a column's data type and a 'spinner' ❷ is used for setting a column's width. Table definition is fast, accurate, and the process is easy to remember. Inserting data is very straightforward, as shown in Figure 3–5. The familiar spreadsheet format facilitates data entry.

Almost without exception, microcomputer RDBMSs support a form of QBE. The query shown in Figure 3–6 answers the following question:

○ **List the firm's name, price, dividend, and quantity where share holding is at least 100,000.**

The table to be queried is shown in the Tables box ❶, and the columns to be reported are listed in the Output Fields box ❷. The condition ❸ is shown in the lower part of the window. By clicking on the "Do Query" button ❹, the query is executed. Notice there is also a button ❺ that when clicked will display the generated SQL code.

The output of the foregoing query is presented in spreadsheet format in Figure 3–7.

Debriefing

Now that you have learned how to model a single entity, create a table, and specify queries, you are on the way to mastering the fundamental skills of database design, implementation, and use. Remember, planning occurs before action. A data model is a plan for a database. The action side of a database is inserting rows and running queries.

Figure 3–4   Table definition with FoxPro

Figure 3–5   Spreadsheet style data entry with FoxPro

Figure 3–6 Querying with FoxPro

Figure 3–7 Query output

SUMMARY

The relational database model is an effective means of representing real world relationships. Data modeling is used to determine what data must be stored and how data is related. An entity is something in the environment. An entity has attributes, which describe it, and an identifier, which uniquely marks an instance of an entity. Every entity must have a unique identifier. A relational database consists of tables with rows and columns. A data model is readily translated to a relational database. The SQL statement CREATE is used to define a table. Rows are added to a table using INSERT. In SQL, queries are written using the SELECT statement. QBE is an alternative to SQL. Project (choosing columns) and restrict (choosing rows) are common table operations. The WHERE clause is used to specify row selection criteria. WHERE can be combined with IN and NOT IN, which specify values for a single column. The rows of a report are sorted using the ORDER BY clause. Arithmetic expressions can appear in SQL statements, and SQL has built-in functions for common arithmetic operations. A subquery is a query within a query. The LIKE clause is used for pattern matching of character strings. Duplicate rows are eliminated with the DISTINCT clause. Rows can be erased using DELETE.

KEY TERMS AND CONCEPTS

Attribute	MAX
AVG	MIN
Column	NOT IN
COUNT	ORDER BY
CREATE	Primary key
Data modeling	Project
Data type	Query-By-Example (QBE)
Database	Relational database
DELETE	Restrict
DISTINCT	Row
Entity	SELECT
Identifier	SQL
IN	Subquery
INSERT	SUM
Instance	Table
LIKE	WHERE

EXERCISES

1. Draw data models for the following entities. In each case, make certain that you show the attributes and identifiers.

   a. Ship: A ship has a name, registration code, gross tonnage, and a year of construction. Ships are classified as cargo or passenger.

    b. Car: A car has a manufacturer, range name, and style code (e.g., a Honda Accord DX, where Honda is the manufacturer, Accord is the range, and DX is the style). A car also has a vehicle identification code, registration code, and color.

    c. Restaurant: A restaurant has an address, seating capacity, phone number, and style of food (e.g., French, Russian, Chinese).

    d. Cow: A dairy cow has a name, date of birth, breed (e.g., Holstein), and a numbered plastic ear tag.

2. Take each of the entities you have modeled, create a relational database, and insert some rows.

3. Do the following queries using SQL or QBE.

    a. List a share's name and its code.

    b. List full details for all shares with a price less than one dollar.

    c. List the name and price of all shares with a price of at least $10.

    d. Create a report showing firm name, share price, share holding, and total value of shares held. (Value of share held is price times quantity.)

    e. List the name of all shares with a yield exceeding 5 percent.

    f. Report the total dividend payment of Patagonian Tea. (The total dividend payment is dividend times quantity.)

    g. Find all shares where the price is less than 20 times the dividend.

    h. Find the share with the minimum yield.

    i. Find the total value of all shares with a PE ratio > 10.

    j. Find the share with the maximum total dividend payment.

    k. Find the value of the holdings in Abyssinian Ruby and Sri Lankan Gold.

    l. Find the yield of all firms except Bolivian Sheep and Canadian Sugar.

    m. Find the total value of the portfolio.

    n. List firm name and value in descending order of value.

    o. List shares with a firm name containing 'Gold.'

    p. Find shares with a code starting with 'B.'

4. Run the following queries and explain the differences in output. Write each query as a manager might state it.

    a. SELECT SHRFIRM FROM SHR WHERE SHRFIRM NOT LIKE '%s%'

    b. SELECT SHRFIRM FROM SHR WHERE SHRFIRM NOT LIKE '%S%'

    c. SELECT SHRFIRM FROM SHR WHERE SHRFIRM NOT LIKE '%s%' AND SHRFIRM NOT LIKE '%S%'

    d. SELECT SHRFIRM FROM SHR WHERE SHRFIRM NOT LIKE '%s%' OR SHRFIRM NOT LIKE '%S%'

    e. SELECT SHRFIRM FROM SHR WHERE (SHRFIRM NOT LIKE '%s%' AND SHRFIRM NOT LIKE '%S%') OR SHRFIRM LIKE 'S%'

5. A weekly newspaper, sold at supermarket checkouts, frequently reports stories of aliens visiting Earth and taking humans on short trips. Sometimes a captured human sees Elvis commanding the spaceship. Well, to keep track of all these reports, the newspaper has created the following data model.

The paper has also supplied some data for the last few sightings and asked you to create the database and add details of these aliens.

al#	alname	alheads	alcolor	alsmell
1	Foozelgiga	1	vermilion	ambrosial
2	Koofoopsiepus	3	amethyst	putrid
3	Bunyippa	1	chartreuse	perfumed
4	Meekamuncha	7	lavender	old cabbage
5	Eop	0	chartreuse	new car

When you have created the database, answer the following queries:
a. What's the average number of heads for an alien?
b. Which alien has the most heads?
c. Are there any aliens with a double *o* in their names?
d. How many aliens are chartreuse?
e. Report details of all aliens sorted by smell and color.

6. If you have a database system on your personal computer, create the SHARE table and insert some rows. Compare the approach of standard SQL to your database system. Which was easier to use for defining a table and inserting some rows? Next, do some queries. How do the two systems compare?

7. Eduardo, an avid music fan, has a collection of several hundred CDs. Being a little disorganized, he has his CDs scattered around his den. They are piled on the floor, some are in racks, and others sit on top of the CD player. Because he has so many CDs, he finds it difficult to remember what he has, and sometimes he cannot find the CD he wants.
Eduardo has a simple personal computer file system which is fine for a single entity

or file.[8] He has decided that he would like to list each CD by performer(s)' name, and type of music (e.g., classical, new age, jazz). Draw a data model for this problem, create a single entity table, and write some SQL queries.

How do you identify each instance of a CD? (It might help to look at a few CDs.)

How should Eduardo physically organize his CDs to permit fast retrieval of a particular one?

Are there any shortcomings with the data model you have created?

8. What is an identifier? Why does a data model have an identifier?

9. What are entities?

10. What is the entity integrity rule?

---

[8]These types of systems, of which FileMaker Pro is a good example, are called flat-file systems because they store and retrieve single, unrelated files.

Chapter 4

The One-to-Many Relationship

Cow, of many—well milked and badly fed.
Spanish proverb

Learning Objectives

Students completing this chapter will be able to:
* model a one-to-many relationship between two entities;
* define a database with a one-to-many relationship;
* write queries for a database with a one-to-many relationship.

The Expeditioner

Alice sat with a self-satisfied smirk on her face. Her previous expedition into her attaché case had revealed the extent of her considerable stock holdings. She was wealthy beyond her dreams. What else was there in this marvelous, magic attaché case? She rummaged further into the case and retrieved a folder labeled "Stocks—foreign." More shares!

On the inside cover of the folder was a note stating that the stocks in this folder were not listed in the United Kingdom. The folder contained three sheets of paper. Each was headed by the name of a country and followed by a list of stocks and the number of shares. The smirk became the cattiest of Cheshire grins. Alice ordered another bottle of champagne and turned to the *Financial Times* page that listed foreign stock prices. She wanted to calculate the current value of each stock and then use current exchange rates to convert the values into British currency.

RELATIONS

Entities are not isolated; they are related to other entities. When we move beyond the single entity, we need to identify the relationship between entities to accurately represent the real world. Once we recognize that all stocks in our case study are not listed in the United Kingdom, we need to introduce an entity called NATION. We now have two entities, STOCK[1] and

---

[1]Why have we changed the label to STOCK when it seems to be the same as SHR? Because, as you will see shortly, STOCK is related to another entity, whereas SHR stands alone.

Figure 4–1   A 1:m relationship between NATION and STOCK

NATION. Consider the relationship between them. A NATION can have many listed stocks. A stock, in this case, is listed in only one nation. There is a 1:m (one-to-many)[2] relationship between NATION and STOCK.

A 1:m relationship between two entities is depicted by a line connecting the two with a crow or chicken foot at the many end of the relationship. Figure 4–1 shows the 1:m relationship between STOCK and NATION. This can be read as: "a nation can have many stocks, but a stock belongs to only one nation." The entity NATION is identified by a nation code and has attributes nation name and exchange rate.

The 1:m relationship occurs frequently in business situations. Sometimes it occurs in a tree or hierarchical fashion. Consider a firm. It has many divisions, but a division belongs to only one firm. A division has many departments, but a department belongs to only one division. A department has many sections, but a section belongs to only one department (see Figure 4–2). We see a similar tree structure in the reporting of sales by country, region, and state.

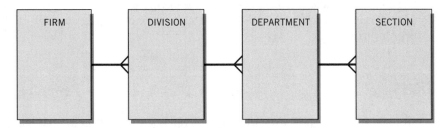

Figure 4–2   A series of hierarchical 1:m relationships

---

[2]One-to-many is the common interpretation of 1:m. You can also think of it as one-and-many, however, because there are two relationships—STOCK is related to one NATION, and NATION is related to many STOCKs. While we believe one-and-many is more precise, we have adopted the common usage.

Why Did We Create an Additional Entity?

Another approach to adding data about listing nation and exchange rate is to add two attributes to STOCK: nation name and exchange rate. At first glance, this seems a very workable solution; however, this will introduce considerable redundancy, as Table 4–1 illustrates.

The same nation name and exchange rate pair occurs ten times for stocks listed in the United Kingdom. Redundancy presents problems when we want to insert, delete, or update data. These problems, generally known as **update anomalies**, occur with three basic operations:

Insert

We cannot insert a fact about a nation's exchange rate unless we first buy a stock that is listed in that nation. Consider the case where we want to keep a record of France's exchange rate and we have no French stocks. We cannot skirt this problem by putting in a null entry for stock details because STKCODE, the identifier, would be null, and this is not allowed. If we have a separate table for facts about a nation, then we can easily add new nations without having to buy stocks. This is particularly useful when other parts of the organization, say International Trading, also need access to exchange rates.

Delete

If we delete data about a particular stock, we might also lose a fact about exchange rates. For example, if we delete details of "Bombay Duck," we also erase the Indian exchange rate.

Update

Exchange rates are volatile. Many companies need to update them every day. What happens when the Australian exchange rate changes? Every row in STOCK with NATION = "Australia" will have to be updated. In a large portfolio, many rows will be changed. There is also the danger of someone forgetting to update all the instances of the nation and exchange rate pair. As a result, there could be two exchange rates for the one nation. If exchange rate is stored in NATION, however, only one change is necessary, there is no redundancy, and no danger of inconsistent exchange rates.

CREATING A DATABASE WITH A 1:M RELATIONSHIP

As before, each entity becomes a table in a relational database, the entity name becomes the table name, each attribute becomes a column, and each identifier becomes a primary key. The 1:m relationship is mapped by adding a column to the entity of the many end of the relationship. The additional column contains the identifier of the one end of the relationship. Consider the relationship between the entities STOCK and NATION (see Figure 4–1). The relational database (see Table 4–2) has two tables, STOCK and NATION. STOCK has an additional column,

Table 4–1   The Table STOCK with Additional Columns

STOCK							
STKCODE	STKFIRM	STKPRICE	STKQTY	STKDIV	STKPE	NAT NAME	EXCHRATE
FC	Freedonia Copper	27.50	10,529	1.84	16	United Kingdom	1.00
PT	Patagonian Tea	55.25	12,635	2.50	10	United Kingdom	1.00
AR	Abyssinian Ruby	31.82	22,010	1.32	13	United Kingdom	1.00
SLG	Sri Lankan Gold	50.37	32,868	2.68	16	United Kingdom	1.00
ILZ	Indian Lead & Zinc	37.75	6,390	3.00	12	United Kingdom	1.00
BE	Burmese Elephant	.07	154,713	0.01	3	United Kingdom	1.00
BS	Bolivian Sheep	12.75	231,678	1.78	11	United Kingdom	1.00
NG	Nigerian Geese	35.00	12,323	1.68	10	United Kingdom	1.00
CS	Canadian Sugar	52.78	4,716	2.50	15	United Kingdom	1.00
ROF	Royal Ostrich Farms	33.75	1,234,923	3.00	6	United Kingdom	1.00
MG	Minnesota Gold	53.87	816,122	1.00	25	USA	0.67
GP	Georgia Peach	2.35	387,333	.20	5	USA	0.67
NE	Narembeen Emu	12.34	45,619	1.00	8	Australia	0.46
QD	Queensland Diamond	6.73	89,251	.50	7	Australia	0.46
IR	Indooroopilly Ruby	15.92	56,147	.50	20	Australia	0.46
BD	Bombay Duck	25.55	167,382	1.00	12	India	0.0228

Table 4–2   Relations Tables NATION and STOCK

NATION		
NATCODE	NATNAME	EXCHRATE
UK	United Kingdom	1.00
USA	United States	0.67
AUS	Australia	0.46
IND	India	0.0228

STOCK						
STKCODE	STKFIRM	STKPRICE	STKQTY	STKDIV	STKPE	*NATCODE*
FC	Freedonia Copper	27.50	10,529	1.84	16	UK
PT	Patagonian Tea	55.25	12,635	2.50	10	UK
AR	Abyssinian Ruby	31.82	22,010	1.32	13	UK
SLG	Sri Lankan Gold	50.37	32,868	2.68	16	UK
ILZ	Indian Lead & Zinc	37.75	6,390	3.00	12	UK
BE	Burmese Elephant	.07	154,713	0.01	3	UK
BS	Bolivian Sheep	12.75	231,678	1.78	11	UK
NG	Nigerian Geese	35.00	12,323	1.68	10	UK
CS	Canadian Sugar	52.78	4,716	2.50	15	UK
ROF	Royal Ostrich Farms	33.75	1,234,923	3.00	6	UK
MG	Minnesota Gold	53.87	816,122	1.00	25	USA
GP	Georgia Peach	2.35	387,333	.20	5	USA
NE	Narembeen Emu	12.34	45,619	1.00	8	AUS
QD	Queensland Diamond	6.73	89,251	.50	7	AUS
IR	Indooroopilly Ruby	15.92	56,147	.50	20	AUS
BD	Bombay Duck	25.55	167,382	1.00	12	IND

NATCODE, which contains the identifier of NATION. If NATCODE is not stored in STOCK, then there is no way of knowing the identity of the nation where the stock is listed.

Notice that the column name NATCODE appears in both the STOCK and NATION tables. In NATION, NATCODE is the primary key; it is unique for each instance of nation. In STOCK, NATCODE is a **foreign key** because it is the primary key for the table, NATION, the one end of the 1:m relationship. NATCODE is a foreign key in STOCK because it is a primary key in NATION. Primary and foreign keys are the method for recording the 1:m relationship between the two tables. This method of representing a relationship is graphically illustrated in

Table 4–2 for the two USA stocks. In the STOCK table, NATCODE is italicized to indicate that is a foreign key. We find this method, like underlining the primary key, is a useful reminder.

Although the same name has been used for the primary key and the foreign key in this example, it is not mandatory. The two columns can have different names, and in some cases, you are forced to use different names. We find it convenient to use identical column names to help us remember that the tables are related.

The table STOCK shows that there is a total of sixteen stocks, ten listed in the United Kingdom, two in the United States, three in Australia, and one in India. Although a nation can have many stocks, it is not mandatory to have any. That is, in data modeling terminology, many can be zero, one, or more, but it is mandatory to have a value for NATCODE in NATION for every value of NATCODE in STOCK. This requirement, known as the **referential integrity constraint**, maintains the accuracy of a database. Its application means that every foreign key in a table has an identical primary key in that same or any other table. In this example, it means that for every value of NATCODE in STOCK, there is a corresponding entry in NATION. As a result, a primary key row must be created before its corresponding foreign key row. So details for a NATION must be added before data about the stocks listed in that nation can be entered.

Why is the foreign key in the table at the many end of the relationship? Because each instance of STOCK is associated with exactly one instance of NATION. The rule is that a stock must be listed in one and only one nation. Thus, the foreign key field is single-valued when it is at the many end of a relationship. The foreign key is not at the one end of the relationship because each instance of NATION can be associated with more than one instance of STOCK, and this implies a multivalued foreign key. The relational model does not support multivalued fields because of the processing problems they can cause.

Using SQL, the two tables are defined in a similar manner to the way we created a single table in Chapter 3. The CREATE TABLE command is used twice, once for each table. Here are the SQL statements:

```
CREATE TABLE NATION
    (NATCODE       CHAR(3)      NOT NULL,
    NATNAME        CHAR(20),
    EXCHRATE       DECIMAL(9,5),
      PRIMARY KEY (NATCODE))


CREATE TABLE STOCK
    (STKCODE       CHAR(3)      NOT NULL,
    STKFIRM        CHAR(20),
    STKPRICE       DECIMAL(6,2),
    STKQTY         DECIMAL(8),
    STKDIV         DECIMAL(5,2),
    STKPE          DECIMAL(5),
    NATCODE        CHAR(3),
      PRIMARY KEY(STKCODE),
      FOREIGN KEY NATIONCODE(NATCODE) REFERENCES NATION
        ON DELETE RESTRICT)
```

Notice that the definition of STOCK includes additional information to specify the foreign key and the referential integrity constraint. The FOREIGN KEY clause defines the column or columns in the table being created that comprise the foreign key. Constraints can be named, and in this case, its name is NATIONCODE. The foreign key is the column NAT-CODE, and it references the primary key of the table NATION. There is no need to specify the matching primary key's name because this can be derived from the definition of the table (NATION in this case) in which the primary key is found.

The ON DELETE clause specifies what processing should occur if an attempt is made to delete a row in NATION with a primary key that is a foreign key in STOCK. In this case, the ON DELETE clause specifies that it is not permissible (the meaning of RESTRICT) to delete a primary key row in NATION while a corresponding foreign key in STOCK exists. In other words, the system will not execute the delete. The user must first delete all corresponding rows in STOCK before attempting to delete the row containing the primary key.

QUERYING A TWO-TABLE DATABASE

A two-table database offers the opportunity to learn more SQL and join, another relational algebra operation.

Join

Join creates a new table from two existing tables by matching on a column common to both tables. Often the common column is a primary key–foreign key combination: the primary key column of one table is matched with the foreign key column of another table. Join is frequently used to get the data for a query into a single row. Consider the tables NATION and STOCK shown in Figure 4–1. If we want to calculate the value—in British pounds—of a stock, we multiply stock price by stock quantity and then exchange rate. To find the appropriate exchange rate for a stock, get its NATCODE from STOCK and then find the exchange rate in the matching row in NATION, the one with the same value for NATCODE. For example, to calculate the value of Georgia Peach, which has NATCODE = 'US', find the row in NATION that also has NATCODE = 'US'. In this case, the stock's value is 2.35*387333*0.67 = £609,855.81.

Calculation of stock value is very easy once join is used to get the three values in one row. The SQL command for joining the two tables is:

```
SELECT * FROM STOCK, NATION
   WHERE STOCK.NATCODE = NATION.NATCODE
```

and the result is:

STKCODE	STKFIRM	STKPRICE	STKQTY	STKDIV	STKPE	NATCODE	NATCODE1	NATNAME	EXCHRATE
NE	Narembeen Emu	12.34	45619	1.00	8	AUS	AUS	Australia	0.46000
IR	Indooroopilly Ruby	15.92	56147	0.50	20	AUS	AUS	Australia	0.46000
QD	Queensland Diamond	6.73	89251	0.50	7	AUS	AUS	Australia	0.46000
BD	Bombay Duck	25.55	167382	1.00	12	IND	IND	India	0.02280
ROF	Royal Ostrich Farms	33.75	1234923	3.00	6	UK	UK	United Kingdom	1.00000
CS	Canadian Sugar	52.78	4716	2.50	15	UK	UK	United Kingdom	1.00000
FC	Freedonia Copper	27.50	10529	1.84	16	UK	UK	United Kingdom	1.00000
BS	Bolivian Sheep	12.75	231678	1.78	11	UK	UK	United Kingdom	1.00000
BE	Burmese Elephant	0.07	154713	0.01	3	UK	UK	United Kingdom	1.00000
ILZ	Indian Lead & Zinc	37.75	6390	3.00	12	UK	UK	United Kingdom	1.00000
SLG	Sri Lankan Gold	50.37	32868	2.68	16	UK	UK	United Kingdom	1.00000
AR	Abyssinian Ruby	31.82	22010	1.32	13	UK	UK	United Kingdom	1.00000
PT	Patagonian Tea	55.25	12635	2.50	10	UK	UK	United Kingdom	1.00000
NG	Nigerian Geese	35.00	12323	1.68	10	UK	UK	United Kingdom	1.00000
MG	Minnesota Gold	53.87	816122	1.00	25	US	US	United States	0.67000
GP	Georgia Peach	2.35	387333	0.20	5	US	US	United States	0.67000

There are several things to notice about the SQL command and the result:

- To avoid confusion because NATCODE is a column name in both STOCK and NATION, it needs to be qualified. Qualification means you precede a column name with its table name and separate the two by a period (e.g., NATION.NATCODE). If NATCODE is not qualified, the system will reject the query because it cannot distinguish between the two columns titled NATCODE.

- The new table has the NATCODE column replicated. It is called both NATCODE and NATCODE1.

- The SQL command specifies the names of the tables to be joined, the columns to be used for matching, and the condition for the match (equality in this case).

- The number of columns in the new table is the sum of the columns in the two tables joined.

- The stock value calculation is now easily specified in an SQL command because all the data are in one row.

The join operation can be streamlined to report only the columns required for decision making and also show the results of the value calculation. In addition, it is useful to sort or order the report. The SQL features that you have used previously can be used with a join.

Join comes in several flavors. The matching condition can be =, <>, <=, <, >=, and >. Generally when people refer to join, however, they mean **equijoin**, when the matching condition is equality.

○ **Report the value of each stock holding in UK pounds. Sort the report by nation and firm.**

```
SELECT NATNAME, STKFIRM, STKPRICE, STKQTY, EXCHRATE,
   STKPRICE*STKQTY*EXCHRATE
     FROM STOCK,NATION
        WHERE STOCK.NATCODE = NATION.NATCODE
           ORDER BY NATNAME, STKFIRM
```

NATNAME	STKFIRM	STKPRICE	STKQTY	EXCHRATE	EXPRESSION 1
Australia	Indooroopilly Ruby	15.92	56147	0.46000	411175.71
Australia	Narembeen Emu	12.34	45619	0.46000	258951.69
Australia	Queensland Diamond	6.73	89251	0.46000	276303.25
India	Bombay Duck	25.55	167382	0.02280	97506.71
United Kingdom	Abyssinian Ruby	31.82	22010	1.00000	700358.20
United Kingdom	Bolivian Sheep	12.75	231678	1.00000	2953894.50
United Kingdom	Burmese Elephant	0.07	154713	1.00000	10829.91
United Kingdom	Canadian Sugar	52.78	4716	1.00000	248910.48
United Kingdom	Freedonia Copper	27.50	10529	1.00000	289547.50
United Kingdom	Indian Lead & Zinc	37.75	6390	1.00000	241222.50
United Kingdom	Nigerian Geese	35.00	12323	1.00000	431305.00
United Kingdom	Patagonian Tea	55.25	12635	1.00000	698083.75
United Kingdom	Royal Ostrich Farms	33.75	1234923	1.00000	41678651.25
United Kingdom	Sri Lankan Gold	50.37	32868	1.00000	1655561.16
United States	Georgia Peach	2.35	387333	0.67000	609855.81
United States	Minnesota Gold	53.87	816122	0.67000	29456209.73

Remember that we created two entities when data modeling, STOCK and NATION, and defined the relationship between them. We showed that if the information was stored in one table, there could be updating problems. Now, with a join, we have combined this data. So why separate the data only to put it back together later? There are two reasons. First, we want to avoid update anomalies. Second, as you will discover, we do not join the same tables every time.

Target Marketing

Many American shoppers carry plastic, check-cashing cards issued by supermarkets. The magnetic stripe on the card is read at the checkout prior to approval of the customer's check. These cards offer a tremendous opportunity for supermarkets to promote their wares.

Vons, the largest supermarket chain in Southern California, has converted its check-approval card into an electronic checking card. Holders of the new card receive automatic discounts on promotional items. More recently, Vons started to capture card holders' purchase data. The captured information is tabulated by customer and product category so that promotions can be focused on the most appropriate and receptive customers.

The shot gun approach of coupons in newspapers and the mail has been replaced by careful targeting of prospective customers. Mass promotions are ill-directed and wasteful; most coupons are thrown away. Vons uses target marketing to reach customers most likely to respond to a coupon or promotional offer. For example, mass marketing is putting a coupon for 50 cents off a roll of film in the

(continued)

Sunday paper's coupon supplement. Target marketing is printing a coupon with the sales receipt for the customer who regularly buys three rolls of film per month.

Successful target marketing requires four key factors. First, the firm must be able to link buyer data and sales data. It must know which buyers purchased which products. Second, it needs to know some demographic details of the customer (age, income range, and so on). Third, the firm must build and maintain a database system to collect and store gigabytes of sales data. Finally, it must analyze the data to determine customer buying patterns.

In the new age of targeted marketing, database technology plays a key role in helping firms move from mass promotions to personalized, directed messages.[3]

Control Break Reporting

The purpose of a join is to collect the necessary data for a report. When two tables in a 1:m relationship are joined, the report will contain repetitive data. If you re-examine the report from the join, you will see that NATION and EXCHRATE are often repeated because the same values apply to many stocks. A more appropriate format for the report is:

Nation	Exchange rate		
Firm	Price	Quantity	Value
Australia 0.4600			
Indooroopilly Ruby	15.92	56147	411175.71
Narembeen Emu	12.34	45619	258951.69
Queensland Diamond	6.73	89251	276303.25
India 0.02280			
Bombay Duck	25.55	167382	97506.71
United Kingdom 1.0000			
Abyssinian Ruby	31.82	22010	700358.20
Bolivian Sheep	12.75	231678	2953894.50
Burmese Elephant	0.07	154713	10829.91
Canadian Sugar	52.78	4716	248910.48
Freedonia Copper	27.50	10529	289547.50
Indian Lead & Zinc	37.75	6390	241222.50
Nigerian Geese	35.00	12323	431305.00
Patagonian Tea	55.25	12635	698083.75
Royal Ostrich Farms	33.75	1234923	41678651.25
Sri Lankan Gold	50.37	32868	1655561.16
United States 0.6700			
Georgia Peach	2.35	387333	609855.81
Minnesota Gold	53.87	816122	29456209.73

[3]Adapted from L. Armstrong, "Coupon Clippers, Save Your Scissors," *Business Week*, 20 June 1994, 164, 166.

The preceding is an example of a **control break report**, which takes advantage of the fact that the values in a particular column or columns seldom change. In this case, NATNAME and EXCHRATE are often the same from one row to the next so it makes sense to report these data only when they change. The report is also easier to read. NATNAME is known as a control field. Notice that there are four groups of data because NATNAME has four different values.

Many RDBMS packages have report writing languages that make it easy to create a control break report. These languages typically support summary reporting for each group of rows having the same value for the control field(s). Remember, however, that a table must be sorted on the control break field(s) before the report is created.

GROUP BY—Reporting By Groups

The SQL **GROUP BY** clause is an elementary form of control break reporting. It permits grouping of rows that have the same value for a specified column or columns, and produces one row for each different value of the grouping column(s).

○ **Report by nation the total value of stockholdings.**

```
SELECT NATNAME, SUM(STKPRICE*STKQTY*EXCHRATE)
   FROM STOCK, NATION WHERE STOCK.NATCODE = NATION.NATCODE
      GROUP BY NATNAME
```

gives:

NATNAME	SUM(EXPRESSION 1)
Australia	946430.65
India	97506.71
United Kingdom	48908364.25
United States	30066065.54

SQL's **built-in functions** (COUNT, SUM, AVERAGE, MIN, and MAX) can be used with the GROUP BY clause. They are applied to a group of rows having the same value for a specified column. You can specify more than one function in the select statement. For example, we can compute total value and number of different stocks and group by nation using:

○ **Report the number of stocks and their total value by nation.**

```
SELECT NATNAME, COUNT(*), SUM(STKPRICE*STKQTY*EXCHRATE)
   FROM STOCK, NATION WHERE STOCK.NATCODE = NATION.NATCODE
      GROUP BY NATNAME
```

NATNAME	COUNT(EXPRESSION 2)	SUM(EXPRESSION 1)
Australia	3	946430.65
India	1	97506.71
United Kingdom	10	48908364.25
United States	2	30066065.54

You can group by more than one column name; however, all column names appearing in the SELECT clause must be associated with a built-in function or be in a GROUP BY clause.

○ **List stocks by nation and for each nation show the number of stocks for each PE ratio and the total value of those stock holdings in UK pounds.**

```
SELECT NATNAME,STKPE,COUNT(*),SUM(STKPRICE*STKQTY*EXCHRATE)
   FROM STOCK, NATION WHERE STOCK.NATCODE = NATION.NATCODE
      GROUP BY NATNAME, STKPE
```

NATNAME	STKPE	COUNT(EXPRESSION 1)	SUM(EXPRESSION 2)
Australia	7	1	276303.25
Australia	8	1	258951.69
Australia	20	1	411175.71
India	12	1	97506.71
United Kingdom	3	1	10829.91
United Kingdom	6	1	41678651.25
United Kingdom	10	2	1129388.75
United Kingdom	11	1	2953894.50
United Kingdom	12	1	241222.50
United Kingdom	13	1	700358.20
United Kingdom	15	1	248910.48
United Kingdom	16	2	1945108.66
United States	5	1	609855.81
United States	25	1	29456209.73

In this example, stocks are grouped by both NATNAME and STKPE. In most cases, there is only one stock for each pair of NATNAME and STKPE; however, there are two situations (United Kingdom stocks with PEs of 10 and 16) where details of multiple stocks are grouped into one report line. Examining the values in the COUNT column helps you to identify these stocks.

HAVING—the WHERE Clause of Groups

HAVING is the WHERE clause of GROUP BY. It restricts the number of rows considered for grouping. Used with built-in functions, HAVING is always preceded by GROUP BY and is always followed by a function (SUM, AVG, MAX, MIN, or COUNT).

○ **Report the total value of stocks for nations with two or more listed stocks.**

```
SELECT NATNAME, SUM(STKPRICE*STKQTY,EXCHRATE)
   FROM STOCK, NATION WHERE STOCK.NATCODE = NATION.NATCODE
      GROUP BY NATNAME
         HAVING COUNT(*) >= 2
```

NATNAME	SUM(EXPRESSION 1)
Australia	946430.65
United Kingdom	48908364.25
United States	30066065.54

Subqueries

A **subquery**, or nested SELECT, is a SELECT nested within another SELECT. A subquery is often used to return a list of values subsequently searched with an IN clause.

○ **Report the name of all Australian stocks.**

```
SELECT STKFIRM FROM STOCK
   WHERE NATCODE IN
      (SELECT NATCODE FROM NATION
         WHERE NATNAME = 'AUSTRALIA')
```

STKFIRM
Narembeen Emu
Queensland Diamond
Indooroopilly Ruby

Conceptually, the subquery is evaluated first. It returns a list of NATCODES ('AUS') so that the query then is the same as:

```
SELECT STKFIRM FROM STOCK
   WHERE NATCODE IN ('AUS')
```

Note that in this case we do not have to qualify NATCODE. There is no identity crisis because NATCODE in the subquery, or inner query, is implicitly qualified as NATION.NATCODE and NATCODE in the outer query is understood to be STOCK.NATCODE.

This query also can be run as a join by writing:

```
SELECT STKFIRM FROM STOCK, NATION
   WHERE STOCK.NATCODE = NATION.NATCODE
      AND NATNAME  = 'AUSTRALIA'
```

Correlated Subquery

A correlated subquery is yet another approach to solving the query:

⭕ **Report the name of all Australian stocks.**

The correlated subquery approach is:

```
SELECT STKFIRM FROM STOCK
   WHERE 'AUSTRALIA' IN
      (SELECT NATNAME FROM NATION
         WHERE NATION.NATCODE = STOCK.NATCODE)
```

Conceptually, think of this query as stepping through STOCK one row at a time and then executing the inner query each time. The first row has NATCODE = 'UK' so the subquery becomes

```
SELECT NATNAME FROM NATION
   WHERE NATION.NATCODE = 'UK'
```

This query returns 'United Kingdom,' and since this does not match 'Australia,' the name of the stock is not reported.

The query then proceeds to the second row of STOCK and executes the inner query again with the value of STOCK.NATCODE for the second row, and so on for all rows of STOCK.

For rows 13 through 15, the inner query becomes

```
SELECT NATNAME FROM NATION
   WHERE NATION.NATCODE = 'AUS'
```

and returns 'Australia,' which matches the IN clause value. Thus, the name of the stock for these three rows is reported.

The term **correlated subquery** is used because its value depends on a variable that receives its value from an outer query (STOCK.NATCODE in this instance). A correlated subquery thus cannot be evaluated once and for all. It must be evaluated repeatedly—once for each value of the variable received from the outer query. In this respect, a correlated subquery is different from a subquery, which only needs to be evaluated once.

Views—Virtual Tables

You have noticed that in these examples we repeated the join and stock value calculation for each query. Ideally, we should do this once, store the result, and be able to use it with other queries. We can do so if we create a **view**, a virtual table. A view does not physically exist as stored data; it is an imaginary table constructed from existing tables as required. In most cases, however, you can treat a view as if it were a table and run the same queries as if it were a real table.

A view contains selected columns from one or more tables. The selected columns can be renamed and rearranged. New columns based on arithmetic expressions can be created. GROUP BY can also be used to create a view. Remember, a view contains no actual data—it is a virtual table.

The following SQL command does the join and stock value calculation and saves the result as a view:

```
CREATE VIEW STKVALUE
   (NATION, FIRM, PRICE, QTY, EXCHRATE, VALUE)
     AS SELECT NATNAME, STKFIRM, STKPRICE, STKQTY, EXCHRATE
        STKPRICE*STKQTY*EXCHRATE
          FROM STOCK, NATION
             WHERE STOCK.NATCODE = NATION.NATCODE
```

There are several things to notice about creating a view:

- The six names enclosed by parentheses are the column names for the view.
- There is a one-to-one correspondence between the names in parentheses and the names or expressions in the SELECT clause. Thus the view column named VALUE contains the result of the arithmetic expression specified in the view creation statement STKPRICE*STKQTY*EXCHRATE.

A view can be used in a query such as find stocks with a value greater than £100,000:

```
SELECT NATION, FIRM FROM STKVALUE WHERE VALUE > 100,000
```

NATION	FIRM
Australia	Narembeen Emu
Australia	Indooroopilly Ruby
Australia	Queensland Diamond
United Kingdom	Royal Ostrich Farms
United Kingdom	Canadian Sugar
United Kingdom	Freedonia Copper
United Kingdom	Bolivian Sheep
United Kingdom	Indian Lead & Zinc
United Kingdom	Sri Lankan Gold
United Kingdom	Abyssinian Ruby
United Kingdom	Patagonian Tea
United Kingdom	Nigerian Geese
United States	Minnesota Gold
United States	Georgia Peach

There are two main reasons for creating a view. First, as we have seen, query writing can be simplified. If you find that you are frequently writing the same section of code for a variety of queries, then isolate the common section and put it in a view. This means that you will usually create a view when a fact, such as stock value, is derived from other facts in the table.

The second reason is to restrict access to certain columns or rows. For example, the person who updates STOCK could be given a view that excludes STKQTY. In this case, changes in stock prices could be updated without revealing confidential information, such as the value of the stock portfolio.

The Microcomputer Approach

As you would expect, micro-based relational databases have a friendlier interface. The screen image (see Figure 4–3) displays a join in FoxPro for the query:

○ **Report the number of stocks and their total value by nation.**

which is written in SQL as

```
SELECT NATNAME, SUM(STKPRICE*STKQTY*EXCHRATE)
   FROM STOCK, NATION WHERE STOCK.NATCODE = NATION.NATCODE
      GROUP BY NATNAME
```

The tables to be joined are shown in the top left of the upper window ❶ of Figure 4–3. The lower window shows the specification of the join ❷. The screen image only shows part of the work done to define the query. For instance, the "Group By" clause ❸ is specified by clicking on the button labeled "Group By," and the partially shown SUM expression is similarly defined by clicking on the "Fields" box ❹.

SUMMARY

Entities are related to other entities by relationships. The 1:m (one-to-many) relationship occurs frequently in data models. An additional entity is required to represent a 1:m relationship to avoid update anomalies. In a relational database, a 1:m relationship is represented by an additional column, the foreign key, in the table at the many end of the relationship. The referential integrity constraint insists that a foreign key must always exist as a primary key in some table. The foreign key constraint can be specified in a CREATE statement.

Join creates a new table from two existing tables by matching on a column common to both tables. Often the common column is a primary key–foreign key combination. The matching conditions for a join can be =, <>, <=, <, >=, and >. An *equijoin* describes the situation where the matching condition is equality. The GROUP BY clause is used to create an elementary control break report. The HAVING clause of GROUP BY is like the WHERE clause of SELECT. A subquery, which has a SELECT statement within another SELECT statement, causes two SELECT statements to be executed—one for the inner query and one for the outer query. A correlated subquery is executed as many times as there are

Figure 4–3   A join with FoxPro

rows selected by the outer query. A view is a virtual table that is created when required. Views can simplify report writing and restrict access to specified columns or rows.

KEY TERMS AND CONCEPTS

Control break reporting

Correlated subquery

Equijoin

Foreign key

GROUP BY

HAVING

Join

One-to-many relationship

Referential integrity constraint

Relationship

Update anomalies

Views

Virtual table

EXERCISES

1. Draw data models for the following situations. In each case, make certain that you show the attributes and feasible identifiers.
   a. A farmer can have many cows, but a cow belongs to only one farmer.
   b. A university has many students, and a student can attend at most one university.
   c. An aircraft can have many passengers, but a passenger can be on only one flight at a time.

    d.   A nation can have many states and a state many cities.

    e.   An art researcher has asked you to design a database to record details of artists and the museums in which their paintings are displayed. For each painting, the researcher wants to know the size of the canvas, year painted, title, and style. The nationality, date of birth and death of each artist must be recorded. For each museum, record details of its location and specialty, if it has one.

2.   (Report all values in British pounds.)

    a.   Report the value of stocks listed in Australia.

    b.   Report the dividend payment of all stocks.

    c.   Report the total dividend payment by nation.

    d.   Create a view containing nation, firm, price, quantity, exchange rate, value, and yield.

    e.   Report the average yield by nation.

    f.   Report the minimum and maximum yield for each nation.

    g.   Report the nations where the average yield of stocks exceeds the average yield of all stocks.

3.   How would you change the queries in exercise 4-2 if you were required to report the values in American dollars, Australian dollars, or Indian rupees?

4.   (This is a continuation of exercise 7 in Chapter 3.)

    Late the other night, after an horrendous statistics exam, Eduardo needed some stress relieving music. He knew there was a piece called *The Girl From Ipanema*, but could not remember the name of the album or the artist. He realized that his simple system for recording details of CDs is missing some important information. He does not keep track of the songs on each CD. Extend the simple data model developed previously to record details of the music on each CD.

    Are there any shortcomings with the data model you have created?

5.   What is a foreign key and what role does it serve?

6.   What is the referential integrity constraint? Why should it be enforced?

7.   Kisha, against the advice of her friends, was simultaneously studying data management and Shakespearian drama. She thought the two subjects would be an interesting contrast. However, the classes are very demanding and often enter her midsummer dreams. Last night, she dreamt that William Shakespeare wanted her to draw a data model. He explained, before she woke up in a cold sweat, that a play had many characters but the same character never appeared in more than one play. "Methinks," he said, "the same name may have appeareth more than the once, but twas always a person of a different ilk." He then, she hazily recollects, went on to spout about the quality of data dropping like the gentle rain.

    Draw a data model to keep old Bill quiet and help Kisha get some sleep.

8.   An orchestra has four broad classes of instruments (strings, woodwinds, brass, and percussion). Each class contains musicians who play different instruments. For example, the strings section of a full symphonic orchestra contains 2 harps, 16 to 18 first violins, 14 to 16 second violins, 12 violas, 10 cellos, and 8 double basses.

    A city has asked you to develop a database to store details of the musicians in its three orchestras. All the musicians are specialists and play only one instrument for one orchestra.

9. Answer the following queries based on the described relational database for a car dealer.

PERSON		
PERSONID	PERSFNAME	PERSLNAME

CAR				
CARID	CARCOST	CARSELL	CARTYPE	*PERSONID*

    a. What is the personid of Sheila O'Hara?
    b. List sales personnel sorted by last name and within last name, first name.
    c. List details of the sales made by Bruce Bush.
    d. List details of all sales showing the gross profit (selling price minus cost price).
    e. Report the number of cars sold of each type.
    f. What is the average selling price of cars sold by Sue Lim?
    g. Report details of all sales where the gross profit is less than the average.
    h. What was the maximum selling price of any car?
    i. What is the total gross profit?
    j. Report the gross profit made by each salesperson who sold at least three cars.
    k. Create a view containing all the details in the CAR table and the gross profit.

Chapter 5

The Many-to-Many Relationship

Fearful concatenation of circumstances.

Daniel Webster

Learning Objectives

On completion of this chapter, you will be able to:

- model a many-to-many relationship between two entities;
- define a database with a many-to-many relationship;
- write queries for a database with a many-to-many relationship.

The Expeditioner

*A*lice was deeply involved in uncovering the workings of her firm. She spent hours talking to the staff, wanting to know everything about the products sold. She engaged many a customer in conversation to find out why they shopped at The Expeditioner, what they were looking for, and how they thought the business could improve. She examined all the products herself and pestered the staff to tell her who bought them, how were they used, how many were sold, who supplied them, and a host of other questions. She plowed (or should that be 'ploughed') through accounting journals, sales reports, and market forecasts. She was more than a new broom; she was a giant vacuum cleaner sucking up data about the firm so that she would be prepared to manage it successfully.

Ned, the marketing manager, was a Jekyll and Hyde character. By day he was a charming, savvy, marketing executive. Walking to work in his three-piece suit, bowler hat, and furled umbrella, he was the epitome of the conservative English businessman. By night he became a computer nerd with ragged jeans, a t-shirt, thick, black-framed glasses, and unruly hair. Ned had been desperate to introduce computers to The Expeditioner for years, but he knew that he could never reveal his second nature. The other staff at The Expeditioner just would not accept such a radical change in technology. Why, they had not even switched to fountain pens until their personal stock of quill pens was finally depleted. Ned was just not prepared to face the indignant silence and contempt that would greet his mere mention of computers. It was better to continue a secret double life than admit to being a cyber punk.

But times were changing, and Ned saw the opportunity. He furtively suggested to Lady Alice that perhaps she needed a database of sales facts. Her response was instantaneous: "Yes, and do it as soon as possible." Ned was ecstatic. This was truly a wonderful woman.

| The Expeditioner |
| **Sale of Goods** |

Sale# 123456   Date:

	Item #	Description	Quantity	Unit price	Total
1					
2					
3					
4					
5					
6					
				Grand total	

Figure 5-1   A sales form

THE MANY-TO-MANY RELATIONSHIP

Consider the case when items are sold. We can immediately identify two entities: SALE and ITEM. A sale can consist of many items, and an item can appear in many sales. We are not saying the same item can be sold many times, but the particular type of item (e.g., a compass) can be sold many times; thus we have a **many-to-many (m:m) relationship** between SALE and ITEM. When we get an m:m relationship, we create a third entity to link the entities through two 1:m relationships. Usually, it is fairly easy to name this third entity. In this case, this third entity, sometimes known as an **intersection entity**, is called LINEITEM. A typical sales form (see Figure 5–1 for an example) lists the items purchased by a customer. Each of the lines appearing on the order form is generally known in retailing as a line item, which links an item and a sale.

The representation of this m:m relationship is shown in Figure 5–2. We say many-to-many because there are two relationships—ITEM is related to many SALEs, and SALE is related to many ITEMs. This data model can also be read as: "a sale has many line items, but a line item refers to only sale. Similarly, an item can appear as many line items, but a line item references only one item."

The entity SALE is identified by saleno (sale number) and has the attributes saledate and saletext (a brief comment on the customer—soft data). LINEITEM is partially identified by lineno (line number) and has attributes lineqty (line quantity—the number of units sold), and lineprice (sales price—the unit selling price for this sale). ITEM is identified by itemno

Figure 5-2   An m:m relationship

(item number) and has attributes itemname (item name), itemtype (item type, e.g., clothing, equipment, navigation aids, furniture, and so on), and itemcolor (item color).

If you look carefully at Figure 5–2, you will notice that we added a vertical bar to the crow's foot at the many end of the 1:m relationship between SALE and LINEITEM. This vertical bar provides information about the identifier of LINEITEM. As you know, every entity must have a unique identifier; in this case, it is lineno (remember, the asterisk prefix denotes an identifier). A sales order (see Figure 5–1) is a series of lines, and lineno is unique only within a particular order. If we just use lineno as the identifier, we cannot guarantee that every instance of LINEITEM is unique. But if we use saleno and lineno together, however, we have a unique identifier for every instance of LINEITEM. Saleno is unique for every sale and lineno is unique within any sale. The vertical bar indicates that LINEITEM's unique identifier is the concatenation of saleno and lineno.

Why Did We Create a Third Entity?

When we have an m:m relationship, we create an intersection entity to store data about the relationship. In this case, we have to store data about the items sold. We cannot store the data with SALE because a sale can be many items, and an entity only stores single-value facts. Similarly, we cannot store data with ITEM because an item can appear in many sales. Since we cannot store data in SALE or ITEM, we must create another entity to store data about the m:m relationship.

You might find it useful to think of the m:m relationship as two 1:m relationships. An item can appear on many line item listings, and a line item entry refers to only one item. A sale has many line items, and each line item entry refers to only one sale.

Social Security Number is Not Unique!

Two girls named Sarah Lee Ferguson were born on May 3, 1959. The U.S. government considered them one and the same and issued both the same Social Security number (SSN), a nine-digit identifier of U.S. residents. Now Sarah Lee Ferguson Boles and Sarah Lee Ferguson Johnson share the same SSN.

Mrs. Boles became aware of her SSN twin in 1987 when the Internal Revenue Service claimed there was a discrepancy in her reported income. Because SSN is widely used as an attribute or identifier in many computer systems, Mrs. Boles encountered other incidents of mistaken identity. Some of Mrs. Johnson's purchases appeared on Mrs. Boles credit reports.

In late 1989, the Social Security Administration notified Mrs. Boles that her original number was given to her in error and she had to provide evidence of her age, identity, and citizenship to get a new number. When Mrs. Boles gets her new SSN, it is likely she will have to get a new driver's license and establish a new credit history.[1]

---

[1] Adapted from "Two women share a number, birthday, and S. S. number!," *Athens* [*Georgia*] *Daily News*, 29 January 1990, 7A.

CREATING A RELATIONAL DATABASE WITH AN M:M RELATIONSHIP

As before, each entity becomes a table in a relational database, the entity name becomes the table name, each attribute becomes a column, and each identifier becomes a primary key. Remember, a 1:m relationship is mapped by adding a column to the entity of the many end of the relationship. The new column contains the identifier of the one end of the relationship.

Conversion of the foregoing data model results in the three tables shown in Table 5–1. Note the one-to-one correspondence between attributes and columns for SALE and ITEM. Observe the LINEITEM has two additional columns, SALENO and ITEMNO. Both of these columns are foreign keys in LINEITEM (remember the use of italics to signify foreign keys). Two foreign keys are required to record the two 1:m relationships. Notice in LINEITEM that SALENO is both part of the primary key and a foreign key.

The SQL commands to create the three tables are:

```
CREATE TABLE SALE
   (SALENO     INTEGER    NOT NULL,
    SALEDATE   DATE,
    SALETEXT   CHAR(50),
      PRIMARY KEY (SALENO))


CREATE TABLE ITEM
   (ITEMNO     INTEGER    NOT NULL,
    ITEMNAME   CHAR(30),
    ITEMTYPE   CHAR(1),
    ITEMCOLOR  CHAR(10),
      PRIMARY KEY (ITEMNO))


CREATE TABLE LINEITEM
   (LINENO     INTEGER    NOT NULL,
    LINEQTY    INTEGER,
    LINEPRICE  DECIMAL(7,2),
    SALENO     INTEGER    NOT NULL,
    ITEMNO     INTEGER    NOT NULL,
      PRIMARY KEY(LINENO,SALENO),
      FOREIGN KEY SALE(SALENO) REFERENCES SALE
         ON DELETE RESTRICT,
      FOREIGN KEY  ITEM(ITEMNO) REFERENCES ITEM
         ON DELETE RESTRICT)
```

While the SALE and ITEM tables are created in a similar fashion to previous examples, there are two things to notice about the definition of LINEITEM. First, the primary key is a composite of LINENO and SALENO. Remember, to uniquely identify an instance of LINEITEM, you need both LINENO and SALENO. Second, there are two foreign keys because LINENO is at the many end of two 1:m relationships.

Table 5–1   Relation tables SALE, LINEITEM, and ITEM

SALE		
SALENO	**SALEDATE**	**SALETEXT**
1	1995-01-15	Scruffy Australian—called himself Bruce.
2	1995-01-15	Man. Rather fond of hats.
3	1995-01-15	Woman. Planning to row Atlantic—lengthwise!
4	1995-01-15	Man. Trip to New York—thinks NY is a jungle!
5	1995-01-16	Expedition leader for African safari.

LINEITEM				
LINENO	**LINEQTY**	**LINEPRICE**	***SALENO***	***ITEMNO***
1	1	4.50	1	2
1	1	25.00	2	6
2	1	20.00	2	16
3	1	25.00	2	19
4	1	2.25	2	2
1	1	500.00	3	4
2	1	2.25	3	2
1	1	500.00	4	4
2	1	65.00	4	9
3	1	60.00	4	13
4	1	75.00	4	14
5	1	10.00	4	3
6	1	2.25	4	2
1	50	36.00	5	10
2	50	40.50	5	11
3	8	153.00	5	12
4	1	60.00	5	13
5	1	0.00	5	2

Table 5–1   Relation tables SALE, LINEITEM, and ITEM (continued)

ITEM			
ITEMNO	ITEMNAME	ITEMTYPE	ITEMCOLOR
1	Pocket knife–Nile	E	Brown
2	Pocket knife–Avon	E	Brown
3	Compass	N	—
4	Geo positioning system	N	—
5	Map measure	N	—
6	Hat–Polar Explorer	C	Red
7	Hat–Polar Explorer	C	White
8	Boots–snake proof	C	Green
9	Boots–snake proof	C	Black
10	Safari chair	F	Khaki
11	Hammock	F	Khaki
12	Tent–8 person	F	Khaki
13	Tent–2 person	F	Khaki
14	Safari cooking kit	E	—
15	Pith helmet	C	Khaki
16	Pith helmet	C	White
17	Map case	N	Brown
18	Sextant	N	—
19	Stetson	C	Black
20	Stetson	C	Brown

QUERYING AN M:M RELATIONSHIP

A Three–Table Join

The join operation can be easily extended from two tables to three or more merely by specifying the tables to be joined and the matching conditions. For example, to join the three tables shown in Table 5–1, use

```
SELECT * FROM SALE, LINEITEM, ITEM
   WHERE SALE.SALENO = LINEITEM.SALENO
     AND ITEM.ITEMNO = LINEITEM.ITEMNO
```

Note that the three tables to be joined are listed after the FROM clause. There are two matching conditions: one to match the SALE and LINEITEM tables (SALES.SALENO = LINEITEM.SALENO) and one to match the ITEM and LINEITEM tables (ITEM.ITEMNO = LINEITEM.ITEMNO). The intersection table, LINEITEM, is the link between the SALE and ITEM and must be referenced in both matching conditions.

Of course, we can tailor the join to be more precise and report some columns rather than all.

○ **List the names of items, quantity, and value of items sold on January 16, 1995.**

```
SELECT ITEMNAME, LINEQTY, LINEPRICE, LINEQTY*LINEPRICE
   FROM SALE, LINEITEM, ITEM
   WHERE LINEITEM.SALENO = SALE.SALENO
      AND ITEM.ITEMNO = LINEITEM.ITEMNO
      AND SALEDATE = '1995-01-16'
```

ITEMNAME	LINEQTY	LINEPRICE	EXPRESSION 1
Pocket knife—Avon	1	0.00	0.00
Safari chair	50	36.00	1800.00
Hammock	50	40.50	2025.00
Tent—8 person	8	153.00	1224.00
Tent—2 person	1	60.00	60.00

EXISTS—Does a Value Exist

EXISTS is used in a WHERE clause to test whether a table contains at least one row satisfying a specified condition. It returns the value *true* if and only if some row satisfies the condition, otherwise it returns *false*. EXISTS represents the **existential quantifier** of formal logic. The best way to get a feel for EXISTS is to examine a query.

○ **Report all clothing items for which a sale is recorded.**

```
SELECT ITEMNAME, ITEMCOLOR FROM ITEM
   WHERE ITEMTYPE = 'C'
      AND EXISTS (SELECT * FROM LINEITEM
         WHERE LINEITEM.ITEMNO = ITEM.ITEMNO)
```

ITEMNAME	ITEMCOLOR
Hat—Polar Explorer	Red
Boots—snake proof	Black
Pith helmet	White
Stetson	Black

Conceptually, we can think of this query as evaluating the subquery for each row of ITEM. The first clothing item, Hat–Polar Explorer (red), in ITEM has LINENO = 6. Thus, the query becomes

```
SELECT ITEMNAME, ITEMCOLOR FROM ITEM
  WHERE ITEMTYPE = 'C'
    AND EXISTS (SELECT * FROM LINEITEM
    WHERE LINEITEM.ITEMNO = 6)
```

Because there is at least one row in LINEITEM with ITEMNO = 6, the subquery returns *true*. The item has been sold and should be reported. The second clothing item, Hat–Polar Explorer (white), in ITEM has ITEMNO = 7. There are no rows in LINEITEM with ITEMNO = 7 so the subquery returns *false*. That item has not been sold and should not be reported.

You can also think of the query as: "Select clothing items for which a sale exists." Also remember, for EXISTS to return *true*, there need be only one row for which the condition is *true*.

NOT EXISTS — Select a Value if It Does Not Exist

NOT EXISTS is the negative of EXISTS. It is used in a WHERE clause to test whether all rows in a table fail to satisfy a specified condition. It returns the value *true* if there are no rows satisfying the condition; otherwise it returns *false*.

○ **Report all clothing items that have not been sold.**

```
SELECT ITEMNAME, ITEMCOLOR FROM ITEM
  WHERE ITEMTYPE = 'C'
    AND NOT EXISTS
      (SELECT * FROM LINEITEM
      WHERE ITEM.ITEMNO = LINEITEM.ITEMNO)
```

If we consider this query as the opposite of that used to illustrate EXISTS, it seems logical to use NOT EXISTS. Conceptually, we can also think of this query as evaluating the subquery for each row of ITEM. The first clothing item, Hat–Polar Explorer (red), in ITEM has LINENO = 6, thus the query becomes:

```
SELECT ITEMNAME, ITEMCOLOR FROM ITEM
  WHERE ITEMTYPE = 'C'
    AND NOT EXISTS
      (SELECT * FROM LINEITEM
      WHERE LINEITEM.ITEMNO = 6 )
```

There is at least one row in LINEITEM with ITEMNO = 6, so the subquery returns *true*. The NOT before EXISTS then negates the *true* to give *false*; the item will not be reported because it has been sold.

The second clothing item, Hat–Polar Explorer (white), in ITEM has ITEMNO = 7. The query becomes:

```
SELECT ITEMNAME, ITEMCOLOR FROM ITEM
    WHERE ITEMTYPE = 'C'
      AND NOT EXISTS
        (SELECT * FROM LINEITEM
          WHERE LINEITEM.ITEMNO = 7)
```

Because there are no rows in LINEITEM with ITEMNO = 7, the subquery returns *false*, and this is negated by the NOT before EXISTS to give *true*. The item has not been sold and should be reported.

```
ITEMNAME                   ITEMCOLOR
------------------------   ------------
Hat—Polar Explorer         White
Boots—snake proof          Green
Pith helmet                Khaki
Stetson                    Brown
```

You can also think of the query as: "Select clothing items for which no sales exists." Also remember, for NOT EXISTS to return *true*, no rows should satisfy the condition.

Data and Customer Service

In mid–1993, a computer system at Whirlpool Corp. alerted managers to a problem in a brand-new washing machine. After a few loads of washing, the machines were leaking badly. The cause—a faulty hose clamp—was soon identified. The computer system was then used to locate the few hundred customers who had purchased the faulty machine, and mechanics were sent to repair the problem. Whirlpool kept its customers happy and also avoided potential property-damage liability.

Customer information not only helps Whirlpool pinpoint faulty washing machines, it also helps the firm to lower its spare parts inventories and negotiate better deals with suppliers of motors and other components. For instance, if a particular motor fails too often, Whirlpool can renegotiate the supplier's warranty on the motor.

American corporations spent more than $1 billion in 1994 on computers and related technology for customer service departments because a customer database is an important aid to developing stronger relationships with customers. Indeed, for many American and European companies, customer service is the main focus of their investments in information technology.[2]

---

[2]Adapted from J. W. Verity, "The Gold Mine of Data in Customer Service," *Business Week*, 21 March 1994, 113–114.

Divide (and Be Conquered)

In addition to the existential qualifier that you have already encountered, formal logic has a **universal qualifier** known as *forall* which is necessary for queries such as:

❍ **Find the items that have appeared in all sales.**

If a universal qualifier were supported by SQL, this query could be phrased as: "Select item names where *forall* sales, there *exists* a LINEITEM row recording that this item was sold." A quick inspection of Table 5−1 shows that one item satisfies this condition (ITEMNO = 2).

Unfortunately, SQL does not directly support the universal qualifier. Nonetheless, formal logic shows that *forall* can always be converted into an equivalent statement using *exists*, and the query now becomes "Find items such that there does not exist a sale in which this item does not appear." Because this double negative is difficult to understand, and the conversion to SQL is not easy to follow, here is the correct SQL statement:

```
SELECT ITEMNO, ITEMNAME FROM ITEM
  WHERE NOT EXISTS
    (SELECT * FROM SALE
      WHERE NOT EXISTS
      (SELECT * FROM LINEITEM
        WHERE LINEITEM.ITEMNO = ITEM.ITEMNO
        AND LINEITEM.SALENO = SALE.SALENO))
```

```
        ITEMNO  ITEMNAME
--------------- -------------------------
             2  Pocket knife—Thames
```

You may be convinced that this query is correct by walking through it step by step using the data in Table 5−2 and examining the outcome of each step of the query (see Table 5−3).

Table 5−2   **Condensed Version of Relational Tables SALE, LINEITEM, and ITEM**

SALE
SALENO
1
2
3
4
5

(continued)

Table 5–2   Condensed Version of Relational Tables SALE, LINEITEM, and ITEM (continued)

LINEITEM		
LINENO	**SALENO**	**ITEMNO**
1	1	2
1	2	6
2	2	16
3	2	19
4	2	2
1	3	4
2	3	2
1	4	4
2	4	9
3	4	13
4	4	14
5	4	3
6	4	2
1	5	10
2	5	11
3	5	12
4	5	13
5	5	2

ITEM
ITEMNO
1
2
3
. . .

Step 1.

The first row of ITEM has ITEMNO = 1, and the first row of SALE has SALENO = 1. The innermost query becomes

```
SELECT * FROM LINEITEM
    WHERE LINEITEM.ITEMNO = 1
        AND LINEITEM.SALENO = 1
```

Examination of the LINEITEM tables shows this query returns *false*, which is negated by the NOT before the innermost EXISTS to give *true*.

Step 2.

We now advance to the second row of SALE with SALENO = 2, and execute the innermost query again. This query will also return *false* which will be negated to *true*.

Steps 3–5.

The results of these and other steps are summarized in Table 5–3.

Step 6.

The subquery

```
SELECT * FROM SALE
    WHERE NOT EXISTS (...
```

has now been executed for each value of SALENO for the first value of ITEMNO and returned *true* for each row. Thus this query returns *true*, and the NOT before the EXISTS of this query changes the *true* to *false*. Since the value returned is *false*, the current value of ITEMNO is not reported.

Steps 7–11.

The results of these steps are shown in Table 5–3.

Step 12.

The subquery

```
SELECT * FROM SALE
        WHERE NOT EXISTS (...
```

has now been executed for each value of SALENO for the second value of ITEMNO and returned *false* for each row. Although this query returns *false*, the NOT before the EXISTS changes the *false* to *true*. Since the value returned is *true*, the current value of ITEMNO is reported. Item 2 appears in all sales.

It will take you some time to step through this example to understand how the double NOT EXISTS works. Once you do, you will be convinced that the query does work.

Relational algebra (Chapter 13) has the **divide** operation, which makes these queries easy to write. Be careful: not all queries containing the word "all" are divides. With experience, you will learn to recognize and conquer divide.

Table 5–3 Results of the First 18 Steps of the Divide Statement

Step	ITEMNO	SALENO	SELECT * FROM LINEITEM WHERE LINEITEM.ITEMNO = ITEM.ITEMNO AND LINEITEM.SALENO = SALE.SALENO	NOT EXISTS	SELECT * FROM SALE WHERE NOT EXISTS (SELECT * FROM LINEITEM WHERE LINEITEM.ITEMNO = ITEM.ITEMNO AND LINEITEM.SALENO = SALE.SALENO)	NOT EXISTS
1	1	1	false	true		
2	1	2	false	true		
3	1	3	false	true		
4	1	4	false	true		
5	1	5	false	true		
6					true	false
7	2	1	true	false		
8	2	2	true	false		
9	2	3	true	false		
10	2	4	true	false		
11	2	5	true	false		
12					false	true
13	3	1	false	true		
14	3	2	false	true		
15	3	3	false	true		
16	3	4	true	false		
17	3	5	false	true		
18					true	false

Figure 5-3   A template for divide

To save the tedium of formulating this query from scratch, we have developed a template (see Figure 5–3) for dealing with these sorts of queries. Divide queries typically occur with m:m relationships.

An appropriate generic query and template SQL command are:

○ **Find the target1 that have appeared in all sources.**

```
SELECT TARGET1 FROM TARGET
   WHERE NOT EXISTS
      (SELECT * FROM SOURCE
         WHERE NOT EXISTS
            (SELECT * FROM TARGET-SOURCE
               WHERE TARGET-SOURCE.TARGET# = TARGET.TARGET#
                  AND TARGET-SOURCE.SOURCE# = SOURCE.SOURCE#))
```

SUMMARY

There can be a many-to-many (m:m) relationship between entities, which is represented by creating an intersection entity and two 1:m relationships. An intersection entity stores data about an m:m relationship. The join operation can be extended from two tables to three or more tables. EXISTS tests whether a table has at least one row that meets a specified condition. NOT EXISTS tests whether all rows in a table do not satisfy a specified condition. Both EXISTS and NOT EXISTS return *true* or *false*. The relational operation divide, also known as *forall*, can be translated into a double negative. It is represented in SQL by a query containing two NOT EXISTS statements.

KEY TERMS AND CONCEPTS

Divide	Many-to-many relationship
EXISTS	NOT EXISTS
Intersection entity	

EXERCISES

1. Draw data models for the following situations. In each case, think about the names you give each entity.

    a. Farmers can own cows or share cows with other farmers.

    b. A hamburger shop makes several types of hamburgers, and the same ingredient can be used with several types of hamburgers. This does not literally mean the same piece of lettuce is used many times, but lettuce is used with several types of hamburgers.

    c. A track and field meet can have many competitors, and a competitor can participate in more than one event.

    d. A patient can have many physicians, and a physician can have many patients.

    e. A student can attend more than one class, and the same class can have many students.

    f. *The Marathoner*, a monthly magazine, regularly reports the performance of professional marathon runners. It has asked you to design a database to record the details of all major marathons (e.g., Boston, London, and Paris). Professional marathon runners compete in several races each year. A race may have thousands of competitors, but only about 200 or so are professional runners, the ones *The Marathoner* tracks. For each race, the magazine reports a runner's time and finishing position and some personal details such as name, gender, and age.

2.   Write the following SQL queries for the database described in this chapter:

    a. List the names of items for which the quantity sold is greater than one.

    b. Compute the total value of sales for each item by date.

    c. Report all furniture items that have been sold.

    d. List all furniture that has not been sold.

    e. List all items that appear in sales with SALENO equals 3 or 4.

    f. Compute the total value of each sale.

3.   The data model shown was designed by a golf statistician. Write SQL statements to create the corresponding relational database.

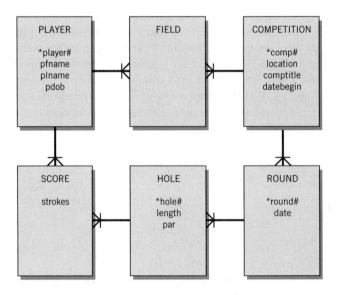

4.   Write SQL statements to create a relational database described by the following data model.

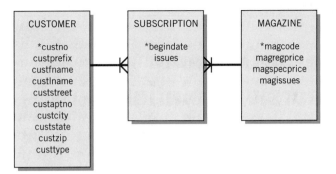

5. Why do you have to create a third entity when you have an m:m relationship?
6. What does a vertical bar on a relationship arc mean?
7. How does EXISTS differ from other clauses in an SQL statement?
8. How is the relational algebra divide statement implemented in SQL? What do you think of this approach?
9. Answer the following queries based on the described relational database.

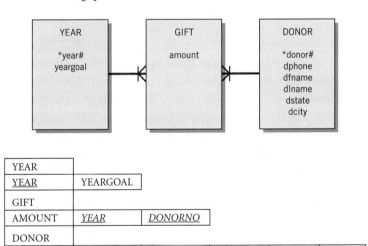

YEAR					
YEAR	YEARGOAL				
GIFT					
AMOUNT	*YEAR*	*DONORNO*			
DONOR					
DONORNO	DLNAME	DFNAME	DPHONE	DSTATE	DCITY

a. List the phone number of donor number 12345.
b. How many donors are there in the donor table?
c. How many people made donations in 1992?
d. What is the name of the person who made the largest donation in 1992?
e. What was the total amount donated in 1993?
f. List the donors who have made a donation every year.
g. List the donors who give twice the average.
h. List the total amount given by each person across all years, sort the report by the donor's name.
i. Report the total donations in 1994 by state.
j. In which years did the total donated exceed the goal for the year?

Chapter 6

One-to-One and Recursive Relationships

Self-reflection is the school of wisdom.

Baltastar Gracián, *The Art of Worldly Wisdom*, 1647

Learning Objectives

On completion of this chapter, you will be able to:
* model one-to-one and recursive relationships;
* define a database with one-to-one and recursive relationships;
* write queries for a database with one-to-one and recursive relationships.

The Expeditioner

A lice was convinced that a database of business facts would speed up decision making. Her initial experience with the sales database had reinforced this conviction. She decided that employee data should be computerized next. When she arrived at The Expeditioner, she found the company lacked an organization chart and job descriptions for employees. One of her first tasks had been to draw an organization chart.

She divided the firm into four departments and appointed a boss for each department. The first person listed in each department was its boss; of course, Alice was paramount.

Ned had finished the sales database, so the time was right to create an employee database. Ned seemed to be enjoying his new role, though his dress standard had slipped. Maybe Alice would have to move him out of Marketing. In fact, he sometimes reminded her of fellows who used to hang around the computer lab all day playing weird games. She wasn't quite ready to sound a "nerd alert," but it was getting close.

MODELING THE ONE-TO-ONE RELATIONSHIP

Initially, the organization chart appears to record two relationships. First, a department has one or more employees, and an employee belongs to one department. Second, a department has one boss, and a person is boss of only one department. That is, boss is a **1:1 relationship** between DEPT and EMP. The data model for this situation is shown in Figure 6–1.

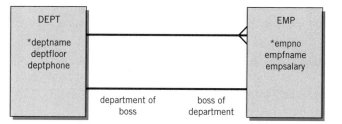

Figure 6–1   A data model illustrating a 1:1 relationship

As a general rule, the 1:1 relationship is labeled to avoid confusion because the meaning of such a relationship cannot always be inferred. This label is called a **relationship descriptor**. The 1:m relationship between DEPT and EMP is not labeled because its meaning is readily understood by reading the model. So use a relationship descriptor when there is more than one relationship between entities or the meaning of the relationship is not readily inferred from the model.

If we think about this problem, we realize there is more to boss than just a department. People also have a boss. Thus, Alice is the boss of all the other employees. In this case, we are mainly interested in who directly bosses someone else. So, Alice is the direct boss of Ned, Todd, Brier, and Sophie. We need to record the person–boss relationship as well as the department–boss relationship.

The person–boss relationship is a **1:m recursive relationship** because it is a relationship between employees—an employee has one boss and a boss can have many employees. The data model is shown in Figure 6–2.

It is a good idea to label the recursive relationship because its meaning is often not obvious from the data model.

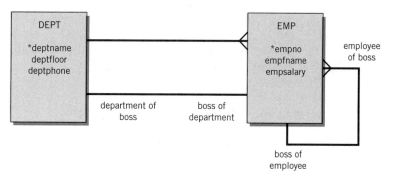

Figure 6–2   A data model illustrating a recursive 1:m relationship

MAPPING A ONE-TO-ONE RELATIONSHIP

Since mapping a 1:1 relationship follows the same rules as for any other data model, the major consideration is where to place the foreign key(s). There are three alternatives:

1. Put the foreign key in DEPT.

    Doing so means that every instance of DEPT will record "empno" of the employee who is boss. Because all departments in this case have a boss, the foreign key will always be non-null.

2. Put the foreign key in EMP.

    Choosing this alternative means that every instance of EMP will record "deptname" of the department this employee bosses. Since many employees are not bosses, the foreign key will generally be null.

3. Put a foreign key in both DEPT and EMP.

    The consequences of putting a foreign key in both tables in the 1:1 relationship is the combination of points 1 and 2.

Although it does not matter where you put the foreign key, a reasonable approach is to select the entity that results in the fewest nulls as this tends to be less confusing to users.

MAPPING A RECURSIVE RELATIONSHIP

A 1:m recursive relationship is mapped like a standard 1:m relationship. An additional column, for the foreign key, is created for the entity at the many end of the relationship. Of course, in this case the one and many end are the same entity, so an additional column is added to EMP. This column contains the key, "empno," of the one end of the relationship. Since EMPNO is already used as a column name, a different name needs to be selected. In this case, it makes sense to call the foreign key column BOSSNO since it stores the boss's employee number.

The mapping of the data model is shown in Table 6–1. Note that "deptname" becomes a column in EMP, the many end of the 1:m relationship, and "empno" becomes a foreign key in DEPT, an end of the 1:1 relationship.

If you examine EMP, you will see that the boss of the employee with EMPNO = 2 (Ned) has BOSSNO = 1. You can then look up the row with EMPNO = 1 to find that Ned's boss is Alice. This 'double lookup' is frequently used when manually interrogating a table that represents a recursive relationship. Soon you will discover how this is handled with SQL.

Here is the SQL to create the two tables:

```
CREATE TABLE DEPT
     (DEPTNAME      CHAR(15)      NOT NULL,
      DEPTFLOOR     SMALLINT      NOT NULL,
      DEPTPHONE     SMALLINT      NOT NULL,
      EMPNO         SMALLINT      NOT NULL,
       PRIMARY KEY(DEPTNAME))
```

Table 6–1   The Relational Tables DEPT and EMP

DEPT			
DEPTNAME	DEPTFLOOR	DEPTPHONE	EMPNO
Management	5	2001	1
Marketing	1	2002	2
Accounting	4	2003	5
Purchasing	4	2004	7
Personnel & PR	1	2005	9

EMP				
EMPNO	EMPFNAME	EMPSALARY	DEPTNAME	BOSSNO
1	Alice	75000	Management	
2	Ned	45000	Marketing	1
3	Andrew	25000	Marketing	2
4	Clare	22000	Marketing	2
5	Todd	38000	Accounting	1
6	Nancy	22000	Accounting	5
7	Brier	43000	Purchasing	1
8	Sarah	56000	Purchasing	7
9	Sophie	35000	Personnel & PR	1

```
CREATE TABLE EMP
   (EMPNO          SMALLINT        NOT NULL,
   EMPFNAME        CHAR(10),
   EMPSALARY       DECIMAL(7,0),
   DEPTNAME        CHAR(15),
   BOSSNO          SMALLINT,
      PRIMARY KEY(EMPNO),
      FOREIGN KEY DEPT(DEPTNAME) REFERENCES DEPT
         ON DELETE RESTRICT)
```

You will notice that some of the foreign keys have not been specified in the CREATE statements. There is no foreign key definition for EMPNO in DEPT and for BOSSNO in EMP (the recursive boss relationship). Why?

First, observe that DEPTNAME is a foreign key in EMP. If we make EMPNO a foreign key in DEPT, then we have a deadly embrace. A new department cannot be added to the DEPT table until there is a boss for that department (i.e., there is a person in the EMP table with the EMPNO of the boss); however, the other constraint states that an employee cannot be added to the EMP table unless there is a department to which that person is assigned. If we have both foreign key constraints, we cannot add a new department until we have added a boss, and we cannot add a boss until we have added a department for that person. Nothing, under these circumstances, can happen if both foreign key constraints are in place. So, only one of the foreign key constraints is specified.

In the case of the recursive relationship for the entity EMPLOYEE, there is no foreign key constraint because some versions of SQL do not allow this constraint to refer to the table being created. Also, observe that the foreign key BOSSNO can be null. This caters to the situation where a person (e.g., Alice) does not have a boss. Similarly, DEPTNAME in EMP is allowed to take null values to handle the situation where a person is not assigned to a department. These two examples illustrate that each foreign key value must match a primary key value or else be null.

As this example shows, the FOREIGN KEY clause provides limited support for ensuring referential integrity. In more complex modeling situations, such as when there are multiple relationships between a pair of entities, use of a FOREIGN KEY clause may result in a deadlock. Always consider the consequences of using a FOREIGN KEY clause before applying it.

QUERYING A ONE-TO-ONE RELATIONSHIP

Querying presents no special difficulties but does allow us to see additional features of SQL.

○ **List the salary of each department's boss.**

```
SELECT EMPFNAME, DEPTNAME, EMPSALARY FROM EMP
    WHERE EMPNO IN (SELECT EMPNO FROM DEPT)
```

or

```
SELECT EMPFNAME, DEPT.DEPTNAME, EMPSALARY
    FROM EMP, DEPT WHERE
    DEPT.EMPNO = EMP.EMPNO
```

EMPFNAME	DEPTNAME	EMPSALARY
Alice	Management	75000
Ned	Marketing	45000
Todd	Accounting	38000
Brier	Purchasing	43000
Sophie	Personnel & PR	35000

QUERYING A RECURSIVE RELATIONSHIP

Handling a query for a recursive relationship is puzzling until you realize that you can join a table to itself. To demonstrate:

○ **Find the salary of Nancy's boss.**

```
SELECT WRK.EMPFNAME, BOSS.EMPSALARY
  FROM EMP WRK, EMP BOSS
    WHERE WRK.EMPFNAME = 'NANCY'
      AND WRK.BOSSNO = BOSS.EMPNO
```

Think of this query as joining two copies of the same table. Notice that there is a suffix (WRK and BOSS) for each copy of the table to distinguish between them. It helps to use a suffix that makes sense. In this case, the WRK and BOSS suffixes can be thought of as referring to worker and boss tables, respectively. You can understand how the query works by examining Table 6–2.

Table 6–2 Joining a Table with Itself

EMP WRK				
__EMPNO__	__EMPFNAME__	__EMPSALARY__	_DEPTNAME_	_BOSSNO_
1	Alice	75000	Management	
2	Ned	45000	Marketing	1
3	Andrew	25000	Marketing	2
4	Clare	22000	Marketing	2
5	Todd	38000	Accounting	1
6	Nancy	22000	Accounting	5
7	Brier	43000	Purchasing	1
8	Sarah	56000	Purchasing	7
9	Sophie	35000	Personnel & PR	1

EMP BOSS				
__EMPNO__	__EMPFNAME__	__EMPSALARY__	_DEPTNAME_	_BOSSNO_
1	Alice	75000	Management	
2	Ned	45000	Marketing	1
3	Andrew	25000	Marketing	2
4	Clare	22000	Marketing	2
5	Todd	38000	Accounting	1
6	Nancy	22000	Accounting	5
7	Brier	43000	Purchasing	1
8	Sarah	56000	Purchasing	7
9	Sophie	35000	Personnel & PR	1

The first step is to find the row in WRK where the employee's name is "Nancy." This row is shaded in WRK. The BOSSNO column of this row contains 5. The second step is to join this row to the row in the BOSS table with EMPNO = 5. This row is also shaded. The result of the SQL query is

```
EMPFNAME        EMPSALARY
--------------  -------------
Nancy               38000
```

○ **Find the names of employees who earn more than their boss.**

```
SELECT WRK.EMPFNAME
   FROM EMP WRK, EMP BOSS
      WHERE WRK.BOSSNO = BOSS.EMPNO
         AND WRK.EMPSALARY > BOSS.EMPSALARY
```

This would be very easy if the employee and boss data were in the same row. We could simply compare the salaries of the two people. To get the data in the one row, we join by matching BOSSNO in WRK with EMPNO in BOSS. The result is

| WRK | | | | | BOSS | | | | |
EMPNO	EMPFNAME	EMPSALARY	DEPTNAME	BOSSNO	EMPNO	EMPFNAME	EMPSALARY	DEPTNAME	BOSSNO
2	Ned	45,000	Marketing	1	1	Alice	75,000	Management	
3	Andrev	25,000	Marketing	2	2	Ned	45,000	Marketing	1
4	Clare	22,000	Marketing	2	2	Ned	45,000	Marketing	1
5	Todd	38,000	Accounting	1	1	Alice	75,000	Management	
6	Nancy	22,000	Accounting	5	5	Todd	38,000	Accounting	1
7	Brier	43,000	Purchasing	1	1	Alice	75,000	Management	
8	Sarah	56,000	Purchasing	7	7	Brier	43,000	Purchasing	1
9	Sophie	35,000	Personnel & PR	1	1	Alice	75,000	Management	

Now the rest of the query is very straightforward. It is easy to compare the salaries of employees and their boss. The result is:

```
EMPFNAME
--------------
Sarah
```

Decision Support at Lands' End

Lands' End uses direct mailing of catalogs to market clothing for adults and children. It has approximately 17 million customers and 1993 sales exceeded $800 million. Printing and delivery of catalogs is expensive, and Lands' End needs to precisely target its mailing to reach the customers who are most likely to buy. Variables such as lifetime customer value, geographic location, and recent purchases can be used to determine who should receive a catalog. To assist in making such decisions, Lands' End has developed a decision support system (DSS) based on IBM's DB2.

Prior to implementing the DSS, Lands' End staff first used data modeling to identify data items and their descriptions. Then the model was converted to a physical design. Because around 150 Gbytes of data or over one billion rows had to be stored, considerable attention was paid to physical design. Indexes were created for frequently accessed columns in some tables. Large tables (those with over two million rows) were partitioned.

A typical business question might be:

What was the return rate for the women's division, grouped by category, in our Christmas catalog? Compare this year to last year.

The SQL query is:

```
SELECT      CATALOG-YEAR,
            CATALOG-DESC,
            PRODUCT-CATEGORY-DESC,
            SUM(RETURNS)/SUM(SHIPMENTS)
FROM        SHIPMENT_TBL D,
            RETURN_TBL R
WHERE       D.ORDER = R.ORDER
AND         DIVISION = 'WOMENS'
AND         CATALOG_YEAR IN (1992,1993)
AND         CATALOG_ID = 'XMAS'
GROUP BY    CATEGORY_YEAR
            CATALOG_DESC,
            PRODUCT_CATEGORY_DESC
```

Queries like these are built by a software tool on the user's workstation and passed to DB2 for execution. DB2 extracts the required data, and the answer is returned to the workstation where it is formatted for presentation.

Lands' End experienced some interesting implementation problems. Data integrity and program bugs are a major problem when a huge volume of data is loaded into a database. When preparing one billion rows of data, the "one-

(continued)

in-a-million" error occurs **1000** times. Errors that may be seen every few years are found and must be corrected before the database can be implemented. It also takes a very long time to load one billion rows of data.

The new DSS means that queries that would have taken hours, or sometimes days, are now satisfied in minutes. Lands' End can use its DSS to market its products more effectively.[1]

The Expeditioner

*A*lice has found several histories of The Expeditioner from a variety of eras. Because many expeditions they outfitted were conducted under royal patronage, it was not uncommon for these histories to refer to British kings and queens. Alice could remember very little about British history, however, let alone when various kings and queens reigned. This sounded like another database problem for Ned. She would ask him to create a database that recorded details of each monarch. She thought it also would be useful to record details of royal succession.

MODELING A ONE-TO-ONE RECURSIVE RELATIONSHIP

The British monarchy can be represented by a simple one entity model. A monarch has one direct successor and one direct predecessor. The sequencing of monarchs can be modeled by a **1:1 recursive relationship** shown in Figure 6–3.

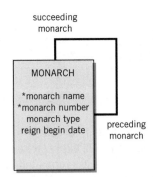

Figure 6–3   A data model illustrating a 1:1 recursive relationship

---

[1] Adapted from G. G. Bustamente and K. Sorenson, "Decision Support at Lands' End—An Evolution," *IBM Systems Journal* 33 (2):228–238 (1994).

Table 6–3   The Relation Table MONARCH

MONARCH							
MONNAME	**MONNUM**	**MONTYPE**	**RGNBEG**	*PRE MONNAME*	*PRE MONNUM*	*SUC MONNAME*	*SUC MONNUM*
Victoria	I	Queen	1837/6/20	William	IV	Edward	VII
Edward	VII	King	1901/1/22	Victoria	I	George	V
George	V	King	1910/5/6	Edward	VII	Edward	VIII
Edward	VIII	King	1936/1/20	George	V	George	VI
George	VI	King	1936/12/11	Edward	VIII	Elizabeth	II
Elizabeth	II	Queen	1952/2/6	George	VI		

MAPPING A ONE–TO–ONE RECURSIVE RELATIONSHIP

The 1:1 recursive relationship is mapped by adding two foreign keys to MONARCH. One foreign key for the succeeding and one for the preceding relationship. Since each instance of a monarch is identified by a composite key, this results in two columns being added to MONARCH for each foreign key. A portion of the resulting table is shown in Table 6–3.

The SQL statements to create the table are very straightforward. Notice that the primary key is a composite, and because the relationship is recursive, the two foreign key constraints cannot be defined. Also notice that the foreign keys are allowed to be null to account for the first monarch, who had no predecessor, and the latest monarch, whose successor is not yet known.

```
CREATE TABLE MONARCH
     (MONNAME        CHAR(15)      NOT NULL,
     MONNUM          CHAR(5)       NOT NULL,
     MONTYPE         CHAR(5)       NOT NULL,
     RGNBEG          DATE,
     PREMONNAME      CHAR(15),
     PREMONNUM       CHAR(5),
     SUCMONNAME      CHAR(15),
     SUCMONNUM       CHAR(5),
        PRIMARY KEY(MONNAME,MONNUM))
```

QUERYING A ONE-TO-ONE RECURSIVE RELATIONSHIP

Some queries on the MONARCH table demonstrate querying a 1:1 recursive relationship.

○   **Who preceded Elizabeth II?**

```
SELECT PREMONNAME, PREMONNUM FROM MONARCH
   WHERE MONNAME = 'ELIZABETH' AND MONNUM = 'II'
```

```
PREMONNAME      PREMONNUM
---------------  -----------
GEORGE           VI
```

This is simple because all the data are in one row. A more complex query is:

○ **Was Elizabeth II's predecessor a king or queen?**

```
SELECT PRE.MONTYPE FROM MONARCH NOW, MONARCH PRE
    WHERE NOW.PREMONNAME = PRE.MONNAME
      AND NOW.PREMONNUM = PRE.MONNUM
        AND NOW.MONNAME = 'ELIZABETH' AND NOW.MONNUM = 'II'
```

```
MONTYPE
---------------
King
```

This is very similar to the query to find the salary of Nancy's boss. The MONARCH table is joined with itself to create a row that contains all the details to answer the query.

○ **List the kings and queens of England in ascending order.**

```
SELECT MONTYPE, MONNAME, MONNUM, RGNBEG
    FROM MONARCH ORDER BY RGNBEG
```

MONTYPE	MONNAME	MONNUM	RGNBEG
Queen	Victoria	I	1837-06-20
King	Edward	VII	1901-01-22
King	George	V	1910-05-06
King	Edward	VIII	1936-01-20
King	George	VI	1936-12-11
Queen	Elizabeth	II	1952-02-06

This is a simple query because RGNBEG is like a ranking column. It would not be enough to store just the year in RGNBEG because two kings started their reigns in 1936, hence the full date is required.

*N*ed quickly finished the Monarch database. It really was straightforward and needed infrequent updating, unless of course Alice decided to keep track of all members of the Royal Family. What with the recent goings-on, he would be as busy as a tabloid reporter if he were required to maintain such a database.

Of course, Alice soon had another project for Ned. The Expeditioner keeps a wide range of products that are sometimes assembled into kits to make other products. For example, the animal photography kit is made up of eight items that The Expeditioner also sells separately. In addition, some kits became part of much larger kits. The animal photography kit is included as one of forty-five items in the East African Safari package. All of the various items are considered products, and each has its own product code. Ned was now required to create a product database that would keep track of all the items in The Expeditioner's stock.

MODELING A MANY-TO-MANY RECURSIVE RELATIONSHIP

The assembly of products to create other products is very common in business. Manufacturing even has a special term to describe it: a bill of materials. Data modeling is relatively simple once you realize that a product can appear as part of many other products and can be composed of many other products; that is, we have an **m:m recursive relationship** for product. As usual, we turn an m:m relationship into two 1:m relationships. Thus, we get the data model displayed in Figure 6-4.

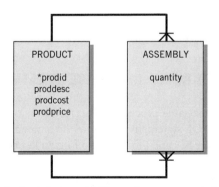

Figure 6−4   A data model illustrating an m:m relationship

Table 6–4   Relational Tables PRODUCT and ASSEMBLY

PRODUCT			
PRODID	**PRODDESC**	**PRODCOST**	**PRODPRICE**
1000	Animal photography kit		725
101	35mm camera	150	300
102	Camera case	10	15
103	70-210 zoom lens	125	200
104	28-85 zoom lens	115	185
105	Photographer's vest	25	40
106	Lens cleaning cloth	1	1.25
107	Tripod	35	45
108	24 exposure, 100 ASA, 35mm color negative film	.85	1

ASSEMBLY		
QUANTITY	*PRODID*	*SUBPRODID*
1	1000	101
1	1000	102
1	1000	103
1	1000	104
1	1000	105
2	1000	106
1	1000	107
10	1000	108

MAPPING A MANY-TO-MANY RECURSIVE RELATIONSHIP

Mapping follows the same procedure described previously, producing the two tables shown in Table 6-4. The SQL statements to create the tables are shown next. Observe that ASSEMBLY has a composite key and there are two foreign key constraints.

```
CREATE TABLE PRODUCT
    (PRODID      INTEGER   NOT NULL,
    PRODDESC     CHAR(30),
    PRODCOST     DECIMAL(9,2),
    PRODPRICE    DECIMAL(9,2),
        PRIMARY KEY(PRODID))
```

```
CREATE TABLE ASSEMBLY
   (QUANTITY INTEGER     NOT NULL,
   PRODID    INTEGER,
   SUBPRODID INTEGER,
     PRIMARY KEY(PRODID, SUBPRODID),
     FOREIGN KEY PROD(PRODID) REFERENCES PRODUCT,
     FOREIGN KEY SUBPROD(SUBPRODID) REFERENCES
          PRODUCT).
```

QUERYING A MANY-TO-MANY RECURSIVE RELATIONSHIP

○ **List the product identifier of each component of the animal photography kit.**

```
SELECT SUBPRODID FROM PRODUCT, ASSEMBLY
   WHERE PRODDESC = 'Animal photography kit'
     AND PRODUCT.PRODID = ASSEMBLY.PRODID
```

```
SUBPRODID
------------
101
106
107
105
104
103
102
108
```

○ **List the product description and cost of each component of the animal photography kit.**

```
SELECT B.PRODDESC, B.PRODCOST FROM PRODUCT A, ASSEMBLY, PRODUCT B
   WHERE A.PRODDESC = 'Animal photography kit'
     AND A.PRODID = ASSEMBLY.PRODID
     AND ASSEMBLY.SUBPRODID = B.PRODID
```

or

```
SELECT PRODDESC, PRODCOST FROM PRODUCT
   WHERE PRODID IN
        (SELECT SUBPRODID FROM PRODUCT, ASSEMBLY
            WHERE PRODDESC = 'Animal photography kit'
                AND PRODUCT.PRODID = ASSEMBLY.PRODID)
```

```
PRODDESC                                PRODCOST
--------------------------------------  ---------------
35mm camera                              150.00
Camera case                               10.00
70-210 zoom lens                         125.00
28-85 zoom lens                          115.00
Photographer's vest                       25.00
Lens cleaning cloth                        1.00
Tripod                                    35.00
24 exp. 100ASA 35mm col neg                0.85
```

Database Design in a High Power Distance Culture: When Recursive Relationships Matter

A Brazilian insurance broker has designed a database to store information about its customers. Along with maintaining data about a customer's claims and premium payments, the database records details of a customer's personal influence and their relationship to powerful people. This database is used to differentiate the service provided to customers. Consider the following two situations.

As a result of a car accident, Maria contacts her insurance broker. On checking her database record, the broker discovers that Maria is not a major customer, she has a single auto insurance policy. However, Maria's husband Joao is a director of Brazilian Industries, a large company, which is one of the broker's important customers. Furthermore, Joao is instrumental in deciding with whom his company insures. Maria is a very important customer because of her husband's influence. Consequently, the insurance broker immediately sends a representative to the accident scene. The representative is authorized to negotiate an agreement and pay damages to the parties involved. Also, the broker's representative will take Maria where she wants to go. In addition, the account manager for Brazilian Industries will be notified immediately, and he will keep Joao informed of the entire process. The particular details of Maria's auto insurance policy are irrelevant. All damages will be paid irrespective of the policy because Maria is connected to a powerful person.

Elizabete, a client of the same insurance broker, has a car accident. When she contacts the insurance broker, the customer service representative checks the database and notes that Elizabete has a single auto insurance policy with it. Because neither Elizabete nor her relatives are influential, the representative advises her of the procedures for submitting a claim and asks her to come to the broker's office to sign the documents. Elizabete's claim will be examined closely to ensure that it is in line with her policy.

It is unlikely that this difference in treatment of ostensibly similar customers would be expected or accepted in Australia or the United States, countries characterized by cultures in which power distance is very low.[2] This means that people in

---

[2]For a comprehensive discussion of national culture and its effects, see G. Hofstede, *Culture and Organizations: Software of the Mind* (London: McGraw–Hill, 1991).

these nations believe everyone has equal rights and should receive the same level of customer service. Brazil, like many Latin American nations, is a high power distance culture. Inequities in the distribution of power are countenanced. Society accepts that powerful people are entitled to privileges and a higher level of customer service.

Building a database that stores details of a customer's potential influence is the smart thing to do if you operate in a high power distance culture. Powerful customers expect deferential treatment. In a low power distance culture, a database also can be used to provide differentiated treatment to a customer, but the key lies in the customer's past or potential profitability to the firm. For example, airlines reward frequent flyers with free tickets when their travel with a particular company exceeds predefined distances.

Interestingly, one of the main design problems for the Brazilian insurance broker was sorting out the many recursive relationships. As you know, people can have a wide variety of relationships to other people. In a high power distance country, expect data models to reflect cultural norms and possibly have more recursive relationships for entities that describe people.[3]

SUMMARY

Relationships can be one-to-one and recursive. A recursive relationship is within a single entity rather than between entities. Recursive relationships are mapped to the relational model in the same way as other relationships. Resolution of queries involving recursive relationships often requires a table to be joined with itself. Many-to-many recursive relationships occur in business in the form of a bill of materials.

KEY TERMS AND CONCEPTS

Joining a table with itself	One-to-one relationship
Many-to-many recursive relationship	Recursive relationship
One-to-many recursive relationship	Relationship descriptor
One-to-one recursive relationship	

EXERCISES

1. Draw data models for the following problems:
   a. (i) A dairy farmer, who is also a part-time cartoonist, has several herds of cows. He has assigned each cow to a particular herd. In each herd, the farmer has one cow that is his favorite—often that cow is featured in a cartoon.
   (ii) A few malcontents in each herd, mainly those who feel they should have appeared in the cartoon, disagree with the farmer's choice of a favorite cow, whom

---

[3]Dr. Eduardo Morgado of the State University of São Paulo, Brazil provided the information for this case.

they disparagingly refer to as the "sacred" cow. As a result, each herd has now elected a herd leader.

b. The originator of a pyramid marketing scheme has a system for selling ethnic jewelry. The pyramid has three levels—gold, silver, and bronze. New associates join the pyramid at the bronze level. They contribute 30 percent of the revenue of their sales of jewelry to the silver chief in charge of their clan. In turn, silver chiefs contribute 30 percent of what they receive from bronze associates to the gold master in command of their tribe. Finally, gold masters pass on 30 percent of what they receive to the originator of the scheme.

c. The legion, the basic combat unit of the ancient Roman army, contained 3000 to 6000 men, consisting primarily of heavy infantry (hoplites), supported by light infantry (velites), and sometimes by cavalry. The hoplites were drawn up in three lines. The hastati (youngest men) were in the first, the principes (seasoned troops) in the second, and the triarii (oldest men) behind them, reinforced by velites. Each line was divided into ten maniples, consisting of two centuries (60 to 80 men per century) each. Each legion had a commander and a century was commanded by a centurion. Julius Caesar, through one of his Californian channelers, has asked you to design a database to maintain details of soldiers. Of course, Julius is a little forgetful at times, and he has not supplied the titles of the officers who command maniples, lines, and hoplites, but he expects that you can handle this lack of fine detail.

d. A travel agency is frequently asked questions about tourist destinations. For example, customers want to know details of the climate for a particular month, the population of the city, and other geographic facts. Also, they often request the flying time and distance between two cities. The manager has asked you to create a database to maintain these facts.

e. The Center for the Study of World Trade keeps track of trade treaties between nations. For each treaty, it records details of the countries signing the treaty and where and when it was signed.

f. Design a database to store details about U.S. presidents and their terms in office. Also, record details of their date and place of birth, gender, and political party affiliation (e.g., Caluthumpian Progress Party). You are required to record the sequence of presidents so the predecessor and successor of any president can be identified. How will you model the case of Grover Cleveland who served non-consecutive terms as president? Is it feasible that political party affiliation may change? If so, how will you handle it?

g. The IS department of a large organization makes extensive use of software modules. New applications are built, where possible, from existing modules. Software modules can also contain other modules. The IS manager realizes that she now needs a database to keep track of which modules are used in which applications or other modules. (Hint: it is helpful to think of an application as a module.)

2. Write SQL to answer the following queries using the DEPT and EMP tables described in this chapter.

a. Find the departments where all the employees earn less than their boss.

  b. Find the names of employees who are in the same department as their boss (as an employee).

  c. List the departments having an average salary greater than $25,000.

  d. List the departments where the average salary of the employees of each boss is greater than $25,000.

  e. List the names and manager of the employees of the Marketing department who have a salary greater than $25,000.

  f. List the names of the employees who earn more than any employee in the Marketing department.

3. Write SQL to answer the following queries using the MONARCH table described in this chapter.

  a. Who succeeded Victoria I?

  b. How many days did Victoria I reign?

  c. How many kings are there in the table?

  d. Which monarch had the shortest reign?

4. Write SQL to answer the following queries using the PRODUCT and ASSEMBLY tables.

  a. How many different items are there in the animal photography kit?

  b. What is the most expensive item in the animal photography kit?

  c. What is the total cost of the components of the animal photography kit?

  d. Compute the total quantity of all items required to assemble fifteen animal photography kits.

Chapter 7

Data Modeling

Man is a knot, a web, a mesh into which relationships are tied. Only those relationships matter.

Saint-Exupéry in *Flight to Arras*

INTRODUCTION

You were introduced to the basic building blocks of data modeling in Chapters 3 through 6. Now it is time to learn how to assemble blocks to build a data model. Data modeling is a method for determining what data and relationships should be stored in the database. It is also a way of communicating a database design.

The goal of data modeling is to identify the facts that must be stored in a database. A data model is not concerned with how the data will be stored. This is the concern of those who implement the database. A data model is not concerned with how the data will be processed. This is the province of process modeling, which is generally taught in systems analysis and design courses. The goal is to create a data model that is an accurate representation of data needs and real world data relationships.

Building a data model is a partnership between a client, a representative of the eventual users of the database, and a designer. Of course, there can be a team of clients and designers. For simplicity, we assume there is one client and one designer.

Drawing a data model is an iterative process of trial and revision. A data model is a working document that will change as you learn more about the client's needs and world. Your early versions are likely to be quite different from the final product. Draw your diagrams with a pencil and keep an extra large eraser handy. Better still, use software for drawing and revising the data model.

THE BUILDING BLOCKS

The purpose of a database is to store data about things. These things can include facts (e.g., an exchange rate), plans (e.g., scheduled production of two-person tents for June), estimates (e.g., forecast of demand for geo positioning systems), and a variety of other data. A data model describes these things and their relationships with other things using four components: entity, identifier, relationship, and attribute.

Entity

The entity is the basic building block of a data model. An **entity** is a thing about which data should be stored, something we need to describe. Each entity in a data model has a unique name that we write in singular form. Why singular? Because we want to emphasize that a data model describes an instance of a thing. Thus, we previously used the word SHARE to define an entity because it describes each instance of a share rather than shares in general.

We have already introduced the convention that an entity is represented by a rectangle and the name of the entity is shown in upper case (see Figure 7–1).

One important distinction to remember is that an entity describes a thing that will be stored in a database. A data model will rarely have more than one hundred entities. A database stores instances of the things described in the model and can easily contain millions of instances (rows) for any one entity (table). Imagine the number of instances in a national tax department's database.

How do you begin to identify entities? One approach is to underline any nouns in the problem description. Most nouns are possible entities and underlining ensures that you do not overlook any potential entities. Start by selecting an entity that seems central to the problem. If you were designing a student database, you might start with the entity student. Once you have picked a central entity, describe it. Then move to the others.

Attributes

An **attribute** describes an entity. When an entity has been identified, the next step is to determine its attributes, or the data that should be kept to describe the entity realistically. An attribute name is singular and unique within the data model. You may need to use a prefix to make an attribute name unique (e.g., "hire date" and "sale date" rather than just "date").

Our convention is that the name of an attribute is recorded in lower case within the entity rectangle. Figure 7–2 illustrates that SHARE has attributes share code, share name, share price, share quantity, share dividend, and share PE. Notice the frequent use of the prefix share. It is possible that other entities in the database might also have a price and quantity, so we use a prefix to create unique attribute names.

Figure 7–1   The entity SHARE

Figure 7–2   The entity SHARE and its attributes

Defining attributes generally takes considerable discussion with the client. You should include any attribute that is likely to be required for present or future decision making. But don't get carried away. Avoid storing unnecessary data. For example, to describe the entity "student" you usually record date of birth, but it is unlikely that you would store height. But, if you were describing an entity "patient," it might be necessary to record height because this is sometimes relevant to medical decision making.

An attribute has a single value, which possibly can be null. Multiple values are not allowed. If you need to store multiple values, it is a signal that you have a 1:m relationship and need to define another entity.

Relationship

Entities are related to other entities. If there were no relationships between entities, there would be no need for a data model and no need for a relational database. A simple, flat file (a single entity database) would be sufficient. A **relationship** is binary. It describes a linkage between two entities and is represented by an arc between them.

Because a relationship is binary, it has two relationship descriptors, one for each entity. Each **relationship descriptor** has a degree stating how many instances of the other entity may be related to each instance of the described entity. Consider the entities STOCK and NATION and their 1:m relationship (see Figure 7–3). We have two relationship descriptors: "stocks of nation" for NATION and "nation of stock" for STOCK. The relationship descriptor "stocks of nation" has a degree of m because a nation may have zero or more listed stocks. The relationship descriptor "nation of stock" has a degree of 1 because a stock is listed in at most one nation.

Because relationship descriptors frequently can be inferred, there is no need to label them; however, each additional arc between two entities must be labeled to clarify meaning. Also, it is a good idea to label 1:1 relationships because the relationship descriptors are not always obvious.

Consider the fragment in Figure 7–4. The descriptors of the 1:m relationship can be in-

Figure 7–3   A 1:m relationship between STOCK and NATION

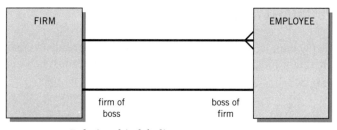

Figure 7–4   Relationship labeling

ferred as "firm has employees" and "employee belongs to firm." The 1:1 relationship is clarified by labeling the arcs.

Identifier

An **identifier** uniquely distinguishes an instance of an entity. An identifier is one or more attributes and may include relationship descriptors. When a relationship descriptor is part of an identifier, a vertical bar is placed on the arc closest to the entity being identified. In Figure 7–5, an instance of the entity LINEITEM is identified by the composite of "lineno" and the relationship descriptor "sale of LINEITEM." "Lineno" does not uniquely identify an instance of LINEITEM because it is simply a number that appears on the order form. Thus, the identifier must include "sale of LINEITEM," which is "saleno" (the identifier of SALE). So any instance of LINEITEM is uniquely identified by the composite "saleno" and "lineno."

Occasionally, there will be several possible identifiers, and these are each given a different symbol. Our convention is to prefix an identifier with an asterisk (*). If there are multiple identifiers, use other symbols such as #, !, or &. Be careful, if you have too many possible identifiers, your model will look like comic book swearing. In most cases, you will have only one identifier.

No part of an identifier can be null. If this were permitted, there would be no guarantee that the other parts of the identifier were sufficiently unique to distinguish all instances in the database.

Figure 7–5   A relationship descriptor as part of the identifier

DATA MODEL QUALITY

Now that you understand the building blocks, you are ready to create a data model. There are two criteria for judging the quality of a data model. It must be well-formed and have fidelity of image.

A Well-Formed Data Model

A **well-formed data model** (see Table 7–1) clearly communicates information to the client. Being well-formed means the construction rules have been obeyed. There is no ambiguity; all entities are named and all entities have identifiers. If identifiers are missing, the client may make incorrect inferences about the data model. All relationships are recorded using the proper notation. Relationship descriptors are noted whenever there is a possibility of confusion.

All the attributes of an entity are listed because any missing attributes create two types of problems. First, it is unclear what data will be stored about each instance. Second, the data model may be missing some relationships. Attributes that can have multiple values become entities. It is only by listing all of an entity's attributes that these additional entities are recognized.

In a well-formed data model, all attribute names are meaningful and unique. The names of entities, identifiers, attributes, and relationship must be meaningful to the client because they are meant to describe the client's world. Indeed, in nearly all cases they are the client's everyday names. Take care in selecting words because they are critical to communicating meaning. The acid test for comprehension is to get the client to read the data model to other potential users. Names need to be unique to avoid confusion.

A High Fidelity Image

Music lovers aspire to own a high fidelity stereo system—one that faithfully reproduces the original performance with minimal or no distortion. A data model is a **high fidelity** image

Table 7–1   Characteristics of a Well-Formed Data Model

All construction rules are obeyed.
No ambiguity.
All entities are named.
Every entity has an identifier.
All relationships are represented, using the correct notation.
Relationship descriptors are used to avoid misunderstanding.
All attributes of each entity are listed.
All attribute names are meaningful and unique.

when it faithfully describes the world it is supposed to represent. All relationships are recorded and are of the correct degree. There are no compromises or distortions. If the real world relationship is m:m, then so is the relationship shown in the data model. A well-formed, high fidelity data model is complete, understandable, accurate, and syntactically correct.

QUALITY IMPROVEMENT

A data model is an evolving representation. Each change should be an incremental improvement in quality. Occasionally, you will find a major quality problem at the data model's core and have to change the data model dramatically.

Detail and Context

The quality of a data model can be determined only by understanding the context in which it will be used. Consider the data model (see Figure 7–6) used in Chapter 4 to discuss the 1:m relationship. This fragment says a nation has many stocks. But is that really what we want to represent? Stocks are listed on a stock exchange, and a nation may have several stock exchanges. For example, each Australian state's capital city has a stock exchange. Australian stocks can be listed on multiple exchanges but have a single home exchange. Furthermore, some Australian stocks are listed on the New York Stock Exchange. If this is the world we have to describe, the data model is likely to differ from that shown in Figure 7–6. Try drawing the revised data model.

As you can see, the data model in Figure 7–7 is quite different from the initial data model of Figure 7–6. Which one is correct? They both can be correct; it just depends on the world you are trying to represent and possible future queries. In the first case, the purpose was to determine the value of a portfolio. There was no interest in where stocks were listed or their home exchange. So the first model has high fidelity for the described situation.

The second data model would be appropriate if the client needed to know the home exchange of stocks and their price on the various exchanges where they were listed. The second data model is an improvement on the first if it incorporates the additional facts and relationships required. If it is not, then the additional detail is not worth the extra cost.

Figure 7–6   A 1:m relationship between NATION and STOCK

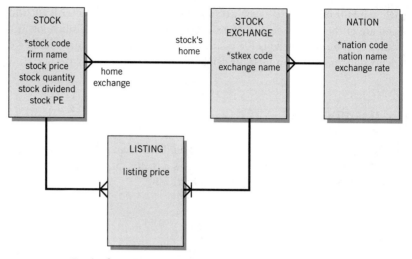

Figure 7–7   Revised NATION–STOCK data model

A Lesson in Pure Geography

A data model must be an accurate representation of the world you want to model. The data model must account for all the exceptions—there should be no impurities. Let's say you want to establish a database to store details of the world's cities. You might start with the data model depicted in Figure 7–8.

Before looking more closely at the data model, let's clarify the meaning of "regtype." Because most countries are divided into regions that are variously called states, provinces, territories, and so forth, "regtype" indicates the type of region (e.g., state).

How many errors can you find in this data model (see Table 7–2)? The revised data model is shown in Figure 7–9.

This geography lesson demonstrates how you often start with a simple model of low fidelity. Additional thinking about relationship and consideration of exceptions gradually creates a high fidelity data model.

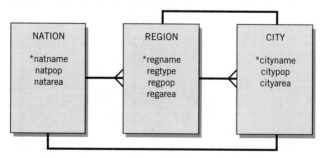

Figure 7–8   A world's cities data model

Table 7–2 Problems and Solutions for the Initial Data Model of World Cities

	Problem	Solution
1.	City names are not be unique. There is an Athens in Greece and the United States has an Athens in Georgia, Alabama, Ohio, Pennsylvania, Tennessee, and Texas.	To uniquely identify a city, you need to specify its region and country. Add a vertical bar to the crow's feet between city and region, and region and nation.
2.	Region names are not necessarily unique. There used to be a Georgia in the old USSR and there is a Georgia in the United States. There is no guarantee that region names will always be unique.	To uniquely identify a region, you also need to know the country in which it is found. Add a vertical bar to the crow's feet between region and nation (already done to solve problem 1).
3.	There are unlabeled 1:1 arcs between city and region and city and nation. What do these mean? They are supposed to indicate that a region has a capital and a nation has a capital.	Label the arcs (e.g., capital city of region).
4.	The assumption is that a region or nation has only one capital, but there are exceptions. The Republic of South Africa has three capitals: Cape Town (legislative), Pretoria (administrative), Bloemfontein (judicial).[1] You only need one exception to significantly lower the fidelity of a data model.	Change the relationship between NATION and CITY to 1:m. Add an attribute "captype" to CITY to distinguish between types of capitals.
5.	Some values can be derived. National population, "natpop," and area, "natarea," are the sum of the regional populations, "regpop," and areas, "regarea," respectively. However, the same rule does not apply to regions and cities because not everyone lives in a city.	Remove the attributes "natpop" and "natarea" from NATION.

[1]You might also look at Bolivia.

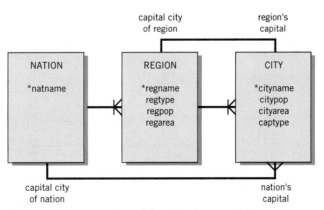

Figure 7–9 A revised world's cities data model

Family Matters

Families can be very complicated. It can be tricky to keep track of all those relations—maybe you need a relational database (this is the worst joke in the book; they improve after this). Before we continue, let's define a family. For the purposes of this book, and mainly to keep the examples simple, we have a very limited view of a family. A family is man and woman united in marriage who may have some children. We need to be restrictive because a very liberal definition will complicate the data model. As we get into exploring marriage, we will become less restrictive. An initial fragment of the data model is shown in Figure 7–10. What do you notice about this fragment? There are several things:

1. There is a 1:1 relationship between man and woman. The labels indicate that this relationship is marriage, but there is no indication of the marriage date. We are left to infer that the data model records the current marriage.

2. MAN and WOMAN have the same attributes. A prefix is used to make them unique. Both have an identifier, (". . . id," in the United States this would probably be a Social Security number), date of birth (". . . dob"), first name (". . . fname"), other names (". . . oname"), and last name (". . . lname").

3. Other names (". . . oname") looks like a multivalued attribute, which is not allowed. Should ". . . oname" be single or multivalue? This is a tricky decision. It depends on how these data will be used. If queries such as find all men whose other names include "Herbert" are likely, then a person's other names—kept as a separate entity that has 1:m relationship for MAN and WOMAN—must be established. That is, a man or woman can have one or more other names. However, if you just want to store the data for completeness and retrieve it in its entirety, then ". . . oname" is fine. It is just a text string. The key question to ask is: What is the lowest level of detail possibly required for future queries? Also, remember that SQL's LIKE clause can be used to search for values within a test string.

The use of a prefix to distinguish attribute names in different entities suggests you should consider combining the entities. In this case, we could combine the entities MAN and WOMAN to create an entity called PERSON. Usually when entities are combined, you have to create a new attribute to distinguish between the different types. In this example, the attribute "gender" is added. We could also generalize the relationship descriptors to "spouse of person." The revised data model appears in Figure 7–11.

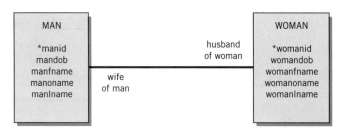

Figure 7–10   Man–woman data model

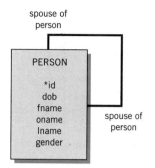

Figure 7–11 A revised man–woman data model

Now for a bit of marriage counseling. Marriage normally is a relationship between two people. Is that so? Well, some societies permit polygamy (one man can have many wives) and others allow polyandry (one woman can have many husbands). So marriage, if we consider all the possibilities, is an m:m relationship. Also, a person can be married more than once. To distinguish between different marriages, we really need to record the start and end date of each relationship and who was involved (see Figure 7–12).

Marriage is an m:m relationship between two persons. It has attributes "begindate" and "enddate". An instance of marriage is uniquely identified by a composite identifier: the two "spouse of person" descriptors and "begindate." This means any marriage is uniquely identified by the composite of two person identifiers and the beginning date of the marriage. We need "begindate" as part of the identifier because the same couple might have more than one marriage (e.g., get divorced and rewed later). Furthermore, we can safely assume that it is impossible for a couple to get married, divorced, and rewed all on the one day. "Begindate" and "enddate" can be used to determine the current state of a marriage. If "enddate" is null the marriage is current, otherwise the couple has divorced.

This data model assumes a couple goes through some formal process to get married or divorced, and there is an official date for both of these events. What happens if they just gradually drift into cohabitation, and there is no official beginning date? Think about it. (The

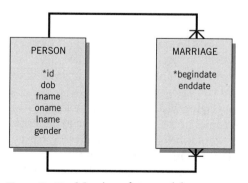

Figure 7–12 Marriage data model

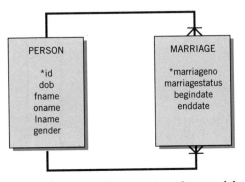

Figure 7–13 A revised marriage data model

data model problem, that is — not cohabitation!) Many countries recognize this situation as a common-law marriage so the data model needs to recognize it. The present data model cannot handle this situation because "begindate" cannot be null—it is an identifier. Instead, a new identifier is needed, and "begindate" should become an attribute.

Two new attributes can handle a common-law marriage. "Marriageno" for marriage number can count the number of times a couple have been married to each other. In the greater majority of cases, "marriageno" will be 1. "Marriagestatus" can record whether a marriage is current or ended. Now, we have a data model that can also handle common-law marriages. This is also a high quality data model in that the user does not have to remember to examine "enddate" to determine a marriage's current status. It is easier to remember to examine "marriagestatus" to check status. Also, we can allow a couple to be married, divorced, and rewed as many times as they like on the one day—which means we can now use the database in Las Vegas. The latest version of the data model is shown in Figure 7–13.

All right, now that we have the couple successfully married, we need to start thinking about its offspring. A marriage has one or more children, but a child belongs to only one marriage, therefore, we have a 1:m relationship between marriage and person to represent the children of a marriage (see Figure 7–14).

When's a Book Not a Book?

Sometimes we have to rethink our ideas of physical objects. Consider a data model for a library.

The fragment (Figure 7–15) assumes that a person borrows a book. What happens if the library has two copies of the book? Do we add an attribute to BOOK called copy number? No, because we would introduce redundancy by repeating the same information for each book. What you need to recognize is that in the realm of data modeling, a book is not really a physical thing but the copy is, because it is what you borrow. The revised data model fragment is illustrated in Figure 7–16.

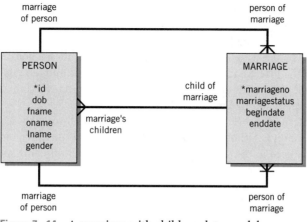

Figure 7–14   A marriage with children data model

Figure 7–15   A library data model fragment

Figure 7–16   A revised library data model fragment

As you can see, a book has many copies and a copy is of one book. A book can be identified by call number "callno," which is usually a Library of Congress number or Dewey number. A copy is identified by a book number, "bookno." This is a unique number allocated by the library to the copy of the book. If you look in a library book, you will generally find it pasted on the inside back cover and shown in numeric and bar code format. Notice that it is called book number despite the fact that it really identifies a copy of a book. This is because most people, including librarians, think of the copy as a book.

The International Standard Book Number (ISBN) uniquely identifies any instance of a book (not copy). Although it sounds like a potential identifier for BOOK, it is not. ISBNs were introduced in the second half of the twentieth century and books published before that do not have an ISBN.

A History Lesson

Many organizations maintain historical data (e.g., a person's job history or a student's enrolment record). A data model can depict historical data relationships just as readily as current data relationships.

Consider the case of a employee who works for a firm that consists of divisions (e.g., production) and departments (e.g., quality control). The firm contains many departments but a department belongs to only one division. At any one time, an employee belongs to only one department. If we were modeling the current situation, the data model fragment would look like that shown in Figure 7–17.

The fragment in Figure 7–17 can be amended to keep track of the divisions and departments in which a person works. While employed with a firm, a person can work in more than one department. Since a department can have many employees, we have an m:m relationship between DEPARTMENT and EMPLOYEE. We might call the resulting intersection entity POSITION (see Figure 7–18).

The revised data model fragment records employee work history. Notice that any instance of POSITION is identified by "begdate" and the relationship descriptors for EMPLOYEE and DEPARTMENT. The fragment is typical of what happens when you move from keeping just current data to recording history. A 1:m relationship becomes an m:m to record history.

People who work get paid. How do we keep track of an employee's pay data? An employee has many pay slips, but a pay slip belongs to one employee. When you look at a pay slip, you

Figure 7–17   Employment history—take 1

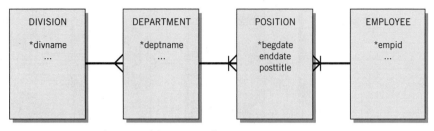

Figure 7–18   Employment history—take 2

will find it contains many items: gross pay and a series of deductions for tax, medical insurance, and so on. Think of pay slip as containing many lines, analogous to an order form. Now look at the revised data model in Figure 7–19.

Typically, an amount shown on a pay slip is identified by a short text field (e.g., gross pay). PAYSLIPLINE contains an attribute "psltype" to identify the text that should accompany an amount, but where is the text? When dealing with codes like "psltype" and their associated text, the fidelity of a data model is improved by creating a separate entity, PSLTEXT, for the code and its text (Figure 7–20).

A Ménage à Trois for Entities

Consider aircraft leasing, for example. An aircraft broker will own many planes that over time will be leased to a variety of airlines. When a lease expires, the broker leases the plane to another airline. So an aircraft can be leased many times and an airline can lease many aircraft. Further-

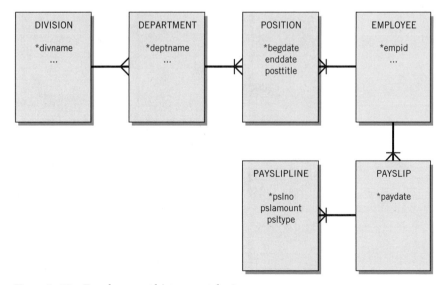

Figure 7–19   Employment history—take 3

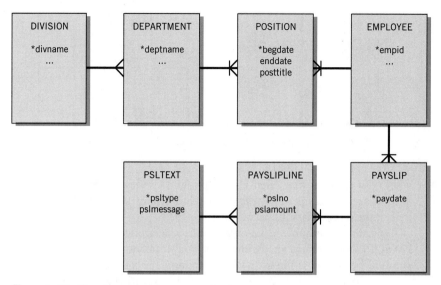

Figure 7–20 Employment history—take 4

more, there is an agent responsible for handling each deal. An agent can lease many aircraft and deal with many airlines. Over time, an airline will deal with many agents. When an agent reaches a deal with an airline to lease a particular aircraft, you have a transaction.

If you analyze the aircraft leasing business, you discover there are three m:m relationships. You might think of these as three separate relationships (see Figure 7–21).

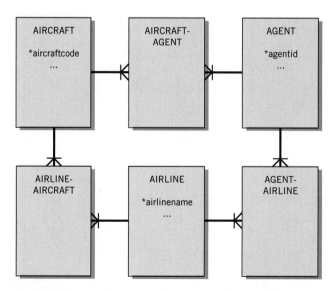

Figure 7–21 An aircraft–airline–agent data model

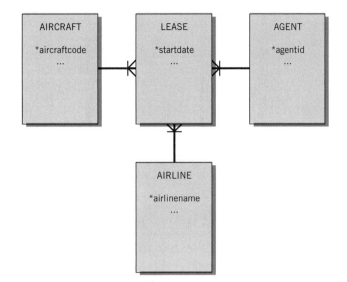

Figure 7–22   A revised aircraft–airline–agent data model

The problem with three separate m:m relationships is that it is unclear where to store data about the lease. Is it stored in AIRLINE-AIRCRAFT? If you store the information there, what do you do about recording the agent who closed the deal? After you read the fine print and do some more thinking, you discover that a lease is the intersection of these three entities in an m:m relationship (see Figure 7–22).

Planning and Doing

Project management involves both planned and actual data. A project is divided into a number of activities that use resources. Planning includes estimation of the resources to be consumed. When a project is being executed, managers keep track of the resources actually used in order to monitor progress and keep the project on budget. Planning data are not as detailed as actual data. Planning data will be fairly broad, such as an estimate of the number of hours that an activity will take. Actual data will be more detailed because they are usually collected by getting those assigned to the project to log a daily account of how they spent their time. Also, resources used on a project are allocated to a particular activity. For the purposes of this data model, we will focus only on recording time and nothing else (see Figure 7–23).

Notice that "planned hours" is an attribute of ACTIVITY, and "actual hours" is an attribute of DAILY WORK. The hours spent on an activity are derived by summing "actual hours" in the associated DAILY WORK entity. This is a high fidelity data model

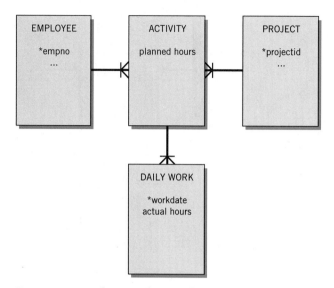

Figure 7-23 A planning data model

if planning is done at the activity level and employees submit daily worksheets. Planning can be done in greater detail, however, if planners indicate how many hours of each day each employee should spend on a project. Figure 7-24 shows the revised data model fragment.

Now you see that "planned hours" and "actual hours" are both attributes of DAILY

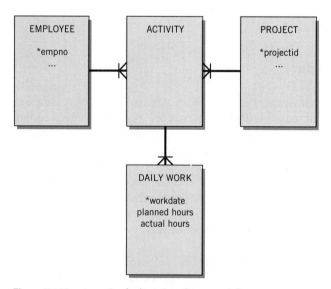

Figure 7-24 A revised planning data model

WORK. The message of this example, therefore, is not to assume that planned and actual data have the same level of detail, but do not be surprised if they do.

ENTITY TYPES

A data model contains different kinds of entities, which are distinguished by the format of their identifiers. Labeling each of these entities by type will help you to determine what questions to ask.

Independent

An **independent entity** is often central to a data model and foremost in the client's mind. Independent entities are frequently the starting points of a data model. Remember that in the investment database, the independent entities are STOCK and NATION. Independent entities typically have clearly distinguishable names because they occur so frequently in the client's world. In addition, they usually have a single, arbitrary identifier, such as "stock code" or "nation code."

Independent entities are often connected to other independent entities in a 1:m or m:m relationship. The data model in Figure 7–25 shows two independent entities linked in a 1:m relationship.

Dependent

A **dependent entity** relies on another entity for its existence and identification. It is recognized by a bar on the dependent entity's end of the arc (see Figure 7–26). CITY cannot exist without REGION. A CITY is uniquely identified by "cityname" and "regname."

Figure 7–25   NATION and STOCK are independent entities

Figure 7–26   CITY is a dependent entity

If the composite identifier becomes unwieldy, creating an arbitrary identifier (e.g., "cityno") will change the dependent entity into an independent one.

Intersection Entity

Intersection entities are byproducts of m:m relationships. They are typically found between independent entities. Intersection entities sometimes have obvious names because they occur in the real world. For instance, the intersection entity for the m:m relationship between DEPARTMENT and EMPLOYEE is usually called POSITION (see Figure 7–27). If the intersection entity does not have a common name, the two entity names are generally hyphenated (e.g., DEPARTMENT–EMPLOYEE). Always search for the appropriate name because it will improve the quality of the data model. Hyphenated names are a last resort.

Intersection entities can show either the current or historic relationship between two entities. If an intersection entity's only identifiers are the two relationship descriptors, then it records the current relationship between the entities. If the intersection entity has some time measure as a partial identifier (e.g., date or hour), then it records the history of the relationship. Whenever you find an intersection entity, ask the client whether the history of the relationship should be recorded.

Creating a single, arbitrary identifier for an intersection entity will change it to an independent one. This is likely to happen if the intersection entity becomes central to an application. For example, if a personnel department does a lot of work with POSITION, it may find it more expedient to give it a separate identifier (e.g., "position number").

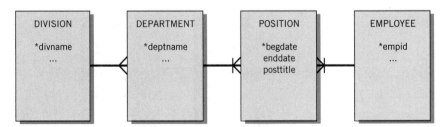

Figure 7–27   POSITION is an intersection entity

Aggregate Entity

An **aggregate entity** is created when several different entities have similar attributes that are distinguished by a prefix or suffix to keep their names unique. For example, because components of an address might occur in several entities (e.g., CUSTOMER and SUPPLIER), an aggregate address entity can be created to store details of all addresses. Aggregate entities usually become independent entities. In this case, we could use "address number" to uniquely identify an instance of address.

Subordinate Entity

A **subordinate entity** stores data about an entity that can vary among instances. A subordinate entity is useful when an entity consists of mutually exclusive classes that have different descriptions. The farm animal database shown in Figure 7–28 indicates that the farmer requires different data for sheep and horses. Notice that each of the subordinate entities is identified by the relationship descriptor. You could avoid subordinate entities by placing all the attributes in ANIMAL but then you make it incumbent on the client to remember which attributes apply to horses and which to sheep. This becomes an important issue for null fields. For example, is the attribute "hay consumption" null because it does not apply to sheep or is it null because the value is unknown?

If a subordinate entity becomes important, it is likely to evolve to an independent entity. The framing of a problem often determines whether subordinate entities are created. Stating the problem as, "A farmer has many animals, and these animals can be horses or sheep," might lead to the creation of subordinate entities. Alternatively, saying that "a farmer has many sheep and horses" might lead to setting up sheep and horse as independent entities.

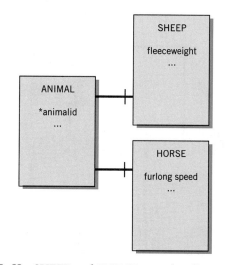

Figure 7–28   SHEEP and HORSE are subordinate entities

DATA MODELING HINTS

A high fidelity data model takes time to develop. The client must explain the problem fully so that the database designer can understand the client's requirements and translate them into a data model. Data modeling is like prototyping; the database designer gradually creates a model of the database as a result of interaction with the client. Some issues will frequently arise in this progressive creation, and the following hints should help you resolve many of the common problems you will encounter.

The Rise and Fall of a Data Model

Expect your data model to both expand and contract. Your initial data model will expand as you extend the boundaries of the application. You will discover some attributes will evolve into entities and some 1:m relationships will become m:m relationships. It will grow because you will add entities, attributes, and relationships to allow for exceptions. Your data model will grow because you are representing the complexity of the real world. Do not try to constrain growth. Let the data model be as large as is necessary. As a rough rule, expect your final data model to grow to about two to three times the number of entities of your initial data model.

Expect your data model to contract as you generalize structures. Consider the abbreviated data model shown in Figure 7 – 29.

Figure 7 – 29   A data model that can shrink

Figure 7–30   The shrunken data model

This fragment is typical of the models produced by novice data modelers. It can be reduced by recognizing that CD, LP, and TAPE are all types of audio recordings. A more general entity, AUDIO RECORDING, could be used to represent the same data. Of course, it would need an additional attribute to distinguish the different types of audio recordings (see Figure 7–30).

As you discover new entities, your data model will grow. As you generalize, your data model will shrink.

Identifier

If there is no obvious simple identifier, invent one. The simplest is a meaningless code (e.g., "person number" or "order number"). If you create an identifier, you can also guarantee its uniqueness.

Don't overwork an identifier. The worst case we have seen is a 22–character product code used by a plastic company that supposedly not only uniquely identified an item but told you its color, its manufacturing process, and type of plastic used to make it! Color, manufacturing process, and type of plastic are all attributes. This product code was unwieldy. Data entry error rates were extremely high, and very few people could remember how to decipher the code.

An identifier has to do only one thing: uniquely identify every instance of the entity. Sometimes trying to make it do double, or even triple, duty only creates more work for the client.

Position and Order

There is no ordering in a data model. Entities can appear anywhere on it. You will usually find a central entity near the middle of the data model only because you tend to start with it (e.g., starting with STUDENT when modeling a student information system). What really matters with entities is that you correctly record all relationships.

Attributes are in no order. You find that you will tend to list them as they are identified. For readability, it is a good idea to list some attributes sequentially. For example, first name, other names, and last name are usually together. This is not necessary, but it speeds up verification of a data model's completeness.

Instances are also assumed to have no ordering. There is no first instance, next instance, or last instance. If you must recognize a particular order, create an attribute to record the order. For example, if ranking of potential investment projects must be recorded, include an attribute ("projrank") to store this data. This does not mean the instances will be stored in "projrank" order, but it does allow you to use the ORDER clause of SQL to report the projects in rank order.

If you need to store details of a precedence relationship (that is, there is an ordering of instances and a need to know the successor and predecessor of any instance), then use a 1:1 recursive relationship. This is illustrated by the Monarch data model in Figure 7–31.

Attributes and Consistency

Attributes must be consistent, retaining the same meaning for every instance. An example of an inconsistent attribute would be an attribute "stock info" that contains a stock's PE ratio or its ROI (return on investment). Another attribute, say "stock info code," is required to decipher which meaning applies to any particular instance. The code could be "1" for PE and "2" for ROI. If one attribute determines the meaning of another, you have inconsistency. Writing SQL queries will be extremely challenging because inconsistent data increase query complexity. It is better to create separate attributes for PE and ROI.

Names and Addresses

An attribute is the smallest piece of data that will conceivably form part of a query. If an attribute has segments (e.g., a person's name), determine whether these could form part of a query. If so, then make them separate attributes and reapply the query test. When you apply

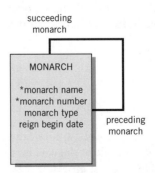

Figure 7–31   Using an attribute to record an ordering of instances

the query test to person name, you will usually decide to create three attributes: "first name," "other name," and "last name."

> ## *The Query Test*
> *If an attribute has parts, are any of the parts ever likely to appear in a query?*

What about titles? There are two sorts of titles: prefix titles (e.g., Mr., Mrs., Ms, and Dr.); and suffix titles (e.g., Jr. and III). These should be separate attributes, especially if you have divided name into separate attributes.

Addresses seem to cause more concern than names because they are more variant. Business addresses tend to be the most complicated, and foreign addresses add a few more twists. The data model fragment in Figure 7–32 works in most cases.

A common feature of every address is city, state, postal code, and nation. Some of these can be null. For example, Singapore does not have states. In the United States, city and state can be derived from the zip code, but this is not necessarily true for other countries. Furthermore, even if this were true for every nation, you would need a different derivation rule for each country, which is beyond the scope of existing relational database technology. If there is a lifetime guarantee that every address in the database will be for one country, then examine the possibility of reducing redundancy by just storing "post code."

Notice that the problem of multiple address lines is represented by a 1:m relationship. An address line is a text string that appears as one line of an address. There is often a set sequence in which these are displayed. The attribute "address rank" records this order. Any instance of ADDRESS LINE is identified by the composite of relationship descriptor and "address rank."

How do you address students? First names may be all right for class, but it is not adequate enough for student records. Students typically have multiple addresses: a home address, a school address, and maybe a summer address. The following data model (see Figure 7–33) fragment shows how to handle this situation.

Figure 7–32 Handling addresses

Figure 7–33   Students with multiple addresses

The identifier "address type" is used to distinguish among the different types of addresses. The same data model fragment works in situations where a business has different mailing and shipping addresses.

When data modeling, can you take a short cut with names and addresses? It is time consuming to write out all the components of name and address for a data model. It creates clutter and does not add much fidelity. Our practical advice is to do two things. First, create a policy for all names and addresses (e.g., all names will be stored as three parts: first name, other names, last name). Second, use shorthand forms of attributes for names and address when they obey the policy. So from now on, we will use name and address as attributes with the understanding that when the database is created, the parts of these attributes will become separate columns.

Single Instance Entities

Do not be concerned about creating an entity with a single instance. Consider the data model fragment in Figure 7–34 which describes a single fast food chain. Because the data model describes only one firm, the entity FIRM will have only one instance. The inclusion of this single instance entity permits facts about the firm to be maintained. Furthermore, it provides flexibility for expansion. If two fast food chains combine, the data model needs no amendment.

Picking Words

Words are very important. They are all we have to make ourselves understood. Let the client choose the words because the data model belongs to that person and describes the client's world. If you try to impose your words on the client, you are likely to create a misunderstanding.

Figure 7–34   FIRM is a single instance entity

Synonyms

Synonyms are words that have the same meaning. For example, task, assignment, and project might all refer to the same real world object. One of these terms, maybe the one in most common use, needs to be selected for naming the entity. Clients need to be told the official name for the entity and encouraged to adopt a single term for describing it. Alternatively, logical views of the database can be created that enable clients to use their own term. Synonyms are not a technical problem. It is a social problem of getting clients to agree on one word.

Homonyms

Homonyms are words that sound the same but have different meanings. Homonyms can create real confusion. "Sales date" is a classic example. In the aircraft manufacturing business it can have several meanings. To the sales people, it is the day that the customer shakes hands and says, "We have a deal." For the lawyers, it is the day when the contract is signed, and for production it is the day the customer takes delivery. In this case, the solution is reasonably obvious, redefine "sales date" to be separate terms for each area (e.g., "sales date," "contract date," and "delivery date" for sales, legal, and production departments, respectively).

Homonyms cause real confusion when clients do not realize that they are using the same word for different entities or attributes. Hunt down homonyms by asking lots of questions and querying a range of clients.

Exception Hunting

Go hunting for exceptions. Keep asking the client questions such as:

Is it always like this?

Would there be any situations where this could be an m:m relationship?

Have there ever been any exceptions?

Are things likely to change in the future?

Always probe for exceptions and look for them in the examples the client uses. Redesigning the data model to handle exceptions increases fidelity.

Relationship Labeling

Relationship labeling clutters a data model. In most cases, relationship descriptors can be correctly inferred. Use labels only when there is a possibility of ambiguity.

Keeping the Data Model in Shape

As you add to a data model, maintain fidelity. Do not add entities without also completing details of the identifier and attributes. By keeping the data model well-formed, you avoid ambiguity, which frequently leads to miscommunication.

Used Entities

Would you buy a used data model? Certainly, because a used data model is more likely to have higher fidelity than a brand new one. A used data model has been subjected to much scrutiny and revision and should be a more accurate representation of the real world.

NORMALIZATION

If data modeling is used for database design and the resulting model is high fidelity, normalization should not be required. Nevertheless, design mistakes may occur and normalization is a useful cross-check for ensuring the soundness of a data model.[2]

Normalization is the process of converting a bad database design into a form that overcomes update anomalies and data inconsistencies. If you model data correctly, you should not get a bad design. The need for normalization seems to have arisen from the conversion of file systems into database format. Often, analysts started with the old file design and used normalization to design the new database.

---

[2]This section is mainly based on W. Kent, "A Simple Guide to Five Normal Forms in Relational Database Theory," *Communications of the ACM* 26 (2):120–125 (1983), and C. J. Date, *An Introduction to Database Systems*, 5th ed., vol. 1. (Reading, MA: Addison–Wesley, 1990).

Normalization gradually converts a file design into normal form by successive application of rules to move the design from first to fifth normal form. But before we look at these steps, it is useful to learn about functional dependency.

Functional Dependency

Functional dependency is a relationship between attributes in an entity. It simply means that one or more attributes determine the value of another. For example, given a stock's code you can determine its current PE ratio. In other words, PE ratio is functionally dependent on stock code. This also means that firm name, stock price, stock quantity, and stock dividend are functionally dependent on stock code. The shorthand way of denoting this is

stockcode→firm name, stock price, stock quantity, stock dividend

An identifier functionally determines all the attributes in an entity. Formulae, such as yield = stock dividend/stock price*100, are a form of functional dependency. In this case, we have (stock dividend, stock price)→yield. This is also an example of **full functional dependency** because yield can be determined only from both attributes.

An attribute, or set of attributes, that fully functionally determines another attribute is called a determinant. Thus, stock code is a determinant because it fully functionally determines stock PE. An identifier, usually called a key when discussing normalization, is a determinant.

First Normal Form

*A relation is in **first normal form** (1NF) if and only if all columns contain atomic values only.* In other words, first normal form states that all occurrences of a row must have the same number of columns. In data modeling terms, this means that an attribute must have a single value. An attribute that can have multiple values must be represented as a 1:m relationship. At a minimum, a data model will be in 1NF because all attributes of an entity are required to be single–valued.

Second Normal Form

Second normal form (2NF) is violated when a non-key column is dependent on a component of the primary key. This can also be stated as *a relation is in second normal form (2NF) if and only if it is in first normal form and all non-key columns are dependent on the key.*

Consider Table 7–3. The primary key of ORDER is a composite of ITEMNO and CUSTOMERID. The problem is that CUSTOMER–CREDIT is a fact about CUSTOMERID (part of the composite key) rather than the full key (ITEMNO+CUSTOMERID), or in other words, it is not fully functionally dependent on the primary key. Analyzing this problem, you realize an item can be in many orders and a customer can order many items—an m:m rela-

Table 7–3   Second Normal Form Violation

ORDER			
<u>ITEMNO</u>	<u>CUSTOMERID</u>	QUANTITY	CUSTOMER-CREDIT
12	57	25	OK
34	679	3	POOR

tionship. By drawing the data model in Figure 7–35 you realize that "customer–credit" is an attribute of CUSTOMER, and you get the correct relational map.

Third Normal Form

Third normal form (3NF) is violated when a non-key column is a fact about another non-key column. Alternatively, *a relation is in third normal form if and only if it is in second normal form and has no transitive dependencies.*

The problem in Table 7–4 is that EXCHANGE RATE is a fact about NATION, a non-key

Figure 7–35   Resolving second normal form violation

Table 7–4 Third Normal Form Violation

STOCK		
__STOCKCODE__	NATION	EXCHANGE RATE
MG	USA	0.67
IR	AUS	0.46

field. In the language of functional dependency, EXCHANGE RATE is not fully functionally dependent on STOCK CODE, the primary key. The functional dependencies are STOCKCODE→NATION→EXCHANGE RATE. In other words, EXCHANGE RATE is transitively[3] dependent on STOCK, since EXCHANGE RATE is dependent on NATION and NATION is dependent on STOCKCODE. When you think about it, you realize that a nation has many stocks and a stock belongs to only one nation. Now the data model and relational map can be created readily (see Figure 7–36).

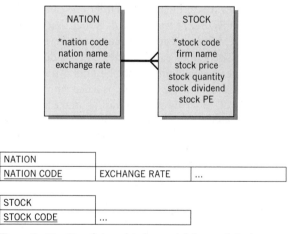

NATION		
NATION CODE	EXCHANGE RATE	...

STOCK	
STOCK CODE	...

Figure 7–36 Resolving third normal form violation

---

[3]Transitivity means that if one object bears a relation to a second object that bears the same relationship to a third object, then the first object bears this relationship to the third. For example, if x = y and y = z, then x = z.

Boyce–Codd Normal Form[4]

The original definition of 3NF did not cover a situation that, although rare, can occur. So **Boyce-Codd normal form** (BCNF), a stronger version of 3NF, was developed. BCNF is necessary because 3NF does not cover the case when a relation

a. has multiple candidate keys, where

b. those candidate keys are composite, and

c. the candidate keys overlap because they have at least one column in common.

Before considering an example, candidate key needs to be defined. Earlier we introduced the idea that an entity could have more than one unique identifier. These identifiers become candidate keys when the data model is mapped to a relational database. One of these candidates is selected as the primary key.

Consider the following case from a management consulting firm. A client can have many problems (e.g., finance, personnel), and the same problem can be an issue for many clients. Consultants specialize and advise on only one problem type, but several consultants can advise on one problem. A consultant advises a client. Furthermore, for each problem, the client is advised by only one consultant. If you did not use data modeling, you might be tempted to create Table 7–5.

CLIENT cannot be the primary key because a client can have several problems; however, a client is advised by only one consultant for a specific problem, so the composite key CLIENT+PROBLEM determines CONSULTANT. Also, because a consultant handles only one type of problem, the composite key CLIENT+CONSULTANT determines PROBLEM. So, both of these composites are candidate keys. Either one can be selected as the primary key, and in this case, CLIENT+PROBLEM was selected. Notice that all the previously stated conditions are satisfied—there are multiple, composite candidate keys that overlap. This means the table is 3NF, but not BCNF. This can be easily verified by considering what happens if the firm adds a new consultant. A new consultant cannot be added until there is a client—an insertion anomaly. The problem is that CONSULTANT is a determinant, CONSULTANT→PROBLEM, but is not a candidate key. In terms of the phrasing used earlier, the problem is that part of the key column is a fact about a non-key column. The precise definition is *a relation is in Boyce–Codd normal form if and only if every determinant is a candidate key.*

Table 7–5   Boyce–Codd Normal Form Violation

ADVISOR		
CLIENT	PROBLEM	CONSULTANT
Alpha	Marketing	Gomez
Alpha	Production	Raginiski

---

[4]Based on Date, *Database Systems*, 543.

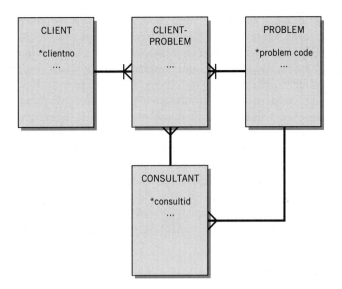

Figure 7–37   Resolving Boyce–Codd normal form violation

This problem is avoided by creating the correct data model (see Figure 7–37), and then mapping to a relational model.

Fourth Normal Form

Fourth normal form (4NF) requires that a row should not contain two or more independent multivalued facts about an entity. This requirement is more readily understood after investigating an example.

Consider students who play sports and study subjects. One way of representing this information is shown in Table 7–6.

Table 7–6   Fourth Normal Form Violation

STUDENT			
STUDENTID	**SPORT**	**SUBJECT**	...
50	Football	English	...
50	Football	Music	...
50	Tennis	Botany	...
50	Karate	Botany	...

This table is not in 4NF because sport and subject are independent multivalued facts about a student. There is no relationship between sport and subject. There is an indirect connection because sport and subject are associated with a student. In other words, a student can play many sports and the same sport can be played by many students—an m:m relationship between student and sport. Similarly, there is an m:m relationship between student and subject. It makes no sense to store information about a student's sports and subjects in the same table because sport and subject are not related. Consider the consequence of trying to insert a student who did not play a sport. Subject would be null, and this is not permissible because part of the composite primary key would then be null—a violation of the entity integrity rule. The problem arises because sport and subject are multivalued dependencies of student. The solution is to convert multivalued dependencies to functional dependencies. More formally, *a relation is in fourth normal form if it is in Boyce-Codd normal form and all multivalued dependencies on the relation are functional dependencies.* A data model (see Figure 7–38) sorts out this problem although the correct relational mapping requires five tables.

Fifth Normal Form

Fifth normal form (5NF) deals with the case where a table can be reconstructed from other tables. The reconstruction approach is preferred because it means less redundancy and fewer maintenance problems.

The consultants, firms, and skills problem is used to illustrate the concept of 5NF. The problem is: consultants provide skills to one or more firms and firms can use many consul-

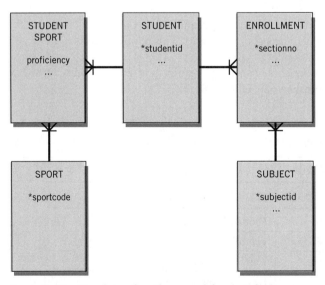

Figure 7–38   Resolving fourth normal form violation

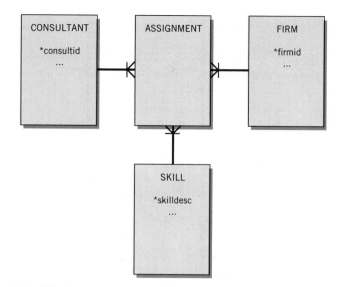

Figure 7–39   The CONSULTANT–FIRM–SKILL data model without a rule

tants; a consultant has many skills and a skill can be used by many firms; and a firm can have a need for many skills and the same skill can be required by many firms. The data model (see Figure 7–39) for this problem has the ménage à trois structure introduced earlier in this chapter.

The relational mapping of the three–way intersection results in four tables, with the intersection entity mapping shown in Table 7–7.

The table is 5NF because the combination of all three columns is required to identify which consultants supply which firms with which skills. For example, we see that Tan advises IBM on database and Apple on data communications. The data in this table cannot be reconstructed from other tables.

Table 7–7 is not in 5NF if there is a rule of the following form: if a consultant has a certain skill (e.g., database), and has a contract with a firm that requires that skill (e.g., IBM), then the consultant advises that firm on that skill (i.e., he advises IBM on database). Notice that this rule means we can infer a relationship, and we no longer need the combination of the three columns. As a result, we break the single three–entity m:m relationship into three two–entity m:m relationships. The revised data model is shown in Figure 7–40.

Table 7–7   The Relation Table ASSIGNMENT

ASSIGNMENT		
CONSULTID	**FIRMID**	**SKILLDESC**
Tan	IBM	Database
Tan	Apple	Data Comm

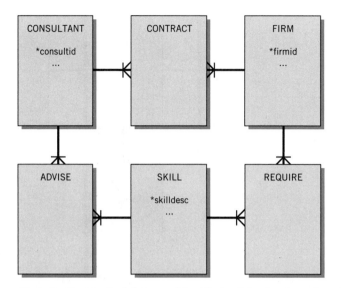

Figure 7−40 Revised data model with the introduction of a rule

Further understanding of 5NF is gained by examining the relational tables resulting from these intersection entities. Notice the names given to each of the intersection entities. CONTRACT records data about the firms a consultant advises; ADVISE describes the skills a consultant has; and REQUIRE stores data about the types of skills each firm requires. To help understand this problem, examine Tables 7−8, 7−9, and 7−10.

Consider the results of joining CONTRACT and ADVISE, the outcome of which we call COULD ADVISE (see Table 7−11) because it lists skills the consultant could provide if the firm required them. For example, Tan has skills in database and data communications, and Tan has a contract with IBM. If IBM required database skills, Tan could handle it. We need to look at REQUIRE to find if IBM requires advice on database; it does not.

Table 7−8 Relational Table CONTRACT

CONTRACT	
CONSULTID	**FIRMID**
Gonzales	Apple
Gonzales	IBM
Gonzales	NEC
Tan	IBM
Tan	NEC
Wood	Apple

Table 7−9 Relational Table ADVISE

ADVISE	
CONSULTID	**SKILLDESC**
Gonzales	Database
Gonzales	Data comm
Gonzales	Groupware
Tan	Database
Tan	Data comm
Wood	Data comm

Table 7–10   Relational Table REQUIRE

REQUIRE	
FIRMID	**SKILLDESC**
IBM	Data comm
IBM	Groupware
NEC	Data comm
NEC	Database
NEC	Groupware
Apple	Data comm

The join of COULD ADVISE with REQUIRE gives details of a firm's skill needs that a consultant can provide. The table named CAN ADVISE (see Table 7–12) is constructed by directly joining the tables CONTRACT, ADVISE, and REQUIRE. Because we can construct CAN ADVISE from three other tables, the data are in 5NF.

Since data are stored in three separate tables, updating is easier. Consider the case where

Table 7–11   Relational Table COULD ADVISE

COULD ADVISE		
CONSULTID	**FIRMID**	**SKILLDESC**
Gonzales	Apple	Database
Gonzales	Apple	Data comm
Gonzales	Apple	Groupware
Gonzales	IBM	Database
Gonzales	IBM	Data comm
Gonzales	IBM	Groupware
Gonzales	NEC	Database
Gonzales	NEC	Data comm
Gonzales	NEC	Groupware
Tan	IBM	Database
Tan	IBM	Data comm
Tan	NEC	Database
Tan	NEC	Data comm
Wood	Apple	Data comm

Table 7–12   Relational Table CAN ADVISE

CAN ADVISE		
CONSULTID	**FIRMID**	**SKILLDESC**
Gonzales	IBM	Data comm
Gonzales	IBM	Groupware
Gonzales	NEC	Database
Gonzales	NEC	Data comm
Gonzales	NEC	Groupware
Tan	IBM	Data comm
Tan	NEC	Database
Tan	NEC	Data comm
Wood	Apple	Data comm

IBM requires database skills. We only need to add one row to REQUIRE to record this fact. In the case of CAN ADVISE, we would have to add two rows, one for Gonzales and one for Tan.

Now we can give 5NF a more precise definition: *a relation is in fifth normal form if and only if every join dependency of the relation is a consequence of the candidate keys of the relation.*

Up to this point, data modeling has enabled you to easily avoid normalization problems. Fifth normal form introduces a complication, however. How can you tell when to use a single three-way intersection or three two-way intersections? If there is a constraint or rule that is applied to the relationships between entities, consider the possibility of three two-way intersections. Question the client carefully whenever you find a ménage à trois. Check to see that there are no rules or special conditions.

Conclusion

We believe data modeling, compared to normalization, is a preferred path to good database design. A high fidelity data model will be of high normal form, and it is unlikely that there will be any need to normalize the resulting relational map. Data modelers who rigorously question the client rarely create a data model that requires normalization. The area that will create most problems is 5NF; show extra vigilance when you get a ménage à trois. Check for the existence of special rules.

The golden rule
Draw the data model

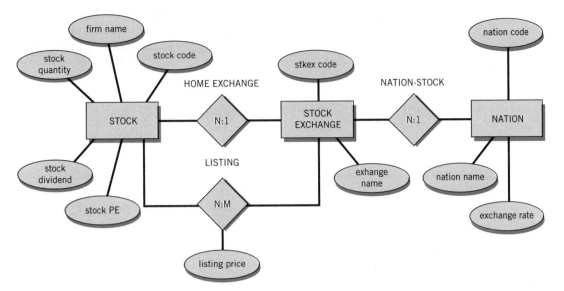

Figure 7–41   An entity–relationship (E-R) diagram

OTHER DATA MODELING METHODS

There are several ways to model data. One of the most widely known methods is the **entity–relationship model** (E-R model) developed by Chen.[5] There is no standard for the E-R model, and it has been extended and modified in a number of ways.

As Figure 7–41 shows, an E-R model looks like the data models with which you are now familiar. Entities are shown by rectangles and relationships are depicted by diamonds within which the cardinality of the relationship is indicated (e.g., there is a 1:m relationship between NATION and STOCK EXCHANGE). Cardinality can be 1:1, 1:m (conventionally shown as 1:N in E-R diagrams), and m:m (shown as M:N). Recursive relationships are also readily modeled. One important difference is that an m:m relationship is not shown as an intersection entity; the database designer therefore must convert this relationship to a table.

Attributes are shown as ellipses connected to the entity or relationship to which they belong (e.g., "firm name" is an attribute of STOCK). If the diagram becomes too cluttered, attributes may be listed below the entity or somewhere else on the diagram. Relationships are named, and the name is shown above, over, or below the relationship symbol. For example, LISTING is the name of the m:m relationship between STOCK and STOCK EXCHANGE.

The underlying concepts of different data modeling methods are very similar. They all

---

[5]P. Chen, "The Entity–Relationship Model—Toward a Unified View of Data," *ACM Transactions on Database Systems* 1 (1): 9–36 (1976).

have the same goal: improving the quality of database design. They share common concepts such as entity and relationship mapping. We have adopted an approach that is simple and effective. The method can be learned rapidly, and novice users can create high quality models. Also, if you have learned one data modeling method, you can quickly adapt to the nuances of other methods. Interestingly, Microsoft uses a method very similar to ours in documentation of its database package, Access. Furthermore, the data modeling method you have learned is very similar to IDEF1X, the U.S. Air Force's standard.[6]

SUMMARY

Data modeling is both a technique for modeling data and its relationships and a graphical representation of a database. It is also a way of communicating a database design. The goal of data modeling is to identify the facts that must be stored in a database. Building a data model is a partnership between a client, a representative of the eventual users of the database, and a designer. The building blocks of data modeling are an entity, attribute, identifier, and relationship. A well-formed data model, which means the construction rules have been obeyed, clearly communicates information to the client. A high fidelity data model faithfully describes the world it is supposed to represent.

A data model is an evolving representation. Each change should be an incremental improvement in quality. The quality of a data model can be determined only by understanding the context in which it will be used. A data model can model historical data relationships just as readily as current ones. The five different types of entities are independent, dependent, intersection, aggregate, and subordinate. Expect a data model to expand and contract. A data model has no ordering. Introduce an attribute if ordering is required. An attribute must have the same meaning for every instance. An attribute is the smallest piece of data that will conceivably form part of a query. Synonyms are words that have the same meaning; homonyms are words that sound the same but have different meanings.

Normalization gradually converts a file design into normal form by successive application of rules to move the design from first to fifth normal form. Functional dependency means that one or more attributes determine the value of another. An attribute, or set of attributes, that fully functionally determines another attribute is called a determinant. First normal form states that all occurrences of a row must have the same number of columns. Second normal form is violated when a non-key column is a fact about a component of the prime key. Third normal form is violated when a non-key column is a fact about another non-key column. Boyce–Codd normal form is a stronger version of third normal form. Fourth normal form requires that a row should not contain two or more independent multivalued facts about an entity. Fifth normal form deals with the case where a table can be reconstructed from data in other tables. Fifth normal form arises when there are special rules or conditions. A high fidelity data model will be of high normal form.

One of the most widely known methods of data modeling is the E-R model. The underlying concepts of most data modeling methods are very similar: all aim to improve database design.

---

[6]T. A. Bruce, *Designing Quality Databases with IDEF1X Information Models* (New York: Dorset House, 1992).

KEY TERMS AND CONCEPTS

A high fidelity image

A well-formed data model

Aggregate entity

Attribute

Boyce-Codd normal form

Data model

Data model quality

Dependent entity

Determinant

Entity

Entity-relationship (E-R) model

Relationship

Relationship descriptor

Second normal form

Fifth normal form

First normal form

Fourth normal form

Full functional dependency

Functional dependency

Homonym

Identifier

Independent entity

Instance

Intersection entity

Normalization

Subordinate entity

Synonym

Third normal form

REFERENCES AND ADDITIONAL READINGS

Bruce, T. A. *Designing Quality Databases with IDEF1X Information Models.* New York: Dorset House, 1992.

Carlis, J. V. *Logical Data Structures.* Minneapolis: University of Minnesota, 1991.

Chen, P. "The Entity–Relationship Model—Toward a Unified View of Data." *ACM Transactions on Database Systems* 1, no. 1 (1976):9–36.

Kent, W. "A Simple Guide to Five Normal Forms in Relational Database Theory." *Communications of the ACM* 26, no. 2 (1983):120–125.

Hammer, M. "Reengineering: Don't Automate, Obliterate. *Harvard Business Review* 68, no. 4 (1990):104–112.

Wetherbe, J. C. "Executive Information Requirements: Getting It Right." *MIS Quarterly* 15, no. 1 (1991):51–65.

EXERCISES

Short answers

1. What is data modeling?
2. What are the building blocks of data modeling?
3. What is a useful technique for identifying entities in a written description of a data modeling problem?
4. When do you label arcs?
5. When is a data model well-formed and when is it high fidelity?
6. How do you handle exceptions when data modeling?
7. Describe the different types of entities.
8. Why might a data model grow?

9. Why might a data model contract?

10. How do you indicate ordering of instances in a data model?

11. What is the difference between a synonym and a homonym?

12. What is normalization?

Data modeling

Create a data model from the following narratives, which are sometimes intentionally incomplete. You will have to make some assumptions. Make certain you state these alongside your data model. Define the identifier(s) and attributes of each entity.

1. The president of a book wholesaler has told you that she wants information about publishers, authors, and books.

2. A university has many subject areas (e.g., MIS, Romance languages). Professors teach in only one subject area, but the same subject area can have many professors. Professors can teach many different courses in their subject area. An offering of a course (e.g., Data Management 457, French 101) is taught by only one professor at a particular time.

3. Kids'n'Vans retails minivans for a number of manufacturers. Each manufacturer offers several models of its minivan (e.g., SE, LE, GT). Each model comes with a standard set of equipment (e.g., the Acme SE comes with wheels, seats, and an engine). Minivans can have a variety of additional equipment or accessories (radio, air, automatic transmission, airbag, etc.), but not all accessories are available for all minivans (e.g., not all manufacturers offer a driver's side airbag). Some sets of accessories are sold as packages (e.g., the luxury package might include stereo, six speakers, cocktail bar, and twin overhead foxtails).

4. Steve operates a cinema chain and has given you the following information:

   "I have many cinemas. Each cinema can have multiple theaters. Movies are shown throughout the day starting at 11 A.M. and finishing at 1 A.M. Each movie is given a two–hour time slot. We never show a movie in more than one theater at a time, but we do shift movies among theaters because seating capacity varies. I am interested in knowing how many people, classified by adults and children, attended each showing of a movie. I vary ticket prices by movie and time slot. For instance, *Lassie Get Lost* at 11 A.M. is 50 cents for everyone, but is 75 cents at 11 P.M."

5. A university gymnastics team can have as many as ten gymnasts. The team competes many times during the season. A meet can have one or more opponents and consists of four events: vault, uneven bars, beam, and floor routine. A gymnast can participate in all or some of these events, though the team is limited to five participants in any event.

6. A famous Greek shipping magnate, Stell, owns many container ships. Containers are collected at one port and delivered to another port. Customers pay a negotiated fee for the delivery of each container. Each ship has a sailing schedule that lists the ports the ship will visit over the next six months. The schedule shows the expected arrival and departure dates. The daily charge for use of each port is also recorded.

7. A medical center employs several physicians. A physician can see many patients and

a patient can be seen by many physicians, though not always on the one visit. On any particular visit, a patient may be diagnosed to have one or more illnesses.

8. A telephone company offers a 10 percent discount to any customer who phones another person who is also a customer of the company. To be eligible for the discount, the pairing of the two phone numbers must be registered with the telephone company. Furthermore, for billing purposes the company records both phone numbers, start time, end time, and date of call.

9. Global Trading (GT), Inc. is a conglomerate. It buys and sells businesses frequently and has difficulty keeping track of what strategic business units (SBUs) it owns, in what nations it operates, and what markets it serves. For example, the CEO was recently surprised to find that GT owns 25 percent of Dundee's Wild Adventures, headquartered in Zaire, that has subsidiaries operating tours of Australia, Zaire, and New York. You have been commissioned to design a database to keep track of GT's businesses. The CEO has provided you with the following information.

    SBUs are head-quartered in one country, not necessarily the United States. Each SBU has subsidiaries or foreign agents, depending on local legal requirements, in a number of countries. Each subsidiary or foreign agent operates in only one country but can operate in more than one market. GT uses the standard industrial code (SIC) to identify a market (e.g., newspaper publishing). The SIC is a unique four-digit code.

    While foreign agents operate as separate legal entities, GT needs to know in what countries and markets they operate. On the other hand, subsidiaries are fully or partly-owned by GT, and it is important for GT to know who are the other owners of any subsidiary and what percentage of the subsidiary they own. It is not unusual for a corporation to have shares in several of GT's subsidiary companies and for several corporations to own a portion of a subsidiary. Multiple ownership can also occur at the SBU level.

10. A real estate investment company owns many shopping malls. Each mall contains many shops. To encourage rental of its shops, the company gives a negotiated discount to retailers who have shops in more than one mall. Each shop generates an income stream that can vary from month to month because rental is based on a flat rental charge and a negotiated percentage of sales revenue. Also, each shop has monthly expenses for scheduled and unscheduled maintenance. The company uses the data to compute its monthly net income per square meter for each shop and for ad hoc querying.

11. Ray, a jazz fan, has an extensive CD collection. He is interested in recording the information about each CD. He has made several observations. A CD can have many tunes or songs (e.g., John Coltrane's *Giant Steps*, released in 1960 by Atlantic, has twelve selections). Any tune or song can feature a number of artists (e.g., *The Girl from Ipanema* on Elaine Elias's *Fantasia* CD features Elaine Elias (piano), Eddie Gomez (bass), Jack DeJohnette (drums), and Nana Vasconcelos (percussion)). Incidentally, did you know the composers of *The Girl from Ipanema* are Antonio Carlos Jobim, Carlos Lyra, and Vinicius De Moraes? Probably the best known recording of this song is that by Astrud Gilberto in 1964. It is available on the CD titled *Getz/Gilberto* under the Verve label (catalog number P2-10048). While it is not

unusual for the same piece to appear on different CDs, it can happen that the same tune appears twice on the same CD. For instance, *Giant Steps* has two takes of *Cousin Mary* (both on May 4, 1959 and featuring the same artists). The second take is nine seconds longer than the first.

Occasionally, artists will perform as a group and release CDs under the group's name. The Modern Jazz Quartet is John Lewis (piano), Milt Jackson (vibraphone), Percy Heath (bass), and Connie Keys (drums). Spryo Gyra consists of six performers.

Chapter 8

Basic Structures and the Relational Model

Few things are harder to put up with than the annoyance of a good example.
Mark Twain, *Pudd'nhead Wilson*, 1894

Every data model is composed of the same basic structures. This is a major advantage because you can just focus on a small part of a full data model without being concerned about the rest of it. As a result, translation to a relational database is very easy because you systematically translate each basic structure. This section describes each of the basic structures and shows how they are mapped to a relational database. Because the mapping is shown as a diagram and SQL CREATE statements, you will use this section frequently. Consequently, the pages are color coded to help you locate them quickly.

ONE ENTITY

No Relationships

The unrelated entity was introduced in Chapter 3. This is simply a flat file, and the mapping is very simple (see Figure 8–1). Although it is unlikely that you will have a data model with a single entity, for completeness it is included in this section.

A Recursive 1:1 Relationship

A recursive 1:1 relationship is used to describe situations like current marriage (see Figure 8–2). A person can have zero or one current spouse. The two relationships must be labeled. Mapping to the relational database requires that the identifier of one end of the relationship become a foreign key. It does not matter which one you select. Notice that when PERSONID is used as a foreign key, it must be given an alias—in this case SPOUSE—because two columns in the same table cannot have the same name. The

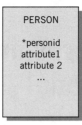

PERSON

PERSON			
PERSONID	ATTRIBUTE1	ATTRIBUTE2	...

```
CREATE TABLE PERSON
    (PERSONID INTEGER NOT NULL,
    ATTRIBUTE1 ... ,
    ATTRIBUTE2 ... ,
    ...
    PRIMARY KEY PERSONID))
```

Figure 8–1 Modeling and mapping a single entity with no relationships

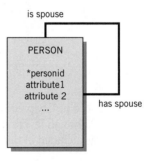

PERSON				
PERSONID	ATTRIBUTE1	ATTRIBUTE2	...	*SPOUSE*

```
CREATE TABLE PERSON
    (PERSONID INTEGER NOT NULL,
    ATTRIBUTE1 ... ,
    ATTRIBUTE2 ... ,
    ...
    SPOUSE INTEGER,
    PRIMARY KEY (PERSONID))
```

Figure 8–2 Modeling and mapping a single entity with a 1:1 recursive relationship foreign key constraint is not defined because this constraint cannot refer to the table being created.

A Recursive 1:m Relationship

A recursive 1:m relationship describes situations like fatherhood or motherhood. Figure 8–3 maps fatherhood. A father may have many biological children, but a child has only one biological father. The relationship is mapped like any other 1:m relationship. The identifier of the one end becomes a foreign key in the many end. Again, we must rename the identifier when it becomes a foreign key in the same row. Also, the foreign key constraint is not defined because it cannot refer to the table being created.

It is possible to have more than one 1:m recursive relationship. For example, details of a mother–child relationship would be represented in the same manner and result in the data model having a second 1:m recursive relationship. The mapping to the relational model would result in an additional column to contain a foreign key MOTHER, the PERSONID of the person's mother.

PERSON				
PERSONID	ATTRIBUTE1	ATTRIBUTE2	...	*FATHER*

```
CREATE TABLE PERSON
    (PERSONID INTEGER NOT NULL,
    ATTRIBUTE1 ... ,
    ATTRIBUTE2 ... ,
    ...
    FATHER INTEGER,
    PRIMARY KEY (PERSONID))
```

Figure 8–3   Modeling and mapping a single entity with a 1:m recursive relationship

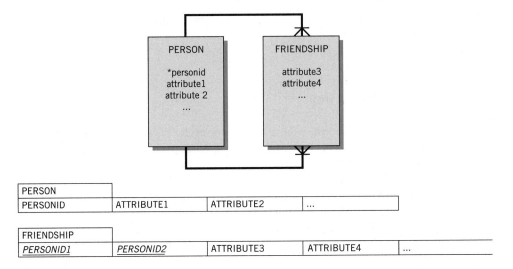

PERSON			
PERSONID	ATTRIBUTE1	ATTRIBUTE2	...

FRIENDSHIP				
PERSONID1	*PERSONID2*	ATTRIBUTE3	ATTRIBUTE4	...

```
CREATE TABLE PERSON
    (PERSONID INTEGER NOT NULL,
    ATTRIBUTE1 ... ,
    ATTRIBUTE2 ... ,
    ...
    PRIMARY KEY (PERSONID))

CREATE TABLE FRIENDSHIP
    (PERSONID1 INTEGER NOT NULL,
    PERSONID2 INTEGER NOT NULL,
    ATTRIBUTE3 ... ,
    ATTRIBUTE4 ... ,
    ...
    PRIMARY KEY(PERSONID1, PERSONID2),
    FOREIGN KEY FRIEND1(PERSONID1) REFERENCES PERSON,
    FOREIGN KEY FRIEND2(PERSONID2) REFERENCES PERSON
```

Figure 8–4 Mapping and modeling a single entity with an m:m recursive relationship

A Recursive m:m Relationship

A recursive m:m relationship can describe a situation like friendship (see Figure 8–4). A person can have many friends and be a friend to many persons. As with m:m relationships between a pair of entities, we convert this relationship to two 1:m relationships and create an intersection entity. The data model fragment is shown in Figure 8–4.

The resulting relational table FRIENDSHIP has a composite primary key based on relational descriptors, which in effect means the two components are based on PERSONID, the primary key of PERSON. To distinguish between them, these components are called PER-SONID1 and PERSONID2. So you can think of FRIENDSHIP as a pair of PERSONIDs. You will see the same pattern occurring with other m:m recursive relationships. Notice both person identifiers are independent foreign keys because they are used to map the two 1:m relationships between PERSON and FRIENDSHIP.

A single entity can have multiple m:m recursive relationships. Relationships such as enmity (not enemyship) or sibling are m:m recursive on PERSON. The approach to recording these relationships is the same as that outlined previously.

TWO ENTITIES

No Relationships

When there is no arc between two entities, the client has decided there is no need to record a relationship between the two entities. When you are reading the data model with the client, be sure that you check whether this assumption is correct now and for the foreseeable future. When there is no relationship between two entities, map them each as you would a single entity with no relationships.

A 1:1 Relationship

A 1:1 relationship usually occurs in parallel with a 1:m relationship between two entities. It signifies that there are some instances of an entity that have an additional role. For example, a department has many employees (the 1:m relationship) and a department has a boss (the 1:1 relationship). The data model fragment shown in Figure 8–5 represents the 1:1 relationship. The guideline, as explained in Chapter 6, is to map the relationship to the relational model by placing the foreign key to minimize the number of instances when it will have a null value. In this case, we place the foreign key in DEPARTMENT.

A 1:m Relationship

The 1:m relationship is possibly the easiest to understand and map (see Figure 8–6). The mapping to the relational model is very simple. The primary key of the one end becomes a foreign key in the many end.

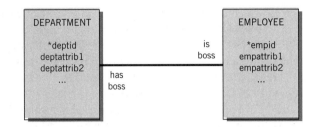

DEPARTMENT				
DEPTID	DEPTATTRIB1	DEPTATTRIB2	...	*BOSSNO*

EMPLOYEE			
EMPID	EMPATTRIB1	EMPATTRIB2	...

```
CREATE TABLE EMPLOYEE
    (EMPID INTEGER NOT NULL,
    EMPATTRIB1 ... ,
    EMPATTRIB2 ... ,
    ...
    PRIMARY KEY (EMPID))


CREATE TABLE DEPARTMENT
    (DEPTID CHAR(3)NOT NULL,
    DEPTATTRIB1 ... ,
    DEPTATTRIB2 ... ,
    ...
    BOSSNO INTEGER,
    PRIMARY KEY(DEPTID),
    FOREIGN KEY DEPTBOSS(BOSSNO) REFERENCES EMPLOYEE)
```

Figure 8–5   Modeling and mapping a 1:1 relationship between two entities

An m:m Relationship

An m:m relationship is transformed into two 1:m relationships. The mapping is then a twofold application of the 1:m rule (see Figure 8–7).

Notice in this example that CALLNO in COPY is specified as NOT NULL. This means every copy must have a corresponding book. BORROWERID, however, can be null because a book need not be borrowed; it can be sitting on the shelf. The BOOK and BORROWER tables must be created first, because the COPY table contains foreign key constraints that refer to BOOK and BORROWER.

Figure 8–6   Mapping and modeling a 1:m relationship between two entities

RELATIONSHIP DESCRIPTORS AS IDENTIFIERS

Relationship descriptors that are used as identifiers tend to cause the most problems for novice data modelers. (A relationship descriptor is an identifier when there is a bar on an arc. The bar is almost always at the crow's foot end of a 1:m relationship.) The relational tables are formed by applying the following rule: the primary key of the table at the other end of the relationship becomes both a foreign key and part of the primary key in the table at the bar end. The application of this rule is demonstrated for several common data model fragments.

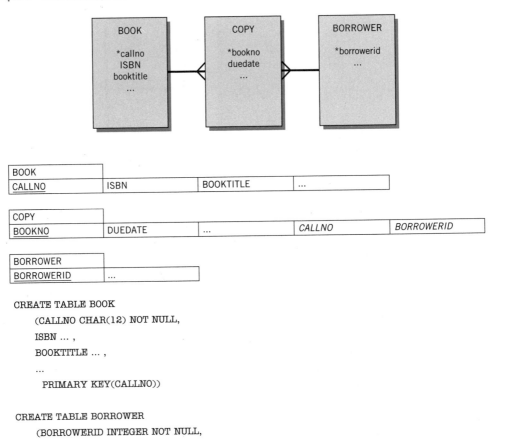

```
BOOK
CALLNO      ISBN        BOOKTITLE      ...
```

```
COPY
BOOKNO      DUEDATE      ...      CALLNO      BORROWERID
```

```
BORROWER
BORROWERID      ...
```

```
CREATE TABLE BOOK
    (CALLNO CHAR(12) NOT NULL,
    ISBN ... ,
    BOOKTITLE ... ,
    ...
    PRIMARY KEY(CALLNO))


CREATE TABLE BORROWER
    (BORROWERID INTEGER NOT NULL,
    ...
    PRIMARY KEY(BORROWERID))


CREATE TABLE COPY
    (BOOKNO INTEGER NOT NULL,
    DUEDATE DATE,
    ...
    CALLNO CHAR(12) NOT NULL,
    BORROWERID INTEGER,
        PRIMARY KEY(BOOKNO),
        FOREIGN KEY BOOK(CALLNO) REFERENCES BOOK,
        FOREIGN KEY BORROWER(BORROWERID) REFERENCE BORROWER)
```

Figure 8–7   Mapping and modeling an m:m relationship between two entities

REGION				
REGNAME	REGTYPE	REGPOP	REGAREA	...

CITY				
CITYNAME	CITYPOP	CITYAREA	...	*REGNAME*

```
CREATE TABLE REGION
    (REGNAME CHAR(20) NOT NULL,
    REGTYPE ... ,
    REGPOP ... ,
    REGAREA ... ,
    ...
    PRIMARY KEY(REGNAME))

CREATE TABLE CITY
    (CITYNAME CHAR(20) NOT NULL,
    CITYPOP,
    CITYAREA ... ,
    ...
    REGNAME CHAR(20) NOT NULL,
    PRIMARY KEY(CITYNAME, REGNAME),
    FOREIGN KEY REGION(REGNAME) REFERENCES REGION)
```

Figure 8–8   Mapping and modeling a dependent entity

A Dependent Entity

Notice that in Figure 8–8 REGNAME becomes both part of the primary key (because the relationship descriptor is part of the identifier) and a foreign key (because of the 1:m relationship between REGION and CITY) of CITY.

An Intersection Entity

In Figure 8–9 observe that CITYNAME and FIRMNAME are both part of the primary key (because they are relationship descriptors) and foreign keys (because of the two 1:m relationships) of STORE.

CITY	
CITYNAME	...

STORE				
STORESTREET	STOREZIP	...	*CITYNAME*	*FIRMNAME*

FIRM			
FIRMNAME	FIRMSTREET	FIRMZIP	...

```
CREATE TABLE CITY
    (CITYNAME CHAR(20) NOT NULL,
    ...
    PRIMARY KEY(CITYNAME))


CREATE TABLE FIRM
    (FIRMNAME CHAR(15) NOT NULL,
    FIRMSTREET ... ,
    FIRMZIP ... ,
    ...
    PRIMARY KEY(FIRMNAME))


CREATE TABLE STORE
    (STORESTREET CHAR(30),
    STOREZIP ... ,
    ...
    CITYNAME CHAR(20) NOT NULL,
    FIRMNAME CHAR(15) NOT NULL,
    PRIMARY KEY(STORESTREET, CITYNAME, FIRMNAME),
    FOREIGN KEY CITY(CITYNAME) REFERENCES CITY,
    FOREIGN KEY FIRM(FIRMNAME) REFERENCES FIRM)
```

Figure 8–9 Mapping and modeling an intersection entity

A Tree Structure

The interesting feature of Figure 8–10 is the primary key. Notice that the primary key of a lower level of the tree is a composite of its identifier and the primary keys of the higher levels. The primary key of DIVISION is a composite of FIRMNAME and DIVNAME, the primary

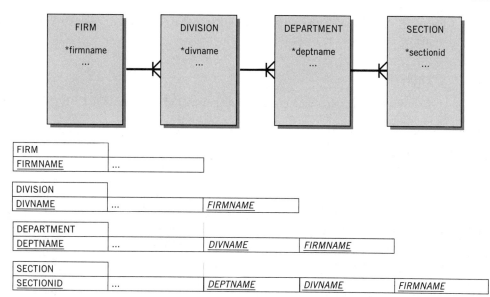

FIRM	
FIRMNAME	...

DIVISION		
DIVNAME	...	*FIRMNAME*

DEPARTMENT			
DEPTNAME	...	*DIVNAME*	*FIRMNAME*

SECTION				
SECTIONID	...	*DEPTNAME*	*DIVNAME*	*FIRMNAME*

```
CREATE TABLE FIRM
    (FIRMNAME CHAR(15) NOT NULL,

        ...

        PRIMARY KEY(FIRMNAME))

CREATE TABLE DIVISION
        (DIVNAME  CHAR(15) NOT NULL,

        ...

        FIRMNAME CHAR(15) NOT NULL,
        PRIMARY KEY(FIRMNAME, DIVNAME),
        FOREIGN KEY FIRM(FIRMNAME) REFERENCES FIRM)

CREATE TABLE DEPARTMENT
        (DEPTNAME CHAR(15) NOT NULL,

        ...

        DIVNAME CHAR(15) NOT NULL,
        FIRMNAME CHAR(15) NOT NULL,
            PRIMARY KEY(FIRMNAME, DIVNAME, DEPTNAME),
            FOREIGN KEY DIVISION(FIRMNAME, DIVNAME) REFERENCES DIVISION)

CREATE TABLE SECTION
        (SECTIONID INTEGER NOT NULL,

        ...

        DEPTNAME CHAR(15) NOT NULL,
        DIVNAME CHAR(15) NOT NULL
        FIRMNAME CHAR(15) NOT NULL,
            PRIMARY KEY(FIRMNAME, DIVNAME, DEPTNAME, SECTIONID),
            FOREIGN KEY DEPARTMENT(FIRMNAME, DIVNAME, DEPTNAME)
                    REFERENCES DEPARTMENT)
```

Figure 8–10 Mapping and modeling a tree structure

key of DEPARTMENT is a composite of FIRMNAME, DIVNAME, and DEPTNAME. Novice modelers often forget to make this translation.

EXERCISES

Convert the following data models to diagrams and write the SQL CREATE statements.

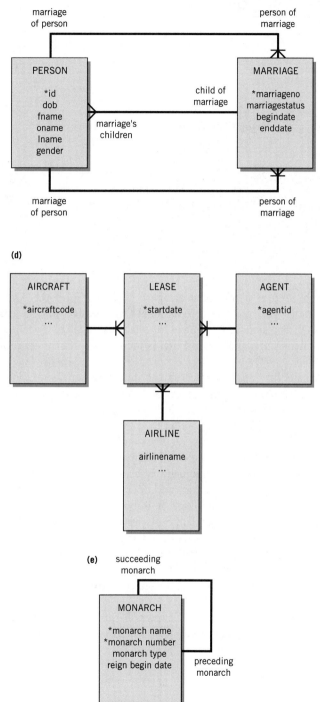

Chapter 9

SQL

The questing beast.
Sir Thomas Mallory, *Le Morte D'Arthur,* 1470

Learning Objectives

Students completing this chapter will have a detailed knowledge of SQL.

INTRODUCTION

SQL is widely used as a relational database language. Both the American National Standards Institute (ANSI) and the International Organization for Standardization (ISO) have designated SQL as a standard language for relational database systems. SQL skills are essential for data management in a world that is increasingly reliant on relational database technology.

SQL originated in the IBM Research Laboratory in San Jose, California. A range of IBM database management products support SQL. Versions of it have also been implemented by many other commercial database vendors for a wide range of operating systems. An ANSI committee, formed in 1978, has guided the definition of an SQL standard. SQL standards were released in 1986, 1989, and 1992. The committee is currently working on object–oriented extensions to SQL that are expected to emerge in 1996 or 1997.[1]

SQL is a **complete database language**. It is used for defining a relational database, creating views, and specifying queries. In addition, it allows for rows to be inserted, updated, and deleted. In database terminology, it is both a **data definition language** (DDL) and **data manipulation language** (DML). SQL, however, is not a complete programming language like COBOL and C. Because SQL statements can be embedded into general purpose programming languages, SQL is often used in conjunction with such languages to create application programs. The **embedded SQL** statements handle the database processing and the statements in the general purpose language perform the necessary tasks to complete the application.

You were introduced to SQL in Chapters 3 through 6. This chapter provides an integrated coverage of the language, pulling together the various pieces that were presented previously.

---

[1]J. Melton, "Changing the Guard: ANSI Makes Its Transition from SQL2 to SQL3," *Database Programming & Design* 6 (3): 31–32 (1993).

DATA DEFINITION

One of the major advantages of relational DBMSs is that DDL statements can be executed at any time. Earlier DBMSs often require halting the entire system to perform maintenance operations such as adding a new table (actually a record type in the terminology of non-relational DBMSs) or creating an index. In many cases, this is extremely difficult to do because many systems are in use 24 hours per day. In some cases, routine maintenance is delayed until the system can be shut down for an extended period. Major holidays, such as Christmas and New Year, are often used for database maintenance. Relational DBMSs greatly alleviate this problem because new tables, views, and indexes can be created without interfering with current operational use.

The DDL part of SQL encompasses statements to operate on tables, views, and indexes. Before we proceed, however, the term base table must be defined. A **base table** is an autonomous, named table. It is autonomous because it exists in its own right, it is physically stored within the database. In contrast, a view is not autonomous because it is derived from one or more base tables and does not exist independently. A view is a virtual table. A base table has a name by which it can be referenced. This name is chosen when the base table is generated using the CREATE statement. Short-lived temporary tables, such as those formed as the result of a query, are not named.

Keys

The concept of a key occurs several times within SQL. In general, a **key** is one or more columns identified as such in the description of a table, an index, or a referential constraint. The same column can be part of more than one key. For example, it can be part of a primary key and a foreign key. A **composite key** is an ordered set of columns of the same table. In other words, the primary key of LINEITEM is always the composite of (SALENO, LINENO) in that order. The order cannot be changed.

Comparing composite keys actually means that corresponding components of the keys are compared. Thus application of the referential integrity rule, "the value of a foreign key must be equal to a value of the primary key" means that each component of the foreign key must be equal to a corresponding component of a composite primary key.

So far, you have met primary and foreign keys. A **unique key** is another type of key. Its purpose is to ensure that no two values of a key are equal. This constraint is enforced by the DBMS during the execution of INSERT and UPDATE statements. A unique key is part of the index mechanism.

Indexes

Indexes are used to accelerate data access and ensure uniqueness. An **index** is an ordered set of pointers to rows of a base table. Think of an index as a table that contains two columns (see Figure 9–1). The first column contains values for the index key and the second

ITEMTYPE INDEX			ITEM			
ITEMTYPE			ITEMNO	ITEMNAME	ITEMTYPE	ITEMCOLOR
C			1	Pocket knife–Nile	E	Brown
C			2	Pocket knife–Thames	E	Brown
C			3	Compass	N	–
C			4	Geo positioning system	N	–
E			5	Map measure	N	–
E			6	Hat–polar explorer	C	Red
F			7	Hat–polar explorer	C	White
N			8	Boots–snakeproof	C	Green
N			9	Boots–snakeproof	C	Black
N			10	Safari hat	F	Khaki

Figure 9–1   An example of an index

column contains a list of pointers or addresses of rows in the table. Since the values in the first column are ordered (i.e., in ascending or descending sequence), the index table can be searched quickly. It's like searching a phone book on a person's last name. This is easy because the telephone book is in last name sequence. In contrast, searching by phone number is extremely time consuming because the telephone book is not in this sequence. Once the required key has been found in the table, the row's address in the second column can be used to quickly retrieve the data. An index can be specified as being unique, in which case the DBMS ensures that the corresponding table does not have rows with identical index keys.[2]

Notation

A short primer on notation is required before we examine SQL commands.

1. Text in upper case is required as is.
2. Text in lower case denotes values to be selected by the user.
3. Statements enclosed within brackets are optional.
4. An ellipsis (. . .) indicates that the immediate syntactic unit may be repeated optionally more than once.

---

[2]Indexes are covered in depth in Chapter 11.

Create Table

CREATE TABLE is used to define a new base table either interactively or by embedding the statement in a host language. The statement specifies a table's name, provides details of its columns, and integrity checks. The format of the command is:

```
CREATE TABLE base-table
   column-definition-block
   [primary-key-block]
   [referential-constraint-block]
   [unique-block]
```

Column Definition

The column definition block defines the columns in a table. Each column definition consists of a column name, data type, and optionally the specification that the column cannot contain null values. The general form is:

```
(column-definition [, ...])
```

where column-definition is of the form

```
column-name data-type [NOT NULL]
```

The **NOT NULL** clause specifies that the particular column must have a value whenever a new row is inserted. This clause should always be defined for a column that is a primary key or a component of a primary key. It is sometimes defined for foreign key, but not always as illustrated by the definition of the MONARCH table in Chapter 6.

Primary Key Definition

The primary key definition block specifies a set of column values comprising the primary key. Once a primary key is defined, the system enforces its uniqueness by checking that the primary key of any new row does not already exist in the table. A table can have only one primary key. While it is not mandatory to define a primary key, it is good practice to always define a table's primary key. The general form of the definition is:

$$\text{PRIMARY KEY (column-name} \begin{bmatrix} \text{ASC} \\ \text{DESC} \end{bmatrix} [, \dots])$$

The optional ASC or DESC clause specifies whether the values from this key are arranged in ascending or descending order respectively.

Referential Constraint Definition

The referential constraint block defines a **foreign key**, which consists of one or more columns in the table that together must match a primary key (or else be null) of the specified table. A foreign key value is null when any one of the columns in the row comprising the foreign key is null. Once the foreign key constraint is defined, the DBMS will check every insert and update to ensure that the constraint is observed. The general form of the definition is:

```
FOREIGN KEY constraint-name (column-name [,...])
   REFERENCES table-name
                ⎡RESTRICT⎤
   ON DELETE    ⎢CASCADE ⎥
                ⎣SET NULL⎦
```

The constraint-name definition supports naming a referential constraint. You cannot use a constraint-name more than once in the same table.

Column-name identifies the column or columns that comprise the foreign key. The data type and length of foreign key columns must match exactly the data type and length of the primary key columns.

The clause REFERENCES table-name specifies the name of the existing table that contains the primary key, which cannot be the name of the table being created.

The ON DELETE clause defines the action taken when a row is deleted from the table containing the primary key. There are three options:

1. RESTRICT prevents deletion of the primary key row until all corresponding rows in the related table, the one containing the foreign key, have been deleted. RESTRICT is the default value for this clause and also the cautious approach for preserving data integrity.
2. CASCADE causes all the corresponding rows in the related table also to be deleted.
3. SET NULLS sets the foreign key to null for all corresponding rows in the related table.

Unique Definition

The unique definition block creates a unique index for the specified column or columns. A unique key is constrained so that no two of its values are equal. Columns appearing in a unique constraint must be defined as NOT NULL. The constraint is enforced by the DBMS during execution of INSERT and UPDATE statements. The general format is:

```
UNIQUE constraint-name (column-name ⎡ASC ⎤ [,...])
                                     ⎣DESC⎦
```

The column-name clause identifies the column or columns that comprise the unique key. Also, these columns should not be the same as those of the table's primary key, which are guaranteed uniqueness by the primary key definition. The ASC and DESC options specify whether the columns of the unique key are arranged in ascending or descending order, respectively.

An example illustrates the use of CREATE TABLE.

```
CREATE TABLE STOCK
   (STKCODE CHAR(3)        NOT NULL,
    STKFIRM  CHAR(20),
    STKPRICE DECIMAL(6,2),
    STKQTY   DECIMAL(8),
    STKDIV   DECIMAL(5,2),
    STKPE    DECIMAL(5),
    NATCODE  CHAR(3),
      PRIMARY KEY(STKCODE),
      FOREIGN KEY NATIONCODE(NATCODE)  REFERENCES NATION
         ON DELETE RESTRICT)
```

Data Types

Some of the variety of data types that can be used for a column are shown in Table 9–1. The choices are also depicted in Figure 9–2.

Table 9–1 Some Allowable Data Types

Numeric	INTEGER	A 31-bit signed binary value
	SMALLINT	A 15-bit signed binary value
	FLOAT(p)	A scientific format number of p binary digits precision
	DECIMAL(p,q)	A packed decimal number of p digits total length; q decimal places to the right of the decimal point may be specified
String	CHAR(n)	A fixed length character string of n characters
	VARCHAR(n)	A variable length character string up to n characters
	LONG VARCHAR	A variable length character string
Date/time	DATE	Date in the form *yyyymmdd*
	TIME	Time in the form *hhmmss*
	TIMESTAMP	A combination of date and time to the nearest microsecond
Graphic	GRAPHIC(n)	A fixed length graphic string of n 16-bit bytes
	VARGRAPHIC(n)	A variable length graphic string of up to n 16-bit bytes
	LONG VARGRAPHIC	A variable length graphic string of 16-bit bytes

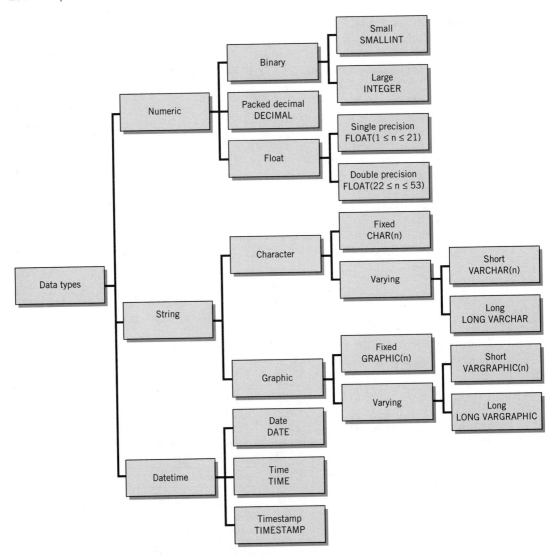

Figure 9-2　Data types

SMALLINT and INTEGER

Most commercial computers have a 32-bit word, where a word is a unit of storage. An integer can be stored in a full word or half a word. If it is stored in a full word (INTEGER) then it can be 31 binary digits in length. If half-word storage is used (SMALLINT) then it can be 15 binary digits long. In each case, one bit is used for the sign of the number. A column defined as INTEGER can store a number in the range $-(2^{31})$ to $(2^{31}-1)$ or $-2{,}147{,}483{,}648$ to $2{,}147{,}483{,}647$. A column defined as SMALLINT can store a number in the range $-(2^{15})$ to $(2^{15}-1)$ or $-32{,}768$ to $32{,}767$. Just remember that INTEGER is good for ±2 billion and SMALLINT for $\pm32{,}000$.

FLOAT

Scientists often deal with numbers that are very large (e.g., Avogadro's number is 6.02252×10^{23}), or very small (e.g., Planck's constant is 6.6262×10^{-34} joule sec). The FLOAT data type is used for storing such numbers, often referred to as floating-point numbers. A single precision floating-point number requires 32 bits and can represent numbers in the range $-7.2E75$ to $-5.4E-79$, 0, $+5.4E-79$ to $7.2E+75$. A double precision floating-point number requires 64 bits. The range is the same as a single precision floating-point number. The extra 32 bits are used to increase precision.

In the specification FLOAT(n), if n is between 1 and 21 inclusive, single precision floating-point is selected. If n is between 22 and 53 inclusive, the storage format is double precision floating-point. If n is not specified, double precision floating-point is assumed.

DECIMAL

Binary is the most convenient form of storing data from a computer's perspective. People, however, work with a decimal number system and do not want to be bothered with thinking in terms of binary numbers. The DECIMAL data type is very convenient for business applications because data storage requirements are defined in terms of the maximum number of places to the left and right of the decimal point. For example, to store the current value of an ounce of gold you would possibly use DECIMAL(6,2) as this would permit a maximum value of $9,999.99. Notice that the general form is DECIMAL(p,q) where p is the total number of digits in the column and q is the number of digits to the right of the decimal point.

CHAR and VARCHAR

Non-numeric columns are stored as character strings. A person's family name is an example of a column that is stored as a character string. CHAR(n) defines a column that has a fixed length of n characters, where n can be a maximum of 255.

Family name might be defined as CHAR(20). This should be enough space to store all the characters of nearly all family names. Of course, it would be a good idea to do some checking because 20 characters might be insufficient for a country like Thailand, where family names can be quite long. It might be too much for Hong Kong because Chinese family names tend to be quite short. There is a trade-off between too many and too few characters. If too few characters are defined, some family names will be truncated, and this could be offensive to some customers. If too many characters are defined, then storage is wasted because a set amount of space is allocated for each column regardless of how many characters are actually required for the column. The rightmost unused portion of a column is filled with the space character. Most database designers err on the side of making a column too long rather than too short—customers are worth more than computer memory.

Of course, there are some columns where there is no trade-off decision because all possible entries are always the same length. U.S. Social Security numbers are always nine characters.

When a column's length can vary greatly, it makes sense to define the field as VARCHAR or LONG VARCHAR. Usually, a column defined as VARCHAR consists of two parts: a header indicating the length of the character string and the character string. If a table contains a column that occasionally stores a long string of text (e.g., a message field) then defining it as VARCHAR makes sense. LONG VARCHAR can store strings up to 32,767 characters long.

Why not store all character columns as VARCHAR and save space? The answer is, because there is a price for using VARCHAR. First, additional space is required for the header to indicate the length of the string. Second, additional processing time is required to handle a variable length string compared to a fixed length string. Depending on the major uses of the database, these can be important considerations.

Data compression programs are another approach to the "space wars" problem. A database can be defined with generous allowances for fixed length character columns so that important columns are not truncated. Then, a data compression program can be used to compress the file to remove the "wasted" space. Again, there is a trade-off, data compression is slow and will increase the time it takes to answer queries. You save space at the cost of time, and save time at the cost of space. When dealing with character fields, the database designer has to decide whether time or space is more important.

TIME and DATE

Columns that have a data type of DATE are stored as *yyyymmdd* (e.g., 1994–11–04). There are several reasons for storing data in this format. First, it is convenient for sorting on chronological order. For example, the common American way of writing dates (*mmddyy*) requires processing before chronological sorting. Second, the full form of the year should be recorded, especially since we are approaching the turn of the century. There is sure to be some confusion in the early days of 2000 because of programs in which year is stored in the abbreviated form of *yy*.

For similar reasons, it makes sense to store times in the form *hhmmss* with the understanding that this is 24-hour time (also known as European time and military time). This is the format used for data type TIME.

Some applications require precise recording of events. For example, transaction processing systems typically record the time a transaction was processed by the computer. Because computer systems operate at such high speeds, the TIMESTAMP data type records date and time with microsecond accuracy. A timestamp has seven parts—year, month, day, hour, minute, second, and microsecond. Date and time are defined as previously described (i.e., *yyyymmdd* and *hhmmss*, respectively). The range of the microsecond part is 000000 to 999999.

Although times and dates are stored in a particular format, they can be reported in a variety of ways. The reporting formatting facilities that generally come with a relational DBMS usually allow tailoring of output to suit local standards; thus for a U.S. firm, date might appear on a report in the form *mm/dd/yy*. For a European firm following the ISO standard, date would appear as *yyyy–mm–dd*.

GRAPHIC and VARGRAPHIC

The CHARACTER data type is fine for storing characters sets, such as that used in English–speaking countries, with less than 256 different symbols (e.g., A, 6, and *). The Chinese and Japanese languages, however, contain thousands of symbols. Chinese contains more than 50,000 distinct characters, although only 3000–4000 are needed for everyday communication. Providing a unique code for each of the many Chinese characters requires 16 bits, which enables representation of 65,536 different symbols (2^{16}). GRAPHIC and VAR-GRAPHIC data types are for storing these double-byte, 16–bit, character sets. LONG VAR-GRAPHIC can store a string of up to 16,834 16–bit characters.

Special Registers

Some implementations of SQL have **special registers** for commonly required data values (e.g., today's date). Some that you might like to use are CURRENT DATE, CURRENT TIME, and CURRENT TIMESTAMP. For example:

```
INSERT INTO SALE
   (SALENO, SALEDATE, SALETEXT)
   VALUES (6, CURRENT DATE, 'Brazilian tourist')
```

BLOB

A new data type has been created for multimedia databases. Multimedia applications typically require the storage of very large but relatively unstructured objects such as images, drawings, audio and video sequences. Binary large objects (BLOBs) define columns that will contain these types of objects. There are two BLOB data types: text and byte. Text BLOBs contain valid text characters, such as reports, correspondence, chapters of a manual, and contracts. Byte BLOBs are binary data that can contain any object, such as a spreadsheet, graph, fax, satellite image, voice pattern, or any digitized data. BLOB is not yet supported by some relational database systems, but you can expect it to appear in the next few years.

Alter Table

The ALTER TABLE statement has two purposes. First, it can add a single column to an existing table. Second, it can add, drop, activate, or deactivate primary and foreign keys constraints.

A base table can be altered by adding one new column, which appears to the right of existing columns. The format of the command is:

```
ALTER TABLE base-table
   ADD column data-type
```

Notice that there is no optional NOT NULL clause for column-definition with ALTER TABLE. It is not allowed because the ALTER TABLE statement automatically fills the additional column with null in every case.[3] Of course, if you want to add multiple new columns,

---

[3]This may not be what happens physically, but it is a good way of visualizing why NOT NULL is an inappropriate clause.

you can repeat the ALTER TABLE command. The following example illustrates the use of ALTER TABLE.

```
ALTER TABLE STOCK ADD STKRATING CHAR(3)
```

Unfortunately, ALTER TABLE does not permit changing the width of a column, amending a column's data type, or deleting an unwanted column. It is strictly for adding a new column.

ALTER TABLE is also used to change the status of referential constraints. There are some occasions when key constraints can cause performance problems. For instance, large volumes of data will be loaded faster if referential integrity constraints are deactivated. You can deactivate constraints on a table's primary key or any of its foreign keys. Deactivation also makes the relevant tables unavailable to all users except the tables' owner or someone possessing database management authority. After loading the data, referential constraints must be reactivated before they can be automatically enforced again. Activating the constraints enables the DBMS to validate the references in the data.

Drop Table

A base table can be deleted at any time by using the DROP statement. The format is:

```
DROP TABLE base-table
```

The table is deleted and any views or indexes defined on the table are also deleted. Naturally, you should think carefully before dropping a table.

Create View

A **view** is a virtual table. It has no physical counterpart but appears to the user as if it really exists. A view is defined in terms of other tables that exist in the database. The syntax for defining a view is:

```
CREATE VIEW view [column [,column] ... )]
    AS subquery
```

There are several reasons for creating a view. First, a view can be used to restrict access to certain rows or columns. This is particularly important for sensitive data. An organization's PERSON table can contain both private data (e.g., annual salary) and public data (office phone number). A view consisting of public data (e.g., person's name, department, and office telephone number) might be provided to many people. Access to all columns in the table, however, might be confined to a small number of people. Here is a sample view that restricts access to a table.

```
CREATE VIEW STKLIST
    AS SELECT STKFIRM, STKPRICE FROM STOCK
```

Handling derived data is a second reason for creating a view. A column that can be computed from one or more other columns should always be defined by a view. For example, a stock's yield is computed by dividing its dividend by its price. Yield would be created by a view rather than being defined as a column in a base table.

```
CREATE VIEW STK
   (STKFIRM, STKPRICE, STKQTY, STKYIELD)
   AS SELECT STKFIRM, STKPRICE, STKQTY, STKDIV/STKPRICE*100
   FROM STOCK
```

A third reason for defining a view is to avoid writing common SQL queries. For example, there may be some joins that are frequently a part of a SQL query. User productivity can be increased by defining these joins as views. Here is an example:

```
CREATE VIEW STKVALUE
   (NATION, FIRM, PRICE, QTY, VALUE)
   AS SELECT NATNAME, STKFIRM, STKPRICE*EXCHRATE, STKQTY,
   STKPRICE*EXCHRATE*STKQTY)
   FROM STOCK, NATION
      WHERE STOCK.NATCODE = NATION.NATCODE
```

The preceding example demonstrates how CREATE VIEW can be used to rename columns, create new columns, and involve more than one table. The view STKVALUE has five columns. The column NATION corresponds to NATNAME, FIRM to STKFIRM, and so forth. A new column, PRICE, is created by multiplying the price of the share by the exchange rate. This calculation converts all share prices from the local currency to British pounds. Also note that the query that defines the view is a join.

Data conversion is a fourth useful reason for using a view. The United States is one of the few countries that does not use the metric system, and reports for American managers often display weights and measures in pounds and feet, respectively. The database of an international company could record all measurements in metric format (e.g., weight in kilograms) and use a view to convert these measures for American reports.

When a CREATE VIEW statement is executed, the definition of the view is entered in the systems catalog, the database about the database. The subquery following AS is executed only when the view is referenced in an SQL command. For example, the following command would enable the subquery to be executed and the view created:

```
SELECT * FROM STKVALUE WHERE PRICE > 10
```

In effect, the following query is executed

```
SELECT NATNAME, STKFIRM, STKPRICE*EXCHRATE, STKQTY,
   STKPRICE*STKVALUE*EXCHRATE
   FROM STOCK, NATION
   WHERE STOCK.NATCODE = NATION.NATCODE
      AND STKPRICE*EXCHRATE > 10
```

Any table that can be defined with a SELECT statement is a potential view. Thus, it is possible to have a view that is defined by another view.

Drop View

DROP VIEW is used to delete a view from the system catalog. The syntax is

```
DROP VIEW view
```

Remember, if a base table is dropped, all views based on that table are also dropped.

A view might be dropped because it needs to be redefined or is no longer used. It must be dropped first before a revised version of the view is created.

Create Index

An index helps speed up retrieval (see Chapter 11 for a complete discussion of indexing). A column that is frequently referred to in a WHERE clause is a possible candidate for indexing. For example, if data on stocks were frequently retrieved using STKFIRM, then this column should be considered for an index. The format for CREATE INDEX is

```
CREATE [UNIQUE] INDEX index
    ON base-table (column [order] [,column, [order]] ...)
    [CLUSTER]
```

This next example illustrates use of CREATE INDEX.

```
CREATE UNIQUE INDEX STKFIRMINDX
    ON STOCK (STKFIRM)
    CLUSTER
```

In the preceding example, an index called STKFIRMINDX is created for the table STOCK. Index entries are ordered by ascending—the default order—values of STKFIRM. The optional clause UNIQUE specifies that no two rows in the base table can have the same value for STKFIRM, the indexed column. Specifying UNIQUE means that the DBMS will reject any insert or update operation that would create a duplicate value for STKFIRM. A clustering index (see Chapter 11) is denoted by the optional CLUSTER.

A composite index can be created from several columns, which is often necessary for intersection entities. The following example illustrates creation of a composite index.

```
CREATE INDEX LINEITEMINDX
    ON LINEITEM (LINENO, SALENO)
```

Drop Index

Indexes can be dropped at any time by using the DROP INDEX statement. The general form of this statement is:

```
DROP INDEX index
```

For example, to drop the index called LINEITEMINDX, use the following statement:

```
DROP INDEX LINEITEMINDX
```

DATA MANIPULATION

SQL supports four DML statements—SELECT, INSERT, UPDATE, and DELETE. Each of these will be discussed in turn, with most attention focusing on SELECT because of the variety of ways in which it can be used. But first, we need to understand why we must qualify column names and temporary names.

Qualifying Column Names

Ambiguous references to column names are avoided by qualifying a column name with its table name, especially when the same column name is used in several tables. Clarity is maintained by prefixing the column name with the table name. The following example demonstrates qualification of the column NATCODE, which appears in both STOCK and NATION.

```
SELECT * FROM STOCK, NATION
   WHERE STOCK.NATCODE = NATION.NATCODE
```

Temporary Names

A table or view can be given a temporary name that remains current for a query. Temporary names were used previously when a table was joined with itself. They were used to clearly establish unique identities for each table. The next example demonstrates how two temporary names, EMP and BOSS, were created for EMP.

```
SELECT WRK.EMPFNAME
   FROM EMP WRK, EMP BOSS
      WHERE WRK.BOSSNO = BOSS.EMPNO
```

A temporary name also can be used as a shortened form of a long table name. For example, *L* might have been used merely to avoid having to enter LINEITEM more than once. If a temporary name is specified for a table or view, any qualified reference to a column of the table or view must also use that temporary name.

Select

The **SELECT** statement is by far the most interesting and challenging of the four DML statements. It is interesting because it reveals a major benefit of the relational model—powerful interrogation capabilities. It is challenging because to master the power of SELECT requires considerable practice with a wide range of queries. The major varieties of SELECT are presented in this section. The SQL Playbook in the next chapter reveals the full power of the command.

The general format of SELECT is

```
SELECT [DISTINCT] item(s)
   FROM table(s)
   [WHERE condition]
   [GROUP BY column(s)]
   [HAVING condition]
   [ORDER BY column(s)]
```

The simplest queries deal with a single table. Chapter 3 provides a complete coverage of single table queries, so refer to that chapter for details. We will now consider more complex queries.

Product

Product, or more strictly Cartesian product, is a fundamental operation of relational algebra. It is rarely used by itself in a query; however, understanding its effect helps in understanding join. The product of two tables is a new table consisting of all rows of the first table concatenated with all possible rows of the second table. An example illustrates how this is expressed in SQL.

○ **Form the product of STOCK and NATION.**

```
SELECT * FROM STOCK, NATION
```

The new table contains 64 rows (16*4), where STOCK has 16 rows and NATION has 4 rows. It has 10 columns (7 + 3), where STOCK has 7 columns and NATION has 3 columns. The result of the operation is shown in Table 9–2. Note that each row in STOCK is concatenated with each row in NATION.

Table 9–2 Product of STOCK and NATION

STKCODE	STKFIRM	STKPRICE	STKQTY	STKDIV	STKPE	NATCODE	NATCODE1	NATNAME	EXCHRATE
FC	Freedonia Copper	27.50	10529	1.84	16	UK	UK	United Kingdom	1.00000
FC	Freedonia Copper	27.50	10529	1.84	16	UK	US	United States	0.67000
FC	Freedonia Copper	27.50	10529	1.84	16	UK	AUS	Australia	0.46000
FC	Freedonia Copper	27.50	10529	1.84	16	UK	IND	India	0.02280
PT	Patagonian Tea	55.25	12635	2.50	10	UK	UK	United Kingdom	1.00000
PT	Patagonian Tea	55.25	12635	2.50	10	UK	US	United States	0.67000
PT	Patagonian Tea	55.25	12635	2.50	10	UK	AUS	Australia	0.46000
PT	Patagonian Tea	55.25	12635	2.50	10	UK	IND	India	0.02280
AR	Abyssinian Ruby	31.82	22010	1.32	13	UK	UK	United Kingdom	1.00000
AR	Abyssinian Ruby	31.82	22010	1.32	13	UK	US	United States	0.67000
AR	Abyssinian Ruby	31.82	22010	1.32	13	UK	AUS	Australia	0.46000
AR	Abyssinian Ruby	31.82	22010	1.32	13	UK	IND	India	0.02280
SLG	Sri Lankan Gold	50.37	32868	2.68	16	UK	UK	United Kingdom	1.00000
SLG	Sri Lankan Gold	50.37	32868	2.68	16	UK	US	United States	0.67000
SLG	Sri Lankan Gold	50.37	32868	2.68	16	UK	AUS	Australia	0.46000
SLG	Sri Lankan Gold	50.37	32868	2.68	16	UK	IND	India	0.02280
ILZ	Indian Lead & Zinc	37.75	6390	3.00	12	UK	UK	United Kingdom	1.00000
ILZ	Indian Lead & Zinc	37.75	6390	3.00	12	UK	US	United States	0.67000
ILZ	Indian Lead & Zinc	37.75	6390	3.00	12	UK	AUS	Australia	0.46000
ILZ	Indian Lead & Zinc	37.75	6390	3.00	12	UK	IND	India	0.02280
BE	Burmese Elephant	0.07	154713	0.01	3	UK	UK	United Kingdom	1.00000
BE	Burmese Elephant	0.07	154713	0.01	3	UK	US	United States	0.67000
BE	Burmese Elephant	0.07	154713	0.01	3	UK	AUS	Australia	0.46000
BE	Burmese Elephant	0.07	154713	0.01	3	UK	IND	India	0.02280
BS	Bolivian Sheep	12.75	231678	1.78	11	UK	UK	United Kingdom	1.00000
BS	Bolivian Sheep	12.75	231678	1.78	11	UK	US	United States	0.67000
BS	Bolivian Sheep	12.75	231678	1.78	11	UK	AUS	Australia	0.46000
BS	Bolivian Sheep	12.75	231678	1.78	11	UK	IND	India	0.02280

continued

213

Table 9–2   Product of STOCK and NATION (Continued)

STKCODE	STKFIRM	STKPRICE	STKQTY	STKDIV	STKPE	NATCODE	NATCODE1	NATNAME	EXCHRATE
NG	Nigerian Geese	35.00	12323	1.68	10	UK	UK	United Kingdom	1.00000
NG	Nigerian Geese	35.00	12323	1.68	10	UK	US	United States	0.67000
NG	Nigerian Geese	35.00	12323	1.68	10	UK	AUS	Australia	0.46000
NG	Nigerian Geese	35.00	12323	1.68	10	UK	IND	India	0.02280
CS	Canadian Sugar	52.78	4716	2.50	15	UK	UK	United Kingdom	1.00000
CS	Canadian Sugar	52.78	4716	2.50	15	UK	US	United States	0.67000
CS	Canadian Sugar	52.78	4716	2.50	15	UK	AUS	Australia	0.46000
CS	Canadian Sugar	52.78	4716	2.50	15	UK	IND	India	0.02280
ROF	Royal Ostrich Farms	33.75	1234923	3.00	6	UK	UK	United Kingdom	1.00000
ROF	Royal Ostrich Farms	33.75	1234923	3.00	6	UK	US	United States	0.67000
ROF	Royal Ostrich Farms	33.75	1234923	3.00	6	UK	AUS	Australia	0.46000
ROF	Royal Ostrich Farms	33.75	1234923	3.00	6	UK	IND	India	0.02280
MG	Minnesota Gold	53.87	816122	1.00	25	US	UK	United Kingdom	1.00000
MG	Minnesota Gold	53.87	816122	1.00	25	US	US	United States	0.67000
MG	Minnesota Gold	53.87	816122	1.00	25	US	AUS	Australia	0.46000
MG	Minnesota Gold	53.87	816122	1.00	25	US	IND	India	0.02280

GP	Georgia Peach	2.35	387333	0.20	5	US	UK	United Kingdom	1.00000
GP	Georgia Peach	2.35	387333	0.20	5	US	US	United States	0.67000
GP	Georgia Peach	2.35	387333	0.20	5	US	AUS	Australia	0.46000
GP	Georgia Peach	2.35	387333	0.20	5	US	IND	India	0.02280
NE	Narembeen Emu	12.34	45619	1.00	8	AUS	UK	United Kingdom	1.00000
NE	Narembeen Emu	12.34	45619	1.00	8	AUS	US	United States	0.67000
NE	Narembeen Emu	12.34	45619	1.00	8	AUS	AUS	Australia	0.46000
NE	Narembeen Emu	12.34	45619	1.00	8	AUS	IND	India	0.02280
QD	Queensland Diamond	6.73	89251	0.50	7	AUS	UK	United Kingdom	1.00000
QD	Queensland Diamond	6.73	89251	0.50	7	AUS	US	United States	0.67000
QD	Queensland Diamond	6.73	89251	0.50	7	AUS	AUS	Australia	0.46000
QD	Queensland Diamond	6.73	89251	0.50	7	AUS	IND	India	0.02280
IR	Indooroopilly Ruby	15.92	56147	0.50	20	AUS	UK	United Kingdom	1.00000
IR	Indooroopilly Ruby	15.92	56147	0.50	20	AUS	US	United States	0.67000
IR	Indooroopilly Ruby	15.92	56147	0.50	20	AUS	AUS	Australia	0.46000
IR	Indooroopilly Ruby	15.92	56147	0.50	20	AUS	IND	India	0.02280
BD	Bombay Duck	25.55	167382	1.00	12	IND	UK	United Kingdom	1.00000
BD	Bombay Duck	25.55	167382	1.00	12	IND	US	United States	0.67000
BD	Bombay Duck	25.55	167382	1.00	12	IND	AUS	Australia	0.46000
BD	Bombay Duck	25.55	167382	1.00	12	IND	IND	India	0.02280

Joins

Join is a very powerful and frequently used operation. Join creates a new table from two existing tables by matching on a column common to both tables. An **equijoin** is the simplest form of join; in this case, columns are matched on equality. You can think of an equijoin as first performing a product of the two tables and then doing a restrict on matching columns. Here is an example:

```
SELECT * FROM STOCK, NATION
    WHERE STOCK.NATCODE = NATION.NATCODE
```

The shaded rows in Table 9–2 shown previously indicate the result of the join.

An equijoin creates a new table that contains two identical columns. If one of these is dropped, then the remaining table is called a **natural join**. It can be expressed as

```
SELECT STKCODE, STKFIRM, STKPRICE, STKQTY, STKDIV, STKPE,
    STOCK.NATCODE, EXCHRATE, NATNAME
    FROM STOCK, NATION
    WHERE STOCK.NATCODE = NATION.NATCODE
```

As you now realize, join is really product with a condition clause. There is no reason why this condition needs to be restricted to equality. There could easily be another comparison operator between the two columns. This general version of join is called a **theta join**, because theta is a variable that can take any value from the set $[=, \neq, >, \geq, <, \leq]$.

A join can involve two or more tables. The extension to three tables is very direct as the following example illustrates:

```
SELECT * FROM SALE, LINEITEM, ITEM
    WHERE SALE.SALENO = LINEITEM.SALENO
      AND ITEM.ITEMNO = LINEITEM.ITEMNO
```

The three tables to be joined are listed after the FROM clause. There are two matching conditions. One to match the SALE and LINEITEM tables (SALE.SALENO = LINEITEM.SALENO) and one to match the ITEM and LINEITEM tables (ITEM.ITEMNO = LINEITEM.ITEMNO). The intersection table, LINEITEM, is the link between the SALE and ITEM and must be referenced in both matching conditions.

As you discovered in Chapter 6, there are occasions when you need to join a table to itself. To do this, make two copies of the table first and give each of these copies a distinguishing name.

○   **Find the names of employees who earn more than their boss.**

```
SELECT WRK.EMPFNAME
    FROM EMP WRK, EMP BOSS
      WHERE WRK.BOSSNO = BOSS.EMPNO
        AND WRK.EMPSALARY > BOSS.EMPSALARY
```

Simple Subquery

A **subquery** is a query within a query. There is a SELECT statement nested inside another SELECT statement. Simple subqueries have been used extensively in Chapters 3 and 4. For reference, here is a simple subquery used in Chapter 4:

```
SELECT STKFIRM FROM STOCK
   WHERE NATCODE IN
      (SELECT NATCODE FROM NATION
         WHERE NATNAME = 'Australia')
```

Correlated Subquery

A **correlated subquery** differs from a simple subquery in that the inner query must be evaluated more than once. Consider the following example described previously in Chapter 4.

```
SELECT STKFIRM FROM STOCK
   WHERE 'Australia' IN
      (SELECT NATNAME FROM NATION
         WHERE NATION.NATCODE = STOCK.NATCODE)
```

Aggregate Functions

SQL's **aggregate functions** increase its retrieval power. These functions are covered extensively in Chapter 3 and are only mentioned briefly here for completeness. The five aggregate functions are:

COUNT   Counts the number of values in a column.

SUM   Sums the values in a column.

AVG   Determines the average of the values in a column.

MAX   Determines the largest value of a column.

MIN   Determines the smallest value of a column.

Nulls in the column are ignored in the case of SUM, AVG, MAX, and MIN. However, COUNT does not distinguish between null and non-null values in a column.

GROUP BY and HAVING

The **GROUP BY** clause is an elementary form of control break reporting and supports grouping of rows that have the same value for a specified column and produces one row for each different value of the grouping column. For example:

○ **Report by nation the total value of stockholdings.**

```
SELECT NATNAME, SUM(STKPRICE*STKQTY*EXCHRATE)
   FROM STOCK, NATION WHERE STOCK.NATCODE = NATION.NATCODE
   GROUP BY NATNAME
```

gives:

NATNAME	SUM(EXPRESSION 1)
Australia	946430.65
India	97506.71
United Kingdom	48908364.25
United States	30066065.54

The **HAVING** clause is often associated with GROUP BY. It can be thought of as the WHERE clause of GROUP BY because it is used to eliminate rows for a GROUP BY condition. Both GROUP BY and HAVING are dealt with in-depth in Chapter 4, where examples demonstrate their use.

LIKE

The **LIKE** clause supports pattern matching to find a defined set of strings in a character column (CHAR or VARCHAR). Refer to Chapter 3 for a detailed discussion and examples of the use of LIKE.

Rattling the Limits of Database Technology

The SABRE system is used by American Airlines and more than 10,000 travel agencies to make flight, rental car, and hotel reservations. The database contains details of flights for over 600 airlines, information on over 10,000 hotel properties, and 20 car rental companies. The computer system consists of 5 IBM 9083s, 70,000 terminals, and over 565,000 miles of communication lines.

The system processes over 110 million air reservations per year, over 5 million car bookings, and over 2.5 million hotel bookings. It handles over 1000 simultaneous input messages per second. On a peak day, there can be more than 256,000 reservations. The number of passenger records on file exceeds 4.5 million.[4]

Scalar Functions

Most implementations of SQL include **scalar functions** that can be used in arithmetic expression, data conversion, or data extraction. Some of these functions are briefly discussed, although you will need to consult the documentation for your particular version of SQL to determine the functions it supports. Some common SQL scalar functions are:

CHAR	Converts a date, time, or timestamp to a character representation.
DAY	Retrieves the day portion of a date or timestamp.
DAYS	Converts a date or timestamp to a number of days. Useful for calculating the number of days between two dates.

---

[4]Source: EaasySabre information screen, June 1993.

DECIMAL	DECIMAL(v,p,d) reports a number v with specified precision p and d decimal place.
FLOAT	Converts a number to floating point representation.
HOUR	Retrieves the hour portion of a time or timestamp.
MICROSECOND	Retrieves the microsecond portion of a time or timestamp.
MINUTE	Retrieves the minute portion of a time or timestamp.
MONTH	Retrieves the month portion of a date or timestamp.
SECOND	Retrieves the second portion of a time or timestamp.
SUBSTR	Extracts a substring from a string. SUBSTR(NATNAME,1,2) gives the first two characters of a nation's name.
YEAR	Retrieves the year portion of a date or timestamp.

To use scalar functions, follow these examples.

```
SELECT      EMPSALARY,
            DECIMAL(EMPSALARY,9,2),
            FLOAT(EMPSALARY)
            FROM EMPLOYEE WHERE BOSSNO = 1
```

EMPSALARY	DECIMAL(EMPSALARY,EXPRESSION	FLOAT(EMPSALARY)
45000	45000.00	4.500000000E+04
38000	38000.00	3.800000000E+04
43000	43000.00	4.300000000E+04
35000	35000.00	3.500000000E+04

○ **How many days' sales are stored in the SALE table?**

This sounds like a simple query, but it is not. Here is one way to solve it. Can you think of any other ways?

```
SELECT DAYS(LATE.SALEDATE)  -  DAYS(EARLY.SALEDATE)
  FROM SALE LATE, SALE EARLY
  WHERE LATE.SALEDATE =
    (SELECT MAX(SALEDATE) FROM SALE)
  AND EARLY.SALEDATE =
    (SELECT MIN(SALEDATE) FROM SALE)
```

EXPRESSION 1
1

The preceding query is based on the idea of joining SALE with a copy of itself. The matching column from LATE is the latest sale's date (or MAX), and the matching column from EARLY is the earliest sale's date (or MIN). As a result of the join, each row of the new table has both the earliest and latest dates.

Insert

There are two formats for **INSERT**. The first format is used to insert a row into a table:

```
INSERT INTO table [(column [,column] ...)]
    VALUES (literal [,literal] ...)
```

The following examples illustrate the use of INSERT.

Inserting a Single Record

```
INSERT INTO STOCK
    (STKCODE,STKFIRM,STKPRICE,STKQTY,STKDIV,STKPE)
    VALUES ('FC','Freedonia Copper',27.5,10529,1.84,16)
```

In this example, STKCODE is given the value 'FC', STKFIRM is 'Freedonia Copper', and so on. In general, the nth column in the table is the nth value in the list.

When the value list refers to all field names in the left-to-right order in which they appear in the table, then the columns list can be omitted. So, it is possible to write

```
INSERT INTO STOCK
    VALUES ('FC','Freedonia Copper',27.5,10529,1.84,16)
```

If some values are unknown, then the INSERT statement can omit these from the list. Undefined columns will have nulls. For example, if a new stock is to be added for which the price, dividend, and PE ratio are unknown, the following INSERT statement would be used:

```
INSERT INTO STOCK
    (STKCODE, STKFIRM, STKQTY)
    VALUES ('EE','Elysian Emeralds',0)
```

Inserting Multiple Records Using a Query

The second form of INSERT operates in conjunction with a subquery; the resulting rows then are inserted into a table. Imagine the situation where stock price information is downloaded from an information service into a table. This table could contain information about all stocks and may contain additional columns that are not required for the STOCK table. The following INSERT statement could be used:

```
INSERT INTO STOCK
   (STKCODE, STKFIRM, STKPRICE, STKDIV, STKPE)
   SELECT CODE, FIRM, PRICE, DIV, PE
   FROM DOWNLOAD WHERE CODE IN
   ('FC','PT','AR','SLG','ILZ','BE','BS','NG','CS','ROF')
```

Think of INSERT with a subquery as a way of copying a table. You can select the rows and columns of a particular table that you want to copy into an existing or new table.

Update

The **UPDATE** command is used to modify a table. The general format is:

```
UPDATE table
   SET column = scalar expression
      [, column = scalar expression] ...
   [WHERE condition]
```

Permissible scalar expressions involve columns, scalar functions (see the section on scalar functions in this chapter), or constants. No aggregate functions are allowable.

Updating a Single Row

UPDATE can be used to modify a single row in a table. Suppose you need to revise your data after 200,000 shares of Minnesota Gold are sold. You would use the command:

```
UPDATE STOCK
   SET STKQTY = STKQTY - 200000
   WHERE STKCODE = 'MG'
```

Updating Multiple Rows

Multiple rows in a table can be updated as well. Imagine the situation where several stocks change their dividend to £2.50, then the following statement could be used:

```
UPDATE STOCK
   SET STKDIV = 2.50
   WHERE STKCODE IN ('FC','BS','NG')
```

Updating All Rows

All rows in a table can be updated by simply omitting the WHERE clause. To give everyone at The Expeditioner a 5 percent raise, use:

```
UPDATE EMPLOYEE
   SET EMPSALARY = EMPSALARY*1.05
```

Updating With a Subquery

A subquery can also be used to specify which rows should be changed. Consider the following example: the employees in the departments on the fourth floor of The Expeditioner have won a productivity improvement bonus of 10 percent. The following SQL statement would update their salaries.

```
UPDATE EMPLOYEE
   SET EMPSALARY = EMPSALARY*1.10
   WHERE DEPTNAME IN
   (SELECT DEPTNAME FROM DEPARTMENT WHERE DEPTFLOOR = 4)
```

Delete

The **DELETE** statement erases one or more rows in a table. The general format is

```
DELETE FROM table
   [WHERE condition]
```

Delete a Single Record

If all stocks in Burmese Elephant are sold, then this row can be deleted using

```
DELETE FROM STOCK
   WHERE STKCODE = 'BE'
```

Delete Multiple Records

If all Australian stocks were liquidated, then the following command would delete all the relevant rows:

```
DELETE FROM STOCK
   WHERE NATCODE = 'AUS'
```

Delete All Records

All records in a table can be deleted by omitting the WHERE clause. The following statement would delete all rows if the entire portfolio were sold.

```
DELETE FROM STOCK
```

This command is not the same as DROP TABLE because although the table is empty, it still exists.

Delete With a Subquery

Despite their sterling efforts in the recent productivity drive, all the employees on the fourth floor of The Expeditioner have been fired. (The rumor is that they were fiddling the tea money.) Their records can be deleted using

```
DELETE FROM EMPLOYEE
   WHERE DEPTNAME =
   (SELECT DEPTNAME FROM DEPARTMENT WHERE DEPTFLOOR = 4)
```

NULLS—MUCH ADO ABOUT MISSING INFORMATION

Nulls are overworked in SQL because they can represent several situations. Null can represent unknown information. For example, you might add a new stock to the database, but lacking details of its latest dividend, you leave the field null. Null can be used to represent a value that is inapplicable. For instance, the EMPLOYEE table contains a null value in BOSSNO for Alice because she has no boss. The value is not unknown; it is not applicable for that field. In other cases, null might mean "no value supplied" or "value undefined." Because null can have multiple meanings, the user must infer which meaning is appropriate to the circumstances.

Do not confuse null with blank or zero, which are values. In fact, null is a marker that specifies that the value for the particular column is null. Thus, null represents no value.

Well-known database expert, Chris Date,[5] has been outspoken in his concern about the confusion caused by nulls. His advice is that nulls should be explicitly avoided by specifying NOT NULL for all columns and by using codes to make the meaning of a value clear (e.g., "U" MEANS "unknown," "I" means "inapplicable," "N" means "not supplied").

SECURITY

Data is a valuable resource for nearly every organization. Just as an organization takes measures to protect its physical assets, it also needs to safeguard electronic assets—its organizational memory, including databases. Furthermore, it often wants to limit the access of authorized users to particular parts of a database and restrict their actions to particular operations.

Two SQL features are used to administer security procedures. A view, discussed earlier in

---

[5]C. J. Date, *Relational Database Writings, 1985–1989* (Reading, MA: Addison–Welsey, 1990), 217–248.

this chapter, can restrict a user's access to specified columns or rows in a table, and authorization commands can establish a user's privileges.

The authorization subsystem is based on the concept of a privilege—the authority to perform an operation. For example, a user cannot update a table unless she has been granted the appropriate update privilege. The database administrator (DBA) is king of the heap and has the highest privilege. The DBA can perform any legal operation. The creator of an object, say a base table, has full privileges for that object. Those with privilege can then use GRANT and REVOKE to extend privileges to or rescind them from other users.

Grant

The **GRANT** command defines a user's privileges. The general format of the statement is:

```
GRANT privileges ON object TO users [WITH GRANT OPTION]
```

where "privileges" can be a list of privileges or the keyword ALL PRIVILEGES, and "users" is a list of list of user identifiers or the keyword PUBLIC. An "object" can be a base table or view.

The following privileges can be granted for tables and views: SELECT, UPDATE, DELETE, and INSERT.

The UPDATE privilege specifies the particular columns in a base table or view that may be updated. Some privileges apply *only* to base tables. These are ALTER and INDEX.

The following examples illustrate the use of GRANT.

○ **Give Alice all rights to the STOCK table.**

```
GRANT ALL PRIVILEGES ON STOCK TO ALICE
```

○ **Permit the accounting staff, Todd and Nancy, to update the price of a stock.**

```
GRANT UPDATE (STKPRICE) ON STOCK TO TODD, NANCY
```

○ **Give all staff the privilege to select rows from ITEM.**

```
GRANT SELECT ON ITEM TO PUBLIC
```

○ **Give Alice all rights to view STK.**

```
GRANT SELECT, UPDATE, DELETE, INSERT ON STK TO ALICE[6]
```

---

[6]In this case, since STK is a view, we cannot use ALL PRIVILEGES because ALL includes ALTER and INDEX privileges, which apply only to base tables and not views.

The WITH GRANT OPTION

This option allows a user to transfer his privileges to another user, as this next example illustrates.

❍   **Give Ned all privileges for the ITEM table and permit him to grant any of these to other staff members who may need to work with ITEM.**

```
GRANT ALL PRIVILEGES ON ITEM TO NED WITH GRANT OPTION
```

This means that Ned can now use the GRANT command to give other staff privileges. To give Andrew permission for select and insert on ITEM, for example, Ned would enter

```
GRANT SELECT, INSERT ON ITEM TO ANDREW
```

Revoke

What GRANT granteth, **REVOKE** revoketh. Privileges are removed using the REVOKE statement. The general format of this statement is:

```
REVOKE privileges ON object FROM users
```

Some examples illustrate the use of REVOKE.

❍   **Remove Sophie's ability to select from ITEM.**

```
REVOKE SELECT ON ITEM FROM SOPHIE
```

❍   **Nancy is no longer permitted to update stock prices.**

```
REVOKE UPDATE ON STOCK FROM NANCY[7]
```

Cascading REVOKE

When a REVOKE statement removes a privilege, it can result in more than one revocation. An earlier example illustrated how Ned used his WITH GRANT OPTION right to authorize Andrew to select and insert rows on ITEM. The following REVOKE command,

```
REVOKE INSERT ON ITEM FROM NED
```

automatically revokes Andrew's insert privilege.

---

[7] A revoked UPDATE privilege cannot be column specific.

SYNONYMS

The CREATE **SYNONYM** command is used to give a base table or view an alternative name. Synonyms can be created for users who prefer to use words with which they are familiar. For example, a column name might be called PROJECT, but some users may prefer to use the word TASK. In this case, CREATE SYNONYM customizes the system to the needs of these particular users. The command also can reduce the number of keystrokes involved when using qualified names. Suppose you frequently access a table owned by Rumplestiltskin containing details of princesses. By creating a synonym, you can give the table a shorter name.

```
CREATE SYNONYM DI FOR RUMPELSTILTSKIN.PRINCESS
```

The query

```
SELECT * FROM DI
```

is equivalent to

```
SELECT * FROM RUMPELSTILTSKIN.PRINCESS
```

and takes fewer keystrokes.

A synonym is deleted with the DROP command, as the following example illustrates:

```
DROP SYNONYM DI
```

THE CATALOG

The **catalog**[8] describes a relational database. It contains the definitions of base tables, views, indexes, and so on. The catalog itself is a relational database and can be interrogated using SQL. Tables in the catalog are called system tables to distinguish them from base tables, though conceptually, these tables are the same. Some important system tables are SYSCATALOG, SYSCOLUMNS, and SYSINDEXES.

SYSCATALOG contains details of all tables in the database. There is one row for each table in the database and the attributes of the rows are table name (TNAME), creator (CREATOR), number of columns (NCOLS), and other data. SYSCATALOG can be queried using SELECT on the qualified name SYSTEM.SYSCATALOG.

○ **Find the table(s) with the most columns.**

```
SELECT TNAME FROM SYSTEM.SYSCATALOG
    WHERE NCOLS = (SELECT MAX(NCOLS) FROM SYSTEM.SYSCATALOG)
```

---

[8]A catalog is similar to a data dictionary, which is discussed in Chapter 19.

SYSCOLUMNS stores details about each column in the database. Each row of SYSCOLUMNS contains data such as column name (CNAME), the table in which the column appears (TNAME), type of data in the column (COLTYPE), column length (LENGTH), column creator (CREATOR), and other items.

○ **I've forgotten the length of a field in table SALE.**

```
SELECT COLNO, CNAME, COLTYPE, LENGTH FROM SYSTEM.SYSCOLUMNS
   WHERE TNAME = 'SALE' AND CREATOR = 'userid'
      ORDER BY COLNO
```

COLNO	CNAME	COLTYPE	LENGTH
1	SALENO	INTEGER	
2	SALEDATE	DATE	
3	SALETEXT	CHAR	50

Sometimes you forget parts of a table definition, such as the length of a text field. The preceding query recalls details of all the columns in a specified table. Notice that you must indicate the userid of the table's creator because others may use the same table name. For convenience, columns are reported in the same order in which they were defined.

○ **What columns in what tables store dates?**

```
SELECT TNAME, CNAME FROM SYSTEM.SYSCOLUMNS
   WHERE COLTYPE = 'DATE'
```

SYSINDEXES contains details of indexes. There is one row for each index. The attributes of SYSINDEXES include index name (INAME), the name of table indexed (TNAME), and other data.

○ **Find all tables that have indexes.**

```
SELECT TNAME FROM SYSTEM.SYSINDEXES
```

As you can see, querying the catalog is the same as querying a database. This is a very useful feature because you can use SQL queries on the catalog to find out more about a database. Most non-relational systems require that you learn another set of commands to access a system dictionary.

EMBEDDED SQL

SQL can be used in two modes. First, SQL is an interactive query language and database programming language. The SELECT command is used to define interactive queries; INSERT,

UPDATE, and DELETE commands are used to define and maintain a database. Second, any interactive SQL statement, including both DDL and DML statements, can be embedded in an application program.

This dual-mode principle is a very useful feature. It means that programmers need learn only one database query language because the same SQL statements apply for both interactive queries and application statements. Programmers can also interactively examine SQL commands before embedding them in a program, a feature that can substantially reduce the time to write an application program.

Because SQL is not a complete programming language, however, it must be used with a traditional programming language to create applications. Common complete programming languages, such as COBOL and C, support embedded SQL. In this case, we assume the host language is COBOL and the relational DBMS is DB2. A source program containing SQL statements must be processed by an SQL preprocessor before it is compiled. The preprocessor checks the syntax of the SQL statements, turns them into host language comments, and generates host language statements to invoke the DBMS. Portions of a sample program follow.

```
FILE SECTION.
*********************************************************************
* Non-database files are defined here
*********************************************************************
WORKING-STORAGE SECTION.
*********************************************************************
* COBOL variables are defined here
*********************************************************************
01  VALUE         PIC S9(8)V99 COMP-3.
01  TOTAL-VALUE   PIC S9(8)V99 COMP-3.
*********************************************************************
* Define the SQL communication area
*********************************************************************
    EXEC SQL INCLUDE SQLCA END-EXEC.
*********************************************************************
* Define variables used to transfer data between the
* application and DB2.
*********************************************************************
    EXEC SQL BEGIN DECLARE SECTION END-EXEC.
01 STOCK-TABLE.
    05 STOCK-CODE    PIC X(3).
    05 STOCK-FIRM    PIC X(20).
    05 STOCK-PRICE   PIC S9(4)V99 COMP-3.
    05 STOCK-QTY     PIC S9(8) COMP-3.
    05 STOCK-DIV     PIC S9(3)V99 COMP-3.
    05 STOCK-PE      PIC S99 COMP-3.
    EXEC SQL END DECLARE SECTION END-EXEC.
*********************************************************************
PROCEDURE DIVISION.
    PERFORM INITIALIZE.
    PERFORM READ-ROW
```

```
            UNTIL SQLCODE NOT = 0.
        PERFORM FINISH.
        STOP RUN.
INITIALIZE.
* Declare cursor
        EXEC SQL
            DECLARE STOCK-CURSOR CURSOR FOR
                SELECT * FROM STOCK
        END-EXEC.
* Set variables
        MOVE ZERO TO TOTAL-VALUE.
* Open the cursor
        EXEC SQL
            OPEN STOCK-CURSOR
        END-EXEC.
* Issue an initial FETCH
        EXEC SQL
            FETCH STOCK-CURSOR INTO :STOCK-TABLE
        END-EXEC.
* Check SQLCODE
        IF SQLCODE = 100
            THEN
                DISPLAY "Table is empty"
                STOP RUN
        END-IF.
READ-ROW.
* Calculate and accumulate value
        VALUE = STOCK-PRICE*STOCK-QTY.
        TOTAL-VALUE = TOTAL-VALUE + VALUE.
* Fetch the next row.
        EXEC SQL
            FETCH STOCK-CURSOR INTO :STOCK-TABLE
        END-EXEC.
FINISH.
        DISPLAY "Total value of stock is" TOTAL-VALUE.
        EXEC SQL
            CLOSE STOCK-CURSOR
        END-EXEC.
```

There are several things to notice about this COBOL program.

1. Every SQL statement is surrounded by the keywords EXEC SQL and END-EXEC. This enables the compiler to identify SQL statements and process them differently from COBOL statements.

2. Only one SQL statement can be included between the EXEC SQL and END-EXEC statements.

3. The DATA DIVISION describes variables that are used to pass data between the application program and DB2 and systems data shared by the application program and DB2.

4. The DECLARE SECTION defines variables that are used to transfer data between the application program and DB2.

5. The SQL table STOCK is defined in the COBOL program as STOCK–TABLE. The columns have been renamed. STKCODE is now STOCK–CODE and so on. The SQL data definitions have been converted to COBOL style. For example, CHAR(3) becomes X(3) and DECIMAL(6,2) becomes S9(4)V99 COMP–3.

6. Systems data is shared through the SQLCA (SQL communications area). SQLCA is defined by the INCLUDE SQLCA statement. SQLCA contains many data items; the most interesting is SQLCODE, which is set by DB2 after each SQL statement is executed. This code has three types of values as shown in the accompanying table:

SQLCODE	Condition	Example
zero	Normal execution	Successful execution of SQL statement
positive	Unusual, but normal condition	End of data (SQLCODE = 100)
negative	Abnormal, unexpected condition	Insufficient file space

7. There is one difference between embedded SQL and interactive SQL statements. The difference is an INTO clause that tells DB2 the name of the variable into which to place the value(s) retrieved from the database.

8. Because it is possible for a DB2 database and application program to both define a variable with the same name, application variables in an SQL statement are distinguished by preceding them with a colon (:).

There is a fundamental difference between application programming languages, such as COBOL and SQL. COBOL processes one record at a time; SQL processes tables. Thus, an SQL statement will return a table that the COBOL application program then has to process a row or record at a time. This incompatibility is handled by defining a cursor within the application program.

Think of a **cursor** as a pointer that indicates the row to be processed. In the preceding example, a cursor is defined for processing the STOCK table. The DECLARE statement defines the cursor associated with a particular query.

Opening the cursor in the INITIALIZE paragraph is like opening a file; it gets the table ready for processing. The FETCH statement in the INITIALIZE paragraph retrieves the first row of the table. FETCH is like the READ statement of COBOL, which retrieves one row. A looping structure, based on the READ–ROWS paragraph is then used to fetch subsequent rows, one at a time, until there are no more rows. Then the cursor is closed, again like a file, and the application program stops.

This brief introduction to embedded SQL was intended to give you an overview of the relationship between SQL and an application development language. Obviously, if you are to write application programs using embedded SQL, you will need considerable training in both the application language and the fine details of how it works in conjunction with SQL.

Daiichi—Customer Service and Data Make a Difference

The Akihabara district of Tokyo is sixteen blocks of consumer electronics stores. It accounts for 10 percent of all electronic sales in Japan. Competition is intense and profits are low, except for Daiichi.

Daiichi customers get a three-year warranty instead of the usual one-year manufacturer warranty. Customers get next-day delivery for large items—competitors normally take a week. Japanese homes are small, and storage space is limited. Daiichi provides space for customers to store seasonal electronic items (e.g., air conditioners in winter and space heaters in summer).

Towards the end of a product's three-year warranty, Daiichi phones the customer and offers to send a technician to the customer's home to check the product before the warranty expires. After inspecting the item, the technician also offers to check all other appliances, regardless of whether these were purchased from Daiichi. Upon completion, the Daiichi technician fills out a detailed report on the condition of all products in the home. These data, stored in the Daiichi database accessible by all sales personnel, are used to identify potential sales. For example, the customer, whose aging refrigerator was noted by the technician, will soon receive a phone call inviting her to the store to inspect the newest refrigerators.

Daiichi collects, analyzes, and uses data to drive its selling efforts. When it makes warranty inspection calls and stores customers' seasonal items, Daiichi collects data about customers' needs. Its employees are trained to use this data to ensure that Daiichi has every opportunity to meet those needs.

About 70 percent of Daiichi's sales are to repeat customers; competitors have a 20 percent rate. Daiichi's response to direct mail is four times that of its competition. The company is outstandingly profitable in a cutthroat business because its knowledge about consumers allows it to provide superior customer service.[9]

SUMMARY

SQL, a widely used relational database language, has been adopted as a standard by ANSI and ISO. It is both a data definition language (DDL) and data manipulation language (DML). A base table is an autonomous, named table. A view is a virtual table. A key is one or more columns identified as such in the description of a table, an index, or a referential constraint. SQL supports primary, foreign, and unique keys. Indexes accelerate data access and ensure uniqueness. CREATE TABLE defines a new base table and specifies primary, foreign, and unique key constraints. Numeric, string, date, or graphic data can be stored in a column. BLOB is a new data type for multimedia databases. ALTER TABLE adds one new column to a table or changes the status of a constraint. DROP TABLE removes a table from a database. CREATE

---

[9]Adapted from G. Stalk, Jr. and A. M. Webber, "Japan's Dark Side of Time," *Harvard Business Review* 71 (4): 93–102 (1993).

VIEW defines a view, which can be used to restrict access to data, report derived data, store commonly executed queries, and convert data. A view is created dynamically. DROP VIEW deletes a view. CREATE INDEX defines an index, and DROP INDEX deletes one.

Ambiguous references to column names are avoided by qualifying a column name with its table name. A table or view can be given a temporary name that remains current for a query. SQL has four data manipulation statements—SELECT, INSERT, UPDATE, and DELETE. INSERT adds one or more rows to a table. UPDATE modifies a table by changing one or more rows. DELETE removes one or more rows from a table. SELECT provides powerful interrogation facilities. The product of two tables is a new table consisting of all rows of the first table concatenated with all possible rows of the second table. Join creates a new table from two existing tables by matching on a column common to both tables. A subquery is a query within a query. A correlated subquery differs from a simple subquery in that the inner query is evaluated multiple times rather than once.

SQL's aggregate functions increase its retrieval power. GROUP BY supports grouping of rows that have the same value for a specified column. The LIKE clause supports pattern matching. SQL includes scalar functions that can be used in arithmetic expression, data conversion, or data extraction. Nulls cause problems because they can represent several situations—unknown information, inapplicable information, no value supplied, or value undefined. Remember, a null is not a blank or zero. The SQL commands GRANT and REVOKE support data security. GRANT authorizes a user to perform certain SQL operations, and REVOKE removes a user's authority. The CREATE SYNONYM command can be used to give a base table or view an alternative name. SYSCATALOG, which describes a relational database, can be queried using SELECT. SQL can be used as an interactive query language and as embedded commands within an application programming language.

KEY TERMS AND CONCEPTS

Aggregate functions	DROP VIEW
ALTER TABLE	Embedded SQL
ANSI	Foreign key
Base table	GRANT
Complete database language	GROUP BY
Complete programming language	Index
Composite key	INSERT
Correlated subquery	ISO
CREATE INDEX	Join
CREATE TABLE	Key
CREATE VIEW	Null
Cursor	Primary key
Data definition language (DDL)	Product
Data manipulation language (DML)	Qualified name
Data types	Referential integrity rule
DELETE	REVOKE
DROP INDEX	Scalar functions
DROP TABLE	Security

SELECT	SYSCOLUMNS
Special registers	SYSINDEXES
SQL	Temporary names
Subquery	Unique key
Synonym	UPDATE
SYSCATALOG	View

REFERENCES AND ADDITIONAL READINGS

Date, C. J. *An Introduction to Database Systems*, 6th ed (Reading, MA: Addison–Wesley, 1995).

Date, C. J. *A Guide to the SQL Standard: A User's Guide to the Standard Relational Language SQL*, 3rd ed. (Reading, MA: Addison–Wesley, 1993).

EXERCISES

1. Why is it important that SQL was adopted as a standard by ANSI and ISO?
2. What does it mean to say "SQL is a complete database language"?
3. Is SQL a complete programming language? What are the implications of your answer?
4. List some operational advantages of a relational DBMS.
5. What is the difference between a base table and a view?
6. What is the difference between a primary key and a unique key?
7. What is the purpose of an index?
8. Consider the three choices for the ON DELETE clause associated with the foreign key constraint. What are the pros and cons of each option?
9. Specify the data type (e.g., DECIMAL(6,2)) you would use for the following columns:
    a. The selling price of a house.
    b. A telephone number with area code.
    c. Hourly temperatures in Antarctica.
    d. A numeric customer code.
    e. A credit card number.
    f. The distance between two cities.
    g. A sentence using Chinese characters.
    h. The number of kilometers from the Earth to a given star.
    i. The text of an advertisement in the classified section of a newspaper.
    j. A basketball score.
    k. The title of a CD.
    l. The X-ray of a patient.
    m. A U.S. zip code.
    n. A British or Canadian postal code.
    o. The photo of a customer.
    p. The date a person purchased a car.
    q. The time of arrival of an e-mail message.

    r. The number of full-time employees in a small business.

    s. The text of a speech.

    t. The thickness of a layer on a silicon chip.

10. How could you add two columns to an existing table? Precisely describe the steps you would take.

11. What is the difference between DROP TABLE and deleting all the rows in a table?

12. Give some reasons for creating a view.

13. When is a view created?

14. Write SQL codes to create a unique index on firm name for the SHR table defined in Chapter 3. Would it make sense to create a unique index for PE ratio in the same table?

15. What is the difference between product and join?

16. What is the difference between an equijoin and a natural join?

17. You have a choice between executing two queries that will both give the same result. One is written as a simple subquery and the other as a correlated subquery. Which one would you use and why?

18. What function would you use for the following situations:

    a. Computing the total value of a column.

    b. Finding the minimum value of a column.

    c. Counting the number of customers in the CUSTOMER table.

    d. Displaying a number with specified precision.

    e. Reporting the month part of a date.

    f. Displaying the second part of a time.

    g. Retrieving the first five characters of a city's name.

    h. Reporting the distance to the Sun in feet.

19. A student database records a home and school term phone number for each student. Some students have a null value for school term phone number. What does this mean?

20. Write SQL statements for the following:

    a. Let Hui-Tze query and add to the NATION table.

    b. Give Lana permission to update the phone number column in the CUS-TOMER table.

    c. Remove all of William's privileges.

    d. Give Chris permission to grant other users authority to select from the AD-DRESS table.

    e. Create a short name for the table PINNOCHIO.FALSEHOODS.

    f. Find the name of all tables that include the word SALE.

    g. List all the tables owned by user CMS5432.

    h. What is the length of the column STREETNAME?

    i. Find all columns that have a data type of SMALLINT.

21. What are the two modes in which you can use SQL?

22. How do COBOL and SQL differ in the way they process data? How is this difference handled in an application program? What is embedded SQL?

Chapter 10

SQL Playbook

Play so that you may be serious.
Anacharsis (c. 600 B.C.)

SQL is a very powerful retrieval language, and most novice users underestimate its capability. Furthermore, mastery of SQL takes considerable practice and exposure to a wide variety of problems. This reference chapter serves the dual purpose of revealing the full power of SQL and providing an extensive set of diverse queries. To make this chapter easier to use, the pages are color coded so you can find them quickly, and we have named each of the queries to make them easy to remember.

Lacroix and Pirotte[1] have defined 66 queries for testing a query language's power, and their work is the foundation of this chapter. Not all their queries are included, some have been kept for the end–of–chapter exercises. Also, many of the queries have been reworded to various extents. Because these queries are more difficult than those normally used in business decision making, they provide a good test of your SQL skills. If you can answer all of them, then you are a proficient SQL programmer. The set of queries also can be used as a test package for evaluating the capability of an implementation of SQL.

You are encouraged to formulate and test your answer to a query before reading the suggested solution.[2] A "Q" has been prefixed to all entity and table names to distinguish them from entities and tables used in earlier problems. The going gets tough after the first few queries, and you can expect to spend some time formulating and testing each one, but remember, this is still considerably faster than using a conventional programming language, such as COBOL, to write the same queries.

The data model accompanying Lacroix and Pirotte's queries is shown in Figure 10–1. You will notice that the complexity of the real world has been reduced; a sale and a delivery are assumed to have only one item. The corresponding relational model is shown in Figure 10–2, and some data that can be used to test your SQL queries are at the end of this chapter.

---

[1]M. Lacroix, and A. Pirotte, *Example Queries in Relational Languages* (Brussels: M.B.L.E., technical report no. 107, 1976).

[2]The author is indebted to Dr. Mohammad Dadashzadeh of Wichita State University in Kansas, who provided valuable assistance by checking each query. Many of his suggestions for writing SQL code to answer these queries have been incorporated. All the queries have been tested with a small database. If you discover a problem with a query or a better way of expressing it, please send an e-mail message to rwatson@uga.cc.uga.edu.

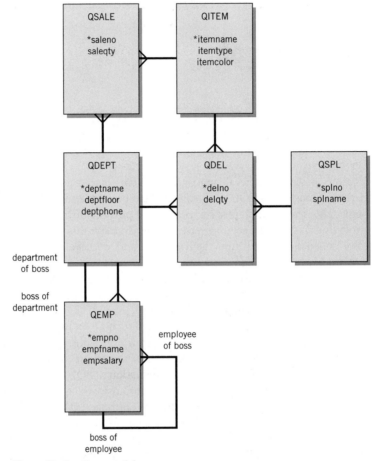

Figure 10–1   Data model

1.   A SLOW FULL TOSS

In cricket, a slow full toss is the easiest ball to hit. The same applies to this simple query.

○   **Find the names of employees in the Marketing department.**

```
SELECT EMPFNAME FROM QEMP WHERE DEPTNAME = 'Marketing'
```

2.   SKINNING A CAT

Queries often can be solved in several ways. For this query, four possible solutions are presented. Also, we indicate the resource units required to answer the query. This resource measure is supplied by SQL/VM when the query is executed.

○   **Find the items sold by the departments on the second floor.**

QSALE			
SALENO	SALEQTY	*ITEMNAME*	*DEPTNAME*

QITEM		
ITEMNAME	ITEMTYPE	ITEMCOLOR

QDEL				
DELNO	DELQTY	*ITEMNAME*	*DEPTNAME*	*SPLNO*

QSPL	
SPLNO	SPLNAME

QDEPT			
DEPTNAME	DEPTFLOOR	DEPTPHONE	*EMPNO*

QEMP				
EMPNO	EMPFNAME	EMPSALARY	*DEPTNAME*	*BOSSNO*

Figure 10−2 Relational tables

2.1 Join (545 units)

```
SELECT DISTINCT ITEMNAME FROM QSALE, QDEPT
   WHERE QDEPT.DEPTNAME = QSALE.DEPTNAME
      AND DEPTFLOOR = 2
```

A join of QSALE and QDEPT is possibly the most obvious way to answer this query. In this case, it is a two−table join because ITEMNAME is a foreign key in QDEPT. If something like ITEMNO were the key of QITEM, a three−way join of QDEPT, QSALE, and QITEM is required.

2.2 In (8)

```
SELECT DISTINCT ITEMNAME FROM QSALE
   WHERE DEPTNAME IN
      (SELECT DEPTNAME FROM QDEPT WHERE DEPTFLOOR = 2)
```

Another simple approach is to use an IN clause. First find all the departments on the second floor and then find a match in QSALE. The subquery returns a list of all departments on the second floor. Then use the IN clause to find a match on department name in QSALE. Notice that this is the most efficient form of the query.

2.3 Correlated subquery (7,780)

```
SELECT DISTINCT ITEMNAME FROM QSALE
   WHERE DEPTNAME IN
```

```
(SELECT DISTINCT DEPTNAME FROM QDEPT
   WHERE QDEPT.DEPTNAME = QSALE.DEPTNAME
      AND DEPTFLOOR = 2)
```

A correlated subquery is another approach. Conceptually, you can think of this query as stepping through QSALE one row at a time. The subquery is executed for each row of QSALE, and if there is a match for the current value of QSALE.DEPTNAME, the current value of ITEMNAME is listed.

2.4   Exists (8,080)

```
SELECT DISTINCT ITEMNAME FROM QSALE
   WHERE EXISTS
      (SELECT * FROM QDEPT
         WHERE QSALE.DEPTNAME = QDEPT.DEPTNAME
            AND DEPTFLOOR = 2)
```

EXISTS works similarly to subselect. Conceptually, think of this query as stepping through each row of QSALE and evaluating whether the existence test is true. Remember, EXISTS returns *true* if there is at least one row in the inner query for which the condition is true.

The difference between a correlated subquery and existence testing is that a correlated subquery returns either the value of a column or an empty table, while EXISTS returns either *true* or *false*. It may help to think of this version of the query as: "Select item names from sale such that there exists a department relating them to the second floor."

3.   ANOTHER FULL TOSS

❍   **Find the names of items sold on floors other than the second floor.**

This straightforward query is a slight adaptation of the second. Just change the equals sign to a not equals sign.

```
SELECT DISTINCT ITEMNAME FROM QSALE, QDEPT
   WHERE QSALE.DEPTNAME = QDEPT.DEPTNAME
      AND DEPTFLOOR <> 2
```

4.   SUBTRACTING FROM ALL

❍   **Find the items sold by no department on the second floor.**

At first attempt, you might be inclined to think this is the same query as the preceding one, but this is not so. The previous query does not exclude an item that is sold on some other floor in addition to the second floor. For example, if polo sticks are sold on both the third and second floors, they will be reported by the preceding query because they are sold on a floor other than the second floor.

The correct way to approach this is, first get a list of all items sold on the second floor (the second query) and then subtract this from all items sold. Clearly, the difference must be all items not sold on the second floor.

```
SELECT DISTINCT ITEMNAME FROM QSALE
   WHERE ITEMNAME NOT IN
      (SELECT DISTINCT ITEMNAME FROM QSALE, QDEPT
         WHERE QSALE.DEPTNAME = QDEPT.DEPTNAME
            AND DEPTFLOOR = 2)
```

5. DIVIDING

○ **Find the items sold by all departments on the second floor.**

This is the relational algebra divide or the SQL double NOT EXISTS encountered in Chapter 5. You can think of this query as:

Select items from sales such that there does not exist a department on the second floor that does not sell this item.

However, it is easier to apply the SQL template described in Chapter 5. Remember, the template is

```
SELECT TARGET1 FROM TARGET
   WHERE NOT EXISTS
      (SELECT * FROM SOURCE
         WHERE NOT EXISTS
            (SELECT * FROM TARGET-SOURCE
               WHERE TARGET-SOURCE.TARGET = TARGET.TARGET
               AND TARGET-SOURCE.SOURCE = SOURCE.SOURCE))
```

The substitutions are straightforward:

TARGET1	=	ITEMNAME
TARGET	=	ITEM
SOURCE	=	QDEPT
TARGET-SOURCE	=	QSALE

Some additional code needs to be added to handle the restriction to items on the second floor. The query becomes:

```
SELECT DISTINCT ITEMNAME FROM QITEM
   WHERE NOT EXISTS
      (SELECT * FROM QDEPT WHERE DEPTFLOOR = 2
         AND NOT EXISTS
            (SELECT * FROM QSALE
               WHERE QSALE.ITEMNAME = QITEM.ITEMNAME
                  AND QSALE.DEPTNAME = QDEPT.DEPTNAME))
```

6.   AT LEAST SOME NUMBER

❍   **Find the items sold by at least two departments on the second floor.**

The GROUP BY and HAVING clauses make it easy for you to count the number of rows that meet some condition.

```
SELECT ITEMNAME FROM QSALE, QDEPT
   WHERE QSALE.DEPTNAME = QDEPT.DEPTNAME AND DEPTFLOOR = 2
      GROUP BY ITEMNAME
         HAVING COUNT(DISTINCT QDEPT.DEPTNAME) > 1
```

7.   A FRIENDLY *IN* FOR AN SQL TRAVELER

❍   **Find the salary of Clare's manager.**

A query that is readily handled with the IN clause. The inner query gets the employee number of Clare's manager, and this locates the row containing that person's salary.

```
SELECT EMPFNAME, EMPSALARY FROM QEMP
   WHERE EMPNO IN
      (SELECT BOSSNO FROM QEMP WHERE EMPFNAME = 'Clare')
```

8.   JOINING A TABLE WITH ITSELF

❍   **Find numbers and names of those employees who make more than their manager.**

This query is a simple play once you realize that you can conceptually create two copies of a table and join them. This type of query is discussed in more depth in Chapter 6.

```
SELECT WRK.EMPNO, WRK.EMPFNAME FROM QEMP WRK, QEMP BOSS
   WHERE WRK.BOSSNO = BOSS.EMPNO
      AND BOSS.EMPSALARY < WRK.EMPSALARY
```

9. A COMBINATION OF SUBTRACT FROM ALL AND A SELF-JOIN

○ **Find the departments where all the employees earn less than their manager.**

The key is to first find the departments where at least one employee earns more than the manager, and then subtract these departments from the set of all departments. What is left must be the departments where no employee earns more than the manager. This query is a combination of queries 4 and 8.

```
SELECT DISTINCT DEPTNAME FROM QEMP
   WHERE DEPTNAME NOT IN
      (SELECT WRK.DEPTNAME FROM QEMP WRK, QEMP BOSS
         WHERE WRK.BOSSNO = BOSS.EMPNO
            AND WRK.EMPSALARY > BOSS.EMPSALARY)
```

10. SELF-JOIN WITH *GROUP BY*

○ **Count the number of direct employees of each manager.**

Join the table with itself by matching employees and their managers and then group by manager's name with a count. Just in case two bosses have the same first name, employee number is included in the selection and grouping clauses.

```
SELECT BOSS.EMPNO, BOSS.EMPFNAME, COUNT(*)
   FROM QEMP WRK, QEMP BOSS
      WHERE WRK.BOSSNO = BOSS.EMPNO
         GROUP BY BOSS.EMPNO, BOSS.EMPFNAME
```

11. A SELF-JOIN WITH TWO MATCHING CONDITIONS

○ **Find the names of employees who are in the same department as their manager (as an employee). Report the name of the employee, the department, and the boss's name.**

There is no reason why a join cannot have matching on more than one common column. Here we have two conditions: one for employee number and one for department name.

```
SELECT WRK.EMPFNAME, WRK.DEPTNAME, BOSS.EMPFNAME
   FROM QEMP WRK, QEMP BOSS
      WHERE WRK.BOSSNO = BOSS.EMPNO
         AND WRK.DEPTNAME = BOSS.DEPTNAME
```

12. AVERAGING WITH GROUPING

○ **List the departments having an average salary over $25,000.**

A gimme for any half-decent SQL programmer.

```
SELECT DEPTNAME, AVG(EMPSALARY) FROM QEMP
    GROUP BY DEPTNAME
        HAVING AVG(EMPSALARY) > 25000
```

13. SELF-JOIN WITH A *GROUP BY* AND *HAVING*

○ **List the departments where the average salary of the employees of each manager is more than $25,000.**

This query is more challenging than simple averaging. Note that the query implies that you should exclude the manager's salary from the calculation. An employee is the manager of a particular department if that person's employee number and the department name are in the same row in QDEPT (i.e., WRK.EMPNO = QDEPT.EMPNO AND WRK.DEPTNAME = QDEPT.DEPTNAME). Once the department manager has been excluded, then use grouping to get the employee data by department.

```
SELECT WRK.DEPTNAME, AVG(WRK.EMPSALARY)
    FROM QEMP WRK, QEMP BOSS
        WHERE WRK.BOSSNO = BOSS.EMPNO
        AND WRK.EMPNO NOT IN
            (SELECT QDEPT.EMPNO FROM QDEPT
                WHERE WRK.EMPNO = QDEPT.EMPNO
                AND WRK.DEPTNAME = QDEPT.DEPTNAME)
                    GROUP BY WRK.DEPTNAME
                        HAVING AVG(WRK.EMPSALARY) > 25000
```

14. AN *IN* WITH *GROUP BY* AND *COUNT*

○ **List the name and salary of the managers who have more than two employees.**

The inner query uses grouping with counting to identify the employee numbers of managers with more than two employees. The outer query then reports details of these managers.

```
SELECT EMPFNAME, EMPSALARY FROM QEMP
    WHERE EMPNO IN
        (SELECT BOSSNO FROM QEMP
            GROUP BY BOSSNO HAVING COUNT(*) > 2)
```

15.   A SELF-JOIN WITH SOME CONDITIONS

○   **List the name, salary, and manager of the employees of the Marketing department who have a salary over $25,000.**

A join gets workers and bosses together in the same row and then the various conditions are applied to restrict the rows reported.

```
SELECT WRK.EMPFNAME, WRK.EMPSALARY, BOSS.EMPFNAME
  FROM QEMP WRK, QEMP BOSS
    WHERE WRK.BOSSNO = BOSS.EMPNO
      AND WRK.DEPTNAME = 'Marketing'
        AND WRK.EMPSALARY > 25000
```

16.   MAKING COMPARISONS

○   **List the name of the employees who earn more than any employee in the Marketing department.**

The first step is to determine the maximum salary of anyone in the Marketing department. Then, find anyone with a larger salary.

```
SELECT EMPFNAME, EMPSALARY FROM QEMP
  WHERE EMPSALARY >
    (SELECT MAX(EMPSALARY) FROM QEMP
      WHERE DEPTNAME = 'Marketing')
```

17.   AN *IN* WITH *GROUP BY* AND *SUM*

○   **Among all the departments with total salary greater than $25,000, find the departments that sell Stetsons.**

This is very similar to query 16. First, find the departments that satisfy the condition, and then select from that list any departments that sell Stetsons.

```
SELECT DISTINCT DEPTNAME FROM QSALE
  WHERE ITEMNAME = 'Stetson'
    AND DEPTNAME IN
      (SELECT DEPTNAME FROM QEMP
        GROUP BY DEPTNAME HAVING SUM(EMPSALARY) > 25000)
```

18. A DOUBLE DIVIDE!

○ **List the items delivered by every supplier who delivers all items of type N.**

SQL programmers who tackle this query without blinking an eye are superheroes. This is a genuinely true–blue, tough query because it is two divides. There is an inner divide that determines the suppliers who deliver all items of type N. The SQL for this query is

```
SELECT * FROM QSPL
   WHERE NOT EXISTS
      (SELECT * FROM QITEM WHERE ITEMTYPE = 'N'
        AND NOT EXISTS
          (SELECT * FROM QDEL WHERE
               QDEL.ITEMNAME = QITEM.ITEMNAME AND
                 QDEL.SPLNO = QSPL.SPLNO))
```

Then there is an outer divide that determines which of the suppliers (returned by the inner divide) provide all these items. If we call the result of the inner query QSPN, the SQL for the outer query is:

```
SELECT DISTINCT ITEMNAME FROM QDEL DEL
   WHERE NOT EXISTS
      (SELECT * FROM QSPN
        WHERE NOT EXISTS
          (SELECT * FROM QDEL
             WHERE QDEL.ITEMNAME = DEL.ITEMNAME
             AND QDEL.SPLNO = QSPN.SPLNO))
```

The complete query is:

```
SELECT DISTINCT ITEMNAME FROM QDEL DEL
   WHERE NOT EXISTS
      (SELECT * FROM QSPL
        WHERE NOT EXISTS
          (SELECT * FROM QITEM WHERE ITEMTYPE = 'N'
            AND NOT EXISTS
              (SELECT * FROM QDEL
                 WHERE QDEL.ITEMNAME = QITEM.ITEMNAME
                 AND QDEL.SPLNO = QSPL.SPLNO))
        AND NOT EXISTS
          (SELECT * FROM QDEL
             WHERE QDEL.ITEMNAME = DEL.ITEMNAME
             AND QDEL.SPLNO = QSPL.SPLNO))
```

19. A SLAM DUNK

○ **Find the suppliers who deliver compasses.**

A simple query to recover from the double divide. It is a good idea to include supplier number since SPLNAME could possible be non-unique.

```
SELECT DISTINCT SPLNO, SPLNAME FROM QSPL, QDEL
   WHERE QSPL.SPLNO = QDEL.SPLNO AND ITEMNAME = 'Compass'
```

20. A 6-INCH PUTT FOR A BIRDIE

○ **Find the suppliers who do not deliver compasses.**

This is a relatively straightforward subtract (and take one off par for a birdie).

```
SELECT DISTINCT SPLNO, SPLNAME FROM QSPL
   WHERE SPLNO NOT IN
      (SELECT SPLNO FROM QDEL WHERE ITEMNAME = 'Compass')
```

21. MAKING THE COUNT

○ **Find the suppliers who deliver an item other than compasses.**

The "other than compasses" clause is tricky. You handle this by finding suppliers who have delivered compasses and more than one item (i.e., COUNT(*) > 1). This means they deliver at least an item other than compasses. Note that the GROUP BY clause includes supplier number to cope with the situation where two suppliers have the same name.

```
SELECT DISTINCT QSPL.SPLNO, SPLNAME FROM QSPL, QDEL
   WHERE QSPL.SPLNO = QDEL.SPLNO
   AND QDEL.SPLNO IN
      (SELECT SPLNO FROM QDEL WHERE ITEMNAME = 'Compass')
   GROUP BY QSPL.SPLNO, SPLNAME HAVING COUNT(*) > 1
```

22. MINUS AND DIVIDE

○ **List the departments that have not recorded a sale for all the items of type N.**

This query has two parts, an inner divide and outer minus. The inner query finds departments that have sold all items of type N. These are then subtracted from all departments to leave only those that have not sold all items of type N.

```
SELECT DEPTNAME FROM QDEPT WHERE DEPTNAME NOT IN
    (SELECT DEPTNAME FROM QDEPT
      WHERE NOT EXISTS
        (SELECT * FROM QITEM WHERE ITEMTYPE = 'N'
          AND NOT EXISTS
            (SELECT * FROM QSALE
              WHERE QSALE.DEPTNAME = QDEPT.DEPTNAME AND
                QSALE.ITEMNAME = QITEM.ITEMNAME)))
```

23. DIVISION WITH COPIES

❍ **List the departments that have at least one sale of all the items delivered to them.**

This is a variation on the divide concept. Normally with a divide, you have three tables representing an m:m relationship. In this case, you only have two tables, QDEL and QSALE. You can still construct the query, however, by creating two copies of QDEL (DEL1 and DEL2 in this case) and then proceeding as if you had three different tables. Also, you must match on DEPTNAME so that you get the correct (DEPTNAME, ITEMNAME) pair for comparing with QSALE.

```
SELECT DISTINCT DEPTNAME FROM QDEL DEL1
    WHERE NOT EXISTS
      (SELECT * FROM QDEL DEL2
        WHERE DEL2.DEPTNAME = DEL1.DEPTNAME
        AND NOT EXISTS
        (SELECT * FROM QSALE WHERE
            DEL2.ITEMNAME = QSALE.ITEMNAME AND
            DEL1.DEPTNAME = QSALE.DEPTNAME))
```

This query can also be written as shown next. Observe how NOT IN functions like NOT EXISTS. We will use this variation on divide with some of the upcoming queries.

```
SELECT DISTINCT DEPTNAME FROM QDEL DEL1
    WHERE NOT EXISTS
      (SELECT * FROM QDEL DEL2
        WHERE DEL2.DEPTNAME = DEL1.DEPTNAME
        AND ITEMNAME NOT IN
        (SELECT ITEMNAME FROM QSALE
          WHERE DEPTNAME = DEL1.DEPTNAME))
```

24. A DIFFICULT PAIRING

○ **List the supplier–department pairs where the department sells all items delivered to it by the supplier.**

This query is yet another variation on divide. An additional complication is that you have to match the department name and item name of sales and deliveries.

```
SELECT SPLNAME, DEPTNAME
   FROM QDEL DEL1, QSPL
      WHERE DEL1.SPLNO = QSPL.SPLNO
      AND NOT EXISTS
         (SELECT * FROM QDEL
            WHERE QDEL.DEPTNAME = DEL1.DEPTNAME
            AND QDEL.SPLNO = DEL1.SPLNO
            AND ITEMNAME NOT IN
               (SELECT ITEMNAME FROM QSALE
                  WHERE QSALE.DEPTNAME = DEL1.DEPTNAME))
```

25. TWO DIVIDES AND AN INTERSECTION

○ **List the items delivered to all departments by all suppliers.**

This query has three parts. First, find the items delivered by all suppliers (the first divide), then find the items delivered to all departments (the second divide). Finally, find the items that satisfy both conditions—the function of the AND connection between the two divides. The items reported must be the ones both delivered by all suppliers and delivered to all departments. The administrative departments (Management, Marketing, Personnel, Accounting, and Purchasing) should be excluded from consideration because they are not involved in selling of items.

```
SELECT ITEMNAME FROM QITEM
   WHERE NOT EXISTS
      (SELECT * FROM QSPL
         WHERE NOT EXISTS
            (SELECT * FROM QDEL WHERE
               QDEL.ITEMNAME = QITEM.ITEMNAME AND
               QDEL.SPLNO = QSPL.SPLNO))
   AND NOT EXISTS
      (SELECT * FROM QDEPT WHERE DEPTNAME
            NOT IN ('Management', 'Marketing', 'Personnel',
            'Accounting', 'Purchasing')
         AND NOT EXISTS
            (SELECT * FROM QDEL WHERE
```

```
            QDEL.ITEMNAME = QITEM.ITEMNAME AND
            QDEL.DEPTNAME = QDEPT.DEPTNAME))
```

Now take a break and have a . . . (this spot is available for your advertisement).[3]

26. A DIVIDE WITH A MATCHING CONDITION

○ **List the items sold only by departments that sell all the items delivered to them.**

Yet another variation on divide—which is why you needed a break. There are two parts to this query. First, look for items sold by departments that sell all items delivered to them, and then make sure that no other department sells the same item.

```
SELECT DISTINCT ITEMNAME FROM QSALE SALE
    WHERE DEPTNAME IN
      (SELECT DEPTNAME FROM QDEPT DEPT1
        WHERE NOT EXISTS
          (SELECT * FROM QDEL
            WHERE QDEL.DEPTNAME = DEPT1.DEPTNAME
            AND ITEMNAME NOT IN
              (SELECT ITEMNAME FROM QSALE
                WHERE QSALE.DEPTNAME = DEPT1.DEPTNAME)))
        AND NOT EXISTS
          (SELECT * FROM QSALE
            WHERE ITEMNAME = SALE.ITEMNAME
            AND DEPTNAME NOT IN
              (SELECT DEPTNAME FROM QDEPT DEPT2
                WHERE NOT EXISTS
                (SELECT * FROM QDEL
                  WHERE QDEL.DEPTNAME = DEPT2.DEPTNAME
                  AND ITEMNAME NOT IN
                    (SELECT ITEMNAME FROM QSALE
                      WHERE QSALE.DEPTNAME = DEPT2.DEPTNAME))))
```

27. RESTRICTED DIVIDE

○ **Who are the suppliers who deliver all the items of type N?**

A slight variation on the standard divide to restrict consideration to the type N items.

```
SELECT SPLNO, SPLNAME FROM QSPL
```

---

[3]Will the information superhighway have billboards?

```
WHERE NOT EXISTS
   (SELECT * FROM QITEM WHERE ITEMTYPE = 'N'
      AND NOT EXISTS
         (SELECT * FROM QDEL WHERE
            QDEL.SPLNO = QSPL.SPLNO AND
            QDEL.ITEMNAME = QITEM.ITEMNAME))
```

28. A *NOT IN* VARIATION ON DIVIDE

○ **List the suppliers who deliver only the items sold by the Books department.**

This query may be rewritten as: *Select suppliers where there does not exist a delivery which does not include the items sold by the Books department.* Note the use of the IN clause to limit consideration to those suppliers who have made a delivery. Otherwise, a supplier who has never delivered an item will be reported as delivering only the items sold by the Books department.

```
SELECT SPLNAME FROM QSPL
   WHERE SPLNO IN (SELECT SPLNO FROM QDEL)
      AND NOT EXISTS
         (SELECT * FROM QDEL
            WHERE QDEL.SPLNO = QSPL.SPLNO
            AND ITEMNAME NOT IN
               (SELECT ITEMNAME FROM QSALE
                  WHERE DEPTNAME = 'Books'))
```

29. ALL AND ONLY

○ **List the suppliers who deliver all and only the items sold by the Equipment department.**

This is one query with three parts. The first part identifies suppliers who deliver all items sold by the Equipment department (they could also deliver other items, but these are not sold in the Equipment department). The second part identifies suppliers who deliver only items sold by the Equipment department (i.e., they do not deliver any other items). This part is similar to the previous query. The third part is the intersection of the first two queries to indicate suppliers who satisfy both conditions.

```
SELECT SPLNAME FROM QSPL
   WHERE NOT EXISTS
      (SELECT * FROM QSALE
         WHERE DEPTNAME = 'Equipment'
            AND ITEMNAME NOT IN
               (SELECT ITEMNAME FROM QDEL
                  WHERE QDEL.SPLNO = QSPL.SPLNO))
   AND NOT EXISTS
```

```
(SELECT * FROM QDEL
   WHERE QDEL.SPLNO = QSPL.SPLNO
   AND ITEMNAME NOT IN
      (SELECT ITEMNAME FROM QSALE
         WHERE DEPTNAME = 'Equipment'))
```

30.   DIVIDE WITH AN EXTRA CONDITION

○   **List the suppliers who deliver every item of type C to the same department on the second floor.**

This is a divide in which there are three WHERE conditions in the innermost query. The extra condition handles the "same department" requirement.

```
SELECT SPLNAME FROM QSPL
   WHERE EXISTS (SELECT * FROM QDEPT
      WHERE DEPTFLOOR = 2
      AND NOT EXISTS (SELECT * FROM QITEM
         WHERE ITEMTYPE = 'C'
         AND NOT EXISTS (SELECT * FROM QDEL
            WHERE QDEL.SPLNO = QSPL.SPLNO
            AND QDEL.ITEMNAME = QITEM.ITEMNAME
            AND QDEL.DEPTNAME = QDEPT.DEPTNAME)))
```

31.   AT LEAST SOME COUNT

○   **List the suppliers who deliver at least two items of type N to departments.**

First, do a three–way join to get the data for deliveries, suppliers, and items. Then group with a COUNT condition. This can be easily extended to a variety of conditions based on counts.

```
SELECT SPLNO, SPLNAME FROM QDEL, QSPL, QITEM
   WHERE ITEMTYPE = 'N'
   AND QDEL.SPLNO = QSPL.SPLNO
   AND QDEL.ITEMNAME = QITEM.ITEMNAME
      GROUP BY SPLNO, SPLNAME
      HAVING COUNT(DISTINCT QDEL.ITEMNAME) > 1
```

32.   DOUBLE DIVIDE WITH A RESTRICTION

○   **List the suppliers who deliver all the items of type B to departments on the second floor who sell all the items of type R.**

Break this query into two parts. First, create a view of departments on the second floor who sell all items of type R.

```
CREATE VIEW V32A AS
  (SELECT DEPTNAME FROM QDEPT
    WHERE DEPTFLOOR = 2
    AND NOT EXISTS (SELECT * FROM QITEM
      WHERE ITEMTYPE = 'R'
      AND NOT EXISTS (SELECT * FROM QSALE
        WHERE QSALE.ITEMNAME = QITEM.ITEMNAME
        AND QSALE.DEPTNAME = QDEPT.DEPTNAME)))
```

Second, report all the suppliers who deliver all the items of type B to the departments designated in the previously created view.

```
SELECT SPLNAME FROM QSPL
  WHERE NOT EXISTS (SELECT * FROM QITEM
    WHERE ITEMTYPE = 'B'
    AND NOT EXISTS (SELECT * FROM QDEL
      WHERE QDEL.ITEMNAME = QITEM.ITEMNAME
      AND QDEL.SPLNO = QSPL.SPLNO
      AND DEPTNAME IN (SELECT DEPTNAME FROM V32A)))
```

Can you write the preceding query without using a view?

33. TRIPLE DIVIDE WITH AN INTERSECTION

❍ **List the suppliers who deliver all the items of type B to the departments that also sell all the items of type N.**

Defeat this by dividing—*that* word again—the query into parts. First, identify the departments that sell all items of type N, and save as a view.

```
CREATE VIEW V33A AS
  (SELECT DEPTNAME FROM QDEPT
  WHERE NOT EXISTS (SELECT * FROM QITEM
    WHERE ITEMTYPE = 'N'
    AND NOT EXISTS (SELECT * FROM QSALE
      WHERE QSALE.DEPTNAME = QDEPT.DEPTNAME
      AND QSALE.ITEMNAME = QITEM.ITEMNAME)))
```

Second, identify the departments to which all items of type B are delivered, and save as a view.

```
CREATE VIEW V33B AS
  (SELECT DEPTNAME FROM QDEPT
 WHERE NOT EXISTS (SELECT * FROM QITEM
   WHERE ITEMTYPE = 'B'
   AND NOT EXISTS (SELECT * FROM QDEL
     WHERE QDEL.DEPTNAME = QDEPT.DEPTNAME
     AND QDEL.ITEMNAME = QITEM.ITEMNAME)))
```

Now, we want to find the suppliers who supply all items of type B to the departments that appear in both views.

```
SELECT SPLNAME FROM QSPL
  WHERE NOT EXISTS (SELECT * FROM QITEM
    WHERE ITEMTYPE = 'B'
    AND NOT EXISTS (SELECT * FROM QDEL
      WHERE QDEL.SPLNO = QSPL.SPLNO
      AND QDEL.ITEMNAME = QITEM.ITEMNAME
      AND EXISTS
        (SELECT * FROM V33A
          WHERE QDEL.DEPTNAME = V33A.DEPTNAME)
      AND EXISTS
        (SELECT * FROM V33B
          WHERE QDEL.DEPTNAME = V33B.DEPTNAME)))
```

34. AN EASY ONE COUNT

○ **List the items delivered by exactly one supplier (i.e., list the items always delivered by the same supplier).**

A reasonably straightforward GROUP BY with an exact count.

```
SELECT ITEMNAME FROM QDEL
  GROUP BY ITEMNAME HAVING COUNT(DISTINCT SPLNO) = 1
```

35. THE ONLY ONE

○ **List the supplier and the item, where the supplier is the only deliverer of some item.**

For each item delivered, check to see if there is no other delivery of this item by another supplier.

```
SELECT DISTINCT QSPL.SPLNO, SPLNAME, ITEMNAME
  FROM QSPL, QDEL DEL1
    WHERE QSPL.SPLNO = DEL1.SPLNO
    AND ITEMNAME NOT IN
```

```
        (SELECT ITEMNAME FROM QDEL
           WHERE QDEL.SPLNO <> DEL1.SPLNO)
```

36.   AT LEAST SOME NUMBER

○   **List the suppliers who deliver at least ten items.**

This is an easy GROUP BY with a count condition.

```
    SELECT SPLNO, SPLNAME FROM QDEL, QSPL
       WHERE QDEL.SPLNO = QSPL.SPLNO
          GROUP BY SPLNO, SPLNAME
             HAVING COUNT(DISTINCT QDEL.ITEMNAME) >= 10
```

37.   A THREE–TABLE JOIN

○   **For each item, give its type, the departments that sell the item, and the floor location of these departments.**

A three–table join is rather easy after all the divides.

```
    SELECT QITEM.ITEMNAME, ITEMTYPE, QDEPT.DEPTNAME, DEPTFLOOR
       FROM QITEM, QSALE, QDEPT
          WHERE QSALE.ITEMNAME = QITEM.ITEMNAME
          AND QSALE.DEPTNAME = QDEPT.DEPTNAME
```

38.   USING *NOT IN* LIKE *NOT EXISTS*

○   **List the departments for which each item delivered to the department is delivered to some other department as well.**

This is another variation on double negative logic. The query can be rewritten as: *Find departments where there is not a delivery where a supplier does not deliver the item to some other department.* In this situation, the NOT IN clause is like a NOT EXISTS.

```
    SELECT DISTINCT DEPTNAME FROM QDEL DEL1
       WHERE NOT EXISTS
          (SELECT * FROM QDEL DEL2
             WHERE DEL2.DEPTNAME = DEL1.DEPTNAME
             AND ITEMNAME NOT IN
                (SELECT ITEMNAME FROM QDEL DEL3
                   WHERE DEL3.DEPTNAME <> DEL1.DEPTNAME))
```

39. MINUS AFTER GROUPING

○ **List each item delivered to at least two departments by each supplier who delivers it.**

The inner query uses grouping to identify items delivered by the same supplier to one department at most. The remaining items must be delivered by the same supplier to more than one department.

```
SELECT DISTINCT ITEMNAME FROM QDEL
   WHERE ITEMNAME NOT IN
      (SELECT ITEMNAME FROM QDEL
         GROUP BY ITEMNAME, SPLNO
            HAVING COUNT(DISTINCT DEPTNAME) < 2)
```

40. SOMETHING TO ALL

○ **List the items that are delivered only by the suppliers who deliver something to all the departments.**

This is a variation on query 25 with the additional requirement, handled by the innermost query, that the supplier delivers to all departments. Specifying that all departments get a delivery means that the number of departments to whom a supplier delivers (GROUP BY SPLNO HAVING COUNT (DISTINCT DEPTNAME)) must equal the number of departments that sell items (SELECT COUNT(*) FROM QDEPT WHERE DEPTNAME NOT IN ('Management', 'Marketing', 'Personnel', 'Accounting', 'Purchasing')).

```
SELECT DISTINCT ITEMNAME FROM QDEL DEL1
   WHERE NOT EXISTS
      (SELECT * FROM QDEL DEL2
         WHERE DEL2.ITEMNAME = DEL1.ITEMNAME
            AND SPLNO NOT IN
               (SELECT SPLNO FROM QDEL
                  GROUP BY SPLNO HAVING COUNT(DISTINCT DEPTNAME) =
                     (SELECT COUNT(*) FROM QDEPT
                        WHERE DEPTNAME NOT IN ('Management',
                        'Marketing', 'Personnel',
                        'Accounting', 'Purchasing'))))
```

41. INTERSECTION *(AND)*

○ **List the items deliverd by Nepalese Corp. and sold in the Navigation department.**

The two parts to the query—the delivery and the sale—are intersected.

```
SELECT ITEMNAME FROM QDEL, QSPL
   WHERE QDEL.SPLNO = QSPL.SPLNO
     AND SPLNAME = 'Nepalese Corp.'
   AND ITEMNAME IN
     (SELECT ITEMNAME FROM QSALE
        WHERE DEPTNAME = 'Navigation')
```

42. UNION *(OR)*

❍   **List the items delivered by Nepalese Corp. or sold in the Navigation department.**

The two parts are the same as query 41, but the condition is *or* rather than *and*.

```
SELECT DISTINCT ITEMNAME FROM QITEM
   WHERE ITEMNAME IN
     (SELECT ITEMNAME FROM QDEL, QSPL
        WHERE QDEL.SPLNO = QSPL.SPLNO
          AND SPLNAME = 'Nepalese Corp.')
   OR ITEMNAME IN
     (SELECT ITEMNAME FROM QSALE
        WHERE DEPTNAME = 'Navigation')
```

43.   INTERSECTION/UNION

❍   **List the departments selling items of type E that are delivered by Nepalese Corp. and/or which are sold by the Navigation department.**

The inner query handles the and/or with OR. Remember *or* can mean that the items are in both tables or one table. The outer query identifies the departments that receive the delivered items, which satisfy the inner query.

```
SELECT DISTINCT DEPTNAME FROM QSALE
   WHERE ITEMNAME IN
     (SELECT QITEM.ITEMNAME FROM QITEM, QDEL, QSPL
        WHERE QITEM.ITEMNAME = QDEL.ITEMNAME
        AND QDEL.SPLNO = QSPL.SPLNO
        AND SPLNAME = 'Nepalese Corp.'
        AND ITEMTYPE = 'E')
   OR ITEMNAME IN
     (SELECT ITEMNAME FROM QSALE
        WHERE DEPTNAME = 'Navigation')
```

44.   AVERAGING WITH A CONDITION

○   **Find the average salary of the employees in the Clothes department.**

This is very easy, especially after conquering the divides.

```
SELECT AVG(EMPSALARY) FROM QEMP
   WHERE DEPTNAME = 'Clothes'
```

45.   AVERAGING WITH GROUPING

○   **Find, for each department, the average salary of the employees.**

Another straightforward averaging query.

```
SELECT DEPTNAME, AVG(EMPSALARY) FROM QEMP
   GROUP BY DEPTNAME
```

46.   AVERAGING WITH A JOIN, CONDITION, AND GROUPING

○   **Find, for each department on the second floor, the average salary of the employees.**

A combination of several averaging queries.

```
SELECT QDEPT.DEPTNAME, AVG(EMPSALARY) FROM QEMP, QDEPT
   WHERE QEMP.DEPTNAME = QDEPT.DEPTNAME
   AND DEPTFLOOR = 2
      GROUP BY QDEPT.DEPTNAME
```

47.   AVERAGING WITH MULTIPLE JOINS

○   **Find, for each department that sells items of type E, the average salary of the employees.**

Four joins, a condition, and grouping—not a particularly challenging query. The multiple joins are needed to get the data required for the answer into a single row.

```
SELECT QDEPT.DEPTNAME, AVG(EMPSALARY)
   FROM QEMP, QDEPT, QSALE, QITEM
      WHERE QEMP.DEPTNAME = QDEPT.DEPTNAME
      AND QDEPT.DEPTNAME = QSALE.DEPTNAME
      AND QSALE.ITEMNAME = QITEM.ITEMNAME
```

```
AND ITEMTYPE = 'E'
   GROUP BY QDEPT.DEPTNAME
```

48. COMPLEX COUNTING

○   **What are the number of different items delivered by each supplier who delivers to all departments?**

First, determine the suppliers who deliver to each department, excluding administrative departments. The inner query handles this part of the main query. Second, count the number of different items delivered by the suppliers identified by the inner query.

```
SELECT SPLNAME, COUNT(DISTINCT ITEMNAME)
   FROM QDEL DEL1, QSPL
      WHERE DEL1.SPLNO = QSPL.SPLNO
      AND NOT EXISTS
         (SELECT * FROM QDEPT
            WHERE DEPTNAME NOT IN
               (SELECT DEPTNAME FROM QDEL
                  WHERE QDEL.SPLNO = DEL1.SPLNO)
               AND DEPTNAME NOT IN
               ('Management', 'Marketing', 'Personnel',
               'Accounting', 'Purchasing'))
      GROUP BY SPLNAME
```

49. SUMMING WITH JOINS AND CONDITIONS

○   **Find the total number of items of type E sold by the departments on the second floor.**

Summing is very similar to averaging (see query 47).

```
SELECT SUM(SALEQTY) FROM QITEM, QSALE, QDEPT
   WHERE QITEM.ITEMNAME = QSALE.ITEMNAME
      AND QDEPT.DEPTNAME = QSALE.DEPTNAME
      AND ITEMTYPE = 'E'
      AND DEPTFLOOR = 2
```

50. SUMMING WITH JOINS, CONDITIONS, AND GROUPING

○   **Find, for each item, the total quantity sold by the departments on the second floor.**

Conceptually, this query is similar to query 47.

```
SELECT QITEM.ITEMNAME, SUM(SALEQTY) FROM QITEM, QSALE, QDEPT
   WHERE QITEM.ITEMNAME = QSALE.ITEMNAME
   AND QDEPT.DEPTNAME = QSALE.DEPTNAME
   AND DEPTFLOOR = 2
      GROUP BY QITEM.ITEMNAME
```

51. ADVANCED SUMMING

❍ **List suppliers who deliver a total quantity of items of types C and N that is altogether greater than 100.**

The difficult part of this query, and it is not too difficult, is to write the condition for selecting items of type C and N. Notice that the original query says C and N,[4] but don't translate this to (ITEMTYPE = 'C' AND ITEMTYPE = 'N') because an item cannot be both types simultaneously. The query means that for any delivery, the item should be type C or type N.

```
SELECT QDEL.SPLNO, SPLNAME FROM QSPL, QDEL, QITEM
   WHERE QSPL.SPLNO = QDEL.SPLNO
   AND QITEM.ITEMNAME = QITEM.ITEMNAME
   AND (ITEMTYPE = 'C' OR ITEMTYPE = 'N')
      GROUP BY QDEL.SPLNO, SPLNAME HAVING SUM(DELQTY) > 100
```

52. COMPARING TO THE AVERAGE WITH A JOIN

❍ **List the employees in the Accounting department and the difference between their salaries and the average salary of the department.**

The key to solving this query is placing the average salary for Accounting employees in the same row as their employee data. This is a two-stage process. You first need to determine the average salary of the employees in all departments and save this as a view. Then, join this view to the QEMP table matching on the Accounting department's name. Once the average departmental salary has been concatenated to each row, the query is straightforward.

```
CREATE VIEW V52(DEPTNAME, DPAVGSAL) AS
   SELECT DEPTNAME, AVG(EMPSALARY) FROM QEMP
      GROUP BY DEPTNAME

SELECT EMPFNAME, (EMPSALARY − DPAVGSAL) FROM V52, QEMP
   WHERE V52.DEPTNAME = QEMP.DEPTNAME
   AND QEMP.DEPTNAME = 'Accounting'
```

---

[4] Aren't you glad that this isn't a bad pun about a TV network?

53. COMPARING TO THE AVERAGE WITH A PRODUCT

❍ **List the employees in the Accounting department and the difference between their salaries and the average salary of all the departments.**

This is a slight variation on the previous query except that a join is not used to combine the data from the view with the employee table. The view is a single row and column table containing the average salary for the organization. To concatenate this row with the data for employees in the Accounting department, we use a product instead of a join. You will remember from Chapter 6 that a product is specified by simply listing the names of the two tables.

```
CREATE VIEW V53(ALLAVGSAL) AS
   SELECT AVG(EMPSALARY) FROM QEMP


SELECT EMPFNAME, (EMPSALARY - ALLAVGSAL) FROM V53, QEMP
   WHERE DEPTNAME = 'Accounting'
```

54. AVERAGING WITH MULTIPLE GROUPING

❍ **What is, for each supplier, the average number of items per department that the supplier delivers?**

Here, the averaging is broken into two levels: department within supplier.

```
SELECT QDEL.SPLNO, SPLNAME, DEPTNAME, AVG(DELQTY)
   FROM QSPL, QDEL
   WHERE QSPL.SPLNO = QDEL.SPLNO
      GROUP BY QDEL.SPLNO, SPLNAME, DEPTNAME
```

55. MORE THAN THE AVERAGE WITH GROUPING

❍ **For each department, find the average salary of the employees who earn more than the average salary of the department.**

The inner query determines the average salary of each department. Look carefully at how it handles matching departments.

```
SELECT DEPTNAME, AVG(EMPSALARY) FROM QEMP OUT
   WHERE EMPSALARY >
      (SELECT AVG(EMPSALARY) FROM QEMP INN
         WHERE OUT.DEPTNAME = INN.DEPTNAME
   GROUP BY DEPTNAME
```

56.   THE SIMPLEST AVERAGE

○   **Give the overall average of the salaries in all departments.**

This is a very simple query.

```
SELECT AVG(EMPSALARY) FROM QEMP
```

Another possible interpretation is that you have to find the total average salary after you determine the average salary for each department. To do this, you would first create a view containing the average salary for each department (see query 52) and then find the average of these average salaries.[5]

```
SELECT AVG(DPAVGSAL) FROM V52
```

57.   DIFFERENCE FROM THE AVERAGE

○   **List each employee's salary, the average salary within that person's department, and the difference between the employees' salaries and the average salary of the department.**

This is a reasonably easy query once you have created a view of departmental average salaries.

```
SELECT EMPFNAME, EMPSALARY,
   DPAVGSAL, (EMPSALARY − DPAVGSAL)
      FROM V52, QEMP
         WHERE V52.DEPTNAME = QEMP.DEPTNAME
```

58.   AVERAGING WITH MULTIPLE JOINS, MULTIPLE GROUPING, AND A CONDITION

○   **What is the average delivery quantity of items of type N delivered by each company who delivers them?**

This is similar to query 54.

```
SELECT QDEL.SPLNO, SPLNAME, QDEL.ITEMNAME, AVG(DELQTY)
   FROM QDEL, QSPL, QITEM
      WHERE QDEL.SPLNO = QSPL.SPLNO
      AND QDEL.ITEMNAME = QITEM.ITEMNAME
      AND ITEMTYPE = 'N'
         GROUP BY QDEL.SPLNO, SPLNAME, QDEL.ITEMNAME
```

---

[5]Some versions of SQL do not permit scalar operations on views, so you may not be able to execute this query.

59. DETAILED AVERAGING

◯ **What is the average delivery quantity of items of type N delivered by each supplier to each department (given that the supplier delivers items of type N to the department)?**

Now we take averaging to three levels—supplier, department, item—although you can take averaging to as many levels as you like.

```
SELECT QDEL.SPLNO, SPLNAME, DEPTNAME, QDEL.ITEMNAME,
  AVG(DELQTY)
  FROM QDEL, QSPL, QITEM
    WHERE QDEL.SPLNO = QSPL.SPLNO
    AND QDEL.ITEMNAME = QITEM.ITEMNAME
    AND ITEMTYPE = 'N'
      GROUP BY QDEL.SPLNO, SPLNAME, DEPTNAME, QDEL.ITEMNAME
```

60. COUNTING PAIRS

◯ **What is the number of supplier–department pairs in which the supplier delivers at least one item of type E to the department?**

First, find all the supplier-department pairs. Without DISTINCT you would get duplicates, which would make the subsequent count wrong.

```
CREATE VIEW V60 AS
  (SELECT DISTINCT SPLNO, DEPTNAME FROM QDEL, QITEM
    WHERE QDEL.ITEMNAME = QITEM.ITEMNAME
    AND ITEMTYPE = 'E'
```

Now, it is a simple count.

```
SELECT COUNT(*) FROM V60
```

61. NO BOOLEANS

◯ **Is it true that all the departments who sell items of type C are located on the third floor? (The result can be a Boolean 1 or 0, meaning yes or no.)**

SQL cannot return "true" or "false"; it always returns a table. But you can get close to Boolean results by using counts. If we get a count of zero for the following query, there are no departments who are not on the third floor who sell items of type C.

```
SELECT COUNT(*) FROM QDEPT
  WHERE DEPTFLOOR <> 3
  AND EXISTS
    (SELECT * FROM QSALE, QITEM
      WHERE QSALE.ITEMNAME = QITEM.ITEMNAME
      AND QSALE.DEPTNAME = QDEPT.DEPTNAME
      AND ITEMTYPE = 'C')
```

Then you need to check that departments on the third floor sell items of type C. If the second query returns a non-zero value, then it is true that departments who sell items of type C are located on the third floor.

```
SELECT COUNT(*) FROM QDEPT
  WHERE DEPTFLOOR = 3
  AND EXISTS
    (SELECT * FROM QSALE, QITEM
      WHERE QSALE.ITEMNAME = QITEM.ITEMNAME
      AND QSALE.DEPTNAME = QDEPT.DEPTNAME
      AND ITEMTYPE = 'C')
```

SUMMARY

Although SQL is a powerful retrieval language, formulation of common business queries is not always, alas, trivial.

KEY TERMS AND CONCEPTS

SELECT

EXERCISES

Here is an opportunity to display your SQL mastery.

1. List the green items of type C.
2. Find the names of green items sold by the Recreation department.
3. Find the items not delivered to the Books department.
4. Find the departments that have never sold a global positioning system.
5. Find the departments that have sold compasses and at least two other items.
6. Find the departments that sell at least four items.
7. Find the employees who are in a different department from their manager's department.
8. Find the employees who have a job status different from their manager's.
9. Find the green items sold by no department on the second floor.
10. Find the items delivered by all suppliers.
11. Find the items delivered by at least two suppliers.

12. Find the items not delivered by Nepalese Corp.
13. Find the items sold by at least two departments.
14. Find the items delivered for which there have been no sales.
15. Find the items delivered to all departments, except Administration.
16. Find the name of the highest paid employee in the Marketing department.
17. Find the names of employees who make 10 percent less than the average salary.
18. Find the names of employees with a salary greater than the minimum salary paid to a manager.
19. Find the names of suppliers who do not supply compasses or global positioning systems.
20. Find the number of employees with a salary under $10,000.
21. Find the number of items of type A sold by the departments on the third floor.
22. Find the number of units sold of each item.
23. Find the green items delivered by all suppliers.
24. Find the supplier who delivers no more than one item.
25. Find the suppliers who deliver to all departments.
26. Find the suppliers who deliver to all the departments that also receive deliveries from supplier 102.
27. Find the suppliers who have never delivered a compass.
28. Find the type A items delivered by Sao Paulo Manufacturing.
29. Find, for each department, its floor and the average salary in the department.
30. If Nancy's boss has a boss, who is it?
31. List each employee and the difference between his (her) salary and the average salary of his (her) department.
32. List the departments on the second floor that contain more than one employee.
33. List the departments on the second floor.
34. List the names of employees who earn more than the average salary of employees in the Shoe department.
35. List the names of items delivered by each supplier. Arrange the report by supplier name, and within supplier name, list the items in alphabetical order.
36. List the names of managers who supervise only one person.
37. List the number of employees in each department.
38. List the green items delivered by exactly one supplier.
39. Whom does Todd manage?
40. List the departments that have not sold all green items.
41. Find the first name of Sophie's boss.
42. Find the names of employees who make less than half their manager's salary.
43. List the names of each manager and their employees arranged by manager's name and employee's name within manager.
44. Who earns the lowest salary?

45. List the names of employees who earn less than the minimum salary of the Marketing department.

46. List the items sold by every department that is delivered all brown items.

47. List the department and the item, where the department is the only seller of that item.

48. List the brown items sold by the Books department and delivered by All Seasons.

49. Which department has the highest average salary?

50. List the supplier who delivers all and only brown items.

APPENDIX—DATA FOR TABLES

QSALE

SALENO	SALEQTY	ITEMNAME	DEPTNAME
1001	2	Boots–snakeproof	Clothes
1002	1	Pith helmet	Clothes
1003	1	Sextant	Navigation
1004	3	Hat–polar explorer	Clothes
1005	5	Pith helmet	Equipment
1006	1	Pocket knife–Nile	Clothes
1007	1	Pocket knife–Nile	Recreation
1008	1	Compass	Navigation
1009	1	Geo positioning system	Navigation
1010	5	Map measure	Navigation
1011	1	Geo positioning system	Books
1012	1	Sextant	Books
1013	3	Pocket knife–Nile	Books
1014	1	Pocket knife–Nile	Navigation
1015	1	Pocket knife–Nile	Equipment
1016	1	Sextant	Clothes
1017	1	Sextant	Equipment
1018	1	Sextant	Recreation
1019	1	Sextant	Furniture
1020	1	Pocket knife–Nile	Furniture
1021	1	Exploring in 10 Easy Lessons	Books
1022	1	How to Win Foreign Friends	Books
1023	1	Compass	Books
1024	1	Pith helmet	Books
1025	1	Elephant polo stick	Recreation
1026	1	Camel saddle	Recreation

QITEM

ITEMNAME	ITEMTYPE	ITEMCOLOR
Boots–snakeproof	C	Green
Camel saddle	R	Brown
Compass	N	—
Elephant polo stick	R	Bamboo
Exploring in 10 Easy Lessons	B	—
Geo positioning system	N	—
Hammock	F	Khaki
Hat–polar explorer	C	White
How to Win Foreign Friends	B	—
Map case	E	Brown
Map measure	N	—
Pith helmet	C	Khaki
Pocket knife–Avon	E	Brown
Pocket knife–Nile	E	Brown
Safari chair	F	Khaki
Safari cooking kit	F	—
Sextant	N	—
Stetson	C	Black
Tent–2 person	F	Khaki
Tent–8 person	F	Khaki

QDEL

DELNO	DELQTY	ITEMNAME	DEPTNAME	SPLNO
51	50	Pocket knife–Nile	Navigation	105
52	10	Pocket knife–Nile	Books	105
53	10	Pocket knife–Nile	Clothes	105
54	10	Pocket knife–Nile	Equipment	105
55	10	Pocket knife–Nile	Furniture	105
56	10	Pocket knife–Nile	Recreation	105
57	50	Compass	Navigation	101
58	10	Geo positioning system	Navigation	101
59	10	Map measure	Navigation	101
60	25	Map case	Navigation	101
61	2	Sextant	Navigation	101
62	1	Sextant	Equipment	105
63	20	Compass	Equipment	103
64	1	Geo positioning system	Books	103
65	15	Map measure	Navigation	103
66	1	Sextant	Books	103
67	5	Sextant	Recreation	102
68	3	Sextant	Navigation	104
69	5	Boots–snakeproof	Clothes	105
70	15	Pith helmet	Clothes	105
71	1	Pith helmet	Clothes	101
72	1	Pith helmet	Clothes	102
73	1	Pith helmet	Clothes	103
74	1	Pith helmet	Clothes	104
75	5	Pith helmet	Navigation	105
76	5	Pith helmet	Books	105
77	5	Pith helmet	Equipment	105
78	5	Pith helmet	Furniture	105
79	5	Pith helmet	Recreation	105
80	10	Pocket knife–Nile	Navigation	102
81	1	Compass	Navigation	102
82	1	Geo positioning system	Navigation	102
83	10	Map measure	Navigation	102

continued

QDEL (Continued)

DELNO	DELQTY	ITEMNAME	DEPTNAME	SPLNO
84	5	Map case	Navigation	102
85	5	Compass	Books	102
86	5	Pocket knife–Avon	Recreation	102
87	5	Tent–2 person	Recreation	102
88	2	Tent–8 person	Recreation	102
89	5	Exploring in 10 Easy Lessons	Navigation	102
90	5	How to Win Foreign Friends	Navigation	102
91	10	Exploring in 10 Easy Lessons	Books	102
92	10	How to Win Foreign Friends	Books	102
93	2	Exploring in 10 Easy Lessons	Recreation	102
94	2	How to Win Foreign Friends	Recreation	102
95	5	Compass	Equipment	105
96	2	Boots–snakeproof	Equipment	105
97	20	Pith helmet	Equipment	106
98	20	Pocket knife–Nile	Equipment	106
99	1	Sextant	Equipment	106
100	3	Hat–polar explorer	Clothes	105
101	3	Stetson	Clothes	105

QSPL

SPLNO	SPLNAME
101	Global Books & Maps
102	Nepalese Corp.
103	All Sports Manufacturing
104	Sweatshops Unlimited
105	All Points, Inc.
106	Sao Paulo Manufacturing

QDEPT

DEPTNAME	DEPTFLOOR	DEPTPHONE	EMPNO
Management	5	34	1
Books	1	81	4
Clothes	2	24	4
Equipment	3	57	3
Furniture	4	14	3
Navigation	1	41	3
Recreation	2	29	4
Accounting	5	35	5
Purchasing	5	36	7
Personnel	5	37	9
Marketing	5	38	2

QEMP

EMPNO	EMPFNAME	EMPSALARY	DEPTNAME	BOSSNO
1	Alice	75000	Management	
2	Ned	45000	Marketing	1
3	Andrew	25000	Marketing	2
4	Clare	22000	Marketing	2
5	Todd	38000	Accounting	1
6	Nancy	22000	Accounting	5
7	Brier	43000	Purchasing	1
8	Sarah	56000	Purchasing	7
9	Sophie	35000	Personnel	1
10	Sanjay	15000	Navigation	3
11	Rita	15000	Books	4
12	Gigi	16000	Clothes	4
13	Maggie	16000	Clothes	4
14	Paul	11000	Equipment	3
15	James	15000	Equipment	3
16	Pat	15000	Furniture	3
17	Mark	15000	Recreation	3

Database Architectures and Implementations

We shape our buildings: thereafter they shape us.
Winston Churchill, *Time*, 12 September 1960

A database architecture is a design for the storage and processing of data. Organizations strive to find an architecture that simultaneously achieves multiple goals:

1. responds to queries in a timely manner;
2. minimizes the cost of processing data;
3. minimizes the cost of storing data;
4. minimizes the cost of data delivery.

This section deals with the approaches that can be used to achieve each of these goals. We begin by tracing the development of schema architectures and conclude with a description of the ANSI/SPARC architecture.

DEVELOPMENT OF DATA ARCHITECTURES

Remember that first program you wrote? It was probably very simple—something that added two numbers and printed the result. More than likely, the two numbers to be added were "hard coded" into the program. If you wanted to add a different pair of numbers, you had to edit the program and rerun it. Most beginners' programs exemplify the situation where programs and data are not separated—also known as a **no-schema architecture** (see Figure S3-1). A schema is a representation of the data's structure.

As your programming skills advanced, you learned it was more efficient to separate a pro-

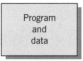

Figure S3–1   No-schema architecture

gram and its data. Instead of hard coding data, you used variable names to represent data values, and your program read data from a file or asked the user to input values. Although you had separated the program and the data, essentially you still saw the data exactly as the program saw it. Your **internal schemas** were identical. This approach is known as a **one-schema architecture** (see Figure S3-2). One advantage of separating the data from a program is that the same data can be used by several different programs, or the same program can run several different sets of data.

Many users, however, do not want to know how data are represented in a program or a file. They simply want a view of the data that matches their needs. As a result, the idea of an **external schema** emerged—charting the users' view of the data. Thus we have a two-schema architecture (see Figure S3-3) that separates the user from the data. Most word processors have a two-schema architecture; your view of the words you type is quite different from what is actually stored.

The major shortcoming of a two-schema architecture is that every time a physical data structure is changed, programs have to be changed.[1] This problem is overcome by introducing a **conceptual schema** and three-level architecture to further separate a program from the data.

ANSI/SPARC

In 1972, ANSI established a committee to examine standardization of database technology. This study group, officially known as the ANSI/X3/SPARC Study Group on Data Base Management, produced a general architecture for describing a database and its various interfaces,

Figure S3–2   One-schema architecture

---

[1]You may notice that some word processing files are not compatible across different versions of the same product. This is an example of how changing the internal schema—the data storage structures—requires the program to change. Of course, conversion programs are usually provided to bridge the gap.

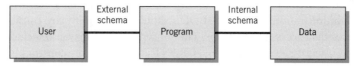

Figure S3–3   Two-schema architecture

the only area which it concluded was suitable for standardization. Its framework for database interfaces is known as the ANSI/SPARC architecture.[2]

The ANSI/SPARC architecture consists of three schemas or levels (the word favored by the group): internal, conceptual, and external (see Figure S3-4).

The External Level

The external level represents a user's view of the system. As the diagram shows, there can be many user views, and as we learned previously, multiple views can be defined for a single SQL table by using CREATE VIEW. These views can be tailored to the needs and data access privileges of any authorized user.

The Conceptual Level

The conceptual level is the database designer's view, which is completely unrestricted and includes all the files and all the fields in each file. The database designer sees everything.

The conceptual level is the mapping of the data model to the DBMS's DDL. In the case of

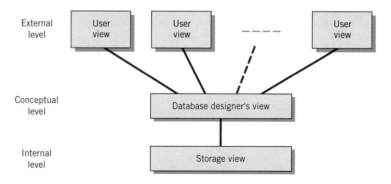

Figure S3–4   The ANSI/SPARC architecture

---

[2]"ANSI/X3/SPARC Study Group on Data Base Management Systems," (Interim report) *ACM SIGMOD Bulletin* 7 (2): (1975); and D.C. Tsichritzis and A. Klug, eds. "The ANSI/X3/SPARC DBMS Framework: Report of the Study Group on Data Base Management Systems," *Information Systems* 3 (1978).

SQL, CREATE TABLE specifies the conceptual level. Because data independence is a key goal of data administration, the selected DDL should not require any consideration of storage structure or data access mechanisms. The conceptual level may also include definitions of security and integrity level checks (e.g., GRANT and foreign key constraints). Ideally, this level completely describes the database without taking physical considerations into account.

The Internal Level

As the chapters in this section will discuss, the internal level—the lowest level description of a database—is concerned with the way data are stored. Although it describes attributes such as types of records stored, indexes, and record sequencing, the internal level does not deal with the device–specific attributes.

Chapter 11 covers database structure and storage alternatives. It provides the knowledge necessary to determine an appropriate data storage structure and device for a given situation. Chapter 12 addresses the fundamental questions of where to store the data and where it should be processed. Alternative choices for data models (relational, hierarchical, network, and object) are considered in the remaining three chapters of this section. The hierarchical and network models are covered jointly in one chapter, however, because they are less widely used now.

Chapter 11

Data Structure and Storage

The modern age has a false sense of superiority because it relies on the mass of knowledge that it can use, but what is important is the extent to which knowledge is organized and mastered.

Goethe, 1810

Learning Objectives

Students completing this chapter will:

* be able to recommend a data storage structure for a given situation;
* be able to recommend a storage device for a given situation.

The Expeditioner

Every quarter, The Expeditioner's IS group measures the quality of its service. It asks users to assess whether their hardware and software are adequate for their jobs, whether IS service is reliable and responsive, and if they thought the IS staff were helpful and knowledgeable.[1] The most recent survey revealed that some users were experiencing unreasonably long delays for what were relatively simple queries. How could the IS group "tune" the database to reduce response time?

As though some grumpy users were not enough, Alice dumped another problem on Ned's desk. The Marketing department had complained to her that the product database had been down for 30 minutes during a peak selling period. What was Ned going to do to prevent such an occurrence in the future?

Ned had just finished reading Alice's memo about the database problem when the Chief Accountant poked his head in the door. Somewhat agitated, he was waving an article from his favorite accounting journal that claimed that data stored on magnetic tape decayed with time. So what was he to do with all those financial records on magnetic tapes stored in the fireproof safe in his office? Were the magnetic bits likely to disappear tonight, tomorrow, or next week? "This business had lasted for centuries with paper ledgers. Why, you can still read

---

[1]Perhaps the source of this idea is L. F. Pitt and others, "Service Quality: A Measure of Information Systems Effectiveness," *MIS Quarterly,* 19 (2), 1995.

the financial transactions for 1527," declared the Chief Accountant, which he did whenever he had a few moments to spare. "But, if what I read is true, I soon won't be able to read the balance sheet from last year!"

It was just after 10 A.M. on a Monday, and Ned was faced with finding a way to improve response time, ensure that databases were continually available during business hours, and protect the long-term existence of financial records. It was going to be a long week.

INTRODUCTION

The following pages explore territory that is not normally the concern of application programmers or database users. Fortunately, the relational model keeps data structures and data access methods hidden. Nevertheless, an overview of what happens "under the hood" is part of a well-rounded education in database management.

Data structures and access methods are the province of the person responsible for physically designing the database so that it responds in a timely manner to both queries and maintenance operations. Of course, there may be installations where application programmers have such responsibilities, and in these situations you will need to know physical database design.

DATA STRUCTURES

An in-depth consideration of the internal level of database architecture provides an understanding of the basic structures and access mechanisms underlying database technology. As you will see, the overriding concern of the internal level is to minimize disk access. In dealing with this level, we will speak in terms of files, records, and fields rather than the relational database terms of tables, rows, and fields. We do this because the discussion extends beyond the relational model to file structures in general.

The time required to access data on a magnetic disk, the usual storage device for databases, is relatively long compared to main memory. Disk access times are measured in milliseconds (10^{-3}), and main memory access times are referred to in nanoseconds (10^{-9}). There are generally around five orders of magnitude difference between disk and main memory—it takes about 10^5 times longer. This distinction is more meaningful if placed in everyday context; it is like asking someone a question by phone or writing them a letter. The phone response takes seconds, and the written response takes days.

For many business applications, slow disk drives are a bottleneck. The computer often must wait for a disk to retrieve data before it can continue processing a request for information. This delay means that users and their customers are also kept waiting. Appropriate selection of data structures and data access methods can considerably reduce delays. Database designers have two options: decrease disk read/write head movement or reduce disk accesses. Before considering these options, we need a general model of database access.

Database Access

A three-layer model provides a framework for thinking about minimization of data access (see Figure 11-1). This is a generic model, and a particular DBMS may implement the approach using a different number of layers. For simplicity, the discussion is based on retrieving a single record in a file, although the principles also apply to retrieval of multiple records or an entire file.

1. The DBMS determines which record is required and passes a request to the file manager to retrieve a particular record in a file.

2. The **file manager** converts this request into the address of the unit of storage (usually called a page) containing the specified record. A **page** is the minimum amount of storage accessed at one time, and is typically around 1 k to 4 kbytes. A page will often contain several short records (e.g., 200 bytes), but a long record (e.g., 10 kbytes) might be spread over several pages. In this example, we assume records are shorter than a page.

3. The **disk manager** determines the physical location of the page, issues the retrieval instructions, and passes the page to the file manager.

4. The file manager extracts the requested record from the page and passes it to the DBMS.

The Disk Manager

The disk manager is that part of the operating system responsible for physical I/O. It maintains a directory of the location of each page on the disk, with all pages identified by a unique page number. The disk manager's main functions are to retrieve pages, replace pages, and keep track of free pages.

Page retrieval requires the disk manager to convert the page number to a physical address and issue the command to read the physical location. Since a page can contain multiple records, when a record is updated, the disk manager must retrieve the appropriate page, up-

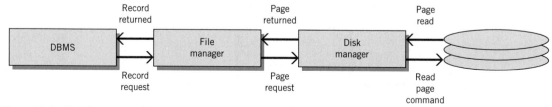

Figure 11-1   Database access layers

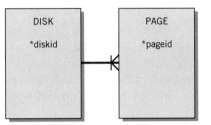

Figure 11-2 Disk manager's view of the world

date the appropriate portion containing the record, and then replace the page without changing any of the other data on it.

The disk manager thinks of the disk as a collection of uniquely numbered pages (see Figure 11-2). Some of these pages are allocated to the storage of data and others are unused. When additional storage space is required, the disk manager allocates a page address from the set of unused page addresses. When a page becomes free because a file or some records are deleted, the disk manager moves that page's address to the unallocated set.

The File Manager

The file manager, a level above the disk manager, is concerned with the storage of files. It thinks of the disk as a set of stored files (see Figure 11-3). Each file has a unique file identifier and each record within a file has a record identifier that is unique within that file.

The file manager can:

- create a file,
- delete a file,

Figure 11-3 File manager's view of the world

- retrieve a record from a file,
- update a record in a file,
- add a new record to a file,
- delete a record from a file.

Techniques For Reducing Head Movement

All disk storage devices have some common features. They have one or more recording surfaces; a commercial magnetic disk pack, for example, typically has twenty recording surfaces, and a removable magneto-optical disk has one surface. Data are stored on tracks on each surface.

The key characteristics of disk storage devices that affect database access **are rotational speed** and **access arm speed.** All disks spin at high speed. The typical rotational speed of a magnetic disk is around 3500 rpm. Reading or writing a page to disk requires moving the read/write head to the destination track and waiting for the storage address to come under the head. Because moving the head usually takes more time (e.g., about 15 msec) than waiting for the storage address to appear under it (e.g., about 6 msec), data access times can be reduced by minimizing the movement of the read/write head or rotating the disk faster. Since rotational speed is set by the disk manufacturer, minimizing read/write head movement is the only option available to database designers.

Cylinders

Head movement is curtailed by storing data that are likely to be accessed at the same time, such as records in a file, on the same track on a single surface, or on a **cylinder,** data stored on the same track on different surfaces. The advantage of cylinder storage is that all tracks can be accessed without moving the read/write head. When a cylinder is full, remaining data are stored on adjacent cylinders. Adjacent cylinders are ideal for sequential file storage be-

A disk drive.

cause the record retrieval pattern is predefined—the first record is read, then the second, and so on.

Clustering

Cylinder storage can also be used when the record retrieval pattern has some degree of regularity to it. Consider the following familiar data model of Figure 11-4. Converting this data model to a relational database creates two tables. Conceptually, we may think of the data in each of the tables as being stored in adjacent cylinders. If, however, you frequently need to retrieve one row of NATION and all the corresponding rows of STOCK, then NATION and STOCK rows should be intermingled to minimize access time.

The term **clustering** describes the concept that records that are frequently used together should be physically close together on a disk. Some DBMSs permit the database designer to specify clustering of different files to tune the database to reduce average access times. If usage patterns change, clustering specifications should be altered. Of course, clustering should be totally transparent to application programs and users.

Techniques For Reducing Disk Accesses

Several techniques are used to accelerate retrieval by reducing disk accesses. The ideal situation is when the required record is obtained with a single disk access. In special circumstances, it may be possible to create a file where the primary key can convert directly to a unique disk address (e.g., the record with primary key 1 is stored at address 1001, the record with primary key 2 is stored at address 1002, and so on). If possible, this method of **direct addressing** should be used because it is the fastest form of data access; however, it is most unusual to find such a direct mapping between the primary key and a disk address. For example, it would be infeasible to use direct addressing with a student file that has a Social Security number as the primary key because so many disk addresses would be wasted. Furthermore, direct addressing can work only for the primary key. What happens if there is a need for rapid retrieval on another field?

In most cases, database designers use features such as indexing, hashing, and linked lists.

Figure 11-4 NATION and STOCK data model

Indexing, a flexible and commonly used method of reducing disk accesses when searching for data, centers on the creation of a compact file containing the index field and the address of its corresponding record. The **B-tree** is a particular form of index structure that is widely used as the storage structure of relational DBMSs. **Hashing** is a direct access method based on using an arithmetic function to compute a disk address from a field within a file. A **linked list** is a data structure that accelerates data access by using pointers to show relationships existing between records.

Indexing

Consider the ITEM file partially shown in Table 11-1. Let's assume that this file has 10,000 records and each record requires 1 kbyte, which is a page on the particular disk system used. Suppose a common query is to request all the items of a particular type or color. Such a query might be:

○   **Find all items of type E.**

Regardless of the number of records with ITEMTYPE = 'E', this query will require 10,000 disk accesses. Every record has to be retrieved and examined to determine the value of ITEM-TYPE. For instance, if 20 percent of the items are of type E then 8000 of the disk accesses are wasted because they retrieve a record that is not required. The ideal situation would be to retrieve only those 2000 records that contain an item of type E. We get closer to this ideal situation by creating a small file containing just the value of ITEMTYPE for each record and the address of the full record. This small file is called an index. Part of the ITEMTYPE index for ITEM and ITEM file is shown in Figure 11-5.

The ITEMTYPE index is a file. It contains 10,000 records and two fields. There is one record in the index for each record in ITEM. The first field contains a value of ITEMTYPE

Table 11–1   Portion of a 10,000 Record File

ITEMNO	ITEMNAME	ITEMTYPE	ITEMCOLOR
1	Pocket knife – Nile	E	Brown
2	Pocket knife – Avon	E	Brown
3	Compass	N	—
4	Geo positioning system	N	—
5	Map measure	N	—
6	Hat – polar explorer	C	Red
7	Hat – polar explorer	C	White
8	Boots – snake proof	C	Green
9	Boots – snake proof	C	Black
10	Safari chair	F	Khaki

ITEMTYPE INDEX		ITEM				
ITEMTYPE		ITEMNO	ITEMNAME	ITEMTYPE	ITEMCOLOR
C		1	Pocket knife–Nile	E	Brown
C		2	Pocket knife–Thames	E	Brown
C		3	Compass	N	–
C		4	Geo positioning system	N	–
E		5	Map measure	N	–
E		6	Hat–polar explorer	C	Red
F		7	Hat–polar explorer	C	White
N		8	Boots–snakeproof	C	Green
N		9	Boots–snakeproof	C	Black
N		10	Safari chair	F	Khaki

Figure 11-5   Part of the ITEMTYPE index

and the second contains a pointer—an address—to the matching record of ITEM. Notice that the index is in ITEMTYPE sequence. Storing the index in a particular order is another means of reducing disk accesses, as we will see shortly. The index is quite small. One byte is required for ITEMTYPE and four bytes for the pointer. So the total size of the index is 50 kbytes, which is 50 pages of disk space.

Now consider finding all records with an item type of E. One approach is to read the entire index into memory, search it for type E items, and then use the pointers to retrieve the required records from ITEM. This method requires 2050 disk accesses—50 to load the index and 2000 accesses of ITEM. Creating an index for ITEM results in substantial savings in disk accesses for this example. In this example, we assume that 20 percent of the records in ITEM contained ITEMTYPE = 'E'. The number of disk accesses saved varies with the proportion of records meeting the query's criteria. If there are no records meeting the criteria, 9950 disk accesses are avoided. At the other extreme, when all records meet the criteria, it takes 50 extra disk accesses to load the index.

The SQL (see Chapter 9 for a detailed discussion of the syntax of the command) for creating the index is

```
CREATE INDEX ITEMTYPEINDX
  ON ITEM (ITEMTYPE)
```

The entire index need not be read into memory. As you will see when we discuss tree structures, we can take advantage of the index's ordering to further reduce disk accesses. Nevertheless, the clear advantage of an index is evident: it speeds up retrieval by reducing disk accesses. Like many aspects of database management, however, indexes have a drawback. Adding a record to a file without an index requires a single disk write. Adding a record to an indexed file requires at least two, and maybe more, disk writes since an entry has to be added to both the file and its index. The trade-off is between faster retrievals and slower updates. If there are many retrievals and few updates, then opt for an index, especially if the indexed field can have a wide variety of values. Avoid indexes if the file is very volatile and updates are frequent and retrievals few.

Indexes can be used for both sequential and direct access. Sequential access means that records are retrieved in the sequence defined by the values in the index. In our example, this means retrieving records in ITEMTYPE sequence with a range query such as

○ **Find all items with a type code in the range E to K.**

Direct access means records are retrieved according to one or more specified values. A sample query requiring direct access would be:

○ **Find all items with a type code of E or N.**

Indexes are also handy for existence testing. Remember, the EXIST clause of SQL returns true or false and not a value. An index can be searched to check whether the indexed field takes a particular value, but there is no need to access the file because no data are returned. The following query can be answered by an index search.

○ **Are there any items with a code of R?**

Multiple Indexes

Multiple indexes can be created for a file. The ITEM file could have an index defined on ITEMCOLOR or any other field. Multiple indexes may be used independently, as in this query:

○ **List red items**

or jointly, with a query such as

○ **Find red items of type C.**

The above query can be resolved by using the indexes for ITEMTYPE and ITEMCOLOR (see Figure 11-6).

Examination of the ITEMTYPE index indicates that items of type C are stored at addresses d6, d7, d8, and d9. The only red item recorded in the ITEMCOLOR index is stored at address d6, and since it is the only record satisfying the query, it is the only record that needs to be retrieved.

Multiple indexes, as you would expect, involve a trade-off. Whenever a record is added or updated, each index must also be updated. Savings in disk accesses for retrieval are exchanged for additional disk accesses in maintenance. Again, you must consider the balance between retrieval and maintenance operations.

Indexes are not restricted to a single field. It is possible to specify an index that is a combination of several fields. For instance, if item type and color queries were very common, then an index based on the concatenation of both fields could be created. As a result, such queries could be answered with a search of a single index, rather than scanning two indexes as in the example above. The SQL for creating the combined index is:

```
CREATE INDEX TYPECOLORINDX
  ON ITEM (ITEMTYPE, ITEMCOLOR)
```

ITEMTYPE INDEX			ITEMCOLOR INDEX	
ITEMTYPE	Disk address		ITEMCOLOR	Disk address
C	d6		Black	d9
C	d7		Brown	d1
C	d8		Brown	d2
C	d9		Green	d8
E	d1		Khaki	d10
E	d2		Red	d6
F	d10		White	d7
N	d3		–	d3
N	d4		–	d4
N	d5		–	d5

Figure 11-6   Indexes for fields ITEMTYPE and ITEMCOLOR

Sparse Indexes

Indexes are used to reduce disk accesses to accelerate retrieval. The simple model of an index introduced earlier suggests that the index contains an entry for each record of the file. If we can shrink the index to eliminate an entry for each record, we can save more disk accesses. Indeed, if we can get an index small enough, it—or key parts of it—can be retained continuously in primary memory.

There is a physical sequence to the records in a file. Records within a page are in a physical sequence, and pages on a disk are in a physical sequence. A file can also have a logical sequence, the ordering of the file on some field within a record. For instance, the ITEM file could be ordered on ITEMNO. Making the physical and logical sequences correspond is a way to save disk accesses. Remember, the ITEM file was assumed to have a record size of 1024 bytes, the same size as a page, and one record was stored per page. If we now assume that the record size is 512 bytes, then two records are stored per page. Furthermore, suppose that ITEM is physically stored in ITEMNO sequence. The index can be compressed by storing ITEMNO for the second record on each page and that page's address. The new index is shown in Figure 11-7.

Consider the process of finding the record with ITEMNO = 7. First, the index is scanned to find the first value for ITEMNO that is greater than or equal to 7—the entry for ITEMNO = 8. Second, the page on which this record is stored (page $p + 3$) is loaded into memory. Third, the required record is extracted from the page.

Indexes that take advantage of the physical sequencing of a file are known as sparse or non-dense, because they do not contain an entry for every value of the indexed field. (A dense index is one that contains an entry for every value of the indexed field.)

As you would expect, sparse indexes have pros and cons. One major advantage is that it takes less storage space and so requires fewer disk accesses for reading. One disadvantage is that it can no longer be used for existence tests because it does not contain a value for every record in the file.

ITEMNO INDEX			ITEM				
ITEMNO			ITEMNO	ITEMNAME	ITEMTYPE	ITEMCOLOR	
2			1	Pocket knife–Nile	E	Brown	page p
4			2	Pocket knife–Thames	E	Brown	
6			3	Compass	N	–	page p + 1
8			4	Geo positioning system	N	–	
10			5	Map measure	N	–	page p + 2
			6	Hat–polar explorer	C	Red	
			7	Hat–polar explorer	C	White	page p + 3
			8	Boots–snakeproof	C	Green	
			9	Boots–snakeproof	C	Black	page p + 4
			10	Safari chair	F	Khaki	

Figure 11-7   A sparse index for ITEM

A file can have only one sparse index because it can have only one physical sequence. This field on which a sparse index is based is often called the primary key. Other indexes, which must be dense, are called secondary indexes.

In SQL, a sparse index is created using the CLUSTER option. For example, to define a sparse index on ITEM the command is

```
CREATE INDEX ITEMNOINDX
   ON ITEM (ITEMNO) CLUSTER
```

B-trees

The B-tree is a particular form of index structure that is frequently the main storage structure for relational systems. It is also the basis for IBM's VSAM (Virtual Storage Access Method), the file structure underlying DB2. A B-tree is an efficient structure for both sequential and direct accessing of a file. It consists of two parts, the sequence set and the index set.

The **sequence set** is a single-level index to the file with pointers to the records (the vertical arrows in the lower part of Figure 11-8). It can be sparse or dense, but is normally dense. Entries in the sequence set are grouped into pages, and these pages are linked together (the horizontal arrows in Figure 11-8) so that the logical ordering of the sequence set is the physical ordering of the file. Thus, the file can be processed sequentially by processing the records pointed to by the first page (records with identifiers 1, 4, and 5), the records pointed to by the next logical page (6, 19, and 20), and so on.

The **index set** is a tree-structured index to the sequence set. The top of the index set is a single node called the root. In this example, it contains two values (20 and 57) and three pointers. Records with an identifier less than or equal to 29 are found in the left branch, records with an identifier greater than 29 and less than or equal to 57 are found in the middle

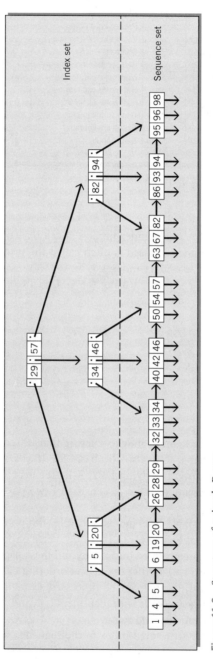

Figure 11-8 Structure of a simple B-tree

branch, and records with an identifier greater than 57 are found in the right branch. The three pointers are the page numbers of the left, middle, and right branches. The nodes at the next level have similar interpretations. The pointer to a particular record is found by moving down the tree until a node entry points to a value in the sequence set; this value can be used to retrieve the record. Thus, the index set provides direct access to the sequence set and then the data.

The index set is a B-tree. The combination of index set and sequence set is generally known as a B+ tree (**B-plus tree**). The B-tree shown in Figure 11-8 simplifies the concept in two ways. First, the number of data values and pointers for any given node is not restricted to 2 and 3, respectively. In its general form, a B-tree of order n can have at least n and no more than $2n$ data values. If it has k values, the B-tree will have $k + 1$ pointers. Second, B-trees typically have free space to permit rapid insertion of data values and possible updating of pointers when a new record is added.

As usual, there is a trade-off with B-trees. Retrieval will be fastest when each node occupies one page and is packed with data values and pointers. This lack of free space will slow down addition of new records, however. Most implementations of B+ tree permit a specified portion of free space to be defined for both the index and sequence set.

Hashing

Hashing reduces disk accesses by allowing direct access to a file. As you know, direct accessing via an index requires at least two or more accesses. The index must be loaded and searched, and then the record retrieved. For some applications, direct accessing via an index is too slow. Hashing can reduce the number of accesses to almost one by using the value in some field—the **hash field**, which is usually the primary key—to compute a record's address. A **hash function** converts the hash field into a **hash address.**

Consider the case of a university that uses the 9–digit Social Security number (SSN) as the student key. If the university has 10,000 students it could simply use the last four digits of the SSN as the address. In effect, the file space is broken up into 10,000 slots with one student record in each slot. For example, the data for the student with SSN 417-03-4356 would be stored at address 4356. In this case, the hash field is SSN, the hash function is

$$\text{hash address} = \text{remainder after dividing SSN by 10,000.}$$

What about the student with SSN 532-67-4356? Unfortunately, the hashing function will give the same address because most hashing schemes cannot guarantee a unique hash address for every record. When two hash fields have the same address, they are called synonyms, and a collision is said to have occurred.

There are techniques for handling synonyms. Essentially, you store the colliding record in an overflow area and point to it from the hash address. Of course, more than two records can have the same hash address, which in turn creates a synonym chain. Figure 11-9 shows an example of hashing with a synonym chain. Three SSNs hash to the same address. The first record (417-03-4356) is stored at the hash address. The second record (532-67-4356) is stored in the overflow area and is connected by a pointer to the first record. The third record

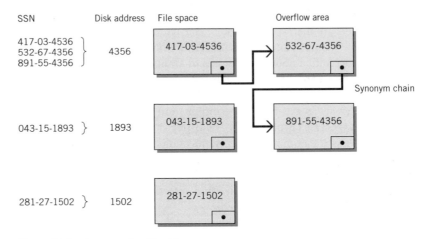

Figure 11-9   An example of hashing

(891-55-4356) is also stored in the overflow area and connected by a pointer from the second record. Because each record contains the full key, SSN in this case, during retrieval the system can determine whether it has the correct record or should follow the chain to the next record.

If there are no synonyms, hashing gives very fast direct retrieval, taking only one disk access to retrieve a record. Even with a small percentage of synonyms, retrieval via hashing is very fast. Access time degrades, however, if there are long synonym chains.

There are a number of different approaches to defining hashing functions. The most common method is to divide by a prime and use the remainder as the address. Before adopting a particular hashing function, test several functions on a representative sample of the hash field. Compute the percentage of synonyms and the length of synonym chains for each potential hashing function and compare the results.

Of course, hashing has trade-offs. There can be only one hashing field. In contrast, a file can have many indexed fields. The file can no longer be processed sequentially because its physical sequence loses any logical meaning if the records are not in primary key sequence or sequenced on any other field.

Linked Lists

A **linked list** is a useful data structure for inter-file clustering. Suppose that the query "Find all stocks of country X" is a frequent request. Disk accesses can be reduced by storing a nation and its corresponding stocks together in a linked list (see Figure 11-10).

In this example, we have two files: NATION and STOCK. Records in NATION are connected by pointers (e.g., the horizontal arrow between 'Australia' and 'USA'). The pointers

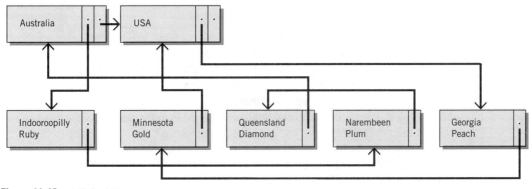

Figure 11-10   A linked list

are used to maintain the NATION file in logical sequence (by nation, in this case). Each record in NATION is linked to its STOCK records by a forward–pointing chain. The NATION record for 'Australia' points to the first STOCK record (Indooroopilly Ruby), which points to the next (Narembeen Plum), which points to the final record in the chain (Queensland Diamond). Notice that the last record in this STOCK chain points to the STOCK record to which the chain belongs (i.e., 'Australia'). Similarly, there is a chain for the two 'USA' stocks. In any chain, the records are maintained in logical sequence (by firm name, in this case).

This linked list structure is also known as a parent/child structure. (The parent in this case is NATION, and the child is STOCK.) Although it is a suitable structure for representing a 1:m relationship, it is possible to depict more than one parent/child relationship. For example, stocks could be grouped into classes (e.g., high, medium, and low risk). A second chain linking all stocks of the same risk class can run through the file. Inter-file clustering of a nation and its corresponding stocks will speed up access, so the record for the parent 'Australia' and its three children should be stored on one page. Similarly, all American stocks could be clustered with the 'USA' record, and so on for all other nations.

Of course, you expect some trade-offs. What happens with a query like "Find the country in which 'Minnesota Gold' is listed?" There is no quick way to find 'Minnesota Gold' except by sequentially searching the STOCK file until the record is found, and then following the chain to the parent NATION record. This could take many disk accesses. One way to circumvent this is to build an index or hashing scheme for STOCK so that any record can be found directly. Building an index for the parent, NATION, will speed up access as well.

Linked lists come in a variety of flavors. Some variations are:

- There can be two-way pointers, both forward and backward. These speed up deletion.
- Every child record can have a parent pointer. This helps prevent chain traversal when the query is concerned with finding the parent of a particular child.

The Tera Database That Is Eating Chicago

Information Resources, Inc.'s (IRI) proprietary database of supermarket data hit 1.7 Tbytes in May 1993. The T stands for tera—the prefix for one trillion or 10^{12}. It would take about 1.5 million 3.5-inch (9 cm) diskettes, each holding 1.2 Mbytes, to store 2 Tbytes. That amounts to a stack of diskettes about three miles (5 km) high! Fed by scanners in 3000 supermarkets, the database is growing at the rate of 100 Gbytes per month. Supermarket suppliers use a consolidated version of the database to track regional buying patterns for the one million products available nationwide.

To prevent the database from becoming unwieldy, IRI carves it into 10 to 20 G slices. Each slice contains data about hundreds of product categories. IRI must balance the value of storing consolidated data in one huge database against the personnel and equipment associated with operating it.

IRI is not alone. United Parcel Services, Inc. (UPS) has a database exceeding 1.5 Tbytes that keeps track of 12 million packages each day. The marketing intelligence database that NYNEX uses in the development of new products and services exceeds 400 Gbytes.[2]

DATA STORAGE DEVICES[3]

Database designers must make three important decisions in choosing which data storage devices will be used for:

1. on-line data;

Table 11–2   A Byte Size Table

Prefix	Size
k - kilo	10^3
M - mega	10^6
G - giga	10^9
T - tera	10^{12}
P - peta	10^{15}
E - exa	10^{18}

---

[2]Adapted from J. S. Bozman, "Grappling with Huge Databases," *Computerworld*, 31 May 1993, 57.

[3]Caveat: This section details characteristics of various devices such as storage capacity, access time, and transfer speed, but technological change can quickly date this information. Use the figures as comparative measures rather than absolute values.

2. backup files;

3. archival storage.

Many systems require data to be on-line—continually available. Here the prime concerns are usually access speed and capacity because many users require rapid response to large volumes of data. Backup files are required to provide security against data loss. Ideally, backup storage is high volume capacity at low cost. Archived data may need to be stored for many years, so the archival medium should be highly reliable, with no data decay over extended periods, and low cost.

In deciding what data will be stored where, database designers need to consider a number of variables:

1. volume of data;

2. volatility of data;

3. required speed of access to data;

4. cost of data storage;

5. reliability of the data storage medium;

6. legal standing of stored data.

These design choices are discussed and considered in terms of the variables just identified.

Magnetic Technology

More than $50 billion is spent annually on magnetic storage devices. Between one-third and one-half of IS hardware budgets are spent on magnetic storage. On-line storage growth rates are in the region of 15 (mid–range and mainframes) to 40 percent (supercomputers and networks) per year.[4] Magnetic technology, the backbone of data storage for four decades, is based on magnetization and demagnetization of spots on a magnetic recording surface. The same spot can be magnetized and demagnetized repeatedly, so spots can be altered many times. Magnetic recording materials may be coated on rigid platters (hard disks), flexible circular substrates (floppy disks), thin ribbons of material (magnetic tapes), or rectangular sheets (magnetic cards).

The main advantages of magnetic technology are its relative maturity and widespread use. For example, nearly every personal computer has a floppy disk drive, and most mainframe computers have a nine–track magnetic tape drive. Thus, floppy disks and nine–track tapes are common distribution media for micro and mainframe computer files and programs. A major disadvantage is susceptibility to strong magnetic fields, which can corrupt data stored on a disk. Another shortcoming is data storage life. Magnetization decays with time, and magnetic tape and disks are not suitable for long-term archival storage.

As organizations convert paper to images, they need a very long-term, unalterable storage medium for documents that could be tabled in legal proceedings (e.g., a customer's

---

[4]D. Vellante, *RAID: The Future of Intelligent Storage Subsystems.* (White paper), International Data Corporation, 1993.

A disk storage unit.

handwritten insurance claim or a client's completed form for a mutual fund investment). Because data resident on magnetic media can be readily changed and decays with time, it is not a good medium for storing archival data or legal documents.

Fixed Magnetic Disk

A **fixed magnetic disk** containing one or more recording surfaces is permanently mounted in the disk drive and cannot be removed. The recording surfaces and access mechanism are assembled in a clean room and then sealed to eliminate contaminants, making the device more reliable and permitting higher recording density and transfer rates. Access time is typically between 10 to 30 ms and transfer rates can be as high as 10 Mbytes per second. Disk unit capacities range from 40 Mbytes to 1 Tbytes. Magnetic disk units are often called direct-access storage devices or DASD (pronounced "dasdee").

High Drives From EMC

In May 1994, EMC Corp. announced a series of mainframe disk arrays with capacities ranging from 45 Gbytes to 1 Tbytes (see the adjoining table). EMC claims that average access time is 17.5 ms.

EMC's disk arrays are aimed at firms for whom capacity is more important than speed. In some cases, they replace tape libraries. For example, General Accident plans to move some of its claims and customer records from tape to a disk array to provide faster access to data.[5]

Model	Disk capacity	I/O per second	Starting price
5200-3	45G-90 Gbytes	2,000	$450,000
5200-9	68G-272 Gbytes	2,000	$549,450
5500-9	272G-1 Tbytes	4,000	$1,525,300

Fixed disk is the medium of choice for most systems, from personal computers to super-computers. It gives rapid, direct access to large volumes of data, and is ideal for highly volatile files. The major disadvantage of magnetic disk is the possibility of a head crash that destroys the disk surface and data. With the read/write head of a disk just 15 millionths of an inch (40 millionths of a centimeter) above the surface of the disk, there is little margin for error. Hence, it is crucial to regularly make backup copies of hard disk files.

RAID

RAID (redundant arrays of inexpensive or independent drives) is a recent development that takes advantage of the economies of scales in manufacturing disks for the personal comput-ing market. The cost of hard drives increases with their capacity and speed. RAID's idea is to use several cheaper drives whose total cost is less than one high capacity drive. As well as lower cost, RAID offers greater data security. All RAID levels (except level 0) can reconstruct the data on any single disk from the data stored on the remaining disks in the array in a man-ner that is quite transparent to the user.

RAID uses a combination of **mirroring** or **striping** to provide greater data protection. When a file is written to a mirrored array (see Figure 11-11), the disk controller writes identi-cal copies of each record to each drive in the array. When a file is read from a mirrored array, the controller reads alternate pages simultaneously from each of the drives. It then puts these pages together in the correct sequence before delivering them to the computer. Mirroring re-duces data access time by approximately the number of drives in the array. Access times are halved for a two-drive array, quartered for a four-drive array, and so on. If a read error oc-curs on a particular disk, the controller can always read the required page from another drive in the array since each drive has a full copy of the file. Mirroring, which requires at least two drives, improves response time and data security; however, it does take considerably more space to store a file because multiple copies are created.

When a file is written to a striping array (see Figure 11-12) of three drives, for instance, one half of the file is written to the first drive and the second half to the second drive. The third drive

[5]Adapted from C. Stedman, "EMC Boosts DASD Performance with Symmetrix Series," *Computerworld*, 6 June 1994, 67.

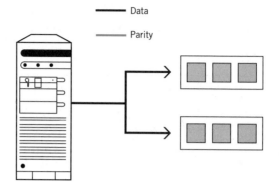

Figure 11-11   Mirroring

is used for error correction. A parity bit is constructed for each corresponding pair of bits written to drives one and two and written to the third drive. When a file is read by a striping array, portions are retrieved from each drive and assembled in the correct sequence by the controller. If a read error occurs, the lost bits can be reconstructed by using the parity data on the third drive. If a drive fails, it can be replaced, and the missing data restored on the new drive. Striping requires at least three drives. Normally data are written to every drive but one, and that remaining drive is used for the parity bit. Striping gives added data security without requiring considerably more storage, but it does not give the same response time increase as mirroring.

RAID subsystems are divided into six levels labeled 0 through 5. All RAID levels, except level 0, have common features:

- There is a set of physical disk drives viewed by the operating system as a single, logical drive.
- Data are distributed across corresponding physical drives.
- Parity information is used to recover data in the event of a disk failure.

Level 0 has been in use for many years. Data are broken into blocks that are interleaved or "striped" across disks. By spreading data over multiple drives, read and write operations can

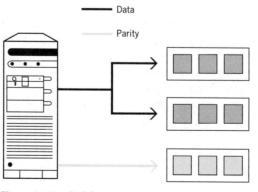

Figure 11-12   Striping

occur in parallel. As a result, I/O rates are higher, which makes level 0 ideal for I/O intensive applications such as recording video. There is no additional parity information, and thus no data recovery when a drive failure occurs.

Level 1 implements mirroring, as described previously. This is possibly the most popular form of RAID because of its effectiveness for critical non-stop applications, although high levels of data availability and I/O rates are counteracted by higher storage costs. Another disadvantage is that every write command must be executed twice (assuming a two–drive array), and thus level 1 is inappropriate for applications that have a high ratio of writes to reads.

Level 2 implements striping by interleaving blocks of data on each disk and maintaining parity on the check disk. This is a poor choice when an application has frequent, short random disk accesses because every disk in the array is accessed for each read operation, but it provides excellent data transfer rates for large sequential data requests. It is therefore suitable for CAD/CAM and multimedia applications, which typically use large sequential files. RAID 2 is rarely used, however, because the same effect can be achieved with level 3 at lower cost.

Level 3 utilizes striping at the bit or byte level, so only one I/O operation can be executed at a time. Compared to level 1, RAID level 3 gives lower cost data storage at lower I/O rates, and tends to be most useful for the storage of large amounts of data common with CAD/CAM and imaging applications.

Level 4 uses sector level striping, thus only a single disk needs to be accessed for a read request. Write requests are slower, however, because there is only one parity drive.

Level 5 (see Figure 11-13), a variation of striping, reads and writes data to separate disks independently and permits simultaneous reading and writing of data. Data and parity are written on the same drive. Spreading parity data evenly across several drives avoids the bottleneck that can occur when there is only one parity drive. RAID 5 is well designed for the high I/O rates required by transaction processing systems and servers. It is the most balanced implementation of the RAID concept in terms of price, reliability, and performance. It requires less capacity than mirroring with level 1 and higher I/O rates than striping with level 3, although performance can decrease with update-intensive operations. RAID 5 is frequently found in LAN environments.

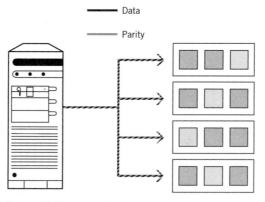

Figure 11-13   RAID level 5

RAID does have drawbacks. It often lowers systems performance in return for greater reliability and increased protection against data loss. Extra disk space is required to store redundant information. Extra disk accesses are required to access and update redundant information. You should remember that RAID is not a replacement for standard backup procedures; it is a technology for increasing the fault tolerance of critical on-line systems. Smaller RAID systems are in the 5 to 10 Gbytes range, and large systems can offer as much as a terabyte of storage.

Lost Time Is Lost Money

Investment banking at Lehman Brothers is a 24-hour-a-day, seven-day-a-week business. There is no time for downtime. A missed deadline can mean the loss of a billion-dollar deal. Although disk mirroring protects data, it does not ensure non-stop operations. A drive failure, which can crash a server, usually forces a server to be taken off-line while the failed drive is replaced.

To hedge against this possibility, Lehman Brothers has installed 4 Gbyte RAID 5 systems on its some 20 LAN servers. It now has a storage system that has a very low probability of failure. There is still the danger that two drives may fail at the same time, but Lehman takes extra efforts to protect against dual failures. Lehman selected a RAID system that its off-hours support staff could easily maintain. If a drive fails, the support staff simply replaces it. There is no need to wait for an engineer to arrive. Furthermore, when a drive fails, the system automatically pages a technician. Lehman Brothers would also like each drive to have dual power supplies, with dual plugs connected to different power sources.[6]

Removable Magnetic Disk

A **removable disk** comes in two formats: single disk and disk pack. The single disk of 40 to 100 Mbytes capacity is used with personal computers, and is typically inserted, like a floppy disk, into a drive.

Disk packs consist of multiple disks mounted together on a common spindle in a stack, usually on a disk drive with retractable read/write heads. Because they are unsealed and exposed to possible contamination, storage densities and transfer rates are considerably lower than fixed disk.

The disk's removability is its primary advantage, making it ideal for backup. For example, an organization may regularly copy its fixed disk storage to multiple disk packs. Removable disk is also useful when applications need not be continuously on-line. For instance, the monthly payroll system can be stored on a removable disk pack and mounted when required.

---

[6]Adapted from S. Marks, "Why I Use RAID," *Computerworld*, 14 March 1994, 99.

Removable magnetic media.

Floppy Disk

Floppy disks are used primarily with microcomputers. Currently the most popular format, the 3.5 inch (9 cm) disk has a storage capacity of 1.44 Mbytes. Transfer rates are very low when compared to fixed disk. Their inexpensiveness makes them ideal for storing and transporting small files and programs, but because people are careless about handling or storing them, floppies do not score highly on reliability. A speck of dust can easily cause a read error.

Magnetic Tape

A **magnetic tape** is a thin ribbon of plastic coated with ferric oxide. The commonly used nine-track 2400 foot (730 m) tape has a capacity of around 160 Mbytes and a data transfer rate of 2 Mbytes per second. The designation nine-track means nine bits are stored across the tape (8 bits plus one parity bit). Magnetic tape was used extensively for archiving and backup in early database systems; however, its limited capacity and sequential nature have resulted in its replacement by other media.

Magnetic Tape Cartridges

Tape cartridges, with a capacity exceeding 200 Mbytes and transfer rates of up to 3 Mbytes per second, have replaced magnetic tape. Easier handling is another feature favoring them over magnetic tape reels. The more recently developed digital data storage (DAT) cartridge offers storage capacity of 1 to 5 Gbytes for between $1000 and $2500 per unit and transfer rates of up to 500 kbytes per second.

Mass Storage

There exist a variety of **mass storage** devices that automate labor-intensive tape and cartridge handling. The storage medium, with capacities of hundreds of Gbytes, is typically located and mounted by a robotic arm.

Optical Technology

Optical technology is a more recent development than magnetic. Its advantages are high storage densities, low cost medium, and direct access. There are three storage media based on optical technology: CD-ROM, WORM, and magneto-optical (see Figure 11-14). All use a laser for reading and writing data, but because the method of recording data differs, media are not interchangeable. For instance, a CD-ROM drive cannot read a magneto-optical disk.

Most optical disks can reliably store records for at least 10 years under prescribed conditions of humidity and temperature. Actual storage life may be in the region of 30 to 50 years. Optical technology is extremely reliable because it is not susceptible to head crashes.

CD-ROM

In the early 1980s, engineers at Phillips and Sony independently recognized that compact disks (CD) could store data as well as sound. In 1986, these two companies introduced the **CD-ROM** format. (ROM stands for read-only memory.) The storage capacity of a CD-ROM is significantly greater than a floppy diskette. Measuring around 5 inches (12 cm) in diameter, a CD-ROM stores some 650 Mbytes of data, whereas a typical floppy diskette of around the same physical dimensions has an upper limit of about 1 Mbyte. CD-ROM drives, with access times in the region of 200 to 300 ms, are relatively slow devices. Transfer rates vary from 300 to 600 kbytes per second.

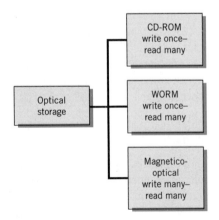

Figure 11-14   Optical storage media

There are considerable gains from using the same medium for both music and data. In particular, many of the same components and technology can be used for CD players and CD-ROM drives. Economies of scale can be exploited, and the cost of both products lowered. CD-ROM drives cost between $250 and $500. They can be somewhat cheaper, however, when purchased as part of a personal computer system.

CD-ROM is a compact, robust, high capacity medium for the storage of permanent data. Initial thinking was that it would be used for storing relatively non-volatile databases, documents, directories, and other archival information. It was anticipated that major customers for these mainly text data stores would be libraries and businesses (e.g., a CD-ROM containing state-by-state details of 118 million registered voters). Indeed, this market has developed, but the major growth is in the consumer market for multimedia encyclopedias, games, and educational material. *The New Grolier Multimedia Encyclopedia,* costing around $100, contains the text of all 21 volumes of the *Academic American Encyclopedia* and includes thousands of pictures, hundreds of maps, sound, animation, and video. The full 633 Mbytes of information come on a single CD.

As indicated previously, organizations can use CD-ROM for low-volatility databases and archival information. A recording CD drive costs about $8000, and a blank CD-ROM is around $25. CD-ROM's main advantage is that the format can be read by the large number of CD-ROM drives now installed. CD-ROM is becoming the preferred medium for information distribution and multimedia applications.

Data stored on CD-ROM possibly has the highest legal standing of any of the forms discussed because once written, the data cannot be altered. Thus, it is ideal for storage of documents that potentially may be used in court.

Feds Cut Magnetic Tape

Federal government agencies are moving from magnetic tape to CD-ROM for storing archival data. At one NASA facility, 200 magnetic tapes per day are copied to CD-ROMs. NASA is also attaching two CD-ROM jukeboxes to the Internet so that more than 2500 Gbytes of data will be available to scientists worldwide.

CD-ROMs are a more cost-effective way of distributing large databases. Previously, the U.S. Geological Survey (USGS) had used magnetic tape; now it sells data on CD-ROMs. Seismic data that once required 640 magnetic tapes and cost $89,000 is now available on 39 CD-ROMs for $1248. The USGS also publishes a CD-ROM containing 560 high-resolution color photographs of natural disasters—earthquakes, volcanoes, and so forth. All 560 pictures can be purchased on a single CD-ROM for $32. Before, the pictures cost $10 each.[7]

---

[7]Adapted from G. H. Anthes, "Feds Moving Data to CD-ROM," *Computerworld,* 7 February 1994, 72.

WORM

WORM (write-once read-many) is the major storage device for images. Information once written to a blank disk cannot be altered. This is a particularly useful feature for data that must be stored for long periods. From a legal standpoint, it is important to have a storage medium that cannot be easily altered. Thus, WORM is an ideal medium for storing correspondence and legal documents.

Access time for WORM disks is around 150 to 250 ms, with data transfer rates of 256 kbytes per second. Three common disk sizes are available: 5.25 inches (13 cm), 12 inches (30 cm), and 14 inches (36 cm). The 14-inch disk can store as many as 10 Gbytes.

WORM *jukeboxes* are used to store high volumes of data. A jukebox may contain up to 2000 WORM disks. Just like a conventional jukebox, a particular WORM disk can be loaded onto the drive, spun up to speed, and read. A WORM jukebox makes terabytes of data available in about 10 seconds.

WORM does not quite have the legal standing of CD-ROM because it is possible for a smart hacker to selectively add a document or modify an existing image. Although there are some techniques to prevent this from happening, WORM nevertheless is not as secure as CD-ROM.

A WORM disk unit.

An optical disk system.

Magneto-Optical Disk

Magneto-optical disks are a high capacity read–write medium. Drives and media come in two sizes—3.5 inches (9 cm) and 5.25 inches (13.5 cm). Respectively, the disks store 128 Mbytes and 650 Mbytes on one side. While most drives are single-sided, there are some double-sided drives that effectively double the capacity of a magneto-optical disk. An ISO standard for 3.5 inch and 5.25 inch optical-disk media makes for free exchange of disks across same size drives of manufacturers who follow this standard.

Magneto-optical disks are a compact, high capacity, reliable, data transfer and archival storage medium. The smaller disks are suitable for personal computer storage and backup. Also, they can be used to distribute data within an organization. The 5.25-inch disks are particularly well-suited for backup of databases under about 5 Gbytes or transfer of large files.

Optical technology is also highly reliable since there is no possibility of a head crash, and stored data has a life of around 30 years. At this stage, access speeds are two to three times longer than magnetic disk.

It's Clearly Optical, Dr. Watson

University professors, especially in MIS, typically have a computer at their office and another at home because they work in both places. There tend to be many interruptions at a faculty office that interfere with time-consuming tasks, such as writing a database book. Thus, many professors do much of their writing at home. With the advent of personal computers, quite a few faculty have moved to direct composition at their personal computer.

Naturally, this means transporting files to and from the two personal computers. Floppy diskettes are a suitable transport medium for a while, but eventually files get scattered across too many diskettes, and the author forgets where they are. Even worse, the project may get too large for all the files to fit on one floppy. For example, the text and graphics for this book occupy about 4 Mbytes. After a few too many frustrating floppy shuffles in loading each floppy to check its directory or loading files to the hard disk, it is time to find a better solution.

The author of this book uses 3.5-inch magneto-optical disks for data transfer and backup. He has a 3.5-inch magneto-optical drive on each machine and all his files on a single disk, which makes transfer between university and home offices very easy.

This problem is not endemic to university professors. Many knowledge workers and business professionals have personal computers at work and home, so magneto-optical disks seem particularly well-suited for personal data transfer.

Details of the various storage devices are summarized in Table 11-3. A simple three star rating system has been used for each device—the more stars, the better. In regard to access speed, RAID gets more stars than floppy disk because it retrieves a stored record more quickly. Similarly, magneto-optical rates three stars because it costs less per megabyte to store data on a magneto-optical disk than a fixed disk. The scoring system is relative. The fact that floppy disk gets a low score for reliability does not mean it is an unreliable storage medium; it simply means that it is not as reliable as other media.

CONCLUSION

The internal and physical aspects of database design are a key determinant of system performance. Selection of appropriate data structures can substantially curtail disk accesses and reduce response times. In making data structure decisions, the database administrator needs to weigh the pros and cons of each choice. Similarly, in selecting data storage devices, the designer needs to be aware of the trade-offs. Various devices and media have both strengths and weaknesses, and these need to be considered.

Table 11–3   Relative Merits of Data Storage Devices

Device	Access speed	Volume	Volatility	Cost per megabyte	Reliability	Legal standing
Fixed disk	***	***	***	**	**	*
RAID	***	***	***	**	***	*
Removable disk	**	**	***	**	**	*
Floppy	*	*	***	*	*	*
Tape	*	**	*	***	**	*
Cartridge	**	***	*	***	**	*
Mass storage	**	***	*	***	**	*
CD-ROM	*	***	*	***	***	***
WORM	*	***	*	***	***	**
Magneto-optical	**	***	**	***	***	*

Legend

Characteristic	More stars means . . .
Access speed	faster access to data
Volume	more suitable for large files
Volatility	more suitable for files that change frequently
Cost per megabyte	less costly form of storage
Reliability	less susceptible to an unrecoverable read error
Legal standing	more acceptable as evidence in court

SUMMARY

It takes considerably longer to retrieve data from a magnetic disk than from main memory. Appropriate selection of data structures and data access methods can considerably reduce delays by reducing disk accesses. The key characteristics of disk storage devices that affect database access are rotational speed and access arm speed. Access arm movement can be minimized by storing frequently used data on the same track on a single surface, or on the same track on different surfaces. Records that are frequently used together should be clustered together. Intra-file clustering applies to the records within a single file. Inter-file clustering applies to multiple files. The disk manager, the part of the operating system responsible for physical I/O, maintains a directory of pages. The file manager, a level above the disk manager, contains a directory of files.

Indexes are used to speed up retrieval by reducing disk accesses. An index is a file containing the value of the index field and the address of its full record. The use of indexes involves a trade-off between faster retrievals and slower updates. Indexes can be used for both sequential and direct access. A file can have multiple indexes. A sparse index does not contain an entry for every value of the indexed field. The B-tree is a particular form of index structure. It is the basis for IBM's VSAM, the file structure underlying DB2, and is an efficient structure for both sequential and direct accessing. It consists of two parts, the sequence set and the index set. Hashing is a technique for reducing disk accesses that allows direct access to a file. There can be only one hashing field. A hashed file can no longer be processed sequentially because its physical sequence has lost any logical meaning. A linked list is a useful data structure for inter-file clustering. It is a suitable structure for representing a 1 : m relationship. Pointers between records are used to maintain a logical sequence. Lists can have forward, backward, and parent pointers.

Systems designers have to decide what data storage devices will be used for on-line data, backup files, and archival storage. In making this decision, they must consider the volume of data, volatility of data, required speed of access to data, cost of data storage, reliability of the data storage medium, and the legal standing of the stored data. Magnetic technology, the backbone of data storage for four decades, is based on magnetization and demagnetization of spots on a magnetic recording surface. Fixed disk, removable disk, magnetic tape, floppy disk, tape cartridge, and mass storage are examples of magnetic technology. RAID, a recent magnetic technology development, uses several cheaper drives whose total cost is less than one high capacity drive. RAID uses a combination of mirroring or striping to provide greater data protection. RAID subsystems are divided into six levels labeled 0 through 5. Optical technology, a more recent development, offers high storage densities, low cost medium, and direct access. CD-ROM, WORM, and magneto-optical are examples of optical technology. Optical disks can reliably store records for at least 10 years and possibly up to 30 years. Optical technology is not susceptible to head crashes.

KEY TERMS AND CONCEPTS

Access time	Hashing
Archival file	Index
B-tree	Index set
Backup file	Inter-file clustering
CD-ROM	Internal schema
Clustering	Intra-file clustering
Conceptual schema	Linked list
Cylinder	Magnetic disk
Data storage device	Magnetic tape
Database architecture	Magneto-optical disk
Disk manager	Mass storage
External schema	Mirroring
File manager	Page
Hash address	Parity
Hash field	Pointer
Hash function	RAID

Sequence set   Track
Sparse index   VSAM
Striping   WORM

EXERCISES

1. Why is a disk drive considered a bottleneck?
2. What is the difference between a record and a page?
3. Describe the two types of delay that can occur prior to reading a record from a disk. What can be done to reduce these delays?
4. What is clustering? What is the difference between intra-file and inter-file clustering?
5. Describe the differences between a file manager and a disk manager.
6. What is an index?
7. What are the advantages and disadvantages of indexing?
8. Write the SQL to create an index on the column NATCODE in the NATION table.
9. A Paris insurance firm keeps paper records of all policies and claims made on it. The firm now has a vault containing 100 filing cabinets full of forms. Because Paris rental costs are so high, the CEO has asked you to recommend a more compact medium for long-term storage of these documents. Because some insurance claims are contested, she is very concerned with ensuring that documents, once stored, cannot be altered. What would you recommend and why?
10. The national weather research center of a large South American country has asked you to recommend a data storage strategy for its historical weather data. The center electronically collects hourly weather information from 2000 sites around the country. This database must be maintained indefinitely. Periodically, weather researchers extract a portion of these data for their use. A researcher must submit a written request detailing what data are required and the purpose of the study. After review of the request, the center sets up a data file on a file server. The center's director is very concerned with cost and wants to minimize the cost of data storage. What would you recommend and why?
11. The national aviation authority in your country has asked you to recommend a data storage device for its air traffic control system. The specification states that the file is relatively small (around 500 megabytes) and system reliability is the foremost criterion. What would you recommend and why?
12. A magazine subscription service has a toll-free number for customers, who may dial the company to place orders, inquire about existing orders, or check subscription rates. All customers are uniquely identified by a 11-digit numeric code. All magazines are identified by a 2 to 4-character code. The company has approximately 10 million customers who subscribe to an average of 4 magazines. Subscriptions are available to 126 magazines. Draw a data model for this situation. Decide what data structures you would recommend for the storage of the data for each entity. The management of the company prides itself on its customer service and strives to answer customer queries as rapidly as possible.

13. A German consumer research company collects scanning data from supermarkets throughout central Europe. The scanned data include product code identifier, price, quantity purchased, time, date, supermarket location, and supermarket name, and in some cases where the supermarket has a frequent buyer plan, it collects a consumer identification code. It has also created a table containing details of the manufacturer of each product. The database is very large and contains nearly one terabyte of data. The data are used by market researchers in consumer product companies. A researcher will typically request access to a slice of the database (e.g., sales of all detergents) and analyze these data for trends and patterns. The consumer research company promises rapid access to its data. Its goal is to give clients access to requested data within one to two minutes. Once clients have access to the data, they expect very rapid response to queries. What data storage and retrieval strategy would you recommend?

14. The navy of a large industrial power has many modern ships. Because of the technology and complexity of these ships, many thick, paper manuals are required to describe how to operate, maintain, and repair the many shipboard electronic and mechanical devices. In fact, there are so many manuals, one wag suggested ships could be 10 percent smaller if they did not have to carry so much paper. What advice do you have for this navy?

15. A video producer has asked for your advice on a data storage device. She has specified that she must be able to record video at 5 to 7 Mbytes per second. What would you recommend and why?

Chapter 12

Data Storage and Data Processing Architectures

The difficulty in life is the choice.

George Moore, *The Bending of the Bough,* 1900

Learning Objectives

On completion of this chapter, you will be able to:

- recommend a data storage and data processing architecture for a given situation;
- discuss the fundamental principles that a hybrid architecture should satisfy.

On a recent transatlantic flight, Sophie, the Personnel and PR manager, had been seated next to a very charming young man who had tried to impress her with his knowledge of computing. He worked for a large systems consulting firm, and his speech was sprinkled with words like "client/server," "gooey," "host," "LAN," and "distributed database." In return, Sophie responded with some "ums," "aahs," and a sprinkling of "that's interesting." Of course, this was before the third glass of champagne. After that, he was more intent on finding out how long Sophie would be in New York and what restaurants and shows piqued her curiosity.

After an extremely pleasant week of wining, dining, and seeing the town—amidst, of course, many hours of valuable work for The Expeditioner—Sophie returned to London. Now, she must ask Ned what all these weird terms meant. After all, it was difficult to carry on a conversation when you did not understand the language. That's the problem with IS, she thought, new words and technologies were always being invented. It makes it very hard for the rest of us to make sense of what's being said.

INTRODUCTION

The ANSI/SPARC architecture was developed during an earlier era of information systems. It is a product of the period when mainframe computers were dominant and personal computers were nonexistent. Now, personal computers have extended the range of architectures available for implementing the ANSI/SPARC model. The three levels of internal, conceptual, and external are still valid, but the internal level needs to be extended to include data processing in addition to data storage.

In the mainframe era, all data were stored and processed on the mainframe. The advent of personal computers on users' desks provides a choice for data storage and processing. In general terms, data can be stored and processed locally or remotely. Combinations of these two options provide four basic architectures (see Figure 12-1). Client/server, which is not exclusively local data processing and remote storage, is shown as overlapping adjacent quadrants.

Remote Job Entry

Remote job entry describes the situation where data are stored locally and processed remotely. Data are sent over a communication link to a remote computer for processing and the output is returned the same way. This fairly common form of data processing is still being used today because remote job entry can overcome three shortcomings of personal computers. First, a personal computer may be too slow. Scientists and engineers need occasional access to a supercomputer for computationally intensive applications. Second, a personal computer may have insufficient main memory. Mainframe computers typically have larger amounts of main memory and can handle larger problems more easily. Third, highly specialized software is not available on the user's personal computer. For example, some statistical and mathematical modeling routines have not been ported to personal computers.

Local storage is used for several reasons. First, it may be cheaper than storing on a mainframe, whose management will charge for storage space. Second, the user may be able to do some local processing and preparation of the data before sending it to the mainframe. Mainframe and supercomputing time can be expensive and, where possible, local processing is used for tasks such as data entry, validation, and reporting. Third, users may feel that local data storage is more secure for particularly sensitive data.

Figure 12-1   Basic architectures

A supercomputer.

Personal Database

Users can store and process their data locally when they have their own computers. Many personal computer database systems now permit users to develop their own applications, and there are many programs available for common applications that require database facilities.

There are a number of reasons favoring personal databases. First, the competitiveness and economies of scale of the microcomputer market make personal computers a low cost alternative for data storage and processing. Second, users are independent of the mainframe and the information systems department. They have greater control and can develop their own

A mainframe computer.

software. The application backlog of most IS departments means that users often have a very long wait for IS department-developed systems. Third, personal computing software is generally friendlier than mainframe systems. The Windows and Macintosh operating systems make personal computers far easier to use. Fourth, the size of the personal computing market has attracted many software companies, and most leading-edge applications are written for personal computers. So, personal computer users have a wide choice of user-friendly software for a wide range of applications.

Of course, there is a downside to personal databases. First, there is a great danger of repetition and redundancy. The same application gets developed in a slightly different way by many users. The same data get stored on many different systems. (It is not always the same, however, because data entry errors or maintenance inconsistencies result in discrepancies across personal databases.) Second, data are not readily shared because various users are not aware of what is available or find it inconvenient to share data. Personal databases are exactly that; but much of the data may be of corporate value and should be shared. Third, data integrity procedures are often quite lax for personal databases. Users rarely make backups, databases are not secured from unauthorized access, and data validation procedures are often ignored. Fourth, often when the user leaves the organization or moves to another role, the application and data are lost because they are not documented and the organization is unaware of their existence. Fifth, there is a danger that users get addicted to developing software and ignore their assigned work. The job of managers is to manage, not write software or

A personal computer.

build personal databases. Personal databases are clearly very important for many organizations—when used appropriately. Data that are shared require a different processing architecture.

Host/Terminal

The **host/terminal** approach was the initial solution to making data accessible to many users. Under this architecture, data storage and processing occur at one location, typically a mainframe computer. In smaller organizational units, this might be a mini or midframe computer. Users have terminals linked to the central computer by communication lines. These terminals have minimal processing capability and are used to display data and may do some limited formatting. More recently, personal computers have been substituted for terminals, but they are usually emulating a terminal and so have the same restricted processing capabilities. Host/terminal architecture was the basis of IBM's success for many years. Its mainframe computers, terminals, communication system, and supporting software were well-suited to handling large volumes of data and high transaction processing rates.

A generic host/terminal architecture consists of several key components (see Figure 12-2). Requirements include the operating system, a Data Communications manager (usually abbreviated to DC manager), and Database Management System (DBMS). The DC manager handles the transfer of data between application programs and terminals. This is sometimes called a Transaction Processing (TP) monitor. For example, when a user enters a query at a terminal, the DC manager handles its transmission from the terminal to the relevant application program. Next, after some processing (e.g., validating the query), the application program passes the query to the DBMS, which retrieves the required data and returns it to the application program. The application program may then do some additional processing of the data before passing it to the DC manager for transmission to the user's terminal. As you can see from this example, mainframe-resident software does all the work.

In a host/terminal setting, all shared resources are managed by the host. When additional processing capacity is required, the host must be upgraded or replaced. As a result, capacity changes tend to be very lumpy and required capacity is often out of balance with actual needs.

LAN-Based Architectures

File/server and DBMS/server systems are variations on client/server found on a local area network (LAN). Before we delve into these architectures, however, you need a brief overview of LANs. A **LAN** connects computers and devices within the same limited geographic area (e.g., a building). High performance communication connections enable data to be transferred on the LAN at speeds of up to 100 Mbytes per second. A LAN enables users to share expensive devices (e.g., laser printers), access shared files, and transfer files to others on the LAN. Its basic components include cabling to connect computers and devices, a card for each computer or device to connect it to the network, a file server for storing shared data, a network operating system (e.g., Novell's NetWare), and the computer and devices.

LAN technology is a direct result of the massive influx of personal computers into organi-

Figure 12-2   Host/terminal architecture

zations. People with personal computers soon discovered they wanted to access corporate databases, share data with colleagues, and share expensive devices—such as a laser printer—within a work group.

A server is a general purpose computer that provides and controls access to shareable resources such as applications, files, printers, fax machines, communication lines, and databases. A server must be able to support multiple, simultaneous requests for shared resources. A server can have a single purpose (e.g., a database server and nothing else) or manage multiple shared resources (e.g., a server handles sharing of a printer and multiple files).

In a client/server environment, shared resources are often managed by several servers. Capacity increases can be very gradual as additional servers are added or some servers upgraded. Compared to a host/terminal architecture, it is far easier to keep required and actual capacity in balance.

A file/server system.

File/Server

A **file/server** is a LAN computer with a large disk file (see Figure 12-3). It is a central data store for the network's users. Files are kept on the file server and processing occurs at the user's personal computer. This means that entire files are transferred on the LAN to an application running on a personal computer. For example, updating a file requires transfer of the file to the personal computer running the application, processing the update, and transferring the revised file to the file/server. Also, when a file is retrieved for update, it is locked. Other users cannot access the file until the changes have been made and the file rewritten to the server. Clearly, this approach is limited to small files and low demand. Network congestion occurs when file sizes are large, and there are multiple, active users.

File/server architecture is a relatively simple solution to data sharing on a local area network. Its shortcomings are addressed by DBMS/server architecture.

DBMS/Server

Another LAN approach to client/server architecture operates a DBMS on the server, which can run on the file server or a separate computer. It does most of the DBMS processing so that only necessary records are transferred across the network, thus reducing network traffic substantially. In addition, with a DBMS/server, locking can take place at the record rather than file level (see Chapter 18 for a more detailed discussion of locking).

There are two separate programs: the **DBMS/server,** sometimes known as the back-end, and the client part, the front-end, which resides on the user's personal computer. The follow-

Figure 12-3   File/server architecture

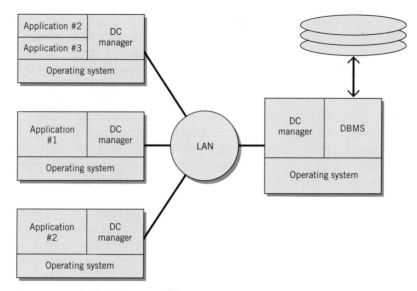

Figure 12-4   DBMS/server architecture

ing example illustrates how the processing load can be shared in a DBMS/server environment (see Figure 12-4). When a user enters a query at a personal computer, it is handled by the resident application program, which will do local processing such as query validation. The application program then hands, for example, an SQL query to the client DC manager for transmission to the server. At the server, the server DC manager picks up the query and passes it to the DBMS, which executes the query. The result of the query is passed to the server's DC manager for transmission to the client's DC manager. The client's DC manager then passes the result to the client application program for processing. Finally, the result of the query appears on the user's personal computer.

CLIENT/SERVER

File/server and DBMS/server are examples of **client/server** architecture, in which two processes interact as superior and subordinate. The client process initiates requests and the server responds. The client is the dominant partner because it initiates a request. Client and server processes can run on the same computer, but generally they run on separate, linked computers. Typically the client is a microcomputer and the server is a more powerful machine.

Client/server aims to take advantage of the lower processing cost of microcomputer technology. It is generally far cheaper to process data on a microcomputer than mainframe. Client/server exploits this cost differential by moving processing from the mainframe to minicomputers and personal computers. A mainframe can be a server, but generally it is cheaper to use high-speed microcomputers or minicomputers as servers. Generally, processing is split between the client and the server, with most of the processing performed by the client. It is also possible that some infrequently changed data is stored locally. For example, the company logo might appear on all screens. As a logo changes rarely, the image file containing the logo should be stored locally rather than transmitted across the network.

Because the client generally has a graphical user interface (GUI), cost savings also come from ease of use, reduced training costs, and productivity gains. Typically, client user interfaces, such as Windows and Macintosh, overcome many of the problems users have with the less friendly, character-based interface of older operating systems.

Lower processing costs are extolled as a major advantage of client/server systems, but this advantage can be gained only if processing can be shifted from a mainframe to clients. When minimal processing is required and there are a few common transactions, a mainframe can be a cheaper solution. If the mainframe is primarily a data store and does little processing, then there is little to be gained in shifting processing to a client. Furthermore, because there are only a few common transactions, there is little to be saved from reduced training and productivity increases. Many large scale transaction processing systems (e.g., an airline reservation system) fit this description. Also, these systems are very stable and have been running for many years. The cost of replacing thousands of terminals with personal computers and rewriting and testing software for a client/server setting is prohibitive.

Mainframe applications are appropriate for transfer to client/server when they are computationally intensive and have a small number of terminals. Processing can be shifted to the client and the cost of replacing a small number of terminals with personal computers is not too high. Some companies are replacing mainframe hardware with client/server technology when upgrading old systems or because they want to use workflow technology (see Chapter 16).

Architecture Arithmetic[1]

The key parameters to consider when comparing host/terminal with client/server are terminal versus personal computer costs, mainframe MIPS (millions of instructions per second) versus personal computer MIPS, and mainframe storage versus server storage. Terminals are about one-third the price of personal computers. Mainframe MIPS cost about 100 times more than personal computer costs. Mainframe storage costs are about double the server costs. Remember, personal computer and server characteristics are becoming far more favorable in terms of costs and over time more mainframe applications become candidates for client/server.

Host/terminal systems on mainframes provide a number of non-hardware related cost savings over client/server. Security, communication, and control are simpler and less costly when processing is mainframe resident. Backup and recovery are simpler for a few mainframes compared to many client/server networks. Mainframe expertise abounds, but few people have extensive client/server knowledge.

Client/server computing offers a number of important advantages over host/terminal.

---

[1]M. Kennedy and A. Gurbaxani, "When Client/Server Isn't Right," *Computerworld*, 19 April 1993, 99, 101.

There can be substantial cost savings by moving from a mainframe to client/server. A large construction company, Turner Corp., reports paring its $5 million IS budget in half by moving to client/server, and United Airlines expects to save $10 million over the next five years.[2] Many of these savings result from exchanging proprietary mainframes for open, or non-proprietary, servers and networked personal computers. Mainframe users were frequently locked into a single vendor's hardware and software whereas in client/server computing there is generally a choice of servers and clients in a highly competitive market. For instance, there are multiple suppliers of UNIX, a popular operating system for servers. So for many companies, the migration to client/server is more than just changing to lower cost hardware, it is an opportunity to escape an undue reliance on the products of a single vendor.

There are other cost savings. The friendly interface of personal computing operating systems lowers training costs and increases worker productivity. A versatile interface that supports a wide variety of tasks is necessary for applications such as decision support and workflow. A client/server application can give decision makers greater flexibility to analyze and present data. Development costs can be lower because personal computer GUI development software is more powerful than text-driven mainframe programming languages. Because these savings are also likely to transfer to software quality and application maintenance, client/server applications should be less expensive, have fewer bugs, and cost less to maintain.

New York State Department of Civil Service[3]

The Employee Benefits division of the New York State Department of Civil Service handles 1.2 million claims per year using a client/server architecture. The system replaces a paper- and mainframe-based system developed in the 1970s.

The server portion of the software runs on an IBM mainframe using IBM's DB2 DBMS at a Nebraska time-sharing service. The clients, PCs running Windows, are linked by leased lines to the mainframe. There are 150 networked PCs at the main office in Albany, NY. There are another 275 clients at other state agencies and local municipalities linked to the Albany office via 9600 baud modems. The department reduces server access costs by processing data at the client.

The result is a more flexible system that offers tighter controls and quicker response to employee claims. Estimated savings are around $1 million per year. Increased flexibility has come at the expense of speed, however. The client/server system is not considered as fast as an equivalent host/terminal architecture. It has also taken time to make people PC-literate.

This case, as with many that demonstrate the application of client/server, probably overstates the savings. When moving to client/server, many organizations redesign existing systems and these contribute to savings as well as hardware cost reductions.

---

[2]E. I. Schwartz, "Finally, Software That Slays Giants," *Business Week,* 15 March 1993, 96–98.

[3]Adapted from M. Vizard, "N.Y. Saves Big with Client/Server," *Computerworld,* 8 March 1993, 87, 89.

Table 12–1   Architecture Summary

Architecture	Main use
Remote job entry	Large scale scientific or engineering work
Personal	Stand-alone, small, personal systems
Host/terminal	Large scale transaction processing
Client/server	Flexible, friendly decision support and workflow

Most data management decisions require a trade-off. The decision to move from host/terminal architecture to client/server is no different. The costs and benefits of different architectures need to be closely investigated (see Table 12-1 for a summary).

Client/Server Designs

Client/server is a general approach to developing an architecture, consequently, there are many ways to do it. After studying more than 100 sites that had implemented a client/server architecture, IBM researchers were able to identify six major designs.[4] The first three patterns emerged from growing PC/workstation applications (see Table 12-2). The second set developed from downsizing mainframe applications (see Table 12-3).

Table 12–2   Client/Server Workstation Focus

Type	Description	Example
Resource centered	Workstation based applications with direct access to the data.	A hospital with clients accessing a relational database server.
Internetting	Application is split between the front- and back-end processors. Data is stored on the back-end.	Gopher information servers on the Internet.
Distributed data	Application is split between the front- and back-end processors. Data "snapshots" are taken periodically and downloaded to local servers.	Financial traders accessing data feeds from stock quotation services.

[4]D. A. Kelly, "Client/Server Journal," *Computerworld,* 11 August 1993, 6.

Table 12–3   Client/Server Mainframe Focus

Type	Description	Example
Front ending	Mainframe applications and database unchanged. Front-end applications add new business logic and possibly a GUI interface.	A customer service center for a credit card operation.
Distributed logic	Mainframe work is off-loaded as the application is split between front and back ends. Data is stored on the back-end processor.	A retail store.
Distributed data	Application is split between the front- and back-end processors, but the majority of the work load is handled by intermediate servers.	A retail bank with mission-critical data on the back-end mainframe and daily download of replicated data to branch offices.

DISTRIBUTED DATABASE

Client/server architecture is concerned with minimizing processing costs by distributing processing between the server and multiple clients. Another factor in the total processing cost equation is communication. The cost of transmitting data usually increases with distance, and there can be substantial savings by locating data close to those most likely to use it. The trade-off for a distributed database is lowered communication costs versus increased complexity.

Distributed database architecture describes the situation where a database is in more than one location but still accessible as if it were centrally located. For example, a multinational organization might locate its Indonesian data in Djakarta, Japanese data in Tokyo, and Australian data in Sydney (see Figure 12-5). If most queries deal with the local situation, communication costs are substantially lower than if the database were centrally located. Furthermore, since the database is still treated as one logical entity, queries that require access to different physical locations can be processed. For example, the query "Find total sales of red hats in Australia" is likely to originate in Australia and be processed using the Sydney part of the database. A query of the form "Find total sales of red hats" is more likely to come from a headquarters user and is resolved by accessing each of the local databases, though the user need not be aware of where the data are stored since the database appears as a single logical entity.

A distributed database system (DDBMS) is a federation of individual DBMSs. Each site has a local DBMS and DC manager. In many respects, each site acts semi-independently. Each site also contains additional software that enables it to be part of the federation and act as a single database. It is this additional software that creates the DDBMS and enables the multiple databases to appear as one.

Figure 12-5   A distributed database system in a multinational firm

A HYBRID ARCHITECTURE

Any organization of a reasonable size is likely to have a mix of the data processing architectures previously described. Databases will exist on stand-alone personal computers, multiple client/server networks, distributed mainframes, and so on. Architectures continue to evolve because information technology is so dynamic. Today's best solutions for database processing can become obsolete very quickly. Yet, organizations have invested large sums in existing systems that meet their current needs and do not warrant replacement. As a result, organizations evolve a **hybrid architecture**—a mix of the various forms. The concern of the IS department is to patch this hybrid together so that users see it as a seamless system that readily provides needed information. In creating this ideal system, there are some underlying key concepts that should be observed. These fundamental principles (see Table 12-4) were initially stated in terms of distributed database,[5] however, they can be considered to apply broadly to the evolving, hybrid architecture that organizations must continually fashion.

Transparency

The user should not have to know where data are stored and how they are processed. The location of data, its storage format, and access method should be invisible to the user. The system should accept queries and resolve them expeditiously. Of course, the system should check that the user is authorized to access the requested data. Transparency is also known as location independence—the system can be used independently of the location of data.

Table 12–4   The Fundamental Principles of a Hybrid Architecture

Principle
Transparency
No reliance on a central site
Local autonomy
Continuous operation
Distributed query processing
Distributed transaction processing
Fragmentation independence
Replication independence
Hardware independence
Operating system independence
Network independence
DBMS independence

[5]C. J. Date, "What is a Distributed Database System?" in C. J. Date, *Relational Database Writings 1985–1989* (Reading, MA: Addison–Wesley, 1990).

No Reliance on a Central Site

Reliance on a central site for management of a hybrid architecture creates two major problems. First, because all requests are routed through the central site, bottlenecks develop during peak periods. Second, if the central site fails, the entire system fails. A controlling central site is too vulnerable, and control should be distributed throughout the system.

Local Autonomy

A high degree of local autonomy avoids dependence on a central site. Data are locally owned and managed. The local site is responsible for the security, integrity, and storage of local data. There cannot be absolute local autonomy because the various sites must cooperate in order for transparency to be feasible. Cooperation always requires relinquishing some autonomy.

Continuous Operation

The system must be accessible when required. Since business is increasingly global and users are geographically dispersed, the system must be continuously available.

Distributed Query Processing

The time taken to execute a query should be generally independent of the location from which it is submitted. Deciding the most efficient way to process the query is the system's responsibility, not the user's. For example, a Sydney user could submit the query "Find sales of wombat coats in Japan." The system is responsible for deciding which messages to send between Sydney and Japan.

Distributed Transaction Processing

In a hybrid system, a single transaction can require updating of multiple files at multiple sites. The system must ensure that a transaction is successfully executed for all sites. Partial updating of files will cause inconsistencies.

Fragmentation Independence

Fragmentation independence means that any table can be broken into fragments and then stored in separate physical locations. For example, the sales table could be fragmented so that Indonesian data is stored in Djakarta, Japanese data in Tokyo, and so on. A fragment is any piece of a table that can be created by applying restriction and projection operations. Using join and union, fragments can be assembled to create the full table. Fragmentation is the key to a distributed database. Without fragmentation independence, data cannot be distributed.

Replication Independence

Fragmentation is good when local data are mainly processed locally, but there are some applications that also frequently process remote data. For example, the New York office of an international airline may need both American (local) and European (remote) data, and its London office may need U.S. (remote) and European (local) data. In this case, fragmentation into American and European data may not substantially reduce communication costs.

Replication means that a fragment of data can be copied and physically stored at multiple sites, thus the European fragment could be replicated and stored in New York, and the American fragment replicated and stored in London. As a result, applications in both New York and London will reduce their communication costs. Of course, the trade-off is that when a replicated fragment is updated, all copies also must be updated. Reduced communication costs are exchanged for increased update complexity.

Replication independence implies replication happens behind the scenes. The user is oblivious to replication and requires no knowledge of this activity.

There are two major approaches to replication: synchronous or asynchronous updates. Synchronous replication means all databases are updated at the same time. Although this is ideal, it is not a simple task and is resource intensive. Asynchronous replication occurs when changes made to one database are relayed to other databases within a certain period established by the database administrator. It does not provide real-time updating but it takes fewer IS resources. Asynchronous replication is a compromise strategy for distributed DBMS replication. When real-time updating is not absolutely necessary, asynchronous replication can save scarce IS resources.

Hardware Independence

A hybrid architecture should support hardware from multiple suppliers without affecting users' capacity to query files. Hardware independence is a long-term goal of many MIS managers.

Operating System Independence

Operating systems independence is another goal much sought by MIS executives. Ideally, the various DBMSs and applications of the hybrid system should work on a range of operating systems on a variety of hardware.

Network Independence

Clearly, network independence is desired by organizations that wish to avoid the electronic shackles of being committed to any single hardware or software supplier.

DBMS Independence

Independence is contagious and has been caught by the DBMS as well. Since SQL is a standard for relational databases, organizations may well be able to achieve DBMS independence. By settling on the relational model as the organizational standard, ensuring that all DBMSs installed conform to this model, and using only standard SQL, an organization may approach DBMS independence. Nevertheless, do not forget all those old systems from the pre—relational days—a legacy that must be supported in a hybrid architecture.

Conclusion

For data managers, the twelve principles just outlined are ideal goals. In the hurly-burly of everyday business, incomplete information, and an uncertain future, data managers struggle valiantly to meet users' needs with a hybrid architecture that is an imperfect interpretation of MIS paradise. It is unlikely that these principles will ever be totally achieved. They are guidelines and something to reflect on when making the inevitable trade-offs that occur in data management.

SUMMARY

Data can be stored and processed locally or remotely. Combinations of these two options provide four basic architectures: remote job entry, host/terminal, personal database, and client/server. Under remote job entry, data are sent over a communication link to a remote computer for processing and the output is sent back. With a personal database, users store and process their data locally. Under host/terminal architecture, data storage and processing occur at one location, typically a mainframe computer. Client/server supports remote storage and data are mainly processed locally. A LAN connects computers and devices within a limited geographic area. A server is a general purpose computer that provides and controls access to shareable resources. A file/server is a central data store for users attached to a LAN. It is a relatively simple solution to data sharing on a local area network. A DBMS/server, a server with a DBMS installed, does query processing so that only necessary records are transferred across a network. In a client/server architecture, the client process initiates requests and the server responds. The client is the dominant partner because it initiates a request. Client/server exploits cost savings that result from moving processing from a mainframe to less expensive minicomputers and personal computers. The key parameters to consider when comparing host/terminal with client/server are terminal versus personal computer costs, mainframe MIPS versus personal computer MIPS, and mainframe storage versus server storage. Six major variations on client/server architecture have been identified.

Under distributed database architecture, a database is in more than one location but still accessible as if it were centrally located. The trade-off is lowered communication costs versus increased complexity. A hybrid architecture is a mix of data processing architectures. The concern of the IS department is to patch this hybrid together so that users see a seamless system that readily provides needed information. The fundamental principles that a hybrid architecture should satisfy are: transparency, no reliance on a central site, local autonomy, continuous operation, distributed query processing, distributed transaction processing, fragmentation independence, replication independence, hardware independence, operating system independence, network independence, and DBMS independence.

KEY TERMS AND CONCEPTS

Client/server	Hardware independence
Continuous operation	Host/terminal
Data communications manager	Hybrid architecture
Data processing	Local area network (LAN)
Data storage	Local autonomy
Database architecture	Mainframe
Database management system (DBMS)	Network independence
DBMS independence	Personal database
DBMS/server	Remote job entry
Distributed database	Replication independence
Distributed query processing	Server
Distributed transaction processing	Software independence
File manager	Transaction processing monitor
File/server	Transparency
Fragmentation independence	Workstation
Graphical user interface (GUI)	

REFERENCES AND ADDITIONAL READINGS

Smith, P. *Client/Server Computing.* Indianapolis: Sams, 1992.

Morris, C. R., and C. H. Ferguson, "How Architecture Wins Technology Wars." *Harvard Business Review* 71, no. 2 (1993): 86–96.

EXERCISES

1. How does remote job entry differ from host/terminal?
2. How does client/server differ from host/terminal computing?
3. How have personal computers affected data architecture decisions?
4. In what situations are you likely to use remote job entry?
5. What are the disadvantages of personal databases?
6. What is a server?
7. What is a potential major problem with a file/server system?

8. Describe the difference between a file/server and a DBMS/server.

9. Define client/server computing.

10. When is client/server likely to be a cheaper information processing solution than host/terminal?

11. What factors are likely to inhibit a company's move from host/terminal to client/server?

12. What is a firm likely to gain when it moves from a centralized to distributed database? What are the potential costs?

13. In terms of a hybrid architecture, what does transparency mean?

14. In terms of a hybrid architecture, what does fragmentation independence mean?

15. In terms of a hybrid architecture, what does DBMS independence mean?

16. A university professor is about to develop a large simulation model for describing the global economy. The model uses data from 65 countries to simulate alternative economic policies and their possible outcomes. In terms of volume, the data requirements are quite modest, but the mathematical model is very complex, and there are many equations that must be solved for each quarter the model is run. What data processing/data storage architecture would you recommend?

17. A large retailer is about to establish a mail–order catalog division. Initially, it plans to hire 500 people to answer telephones. The system will have a few standard transactions (e.g., take an order, query the status of the order, and check inventory). It is anticipated that within two years the database will need to maintain details of two million customers and 10,000 products. What data processing/data storage architecture would you recommend?

18. A small bank has reformulated its strategy to focus on serving the wealthiest 25 percent of the population in its reasonably affluent region. Customers will have a personal banker who will offer a wide range of services. For example, a personal banker will be able to analyze an investment portfolio, organize foreign currency transfers, and book foreign travel. The bank expects to appoint 22 personal bankers and will provide each person with extensive training in a wide range of transactions. What data processing/data storage architecture would you recommend?

19. The advertising manager of a small veterinary pharmaceutical supplier wants to track the firm's advertising in the journal and at the conference of each of the 50 U.S. state veterinary societies. Each state has one journal, which is published at most 12 times per year, and one annual conference. What data processing/data storage architecture would you recommend?

20. A multinational company has operated relatively independent organizations in 15 countries. The new CEO wants greater coordination and believes that marketing, production, and purchasing should be globally managed. As a result, the corporate IS department must work with the separate IS national departments to integrate the various national applications and databases. What are the implications for the corporate data processing and database architecture? What are the key facts you would like to know before developing an integration plan? What problems do you anticipate? What is your intuitive feeling about the key features of the new architecture?

Chapter 13

The Relational Model

Nothing is so practical as a good theory.

K. Lewin, 1945

Learning Objectives

On completion of this chapter, you will:

- know the structures of the relational model;
- understand relational algebra commands;
- be able to determine whether a DBMS is completely relational.

BACKGROUND

The relational model,[1] developed as a result of recognized shortcomings of hierarchical and network DBMSs (see Chapter 14), was introduced by Codd in 1970 in an article published in the *Communications of the ACM*.[2] Part of the practical value of the relational model is its strong theoretical base. As the model's major developer, Codd believed that a sound theoretical model would solve most practical problems that could potentially arise.

In another article,[3] Codd expounds the case for adopting the relational model over other database models. There is a threefold thrust to his argument. First, other database models force the application programmer to code at a low level of structural detail. As a result, application programs are more complex and take longer to write and debug. Second, no commands are provided for processing multiple records at one time. Other models do not provide the set processing capability of the relational model, which means that queries can be much more concisely expressed. Third, only the relational model, through a query language such as SQL, recognizes the users' need to make ad hoc queries. Adoption of the relational

---

[1]Under the spiral approach to teaching data modeling and SQL, many aspects of the relational model were introduced in Section 2. This chapter consolidates and extends the earlier work to provide formal coverage of this most widely used database model.

[2]E. F. Codd, "A Relational Model for Large Shared Data Banks," *Communications of the ACM* 13 (6): 377–387 (1970).

[3]E. F. Codd, "Relational Database: A Practical Foundation for Productivity," *Communications of the ACM* 25 (2): 109–117 (1982).

model and SQL permits an MIS department to respond far more rapidly to users' unanticipated requests. It can also mean that users write and execute their own queries. Thus, Codd's assertion that the relational model is a practical tool for increasing the productivity of MIS departments is well founded.

The productivity increase arises from three of the objectives that drove his research. The first objective was to provide a clearly delineated boundary between the logical and physical aspects of database management. Application programmers could then be divorced from considerations of the physical representation of data. Codd labels this the **data independence objective.** The second objective was to create a simple model that was readily understood by a wide range of users and programmers. This **communicability objective** promotes effective and efficient communication between users and MIS personnel. The third objective was to increase processing capabilities from record-at-a-time to multiple records-at-a-time—**the set processing objective.** Achievement of these objectives means fewer lines of code are required to write an application program and there is less ambiguity in user–analyst communication.

The relational model has three major components:

- Data structures;
- Integrity rules;
- Operators used to retrieve, derive, or modify data.

DATA STRUCTURES

Like most theories, the relational model is based on some key structures or concepts. We need to understand these in order to understand the theory.

Domain

A **domain** is a set of values all of the same data type. For example, the domain of nation name is the set of all possible nation names. The domain of all stock prices is the set of all currency values in, say, the range $0 to $10,000,000. You can also think of a domain as all the legal values of an attribute.

In specifying a domain, you also need to think about the smallest unit of data for an attribute defined on that domain. In Chapter 7, we discussed how a candidate attribute should be examined to see if it should be segmented (e.g., we divide name into first name, other name, and last name, and maybe more). While it is unlikely that name will be a domain, it is likely that there will be a domain for first name, last name, and so on. Thus a domain contains values that are in their atomic state; they cannot be decomposed further.

The practical value of a domain is to define what comparisons are permissible. Only attributes drawn from the same domain should be compared; otherwise it is a bit like comparing apples and oranges. For example, it makes no sense to compare a stock's PE ratio to its price. They do not measure the same thing; they belong to different domains. Although the domain concept is useful, it is rarely supported by relational model implementations.

Relations

A **relation** is a table of n columns (or attributes) and m rows (or tuples). Each column has a unique name, and all the values in a column are drawn from the same domain. Each row of the relation is uniquely identified. The order of columns and rows is immaterial.

The **cardinality** of a relation is its number of rows. The **degree** of a relation is the number of columns. For example, the relation NATION (see Table 13-1) is of degree 3 and has a cardinality of 4. Because the cardinality of a relation changes every time a row is added or deleted, you can expect cardinality to change frequently. The degree changes if a column is added to a relation, but in terms of relational theory, it is considered to be a new relation. So, only a relation's cardinality changes.

Relational Database

A relational database is a collection of relations. This definition really applies to the external and conceptual levels. Internally, the data could have some other representation. What really matters is that users of the database think of it as a collection of relations or tables.

The distinguishing feature of the relational model, when compared to hierarchical and network, is that there are no explicit linkages between tables. Tables are linked by common columns drawn on the same domain; thus the portfolio database (see Table 13-1) consists of tables STOCK and NATION. The 1:m relationship between the two tables is represented by the column NATCODE that is common to both tables. Note that the two columns need not have the same name, but they must be drawn on the same domain so that comparison is possible. In the case of an m:m relationship, while a new table must be created to represent the relationship, the principle of linking tables through common columns on the same domain remains in force.

Primary Key

A relation's **primary key** is its unique identifier; for example, the primary key of NATION is NATCODE. As you already know, a primary key can be a composite of several columns. The primary key guarantees that each row of a relation can be uniquely addressed. A primary key need not be indexed, though it often is.

Table 13–1 The Relational Tables NATION and STOCK

NATION		
NATCODE	**NATNAME**	**EXCHRATE**
UK	United Kingdom	1.00
USA	United States	0.67
AUS	Australia	0.46
IND	India	0.0228

STOCK						
STKCODE	**STKFIRM**	**STKPRICE**	**STKQTY**	**STKDIV**	**STKPE**	*NATCODE*
FC	Freedonia Copper	27.50	10,529	1.84	16	UK
PT	Patagonian Tea	55.25	12,635	2.50	10	UK
AR	Abyssinian Ruby	31.82	22,010	1.32	13	UK
SLG	Sri Lankan Gold	50.37	32,868	2.68	16	UK
ILZ	Indian Lead & Zinc	37.75	6,390	3.00	12	UK
BE	Burmese Elephant	.07	154,713	0.01	3	UK
BS	Bolivian Sheep	12.75	231,678	1.78	11	UK
NG	Nigerian Geese	35.00	12,323	1.68	10	UK
CS	Canadian Sugar	52.78	4,716	2.50	15	UK
ROF	Royal Ostrich Farms	33.75	1,234,923	3.00	6	UK
MG	Minnesota Gold	53.87	816,122	1.00	25	USA
GP	Georgia Peach	2.35	387,333	.20	5	USA
NE	Narembeen Emu	12.34	45,619	1.00	8	AUS
QD	Queensland Diamond	6.73	89,251	.50	7	AUS
IR	Indooroopilly Ruby	15.92	56,147	.50	20	AUS
BD	Bombay Duck	25.55	167,382	1.00	12	IND

Candidate Key

In some situations, there may be several attributes—known as **candidate keys**—that are potential primary keys. NATNAME is unique in the NATION relation, for example. We also can be fairly certain that two nations will not have the same name, therefore, NATION has multiple candidate keys: NATCODE and NATNAME.

Alternate Key

When there are multiple candidate keys, one is chosen as the primary key and the remainder are known as **alternate keys.** In this case, we selected NATCODE as the primary key, and NATNAME is an alternate key.

Foreign Key

The foreign key is an important concept of the relational model. It is the way relationships are represented and can be thought of as the glue that holds a set of tables together to form a relational database. A **foreign key** is an attribute (possibly composite) of a relation that is also a primary key of a relation. The foreign key and primary key may be in different relations or the same relation, but both keys should be drawn from the same domain.

INTEGRITY RULES

The integrity section of the relational model consists of two rules. The **entity integrity rule** ensures that each instance of an entity described by a relation is identifiable in some way. Its implementation means that each row in a relation can be uniquely distinguished. The rule is:

No component of the primary key of a relation may be null.

Null in this case means that the component cannot be undefined or unknown—it must have a value. Notice that the rule says *component of a primary key.* This means every part of the primary key must be known; if a part cannot be defined, it implies that the particular entity it describes cannot be defined. In practical terms, it means you cannot add a nation to NATION unless you also define a value for NATCODE.

The definition of a foreign key implies that there is a corresponding primary key. The **referential integrity rule** ensures that this is the case. It states:

A database must not contain any unmatched foreign key values.

Simply, this rule means that you cannot define a foreign key without first defining its matching primary key. In practical terms, it would mean you could not add a Canadian stock to the STOCK relation without first creating a row in NATION for Canada.

Notice that the concepts of foreign key and referential integrity are intertwined. There is not much sense in having foreign keys without having the referential integrity rule. Permitting a foreign key without a corresponding primary key means the relationship cannot be determined.

MANIPULATION—RELATIONAL ALGEBRA

The relational model includes a set of operations (see Table 13-2), known as **relational algebra,** for manipulating relations. Relational algebra is a standard for judging data retrieval languages. If a retrieval language, such as SQL, can be used to express every relational algebra operator, it is said to be **relationally complete.**

Table 13–2   Relational Algebra Operators

Restrict	Creates a new table from specified rows of an existing table.
Project	Creates a new table from specified columns of an existing table.
Product	Creates a new table from all the possible combinations of rows of two existing tables.
Union	Creates a new table containing rows appearing in one or both tables of two existing tables.
Intersect	Creates a new table containing rows appearing in both tables of two existing tables.
Difference	Creates a new table containing rows appearing in one table but not in the other of two existing tables.
Join	Creates a new table containing all possible combinations of rows of two existing tables satisfying the join condition.
Divide	Creates a new table containing x_i such that the pair (x_i, y_i) exists in the first table for every y_i in the second table.

There are eight relational algebra operations that can be used with either one or two relations to create a new relation. The assignment operator $(: =)$ indicates the name of the new relation. The relational algebra statement to create relation A, the union of relations B and C, is expressed as

```
A : =  B UNION C
```

Before we begin our discussion of each of the eight operators, note that the first two—restrict and project—operate on a single relation and the rest require two relations.

Restrict

Restrict extracts specified rows from a single relation. As the shaded rows in Figure 13-1 depict, restrict takes a horizontal slice through a relation.

The relational algebra command to create the new relation using restrict is

```
tablename WHERE column1 theta column2
OR
tablename WHERE column1 theta literal
```

where theta can be $=, <>, >, \geq, <, \leq$.

For example, the following relational algebra command creates a new table from STOCK containing all rows with a nation code of US:

```
USSTOCK : = STOCK WHERE NATCODE =  'US'
```

You will sometimes see restrict referred to as select. Nowadays, to avoid confusion with SQL's SELECT statement, restrict is the preferred term.

Figure 13-1   Relational operation restrict—a horizontal slice

Project

Project extracts specified columns from a table. As Figure 13-2 shows, project takes a vertical slice through a table.

The relational algebra command to create the new relation using project is

```
tablename [columnname, . . .]
```

So, in order to create a new table from NATION that contains the nation's name and its exchange rate, for example, you would use this relational algebra command:

```
RATES : =  NATION[NATNAME, EXCHRATE]
```

Product

Product creates a new relation from all possible combinations of rows in two other relations. It is sometimes called TIMES or MULTIPLY. The relational command to create the product of two tables is

```
tablename1 TIMES tablename2
```

The operation of product is illustrated in Figure 13-3, which shows the result of A TIMES B.

Figure 13-2   Relational operation project—a vertical slice

A			
V	W		
v_1	w_1		
v_2	w_2		
v_3	w_3		

B		
X	Y	Z
x_1	y_1	z_1
x_2	y_2	z_2

A TIMES B				
V	W	X	Y	Z
v_1	w_1	x_1	y_1	z_1
v_1	w_1	x_2	y_2	z_2
v_2	w_2	x_1	y_1	z_1
v_2	w_2	x_2	y_2	z_2
v_3	w_3	x_1	y_1	z_1
v_3	w_3	x_2	y_2	z_2

Figure 13-3   Relational operation product

Union

The **union** of two relations is a new relation containing all rows appearing in one or both relations. The two relations must be **union compatible,** which means they have the same column names, in the same order, and drawn on the same domains. Duplicate rows are automatically eliminated—they must be, or the relational model is no longer satisfied. The relational command to create the union of two tables is

```
tablename1 UNION tablename2
```

Union is illustrated in Figure 13-4. Notice that corresponding columns in tables A and B have the same names. While the sum of the number of rows in relations A and B is five, the union contains four rows because one row (x_2, y_2) is common to both relations.

A	
X	Y
x_1	y_1
x_2	y_2
x_3	y_3

B	
X	Y
x_2	y_2
x_4	y_4

A UNION B	
X	Y
x_1	y_1
x_2	y_2
x_3	y_3
x_4	y_4

Figure 13-4   Relational operation union

Intersect

The **intersection** of two relations is a new relation containing all rows appearing in both relations. The two relations must be union compatible. The relational command to create the intersection of two tables is

```
tablename1 INTERSECT tablename2
```

Figure 13-5 shows that the result of A INTERSECT B is one row because only one row (x_2, y_2) is common to both relations A and B.

Difference

The **difference** of two relations is a new relation containing all rows appearing in the first relation but not in the second. The two relations must be union compatible. The relational command to create the difference of two tables is

```
tablename1 MINUS tablename2
```

The result of A MINUS B is two rows (see Figure 13-6). Both of these rows are in relation A but not in relation B. The row containing (x_2, y_2) appears in both A and B, and thus is not in A MINUS B.

Join

Join creates a new relation from two relations for all combinations of rows satisfying the join condition. The general format of join is

```
tablename1 JOIN tablename2 WHERE tablename1.columnname1 theta
    tablename2.columnname2
```

where theta can be $=, <>, >, \geq, <, \leq$.

A	
X	Y
x_1	y_1
x_2	y_2
x_3	y_3

B	
X	Y
x_2	y_2
x_4	y_4

A INTERSECT B	
X	Y
x_2	y_2

Figure 13-5   Relational operation intersect

A	
X	Y
x_1	y_1
x_2	y_2
x_3	y_3

B	
X	Y
x_2	y_2
x_4	y_4

A MINUS B	
X	Y
x_1	y_1
x_3	y_3

Figure 13-6   Relational operation minus

Figure 13-7 illustrates A JOIN B where W = Z, which is an equijoin because theta is an equals sign. Tables A and B are matched when values in columns W and Z in each relation are equal. The matching columns should be drawn from the same domain. You can also think of join as a product followed by restrict on the resulting relation. So the join can be written:

```
(A TIMES B) WHERE W THETA Z
```

Divide

Divide is the hardest relational operator to understand. Division requires that A and B have a set of attributes, in this case Y, that are common to both relations. Conceptually, A divided by B asks the question, "Is there a value in the X column of A (e.g., x_1) that has a value in the Y column of A for every value of y in the Y column of B?" Look first at B, the Y column has val-

A	
V	W
v_1	wz_1
v_2	wz_2
v_3	wz_3

B		
X	Y	Z
x_1	y_1	wz_1
x_2	y_2	wz_3

A EQUIJOIN B				
V	W	X	Y	Z
v_1	wz_1	x_1	y_1	wz_1
v_3	wz_3	x_2	y_2	wz_3

Figure 13-7   Relational operation join

ues y_1 and y_2. When you examine the X column of A, you find there are rows (x_1, y_1) and (x_1, y_2). That is, for x_1, there is a value in the Y column of A for every value of y in the Y column of B. Thus, the result of the division is a new relation with a single row and column containing the value x_1 (see Figure 13-8).

A PRIMITIVE SET OF RELATIONAL OPERATIONS

The full set of eight relational operators is not required. As you have already seen, join can be defined in terms of product and restrict. Intersection and divide can also be defined in terms of other commands. Indeed, only five operators are required—restrict, project, product, union, and difference. These five operators are known as **primitives** because these are the minimal set of relational operations. None of the operations in the primitive set can be defined in terms of the other operations. Table 13-3 illustrates how each primitive can be expressed as an SQL command, which implies that SQL is relationally complete.

A FULLY RELATIONAL DATABASE

The three components of a relational database system are structures (domains and relations), integrity rules (primary and foreign keys), and a manipulation language (relational algebra). A **fully relational database** system provides complete support for each of these components. Many commercial systems support SQL, but do not provide support for domains or integrity rules. Such systems are not fully relational, but are relationally complete.

A	
X	Y
x_1	y_1
x_1	y_3
x_1	y_2
x_2	y_1
x_3	y_3

B
Y
y_1
y_2

A
DIVIDE
B
X
x_1

Figure 13-8 Relational operation divide

Table 13–3   Comparison of Relational Algebra Primitive Operations and SQL

	Relational algebra	SQL
Restrict	A where condition	SELECT * FROM A WHERE condition
Project	A [X]	SELECT X FROM A
Product	A times B	SELECT * FROM A, B
Union	A union B	SELECT * FROM A UNION SELECT * FROM B
Difference	A minus B	SELECT * FROM A WHERE NOT EXISTS (SELECT * FROM B WHERE A.X = B.X AND A.Y = B.Y AND . . .)[4]

In 1985, Codd[5] established the 12 commandments of relational database systems (see Table 13-4). In addition to providing some insights into Codd's thinking about the management of data, these rules can also be used to judge how well a database fits the relational model. The major impetus for these rules was uncertainty in the market place about the meaning of relational DBMS. Unfortunately, some DBMS vendors used the term *relational* somewhat freely, and this created misunderstanding about what relational database really meant. Codd's rules are a checklist for establishing the authenticity of a DBMS that claims to be relational.

Table 13–4   Codd's Rules for a Relational DBMS

The information rule
The guaranteed access rule
Systematic treatment of null values
Active on-line catalog of the relational model
The comprehensive data sublanguage rule
The view updating rule
High level insert, update, and delete
Physical data independence
Logical data independence
Integrity independence
Distribution independence
The nonsubversion rule

[4]Essentially, where all columns of A are equal to all columns of B.

[5]E. F. Codd, "Is Your DBMS Really Relational?" *Computerworld,* 14 October 1985, and "Does Your DBMS Run By the Rules?" *Computerworld,* 21 October 1985.

The Information Rule

This rule stimulates that there is only one logical representation of data in a database. All data must appear to be stored as values in a table.

The Guaranteed Access Rule

Every value in a database must be addressable by specifying its table name, column name, and the primary key of the row in which it is stored.

Systematic Treatment of Null Values

There must be a distinct representation for unknown or inappropriate data.[6] This must be unique and independent of data type. The DBMS should handle null data in a systematic way. For example, a zero or a blank cannot be used to represent a null. As we saw earlier, this is one of the more troublesome areas because null can have several meanings (e.g., missing or inappropriate).

Active On-Line Catalog of the Relational Model

There should be an on-line catalog that describes the relational model (see Chapter 9 for details of the DB2 catalog). Authorized users should be able to access this catalog using the standard query language.

The Comprehensive Data Sublanguage Rule

There must be a relational language that supports data definition, data manipulation, security and integrity constraints, and transaction processing operations. Furthermore, this language must support both interactive querying and application programming and be expressible in text format. SQL fits these requirements.

---

[6]In DB2, each column has an associated one byte field that denotes whether the column is null.

The View Updating Rule

The DBMS must be able to update any view that is theoretically updatable.

High-Level Insert, Update, and Delete

The system must support set-at-a-time operations. For example, multiple rows must be updatable with a single command.

Physical Data Independence

Changes to storage representation or access methods will not affect application programs. For example, application programs should remain unimpaired even if a database is moved to a different storage device or an index is created for a table.

Logical Data Independence

Information preserving changes to base tables will not affect application programs. For instance, no applications should be affected when a new table is added to a database.

Integrity Independence

Integrity constraints should be part of a database's definition rather than embedded within application programs. It must be possible to change these constraints without affecting any existing application programs.

Distribution Independence

Introduction of a distributed DBMS or redistributing existing distributed data should have no impact on existing applications (see the discussion of distributed database in Chapter 12).

The Nonsubversion Rule

It must not be possible to use a record-at-a-time interface to subvert security or integrity constraints. You should not be able to write a COBOL program with embedded SQL commands to bypass security features.

Codd issued an additional higher level rule, rule 0, that states that a relational DBMS must be able to manage databases entirely through its relational capacities. In other words, a DBMS is either totally relational or it is not relational.

Shrinking Data[7]

Compression technology finds the redundant information in a data set and removes it. Compression techniques can be used with text, pictures, sound, and video data. When analog signals, such as with video, are converted to digital they require considerably more storage space—approximately 45 times the storage capacity. However, compression technology means digital TV signals can actually require less space than analog ones. For instance, it is possible to transmit 150 channels of compressed digital TV in the same space as 32 uncompressed analog channels. Compression is everywhere: videoconferencing, relational databases, CD-ROM encyclopedias, and video games. A compressed two-hour movie can fit on two CD-ROMS; uncompressed, it might take 360 disks.

Compression lowers the cost of data storage and transmission. It means the copper wires that connect your telephone to the phone company's high speed lines can carry massive amounts of data, including high-quality video. Compression means the information superhighway can extend to your house, without the need to replace existing copper wires with fiber optic cable.

The leading standards in visual compression are JPEG (jay-peg) for still images and MPEG (em-peg) for moving images. Other compression techniques are currently being studied in leading research labs.

SUMMARY

The relational model developed as a result of recognized shortcomings of hierarchical and network DBMSs. Codd created a strong theoretical base for the relational model. Three objectives drove relational database research: data independence, communicability, and set processing. The relational model has domain structures, integrity rules, and operators used to retrieve, derive, or modify data. A domain is a set of values all of the same data type. The practical value of a domain is to define what comparisons are permissible. A relation is a

---

[7]Adapted from P. Coy, "Invasion of the Data Shrinkers: Compressed Digital Signals Could Open the Information Superhighway, Cheaply," *Business Week,* 14 February 1994, 115–116.

table of n columns and m rows. The cardinality of a relation is its number of rows. The degree of a relation is the number of columns.

A relational database is a collection of relations. The distinguishing feature of the relational model is that there are no explicit linkages between tables. A relation's primary key is its unique identifier. When there are multiple candidates for the primary key, one is chosen as the primary key and the remainder are known as alternate keys. The foreign key is the way relationships are represented and can be thought of as the glue that binds a set of tables together to form a relational database. The purpose of the entity integrity rule is to ensure that each entity described by a relation is identifiable in some way. The referential integrity rule ensures that you cannot define a foreign key without first defining its matching primary key.

The relational model includes a set of operations, known as relational algebra, for manipulating relations. There are eight operations that can be used with either one or two relations to create a new relation. These operations are: restrict, project, product, union, intersect, difference, join, and divide. Only five operators, known as primitives, are required to define all eight relational operations. An SQL statement can be translated to relational algebra and vice versa. If a retrieval language can be used to express every relational algebra operator, it is said to be relationally complete. A fully relational database system provides complete support for domains, integrity rules, and a manipulation language. Codd set forth 12 rules that can be used to judge how well a database fits the relational model. He also added rule 0—a DBMS is either totally relational or it is not relational.

KEY TERMS AND CONCEPTS

Alternate key
Candidate key
Cardinality
Catalog
Communicability objective
Data independence
Data structures
Data sublanguage rule
Degree
Difference
Distribution independence
Divide
Domain
Entity integrity
Foreign key
Fully relational database
Integrity independence
Integrity rules
Intersect
Join

Logical data independence
Nonsubversion rule
Null
Operators
Physical data independence
Primary key
Product
Project
Referential integrity
Relational algebra
Relational database
Relational model
Relationally complete
Relations
Restrict
Set processing objective
The guaranteed access rule
The information rule
Union
View updating rule

REFERENCES AND ADDITIONAL READINGS

Bustamente, G. G. and K. Sorenson, Decision Support at Lands' End—An Evolution." *IBM Systems Journal* 33, no. 2 (1994):228–238.

Codd, E. F. "Does Your DBMS Run By the Rules?" *Computerworld*, 21 October 1985.

Codd, E. F. "Fatal Flaws in SQL." *Datamation*, 15 August and 1 September 1988.

Codd, E. F. "Is Your DBMS Really Relational?" *Computerworld*, 14 October 1985.

Codd, E. F. "Relational Database: A Practical Foundation for Productivity." *Communications of the ACM*, 25 no. 2 (1982): 109–117.

Rozen, S. and D. Shasha, "Using a Relational System on Wall Street: The Good, The Bad, The Ugly, and The Ideal." *Communications of the ACM* 32, no. 8 (1989): 988–994.

EXERCISES

1. What reasons does Codd give for adopting the relational model?
2. What are the major components of the relational model?
3. What is a domain? Why is it useful?
4. What are the meanings of cardinality and degree?
5. What is a simple relational database?
6. What is the difference between a primary key and an alternate key?
7. Why do we need an entity integrity rule?
8. Why do we need a referential integrity rule?
9. What is the meaning of union compatible? Which relational operations require union compatibility?
10. What is meant by the term "a primitive set of operations?"
11. What is a fully relational database?
12. Take a microcomputer relational database package and examine how well it satisfies Codd's rules.

Chapter 14

Hierarchical and Network Models

Thinking means connecting things, and stops if they cannot be connected.

G. K. Chesterton, *Orthodoxy*

Learning Objectives

On completion of this chapter, you will be able to:
- describe the main features of the hierarchical and network models;
- compare and contrast the relational model to the hierarchical and network models.

The Expeditioner

The Expeditioner has continued to expand its retailing business and now has stores in major cities in several countries. For some time, it has been looking for an opportunity to expand into France. A famous, well-established Paris based firm, L'Explorateur, has become available for acquisition. Like The Expeditioner, L'Explorateur has been operating for many years and was extremely successful in the nineteenth century when France was a major colonial power. In the last few years, sales have dwindled and the company is marginally profitable. L'Explorateur has stores in several major French cities, including Paris and Lyon, and in French-speaking regions of the world (e.g., Tahiti and Madagascar).

Although the acquisition looks fine from a financial perspective, the management committee has some concerns about integrating the information systems of the two companies. Due to financial problems, L'Explorateur has invested very little in information systems over the last few years, and most of its data are still stored on a ten-year-old mainframe. Further investigation shows that nearly all the systems are written in COBOL and use a hierarchical DBMS. In contrast, The Expeditioner uses relational DBMS on a client/server platform. What should The Expeditioner do? Should it convert L'Explorateur's existing systems to its own systems or maintain the existing ones?

Fortunately, L'Explorateur's systems are very solid and with a little updating could continue to process business transactions and provide managers with some useful reports. For a small expenditure, the existing systems could be used for another few years, when the mainframe would definitely have to be replaced. Avoiding the cost of conversion certainly makes the acquisition less costly and avoids a major disruption of the French business.

The Expeditioner's management, however, is concerned that if does not make the conversion, it would not be easy to integrate data from the two quite separate information systems.

Furthermore, L'Explorateur's systems are not very user-friendly and ad hoc reporting is difficult and usually requires writing new programs. Conversion of L'Explorateur's systems would give managers better reporting and querying capability, which could be vital when they are learning how to manage the new French business. It may be worthwhile to pay the cost of conversion to get a better information system. After all, if managers are better informed about the business, they are more likely to make better decisions and quickly improve the profitability of L'Explorateur.

What should the management team do? Should it keep L'Explorateur's systems or replace them? Before you answer this question, you might find it helpful to know more about database systems that preceded the relational model.

INTRODUCTION

Hierarchical and network data models underlie most DBMSs developed between the late 1960s and the early 1980s. Systems such as IBM's IMS are hierarchical and Computer Associates' IDMS are network. Many of these systems are still operational, and must be maintained as long as they continue to meet organizational needs. Applications based on the hierarchical and network models are often referred to as **legacy systems** handed down from a previous era of information technology. Nevertheless, these applications and databases cannot be abandoned while they continue to process key business transactions and provide important managerial data; therefore, data management professionals need an awareness of the hierarchical and network models. This chapter is intended to give you a feel for the major features of these two models by discussing each data model and key features of its implementation.

A Legacy of Maintenance

MIS managers are overwhelmed by a constant need to care for and attend to legacy systems. Executives revealed that nearly half of their department's manpower goes to simply maintaining host-based systems. The majority of managers surveyed, all from Fortune 500 companies, said they feel that the picture will not change in the immediate future. Large companies will possibly take five to seven years to migrate from inflexible host-based systems to more responsive client/server technology.[1]

The data modeling technique that you learned in Section 2 applies to the design of hierarchical and network databases. The relationships between data don't change just because you are using another network model. Regardless of whether the target data model is hierarchi-

---

[1]Adapted from "Managing Mainframe Maintenance Madness," *Computerworld,* February 1994, 81.

cal, network, or relational, you should create a data model in exactly the same fashion as you previously learned. The difference comes in the mapping of the data model. In the case of the relational model, it is very direct. Mapping to hierarchical and network models is not as simple, but you will be able to adjust quickly.

Because of its familiarity, the relational model will be the benchmark for comparing data structures, language interface, and programming of the hierarchical and network models. The relational model is clearly the simplest database model because it is founded on the table, a simple and familiar data structure, and has a very high-level retrieval language, SQL. Together, the set processing capability of SQL and the foreign key concept make programming relatively easy. In contrast, the data structures of the hierarchical and network models are more complex, and as a result, programming is more complex.

The relational model is easier to use and understand because it is further removed from physical considerations than the other two models. If you examine each approach at the physical level, you may find they employ similar data structures and ways of processing records. A table could be stored as part of a linked list and a join executed using record at-a-time processing. The great advantage of the relational model is it leaves issues of data storage to the DBMS and navigation of data structures to SQL, while this is not the case with the hierarchical and network models. It is this relatively higher level of abstraction from physical details that makes the relational model simpler.

It is not our intention to cover exhaustively the fine detail of the hierarchical and network models. Instead, by focusing on a broad coverage, you will gain the necessary insights to appreciate a comparative analysis of the three models without getting enmeshed in details.

HIERARCHICAL MODEL

Unlike the relational model, the hierarchical model did not start as a research project in a laboratory. It arose from the American space program's need to rapidly access large volumes of stored data. Engineers needed to manage data describing millions of parts that were related to each other hierarchically, and so the model emerged from a practical solution to a very significant data management problem.

The basic structure of the hierarchical model is a hierarchy or tree relationship. The tree image follows from the restriction on the 1:m relationship (called parent–child in this case) between entities—a parent can have many children, but a child can have only one parent. When drawn, this structure looks like a tree, although most of the time the root is at the top rather than the bottom. Figure 14-1 shows the relational and hierarchical designs of the same data model.

The major difference to note in the mapping of the data model to the two designs is the use of foreign keys in the relational design and pointers in the hierarchical design. For the relational design, the 1:m relationship between NATION and STOCK is represented by NAT-CODE as a foreign key in STOCK. In the case of the hierarchical design, the same relationship is represented by a pointer from NATION to STOCK.

The lower portion of Figure 14-1 illustrates some of the principles of the hierarchical model. Notice that fields are grouped into segments or records. The three fields describing a

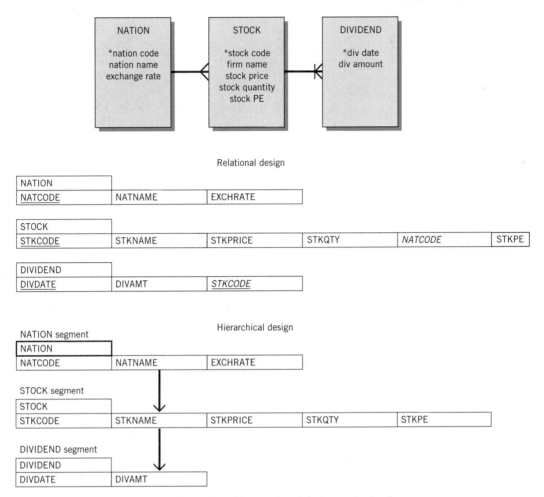

Figure 14-1 Comparison of relational and hierarchical designs of a database

nation comprise the NATION segment. The nodes of a tree are segments. Each segment has only one parent (e.g., NATION is the parent of STOCK). Each segment also has a sequence field defining the ordering to be maintained. The sequence field for NATION is NATCODE, so these segments are maintained in NATCODE order (i.e., India will appear before United States). STKCODE is the sequence field for the STOCK, and within a particular nation, stock segments are in STKCODE order (i.e., within the U.S. stocks, Alaska Gold appears before Georgia Peach).

By considering some instances of database trees, we understand additional principles of the hierarchical model (see Figure 14-2). Each nation is the root of a distinct tree for exactly one instance of a nation. In Figure 14-2, you see separate trees for India and the United States. There will be as many trees as there are instances of the root segment. Thus, you can think of a hierarchical database as a set of trees. Figure 14-2 also illustrates the concept of a

Figure 14-2   Instance trees for the investments database

twin. All segments having the same parent are termed twin segments. In the U.S. segment, Alaska Gold and Georgia Peach are twins. Observe that the Bombay Duck segment has three twins.

The hierarchical model supports several methods for storing a tree. The child and twin pointer approach is shown in Table 14-1. The data for a tree are stored together (e.g., the data for the India tree are stored contiguously in records 1 through 5). Within a parent, twins are stored together (e.g., Alaska Gold and Georgia Peach are stored in records 7 and 8). Pointers keep track of children and twins. If you look at record 7, the child pointer is 9 (record 9 contains details of the stock's dividend) and the twin pointer is 8 (record 8 contains details of another stock, Georgia Peach). Notice that India has a twin pointer of 6, the address of the record containing the root segment for the United States, the next tree. Thus, you can think of the hierarchical model as an ordered set of trees.

Table 14-1   Storage Layout of the Investment Database

Record number	Key data	Non-key data	Pointers	
			Child	Twin
1	India	. . .	2	6
2	Bombay Duck	. . .	3	—
3	1/1/92	. . .	—	4
4	1/1/93	. . .	—	5
5	1/1/94	. . .	—	—
6	US	. . .	7	—
7	Alaska Gold	. . .	9	8
8	Georgia Peach	. . .	11	—
9	1/1/92	. . .	—	10
10	1/1/94	. . .	—	—
11	1/1/90	. . .	—	—

Table 14–2 Comparison of Hierarchical and Relational Models Based on DL/I and SQL as the DMLs

Hierarchical	Relational
Complex conceptual structure (tree)	Simple conceptual structure (table)
Relationship represented by a pointer	Relationship represented by a foreign key
Optimized for 1:m relationships	Not optimized for any particular relationship
Handles m:m relationships by creating two trees	Handles m:m relationships by creating an additional table
DML (DL/I) is a low level language	DML (SQL) is a high level language
DML (DL/I) is a sequential record processing language	DML (SQL) is a set processing language
Programming is more difficult because the programmer has to navigate the data structure	Programming is easier because SQL always returns a single table that is easily navigated
IBM is the dominant vendor	Many vendors
Not a standard	ANSI standard

Now that you have an idea of the main features of the hierarchical model, it is useful to compare it to the relational model (see Table 14-2). This comparison also considers the DML primarily used with each model: DL/I in the case of the hierarchical model and SQL for the relational. Remember, the DML is the programmer's—or in the case of SQL also the user's—interface to the data model. It is often the DMLs that become the focus of comparison because this is the most common interface. In the case of both languages, there can be third-party products that change this perspective. For example, an interactive query language for a hierarchical database is likely to be friendly and easier to use than DL/I.

Compared to implementing a relational database, the designer of a hierarchical database must be more concerned with physical storage considerations (e.g., what method should be used for representing trees?). This is not surprising, since the hierarchical model was developed during an era when computing resources were more expensive and disks much slower. As a result, designers needed to be very conscious of the manner in which data were accessed. For instance, if common transactions require the retrieval of a parent and its children, then storing this data contiguously saves disk accesses. Of course, this is not always the case. When dealing with ad hoc queries that run across trees rather than down them, the hierarchical model can lose its efficiency advantage and programming is more complex. In contrast, the relational model easily handles ad hoc queries.

Another problem with the hierarchical model is its inability to directly model m:m relationships because of the restriction that a child can have only one parent. As your data modeling experience confirms, m:m relationships occur frequently in the real world. Thus, many designers find hierarchical databases frustrating because they cannot represent data relationships as they truly exist. The way to circumvent this shortcoming is to create two trees. In Figure 14-3, a data model depicting an m:m relationship between SALE and ITEM is converted into two trees or two 1:m relationships.

Two separate trees could mean storing the data for LINEITEM twice, once in each tree. The way around this problem is to store the data in one tree and point to it from the other tree. In Figure 14-4, the data for LINEITEM are stored in the SALE tree and the child segments of ITEM contain pointers to data, rather than the data. One key question for database designers is, "Which tree should store data and which should store pointers?" The answer is determined by considering which tree is likely to be accessed most often. If the SALE tree is accessed most frequently, then storing data there will minimize disk accesses.

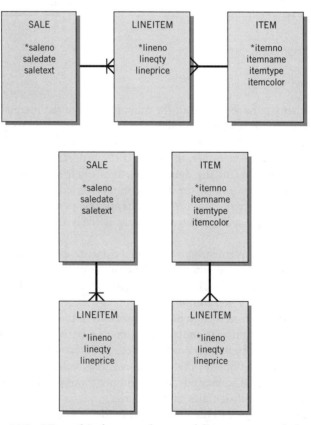

Figure 14-3 Hierarchical approach to modeling an m:m relationship

Figure 14-4 Hierarchical representation of an m : m relationship

IMS

The most popular implementation of the hierarchical model is IBM's IMS, which was released in 1968. Because of IBM's dominance in the market place, IMS was probably the most popular DBMS for a long time.

DL/I, the data manipulation language for IMS, is not an interactive query language. Because commands are embedded in a host application programming language such as COBOL, use of DL/I is reserved for computer programmers. DL/I processes data sequentially, a segment at a time. Regardless of actual storage format, DL/I presumes a database is a set of ordered trees (see Table 14-1). Remember, when SQL commands are embedded in a COBOL program (see Chapter 9), the COBOL program also has to process records sequentially. This processing is relatively direct because SQL always returns a single, flat file. In contrast, when DL/I is embedded in COBOL, the programmer must navigate the data structure, which is a more complex task than processing a simple file.

The hierarchical database model shown in Figure 14-1 can be translated into the DDL of DL/I (see Figure 14-5). The name of the database is described in the DBD statement. Each segment of the database is defined by a SEGM statement. For instance, the root segment, NATION, has a length of 28 bytes. Fields are defined by a FIELD statement. The three fields of NATION are defined in statements 3 through 5. Notice that the code word SEQ defines NATCODE as the sequence field. The parent–child relationship between NATION and STOCK is defined in statement 6 by the phrase PARENT = NATION in the definition of the STOCK segment.

```
1.  DBD    NAME=PORTFOLIO
2.  SEGM   NAME=NATION,BYTES=28
3.  FIELD  NAME=(NATCODE,SEQ),BYTES=3,START=1
4.  FIELD  NAME=NATNAME,BYTES=20,START=4
5.  FIELD  NAME=EXCHRATE,BYTES=5,START=24
6.  SEGM   NAME=STOCK,PARENT=NATION,BYTES=33
7.  FIELD  NAME=(STKCODE,SEQ),BYTES=3,START=1
8.  FIELD  NAME=STKNAME,BYTES=20,START=4
9.  FIELD  NAME=STKPRICE,BYTES=3,START=24
10. FIELD  NAME=STKQTY,BYTES=4,START=27
11. FIELD  NAME=STKPE,BYTES=3,START=31
12. SEGM   NAME=DIVIDEND,PARENT=STOCK,BYTES=9
13. FIELD  NAME=(DIVDATE,SEQ),BYTES=6,START=1
14. FIELD  NAME=DIVAMT,BYTES=3,START=7
```

Figure 14-5 An abbreviated DL/I description of a database

There are several noticeable differences between a DL/I and SQL definition of a database. For starters, there are no foreign keys in the DL/I definition. The 1 : m parent–child relationship is explicitly defined by a SEGM statement. Second, there are no data field types. The length of the field in bytes is given without any indication of the type of data stored in the field. This information is supplied by the program accessing the database.

Examination of a few DL/I commands gives you some idea of the power of the language (see Table 14-3 for a summary). The intention is not to give you DL/I skills, but provide enough knowledge to understand the differences between DL/I and SQL and their consequences. One obvious difference is the additional commands required to retrieve data. SQL

Table 14–3   A Summary of Dl/I Commands

DL/I	Meaning	Operation
GU	Get unique	Retrieves the first segment satisfying the condition
GN	Get next	Retrieves the next segment
GNP	Get next within parent	Retrieves the next segment within the current parent
GHU	Get hold unique	Same as GU but holds the segment for subsequent DLET or REPL
GHN	Get hold next	Same as GN but holds the segment for subsequent DLET or REPL
GHNP	Get hold next within parent	Same as GNP but holds the segment for subsequent DLET or REPL
ISRT	Insert	Inserts a new segment
DLET	Delete	Deletes the existing segment being held
REPL	Replace	Replaces the existing segment being held

has one command (SELECT); DL/I has a number of retrieval commands (e.g., GU, GN, GNP, GHU, GHN, and GHNP).

Get Unique (GU)

GU reads a segment. For example, to read the segment containing SALENO = 10001, you write GU SALE (SALENO = 10001). This command retrieves the first SALE segment with SALENO = 10001. The DL/I programmer also has to write the instructions to format and display the data because the GU command only retrieves the segment.

DL/I requires the programmer to specify how to get to a particular record. Consider the DL/I code for the following query:

○ **What was the amount per share of the dividend paid on 1/1/92 to the Indian stock Bombay Duck?**

```
GU NATION (NATNAME = 'India');
   STOCK (STKNAME = 'Bombay Duck');
   DIVIDEND (DIVDATE = 1/1/92);
```

Get Next (GN)

Once GU gets you to a particular place in a database, GN then supports sequential retrieval of segments from that point. Consider the following query:

○ **List all stocks, starting with the first U.S. stock.**

The DL/I code is embedded in a loop in the host language (in this case, a generalized programming language or pseudo-code is used). The first segment meeting the requirement is retrieved using GU, and subsequent segments are retrieved using GN until there are no more (STATUS = 0). Remember, IMS databases have a sequential structure, so this program does not just retrieve American stocks. It retrieves all stocks, regardless of NATNAME, until there are no more STOCK segments.

```
GU NATION (NATNAME = 'US');
   do while (STATUS = 0)
     GN STOCK;
   end;
```

Get Next Within Parent (GNP)

GNP confines retrieval of segments to a particular parent record. It is useful for queries such as:

○ **List all U.S. stocks**

```
GU NATION (NATNAME = 'US')
   do while (STATUS = 0)
     GNP STOCK;
   end;
```

Now, compare the query with the corresponding SQL command:

```
SELECT * FROM STOCK, NATION
  WHERE NATNAME = 'US'
  AND STOCK.NATCODE = NATION.NATCODE
```

Since DL/I works with a record at a time, a loop is needed to retrieve each of the records meeting the condition. In contrast, SQL works with sets of records, and a join is required to get the required data from two tables. If either statement is embedded in a host language, the programmer will also have to write code to format and display the retrieved records—around two pages of COBOL programming. Of course, the advantage of SQL is that you can run the command interactively, and SQL will automatically format and display the results. Similar features are available with interactive query languages designed to work with DL/I databases.

Secondary Indexes

The order of a hierarchical database is defined by the root segment sequence field, the primary key sequence. Using the primary key enables a segment to be retrieved directly (e.g., finding details of the American stocks); however, there are many cases where it may be necessary to quickly retrieve records based on some other field in a segment. For example, there may be a need to frequently report all stocks paying a dividend on a certain date. Such a request means that each DIVIDEND segment in the database would have to examined—a very arduous process. Alternatively, a secondary index could be defined for DIVDATE to increase retrieval efficiency, but this means that the programmer must explicitly command DL/I to use the index, which is not the case with SQL. Obviously, secondary indexes are not transparent in a hierarchical database.

IMS—Still Going

Diligently trying to retain its many IMS customers, IBM has announced plans to build object-oriented capabilities into IMS, add support for common communication network protocols, and shorten the gap between new releases. Although many organizations are unlikely to undertake new development using IMS, some current applications may benefit from the changes, and it will make it easier to link IMS databases to client/server applications. The changes will also extend the useful life of some legacy systems. IMS generally outperforms IBM's DB2 and other relational databases for applications with simple, high-volume transactions. As a result, it usually has lower costs per transaction. Although IMS licenses are declining about 3 percent per annum, the installed base is very large, and it was only in 1993 that DB2 supplanted IMS as IBM's leading mainframe database.[2]

---

[2]C. Stedman, "IBM Tries to Keep IMS Vibrant," *Computerworld*, 21 March 1994, 83.

Conclusion

The hierarchical model was a successful replacement for the simple flat file. It enabled organizations to store relationships between data. Nevertheless, database technology, like all technology, continues to advance. Each new technology provides the impetus for its successor. Although a new technology may be superior to its predecessor, there is no wholesale replacement of the old because in many cases, it simply costs too much and is too disruptive to replace the old with the new. Consequently, many IMS databases may remain in use for some years.

THE NETWORK DATA MODEL AND CODASYL/DBTG

Some serious shortcomings of the hierarchical model—that it does not readily represent m:m relationships and it is not an industry standard—fostered interest in developing a better data model and database technology. Both customers and vendors, except IBM, were concerned about the lack of portability of IMS databases. Similar concerns about portability had driven the development and standardization of COBOL. So, in the late 1960s, the organization responsible for COBOL, the Conference on Data Systems Languages (CODASYL), established the Database Task Group (DBTG) to investigate a standard DBMS.

In 1971, DBTG released its official report, which it forwarded to ANSI as a proposed standard DBMS. ANSI's failure to accept or reject the proposal is possibly why the DBTG model never enjoyed the same success as COBOL. Nevertheless, several major vendors used the DBTG report as a basis for developing a commercial DBMS. Some of these systems are Computer Associates IDMS/R, DMS1100 from Unisys, and DBMS 10 and DBMS 11 from DEC.

There are other reasons that contributed to this lack of success. First, it was a very complex model without a clear theoretical base. Second, it was overtaken by the relational model, which has a number of clear advantages over the network model, including becoming an ANSI standard in 1986. Third, portability was not realistic because vendors added enhancements to their individual versions in order to differentiate themselves from their competitors. Fourth, IBM's dominance in the market made it very hard for competitors to make headway against IMS.

The network model extends the hierarchical model by permitting a child to have zero, one, or more parents. The DBTG model also introduced the notions of a DDL and DML. Once again, we will use the relational model as a reference point for understanding the network model. Major differences between the two models are summarized in Table 14-4.

DDL

The three building blocks of the DDL are data-items, records, and sets. A **data-item** is a field or attribute. It has a name and format (e.g., STKNAME, Character 20). A **record** is a collection of data-items (e.g., all the facts describing a stock). Permitting repetitions of a data-item

Table 14–4   Comparison of Network and Relational Models Based on Standard DMLs

Network	Relational
Complex conceptual structure (network)	Simple conceptual structure (table)
1:m relationship represented by a set	1:m relationship represented by a foreign key
m:m relationship represented by a member contained in two sets	m:m relationship represented by creating an additional table and using foreign keys
Repeating groups supported	Repeating groups not supported (a repeating group is against the principles of the relational model)
DML is a low level language	DML (SQL) is a high level language
DML is a sequential record processing language	DML (SQL) is a set processing language
Programming is more difficult because the programmer has to navigate the data structure	Programming is easier because SQL always returns a single table that is easily navigated
Domain, intra-record, and inter-record constraints	Entity and integrity constraints
Many vendors	Many vendors
A partial standard	ANSI standard

is a distinct feature of the DBTG model. For example, a single record could be used to store the data about a nation and its stocks, where the stock data can be repeated many times in a record (see Figure 14-6). Although permitted, it is unwise to use repeating groups because they violate the principles of good database design. You should maintain the data model's separation of NATION and STOCK as distinct entities.

A **set**, a key concept of the network model, is a 1:m relationship between records. A set has two parts: an owner and member. The "1" end of the relationship, the parent, is the **owner** of the set. The "m" end contains a **member** of a set. Thus for the share portfolio example, NATION and STOCK form a set (see Figure 14-7); NATION is the owner and STOCK is a member.

There are several parallels between the relational and network models. First, in the relational model, all the columns in a table describe one type of entity (e.g., STOCK), and in the network model, all the records in an owner also describe only one type of entity. Second, 1:1 and 1:m relationships can be readily represented by both models, though the representation method differs. The relational model uses foreign keys, and the network

					Repeating group			
NATCODE	NATNAME	EXCHRATE	SHRCODE	SHRFIRM	SHRPRICE	SHRQTY	SHRDIV	SHRPE

Figure 14-6   Record with a repeating group

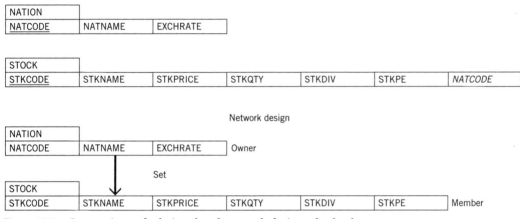

Figure 14-7   Comparison of relational and network design of a database

model has the concept of a set and the DBMS-maintained pointers. For comparison, Figure 14-7 shows the relational and network designs of the same database. Notice how the 1:m relationship is represented. In the relational model, it is through the foreign key, NATCODE. In the network model, the relationship is represented by a set, which is implemented using pointers.

A third similarity is in the representation of m:m relationships. In the data modeling that precedes definition of the relational database, an intersection entity is created. In the network model, a member is created that appears in two sets (see Figure 14-8). In the relational model, the intersection entity becomes the table LINEITEM, while in the network model, it becomes the member LINEITEM and appears in the two sets with owner's SALE and ITEM. Again, notice that there are no foreign keys in the network model, but there are pointers from SALE and ITEM to LINEITEM.

Not surprisingly, the description of a database using the CODASYL/DBTG DDL looks somewhat like a COBOL data definition (see Figure 14-9). The relationship between NATION and STOCK is specified explicitly by the SET statement, in which the owner and member are defined.

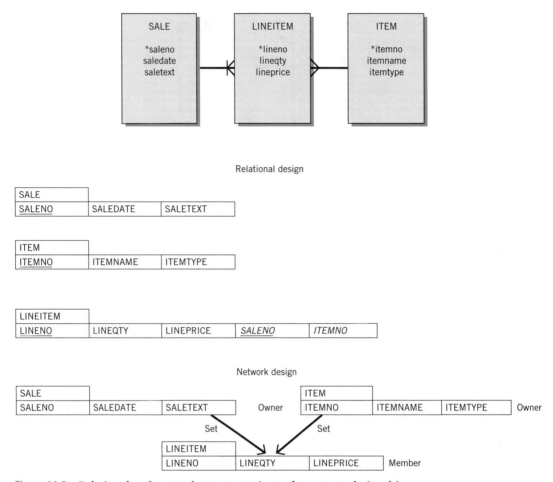

Figure 14-8 Relational and network representations of an m:m relationship

Database Integrity

The DBTG model supports three constraints that can be used to maintain data integrity.

Domain Constraints

There are two forms of domain constraints. First, the format description of a data-item is a constraint (e.g., you cannot enter an alphabetic value in a data-item defined as numeric). Second, some implementations of the network model support a CHECK statement, which can be used for range checking (e.g., LINENO IS LESS THAN 10) and checking that a value is not null (e.g., SALENO IS NOT NULL).

```
SCHEMA NAME IS INVESTMENTS.
RECORD NAME IS NATION.
   DUPLICATES ARE NOT ALLOWED FOR NATCODE.
   05 NATCODE        PIC X(3) CHECK IS NOT NULL.
   05 NATNAME        PIC X(20).
   05 EXCHRATE       PIC 9(4)V9(5).
RECORD NAME IS STOCK.
   DUPLICATES ARE NOT ALLOWED FOR STKCODE.
   05 STKCODE        PIC X(3) CHECK IS NOT NULL.
   05 STKNAME        PIC X(20).
   05 STKPRICE       PIC 9(4)V99.
   05 STKQTY         PIC 9(8).
   05 STKPE          PIC 9(5).
SET NAME IS NATSTK.
OWNER IS NATION.
MEMBER IS STOCK.
```

Figure 14-9   An abbreviated CODASYL/DBTG description of a database

Intra-Record Constraints

The uniqueness constraint is the only type of intra-record constraint supported. It enforces the rule that one or more data items must be unique (e.g., DUPLICATES NOT ALLOWED FOR STKCODE). Composite data items also can be covered by a uniqueness constraint (e.g., DUPLICATES NOT ALLOWED FOR SALENO, LINENO). The uniqueness constraint is similar to the unique key feature of indexes within SQL.

Inter-Record Constraints

There is support for referential integrity through the inter-record constraint. The CHECK statement can be used to check that a data-item in a child record is the same as a data-item in a parent record (e.g., CHECK IS SALENO IN SALE = SALENO IN LINEITEM). This is similar to the FOREIGN KEY clause in the SQL CREATE statement.

The CODASYL/DBTG Data Manipulation Language

The data manipulation language supports record retrieval (see Table 14-5 for a summary). Most commands have two steps. First, a FIND is issued to identify the required record. Then, a command is issued for the required operation (e.g., GET to read the record). This seems to be an unnecessary addition without any real gains. Some implementations of the DBTG model combine FIND and GET into a single command called OBTAIN.

A few examples demonstrate the general features of the DML. Remember, you are seeing only a small portion of a program. More code has to be written to format and report the data.

Table 14–5   A Summary of CODASYL/DBTG Commands

Command	Operation
FIND	Locate a record
GET	Retrieve a record
OBTAIN	Locate and retrieve a record
MODIFY	Update a record
ERASE	Delete a record
STORE	Insert a record

○ **Read the record for the stock with code = 'FC'**

```
MOVE 'FC' TO STKCODE IN STOCK
FIND ANY STOCK USING STKCODE
GET STOCK
```

These commands set the value of STKCODE to that of the record sought, find it, and then read it.

○ **List all stocks with a PE of 10.**

```
MOVE 10 TO STKPE IN STOCK
FIND ANY STOCK USING STKPE
DOWHILE DB-STATUS = 0
  GET STOCK
  (format and display the record)
  FIND DUPLICATE STOCK USING STKPE
END-DO
```

A loop is established to process all records meeting the criterion. When there are no more records with STKPE = 10, then DB-STATUS is set to zero by the DBMS.

○ **List all United States stocks.**

```
MOVE 'US' TO NATCODE IN NATION
FIND ANY NATION USING STKCODE
FIND FIRST STOCK WITHIN INVESTMENT
DOWHILE DB-STATUS = 0
  GET STOCK
  (format and display the record)
  FIND NEXT STOCK WITHIN INVESTMENT
END-DO
```

We can take advantage of set membership to code this command. The set has NATION as the owner and STOCK as the member. Furthermore, records in NATION are maintained in STKCODE sequence. The first FIND locates the record in NATION containing details of the United States, then the loop processes each of the American stocks.

These examples clearly demonstrate the economy of SQL. For example, the preceding query is equivalent to SELECT * FROM STOCK WHERE STKCODE = 'US'.

There are also commands for inserting and removing records from sets. CONNECT places a record in a set, DISCONNECT removes a record from a set, and RECONNECT changes set membership. The use of these commands depends on set insertion and retention status. A set can have a retention status of FIXED, MANDATORY, or OPTIONAL. Insertion status can be AUTOMATIC or MANUAL. Let's dwell on these complications long enough to realize that the CODASYL/DBTG model is more complicated than the relational model.

Conclusion

The CODASYL/DBTG model is very comprehensive and addresses many of the problems of the hierarchical model. It is also complicated, especially when compared with the simplicity of the relational model. In addition, because there were so many committees and stakeholders involved in the development of the model, the specifications are sometimes inconsistent and vague because they often represent a compromise of competing viewpoints. Loose specifications enable different vendors to interpret the model so that their implementation is compliant. Compatibility, however, is a victim of loose specification. Thus, portability across vendors, an important goal, was not achieved because the specifications were too open to interpretation. DBTG-based versions of the network model were released by a number of major software vendors. Possibly the most successful of these was IDMS by Cullinet (now Computer Associates). Although the various versions of the network model achieved some market success, they never replaced IMS as the main model. Finally, the relational model appeared, and its obvious advantages effectively killed the DBTG effort.

DATA EXTRACTION

Organizations that have a significant investment in hierarchical or network databases can still enjoy some of the benefits of the relational model. Extraction programs can be run periodically, say daily, to extract data from hierarchical or network databases and convert the extracted data to relational format. The resulting data then can be used for less time-critical managerial operations and decisions for which day-old data are acceptable. For many organizations, it makes sense to continue to operate existing hierarchical or network databases for well-established transaction processing systems and regularly use data extraction to give managers the flexible, ad hoc querying capability of a relational database.

SUMMARY

Hierarchical and network data models underlie most DBMSs developed in the late 1960s through to the early 1980s. Many of these systems, often referred to as legacy systems, are still operational, and while they continue to meet organizational needs, must be maintained. The hierarchical model emerged from a practical solution to a very significant data management problem. The basic structure of the hierarchical model is a tree or parent–child relationship.

A hierarchical database is a set of trees. A tree data structure is composed of segments. The hierarchical model has a well-defined order for storing data and uses pointers for navigation. A problem of the hierarchical model is its inability to directly model m : m relationships because of the restriction that a child can have only one parent. The most popular implementation of the hierarchical model is IBM's IMS. DL/I, which processes data a segment at a time, is the data manipulation language for IMS. In IMS, secondary indexes increase retrieval efficiency.

Concerned about shortcomings of the hierarchical model, CODASYL established the Database Task Group (DBTG) to investigate a standard DBMS. The proposed standard model was never accepted by ANSI, and the DBTG model enjoyed limited success. It was a very complex model without a clear theoretical base, the relational model outweighed it in number of clear advantages, portability was not achieved, and IBM dominated the marketplace with IMS. The three building blocks of the DDL are data-items, records, and sets. The DBTG model introduced the idea of a set with an owner and members. Relationships are represented using pointers. The DBTG model supports domain, intra-record constraints, and inter-record constraints. The DML supports record-at-a-time retrieval. Although the various versions of the network model achieved some market success, they never replaced IMS as the main model. The advent of the relational model effectively killed the DBTG effort.

Data extraction programs can be used to convert data from currently operational hierarchical or network databases to relational format. This is often an acceptable alternative to wholesale conversion of existing systems.

KEY TERMS AND CONCEPTS

Child	Member
CODASYL/DBTG	Network model
Data definition language (DDL)	Owner
Data manipulation language (DML)	Parent
Data-item	Pointer
DL/I	Record
Domain constraints	Root segment
Hierarchical model	Secondary index
IMS	Segment
Intra-record constraints	Set
Legacy system	Tree structure

EXERCISES

1. What is a legacy system?
2. What is the basic data model of the hierarchical model?
3. What data structure might you use for storing details of a tree?
4. What is the difference between a child and twin pointer?
5. What is a secondary index?
6. What are the advantages and disadvantages of the hierarchical model?
7. What were the goals of the CODASYL/DBTG project?
8. What is the difference between a DDL and DML?

9. What is a set?

10. Why did the network data model have limited success?

11. Convert the following data models to hierarchical and network designs.

(a)

(b)

(c)

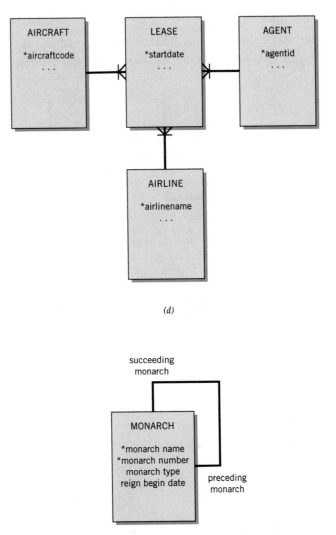

(d)

(e)

Chapter 15

Object-Oriented Database Management Systems

The goal of all inanimate objects is to resist man and ultimately to defeat him.
Russell Baker, "Observer," *The New York Times,* June 18, 1968

Learning Objectives

On completion of this chapter, you will be able to:

* explain the main concepts of object-orientation;
* compare and contrast the object-oriented model to the relational model;
* develop a simple object-oriented model.

INTRODUCTION

Information systems managers are continually searching for better ways to develop and maintain information systems. They want to deliver on time, on budget, fully functional information systems that meet clients' needs. In recent years, object orientation (OO) has attracted considerable attention because it offers the prospect of lowering systems development and maintenance costs. OO concepts are being applied to analysis, design, programming, and database. Furthermore, now that information systems have moved beyond storing only numbers and text, new applications are often required to support multimedia, CAD/CAM, economic models, document management systems, and other complex data structures. Procedural languages and relational databases are not designed to manipulate and store these data forms, but OO programming languages (OOPLs) and object-oriented database management systems (ODBMSs) are capable of doing so.

The proponents of OO[1] maintain that an ODBMS offers several advantages over current implementations of relational database technology. They assert that the shortcomings of the relational model are:

1. It cannot handle complex objects, such as multimedia;

Tore Ørvik of Agder College (Kristiansand, Norway) was the co-author of this chapter.

[1]There is considerable disagreement between the OO and relational adherents. This chapter tries to present a balance of the two viewpoints, but in describing the OO approach, it is often easier to present the OO proponents' perspective. Also, you need to remember we are comparing implementations of the two concepts and not the theoretical models. For example, if the domain concept of the relational model was broadly implemented, then some deficiencies of present relational implementations would disappear.

2. There is no support for general data types found in some programming languages;

3. Performance degrades when large numbers of tables must be joined to respond to a query;

4. There is a mismatch between the relational data model's set-at-time processing and the record-at-a-time processing of programming languages;

5. There is no support for representing and recording change, such as different versions of objects.

ODBMS technology addresses these shortcomings. In this chapter, we explain the concept of OO by demonstrating OO modeling and then exploring the current state of ODBMS.

Florida Utility: An Object Example

Florida Power & Light's (FP&L) facilities management system is based on ODBMS technology. The system displays geographic features like streets, buildings, properties, and power lines. There are object symbols for poles, switches, and transformers. Engineers can view a map showing the details of utilities in the area where they are working. Information in the database is used to estimate labor and materials costs, and to produce drawings for use by construction crews. Object technology permits ready modeling of the electrical network and connectivity between electrical devices. Connectivity can be handled more easily than with a relational structure. The application was built using Gemstone, an ODBMS, and Smalltalk, a programming language.[2]

HISTORICAL DEVELOPMENT

Although its underlying concepts have been known and used for a relatively long time, the notion of OO has only recently become commonplace and popular. The first OOPL (object-oriented programming language), SIMULA, was developed in Norway in the mid–sixties. The development of the Smalltalk language at Xerox PARC in the seventies introduced the terms object and OO and was a major step towards popularizing OO programming language. In the eighties, several existing programming languages were extended to embrace OO. Now, languages like C++ and COBOL support OO. In addition to these hybrid languages, several pure OO languages were developed.

In the late eighties, the graphical user interface (GUI), with its support for windows, icons, mouse, and pointers (WIMP), became increasingly common. OOPLs are invaluable for the development of GUI applications, which further enhanced the popularity of OO. As OO programming languages matured, OO found its way into the realms of database, and systems analysis and design.

---

[2]Adapted from E. Eldred, "Entering the Realm of Complex Data," *Client/Server Today,* May 1994, 47–63.

KEY OO CONCEPTS

It is useful to first become familiar with some key OO concepts before examining the benefits of applying OO ideas. OO applications are created by assembling and using objects—self-contained units that can contain data—very much like entities in data modeling. An object is something in the real world. Like an entity, it can be physical (e.g., a car) or conceptual (e.g., a job). Objects also contain the necessary instructions—the algorithm—to transform data. Thus, an object contains both data and methods, which are also known as procedures, operations, or services. Objects, therefore, can be thought of as application development building blocks.

OO modeling and data modeling have a common objective of creating a representation of a real world information system. Consequently, they frequently deal with the same concepts but use different terminology. A comparison of some of the key concepts is shown in Table 15-1.

Encapsulation

Encapsulation is a central concept of OO. It means that all processing that changes the state of an object (i.e., changes the value of any of its attributes) is done within that object. Encapsulation implies that an object is shielded from interference from other objects; that is, an object cannot directly change any other objects.

Classes or Object Types

In information systems, objects are individual occurrences, often corresponding to objects in the real world. For example, a teacher's grading system includes objects for Ida, Per, and every other student in the class. There usually will be several objects of the same type, and these are called an object class or, simply, class. In the grading system there will be an object class, which we will call STUDENT. Ida, Per, and the others are student objects belonging to the student object class.

Table 15–1   A Comparison of Data Modeling and OO
Modeling Terminology

Data Modeling Term	OO Modeling Term
Entity	Object class or classes
Instance	Object
Attribute	Attribute

Figure 15-1   The object class STUDENT

We will represent a class by a rounded rectangle divided into three parts (see Figure 15-1). The upper part contains the name of the class, the attributes of the class are in the middle, and the methods appear in the lower part. Because attributes and methods may need more specification detail than can fit into the available block, each block can be visualized as an expandable window that when fully opened shows additional detail. This will certainly be the case if we use special purpose OO modeling software (e.g., a CASE[3] tool). In order to focus on the higher level aspects of an OO model, however, the following examples will not specify attributes and methods even though this additional detail is required to fully define an OO model.

Message Passing

Objects communicate with each other by sending and receiving messages. For example, an object may send a message to request particular data from another object. Provided a relevant method has been established for the receiving object, the requested data value is sent back to the object issuing the request. This way of communicating is usually referred to as message passing. A message can also trigger a change in the receiving object. Again, an appropriate method must be defined for the object receiving the message.

Generalization/Specialization Hierarchies

Classes can be specializations or generalizations of other classes. The STUDENT class, for example, may be viewed as a specialization of a ACADEMIC PERSON. A super-class, in turn, might have several subclasses which, as Figure 15-2 shows, include STAFF and STUDENT. The ACADEMIC PERSON class is a generalization of the two subclasses STUDENT and STAFF.

---

[3]Computer-aided software engineering (CASE) is a set of tools to automate the tasks involved in designing and developing large-scale or complex software projects. Included are data dictionaries, diagram generators, prototyping tools, and consistency-checking tools.

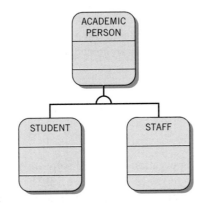

Figure 15-2   An example of a generalization/specialization hierarchy

Inheritance

An important feature of OO is that classes in a generalization/specialization hierarchy will inherit data and methods from the superclass. The ACADEMIC PERSON class in the preceding example probably will have attributes such as person name, address, and Social Security number. These attributes will be inherited by both the STUDENT and STAFF classes. In addition, we may specify some additional attributes for the STUDENT class, such as GPA and major, which are not relevant for the superclass. Inheritance simplifies specification and programming and is especially important for creating reusable objects.

The ideas of inheritance and generalization/specialization hierarchy are conceptually similar to the independent/subordinate entities structure (see Figure 15-3) of data modeling. The independent entity, ANIMAL, contains general attributes common to all subordinate entities,

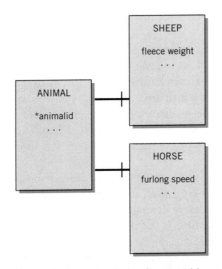

Figure 15-3   An independent/subordinate entities structure

which have specific attributes appropriate to the entity (e.g., "fleece weight" for SHEEP). Thus, you can think of SHEEP inheriting the attributes of ANIMAL, with this inheritance occurring when the two entities are joined. Of course, there are no methods associated with this data model.

Reuse

When building new applications with OO software tools, the programmer usually looks for existing object classes to use as building blocks. The exact required class may not be found, but by creating new subclasses and using the inheritance feature, new classes can be created with little effort. For example, if you are writing a drawing program, you may avoid writing a new spelling checker by reusing the existing object class written for a word processing program. This leads to a development strategy where recognizing and exploiting similarities in classes is a major means of increasing programmer productivity.

WHY OO?

Many organizations have a substantial backlog of applications because it takes significant resources to build new applications and maintain existing systems. The need to increase programmer productivity and reduce the cost of maintaining systems are the major reasons for adopting the OO approach.

Productivity

The productivity for software development has not increased substantially over the years, maybe as little as a four to sevenfold increase since the early sixties. This is trivial compared to the massive increases in hardware productivity over the same period. As a result, many potential applications, which are economically feasible because of reduced hardware costs, are piled up in the IS department waiting the attention of software developers. Software productivity has not kept pace with the increase in demand for new software. Furthermore, many of the projects in the pipeline tend to be larger and more complex than those already undertaken.

Many problems, such as WIMP-based applications, are not easily programmed using traditional, functional languages. In most cases, use of an OOPL makes programming easier and also produces more compact and efficient code. This in itself enhances productivity. More importantly, there is the possibility of creating reusable objects which, if this feature were exploited, could precipitate significant increases in productivity.

The potential reuse of objects has stimulated widespread interest in OO. Organizations can create or purchase libraries of objects that can become an important source of objects for new applications. Consequently, application development time and cost will be reduced because significant portions of new systems can be built using existing objects.

Maintenance

The slow growth in programmer productivity is exacerbated by the massive effort required to keep operational software systems current. Some companies spend as much as 80 percent of their potential development resources on maintenance of old systems. There are five main reasons for the maintenance problem:

1. Programming is a very difficult, intellectual task, and one that is prone to logic and syntax errors.
2. Determining the client's true needs is a major challenge. Too often, the specified requirements do not reflect the client's real needs, and these needs sometime do not clearly emerge until after the first version of the software is released.
3. Additional features that could not be accommodated in the original development schedule might be needed once the system is introduced.
4. The business environment changes.
5. Hardware changes.

The first two problems are strictly maintenance, and we can alleviate them by using better programming tools and by determining requirements more precisely. Items three and four are more correctly called enhancements or extensions, and we want to handle these more speedily. The fifth item, hardware changes, we try to avoid by adhering to common architectural standards, which should result in smooth transitions when hardware is replaced.

Changing large programs is very complicated, and new errors will often be introduced in the process. Because of the tendency not to document all changes properly, the actual software and the documentation become inconsistent as time passes. As developers move on to new assignments, or new careers, and documentation becomes outdated, it becomes increasingly complicated for maintenance programmers to get a thorough understanding of how existing programs work, therefore making it difficult to change or correct items without introducing unwanted side effects.

To resolve the software crisis, we must build quality software faster and reduce the cost of its maintenance and enhancement. Many believe OO directly addresses several major causes of maintenance problems.

Logical and Syntactical Errors

OO software is constructed by creating self-contained object classes. Most objects require a small number of programming statements. As a result, a program is broken into manageable units and the overall complexity of the software is reduced. Less complexity means fewer errors.

Errors will still occur, but changes can be made to the interior structure or processing rules of the object class without creating unforeseen changes throughout the system. Because each object is relatively independent, there is no ripple effect, which often occurs with traditional programming methods. This makes the existing code easy to understand, even if documentation is sparse or the maintenance programmer has little knowledge of the application.

Missing or Incorrect Specifications

Traditionally, information systems have been developed using some variation of a structured development methodology, in which the most common modeling techniques used are data flow diagramming and data modeling. OO advocates argue these techniques force clients to adopt abstract modes of thinking too remote from the way they usually think about their work, and therefore these are unsuitable for facilitating communication between the client and designer. Proponents of OO modeling claim OO alleviates this by using concepts and structuring techniques that are closer to the way people think about their work. In the everyday world, we usually think about objects like people, cars, and computers, and we also think about what these objects can do. The argument is that specifications will be more accurate because OO modeling is similar to the client's model of the world.[4]

Adding features

Methods and attributes can be easily added to existing object classes, without the risk of disrupting the rest of the system. By exploiting inheritance, new classes often can be created with minimal programming effort. Thus, OO is suitable for evolutionary development in which the main features of the system are first developed and less critical elements added as development resources become available.

Accommodating Business Change

In a competitive world, it is very important that information systems can be easily modified to reflect changes in the business environment. This requirement has become more apparent in recent years. The self-contained nature of the object classes and the inheritance feature of OO systems are expected to make it easier to change and expand OO–based systems than those developed using traditional methods.

Summary

As we have shown, OO can address the software crisis—slow development of new applications and expensive maintenance. OO systems development methods have yet to mature, but as this happens, OO is likely to move into the mainstream of software development. Many of the claims made for adopting OO modeling, however, echo Codd's rationale for introducing the relational model (see Chapter 13). Data modeling and the relational model are tools for increasing programmer productivity and reducing maintenance. Codd argued for the separation of data and procedures (or methods in OO terminology) to increase productivity; the

---

[4]As far as we are aware, there is little empirical research to support these claims.

OO school claims that encapsulating both in an object will improve productivity. So who is right? We believe there is still not enough evidence to make a judgment, and there probably will be no overall advantage for either approach. OO modeling may be better suited for some applications and process modeling/data modeling for others. With research and experience, we will discover when to use each approach.

OBJECTS AND INFORMATION SYSTEM MODELING

Modeling, as you discovered in Section 2, is a central activity of systems development. Models allow us to describe and understand information systems and to explore possible changes to such systems without interfering with or disrupting the actual system. Many different modeling techniques exist, some deal with different aspects of information systems description (e.g., procedure modeling as compared to data modeling) and some others deal with the same aspect differently (e.g., different methods of data modeling).

Models and Abstraction Levels

A model is by definition an abstraction of something else. When modeling, we leave out some of the features or detail we find in the real world, and incorporate only those we find useful for the client's needs. For instance, there are many attributes necessary to describe a person completely — height, weight, shoe size, color of eyes — but we only select those that are pertinent to the current problem.

A city map is a model of some aspects of a city's streets. For the tourist, it conveys the layout of a city very concisely and effectively. It is also an abstract model of the city, many features and details are left out. Only that information which is useful for the intended purpose is depicted. As we develop software systems, we start out with quite abstract models, concentrating on understanding required functionality. As we progress, more detail is needed, and our models become more elaborate and concrete. Eventually, they become a functioning system.

The Client–Developer Mind-Frame Gap

Clients frequently have problems defining what they want from an information system.[5] Even when they are reasonably certain, it is very difficult to capture all the necessary details. Modeling techniques used to capture and record details often include methods for prompting clients about their needs and to ensure that no details are overlooked. Nonetheless, if clients

---

[5]For an excellent discussion of this problem, see J. C. Wetherbe, "Executive Information Requirements: Getting It Right," *MIS Quarterly* 15 (1): 51–65 (1991).

are not trained in data modeling techniques, their way of thinking about their information needs may not relate closely to the way the systems analysts try to model their requirements.

This communication gap between clients and systems developers is purportedly the main reason for low quality, overdue, and over budget projects. OO supporters assert that dealing with systems objects, which closely resemble real life objects, is more natural than dealing with entities, relationships, and data flows. They argue that the OO approach narrows the communication gap because it uses modeling concepts and techniques that are more closely related to the clients' way of thinking.

Data and Procedures

Data modeling, covered in Section 2, deals with what the system needs to remember. A data model is often called static because it tends to be fairly stable and requires little change over time. This does not mean, however, that it will never change. The procedural model describes what the system needs to do, and how to do it. Often referred to as the dynamic part of an information systems model, a procedural model has two main parts: processing and control.

The processing model records the instructions—the algorithms—for processing data. Traditionally, this has been described using data flow diagrams (DFDs) or pseudo code (a structured English description of a procedure). Several other techniques can be used for this purpose, but the DFD is by far the most common. The control model deals with sequencing and timing control of processing. It also specifies any conditions that must exist in order for processing to occur.

Imagine a simple banking system with accounts for the deposit or withdrawal of money. The processing model deals with identifying and describing processes such as establishing an account, processing a withdrawal, and depositing funds; the control model defines sequencing requirements such as "a deposit cannot be made until after an account has been established." State transition diagrams and entity life history diagrams are the predominant tools for control modeling.

Some form of structured analysis and design has been the dominant systems development paradigm for about two decades. Initially, structured analysis dealt primarily with the processing model. Later versions tried to address both the data and control side by incorporating data modeling and state transition diagramming. The different models tend to become inconsistent, however, and for large complex systems, may not convey a unified model of the system.

Statics and Dynamics

In OO analysis (OOA), the terms static and dynamic assume a slightly different meaning than that used in other analysis methods. The static aspects are modeled in the main class and object model, which shows the potential or the capabilities of the system as opposed to what the system will actually do in a given circumstance. The model is static in the sense that it shows what the objects are capable of doing and remembering (like a data model), and these are fairly stable characteristics. In this case, static is a relative term, and both the capability for remembering and doing may change over time. Methods—the capability for doing—is possibly the more volatile. The dynamic aspect of a model deals with what the system actually does for any particular event.

Scenarios

A scenario is a typical event or sequence of events in the problem domain and the related behavior of the information system. In a simple banking system, some key scenarios are a customer making a withdrawal or a deposit, and a manager requesting the day's total withdrawals and deposits. Although the same classes might be involved in the different scenarios, different data and methods will be invoked and different messages will be transmitted. For each scenario, a subset of the potential capabilities are used and combined to yield the desired system behavior. We usually start by developing the static model, which also incorporates the main methods. We gain sufficient knowledge of all the needed methods only after a thorough analysis of all relevant scenarios.

Traditional systems have an overall control structure or main application program. There is no such parallel in OO because each scenario is associated with a sequence of actions and interactions that define system behavior in that particular context.

Static OO Modeling

The basic data modeling concepts learned earlier apply to OO modeling of the static part of a system. It may help to think of object classes as entities with integrated procedural rules. Like entities, object classes can be related to other object classes. One distinction is the kinds of relationships or structures that are defined in an OO model.

Two broad types of possible relationships are depicted in an OO model: relationships between classes and relationships between individual objects. Classification or inheritance relationships are between classes; composition or aggregation, association, and user or communication relationships are between individual objects. Each of these relationships will be demonstrated with an OO modeling exercise.

Finding Objects and Classes

Usually the initial activity in OO analysis, finding objects and classes is, in many respects, very similar to identifying entities in data modeling. Which classes to include in a system is highly dependent on the context, the client, and the modeler. Although there is no "correct" set of classes (or entities, in the case of data modeling), the OO analyst should strive to create a high fidelity model of the client's world. Careful questioning and looking for exceptions are key skills for an analyst. Domain area knowledge and experience also play an important role in the development of high fidelity models.

One approach is to underline any nouns in the problem description. Most nouns are possible classes and underlining ensures that you do not overlook any potential classes. These suggestions for OO modeling also apply to data modeling. Finding entities and finding classes are quite similar exercises.

Coad and Yourdon[6] present a five-layer model of OO analysis:

Class and object layer – object classes;

Structure layer – structural relations between classes;

Subject layer – the clustering of object classes into units of a higher level of abstraction;

Attribute layer – the attributes of each class;

Service layer – the methods for each class.

Although presented sequentially, actual analysis will usually not strictly follow such a serial pattern. The sequence does suggest a main order of activities, however, because the tendency is to work in an iterative fashion rather than finishing all the activities associated with one layer before undertaking the next.

We will now explore these concepts in more depth through an example that will gradually build the layers of an OO model. The notation used for this modeling is adopted from Coad and Yourdon and is also influenced by Booch.[7]

The Expeditioner

The Expeditioner has arranged many diving safaris to the Great Barrier Reef off Australia's northeast coast. The customers have been extremely pleased with these expeditions, which were handled by a local operator, Dick's Dive 'n Thrive, or DDT for short. Stories in diving magazines and word of mouth among diving devotees have generated tremendous growth for DDT. Although he is a great diver, Dick unfortunately is a poor manager. The company has been unable to handle the growth, and is now in serious financial trouble. As a result, Dick has turned to one of his major customers, The Expeditioner, for help. After a thorough investigation of the business opportunities, The Expeditioner decides to take a major interest in DDT. Its management team recognizes that new business practices have to be established, especially for the rental side of DDT, which generates most of the business, and is currently losing money.

The management team concludes that existing procedures need to be automated to provide better control and information for managerial decision making, and so they hire a local systems analyst to develop and install an information system. A young lad from Townsville, Bruce "Shark" Dundee,[8] is hired. Shark has had considerable success using OO concepts and

---

[6]P. Coad and E. Yourdon, *Object-Oriented Analysis* (Englewood Cliffs, NJ: Prentice–Hall, 1990).

[7]G. Booch, *Object Oriented Design with Applications* (Redwood City, CA: Benjamin/Cummings, 1991).

[8]Although his father is a famous crocodile hunter, Shark prefers the ocean.

decides to create an OO model of DDT's rental business. He starts by writing a statement of the business and underlining the nouns.

Customers can rent diving equipment and boats from DDT. When a customer has seen what is available and decided what to rent, a rental agreement or contract is produced and signed.

Class and Object Layer

The brief description of DDT's rental business is a starting point for modeling. By underlining the nouns, we see that customer, diving equipment, contract, and boat all are prime candidates for classes (see Figure 15-4).

Structure Layer

There are two types of structures: generalization/specialization and whole/part. Each of these will be discussed in turn.

Generalization/Specialization Structures

Depending on how and with which classes we start, OO modeling can be top down or bottom up. In this example, we first look at the classes[9] BOAT and DIVING EQUIPMENT, both of which may be regarded as types of rental equipment. Thus, it is useful to establish a generalized class, which we call RENTAL EQUIPMENT. The attributes and methods established for RENTAL EQUIPMENT are inherited by the classes DIVING EQUIPMENT and BOAT. In this case, we have done bottom up modeling (see Figure 15-5). If we had started with RENTAL EQUIPMENT, we would have done top down modeling.

If DIVING EQUIPMENT and BOAT are exhaustive classes—that is, DDT only rents boats and diving equipment—the RENTAL EQUIPMENT class will not contain any objects. It will serve solely as a vehicle for specifying the common attributes and methods of DIVING EQUIPMENT and BOAT. If, on the other hand, DDT rents other items which could be

Figure 15-4   Some classes

---

[9]The names of classes are shown in uppercase.

Figure 15-5 A generalization/specialization structure

totally described within the RENTAL EQUIPMENT class, then it would contain objects.[10] Classes with non-exhaustive subclasses, or no subclasses at all, contain objects. Classes containing objects—instances of a class—are depicted by a darker line around the class symbol (see Figure 15-6).

Figure 15-6 shows that DIVING EQUIPMENT and BOAT are exhaustive. They contain objects, but RENTAL EQUIPMENT stores none, which reflects the current DDT situation. If DDT gets other types of equipment that it rents, RENTAL EQUIPMENT could become an object-containing class, provided it does not need to store any special information about the equipment. Alternatively, if extra information must be remembered, a new subclass must be established.

If we look more closely at DIVING EQUIPMENT, we see that more detail may be re-

Figure 15-6 Exhaustive classes DIVING EQUIPMENT and BOAT

---

[10]Strictly speaking, we should write "classes that have corresponding objects" in place of "classes contain objects." Nevertheless, it is useful to think of objects as being contained within classes, and it certainly makes writing about them less contorted.

quired. DDT rents the usual diving gear such as tanks, regulators, weights, wet suits, and depth gauges, but it needs to store additional specialized information about some of this equipment. For example, diving suits are described by size, thickness, and type. Although we have not specified attributes yet, it is still necessary to think about them (or what must be re-membered) to determine what subclasses to create. An analyst who understands the business and the intended use of the system will soon gain a good idea of the required attributes. As with data modeling, when attributes are specified, some changes in structure often occur. Thus, it makes sense to define attributes as you develop the OO model.

In this case, we recognize the need for a subclass SUIT (see Figure 15-7). Later, we might have to refine DIVING EQUIPMENT, but for now, it will have only one subclass. This means that all diving equipment we rent, except suits, will be called DIVING EQUIPMENT, with an attribute identifying the type of rental equipment (e.g., tank, regulator, etc.). DIVING EQUIPMENT contains objects (the subclass is not exhaustive) and retains the darker line of a class symbol. In addition to the services and attributes we will later specify for it, the SUIT class will inherit all specified attributes and services from DIVING EQUIPMENT and RENTAL EQUIPMENT.

We have now seen an example of generalization and specialization in which inheritance flows from the superclass to the subclass. This is sometimes referred to as an inheritance rela-tion or an "is a kind of" relation; for instance, SUIT is a kind of DIVING EQUIPMENT. An inheritance relation is depicted by and distinguished from the other types of relationships by the semicircle annotation shown in Figure 15-7. We recommend placing the superclass above the subclasses to increase readability.

An inheritance relation is between classes, but inheritance is not like a relationship in data modeling. The inheritance relationship between SUIT and DIVING EQUIPMENT does not

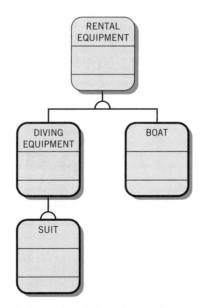

Figure 15-7   SUIT as a subclass of DIVING EQUIPMENT

imply that a SUIT object (one specific suit) is linked to a corresponding DIVING EQUIP-MENT object. Here, inheritance means SUIT has the same methods and attributes as DIV-ING EQUIPMENT and some other methods and attributes that are unique to SUIT.

Multiple Inheritance

So far, generalization/specialization structures have been simple tree structures. Each subclass has one superclass from which it inherits methods and attributes. Multiple inheritance means a class can inherit attributes and methods from more than one superclass. The generalization/specialization structure then becomes more like a lattice than a tree.

Looking at DDT's customers, we see a difference (see Figure 15-8). Some customers rent boats and others rent diving equipment. If this difference is significant in DDT's context (due to different licensing and insurance requirements, for example), we could create a class for each group.

DIVING CUSTOMER and BOAT CUSTOMER are exhaustive subclasses so there will be no customer objects, hence the thin and thick lines in the figure. Some customers probably will be both diving customers and boat customers (see the model in Figure 15-9), so COM-BINED CUSTOMER inherits methods and attributes from both DIVING CUSTOMER and BOAT CUSTOMER.

As you may anticipate, multiple inheritance can create problems when an application is executed. There may be conflicts between the inherited methods and attributes. Although there are different strategies for dealing with this problem, the issue remains unresolved. One strategy is not to support multiple inheritance, which is the approach taken by some OOPLs. From a modeling perspective, it is certainly possible to model multiple inheritance and defer considerations about conflict resolution until time for design. Some modelers recommend avoiding multiple inheritance altogether, especially if the implementation environment does not support it.

Whole/Part Structures

Now, let us now look more closely at the class BOAT. Some of DDT's boats are rented with a trailer, and some with zero, one, or two motors. Trailers and motors always stay with the same boats. Motors are never rented without boats or taken away from the boats to which

Figure 15-8 Classes of CUSTOMER

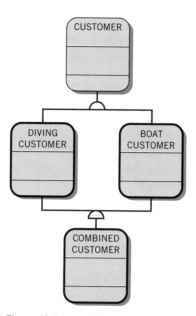

Figure 15-9   Multiple inheritance

they belong, except to be serviced or replaced. We now have a BOAT ASSEMBLY which includes BOAT, TRAILER, and MOTOR classes, as shown in Figure 15-10. This is a whole/part structure, depicting the whole (the boat assembly) and its parts.

We have a relationship between objects that implies that there is one specific boat assembly for a particular trailer. The relationship for the whole/part structure is usually referred to as composition, aggregation, or "part of" relationship, i.e., a TRAILER is a "part of" BOAT ASSEMBLY. The composition relationship is distinguished from the other types of relation-

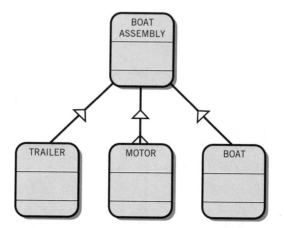

Figure 15-10   A whole/part structure

ships by a broad arrow. Conventionally, the whole class (BOAT ASSEMBLY in this case) is placed above the components to enhance readability.

An OO model, like a data model, records details of the composition relationship. In the case of an OO model, the relationship is between objects. Since a boat assembly can have one or more motors, this must be shown on the OO model. The notation used is similar to that of data modeling—a crow's foot is used to show a 1:m relationship between BOAT ASSEMBLY and BOAT. As in data modeling, this means that a boat assembly can have zero, one, or more motors. Furthermore, a motor belongs to one and only one boat assembly.

We can now combine the completed pieces to illustrate the current state of our OO model (Figure 15-11). Observe that the model is incomplete at this stage because it does not include CUSTOMER or CONTRACT.

Subject Layer

Because most people have difficulty handling more than seven, plus or minus two, objects at a time,[11] partitioning or clustering is needed to reduce complexity in large OO models. These clusters are usually called subjects. For small models, the subject layer is hardly needed, and

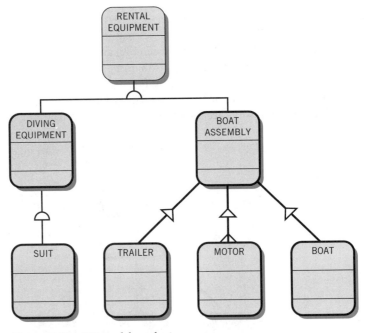

Figure 15-11 OO model—take 1

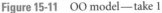

[11]G. A. Miller, "The Magical Number Seven, Plus or Minus Two: Some Limits On Our Capacity for Processing Information," *The Psychological Review* 63 (2): 81–97 (1956).

for medium-sized models, it is best developed after the structure layer. For large models, it is often necessary to start with the subject layer in order to facilitate project planning and work assignment, partitioning, and scheduling.

In an existing model, the general classes in generalization/specialization and whole classes in whole/part structures are prime candidates for subjects. In our example, the RENTAL EQUIPMENT class would be a subject. Classes not belonging to generalization/specialization or whole/part structures may be candidates by themselves or combined with other non-generalization/specialization or whole/part classes to which they are related. In our example, the combination of CUSTOMER and CONTRACT classes is another likely candidate. Subjects, represented by rectangles, may be shown in a separate figure (see Figure 15-12).

Another approach represents subjects by enclosing the object classes belonging to a subject (see Figure 15-13) within a rectangle.

Attribute Layer

The attribute layer has two purposes: specification of attributes and specification of association relationships.

Attributes

Attributes are the facts to be remembered by the object. Some OO proponents argue that definition of attributes is not needed until physical design or implementation. We recommend that you specify attributes as you discover them. It is only by recording attributes that you really understand the nature of the object classes. As a result, you may have to revise some classes and structures to improve the fidelity of your OO model. Attribute names are listed in the middle segment in the class representation (see Figure 15-14).

As in data modeling, more information (e.g., range, length, and validation criteria) about an attribute than is provided in the model will be needed before a system can be fully described. Attribute names serve as references to more detailed descriptions that we store elsewhere, on paper or in the database associated with a CASE tool. Due to space limitations, we might also want to show aggregate attributes in the model and then completely specify them elsewhere. Address, for example, is usually an aggregate of address lines, city, state, and zip code. By specifying only "address" in the model, we avoid cluttering it with too much detail—although we still convey an impression of what is included—which is sufficient to allow us to proceed with the modeling activity.

Figure 15-12 Subjects RENTAL EQUIPMENT and CUSTOMER/CONTRACT—a higher level diagram

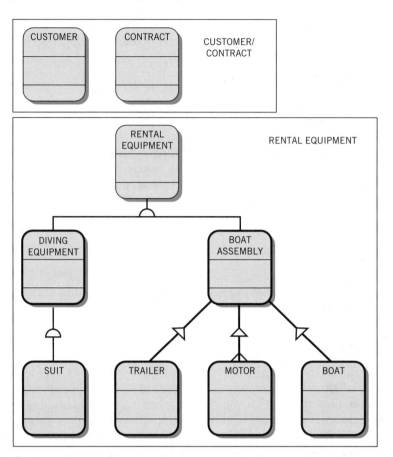

Figure 15-13 Subjects RENTAL EQUIPMENT and CUSTOMER/CONTRACT
—a lower level diagram

When deciding which attributes to include, the same principles that are used in data modeling apply to OO modeling. The selection of attributes is based on understanding how objects are described in the actual problem domain, the responsibilities they will have in the information system, and what they need to remember and do. For example, a student object is

Figure 15-14 Attributes of CUSTOMER

unlikely to include details of the student's hair color. Although this is an attribute of a student, this fact probably will not be used by any object and need not be remembered by the system.

If an attribute is only relevant for some of the objects in a class, another class—a specialization—might be needed. For example, diving certificate issue date may be an attribute, but it is not relevant for customers who only rent a boat assembly. We then must differentiate between different types of customers by introducing specialized classes for diving equipment customers and boat assembly customers. To keep the model simple, attribute names are not shown in our examples, except where needed for illustration purposes.

Association Relationships

Association relationships depict links between occurrences of object. Sometimes called instance connections, they are conceptually the same as relations in data modeling. For example, a specific contract or rental agreement is associated with a specific customer. A CUSTOMER can be associated with many CONTRACTs. A CONTRACT is related to one and only one CUSTOMER (see Figure 15-15). This is the familiar notation of data modeling. A CONTRACT is also related to RENTAL EQUIPMENT, because a CONTRACT describes the RENTAL EQUIPMENT rented (see Figure 15-16).

As you can see, there is an m:m association between CUSTOMER and RENTAL EQUIPMENT objects. A customer can rent many pieces of equipment and a piece of equipment can be rented by many customers. When a customer rents equipment, a contract is created, and this typically includes many items. Because there is an m:m association between CONTRACT and RENTAL EQUIPMENT objects, the model should include another object class, CONTRACT ITEM, which is related to CONTRACT. We have shown this as an aggregation relationship because it reflects the client's thinking that an item on a contract is logically part of a contract (see Figure 15-17).

The aggregation relationship is actually a special version of the association relationship. It reflects a strong tie between objects and also resembles a fundamental way of thinking about objects in the real world—an object as part of another object. All aggregation relationships conceivably can be modeled with association relationships although some OO proponents discard the aggregation relationship altogether. By using it, we obtain a model that is less abstract and closer to the way we usually think about objects. The latest version of the model is shown in Figure 15-18.

Figure 15-15 A 1:m association between CUSTOMER and CONTRACT

Figure 15-16   An association between CUSTOMER,
CONTRACT, and RENTAL EQUIPMENT

Service Layer

The required processing for each object is specified in the service layer. Simple and complex services are distinguished. Simple services are the standard services that nearly all objects need to be able to perform. These are usually implied as always being available and are not shown in the model. Simple services typically include: create, connect, access, and release.

Complex or non-standard services, which are shown explicitly, fall into two categories: calculate and monitor. For example, the object class CONTRACT needs to calculate a rental fee. This non-standard service is shown in the services window (see Figure 15-19). The service name shown in the model is also a reference to a detailed specification of the rental fee calculation algorithm. The actual specification is usually deferred until the static model has stabilized after a few iterations.

Message Connections and Use Relationships

DDT's rental policy includes a 30 percent surcharge on the daily rent for any holiday, weekend day, or any day during the main vacation season. Thus, for a CONTRACT object to calculate rent, it has to refer to a calendar. CALENDAR is an example of a class with only one

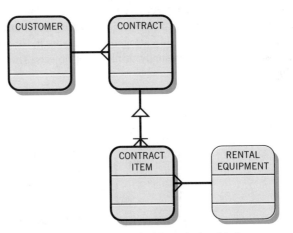

Figure 15-17   An aggregation relationship between
CONTRACT and CONTRACT ITEM

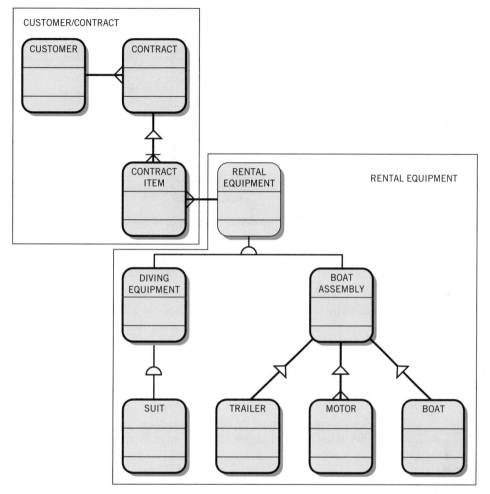

Figure 15-18   OO model—take 2

object, something which is feasible but not common. The CALENDAR class is required to support the "calculate days" procedure. Think of CALENDAR as a collection of days, each having the attributes date and type, which indicates if a surcharge applies to the particular day. So we add a new object class, DAY, in a whole/part structure (see Figure 15-20).

A CONTRACT object is not associated with a CALENDAR object in the usual sense because

Figure 15-19   The service "Calculate rent"

Figure 15-20 Representing CALENDAR as aggregation of DAY

it uses information from the CALENDAR object, hence the broken line in Figure 15-21 denotes a use or communication relationship. Communication is usually in both directions: CONTRACT sends a message to CALENDAR for the number of days of each type between two given dates, and CALENDAR responds (see Figure 15-21). The arrow indicates the direction of the main result of the interchange. The provider of the information is often referred to as a server object and the receiver as a client object, with the arrow pointing to the client object. Of course, an object might serve the role of client in one interaction sequence and a server in another.

This completes the first iteration of the static class and object model. You now have seen examples of the four types of relationships—inheritance, aggregation, association, and

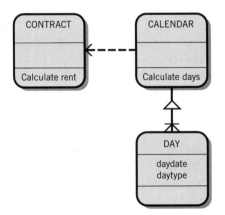

Figure 15-21 Communication between CONTRACT and CALENDAR

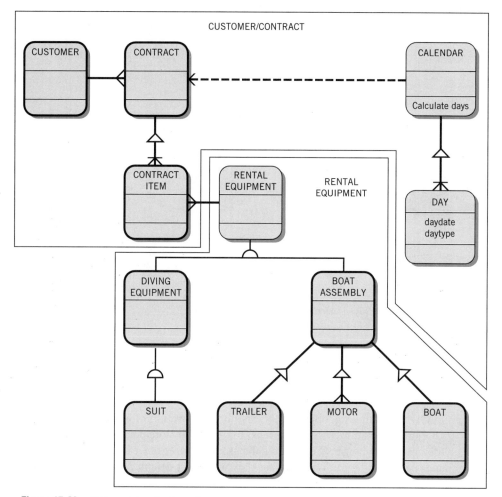

Figure 15-22   OO model—final version

use—which are the basic features of OO modeling. Figure 15-22 shows the final version of our OO model.

Summary

Many concepts were introduced in the preceding discussion on OO modeling. Figure 15-23 maps the links between some key OO ideas. A subject is a cluster of object classes. An object class, composed of individual occurrences of objects, has attributes and methods. Attributes are the facts an object remembers, and methods are the actions an object can perform. Associations describe the links between object occurrences. Objects can participate in two types of structures: generalization/specialization ("is a kind of") and whole/part ("is part of").

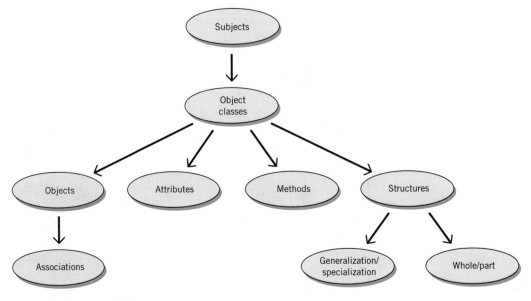

Figure 15-23   A map of OO concepts

PERSISTENT OBJECTS

In OO programming, objects only exist for the duration of a program's execution. If we use OO for information systems, we need to be able to store details of *persistent* objects — those that last much longer. We need a database that stores objects and has facilities for accessing and executing them. What we need is an object-oriented database management system (ODBMS).

OBJECT-ORIENTED DATABASE MANAGEMENT SYSTEMS

An ODBMS stores simple and complex objects. It also supports the creation of abstract data types, encapsulation, and inheritance. An ODBMS is the database extension of OO concepts. It stores data when the OO application is no longer executing. ODBMSs also are designed to work closely with OOPLs, and the linkage is tighter than that between a RDBMS and procedural languages. Because of the consistent use of OO concepts, OO applications are more suited to manage data using ODBMS rather than RDBMS technology. As you would expect, ODBMSs also manage data sharing, concurrent data access, and recovery control, which are necessary features of any database technology.

There are some fundamental differences between ODBMS and RDBMS technology. An ODBMS has pointers, like the hierarchical and network models, for quickly accessing data.

Every object has a system-generated unique object identifier, which contains the address of the pointer to the data. This is a significant difference from the approach of the relational data model, where relationships are maintained by foreign keys. As a result, the system can directly access the required data. An ODBMS does not require joins.

Volkswagen Selects Versant

Volkswagen GmbH, the manufacturer of Volkswagen and Audi cars, is planning a single on-line system that will monitor every task involved in the life cycle of a car—building, distributing, selling, servicing, and recycling. The system will link car dealerships and factories across several continents, and is expected to reach some 110,000 users by 1997.

Volkswagen has selected Versant Object Technology Corp.'s object-oriented database as the basis for the system. The selection of Versant followed assessment of several systems in late 1992 and early 1993. Potential relational and object databases were evaluated by building a prototype of part of the system. Among other reasons, Versant was chosen because object technology outperformed relational technology when dealing with unstructured data and many of the staff were already familiar with object-oriented applications.

When implemented, the system will permit sales staff to search 10,000 dealerships for a car that precisely matches a customer's requirements. Currently, such searches are very time consuming and require many telephone calls and manual checking of production records.

As the costliest high-volume car maker in the world, Volkswagen must find ways to reduce its costs and increase market share. In 1992, the company sold 3.5 million cars and made a profit of about $26 on each sale. Volkswagen predicts the new system will reduce inventory and improve customer service.[12]

The so-called impedance problem, the mismatch between RDBMS set-at-time processing and procedural language record-at-time processing, is cited as a shortcoming of relational technology. If you look back at the COBOL program in Chapter 9, you will see how the cursor handles the impedance problem. OOPLs and ODBMSs do not have this problem because all operations are at the record level. Of course, this also means the relational model advantages of set-at-time processing are lost. Furthermore, some procedural languages do not handle RDBMS data types and arithmetic. For example, SQL permits the definition of date as a data type and supports arithmetic on dates, but not all procedural languages support all SQL data types or may store them differently, which can cause additional work when programming. There is no mismatch between ODBMS and OOPL data types.

---

[12]Adapted from K. S. Nash, "VW Picks Single System," *Computerworld*, 10 January 1994, 57, 61.

ODBMS Standards

Information systems managers are reluctant to adopt technology that ties them to a particular vendor. They seek compatibility and standardization because it gives them greater flexibility when buying new hardware and software. Consequently, OO technology vendors have established the Object Management Group (OMG) to create and promulgate standards for OO technology and object interaction. The OMG is also working on ODBMS issues. Its objective is to minimize incompatibilities across various implementations of the ODBMS idea and standardize some of the features.

OMG has released ODMG-93, an object database standard, which it intends to promote as an ANSI/ISO standard. Adoption of this standard by ANSI and ISO will certainly help the growth of the ODBMS market because it assures potential adopters that they will avoid future incompatibility problems. ODMG-93 has four major components: object data model, object definition language, object query language, and application program interfaces.

The object data model (ODM) defines a set of built-in types that are used to create and represent composite structures that mirror real world entities. Its support for the definition of arbitrary objects (i.e., user-defined objects that are not part of the standard language) is a major advantage over the relational model. ODM corresponds to the data modeling methods of the relational model.

Once the object data model is prepared, the object data language (ODL) is used to define objects. It parallels the CREATE statement of SQL. An ODL precompiler can translate object definitions into C++ and Smalltalk source code for use in writing application programs. Unlike the relational model, ODL does not have a rigorous mathematical underpinning.

There is an SQL-like query language—object query language (OQL)—for operating directly on objects and their attributes. For example, OQL can be used to join and compare objects. OQL is not restricted to SQL's tabular structure of rows and columns and can work with more complex structures.

A Commercial System—UniSQL/X

UniSQL/X is an object-relational, client server database. Object orientation is provided by extending SQL. A database can be created and used without writing a line of OOPL code. Defining a class is very similar to defining a table. Part of the code for describing an OO model is shown in Figure 15-24. As you can see, it has a similar structure to the SQL CREATE statement. UniSQL/X is highly compatible with SQL once you use class as a substitute for table.

In addition, UniSQL/X makes some major extensions to the relational model: user-defined data types, multiple values, encapsulation, inheritance, and polymorphism.[13] These useful extensions will possibly appear in the next SQL standard.

---

[13]Polymorphism is the capability to send a common message to objects of different types, with each object responding in its own particular way.

```
create class academic_person
  (acperid    integer         unique,
  acperfname    string,
  acperlname    string);
method     class      add_academic_person       (acperid,      acperfname,
acperlname)...;
create class student as subclass of academic_person
  (major string,
  ...);
create class staff as subclass of academic_person
  (department string,
  ...);
```

Figure 15-24   Describing an OO model with UniSQL/X

User-Defined Data Types

This extension permits new data types to be defined. For example, a table can be defined as a data type and as a result, nested tables can be defined. Nested tables can be useful when complex or composite objects must be defined. Also, retrieval should be faster because multiple joins are unnecessary when one table is nested within another. The use of nested tables means a bill of materials structure can be exploded very rapidly.

Multiple Values

The relational model restricts a column in a row to one value—the so-called notion of atomic values. UniSQL/X relaxes this constraint and permits a row–column unit to contain sets, multisets (called bags), sequences (lists), and even heterogeneous domains (a mixture of data types). Consequently, fewer tables are needed to describe data relationships and response times are reduced, but this flexibility is gained via a more complex structure that may be more difficult for the user to comprehend and harder for the programmer to code.

Encapsulation

UniSQL/X also supports the OO notion of encapsulation. Methods, written in an OOPL, can be embedded in tables.

Inheritance and Polymorphism

Inheritance and polymorphism, important OO concepts, are supported by UniSQL/X. There is explicit support for hierarchical structures. A table can be a parent or child of another table. Polymorphism is supported because a child can have many parents.

THE FUTURE OF ODBMS

A question that many data managers ask is "Will ODBMS replace RDBMS in the next five years?" Based on the slowness with which the RDBMS technology was adopted, this is unlikely. RDBMS technology first appeared in 1979, and it took many years for it to replace hierarchical and network systems and become the major database model. Organizations have a heavy investment in relational database systems and have learned how to build and manage such systems. They are unlikely to discard this large investment quickly and switch to the object-oriented model. Many companies still maintain hierarchical and network systems—a legacy of the past, so do not expect ODBMSs to become a dominant force in the next few years. RDBMSs are likely to remain the predominant choice, especially for non-complex data stores.

Furthermore, there is no single database system that is "right" for all applications. Instead of generally adopting a single model, database designers need to consider the characteristics of the data, data structures, and the system's goals before deciding on which DBMS is appropriate. Clearly, applications that must handle complex objects are well-suited to ODBMS. Our prognosis is that relational systems will dominate over the next few years, with object-oriented sales increasing and those of hierarchical and network declining. We also expect some merging of object and relational concepts. ODBMSs may incorporate some relational concepts without losing OO advantages, and RDBMSs may add some OO concepts without compromising the relational model. Eventually, we may see the emergence of a hybrid object relational model.

SUMMARY

OO has attracted considerable attention because it offers the prospect of lowering systems development and maintenance costs. OO concepts are being applied to analysis, design, programming, and database. OO modeling creates a representation of a real world information system. An ODBMS with an OOPL can overcome some of the shortcomings of relational database technology. OOPLs are invaluable for the development of GUI applications.

OO applications are created by assembling and using objects, self-contained units that can contain data. Objects also contain the necessary instructions to transform data. Encapsulation means that all processing that changes the state of an object is done within an object. Objects are individual occurrences, often corresponding to objects in the real world. Objects of the same type are called an object class. Objects communicate with each other by sending and receiving messages.

Classes can be specializations or generalizations of other classes. Classes in a generalization/specialization hierarchy will inherit data and methods from the superclass. Inheritance simplifies specification and programming and is especially important for creating reusable objects. Recognizing and exploiting similarities in classes is a major means of increasing programmer productivity.

Modeling is a central activity of systems development. A model is an abstraction of something. OO supporters argue that their approach narrows the communication gap between client and analyst because it uses modeling concepts and techniques that are more closely related to the clients' way of thinking. It is necessary to describe two aspects of an information system—data and procedures. The static part of a model shows what objects are capable of doing and remembering; the dynamic aspect deals with what the system actually does for any particular event. A scenario is a typical event or sequence of events in the problem domain and the related behavior of the information system.

Two broad types of possible relationships are shown in an OO model: relationships between classes and relationships between individual objects. Finding objects and classes is usually the initial activity in OO analysis. One approach is to underline any nouns in the problem description. A five-layer model of OO analysis includes: class and object layer, structure layer, subject layer, attribute layer, and service layer.

The two types of structures are generalization/specialization and whole/part. A generalization/specialization structure is sometimes referred to as an inheritance relation or an "is a kind of" relation. Multiple inheritance means a class can inherit attributes and methods from more than one superclass. The relationship for the whole/part structure is usually referred to as composition, aggregation, or "part of" relationship. Partitioning or clustering reduces the complexity of large OO models. These clusters are usually called subjects.

The attribute layer has two purposes: specification of attributes and specification of association relationships. Attributes are the facts to be remembered by the object. Association relationships depict links between actual object occurrences. They are conceptually the same as relations in data modeling. The aggregation relationship is a special version of the association relationship. The processing required for each object is specified in the service layer. Simple services are the standard services that nearly all objects need to be able to perform. Complex or non-standard services fall into two categories: calculate and monitor. Objects can have message connections and use relationships.

An ODBMS stores details of persistent objects; it is the database extension of OO concepts. ODBMSs have high synergy with OOPLs. ODBMSs manage data sharing, concurrent data access, and recovery control. Every object has a system-generated unique object identifier, which contains the address of the pointer to the data. All operations are at the record level. OO technology vendors have established the Object Management Group (OMG) with the goal of creating and promulgating standards for OO technology and object interaction. OMG has released ODMG-93 with four major components: object data model, object definition language, object query language, and application program interfaces.

Relational systems will dominate over the next few years, with object-oriented sales increasing and those of hierarchical and network declining. ODBMSs may incorporate some relational concepts without losing OO advantages, and RDBMSs may add some OO concepts without compromising the relational model. Eventually, we may see the emergence of a hybrid object relational model.

KEY TERMS AND CONCEPTS

Aggregation	Dynamic model
Association	Encapsulation
Attribute	Exhaustive class
Complex objects	Generalization/specialization structure
Complex service	Hybrid object relational model
Composition	Impedence problem

Information engineering	Persistent object
Inheritance	Polymorphism
Layer	Relationship
Message passing	Reusable objects
Methods	Scenario
Object	Service
Object class	Simple service
Object data language (ODL)	Software productivity
Object data model (ODM)	Specialization
Object identifier	Static model
Object Management Group (OMG)	Structured analysis
Object-orientation (OO)	Subclass
ODBMS	Subject
OO analysis (OOA)	Superclass
OO design (OOD)	Use relationship
OO modeling	Whole/part structure
OO programming language (OOPL)	Windows, icon, mouse, pointer (WIMP)

REFERENCES AND ADDITIONAL READINGS

Booch, G. *Object-Oriented Design with Applications.* Redwood City, CA: Benjamin/Cummings, 1991.

Cattell, R. G. G. "Next-Generation Database Systems." *Communications of the ACM* 34, no. 10 (1991): 31–33.

Coad, P., and E. Yourdon. *Object-Oriented Analysis.* Englewood Cliffs, NJ: Prentice–Hall, 1990.

Pascal, F. "Objection!" *ComputerWorld*, 14 June 1993, 127–128, 130.

EXERCISES

1. What circumstances have stimulated interest in OO concepts?
2. What is encapsulation? Why is it desirable?
3. Draw a generalization/specialization hierarchy to describe audio recording media (e.g., cassette, CD, LP).
4. Draw a generalization/specialization hierarchy to describe farm animals.
5. What are the advantages of inheritance?
6. Draw a generalization/specialization hierarchy to describe transport choices (e.g., bus, car, plane, boat). What attributes are common to all object classes? What are some unique attributes of a plane?
7. What are the advantages of the OO approach?
8. How does OO reduce maintenance costs?
9. How does a data model differ from a procedural model?
10. Why do objects pass messages?

11. What is the difference between association and aggregation relationships?

12. Why is an ODBMS required?

13. How do an ODBMS and RDBMS differ in the way they handle recording relationships?

14. What are ODBMS vendors doing to increase the likelihood of the adoption of ODBMS technology?

15. What is the likely future for ODBMS and RDBMS?

16. A travel company sells two types of trips: ship cruises and bus tours. Customers fall into two categories: group and individual. Group customers belong to an affinity group (e.g., a birdwatchers' club), which will book a block of tickets on a trip. Individual customers make personal bookings. Some individual customers, because of their frequent use of the travel company, are designated "gold star travelers" and get additional benefits when traveling. Draw a class and object layer model.

17. Night-on-the-Town offers a package deal to New York tourists. For a flat fee, a person can select a Broadway play, dinner at a fancy restaurant, and jazz at a nightclub. Night-on-the-Town offers a choice in each category, and the customer selects one from each of the three categories (i.e., the customer goes to a play, eats dinner, and then listens to jazz). Draw a class and object layer model.

18. An agent can represent many bands, but a band has only one agent. A band consists of many musicians, but a musician belongs to only one band. Model this situation, using association and aggregation relationships.

19. A government treasury bond provides a guaranteed stream of future payments. The date and amount of each of these payments is known. Model this relationship first, and then add to your model the information that the BOND object can use an object called NET PRESENT VALUE to calculate the current value of this stream of payments. Show relevant attributes.

20. An educational software developer has asked you to develop a database of orchestral musical instruments. An orchestra consists of four broad classes (strings, woodwinds, brass, and percussion). What data would you store for each musical instrument? How would the data describing a drum differ from a violin? Draw a class and object layer model. Consider one of the microcomputer databases with which you are familiar. How suitable would it be for this database?

Organizational Memory Technologies

Science and technology revolutionize our lives, but memory, tradition and myth frame our response.
Arthur M. Schlesinger, Jr.
"The Challenge of Change" in *New York Times Magazine*, 27 July 1986

F acts stored in organizational memory come in a variety of formats. Facts that are numbers or short text strings can be readily converted to electronic format and stored in databases; hence, databases are a main form of organizational memory technology for many organizations. Numbers and short text strings represent only a portion of the data that an organization needs to maintain, however, and it is often a costly process to convert numbers and short text to a format suitable for database storage. As a result, other technologies have been developed to capture a wide range of the data that organizations need to maintain. Also available are organizational memory technologies that enable organizations to share data more effectively.

Groupware is a technology that has emerged in the last decade. The term groupware covers a range of technologies from e-mail to group decision support. In its various forms, groupware allows people to share information. Thus, groupware can be viewed as an organizational memory technology because it enables sharing of the people component of organizational memory.

For many years, organizations have relied on paper as the prime medium for data storage. Inherently, paper is a linear medium. Although you can scan a document, you are generally forced to read it in a particular sequence, that is, you start at the beginning of some physical break (e.g., a chapter) and read from that point onward. Readers often do not want to process data sequentially, however. Sometimes they need to jump to other sections of a document. For example, a reader of this book may come across an unfamiliar term and want to check its meaning. If this book were in hypertext format, you could simply click on the word and bring up the definition or maybe even a photo or diagram illustrating the term. As an organizational memory technology, hypertext enables readers to rapidly find the information they require.

Data generated internally are often the easiest to capture in electronic format. For example, a clerk taking an order over the phone can key the data directly into an electronic form that then becomes a transaction to update a database. But there can be a considerable volume of data that originates outside an organization. An insurance company, for instance, will receive many forms and letters from customers. The company could key all these data into its database at considerable cost, however, it would still need to store the original paper versions of customer communications because they might be required for future legal proceedings. Alternatively, the firm could use imaging, an organizational memory technology that captures a digital copy of a document and stores it electronically. Because it is an exact copy of a document, an image is widely accepted as an accurate replica of the original paper version. Data managers need to understand the characteristics of imaging in order to decide when this technology can be used to capture organizational memory electronically.

Organizations face two important problems in building an effective organizational memory. First, they cannot possibly capture all the data they potentially might need in the future. As a result, many organizations use the external memories maintained by information service providers. They can then inexpensively gain access to data (e.g., credit worthiness, newspaper articles, and financial statistics) that would be prohibitively costly for a single organization to capture and maintain just for internal use. Second, for all but the largest organizations, it is too costly to build a communications network, so most organizations must use commonly available public networks.

The Internet is the largest public network. Actually, it is really a network of networks. Millions of people in more than 60 countries are connected to the Internet, which will continue to grow at an astonishing pace and will become a major vehicle for the conduct of business and government. The Internet is a communication network, a gateway to gigabytes of data, and a link between an organization and potential and existing customers. Organizations, and particularly data managers, ignore the Internet at their peril. Innovative organizations are already using the Internet to boost sales and customer service.

Information services have existed for many years. Newspapers are a common information service. They collect news and make it available, at a very modest price, to their many readers. In addition, we now have computer–based information services that give rapid access to a wide variety of data. To keep pace, data managers cannot afford to isolate themselves and focus only on internal data management. They must understand that the full scope of their role is to provide the data users need to solve their problems. Consequently, they must be aware of the data available from information services and provide connections to these services so that their organization can be more effective.

As you may have surmised, the intent of this section is to broaden your understanding and knowledge of the role of data management. In our view, a data manager who focuses solely on databases is providing a poor and incomplete customer service. Data managers need to embrace the full gamut of technologies that can support organizational memory.

Chapter 16

Groupware, Hypertext, and Imaging

If computers are the wave of the future, displays are the surfboards.
Ted Nelson, *Communications of the ACM,* July 1988

Learning Objectives

Students completing this chapter will

- understand the role of groupware in organizational memory;
- understand the role of hypertext in organizational memory;
- understand the role of imaging in organizational memory.

INTRODUCTION

Organizations use a variety of information technologies to manage organizational memory. In this chapter, we examine three technologies that provide different types of support for organizational memory. **Groupware** mainly supports communication between persons and thus enhances access to organizational memory residing within people. The groupware notion is so broad that, as you will see, it embraces several aspects of organizational memory. **Hypertext** structures electronic text (often with embedded images, audio, and video) for rapid retrieval. The World Wide Web (see Chapter 17) demonstrates very clearly the power of hypertext. **Imaging** is an information technology for capturing and retrieving written communication. It is particularly useful for maintaining an organizational memory of messages coming from outside the organization (e.g., letters from customers).

The Expeditioner

*A*lice and Angie, the newly appointed Manager of International Operations, were planning the international expansion of The Expeditioner. Several issues resulting from the expansion touched on some key principles that the staff had decided should influence The Expeditioner's management. First, the firm should be a "green" company in terms of both the products it sold and the way it conducted business. Second, The Expeditioner should be an "open" company—employees should have unfettered access to all but the most confidential information, and communication should flow freely within the company. For instance, if they feel it is necessary, the sales staff must be able to communicate directly with the managing director. Third, The Expeditioner should sell high quality products and provide outstanding customer service.

Alice stressed to Angie that these principles should not be compromised by the international expansion. She provided several guidelines to illustrate how these principles would be applied.

Electronic transmission of messages and ideas should be substituted for physical transport of people wherever feasible because business travel is more costly. Employees should be encouraged to use video conferencing, telephone conversations, e-mail, and groupware.

All employees will have equal access to current information. The sales assistant in São Paulo will see the same version of the company policy manual as does the Personnel Manager in London. This means The Expeditioner will accelerate its transition from paper to electronic storage and distribution of information.

The Expeditioner will actively encourage its major suppliers to install communication networks, which will foster interaction between them. The Expeditioner wants to share details of customer complaints, product failures, merchandising plans, and new product ideas with its suppliers. It wants an ongoing dialogue with suppliers so that the combined organizational memory of The Expeditioner and its suppliers can be used to enhance product quality and customer service. For example, if a customer comes to a store with a faulty product, details of the failure should be disseminated to the relevant supplier and appropriate Expeditioner staff within one working day. The sales staff in Sydney should know that a customer of the San Francisco store has reported a defect in a particular navigation aid.

Angie, who had considerable experience in information systems before she switched to international management, knew that some of the software products that fell into the groupware category could meet most of the needs that Alice had outlined.

GROUPWARE

In an information society, many tasks are too complex to be handled by one person. Multiple knowledge bases, skills, and perspectives are often necessary to complete an activity effectively. Consequently, new technologies are required to support the surge in complexity and frequency of group work, which is becoming increasingly important to effective organizational performance. Groupware describes a range of technologies directed at supporting group work. Traditionally, much group work has been performed face-to-face in the same location. Now, networks offer the opportunity for geographically dispersed groups to meet electronically.

We introduced the concept of organizational memory in Chapter 1. You learned that people are the principal component of this memory. To tap the people side of organizational memory, we need to discover what they know, what they think, their ideas and perspectives, their rationale for a particular opinion, and more. Some traditional approaches to this problem are to ask questions, commission reports, establish focus groups, and run brainstorming sessions. Now, groupware presents an opportunity to use information technology to collect and process organizational data from personal memory. It can also assist in the evaluation and dissemination of data extracted from individual memories.

We can gain some initial insights into the use of groupware by considering brainstorming. A brainstorming session is an intense, focused conversation in which participants try to contribute as many ideas as possible. Often, one person's idea will stimulate a flurry of thoughts from other participants. Brainstorming is a means of accessing organizational memories stored in people's personal memory, and the electronic brainstorming tools found in many groupware products are particularly useful for eliciting this information.

Imagine you are participating in an electronic brainstorm. You are seated in front of a microcomputer reading the issue the group will brainstorm, "How can The Expeditioner improve customer service?" After thinking about the question for a few seconds, you type your first idea in the data entry window at the bottom of the screen. Once you press the return key to enter your idea in the system, you glance up at the top half of the screen to see it appear immediately on a rapidly growing list. You realize that as each person in the room contributes an idea, the brainstorming system collects the idea and inserts it in the list. You have so many good ideas, you do not stop to read anyone else's contributions until you have rattled off about another dozen suggestions. Then you pause for a while to scroll through the group's ever-lengthening list. Occasionally someone else's idea stimulates another rush of personal ideas. After about 15 minutes, the meeting organizer asks the group to stop generating ideas and start reviewing the list. You are surprised to discover that in this short period the seven people in the group have produced 147 ideas—and not a word was spoken! You compare this meeting to the previous brainstorming session, where the group sat around a table and talked about the problem. One person spoke for 15 minutes about his favorite suggestion!

The University of Arizona decision room.

Electronic brainstorming has two major advantages over traditional methods. First, group members can be contribute their ideas anonymously. This is particularly valuable when dealing with sensitive topics (why was the last database project six months late?) or when some group members may be reluctant to reveal their true opinion in fear of offending someone in authority. Even in a non-threatening setting, some people hesitate to reveal their ideas because of anxiety about negative feedback. Second, all the ideas are captured and stored electronically. This means the list of ideas can be edited, rearranged, and used for other group activities such as voting. Also, the captured ideas are part of the group's memory, which they can review at a later meeting.

Electronic brainstorming, also called idea generation, usually generates more ideas that the group wants to handle. Consequently, the group needs to sort its list of ideas by evaluating them for importance and relevance. Some methods of evaluation are rating each idea on a seven-point importance scale or ranking items on relevance. Electronic rating and ranking tools can help a group to evaluate quickly the items generated by an electronic brainstorm.

Examination of electronic brainstorming provides some elucidating glimpses into groupware's usefulness. Groupware can be thought of as a general way of structuring, focusing, and facilitating conversations—a key method of accessing people's memory—to make them more productive. The term groupware describes a general class of information technologies designed to assist groups in a wide variety of organizational tasks. Groupware products have three components: computer hardware, computer software, and communications technology. These are combined to provide support for one or more group activities. For example, some groupware products support a single activity such as voting, and others support multiple activities such as idea generation and idea evaluation.

Although groupware is the term most commonly used for information technology that supports group work, there are a host of other names and acronyms in widespread use. Some of the more common ones include: group decision support system (GDSS), group support system (GSS), computer-supported cooperative work (CSCW), electronic meeting system (EMS), decision conferencing, collaborative work support system (CWSS), electronic communities (EC), distributed group support system, and collaborative system. Technologies such as audio and video conferencing are also classified as groupware.

Common Groupware Applications

The groupware designation covers a wide range of products, the most common of which are listed in Table 16–1. Electronic mail (e-mail) and workflow software reduce the amount of time information spends in transit. Workflow software primarily manages the movement of electronic information between people. Workflow documents have more structure than e-mail and often include electronic forms and images. Electronic transfer of documents reduces transmission delays from days to seconds, allowing the organization to react more rapidly to customer needs and environmental change. Some of the potential payoffs of reducing cycle times are improved customer service, reduction in a business's need for cash, and getting products to market faster.

Traditional face-to-face meetings are constrained by geography and size. Some meetings

Table 16–1   Some Classes of Groupware Products

Electronic mail
Bulletin boards
Electronic meeting support/group support systems
Conferencing software
Shared screen systems
Group calendar
Workflow automation
Image management
Desktop videoconferencing

simply include those people who are readily available—the searching under the street lamp syndrome (the drunk who drops his car keys in the street searches under the lamp because the light is better). People who have the expertise to solve the problem may be excluded because they are located elsewhere. Thus, the organization may not make the best use of its memory because some of the key people are missing. In addition, large meetings get unwieldy: too many people who have too much to say. As a result, there is much talk, but little closure.

Groupware can potentially support meetings with anyone, anytime, and anywhere (see Figure 16–1). People don't need to be transported to meetings. It is their thoughts and memory that matter, and these can be transported electronically. Furthermore, groupware permits parallel communication—multiple, simultaneous conversations.

A **face-to-face meeting** usually means a group of people sitting around a table discussing the issue at hand. Information is mainly exchanged by speaking, though occasionally someone may write on a flip chart or white board. The restricted, serial channel of a face-to-face meeting is inefficient when there are many thoughts to be collected. Groupware's parallel, electronic channel means groups can be larger without loss of productivity.

Figure 16–1   Meeting settings supported by groupware

A **team room** is where team members work on a project. For example, a database design team may set up a room containing such items as records of client interviews, documentation of DBMSs, a wall chart of the latest version of the data model, and a computer system with a prototype database. Sometimes the whole team may assemble in the team room; on other occasions, one or two members may go there to work on a section of the project.

Video conferencing is a method of assembling a group of people who are in different locations. Imagine a team meeting where the participants are in Switzerland, Singapore, and New Zealand. Each person is seated in front of a personal computer, equipped with a video camera, microphone, and appropriate software (e.g., CU–SeeMe—shareware video conferencing software that runs on the Internet). Windows on each computer display the image relayed by each video camera and the spreadsheet the group is discussing. As the person in Switzerland moves her mouse around on the spreadsheet to highlight a point, the other team members see the mouse movements replicated on their screens. After a half hour meeting, the group reaches a decision, and the Swiss participant goes back to bed. She likes video conferencing because she can meet with her colleagues without traveling half way round the world, but dislikes staying up late for these meetings at 8 A.M. Singapore time.

Electronic mail, a means of conducting meetings from different times and places, is discussed in detail in Chapter 17. It is very useful when participants have problems synchronizing their activities because of time zone differences (as illustrated in the previous example) or very busy schedules.

A video conference.

Groupware offers many opportunities for organizations to change the nature of team interaction and improve the quality of group decisions and group behavior. Let's consider some of the ways in which organizations can use groupware.

Taking Advantage of Group Diversity

In a global business setting, very few group problems are one dimensional. Different perspectives are needed to examine a problem and explore possible solutions from multiple dimensions. In face-to-face meetings, however, people who think differently or see the world through a different cultural lens are often reluctant to express an opinion through fear of negative evaluation. Adding diversity to a team is often not enough; those who are different require a communication medium that does not suppress their difference.

Because groupware can offer the protection of anonymity, different and controversial opinions are more likely to be expressed. Private perspectives become public with the risk of public evaluation being considerably dampened. Groupware provides a voice for those who are different, enabling the group to tap more effectively its organizational memory.

Uncovering Differences

Groupware voting tools can quickly uncover differences. Compared to traditional face-to-face meetings, a team can quickly and precisely discover its areas of agreement and disagreement. Once diverse opinions have been uncovered, a team can explore the meaning and origin of these differing perspectives.

Sharing Knowledge

Many organizations depend on exploiting their employees' knowledge for their continued success. Groupware is a particularly effective device for sharing knowledge in organizations where there are too many people too widely scattered for the traditional grapevine to be effective. There is an old saying that knowledge is power; however, the wise hermit who never communicates his wisdom has no power. Knowledge becomes power only when it is shared and used to take action. The power of knowledge is contingent upon someone requiring that expertise to initiate action. Groupware enables knowledge sharing because it is an extremely effective and efficient means of connecting the person with the knowledge to the person who needs it. Different time and place systems, such as Lotus Notes, computer conferencing software, and electronic bulletin boards, are being used to facilitate information sharing about customers, solutions to problems, new products, and market changes.

Adding Structure

Groupware adds structure in two ways. First, it forces meeting planners to think about groupware tools and the sequence in which they will be used in a meeting. Second, structuring forces more careful consideration of issues. For example, a pairwise comparison vote forces a group to think about the trade-offs when selecting one item over another. Ordinarily, such an analysis would not occur in the free-for-all of a traditional meeting.

Improving Quality

Groupware improves the quality of meetings, and this change flows through to better decisions about the products and services the organization provides. Improved decision quality is only part of the game, however, and in many ways, a less important aspect. Implementation is what really matters: "A poor decision well implemented is better than a good decision poorly implemented."

Accelerating Implementation

There are several reasons why groupware can accelerate implementation. First, because it permits larger groups without loss of productivity, implementers can be included in decision making. Consequently, decision makers do not spend time communicating and selling a decision to implementers. Implementers understand the spirit and the intent of the decision and can take appropriate action immediately. Second, implementation problems can be anticipated and avoided because implementers participate in decision making.

Remember the high school demonstration of magnetism? The teacher scattered iron filings on a piece of paper and then aligned them by stroking a magnet against the underside of the paper. Groupware is a tool for aligning organizations. It allows more people to be involved in decision making and promotes equality of participation. As a result, there is greater commitment to the decisions of groupware-assisted teams. Individual objectives get aligned with departmental objectives, and departmental objectives get aligned with corporate objectives. There is higher fidelity in the reproduction of organizational goals at lower layers in the organization.

Increasing Information Flow

Groupware permits information to be readily broadcast to many employees. It also supports question and response sessions to organizational messages. Groupware can increase the information flow within the organization so that employees are better informed about the organization and its goals. Informed employees, in turn, are more likely to demonstrate a stronger commitment to the organization.

Enabling Change

Many organizations are implementing new cultures and ways of operating. Ideas such as empowerment, autonomous work groups, and virtual corporations are gaining popularity as organizations seek structures that can respond rapidly in a fast changing global environment. Groupware is an enabler for these concepts. It enables empowerment by supporting knowledge sharing. It enables autonomous work groups by permitting collaborative, egalitarian, electronic communication. It supports virtual corporations through enabling different time and place meetings that cut across organizational, geographic, and temporal boundaries. Thus, groupware can be an agent of change. It can be used to support and propagate an organizational culture based on collaboration, teams, knowledge sharing, and the free-flow of information.

Groupware can be used to enhance an existing culture or change to a new culture. An inherent culture of participative management can be enhanced and extended or changed to allow autonomous work groups. Regardless of which of these two objectives, fit or change, is sought, the relationship of groupware to culture needs to be clearly articulated in the organizational vision. Groupware implementers have rapidly discovered that organizational culture is a key determinant of successful groupware adoption.

Clearly, cultural change is much harder than fitting groupware to an existing social system. Groupware, by itself, cannot create a successful transition. It is one element of an all embracing approach that modifies both the social and technical systems. Implementing groupware and expecting people to cooperate are unlikely to work if the reward system is based on individual performance. But groupware can be a facilitating agent when it is part of a total system.

Rapidly Developing Applications

Some groupware products are viewed as platforms for building groupware applications. Lotus Notes, bulletin boards, enhanced e-mail, and workflow systems are being used to create systems. One organization, for example, replaced its mainframe placement system with an electronic bulletin board.

Because some groupware products are built on client/server architecture and have database facilities, they are being used to circumvent the lack of software for development of client/server applications. Also, server groupware products offer ready support for storing and transporting human data types such as images and sound. These features mean that groupware offers tremendous leverage for accelerated development of time–critical projects—those that must be completed in less than three months. As a result, some organizations are using groupware to develop strategic or mission critical applications such as customer service delivery, product development, and client tracking.

The Downside

The preceding discussion has paraded the potential positive outcomes of using groupware. These benefits cannot be achieved without an investment in hardware and software, and more importantly, in training people to use groupware effectively. Meeting facilitators need to learn how and when to use it. Groupware users must learn how to use the hardware and software and gain skills in participating in group activities now conducted in a non-traditional manner. With adequate preparation and training, many organizations can harvest the advantages of groupware.

Some Groupware Products

To appreciate the breadth of groupware products currently available, we will look at two of the most popular: Lotus Notes and GroupSystems V.

Lotus Notes

Possibly the most popular groupware product, Lotus Notes supports collecting, organizing, and sharing information. Notes' popularity derives from the ease with which applications can be created and data shared across networks. Every Notes application uses a database. Indeed, in Lotus Notes an application and its database are inseparable, and the two terms are used interchangeably.

A Notes **database** is a collection of related documents stored in a single file.[1] A Notes document is like a relational database row. A **form**, which describes the format and layout of a document, can contain fields, static text, graphics, and buttons.

A **field** corresponds to a column of a relational database. It contains data that can change. Like a column, it has a name and data type. Notes supports nine data types for fields, including text, number, time-date, and rich text (used for storing pictures, graphs, and so on). Additionally, Notes supports data types of author names and reader names. An author names field contains a list of names of those who can edit a document; reader names is a list of those who can read it.

Static text labels fields and frequently indicates what should be entered in a particular field. **Graphics** include objects like corporate logos, cartoons, and maps. **Buttons** are used to simplify routine tasks such as opening a database, selecting the value of a particular field, and executing Notes commands. Pressing a button activates the commands associated with it.

As you can see, Notes provides a richer interface than the very plain vanilla standard SQL of relational database. While this same richness is provided by many microcomputer database packages (e.g., Access, Paradox, and Rbase), Notes' client/server design makes it exceptionally powerful for developing applications for teams.

We gain further insights into how Notes can be used by considering the five major categories of applications. Also, we look at some of the screens for a simple application.

Tracking

Tracking applications are highly dynamic; the information is continually changing and many users may contribute information. Tracking applications, containing both hard and soft data, are a way of creating an electronic grapevine.

In keeping track of The Expeditioner's international expansion, a Notes application could be created to gather weekly sales from each store (hard data) along with each manager's written report on local conditions (soft data). This information would be shared by all managers so they have the opportunity to learn from each others' experiences.

There are two main stages to creating a Notes application. First, a form for collecting data must be designed. Figure 16–2 shows the design stage of a form built for the tracking application just described. Fields are indicated by a rectangle. In this example, "Store" is a field that will contain the name of the store making the report. For convenience, the field names are the same as the static text that labels them, but this is not necessary.

---

[1] The Notes definition of a database is quite different from that used when discussing a relational database. In Notes, database and application are used interchangably, but to avoid confusion, we use the term application most of the time.

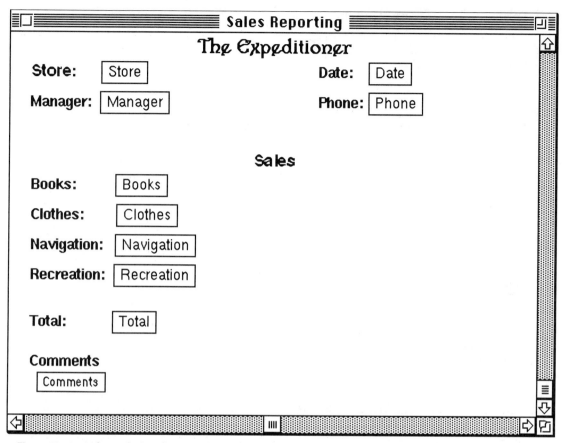

Figure 16–2   A form design for a tracking application

As Figure 16–3 shows, the format of a form changes when it is used for data entry. In Lotus Notes terms, you **compose** a new document when you fill in an electronic form. Observe that the field "Store" is entered by checking one of three boxes. Since The Expeditioner operates in only three cities, a list containing the names of the three cities can be established, and then it is very easy for the person completing the form to click on the appropriate name. This is far faster, friendlier, and less error prone than keying the name of a city. A similar technique is used for the manager's name and the store's phone number. Of course, the field "Total" is automatically calculated when the form is completed.

Forms are the data collection side of Lotus Notes. The data display side is a view, which in this example is data collected from six sales report forms (see Figure 16–4). This view reports sales by date, and within date by store. Notice that a view need not show all the data collected by a form. A useful feature of a view is the ability to "drill down" or go back to the form that supplies the data for a line on a view. Figure 16–4 shows the report line for London selected. Once the line has been selected, the form for this report line can be readily accessed by simply clicking the mouse button. As a result, the form shown in Figure 16–3 would be displayed.

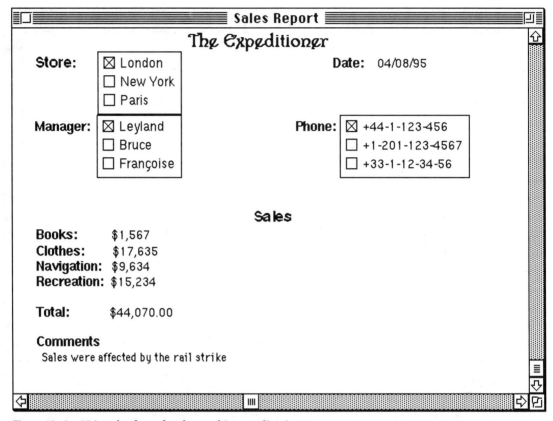

Figure 16-3   Using the form for the tracking application

Broadcast

Broadcast applications disseminate information to many people. Newsletters, company announcements, meeting agendas and minutes are all candidates for broadcast applications. When used in broadcast mode, Notes is an electronic bulletin board.

The distribution of the quarterly employee report within The Expeditioner is a good candidate for a broadcast application. The information is static and must be sent quickly to all employees.

Reference

Written documents are well-suited to reference applications. Policy and procedure handbooks, organizational charts, telephone directories, and software documentation are possible reference applications. The movement from paper to electronic storage and distribution is less expensive and ensures that everyone sees the latest copy. Reference applications are typically written by few and read by many.

The Expeditioner's list of preferred suppliers for each category of items is a typical refer-

```
┌────────────────────────────────────────────────────────────┐
│ ▤▢ ══════════ Sales Tracking - Sale Report ══════════ ▯▯ │
├──────────────────────────────────────────────────────┬─────┤
│  Date       Store            Sales                    │  ⇧  │
│  04/08/95                   $152,128                  │ ▤   │
│ ┌────────────────────────────────────────────────────┤     │
│ │           London          $44,070                  │     │
│             New York         $63,328                  │     │
│             Paris            $44,730                   │     │
│  04/15/95                   $281,115                   │     │
│             London          $181,018                  │     │
│             New York         $41,345                   │     │
│             Paris            $58,752                   │     │
│                             ─────────                 │     │
│                             $433,243                  │     │
│                                                        │  ⇩  │
├─────┬────────────────────────────────────────────────┼──┬──┤
│ ⇦ ▥│░░░░░░░░░░░░░░░░░░░░░░░░░░░░░░░░░░░░░░░░░░░░░░░░░░░│⇨│▤│
└─────┴────────────────────────────────────────────────┴──┴──┘
```

Figure 16-4   A view of the tracking application

ence application. Though the information seldomly changes, all purchasing personnel need to see the latest copy. Also, only the General Manager for Purchasing has authority to edit the database.

Discussion

Discussion applications, like bulletin boards, support information exchange. Their use includes electronic brainstorming, collecting opinions on a topic, and seeking answers to a problem. Discussion applications typically allow anybody to edit a document.

The Expeditioner's goal to increase communication with its suppliers could be handled by a discussion application. Discussion databases could be established for each supplier. Purchasing, marketing, or sales staff could then post comments to the appropriate discussion list for a supplier. For example, a technical problem with Geo Positioning Systems may be quickly solved by posting details of the problem to the appropriate discussion database. Of course, The Expeditioner's suppliers must have at least a Notes client and some method of connecting to The Expeditioner's server.

Workflow

Workflow applications automate routine tasks such as directing documents to certain employees and sending meeting reminders. In addition, certain applications that occur at regular intervals may be suitable for workflow automation. One example of workflow automation is batch updating a newsletter subscriber list each month when the latest issue of a newsletter is dispatched. For each subscriber, the number of the issues received would be increased by one, and the application would automatically generate renewal notices for those whose subscriptions are about to lapse.

Alice keeps tight control over travel expenses, and she encourages her staff to use electronic media to convey their ideas so they spend less time and money traveling. She has directed that all travel claims exceeding £250 be referred automatically to her for approval. Smaller claims can be approved by the Accounting Department. She also wants a weekly report on travel expenses by employee. This is an application appropriate for workflow automation.

Replication

Notes is a distributed application, and as you remember from Chapter 12, a distributed database should support replication independence. Copies of a Notes application can be replicated on multiple Notes servers. Consequently, users on different networks, which could be in different countries, can share information. A change made to one copy of the application will be replicated in all copies.

Deciding the frequency of replication and what data to replicate are key issues for a Notes administrator. Replication may take place every few hours for time-sensitive information (e.g., foreign exchange rates). Information that changes rarely or is not time-sensitive may be replicated daily or less frequently (e.g., procedure manuals). The administrator has to trade-off the cost of frequent replications against the cost of using non-current information.

Replication does not mean that application replicas are always identical. Servers connect with each other to update replicas on a regular basis, after which applications on each server are synchronized. As changes are made to the applications of each server, however, this synchronization disappears and is only restored at the next scheduled replication.

Not all data need to be replicated. Possible candidates for replication are applications that are used frequently by many people on different networks. Large applications that are used less frequently are also good candidates for replication because communication costs should be less when these applications can be accessed from a local server rather than via a remote server.

Notes users who are away from the office a great deal or frequently work at home can take advantage of replication. Before leaving on a trip, a Notes user can replicate selected applications on her notebook computer. During the trip, she can use these applications to process mail and prepare reports. During or at the end of the trip, she can use remote dial-up to connect to a Notes server and exchange updates by replicating the selected applications. This means her changes are replicated in the server database and her local database receives changes made at the server level.

One of Notes's strengths, replication is highly desirable when many organizations are geographically dispersed and use networked personal computers extensively. Replication permits information to be rapidly and conveniently shared by many people.

Conclusion

If you look at the organizational memory hierarchy introduced in Chapter 1 (see Figure 16–5), you can see several places where Notes supports organizational memory. Tracking, broadcast, and discussion applications support the social network. These applications pro-

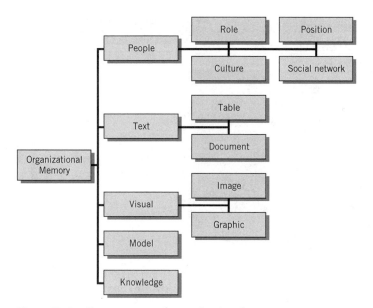

Figure 16–5   Components of organizational memory

mote the exchange of information that is stored in individual memory or not captured by the formalized parts of organizational memory (e.g., databases). Reference applications are well-suited to the document component of organizational memory.

You can also think of Notes as a general delivery service for transporting information on networks. It is a super fast UPS van. For example, the rich text data format can be used to store images within a Notes application, and these are transported to a user's desktop just like any other application. In late 1993, it was announced that Lotus Notes would support access to SQL. Several vendors promised client/server tools supporting the Notes application programmer interface (API)[2] — another example of how Notes is a general delivery service.

GroupSystems V

GroupSystems V, developed in the MIS department at the University of Arizona and marketed by Ventana Corporation, is a good example of a group support system. Although mainly used in face-to-face mode, it can support meetings in which participants are separated by time and place. It is often used for decision making and planning sessions. GroupSystems V provides tools for aiding many phases of a meeting, including generating, organizing, analyzing, evaluating, and establishing priorities for ideas (see Figure 16–6). The tools fall into three categories: idea generation, idea classification, and idea evaluation.

Electronic brainstorming, an idea generation tool, is a quick way for a group to create a list of ideas on a defined topic. Everyone in the group can enter ideas simultaneously. All

---

[2]K. Damore, "Client/Server Tools will Let Notes Users Access SQL Data Next Year," *InfoWorld*, 1 November 1993, 14.

Figure 16–6   GroupSystems V tools

ideas are captured and displayed on a public screen for group viewing. Part of a sample electronic brainstorming screen is shown in Figure 16–7.

The final product of brainstorming is a list of ideas. The meeting facilitator then typically leads the group through a review of these ideas. Ambiguous items are clarified and edited if necessary; redundant statements are deleted. At the end of the review, the group has a shared opinion of the issue under consideration.

Evaluation of ideas typically follows generation. Rating and ranking are examples of techniques often found in a set of evaluation tools. Rating permits group members to rate each alternative based on certain criteria such as the item's importance and its impact on customers. The group may use a pre-established rating scale of 1 to 5, where 1 = low and 5 = high. Ranking is often used to force group members to pick an alternative. Output from a ranking using the Vote tool of GroupSystems V is shown in Figure 16–8. Results from the eleven participants indicate that "Introduce a special telephone number" was the top ranked idea, receiving seven first choices, three second choices, and so on. The mean ranking for this idea was 1.55 with a standard deviation of 0.93. The reported statistics allow a group to determine its collective opinion and the level of consensus for particular ideas.

Conclusion

There are hundreds of groupware products currently available. This tremendous variety reflects increasing interest in the use of organizational teams and the realization that there are vast opportunities to increase the efficiency and effectiveness of group work. Groupware enables teams to communicate and share knowledge.

```
╔══════════════ Electronic Brainstorming ══════════════╗
 ◆ Uncategorized                                Top Line 1 of 4
2.1 Publish guides for buying products (e.g., selecting a tent for Africa).

3.1 Monthly lectures on exotic locations.

4.1 More staff on the floor to answer questions.

1.1 Introduce a special telephone number for customer service.



                                          ↑/↓/PgUp/PgDn/^PgUp/^PgDn
      Participants = 8    Total Comments = 4   Collect On
   F1-Help    F2-Mark   Shift+F4-Search   Ctrl+Ins-Copy   Esc-Return
```

Figure 16–7   Brainstorming with GroupSystems V

```
╔═════════════════════════ Vote ═══════════════════════╗
 File   View   Options   Session   Help
           Rank Order   (4 items)    Total Group - (N - 11)
  Matrix                               1  2  3  4   Mean   STD   n
 ┌──────────────────────────────────┐
 │ 1. Introduce a special telephone number │  7  3  -  1   1.55  0.99  11
   2. More staff on the floor to answer qu    4  6  1       1.73  0.65  11
   3. Publish guides for buying products (    -  2  5  4   3.18  0.75  11
   4. Monthly lectures on exotic locations    -  -  5  6   3.55  0.52  11




                                          ↑/↓/PgUp/PgDn
   F1-Help   F5-Next Screen   F8-Description   Enter-Vote Spread   Alt+F9-Exit
```

Figure 16–8   Evaluating ideas with GroupSystems V

The Expeditioner

For many years, The Expeditioner's staff has provided excellent travel advice to its many customers. Brier, who recently took over the Travel Department, is concerned that the quality of the service is somewhat uneven. The advice you get depends very much on the person with whom you speak. Nancy might be the expert on East Africa, but if she is not available, you have to speak to someone who may know less about that region. Also, it is difficult to get information shared. The staff tell each other about their travels and experiences, but this is a very informal and casual way of exchanging information. Brier knows that the collective travel wisdom of The Expeditioner's staff is very valuable, but she is uncertain of how to share effectively this organizational memory.

Brier is considering creating computer text files to capture each person's expertise about each country and making this information available to customers through several microcomputers scattered around the building. She wants to encourage customers to browse the files. From her personal experience, however, Brier knows that customers' interests jump wildly, and they may become impatient with reading a linear text file. She wants a system that makes it easy for customers to find the topics of interest without scanning a long text file. Is hypertext her answer?

HYPERTEXT

Hypertext is a popular approach to storing irregularly structured information, such as text files. It is used for a variety of applications ranging from repair manuals to information services. Hypertext stores data in a network of nodes connected by links. A node is multimedia—it can contain text, graphics, audio, video, and other forms of data. An interactive viewer (a computer program) is used to browse and manipulate the nodes. The original concept of hypertext can be traced to Vanevar Bush[3] who described "the memex:"

> *A device in which an individual stores his books, records, and communications, and which is mechanized so that it may be consulted with exceeding speed and flexibility. It is an enlarged supplement to his memory.*

Notice that Bush's notion of the memex as a supplement to human memory reflects ideas discussed at the beginning of this book. Bush visualized the memex as working more like the human mind, which he suggests operates by association. Ideas are linked together, and the brain can skip from one to another very rapidly. In contrast, indexing or key word searching has been the approach used by many computer systems for data retrieval.

Hypertext documents differ from conventional paper documents. Paper documents—

---

[3]V. Bush, "As We May Think," *Atlantic Monthly* 176 (1): 101–108 (1945).

books, reports, and instruction manuals—have closely linked physical and logical structures. Most documents are a linear sequence of words divided, for physical reasons, into physical lines and pages. The logical structure is also linear. Words are combined into sentences, sentences into paragraphs, and so forth.

Reference documents such as encyclopedias, dictionaries, and thesauruses do some separating of the logical and physical structure. The physical structure is a set of independent units—topics in an encyclopedia, words in a dictionary, synonyms in a thesaurus. You do not read these documents linearly, but find the topic or word of interest and then read that portion of the document.

When reading an encyclopedia, you may find cross-references to other topics. Perhaps you are interested in learning about Nepal. You will find the article on Nepal in a multi-volume encyclopedia by selecting the volume containing articles beginning with "N," then searching for the required article. When reading about that country, you become intrigued by the brief description of the Gurkha people and decide to read more by accessing the article titled Gurkha. This means selecting the "G" volume of the encyclopedia and searching for the article. As you can visualize, following a sequence of cross-references takes several minutes when using a paper-based encyclopedia. You spend considerable time searching when your main interest is in learning.

Now consider the case of an electronic encyclopedia. To find the article on Nepal in the on-line encyclopedia, you type "Nepal" in the search entry box. The system retrieves and displays the requested article. (A portion of the on-line version of the *New Grolier Multimedia Encyclopedia* article on Nepal is shown in Figure 16–9.) Notice that the words SHERPA and GURKHA are in uppercase. This means that there are articles on each of these topics. Suppose you want to read more about Gurkhas. Double-click on GURKHA to select the word, then select "Hyperlink to selection" from the pull-down Search menu. The article is retrieved in seconds. As you see, linking between references is much faster than with a paper-based multi-volume encyclopedia.

In a hypertext document, a node is the unit of retrieval. Think of it as a topic or subtopic in an encyclopedia or a graphic such as a map or diagram, a sound bite, or a video clip. A node is a discrete, self-contained unit of information. Of course, deciding what is contained within a node is not a trivial design issue. For example, should all the information about Nepal be contained in one node or should there be several nodes as illustrated in Figure 16–10?

People

The people of Nepal are dominantly Indo-Nepalese, and about one-fifth of the population is Tibeto-Nepalese. The Nepali and the Newars, the largest ethnic groups in the country, are the principal inhabitants of the greater Katmandu area. In the Himalayas, SHERPA and Bhutias—ethnologically related to the Tibetans—are in the majority. GURKHA inhabitants introduced Hinduism in the area.

Figure 16–9   Text from a multimedia encyclopedia showing hyperlinks in uppercase

A CD-ROM encyclopedia.

The structure shown has six nodes. One node gives a general overview of Nepal and separate nodes provide more detailed information on geography, history, government, economy, and resources. There are links from the Nepal node to each of the more detailed nodes, and return links from each of them. This design means a person can access the Nepal node first, and then link to the node containing detailed information of interest. This design is better than simply lumping all the information in a single node. For example, if you are just interested in the government of Nepal, you can go to that node without having to linearly scan a single node containing all the information about Nepal.

A key principle of good design is to make each node a self-contained unit of information dealing with one topic. Too much information means readers spend a lot of time linearly searching for the topic of interest. Of course, too little information means readers spend too much time jumping between links and can lose the continuity of a topic.

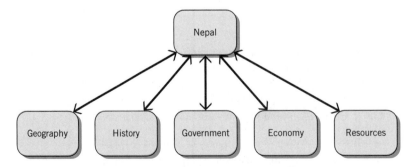

Figure 16–10   Nodes for an article on Nepal

Another key principle is to decide what nodes should be linked. Should we have links between each of the detailed nodes about Nepal? Should a reader be able to jump directly from the geography to the history node, or first have to return to the Nepal node and then link to the history node? Answering these questions requires a sound understanding of how potential readers might navigate a hypertext document.

Identifying which phrases or words in a node should be linked to other nodes is another important consideration. An encyclopedia, for instance, should support links to articles that cover a particular phrase or word in more depth. Thus, the article on Nepal has a link to the article on Gurkha. In the text, phrases or words that have links are denoted in some special way—all capitals or a different color, for example.

Hypertext and the Oxford English Dictionary[4]

The *Oxford English Dictionary (OED)*, the largest and most scholarly of written English dictionaries, was produced between 1884 and 1928. It consists of 12 books containing 41.8 million words, 252,259 entries, and 1.8 million quotations. The four volume *Supplement*, created between 1958 and 1986, contains 14.5 million words, 69,372 entries, and 560,000 quotations. Seventy percent of the entries in the *Supplement* describe words not in the *OED*.

The basic unit of information of the *OED* is an entry, which describes the historical development of a given word. Each entry contains the word, its pronunciation, parts of speech, a list of variant forms, the etymology (an account of the source and development of the word), and a list of senses. Each sense is defined and illustrated by quotations from different sources and time periods.

A hypertext version of the *OED* was considered because it would enable browsing, provide a better interface, support rapid navigation, allow users to annotate their copy, and support statistical analysis of selected variables.

In planning the conversion of the *OED* to hypertext, the analysts had to deal with the issue of fragmentation—deciding on the unit of information to be stored in each node. This is a not a simple task because some possible choices, such as entry, vary in size from a few characters to half a megabyte. Eventually, the designers settled on an approach they call dynamic fragmentation, where fragmentation is controlled by the user.

Another important issue was identifying links between nodes. The *OED* contains 569,000 cross-references, and these were a major source of possible hypertext links. Other links had to be considered as well. For instance, the definition of a word is written in terms of other words, which of these words should be linked to their entry?

(continued)

---

[4]Adapted from D. R. Raymond, and F. W. Tompa, "Hypertext and the Oxford English Dictionary," *Communications of the ACM* 31 (7): 871–879 (1988).

> **Hypertext and the Oxford English Dictionary (continued)**
>
> The second edition of the *OED* was released in March 1989, six decades after the first edition. It consists of 20 volumes and costs $2,500.[5]
>
> The Oxford University Press's $850 *OED* Second Edition on CD-ROM, which runs under Microsoft Windows, contains close to 640 Mbytes of information. The database contains some 600,000 individual references and 2.5 million quotations.[6]

HyperCard

One of the most widely-known implementations of the hypertext concept is HyperCard, which was initially included in the purchase of a Macintosh. Its availability for free made it very popular, particularly in education. There are similar products for the Windows environment.

A HyperCard node is represented by a card, the basic unit of information. An application is a stack of cards. Thus, a deck of index cards is a useful physical analogy to keep in mind when thinking about a HyperCard application. A card contains buttons, fields, and graphics. Fields are used to store information and buttons are used, among other things, to link cards.

Many educational products are based on HyperCard. Figure 16–11 presents a card from a stack called *Exotic Japan*,[7] which contains 165 lessons on Japanese culture and language. This particular card demonstrates several key capabilities of HyperCard. The card contains both visual (the Japanese character for "person") and textual information (a description of the character). Clicking the Start Animation button animates the character and its audible pronunciation.

Layers

A card has two layers—a foreground layer (the card layer) and a background layer. Both layers can contain buttons, fields, and graphics. When you see a card, you cannot distinguish between the card layer and the background layer. So what is the purpose of the background layer?

The background layer is a common template for more than one card. Buttons, fields, and graphics that are to appear on a number of cards are placed on the background layer, and these will appear on all cards that share that background. So the background card incorporates some of the ideas of inheritance that we introduced when discussing ODBMSs. Creating a common background for many cards saves considerable work when editing a deck of cards. One change to the background is inherited by all cards sharing that background. With-

---

[5] D. Fisher, "New Oxford Dictionary—Improving on the Ultimate," *Los Angeles Times,* 25 March 1989, sec. 1, p. 1, col. 1.

[6] A. Redfern, "The Oxford English Dictionary Second Edition on CD-ROM," *Byte,* September 1992, 80–81.

[7] N. Yokokura, *Exotic Japan: an Interactive Introduction to Japanese Culture and Language* (Irvington, NY: Voyager, 1991).

Figure 16–11 A card from a HyperCard stack

out a background layer, you would have to make the same change to each relevant card in the stack. Buttons, fields, and graphics that are specific to a particular card are placed on the card's foreground layer.

Buttons

Buttons are screen areas that make things happen when you click them. Clicking a button may take you to another card, display a video clip, launch an application, perform a calculation, or play music.

A common use of buttons is to link cards. For example, to move from the overview card about Nepal to the card containing details of Nepal's history, you might click the button labeled "History." Often, buttons are represented by meaningful icons. A left pointing arrow indicates that clicking this button links you to the previous card in the stack.

You can also associate a script with a button. A script is a program that is executed when a button is clicked. HyperTalk, the scripting language for HyperCard, considerably increases the power of an application and moves it beyond being a fairly passive collection of linked cards. A particular use of scripts, which is relevant to our interest in data management, is retrieving multimedia information. A card could store a video clip of Katmandu and some

Nepalese music, for example. Clicking the appropriate button will display the scenes of Katmandu or play the music of a Nepalese orchestra.

Fields

Fields are text containers. They are used for both text entry (e.g., collecting customer information) or displaying previously entered text (e.g., information about a tourist destination). The HyperCard designer has considerable control over the characteristics and appearance of a field. One useful feature is a scrolling field,[8] which overcomes the physical limitations of the amount of text that can be displayed on a card. A scrolling field gives you access to the total 30,000 characters that a text field can store.

Conclusion

Hypertext is a very useful technique for linking nodes of information and accelerating an information search. The concept appears in many products. You will probably recognize it in the *help* feature of your word processor or spreadsheet. It is used extensively in the World Wide Web to link pages of information. In the future, you can expect hypertext concepts to be built into many common products.

The Expeditioner

Todd's idea The Expeditioner should begin selling travel insurance has been enthusiastically greeted. The firm's knowledge of travel conditions in many remote and exotic areas of the world enabled it to work with the insurance brokers of Lloyds of London to develop a variety of attractive travel insurance policies.

Of course, a new information system needs to be developed to cater for the travel insurance business. As the new Manager of Travel Insurance, Todd is responsible for defining the new system's requirements. He is really concerned with how he will handle all the documents, especially customer applications and claims. He plans to capture some of the data by using data processing operators to key the information from application and claim forms; customer name and address, policy type, and amount paid will be stored in a relational database. Copies of applications, claims, and customer correspondence, however, must be kept because they often will contain additional data not readily stored in a relational database. For example, a customer's letter will not be stored in the relational data-

---

[8]If you do not know what a scrolling field is, look at the HyperCard example in Figure 16–11. The side bar on the right indicates the text describing the character is a scrolling field. You can scroll the text by clicking on the up and down arrows.

base, but the information must be kept because it may be required when settling the customer's insurance claim.

One approach to storage is to buy some new filing cabinets and set up individual folders in which to keep all forms and correspondence from each customer. Todd dislikes this approach because The Expeditioner has little space to spare in its London office, and high rental costs discourage consideration of additional office space in the city. Furthermore, customers have been told that they can file claims in any of The Expeditioner's offices. Thus, it is unrealistic to have a single physical folder in which all details of a customer are kept.

IMAGING

Paper documents are a large and significant component of the organizational memory of many companies. The number of existing documents in American organizations is in the vicinity of three trillion (10^{12}) items, some 95 percent of which are still in paper form, and the cost of storing a page of paper is around $2.[9] Paper is often particularly important for companies with a large number of customers. Insurance firms, mutual funds, and government agencies are instances of organizations that maintain large paper-based organizational memories.

These massive paper systems have several major shortcomings. First, it is expensive to store and maintain large volumes of paper in filing cabinets and storage boxes. Second, it takes considerable time to retrieve information from paper storage devices. Third, manipulation of information is very difficult and often requires time-consuming manual extraction of data. Fourth, because of high cost, backup and recovery is sometimes nonexistent; fire can destroy a complete sector of organizational memory.

Imaging processing systems overcome these shortcomings by converting documents into digital form with a scanner. The bit-mapped image is then indexed, compressed, and stored in a database. Subsequently, the index can be used to retrieve the image, which can then be distributed electronically and decompressed for display on a computer monitor.

Components of an Imaging System

Imaging systems have many of the components of a typical data processing system. Imaging software may run on a host/terminal or client/server system. Printers attached to the system produce paper copies of documents. An imaging workstation is similar to a data processing workstation. Sometimes a large monitor is used to permit viewing more information. A popular storage device for images is the 12-inch optical disk. An optical disk library works like a jukebox—disks are loaded onto the reader as required.

A *scanner* (see Figure 16–12) is the acquisition device of an imaging system. A standard

---

[9]N. J. Muller, *Computerized Document Imaging Systems: Technology and Applications* (Boston: Artech House, 1993).

An imaging system.

document (letter-sized in the United States and A4 in most other countries) when scanned at 200 dots per inch requires about 0.5 Mbytes of storage, which is roughly 155 times the size required to store the data in text format. Color documents require 10 to 20 times more storage. Optical character recognition (OCR), to convert image text to character format, also may be used during data capture.

Figure 16–12 A scanner

Acquisition of data, as is the case with most information systems, is the most error-prone phase of imaging. For example, an operator might scan only one side of a document, failing to realize information is also written on the reverse. Also, OCR is not 100 percent accurate and some text may be incorrectly converted.

Every stored document, just like a row in a relational database, needs a unique identifier to permit subsequent retrieval. Other information associated with the image can be entered at the time of image acquisition. This additional information can include date and time of acquisition and retrieval keywords.

Advantages of Image Processing

Like most information technologies, image processing has both pluses and negatives, which are summarized in Table 16–2. Let's consider these.

Space Compression

Considerably less space is required to store documents. Paper documents are imaged and stored on optical disk, and the original paper version can be destroyed. Storage space savings are often sufficient to cover initial systems costs in one to three years.

Productivity Gains

It takes less time to retrieve documents. Images distributed electronically help to automate workflow; documents no longer spend days sitting on desks or in transit between offices. The system can also handle automatic routing, ensuring that high priority documents move quickly.

Better Customer Service

Imaging makes it possible to respond to customer queries very rapidly. Indeed, a well-designed imaging system allows a service agent to retrieve a customer's paperwork during their

Table 16–2 Advantages and Disadvantages of Image Processing

Advantages	Disadvantages
Space compression	Cost of installation
Productivity gains	Image quality
Better customer service	Legality of document images
Data sharing	Lack of standards
Tracing use	
Data security and integrity	

conversation. This improved customer service frequently translates into increased market share and greater customer loyalty.

Data Sharing

An imaging system permits more than one person to look at a copy of a document simultaneously, which paper systems cannot do.

Tracking Use

Because they are computer based, imaging systems can easily record which documents are accessed most frequently. As a result, these documents can be placed on a high speed storage device. Also, it is far easier to manage the workflow. Supervisors can readily check the status of documents, and receive exception reports for documents that take too long to process.

Data Security and Integrity

A major problem with paper systems is that repeated handling of documents increases the likelihood of damage. Also, paper documents decay with time because of the acid used in paper manufacturing.

Imaging systems give greater control over who has access to documents, and are more secure than traditional filing cabinets. Furthermore, it is relatively easy and inexpensive to make backup copies of optical disks, the prime storage medium for images. Backup and recovery procedures can be implemented to ensure that images are not permanently lost.

Disadvantages of Image Processing

Cost of Installation

Installing an image processing system requires a considerable investment in equipment, time, and appropriate expertise. In this respect, an image processing system is no different from most other information technology-based organizational memory systems.

Image Quality

Images will not be identical to the originals. Color will be lost and shading may not be as distinct. You notice a similar degradation of image quality when you photocopy an original document.

Legality of Document Images

The legal system lags technological change, and there can be problems regarding the legal acceptability of copies of image documents. The importance of this problem varies between states and countries.

Lack of Standards

Typical of information systems, there is a lack of industry standards. Multiple vendors have resulted in incompatibilities between vendors and systems. This can result in an organization getting locked into a particular vendor's hardware and software.

Imaging in Essex County

"When I came here in 1977, we had 70 employees processing 250 documents per day," said Michael Day, assistant register at Massachusetts's Essex County Registry of Deeds. "Currently, we have 45 employees, processing 600 to 800 documents per day."

These productivity gains result from the county's decision in 1976 to find a more cost-effective means of processing mortgages, liens, and other real estate documents. The county currently uses a LAN-based imaging system and mainframe computer to automate the movement of paper-based information.[10]

Indexing

Each document image has associated data values or descriptors stored in a file or database. These data values, known as indexes, are used for image retrieval. If relational database technology is used to store the index, then apply the data modeling techniques learned earlier to design the database.

At the simplest level, each document has a unique identifier and the storage address of an image. Such a low level of indexing makes little use of information technologies power to find data, however, so more advanced forms of indexing are generally desirable.

Capture Indexing

During document capture, information such as document and page number can be assigned. Each document is numbered chronologically, so a page is uniquely identified by document and page number. Additional information may be date of capture, workstation used, and operator identifier. Because the operators who perform data capture typically are low-level clerical employees who simply scan documents, capture indexing is usually limited to attributes that the system can handle automatically.

Contents Indexing

Contents indexing captures data about the image. Trained personnel, who understand indexing and the contents of the document, are required for this task. Data captured will in-

---

[10]Adapted from R. Knight, "Preserving Investment," *Computerworld*, 5 April 1993, 85.

clude the name of sender and receiver, date of correspondence, and some descriptors of the content. Of course, there is a trade-off in selecting how many descriptors to provide for each document. Many descriptors means document retrieval can be more fine-grained—a search produces a few, highly relevant documents—but indexing takes more time and skill. A few descriptors results in coarse-grained retrieval—many documents that need further manual processing to identify those relevant—but indexing takes less time and skill.

Full Text Indexing

Full text indexing is a low cost method of indexing. There is no formal contents indexing; machine-readable text is processed and stored in text format. This text can then be searched for a given term.

There are several important factors to consider with full text indexing. First, the technique assumes that the subject matter of a document can be derived from the text within the document. Second, searching takes considerably longer. Savings in indexing may be offset by increased processing costs. Third, only machine-readable text can be searched, so this excludes handwritten documents and graphics.

The Relationship Between Image and Character Databases

There are several possible relationships between an imaging processing system and relational databases (we assume the character database is relational). One possibility is that there is no relationship—the two systems exist independently. Clearly, this is undesirable because there is a lack of data integration and an increase in resources expended on information searching.

A second possibility is that attributes or indexes of the image are stored in a relational database, along with other relevant data. For example, a customer database could have a table containing a row describing each document received from a customer. Also, there are cross-links between the image and relational database to speed up retrieval from either database. The relational database could record the image processing system address of an associated image. This approach combines high speed retrieval of index information with low cost optical storage of images. Remember, magnetic disk storage is more expensive than optical disk, but access times are faster. This design is appropriate when the image database is very large.

The third possibility is that the image is stored in the character database as a binary large object (BLOB). Thus, a fragment of a customer database would be a 1:m relationship between customer and document (i.e., a customer has many documents). BLOB gives rapid access to images but increases the cost of image storage if documents are stored on a magnetic disk. BLOB is appropriate when the image component of the database is not too large.

Integration at Genentech

California biotech company Genentech has integrated document management and relational database. The relational database contains pointers to image files, rather than the images, which are stored on optical jukeboxes.

Information stored by the imaging system includes details of FDA approval applications, which are often more than 2 million pages long. Handwritten case-report forms completed by doctors during clinical trials are also stored.[11]

An Apple a Day

A law firm has equipped all its professionals with Apple Macintoshes and 21-inch (53 cm) screens to give them access to 750 Gbyte document image and 30 Gbyte text databases. Each day, between 20,000 to 40,000 new documents are scanned and added to the databases. As documents are scanned, they are coded for future retrieval and indexed in a flat-file database. Scanned images are also passed through an optical character recognition system to create text files, which can be subsequently searched. The search engine uses fuzzy logic to overcome scanning problems and spelling errors.

In a recent court case, the system was used to scan a 700,000-page database. The necessary document was found in 5 minutes. In the past, 50 paralegals would have spent the entire night digging through boxes of documents.[12]

Conclusion

Organizations receive many documents that need to be stored, distributed, and processed. These documents are often a significant component of organizational memory. Imaging technology is extremely powerful in managing this important segment of organizational memory.

SUMMARY

Organizations use a variety of information technologies to manage organizational memory. Groupware mainly supports communication between people and enhances access to organi-

---

[11]Adapted from J. Ubois, "Document–Management Imaging Systems Lead Fight to Stem Paper Glut," *MacWeek*, 15 November 1993, 67.

[12]Adapted from S. Cummings, "Cross-platform Tools Ease Development Tasks," *MacWeek*, 15 November 1993, 67.

zational memory residing within them. It also embraces several other aspects of organizational memory. Multiple knowledge bases, skills, and perspectives are often necessary to complete an activity effectively. Groupware describes a range of technologies directed at supporting group work. Dispersed groups can meet electronically. The electronic brainstorming tools found in many groupware products are particularly useful for eliciting information stored in people's heads. Groupware can be thought of as a general way of structuring, focusing, and facilitating conversations. Groupware products consist of computer hardware and software, and communications technology. Groupware can help reduce cycle times, assemble the right team, take advantage of team diversity, increase the capacity to share knowledge, improve quality, accelerate implementation, improve employee information flow and commitment, facilitate change, and accelerate application development.

Lotus Notes is a popular groupware product. A Notes database is a collection of related documents stored in a single file. Notes is used for tracking, broadcasting, reference, discussion, and workflow applications. Replication is an important feature. Notes is a general delivery service for transporting information on networks.

Hypertext structures formal organizational memory to facilitate rapid retrieval of information. Hypertext stores data in a network of nodes connected by links. A node can contain text, graphics, audio, video, and other forms of data. A key principle of good design is to make each node a self-contained unit of information dealing with one topic. Identifying which phrases or words in a node should be linked to other nodes is an important consideration.

One of the most widely-known implementations of the hypertext concept is Apple's HyperCard, in which a node is represented by a card, the basic unit of information. A HyperCard application is a stack of cards. A card contains buttons, fields, and graphics. Fields store information and buttons link cards.

Paper documents are a significant component of the organizational memory of many companies. Imaging is a technology for capturing and retrieving paper communication. It is particularly useful for maintaining an organizational memory of messages coming from outside the organization. Imaging technology uses a scanner to convert a document into digital form. The bit-mapped image is then indexed, compressed, and stored in a database. Every stored document, just like a row in a relational database, needs a unique identifier to permit subsequent retrieval. On the plus side, image processing reduces document storage space, helps retrieve and distribute documents more rapidly, improves customer service, enhances data sharing, helps track documents, and augments data security and integrity. On the minus side, installation costs must be borne, image quality is lower than the original, images are not always acceptable legal documents, and there is a lack of industry standards. An index is a database that is used to identify the images to be retrieved. Three forms of indexing are capturing, contents, and full text.

KEY TERMS AND CONCEPTS

Collaboration	Electronic brainstorming
Compression	Electronic mail
Culture	Empowerment
Cycle time	Groupware

Hypertext
Imaging system
Indexing
Knowledge sharing
Organizational memory
Rapid application development

Replication
Scanner
Team diversity
Video conferencing
Workflow

REFERENCES

Groupware

Bostrom, R. P.; R. T. Watson; and S. T. Kinney, eds. *Computer Augmented Teamwork: A Guided Tour.* Princeton, NJ: Van Nostrand–Reinhold, 1992.

Grohowski, R.; C. McGoff; D. R. Vogel; B. Martz; and J. F. Nunamaker, Jr. "Implementing Electronic Meeting Systems at IBM: Lessons Learned and Success Factors." *MIS Quarterly* 14, no. 4 (1990): 369–382.

Hypertext

Communications of the ACM 31, no. 7 (1988). This is a special issue on hypertext.

Nielson, J. "Navigating Through Hypertext." *Communications of the ACM* 33, no. 3 (1990): 296–310.

Imaging

Lasher, D. R.; B. Ives; and S. L. Jarvenpaa. "USAA–IBM Partnerships in Information Technology." *MIS Quarterly* 15, no. 4 (1991): 551–565.

Muller, N. J. *Computerized Document Imaging Systems: Technology and Applications.* Boston: Artech House, 1993.

EXERCISES

1. Identify the distinguishing features, respectively, of groupware, hypertext, and imaging. Give characteristics of applications that are best handled by each technology.

2. Give some reasons why an organization might use groupware.

3. What are the advantages of electronic brainstorming?

4. What are some of the benefits of using groupware?

5. How might an organization use Lotus Notes?

6. Lotus Notes is described as a general delivery system for distributing information. Discuss the various components of organizational memory and how they might be distributed using Lotus Notes.

7. When would an organization use a product like GroupSystems V?

8. What advantages does hypertext have over linear text?

9. Why are reference manuals and encyclopedias suitable hypertext applications?

10. What are the key design issues when creating a hypertext file?

11. Compare the design of a relational database with that of a hypertext file. How do they differ?

12. Distinguish between cards, buttons, and fields.

13. What's wrong with storing data on paper and in filing cabinets?

14. What are the components of an imaging system?

15. What is the purpose of indexing and what types can you have?

16. Two recent graduates in landscape architecture want to publish a book describing plants native to the southeast of the U.S. For each plant, they want to show a photo of it in flower, show a map of its preferred habitat, describe its major features and indicate under what conditions it will grow (e.g., full sun). They would also like to provide some cross-reference features. The reader, for instance, should be able to find quickly details of all blue shrubs that grow in partial shade. Should they publish a book or are there other choices? What would you recommend?

17. A small legal firm has asked you to estimate how much optical disk storage space is required for its 15 four-drawer filing cabinets. Describe the procedure you would use to estimate the firm's requirements.

18. A university will be the venue for the Olympic Games soccer finals. The housing manager has recognized that the student dormitories could be used to house spectators. However, he knows that housing soccer spectators is different from accommodating students. He wants his staff to develop a checklist of all the things that must be done to make this a successful venture. What advice would you give him?

19. An international advertising agency often works on projects that involve staff from many offices and countries. It is not unusual for people from the Sydney, Toronto, and Buenos Aires offices to be working on the same project. Consequently, the firm needs to transfer advertisement designs and customer information rapidly between offices. How can the firm do this efficiently?

20. A mutual fund company offers its clients more than 20 funds in which they can invest. Details of customers and their investments are stored in a relational database. When customers open their accounts or make additional investments, they mail appropriate forms to the firm. Also, customers often write letters requesting special action to be taken for a particular fund. All forms and letters are currently stored in filing cabinets and take between 3 to 4 hours to retrieve. Obviously, this means customer representatives often lack necessary information when dealing with clients, who frequently expect prompt service. What action should the firm take to improve customer service?

Chapter 17

Internet and Information Services

Knowledge is of two kinds; we need to know a subject ourselves, or we need to know where you can find information upon it.

Samuel Johnson, quoted in Boswell's *Life of Samuel Johnson,* 1775

Learning Objectives

After completing this chapter, you will:

- have a comprehensive understanding of the role of electronic networks in enhancing organizational memory;
- know how to use some common information services on the Internet;
- be familiar with products provided by commercial information services.

INTRODUCTION

The brain relies on axons and dendrites to communicate between its various components. Similarly, organizations rely on a variety of communication media for connecting their various functions. Memos, reports, telephone conversations, and faxes, are communication media that facilitate the flow of information throughout an organization. Today, the combination of computer and communication technology enables an organization to create an electronic network that resembles the brain's maze of interlaced communication links. These networks are used for a vast variety of tasks: from small, local networks for group decision making to corporate, global networks for e-mail.

Beyond the organization at the national and international level, there are networks connecting tens of millions of people throughout the world. These networks support e-mail, links to information services, and access to remote computers. The considerable flexibility of these networks provides many opportunities for their creative use to enhance and extend organizational memory and support the attainment of organizational goals.

Communication networks extend organizational memory in several ways. Networks support conversations among people by extending their capacity to communicate. We can use electronic networks to increase the number of people with whom we maintain relationships.[1] The telephone serves a similar purpose, but e-mail, the major communication medium on networks, has several advantages. It is cheaper than the telephone because text messages require less bandwidth (communication capacity) than voice. E-mail is more convenient;

---

[1]Electronic friendships can be very strong. A survey at a computer camp for children found that 30 percent had never met their best friend face-to-face.

messages can be retrieved at the receiver's pleasure. This means the sender and receiver do not have to synchronize their activities to have a conversation, which is particularly important when the sender and receiver live in different time zones or spend a lot of time away from their desks. Another advantage of e-mail is that it can be used to broadcast a message. You can create a single message that is automatically sent to all people on a distribution list. For example, a professor can use e-mail to broadcast details of the latest database assignment to all class members.

Bulletin boards (also known as discussion lists and computer conferences) are a very effective device for tapping the people component of organizational memory. When you post a question to an electronic bulletin board, it is automatically sent to all members of that board. A multinational consulting company can distribute details of a client's problem to all of its consultants and use their shared wisdom to resolve the problem. Bulletin boards are a tremendous opportunity for organizations to harness the collective memory and expertise of their staffs.

Bulletin boards can cross national and organization boundaries. For example, the academic community has a board for research methodology questions. A problem posted to the board frequently elicits half a dozen responses in a day.

Networks extend organizational memory by enabling the sharing of text, visual, model, and knowledge elements of memory. Without networks, the user has to go to the memory's physical location (e.g., manually searching a library's card catalog). With networks, data can be transported to the user's computer (e.g., accessing a library's on-line catalog from your desk and using key words to accelerate the search). Sharing data over networks has important implications for organizations and society, and we are only just beginning to observe and understand the ramifications.

Networks extend an organization's reach to people and memories beyond its boundaries. Gateways permit e-mail to cross organizational and international boundaries. For example, a Thai firm can electronically send a technical question and supporting diagnostic data to its Singaporean supplier. Commercial information services maintain memories that have potential value to a wide variety of organizations. A firm wishing to check the credit worthiness of a new customer can access Dun & Bradstreet's credit information service, for example.

Now that you understand the broad relationship between organizational memory and networks, let's examine some aspects of this relationship in more detail. In particular, we will look at the Internet and information services.

THE INTERNET

The Internet is an information highway. It is a series of inter-connected networks communicating over high speed communication lines to give real time access to information. The Internet consists of more than 59,000 connected networks, comprising more than 2.2 million computers, and has over 15 million users. Since 1988, the Internet has doubled in size every year.[2]

---

[2]G. H. Anthes, "Info Highway Hits Technical Detours," *Computerworld,* 6 February 1995, 20.

The Internet is a cooperating system owned by more than 18,000 organizations world-wide. While the American government was influential in initiating the Internet's development, it currently owns only a small portion of the network. The Internet is the Great Barrier Reef of the information world — it is thousands of cooperating systems creating one vast, dynamic organism.

You join the information society when you connect to the Internet. You have access to millions of other Internet users in over 90 countries and gigabytes of data. It is expected that nearly all countries will eventually join. The nations currently with the most hosts are the United States, Australia, Canada, and Germany. The Scandinavian countries have the most hosts per person.

The Internet lets you travel the world's electronic highways. You can check out the contents of a library in Australia or have a conversation with someone in France. There is so much available on Internet that you probably will never have enough time to explore it completely; however, you certainly will have fun just poking around and finding some of the things available. We will give you some basic instructions to equip you for your expedition. We encourage you to explore and discover.

The Physical Connections

Networks are connected by communication lines of varying capacity. The most common carriers for the Internet are 56 kps (56 kilobit-per-second) dedicated leased telephone lines and 1 Mbps T1 links. T3 links, with a capacity of 45 Mbps, are installed between major locations. Some Internet traffic is also transported using high-speed modems. Like most parts of the Internet, these physical connections constantly change as their carrying capacity increases.

Addresses

Every explorer needs some basic navigation aids. Your electronic compass is a computer address. It helps you send someone a message or gets you to your destination computer. Addresses are of two forms: a computer address and a userid.

Computer Addresses

A computer's address is a set of two to five words connected by periods (e.g., uga.cc.uga.edu). The last word in the series is known as the top-level domain, which can describe the nature of the organization or the country. The value of the top-level domain for most American universities is edu. Some common organizational values for top-level domains are given in Table 17–1, and some common country codes for the top-level domain are listed in Table 17–2. There is a country code for the United States (yes, it is "us"), but it is generally not used. This is similar to postage stamps. Great Britain, the birthplace of stamps, is the only

Table 17–1   **Some Top-level Domains**

Domain	Description
com	A commercial organization (e.g., jwiley.com)
edu	An educational institution (e.g., uga.cc.uga.edu)
gov	A government site (e.g., whitehouse.gov)
mil	A military site (e.g., nosc.mil)

country that does not have its name on its stamps. Likewise, American Internet nodes generally do not have a country code.

The words preceding the top-level domain describe mid-level domains—typically, the location or purpose of the computer. Consider the address "iscs.nus.sg." This computer is located in the Department of Information Systems and Computer Science (the "iscs" part) at the National University of Singapore (the "nus" part). Just for interest, here is the address of a machine at the University of Oulu in Finland: rieska.oulu.fi.

Userid

A userid identifies a specific user on a computer. People generally select userids that correspond to their names. For example, this author's userid is "rwatson." Less friendly systems may allocate userids that are not so easy to remember. For example, one university system generates students' userids by combining a student's initials and the last four digits of that person's Social Security number.

Combining a userid and computer address gives you a unique e-mail address. The two parts are combined using the @ symbol. Thus, my e-mail address is rwatson@uga.cc.uga.edu. Even the President of the United States has an e-mail address: president@whitehouse.gov.

Table 17–2   **Some Country Codes**

Code	Country
au	Australia (e.g., a computer in the business school at Edith Cowan University in Western Australia has the address bsmail.bs.ac.cowan.edu.au)
ca	Canada (e.g., a computer at the University of Calgary is called acs.ucalgary.ca)
sg	Singapore (e.g., iscs.nus.sg is the name of a computer at the National University of Singapore)
uk	United Kingdom (e.g., the address of a computer at Henley Management College is henleymc.ac.uk)

Clients and Servers

In reading the section on the Internet, you will find a number of Internet applications that utilize the client/server concept (client/server architecture is discussed in Chapter 12). Typically, the client runs on a personal computer and the server is on a larger machine (e.g., a high-end microcomputer), though this is not necessary. In many cases, client software is available free or at minimum cost as shareware. We encourage you to explore the Internet for such software. Another good source is a book on the Internet. Many of these come with a diskette containing client software for common Internet applications.

The Internet can be used in a wide variety of ways. It is a medium for computer conferencing, provides access to a wide variety of other computers and databases, and is a source of software and documentation. To take advantage of it, however, you need some basic survival technologies (see Table 17–3).

Table 17–3   A Summary of Internet Facilities and Their Use

Service	Use
Communication	
Electronic mail	Electronic communication
Listserv	Computer bulletin board and group discussions
Computer and file access	
Telnet	Accessing a remote computer
FTP	Transferring files between Internet machines
Information searching	
Archie	Searching for files across anonymous FTP sites
Veronica	Searching Gopher sites by key words in menu or document titles
WAIS	Searching WAIS libraries for key words embedded in the text
Information structuring	
and retrieval	
Gopher	Navigating the Internet and retrieving information
World Wide Web	Navigating the Internet and retrieving information
Entertainment	
MUDs	Game playing and virtual space

Electronic Mail

People enjoy communicating and quickly take advantage of technologies that extend the power of their voices. The advent of a reliable postal service in the late 1700s stimulated letter writing in England. The telephone system grew sevenfold in the eight years following the beginning of full-scale competition in 1894.[3] Fax spread like a wind-driven scrub fire in the 1980s. Now, we have e-mail, one of the most popular uses of the Internet.

E-mail messages are delivered within seconds and may contain sound, images, video, and files. To send a message to a person whose electronic mailbox is at a particular computer, you need to know that person's electronic address. Mostly, you find someone's address through personal communication, however, once you get started on the Internet you will find there are directories to help you.

A variety of software packages give you access to e-mail. Most have the same features; they just implement them differently. Have you checked out the e-mail software on your system?

The Credible Editor

Beth, an editor for publisher John Wiley, uses e-mail on the Internet to communicate with authors, prospective authors, and book reviewers. She says, "E-mail makes it easier for professors to find me and for me to reach them. It also keeps me off the telephone in many cases, for which I am thankful." Also, because e-mail is so widely used by MIS faculty, she believes using e-mail enhances her credibility within the MIS academic community.

Discussion Lists

Discussion lists are another common use of the Internet that build on e-mail facilities. An electronic meeting can easily be established for people with a common interest. Information exchange is facilitated by setting up an e-mail address to which anyone in the electronic discussion can send a message. The software then automatically distributes the message to everyone on the list.

Information systems professors have a discussion list called ISWorld, with the address isworld@irlearn.ucd.ie. The list, maintained on a computer at the University College Dublin, Ireland, enables IS professors throughout the world to exchange information. For instance, details of academic conferences are posted to the list for distribution to all subscribers. Pro-

---

[3]C. S. Fischer, *America calling: a social history of the telephone to 1940.* Berkeley, CA: University of California Press, 1992.

fessors wishing to join the list send the following message, after adding their first and last names as indicated, to listserv@irleanr.ucd.ie.[4]

```
SUBSCRIBE ISWORLD FIRSTNAME LASTNAME
```

Be careful when replying to a message sent to a mailing list. The default is often to send a message to all subscribers, not just the person who originated the message. Failure to remember this procedure has frequently resulted in the embarrassment of a few and the amusement of many.

There are thousands of mailing lists; some are very active with lots of traffic and others are dormant. A list of the currently available mailing lists is available in a file on ftp.nisc.sri.com called interest groups under the netinfo/directory.

FTP

FTP (File Transfer Protocol) supports file transfers over the Internet. Files are typically transferred at speeds of 5 to 10 kbytes per second. To make it easy to find the files you might want to copy, FTP also permits listing of directories. To transfer files you generally need permission to access the host machine, but anonymous FTP is available because in many cases seeking approval is burdensome and defeats the information sharing goal of the Internet.

Anonymous FTP opens a portion of the host's file space to all comers and may be freely copied. There are thousands of anonymous FTP hosts. Many contain free software, shareware, and software upgrades. Some popular hosts are shown in Table 17–4.

To use anonymous FTP from your Internet connection, you will need software to make the connection. On most machines, this is called FTP. You create a connection by specifying the address of the machine you want to access (e.g., sumex-aim.stanford.edu) and then logging into the system as user "anonymous" with your e-mail address as your password (see Figure 17–1). There is no password checking, but FTP etiquette is to give your e-mail address.

Table 17–4   Some Anonymous FTP Sites

Host Address	Software
wsmr-simtel20.army.mil	MS-DOS
sumex-aim.stanford.edu	Macintosh
gatekeeper.dec.com	DEC

---

[4]Sometimes it is hard to be grammatically correct and convey e-mail addresses accurately. Remember, the final period terminates the sentence and is not part of the address.

```
OPEN (name of foreign host):
sumex-aim.stanford.edu
Connecting to sumex-aim.stanford.edu 36.44.0.6, port 21
220 SUMEX-AIM FTP server (Version 4.212 Mon May 17 20:58:59
PDT 1995) ready.
USER (identify yourself to the host):
anonymous
>>>USER anonymous
331 Guest login ok, send mail address (user@host) as password.
Password: (not echoed for security reasons)
```

Figure 17-1   Sample login to an anonymous FTP site

Now we will give you a few basic FTP commands to help you get started (see Table 17–5), although you should consult the documentation for your FTP software for particular details.

An FTP client running on your personal computer will give you a graphical user interface and will be easier to use when downloading from an FTP site. So one of the first things you might do with FTP is find a suitable client and download it to your machine.

Chat and Talk

Chat and Talk are common software programs that are the equivalent of the e-mail version of the telephone. You can have a text chat with another user simultaneously connected to the Internet. Check local documentation to see if Chat or Talk is available on your network and how to use it.

IRC

Internet Relay Chat (IRC) is a real time, group conversation system—the Internet equivalent of CB radio. IRC permits a group of people to communicate on one channel, which is usually

Table 17–5   Basic FTP Commands

Command	Purpose
DIR	List the files in the current directory
CD dname	Change to directory called dname
CD ..	Change to higher level directory
GET filename	Copy file called filename from remote system to your local system
PUT filename	Copy file called filename from local system to remote system

devoted to a particular topic. Client programs for many different systems exist. For more information on IRC and a client program, see anonymous FTP at cs.bu.edu in the directory/irc/support.

Telnet

Telnet is the main Internet protocol for connecting to a remote machine. It enables you to work on any another computer on the Internet. Of course, you must have an authorized account on the other computer or be permitted to log in as an anonymous or general user. Fast and error-free, telnet provides a superior connection compared to a modem.

The command for making a telnet connection depends on your computer software. A generic form of the command is

```
telnet address
```

An example of using telnet to connect to another computer is shown in Figure 17–2. The message you get will depend on the local and remote systems you use.

Telnet Ports

A telnet address can also include the connection port. Normally, you do not have to indicate a port number, but some services are available only through a specified port. Entering *telnet computer port* will connect you to the specified port on the machine with address *computer*.

```
Telnet archie.ans.net
VM TCP/IP Telnet V2R2
Connecting to ARCHIE.ANS.NET 147.225.1.10, port TELNET (23)

Using Line Mode. . .

Notes on using Telnet when in Line Mode:
- To hide Password, Hit PF3 or PF15
- To enter Telnet Command, Hit PF4-12, or PF16-24

AIX telnet (forum.ans.net)

IBM AIX version 3 for RISC System/600
  (C) Copyrights by IRM and by others 1982, 1991.
login:
```

Figure 17-2   Sample telnet connection

For instance, to connect to the geographic database server at the University of Michigan, you must enter

```
telnet martini.eecs.umich.edu 3000
```

Incidentally, this command connects you to a database listing information for cities in the United States and some international locations. The database is searchable by city name and zip code, and reports data such as county, state, latitude and longitude, population, elevation, and zip code(s). For example, entering Athens, GA yields the output shown in Figure 17–3. To try this server, telnet to martini.eecs.umich.edu 3000, and read the help instructions.

The Archie Server

Searching for a file across many anonymous FTP sites is like looking for the proverbial needle in a haystack. Fortunately, Archie is a quick and easy way to scan the directories of the many anonymous FTP sites. Containing over a million files, Archie currently tracks the contents of over 1000 anonymous FTP servers worldwide. Collectively, these files represent well over 150 Gbytes of data.

Archie servers periodically connect to a large number of anonymous FTP sites and collect data on what is available at each site and in what directories they are stored. These data are stored in a local database that Archie searches when you make a query.

To access Archie interactively, telnet to one of the servers shown in Table 17–6. At the login: prompt, enter *archie*. Enter a command following the archie> prompt. Type *help* to find out how to use Archie. Type *quit* at the prompt to leave Archie. If you want to find a copy of a program to tell you the location of an area code, you might type *prog areacode*. Figure 17–4 shows part of the response to the search for a program called areacode. The output indicates several FTP sites have a program called areacode, for example, there is a copy in the /pub directory at wilbur.stanford.edu.

```
0 Athens
1 13059 Clarke
2 GA Georgia
3 US United States
R county seat
F 45 Populated place
L 33 57 39 N 83 22 41 W
P 42549
E 662
Z 30601 30602 30603 30604 30605 30606 30607 30609 30610 30612
```

Figure 17-3   Output from the geographic database server at the University of Michigan

Table 17-6   Some Telnet Servers

Address	Location
archie.ans.net	New York, USA
archie.rutgers.edu	New Jersey, USA
archie.mcgill.ca	Archie's birthplace at McGill University, Canada
archie.funet.fi	Finland
archie.au	Australia
archie.doc.ic.ac.uk	Great Britain

Gopher

Gopher, a distributed document search and retrieval system, is another tool for exploring the Internet. Developed at the University of Minnesota (whose mascot is a gopher), this tool helps you find information stored on Gopher servers. A Gopher client has a complete view of all Gopher information, even though it is on many different servers. The beauty of Gopher is its transparency, the client is not concerned with the location of a Gopher server.

```
Host cac.washington.edu  (140.142.100.1)
Last updated 07:51 26 May 1993

   Location: /local/bin.sun386
      FILE       rwxrwxr-x       4807   Nov   7   1991      areacode
   Location: /local/bin.sparc
      FILE       rwxrwxr-x       4807   Nov   7   1991      areacode
   Location: /local/bin.pmax4.0
      FILE       rwxrwxr-x       4807   Nov   7   1991      areacode
   Location: /local/bin.next2.0
      FILE       rwxrwxr-x       4807   Nov   7   1991      areacode

Host wilbur.stanford.edu  (36.14.0.30)
Last updated 04:31 23 May 1993

   Location: /pub
      FILE       r-xr-xr-x       7838   Nov  16   1992      areacode

Host src.doc.ic.ac.uk  (146.169.2.1)
Last updated 20:29 20 May 1993

   Location: /ic.doc/gopher-admin/go4gw
      FILE       rwxr-xr-x       7942   Sep  18   1992      areacode
archie>
```

Figure 17-4   Partial output of an Archie search for areacode

A client/server system, Gopher has been implemented for many hardware platforms. Many of these implementations are in the public domain. You may have a Gopher client installed on your machine. If so, you enter *gopher* to execute the program, pick the Gopher client from a menu, or select the appropriate icon for a GUI interface. Your Gopher client will connect you to a server. For example, Gopher clients on many personal computers at The University of Georgia connect to a server on the University's mainframe.

The main client navigation aid is a hierarchical menu. The top-level menu guides you to data sources at your server and provides connections to other Gopher servers. Figure 17–5 shows the top-level menu for the Gopher server at The University of Georgia. You use the cursor keys to move to the desired menu item and then press *enter*. Of course, navigation techniques depend on your Gopher client. To try Gopher, check your local system or telnet to one of the public Gopher servers listed in Table 17–7.

Gopher servers are connected to create a large gopherspace. Once you access one server, you can access all other registered servers. Universities, government agencies, and commercial organizations have registered their servers with Gopher Central. Those connected include Apple Computer, IBM, Novell, NASA, the Library of Congress, and the Social Security Administration. The U.S. Department of State's travel advisories are available on its server.

Because there are so many Gopher servers, you can easily spend a lot of time navigating from your local server to a remote one. This is particularly annoying if you access the same remote server frequently. Fortunately, you can create "bookmarks," pointers to remote servers.

One source of Gopher client and server software is the /pub/gopher directory at boombox.micro.umn.edu. You can download the software using anonymous FTP. There are other Gopher software sources, and finding these is a good exercise for the reader.

Organizations can use Gopher to disseminate public information such as quarterly and annual reports, product specifications, answers to frequently asked questions about the firm and its products, and technical support material. Some universities place their telephone and e-mail directories on their Gopher server.

Veronica

Information is everywhere in Gopherspace, but how do you find it? It is far too time consuming to visit each server and check what is stored there. Fortunately, Veronica (Very easy rodent-oriented net-wide index to computerized archives) is available for searching Gopher

```
CMS                         Gopher 2.3.0              gopher.uga.edu

                            (root menu)

<menu>      About the University of Georgia (UGA) Gopher
<menu>      Library
<menu>      UGA Campus-Wide Information
<menu>      UGA Departments
<menu>      University System of Georgia
<menu>      Weather
<menu>      Worldwide Information
```

Figure 17-5 The top-level Gopher menu for The University of Georgia

Table 17–7 Some Gopher Sites

Hostname	Login	Region
info.anu.edu.au	info	Australia
gopher.sunet.se	gopher	Europe
consultant.micro.umn.edu	gopher	North America
tolten.puc.cl	gopher	South America

sites. Veronica will search for items, menus or documents containing specified keywords in their titles. Veronica is accessed via Gopher, so look for it on your Gopher server.

Here is an example of a search.

```
Search Gopher sites via Veronica
Enter KEY word(s): Iceland
```

The search returns a screen of menus and documents that contain the key word(s) (see Figure 17–6). Some key words result in many screens of information. One of the shortcomings of Veronica is that the same item can be reported several times because it is stored at different Gopher sites. Furthermore, there is no guarantee that the same title means the same document.

```
<menu>        Iceland
<menu>        Iceland
<menu>        Iceland
<menu>        Iceland
<menu>        Iceland
<document>    Iceland.sd
<menu>        Iceland
<document>    000:112 University of Iceland Exchange Program
<document>     000:112 UNIVERSITY OF ICELAND EXCHANGE PROGRAM
arr
<document>    University of Iceland
<menu>        Iceland
<menu>        Iceland
<menu>        Iceland (country)
<menu>        Iceland
<document>    Red Clay people in Iceland
<document>    Re: Red Clay people in Iceland
<document>    Re: Red Clay people in Iceland
```

Figure 17-6   A Veronica search on "Iceland"

```
000:112 UNIVERSITY OF ICELAND EXCHANGE PROGRAM
arr
Prerequisites: A UI participant must have earned at least 36 s.h.
and a 3.00 cumulative gpa or above.
A UI studient selected to participate in this exchange usually en-
rolls in the University of Iceland's Icelandic for Foreign Students
Program and takes first year language courses. The course work em-
phasizes speaking and writing skills, and covers the most important
aspects of Icelandic phonetics, grammar, and morphology. If the UI
student has studied Icelandic language, placement in more advanced
courses may be arranged.
A participant takes twelve hours of classroom instruction each
week, and must pass two examinations (one in January and one in
May) to earn 24 transfer credits. These credits may fulfill the UI
College of Liberal Arts foreign language requirement. A structured
field study project or independent research on a pre-approved topic
may also be undertaken for credit at the undergraduate or graduate
level.
```

Figure 17-7   Further results of the Veronica search on "Iceland"

You can get further information on any listed item by positioning the cursor on the item and pressing return (see Figure 17–7). Then, if you feel like doing something more challenging, you might consider learning Icelandic.

WAIS

WAIS (Wide Area Information Servers) is a project sponsored by Dow Jones & Co., Apple Computer, KPMG Peat Marwick, and Thinking Machines Corporation. WAIS's objective is to provide an easy to use full-text information retrieval to corporate clients. Each of the participants brings special expertise to the project. Dow Jones is an experienced business information provider, Apple is particularly strong in the area of human–computer interface, KPMG Peat Marwick serves many information-hungry consultants and clients, and Thinking Machines has high-end information retrieval engines.

WAIS is a powerful search tool because it searches the text within a document. Every word within a WAIS document is usually indexed. You give WAIS some keywords, and it searches its libraries. Currently, WAIS contains more than 250 libraries.

WAIS has three separate parts: clients, servers, and a communications protocol. The client handles the user interface, the server indexes and retrieves documents, and the communications protocol transmits queries and responses between client and server. The value of the communications protocol is that it isolates clients and servers. As a result, WAIS can be used with any client capable of translating a user's request into the standard protocol. Similarly, any server capable of answering a request encoded in the protocol can be used. To promote development of both clients and servers, the communication protocol specification is in the public domain, as is its initial implementation.

WAIS has a natural language interface—queries are expressed in English. The server returns a set of document descriptions selected from multiple databases across several platforms. These items, which include text, picture, video, or sound, can be examined. If the initial response is incomplete or insufficient, the query can be refined and resubmitted.

An interesting and very useful feature is that a user can indicate which retrieved documents are relevant to the current search, and then re-run the search. The server attempts to find documents similar to those marked as relevant. In the present WAIS system, "similar" documents are simply ones which share a large number of common words. This method of information retrieval is called "relevance feedback."

Free software for a variety of WAIS clients (e.g., Macintosh and Windows) is available from anonymous FTP think.com, where you will also find documentation on WAIS. To try out WAIS, telnet to quake.think.com. Alternatively, you can access WAIS through most Gopher servers by checking the menu item for other Gopher and Information Services.

A sample WAIS search, using a Macintosh client, is shown in Figure 17–8. The first window shows the keywords used in the search. In this case, information on *optical disk* is sought. The search is to be made in the source called current.cites.src, which contains abstracts of recently published articles. The search lists 15 documents in the order of likely relevance, based on the keywords. The document's size in bytes is on the left side of the screen.

You can read any of the reported articles by clicking on its icon on the left side. The article will then be displayed in a scrollable window, similar to that reporting the results of the search. You may have to scan several articles before finding the one that matches your needs.

Usenet News

Usenet News is a vast set of discussion lists on a wide range of topics. News groups are organized in a tree structure of discussion topics. The number of top level categories vary with the news server to which you gain access; seven common major categories are shown in Table 17–8.

World Wide Web

The World Wide Web (WWW), an initiative started at CERN (the European Laboratory for Particle Physics) in 1989, now has many participants. WWW is a body of software, a set of protocols, and conventions. It uses hypertext and multimedia techniques to make the Internet web easy for anyone to browse and add contributions. WWW extends the idea of Gopher by moving beyond simple, linear text files to hypertext, color, and multimedia. It blends networked information and hypertext to create a user friendly, global information system.

Question-1

Look for documents about

Optical disk

[Run]

Which are similar to

In these sources

⊕ current.cites.src

Results   15 documents

📊	751	Theil, Thomas J. "Integrating CD-ROM and WORM Optical Disk Systems or
📊	751	Theil, Thomas J. "Integrating CD-ROM and WORM Optical Disk Systems or
📊	394	Kaebnick, Gregory. "Rewriting the Future: Putting Rewritable Optical
📊	394	Kaebnick, Gregory. "Rewriting the Future: Putting Rewritable Optical
📊	685	Rizzo, John "Double Duty Drives: Multifunction Optical Storage"
📊	772	Barron, Gary. "The Role of Optical Technology in Megamedia
📊	517	Harvey, David A. "Optical Storage Primer." BYTE IBM Special Edition
📊	517	Harvey, David A. "Optical Storage Primer." BYTE IBM Special Edition
📊	750	"State of the Art: Magnetic vs. Optical." BYTE 15(2) (November
📊	750	"State of the Art: Magnetic vs. Optical." BYTE 15(2) (November

Figure 17-8   Output from a WAIS search

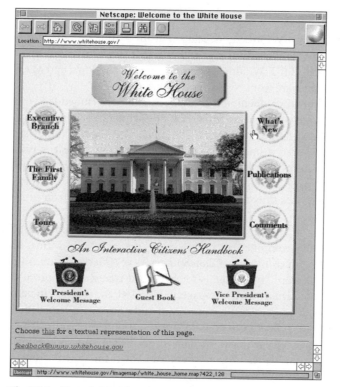

The White House's World Wide Web home page.

Table 17–8   **Common Major News Categories**

Category	Description
comp	Computer science, software sources, and information on hardware and software systems (e.g., comp.databases)
misc	Topics not covered by the other categories (e.g., misc.forsale)
sci	Sciences (e.g., sci.astro.hubble)
soc	Social issues and social communications (e.g., soc.culture.australia)
talk	Discussion and debate on a variety of subjects (e.g., talk.politics.gun)
news	News network maintenance and software (e.g., news.admin.policy)
rec	Hobbies and recreations (e.g., rec.arts.cinema)

NCSA Mosaic

Mosaic is a WWW browser developed at the National Center for Supercomputing Applications (NCSA) at the University of Illinois that was released in September 1993. Mosaic offers WWW clients for X Window System, Microsoft Windows, and Macintosh. You can download the client software from NCSA (ftp.ncsa.uiuc.edu).

WWW breaks a document into pages. Links are embedded within pages so that you can navigate from one page to another. Links, which can be words, icons, or images, are highlighted (the default is blue and underlined). You select a link by simply clicking on it. Once you have viewed a link, the color is changed (the default is red) to help you remember where you have been. As you would expect, there are navigation aids to link to the previous page, next page, and home page. Mosaic includes links to Gopher, Usenet News, and other Internet services thus reducing the number of interfaces you need to learn to access Internet services.

The key to finding pages is the Uniform Resource Locator (URL), which defines the name of the computer and address of the a WWW format document. For example, http://info.cern.ch/hypertext/DataSources/WWW/Servers.html is the URL of a list of WWW servers. The word "http" stands for hypertext transmission protocol, the name of the computer is info.cern.ch, and the page is found at the address hypertext/DataSources/WWW/Servers.html.

WWW documents can contain images, sound, and video. Distinct icons are embedded within a page for each of these data forms. When you click on an icon, the data are transferred from the server to your client and when the downloading is complete, the data are played. For example, you hear a voice, or see an image, or view a video. For large files, such as most video clips, downloading will take some time, especially when Internet traffic is heavy.

There is a case study that will teach you more about WWW and give you a graphic example of how WWW supports commerce. The URL is http://www.cox.smu.edu/mis/cases/webcase/home.html.

Directories—Finding Someone

Before you can communicate with someone, you need to know their e-mail address. Finding an Internet address is not as simple as dialing the telephone company's directory service or flipping through the telephone book. Because Internet is a loose federation of networks, there is no central registry of addresses. Fortunately, the Internet has several databases that contain information about individuals. Here are a few you may want to try.

White Pages

PSI maintains a directory of information on individuals. It lists the person's name, organization, and e-mail address if it is given. Telnet to wp.psi.net and log in as *fred*.

Knowbot

Knowbot contains e-mail address information from several directories, including the PSI X.500 White Pages Pilot Project and MCI Mail. Telnet to info.cnri.reston.va.us on port 185.

Paradise

Paradise is a large X.500 directory at the University College of London. Paradise servers, distributed throughout the world, are searchable via Gopher and WAIS.

MUDs—A New Frontier for Exploration

MUDs (multiple user dimensions) originated in the late 1980s as multiple-user, electronic versions of the game "Dungeons and Dragons." A virtual world populated by the players and their creations, a MUD is an ongoing drama with an electronically assembled cast exploring and interacting in cyberspace.[5]

MUDs are addictive, particularly for students. MUDs were banned in Australia because their introduction sparked a 25 percent increase in Internet traffic out of the country. There was simply not enough bandwidth to carry MUD traffic. Some universities have banned MUDs because they consume too many computing resources and too much student time. You have been warned: be wary of MUDs consuming your time. A list of MUDs is available at caisr2.caisr.cwru.edu in /pub/mud.

Today's MUDs may be prototypes of virtual worlds that will appear in the future. These worlds will move beyond the constrained text interchange of present MUDs to become multimedia. They may also become vehicles for social interaction. A MUD could be an ideal way for a organization to develop team spirit in a group that never meets face-to-face. Teams need playtime if they are to develop the social bonding that is a precursor to goal commitment and successful project implementation. Many teams develop their social dimension outside of formal work assignments. For example, a team might lunch together after a meeting. Virtual teams, those formed by electronic links, need to find ways to socialize, and a MUD might be a convenient way to do it.[6]

---

[5]This term was coined by William Gibson in his 1984 novel *Neuromancer*.

[6]For an expanded discussion of MUDs and their organizational application, see Devereaux, M. O., and Johansen, R. *Bridging distance and diversity: navigating the challenges of distributed and cross-cultural business teams.* Menlo Park, CA: The Institute for the Future, 1993.

Project Gutenberg

Project Gutenberg is converting printed text to electronic text for selected works. These are generally well-known books for which the copyright has expired or copyrighted books for which electronic distribution has been approved. Some of the books available include *Alice's Adventures in Wonderland* by Lewis Carroll, the King James version of *The Bible,* and the *1991 CIA World Fact Book.* One of the project's electronic publications, *Zen and the Art of Internet* by Brendan P. Kehoe, is a source for additional material on the Internet.

Project Gutenberg asserts that it produces about $1 million for each hour of its work. This claim is based on an estimate of 100 hours to take a text, check its copyright, and convert it to electronic format. It then projects its potential audience at 100 million readers and gives each electronic text a nominal value of $1. The current plan is to publish four electronic books per month. The project's long-term goal is to give away one trillion (10^9) electronic books by 2001.

Project Gutenberg is based at Illinois Benedictine College. You can FTP directly to the Project Gutenberg archives at mrcnext.cso.uiuc.edu and login as an anonymous user.

NREN — The Future

The Internet and other such networks are the highways of an information society. The American interstate highway and airline systems are an important national competitive resource because they lower the cost of distributing goods. A high speed electronic superhighway is required for the efficient distribution of information and many information-based services. In 1991, Congress approved funding for The National Research and Education Network (NREN), a five-year project to create a national electronic superhighway 50 times faster than the currently fastest available networks. Using NREN, the entire text of the *Encyclopedia Britannica* could be transported in one second. Further information, including the original text of the bill presented by Vice President (then-Senator) Al Gore, is available through anonymous FTP at nis.nsf.net in the directory nsfnet.

The Internet and Organizational Memory

Many companies have discovered that the World Wide Web, after e-mail the most popular use of the Internet, provides a ready means of giving customers access to information. For example, Promus (http://www.promus.com/) provides descriptions of its hotel chains, hotel directories, and reservation numbers. In addition, its Web site includes photographs of hotel rooms, press releases, and an employee directory. The Web is an inexpensive way for a firm to make some aspects of its organizational memory widely available. As software tools for creating Web sites develop, you can expect to see support for interfaces to organizational memory technologies such as a DBMS or imaging system. For instance, a customer will be able to write a query to search a database to identify products of interest. There is every indication that the World Wide Web will become a widely used interface to those components of memory an organization wants to make available to the general public.

INFORMATION SERVICES

Information services are available to anyone with a personal computer and modem (see Table 17–9). Most services have a minimal monthly connection charge (in the region of $10–$20) that provides several hours of free access to basic services. Advanced services carry surcharges. For example, retrieving the full text of a Wall Street analyst's company report could cost $15. Access to a database of stock and mutual funds prices may cost an additional $20 per month.

America Online

America Online, established in 1985 as Quantum Computer Services, offers a user friendly interface for novice personal computer users. Rather than building its own communication network, America Online uses public networks such as Sprint's SprintNet and British Telecom's Tymnet.

America Online provides a variety of information services, and supports key word searching (see Figure 17–10). If you need to get the latest new stories that mention Malaysia, just type in the key word and then select from the listed stories.

You can use EAAsy Sabre, the consumer version of American Airlines reservation system, to make your own airline, hotel, and rental car reservations. Feeling adventurous? Check out the flight schedules from Atlanta to Ouagadougou (see Figure 17–11). So where *is* Ouagadougou?

Closer to home, the vicarious adventurer can visit the Smithsonian via computer (see Figure 17–12).

Table 17–9   Some Information Services

Information Service	Phone Number
America Online	1-800-827-6364
CompuServe	1-800-848-8199
Dow Jones News/Retrieval	1-800-522-3567
GEnie	1-800-638-9636
LEXIS-NEXIS	1-800-227-4908
Prodigy	1-800-776-3449

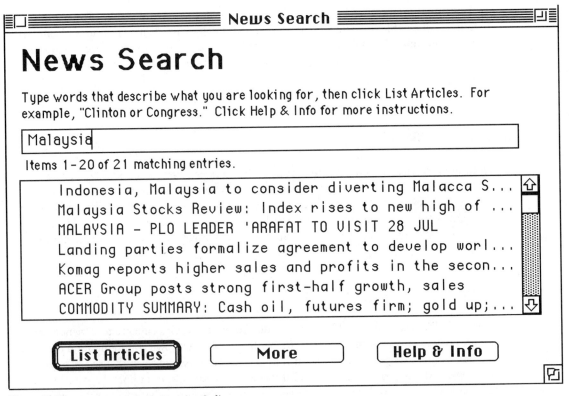

Figure 17-10   A news search on America Online

America Online divides its services into eight departments: computing and software, news and finance, travel and shopping, people connection, lifestyles and interest, learning and reference, entertainment, and members' on-line support. Like most of the information services, you can spend hours exploring these departments and downloading files.

CompuServe

CompuServe provides services for both the corporate and consumer markets through differential pricing for its basic, extended, and premium services. Essentially, the basic service provides facilities similar to those found on America Online and Prodigy; the extended and premium services parallel the offerings of Dow Jones News/Retrieval. Serving both markets through the one system makes good sense because overheads (e.g., the communication network) are shared and customers can easily upgrade to the extended service if desired.

Figure 17-11   Checking out flight details with EAAsy Sabre

The basic service includes news, sports, weather, e-mail, a reference library, an electronic mall, financial information, EAAsy Sabre, travel information, entertainment, and games. A useful feature of the travel department is U.S. Department of State advisories and visa advice. A single monthly charge of approximately US$10 provides unlimited connect time to the basic service.

In addition to the flat monthly charge for the basic service, a fee based on time is levied for extended and premium services, which provide more extensive financial information and news services. For example, you get access to Wall Street analysts' reports, S&P Online earnings projections, Securities and Exchange Commission filings, and access an on-line discount broker. The news service includes Associated Press (part of the basic service), *The Washington Post,* Reuters, United Press International, and a number of other news sources.

An executive service option permits automatic scanning of major news wires, with clipping of related stories and filing for subsequent reading. It also includes investment analysis company research tools, and information on more than 10,000 corporations worldwide.

Figure 17-12 An virtual visit to the Smithsonian

Dow Jones News/Retrieval

Dow Jones, the publisher of *The Wall Street Journal,* has provided information to business since 1882. Thus it is not surprising that Dow Jones News/Retrieval, with its five major services, is geared for the corporate market, financial professionals, and private investors.

The business and world news wires provide up-to-the-second news and coverage that is held for 90 days. The news wires cover national and international news, more than 5000 American stocks, world financial markets, SEC filings, and press releases from major organizations. Subscribers can customize the service to continuously scan and filter incoming news. Alerts can be delivered via on-line, fax, or e-mail. It is also possible to track automatically news on up to 125 companies.

The Dow Jones text library provides access to over 1000 national and regional business and industry-specific publications. It is the exclusive on-line provider of the full text of *The Wall Street Journal,* including European and Asian versions, *Times of London, China Daily,* and more than 70 additional international sources. It also has the full text for selected articles

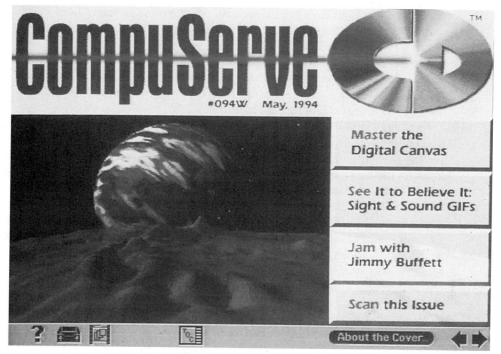

A CompuServe screen.

from *The Los Angeles Times, The Washington Post, Business Week, Time, Fortune,* and other publications. Also available is the full text of nearly 600 trade and business newsletters.

Company and industry information covers major American and Canadian public, private, and government-owned companies. In addition, there are reports on more than 7500 corporations in over 30 countries. The service provides company and market identification data on over 7 million American companies. Up to 15 years of historical information is available for stocks, bonds, mutual funds, and indexes. Real time market quotes are available for a number of stock exchanges.

General services includes book reviews, career management advice, a 32,000 article encyclopedia, movie reviews, and sports news. Also, there is information on airline schedules and fares, hotel/motel information, vacation packages, and on-line reservations booking.

LEXIS–NEXIS

The LEXIS service, started in 1973, claims to have been the first commercial full-text information service. Originally created to support legal research, it now includes news and business information services.

LEXIS–NEXIS subscribers in more than 50 countries can access nearly 4700 databases containing more than 188 million on-line documents. The database, more than 188 Gbytes in size, grows at the rate of 650,000 documents per week.

The LEXIS service contains American federal and state case law, statutes of all 50 states, and federal and state regulations. There are also databases of Canadian, English, and French law, and legal materials from Australia, New Zealand, Ireland, and Scotland. Specialized libraries cover many fields of legal practice.

Introduced in 1979, NEXIS provides full-text news and business information services. It is the exclusive on-line source for *The New York Times,* and other major publications included are *The Washington Post, Business Week, Fortune,* and *The Economist.* It also provides transcripts of radio and television news and features. The major news services of Britain, China, France, Japan, Mexico, and Russia are also available.

NEXIS includes financial information, brokers' reports, and real-time and historical stock quotes from all North American exchanges. There are country reports, and information on elections, political issues, polls, and candidates. The National Automated Accounting Research System covers annual reports of public corporations and government entities. The MEDIS service offers full-text medical information from leading medical journals and government reports. The 1.5 million American patents issued since 1975 are available through the LEXPAT service.

Mead Data Central, Inc., the providers of LEXIS–NEXIS, support a wide range of on-line information services and complementary retrieval aids. Its market includes lawyers, accountants, financial analysts, journalists, and marketing and information specialists.

Prodigy

Prodigy Services Co. is a joint venture of IBM and Sears Roebuck and Co. Started in 1984, Prodigy has invested millions of dollars in a large computer network. The friendly graphical interface is great for beginners, but the advertisements are a bit wearing and consume precious screen space. Prodigy provides services similar to America Online. Indeed, they compete in the same consumer information services market.

Some interesting services provided by Prodigy include on-line investing with a discount broker, a bill paying service, weather maps, and on-line ordering of stamps and envelopes from the U.S. Postal Service. It also has an on-line version of Sesame Street.

Dun & Bradstreet—Profile of An Information Services Company

This section gives a more detailed profile of one of the oldest information service firms, Dun & Bradstreet (D&B). We use it to discuss some key ideas about information services, especially the role of external information services in corporate decision making. Although organizations collect and store data to support decision making, it is too costly and time consuming to collect all the data an organization might require. Some of this hard-to-collect data are used by many organizations (e.g., credit worthiness); hence, specialized information services collect and maintain such data and sell it as required.

Organizations essentially face a make-or-buy decision with a database. Data generated by internal operations are most readily collected and stored by the organization—the make decision. Data created by external organizations are most readily collected and stored by a third-party information service—the buy decision.

D&B has been an information services company for more than 150 years. Founded as The Mercantile Agency in 1841 by Lewis Tappan, the purpose of the original business was to promote and protect trade by providing information on the financial responsibility of firms. While still serving its original purpose, D&B now provides a very broad range of information services (see Figure 17–13).

D&B's core services are business and television audience information, which accounted for about 50 percent of revenue in 1992. Traditionally a supplier of information, D&B is now broadening its service to include decision support software. Because clients[7] must acquire information to support decision making, D&B realizes it can extend its business by providing them with both the information and the software for processing it.

As the world's leading supplier of commercial credit information, D&B has a database covering more than 25 million businesses in over 30 countries. This database has many uses beyond just checking the credit worthiness of a firm. By applying the customer service life cycle,[8] which separates the customer relationship into four major and 15 minor phases (see Figure 17–14), D&B creates new business.

The customer service cycle is a valuable tool for an information services company because it can be used to identify opportunities for extending services. Indeed, it can be doubly valuable. D&B clients want information that enables them to provide products and services to their customers. So D&B is in a double cycle: the client service cycle and the client's customer service cycle. Thus, D&B has twice as many opportunities because it can serve both the client directly and the client's customer indirectly. In terms of the client's customer service life cycle, D&B helps the client to manage its customer relationships in several ways (see Table 17–10).

D&B also uses the service life cycle to gain new clients and service them directly. As Table 17–11 depicts, it uses data in several ways.

If an information services company understands why its clients want information and how they use it, then they can undercover opportunities to augment their service. The service life cycle is a useful model for analyzing both the client relationship and the client's relationship with the customer. Of course, application of the customer service life cycle model is not just limited to information service companies. All organizations can gain from using it as a

---

[7]In this section, we are very careful with the use of the word *client* and *customer* to avoid confusion. We use client to identify a firm using D&B's services. A customer is someone who buys a product or service from the D&B client.

[8]Ives, B. and Learmonth, G. P. The information systems as a competitive weapon. *Communications of the ACM.* 1984; 27(12): 1193–1201.

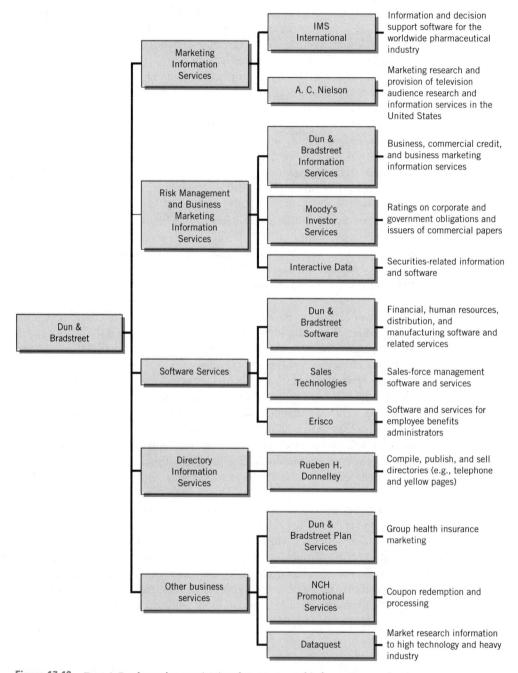

Figure 17-13   Dun & Bradstreet's organizational structure and information services

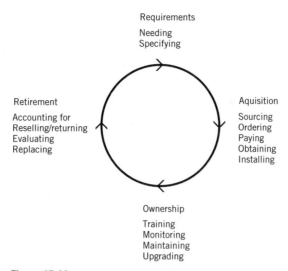

Figure 17-14   Customer service life cycle

tool for recognizing ways to use information effectively. D&B's understanding of how clients can use its information services increases its value to them and simultaneously ties the client more closely to D&B.

For the purposes of decision making, organizations often need to integrate data from internal and external sources. Managers don't care about the data sources, but they do care that they have adequate, highly reliable data. Furthermore, they often want software that helps them analyze the data—a DSS.

Organizations face a make-or-buy decision with a DSS. If they have reasonably unique decision making circumstances, then an in-house DSS may be appropriate. Many business decisions have a high degree of commonality, however, and external vendors can often provide appropriate DSS software at a lower cost.

As an information provider, D&B is situated to meet clients' DSS needs. Understanding how and why customers use data, it is logical for D&B to provide both the data and DSS tools

**Table 17–10   D&B's Use of the Customer Service Life Cycle to Help Clients Manage
Their Customers**

Phase	Example
Requirements	Identifying client's potential customers
Acquisition	Checking credit worthiness of client's customers
Ownership	Selling client accounts receivable software to monitor customer accounts
Retirement	Collecting delinquent customer accounts for clients

Table 17–11   D&B's Use of the Customer Life Cycle with Its Clients

Phase	Example
Requirements	Potential customers are identified by extracting from the credit database those firms whose financial indicators suggest cash flow problems. These firms usually require D&B's accounts receivable services.
Acquisition	If the client does not want to manage its receivables, it can outsource them to D&B, which has the skills, data, and software to handle this task.
Ownership	D&B can provide clients with software to monitor D&B's handling of past due accounts as the account proceeds through varying levels of service—friendly letter reminders to litigation.
Retirement	D&B can provide collection of past due receivables or a report detailing collection efforts. This report can be used to satisfy tax reporting purposes.

to support clients' decision making. Some recent products illustrate how D&B is delving into decision support. There is a service that helps clients compare their performance with others in the industry; and software to help purchasing managers evaluate suppliers.

If D&B is to provide a complete information service to its customers, it needs three core competencies (see Figure 17–15). First, it must maintain highly reliable and extensive databases that meet the full complement of the customers' needs. These databases must be supported by an efficient and effective system for timely collection of data. Second, it must efficiently deliver accurate information to customers when and where required. For a global operation such as D&B, it often means creating and maintaining a worldwide communication network. The low quality and unreliability of some national communication systems can seriously impair the delivery of information. Third, it must solve the client's fundamental requirement: clients acquire information for a purpose, and satisfying this real need increases customer loyalty. D&B's software business can create DSSs that help clients resolve problems.

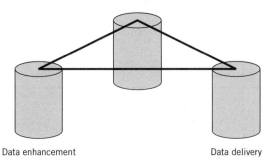

Databases

Data enhancement   Data delivery

Figure 17-15   The foundations of information service

Télétel

Télétel is the most famous and commercially viable national videotex system. It is commonly known as Minitel, the name of the dedicated terminal used by consumers, but the term Télétel refers to the entire system. In 1993, Télétel had over 6 million subscribers and 20,000 services. It handles close to 2 billion calls and 110 million hours of connect time per year. Government-operated Télétel is much larger than privately owned American information services such as America Online.

Télétel initially offered an electronic telephone directory to overcome problems with the printed directory, which was often obsolete when printed and expensive to produce. It now offers a wide range of information services and e-mail. Although the system is used regularly by a broad cross-section of the population in a number of ways, business applications seem to be the most common purpose.

Télétel supports third party providers of information services. All billing for services is done by France Télécom. The customer's regular telephone bill does not identify the specific service used, and France Télécom does not supply the information provider with any customer information. This procedure protects the anonymity of the user and relieves the service provider from the tedious task of billing customers. Variously priced services can be easily provided through different telephone numbers.[9]

Surfing Minitel

Wind surfing is a popular summer sport in France. It is very frustrating, however, to spend two hours driving to the nearest lake, the Mediterranean Sea, or Atlantic Ocean only to find calm water. Wind surfers want to know the current wind conditions on the water before they start the long drive.

Wind surfing MIS Professor Marc Favier of Grenoble created a Minitel service for wind surfers. He has organized vendors of wind surfing equipment at popular waterside sites throughout France, asking them to enter current wind conditions into Télétel each hour. Wind surfers can then retrieve the latest wind data from the Minitel terminal in their homes. Now the informed wind surfer does not spend hours traveling to flat water.

The service costs 60 French francs (about $10) per hour, of which 26 francs ($4) goes to French Télécom, the provider of Minitel terminals and the network, and the remaining 34 francs ($6) goes to Dr. Favier. Usually, a wind surfer spends between 2 to 4 minutes, about 50 cents, checking out the latest wind conditions.[10]

---

[9]Cats-Baril, W. L. and Jelassi, T. The French Videotex System Minitel: A Successful Implementation of a National Information Technology Infrastructure. *MIS Quarterly*. 1994; 18(1): 1–20.

[10]Personal electronic correspondence with Dr. Marc Favier, University of Pierre Mendés France, Grenoble.

SUMMARY

The combination of computer and communication technology enables the creation of electronic networks. There are networks, connecting tens of millions of people throughout the world, that support e-mail, links to information services, and access to remote computers. Communication networks extend organizational memory.

The Internet is a large "network of networks." It is a cooperating system owned by more than 18,000 organizations worldwide. A computer's address is a set of two to five words connected by periods. A userid identifies the name of a specific user on a computer. E-mail is one of the most popular uses of Internet; discussion lists are another common use. FTP supports file transfers over the Internet. Anonymous FTP opens a portion of the host's file space to all comers. Chat and Talk are the e-mail version of the telephone. IRC—the Internet equivalent of CB radio—permits a group of people to communicate on a single channel, which is usually devoted to a particular topic. Telnet is the main Internet protocol for connecting to a remote machine. Archie is a quick and easy way to scan the directories of the many anonymous FTP sites. Gopher is a distributed document search and retrieval system. A Gopher client has a complete view of all Gopher information, even though it is on many different servers. The main client navigation aid is a hierarchical menu. Veronica will search all Gopher sites for items, menus or documents containing specified keywords in their title. WAIS searches the text within a document, since every word within a WAIS document is usually indexed. Usenet news groups are organized in a tree structure of discussion topics.

WWW uses hypertext and multimedia techniques to make the Internet easy for anyone to browse and add contributions. It extends the idea of Gopher by moving beyond simple, linear text files to hypertext, color, and multimedia. WWW documents can contain images, sound, and video. The Internet contains several databases which can be searched to find a person's e-mail address. A MUD is a virtual world populated by the players and their creations. Project Gutenberg is converting printed text to electronic text for selected works. The Internet and other such networks are the highways of an information society.

Information services are available to anyone with a personal computer and modem. Most services have a minimal monthly connection charge that provides several hours of free access to basic services. Advanced services carry surcharges. Some information service providers are America Online, CompuServe, Dow Jones News/Retrieval, Dun & Bradstreet, LEXIS–NEXIS, and Prodigy.

KEY TERMS AND CONCEPTS

Archie	Information service
Bookmark	Internet
Bulletin board	Internet relay chat (IRC)
Computer address	Mosaic
Customer service life cycle	Multiple user dimensions (MUDs)
Discussion list	Network
Electronic mail	NREN
File transfer protocol (FTP)	Organizational memory
Gopher	Project Gutenberg

Talk
Telnet
Userid
Usenet news

Veronica
Wide area information servers (WAIS)
World Wide Web (WWW)

REFERENCES

Engst, A. C. and Dickson, W. *Internet Explorer's Kit for Macintosh*, Indianapolis, IN: Hayden, 1994.

Engst, A. C., Low, C. S. and Simon, M. A. *Internet Explorer's Kit for Windows.* Indianapolis, IN: Hayden, 1994.

Kehoe, B. P. *Zen and the Art of the Internet.* Englewood Cliffs, NJ: Prentice Hall, 1992. Also available from the Project Gutenberg archives through anonymous FTP to mrcnext.cso.uiuc.edu.

Krol, E. *The Whole Internet User's Guide & Catalog.* Sebastopol, CA: O'Reilly & Associates, 1992.

EXERCISES

1. What is the Internet?
2. How does the Internet support maintenance and use of organizational memory?
3. What are the advantages of using e-mail?
4. What is a discussion list? When is it useful?
5. What's FTP? What's different about anonymous FTP?
6. When would you use Telnet?
7. How many cities called Perth are there in the United States?
8. What is the latitude and longitude of Oslo, Norway?
9. How do you find files stored at anonymous FTP sites?
10. Give the name of one FTP site where you can find a program called Anarchie.
11. What is Gopher?
12. Give the name of one Harvard Business School case whose keyword descriptors include Singapore (hint: Harvard Business School is in Massachusetts).
13. What does Veronica do?
14. List one location where you can find the "Hacker's dictionary."
15. According to the Hacker's dictionary, what is a "computer geek?"
16. List the Gopher sites in São Paulo, Brazil.
17. How does WAIS differ from Veronica?
18. How does Usenet news differ from a discussion list?
19. What is WWW? How does it compare to Gopher?

20. What is a URL?
21. Where can you get stock prices on WWW?
22. Find an electronic shopping mall and describe the businesses that operate there.
23. Who are the member organizations of ISWorld Net?
24. How many campuses are there at Japan's Keio University?
25. Where is Karl Franzens University?
26. Describe a MUD.
27. What is the goal of Project Gutenberg?
28. What do you think is the future of the Internet? How will it affect your career?
29. Why might you subscribe to an information service? Why might a firm subscribe to an information service?
30. What is Télétel? How does it differ from America Online?

Managing Organizational Memory

Everyone complains of his memory, none of his judgment.

François Duc de La Rochefoucauld
"Sentences et Maximes," *Morales* No. 89 1678

As you now realize, organizational memory is an important resource that needs to be managed. An inaccurate memory can result in bad decisions and poor customer service. Some aspects of organizational memory (e.g., chemical formulae, marketing strategy, and R&D plans) are critical to the well-being of an organization. The financial consequences can be extremely significant if these memories are lost or fall into the hands of competitors. Consequently, organizations must develop and implement procedures for maintaining data integrity. They need policies to protect the existence of data, maintain its quality, and ensure its confidentiality. Some of these procedures may be embedded in organizational memory technology and others may be performed by data management staff. Data integrity (Chapter 18) is the first issue addressed in this section.

When organizations recognize that a resource is important to their long-term viability, they typically create a formal mechanism to manage this resource. For example, most companies have a human resources department, which is responsible for activities such as compensation, recruiting, training, and employee counseling. People are the major resource of nearly every company, and the human resources department manages this resource. Similarly, the finance department manages a company's financial assets.

In an information age, data, the raw material of information, need to be managed. Consequently, data administration has become a formal organizational structure in many enterprises. Data administration is the focus of Chapter 19.

Dr. Robert P. Bostrom of The University of Georgia was the principal author of this section.

Chapter 18

Data Integrity

Integrity without knowledge is weak and useless, and knowledge without integrity is dangerous and dreadful.

Samuel Johnson, *Rasselas*, 1759

Learning Objectives

After completing this chapter, you will:

- understand the three major data integrity outcomes;
- understand the strategies for achieving each of the data integrity outcomes;
- understand the possible threats to data integrity and how to deal with them;
- realize that successful management of organizational memories requires both making data available and maintaining data integrity.

The Expeditioner

The Expeditioner has become very dependent on its database. The day-to-day operations of the company would be adversely affected if the major operational databases were lost. Indeed, The Expeditioner may not be able to survive a major data loss. Recently, there have also been a few minor problems with the quality and confidentiality of some of the databases. A part-time salesperson was discovered making a query about staff salaries. A major order was nearly lost when it was shipped to the wrong address because the complete shipping address had not been entered when the order was taken. The sales database had been off-line for 30 minutes last Monday morning because of a disk sector read error.

The Expeditioner had spent much time and money creating an extremely effective and efficient management system. It became clear, however, that more attention needed to be paid to maintaining the system and ensuring that high quality data were continuously available to authorized users.

INTRODUCTION

The management of organizational memories is driven by two goals: availability and integrity. **Availability** deals with making data available to whomever needs it, when and where they need it, and in a meaningful form. As illustrated in Figure 18–1, availability deals with

Figure 18–1   Goals of managing organizational memory

the creation, interrogation, and update of organizational memories. Although most of the book, thus far, has dealt with making data available, an organizational memory is of little use to anyone unless it has integrity. Maintaining organizational memory integrity implies three goals:[1]

1. **Protecting existence:**   data are available when needed.
2. **Maintaining quality:**   data are accurate, complete, and current.
3. **Ensuring confidentiality:**   data are accessed only by those authorized to do so.

This chapter deals with strategies for maintaining data integrity within an organizational memory.

There are three types of strategies for maintaining data integrity:

- **Legal** strategies are external imposed laws, rules, and regulations. Privacy laws are an example.
- **Administrative** strategies are organizational policies and procedures. An example is a standard operating procedure of storing all backup files in a locked vault.
- **Technical** strategies are those incorporated in the computer system (e.g., DBMS, application program, or operating system). An example is the inclusion of validation rules (e.g., NOT NULL) in a database definition, which are used to ensure data quality when a database is updated.

A **consistent database** is one in which all data integrity constraints are satisfied.

---

[1]To our knowledge, Everest was the first to define integrity in terms of these three goals. See Everest, G. *Database management: objectives, systems functions, and administration.* New York, New York: McGraw-Hill, 1986.

Our focus is on organizational memories stored in computer databases and technical and administrative strategies for maintaining integrity.[2] The term **database integrity** is commonly used to denote data integrity in computer environments. More and more organizational memories are being captured in computerized databases. From an integrity perspective, this is a very positive development. Computers offer some excellent mechanisms for controlling data integrity, but this does not eliminate the need for administrative strategies. Both administrative and technical strategies are needed.

Who is responsible for database integrity? Some would say the data users, others the database administrator. (We discuss the data administrator's role in the Chapter 19.) Both groups are probably right, database integrity is a shared responsibility, and the way it is managed may differ across organizations. Our focus is on the tools and strategies for maintaining data integrity regardless of who is responsible.

The strategies for achieving the three integrity outcomes are summarized in Table 18–1. We will cover the strategies for protecting existence, followed by those for maintaining quality, and finally those used to ensure confidentiality. Because maintaining integrity is linked to the database environment, we first provide some background on DBMSs.

Stock Market Crash

NASDAQ, which calls itself the "the stock market for the next 100 years," suffered a 34-minute interruption to trading in August 1994 when a squirrel chewed through a power line and NASDAQ's backup power system failed to take over. A circuit board in the uninterruptible power system failed to transfer the network to battery power. In 1987, a squirrel also crashed the system.

About a month before the 1994 crash, outages were caused by two separate incidents: an upgrade to communications software and a disk drive failure. Some NASDAQ users have pointed out that the exchange is vulnerable in the communications area because it relies on a single carrier, MCI, for linking traders to the exchange.

NASDAQ is part way through a $175 million information systems and telecommunications upgrade. When completed in three to five years, the new system will support trading of 900 million shares per day—double the existing transaction capacity.[3]

---

[2]Many of the concepts presented are applicable to non-computerized databases as well.

[3]Hoffman, T. Squirrel crashes stock market. *Computerworld*; August 8, 1994: 4.

Table 18–1   Strategies for Maintaining Database Integrity

Database Integrity Outcome	Strategies for Achieving the Outcome
Protecting existence	Isolation (preventive) Database backup and recovery (curative)
Maintaining quality	Update authorization Integrity constraints/data validation Concurrent update control
Ensuring confidentiality	Access control Encryption

SINGLE-USER AND MULTI-USER DATABASE SYSTEMS

One criterion for classifying a DBMS is by the number of users who can access the system concurrently. A DBMS is **single-user** if only one user at a time can use it. A DBMS is **multi-user** if many users can use the system concurrently. Single-user DBMSs are mainly found in microcomputer environments. DBMSs in most other environments (client/server, mainframe, etc.) are multi-user. For example, a hotel reservation system can be accessed by hundreds of travel agents and reservations clerks at the same time. Firms that provide information services, such as America Online or Prodigy, are likely to have thousands of users accessing their databases concurrently. As you will discover, maintaining integrity is much harder in multi-user environments.

Multiple people can use computer systems concurrently because of the multiprogramming nature of most computer operating systems. **Multiprogramming** allows the computer to process multiple programs or user transactions at the same time. If only a single central processing unit (CPU) is available, the computer can process only one program at a time. Multiprogramming operating systems execute some commands from one program, then suspend or interrupt that program and execute some commands from other programs. A program is resumed or restarted exactly where it was suspended when it gets its turn to use the CPU again. Hence, concurrent execution of the programs is actually interleaved. If the computer system has multiple CPUs, then **multiprocessing** of several programs is possible, leading to simultaneous rather than interleaved concurrency.

In a multi-user DBMS, stored data records and items are accessed by user programs or transactions. A transaction is a series of actions to be taken on the database such that they must be entirely completed or aborted. Transactions are constantly retrieving data from and updating the database. A transaction may consist of a simple SELECT to generate a list of a record's contents, or it may consist of a series of related UPDATE commands. It is referred to as a logical unit of work because no intermediate states of the database are accepted, the database will remained unchanged unless all actions are completed. For example, if you have credit sale of a product, your transaction consists of least two parts: you must update the inventory on hand, and you must update the customer information with the items sold in order to bill the customer later. Updating only the inventory or only the customer information would create a database without integrity or an inconsistent database.

PROTECTING EXISTENCE

As outlined in Table 18–1, one of the three database integrity outcomes is protecting the existence of the database—making sure data are available when needed. Two strategies for protecting existence are isolation and database backup and recovery. **Isolation** is a preventive strategy that involves administrative procedures to insulate the physical database from destruction. Some mechanisms for doing this are keeping data in safe places such as vaults or underground, having multiple installations, and security systems. For example, one organization keeps backup copies of important databases on removable magnetic disks. These are stored in a vault, which is always guarded. To gain access to the vault, employees need a badge with an encoded personal voice print. Many companies are building total backup computer centers, which contain duplicate databases and documentation for system operation. If something should happen at their main center (e.g. a flood), they can be up and running at their backup center in a few hours, or even minutes in some highly critical situations. What isolation strategies do you use to protect the backup medium of your personal computer? Do you backup?

Computer Sabotage

Malicious employees, natural disasters, or technology problems affected more than 25 percent of American companies in the last two years, according to a survey taken by Ernst & Young. Losses exceeded $1 million for 10 of the 870 companies participating in the study. Employees who corrupted data files, infected office computers with viruses, or sabotaged equipment accounted for about 35 percent of the losses. Businesses using computers to downsize often angered employees, who retaliated by attacking computers. Natural disasters caused about 30 percent of the reported losses, and the remainder were due to problems such as telephone service breakdowns and disk drive crashes. Ironically, some companies had curtailed computer security to cut costs and thus were more exposed to employee sabotage when it was more likely to occur. Furthermore, many CIOs believe their employees are the biggest threat to data integrity. The study noted that firms are becoming increasingly vulnerable as wide area networks, electronic data interchange, and the Internet continue to expand.[4]

---

[4]Adapted from Coates, J. (*Chicago Tribune*) from America Online; October 2, 1993.

Backup and Recovery

Database backup and recovery is a curative strategy to protect the existence of a physical database and to re-create or recover the data whenever loss or destruction occurs. The possibility of loss always exists. The use of and choice among backup and recovery procedures depends upon an assessment of the risk of loss and the cost of applying recovery procedures. The procedures in this case are carried out by the computer system, usually the DBMS. Data loss and damage should be expected, no matter how small the probability. There should be a detailed plan for data recovery.

There are several possible causes for data loss or damage, which can be grouped into three categories.

Storage Medium Destruction

In this situation, a portion of or all of the database is unreadable due to catastrophes such as power or air conditioning failure, fire, flood, theft, sabotage, and overwriting disks or tapes by mistake. A more frequent cause is a disk failure. Some of the disk blocks may be unreadable because of a read or write malfunction such as a head crash.

Abnormal Termination of an Update Transaction

In this case, a transaction fails in the middle of execution, leaving the database partially updated. The database will be inconsistent because it does not accurately reflect the current state of the business. The primary causes of an abnormal termination are a transaction error or system failure. Some operation in the transaction, such as division by zero, may cause it to fail. A hardware or software failure will usually result in one or more active programs being aborted. If these programs were updating the database, integrity problems could result.

Incorrect Data Discovered

In this situation, an update program or transaction incorrectly updated the database. This usually happens because a logic error was not detected during program testing.

Most organizations rely heavily on their databases, thus a DBMS must provide the following mechanisms for restoring a database quickly and accurately after loss or damage.

1. **Backup facilities** that create duplicate copies of the database;
2. **Journaling facilities** which provide backup copies or an audit trail of transactions and/or database changes;
3. A **recovery facility** within the DBMS to restore the database to a consistent state and restart the processing of transactions.

Before discussing each of these mechanisms in more depth, let's review the steps involved in updating a database and how backup and journaling facilities might be integrated into this process.

An overview of the database update process is captured in Figure 18–2. The process can be viewed as a series of database state changes. The initial database, state 1, is modified by an

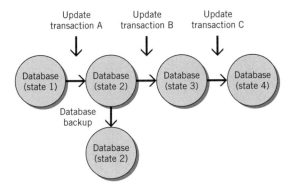

Figure 18–2   Database update procedures

update transaction such as deleting customer Jones, creating a new state (state 2). State 1 reflects the state of the organization with Jones as a customer, while state 2 reflects the organization without this customer. Each update transaction changes the state of the database to reflect changes in organizational memory. Periodically, the database is copied or backed up, possibly onto a different storage medium, and stored in a secure location. In Figure 18–2, the backup is made when the database is in state 2.

A more detailed look at database update procedures and the incorporation of backup facilities is illustrated in Figure 18–3. The updating of a single record is described in the following steps.

1. The user submits an update transaction from a workstation.
2. The transaction is edited and validated by an application program or the DBMS. If it is valid, it is logged or stored in the transaction log or journal. A **journal or log** is a special database or file storing information for backup and recovery.
3. The DBMS obtains the record to be updated.
4. A copy of the retrieved record is logged to the journal file. This copy is referred to as the **before image**, because it is a copy of the database record before the transaction changes it.
5. The transaction is processed by changing the affected data items in the record.
6. The DBMS writes the updated record to the database.
7. A copy of the updated record is written to the journal. This copy is referred to as the **after image**, because it is a copy of the database record after the transaction has updated it.
8. An output message tells the user that the update has been successfully completed.
9. The database is copied periodically. This backup copy reflects all updates to the database up to the time when the copy was made. An alternate strategy to periodic copying is to maintain multiple, usually two, complete copies of the database on-line and update them simultaneously. This technique, known as mirroring, is discussed in Chapter 11.

Figure 18–3 Possible backup procedures for a database update

In order to recover from data loss or damage, it is necessary to store backup data, such as a complete copy of the database or the necessary data to restore the accuracy of a database. Preferably, backup data should be stored on another medium and kept elsewhere from the primary database. As the description of the update process indicates, there are several options for backup data (see Table 18–2), depending on the objective of the backup procedure.

Data stored for backup and recovery are generally some combination of periodic database backups, transaction logs, and before and after image logs. Different recovery strategies use different combinations of backup data to recover a database.

The recovery method is highly dependent on the backup strategy. The database administrator selects a backup strategy based on a trade-off between ease of recovery from data loss or damage and the cost of performing backup operations. For example, keeping a mirror database is more expensive then keeping periodic database backups. But a mirroring strategy is very useful when recovery is needed very quickly, say seconds or minutes. An airline reservations system probably uses mirroring to ensure fast and reliable recovery. In general, the cost of keeping backup data is measured in terms of interruption of database availability

Table 18–2   Backup Options

Objective	Action
Complete copy of database	Dual recording of data (mirroring)
Past states of the database[5]	Database backup
Changes to the database	Before image log or journal After image log or journal
Transactions that caused a change in the state of the database	Transaction log or journal

(e.g., sometimes unavilable when a database is being backed up); storage of redundant data; and degradation of update efficiency (e.g., extra time taken in update processing to save before or after images).

Recovery Strategies

The type of recovery strategy or procedure that is used in a given situation depends on the nature of the data loss, the type of backup data available, and the sophistication of the DBMS's recovery facilities. The following discussion outlines the four major recovery strategies: switch to a duplicate database; backward recovery or rollback; forward recovery or roll forward; and reprocessing transactions.

The recovery procedure of switching to a duplicate database requires the maintenance of the mirror copy. The other three strategies assume a periodic dumping or backing up of the database. Periodic dumps may be made on a regular schedule, triggered automatically by the DBMS or triggered externally by personnel. The schedule may be determined by time (hourly, daily, weekly) or by event (the number of transactions since the last backup).

Switching to a Duplicate Database

This recovery procedure requires maintaining at least two copies of the database and updating both simultaneously. When there is a problem with one database, access is switched to the duplicate. This strategy is particularly useful when recovery must be accomplished in seconds or minutes. This procedure offers good protection against certain storage medium destruction problems, such as disk failures, but none against events which damage or make both databases unavailable, such as a power failure or a faulty update program. This strategy entails additional costs in terms of doubling on-line storage capacity. It can be also be imple-

---

[5]Past states of the database are also referred to as database dumps.

mented in dual computer processors where each computer updates its copy of the database. This duplexed configuration offers greater backup protection at a greater cost.

Backward Recovery or Rollback

Backward recovery (also called rollback or rolling back) is used to back out or undo unwanted changes to the database. For example, Figure 18–2 shows three updates (A, B, and C) to a database. Let's say that update B terminated abnormally, leaving the database, now in state 3, inconsistent. What we need to do is return the database to state 2 by applying the before images to the database. Thus, we would rollback by changing the database to state 2 with the before images of the records updated by transaction B.

Backward recovery reverses the changes made when a transaction abnormally terminates or produces erroneous results. To illustrate the need for rollback, consider the example of a budget transfer of $1000 between two departments.

1. The program reads the account record for Department X and subtracts $1000 from the account balance and updates the database.

2. The program then reads the record for Department Y and adds $1000 to the account balance, but while attempting to update the database, the program encounters a disk error and cannot write the record.

Now the database is inconsistent. Department X has been updated but Department Y has not. Thus, the transaction must be aborted and the database recovered. The DBMS would apply the before image to Department X to restore the account balance to its original value. The DBMS may then restart the transaction and make an another attempt to update the database.

Forward Recovery or Roll Forward

Forward recovery (also called roll forward or bringing forward) involves re-creating a database using a prior database state. Returning to the example in Figure 18–2, suppose state 4 of the database was destroyed and we need to recover it. We would take the last database dump or backup (state 2) and then apply the after image records created by update transactions B and C. This would return the database to state 4. Thus, roll forward starts with an earlier copy of the database and by applying after images (the results of good transactions), the backup copy of database is moved forward to a later state.

Reprocessing Transactions

Although similar to forward recovery, this procedure uses update transactions instead of after images. Taking the same example shown in Figure 18–2, assume the database is destroyed in state 4. We would take the last database backup (state 2) and then reprocess update transactions B and C to return the database to state 4. The main advantage of using this method is its simplicity. The DBMS does not need to create a database after image change journal, and there are no special restart procedures. The one major disadvantage, however, is the length of time to reprocess transactions. Depending on the frequency of database backups and the time needed to get transactions into the identical sequence as previous updates, several hours

Table 18–3   What to do When Data Loss Occurs

Problem	Recovery Procedures
Storage medium destruction (database is unreadable)	*Switch to duplicate database—this can be transparent with RAID Forward recovery Reprocess transactions
Abnormal termination of an update transaction (transaction error or system failure)	*Backward recovery Forward recovery or reprocess transactions—bring forward to the state just before termination of the transaction
Incorrect data detected (database has been incorrectly updated)	*Backward recovery Reprocess transactions (Excluding those from the update program that created incorrect data)

*Preferred strategy

of reprocessing may be required. Processing new transactions must be delayed until the database recovery is complete.

Table 18–3 reviews the three types of data losses and the corresponding recovery strategies one could use. The major problem is to re-create a database using a backup copy, which is a previous state of organizational memory. Recovery is done through forward recovery, reprocessing, or switching to a duplicate database if one is available. With abnormal termination or incorrect data, the preferred strategy is backward recovery, but other procedures could be used.

Recovering After the Flood

A survey of 109 companies affected by the 1993 floods that swept the Midwest showed that less than half had any kind of PC disaster recovery plan. Fortunately, only 5 percent of all the firms interviewed lost any PC data because of the floods or subsequent power outages. Only 2 percent lost data because it was not backed up. About 21 percent of the sites said they backed up their data in advance of the floods; however, 38 percent of the respondents said that prior to the floods, they did not back up data daily. Another third backed up only "some" or "none" of their data, and a slightly greater number stored most of their backup data on-site.

Among those who had a disaster recovery plan, the most frequent solution was to move to another location to process data (26 percent). Just 20 percent of those with a plan said they had a document that told staff who to call and what to do in the event of a disaster.[6]

---

[6]Adapted from Booker, E. Midwest firms without data protection as rains begin. *Computerworld*, 22 November 1993: 42.

Use of Recovery Procedures

Usually the person doing a query or an update is not concerned with backup and recovery. Database administration personnel often implement strategies that are automatically carried out by the DBMS. ANSI has defined standards that govern SQL processing of database transactions that relate to recovery. Transaction support is provided through the use of two SQL statements: COMMIT and ROLLBACK. These commands are employed when a procedural programming language such as COBOL is used to update a database. Consider the program segment in Figure 18–4, which contains the SQL commands to execute an update transaction:

```
MAIN

* If an error occurs perform undo code block

1 EXEC SQL WHENEVER SQL ERROR PERFORM UNDO

* Insert a single row in table A

2 EXEC SQL INSERT

* Update a row in table B

3 EXEC SQL UPDATE

* Successful transaction, all changes are now permanent

4 EXEC SQL COMMIT WORK

5 PERFORM FINISH

UNDO

* Unsuccessful transaction, rollback the transaction

6 EXEC SQL ROLLBACK WORK

FINISH

  EXIT
```

Figure 18–4   Use of COMMIT and ROLLBACK

The programmer wants the two update actions (statements 2 and 3) to be considered as a transaction. If both update actions are not successfully completed, the database would be inconsistent.

In the example, therefore, the programmer issues a COMMIT WORK command to the DBMS (or transaction processing portion of the DBMS) if the program completes the two updates successfully, which will commit the changes to the database and make them permanent. If anything goes wrong, however, the program issues the ROLLBACK WORK command to undo any changes made so far. The ROLLBACK WORK command works just like the backward recovery procedure previously discussed.

MAINTAINING QUALITY

The second integrity goal for organizational memory is to maintain quality, which implies keeping the data accurate, complete, and current. Functions are needed within the DBMS to ensure that update actions are performed by authorized persons, in accordance with stated rules or integrity constraints, and that the results are properly recorded. These functions are accomplished by update authorization, data validation using integrity constraints, and concurrent update control. Each of these functions is discussed in turn.

Update Authorization

Without proper controls, update transactions can diminish the quality of a database. Unauthorized users could sabotage a database by entering erroneous values. The first step is to ensure that anyone who wants to update a database is authorized to do so. Some responsible person, usually the database owner or database administrator, must tell the DBMS who is permitted to initiate particular database operations. The DBMS must then check every transaction to ensure it is authorized. Unauthorized access of a database exposes an organization to many risks, including fraud and sabotage.

Update authorization is accomplished through the same access mechanism used to protect confidentiality. We will discuss access control more thoroughly later in this chapter. In SQL, access control is implemented through the GRANT command, which gives a user a privilege and REVOKE, which removes a privilege. (These commands are discussed in Chapter 9.) A control mechanism may lump all update actions into a single privilege or separate them for greater control. In SQL, they are separated as follows:

UPDATE (Privilege to change field values using UPDATE. This can be column specific);

DELETE (Privilege to delete records from a table);

INSERT (Privilege to insert records into a table).

Separate privileges for each of the update commands allows tighter controls on certain update actions such as updating a salary field or deleting records.

Data Validation Using Integrity Constraints

Once the update process has been authorized, the DBMS must make sure a database is accurate and complete before any updates are applied. Consequently, the DBMS needs to be aware of any integrity constraints or rules that apply to the data. For example, the QDEL table in the relational database described in Chapter 10 would have constraints such as:

Delivery numbers (DELNO) must be unique, numeric, and in the range 1–99999;

Delivered quantity (DELQTY) must be non-zero;

Item names (ITEMNAME) must appear in the QITEM table;

Supplier codes (SPLNO) must appear in the QSPL table.

Once integrity constraints are specified, the DBMS must monitor or validate all insert and update operations to ensure that they do not violate any of the constraints or rules.

The key to update data validation is a clear definition of valid and invalid data. Data validation cannot be performed without integrity constraints or rules. A person or the DBMS must know what the data should look like—valid values, tests to perform, procedures to invoke—to determine their validity. All data validation is based on a prior expression of integrity constraints.

Data validation may not always produce error-free data, however. Sometimes integrity constraints are not known or are not well defined. In other cases, the DBMS does provide a convenient means for expressing and performing validation checks. Sometimes it is decided that the costs of implementing the constraints are too high. Certain checks may take too long or require the storage and management of too much extra data. For example, to validate American state codes, you need to create a table containing the correct codes for all 50 states and Washington, D.C. This is not very expensive to establish. But what if you decided to validate all zip codes? Like most design decisions, establishing integrity constraints involves trade-offs.

Based on how integrity constraints have been defined, data validation can be performed outside the DBMS by people or within the DBMS itself. External validation is usually done by reviewing input documents before they are entered into the system and by checking system outputs to ensure that the database was updated correctly. Maintaining data quality is of paramount importance, and data validation preferably should be handled by the DBMS as much as possible, rather than by the user. The user should handle the exceptions and respond to any data validation checks that fail.

Integrity constraints are usually specified as part of the database definition supplied to the DBMS. For example, the primary key uniqueness and referential integrity constraints can be specified within the SQL CREATE statement (see Chapter 9). DBMSs generally permit some constraints to be stored as part of the database schema and are used by the DBMS to monitor all update operations and perform appropriate data validation checks. Any given database is likely to be subject to a very large number of constraints, but not all of these can be automatically enforced by the DBMS. Some need to handled by application programs.

The general types of constraints applied to a data item are outlined in Table 18–4. Each constraint is explained and illustrated, using the database described in Chapter 10. Not all of these necessarily would be supported by a DBMS, and a particular database may not use all types.

As mentioned, integrity constraints are usually specified as part of the database definition

Table 18–4 Types of Data Item Integrity Constraints

Type of Integrity Constraint	Explanation	Example
TYPE	Validating a data item value against a specified data type.	Supplier number is numeric.
SIZE	Defining and validating the minimum and maximum size of a data item value. (Most DBMSs only check for maximum.)	Delivery number must be at least 3 digits and at most 5.
VALUES	Providing a list of acceptable values for a data item.	Item colors must match the list provided.
RANGE	Providing one or more ranges within which the data item must fall or must NOT fall.	Employee numbers must be in the range 1–100.
PATTERN	Providing a pattern of allowable characters which define permissible formats for data values.	Department phone number must be of the form 542-*nnnn* (stands for exactly four decimal digits).
PROCEDURE	Providing a procedure to be invoked to validate data items.	A delivery must have valid itemname, department, and supplier values before it can be added to the database. (Tables are checked for valid entries.)
CONDITIONAL	Providing one or more conditions to apply against data values.	If item type is 'Y', then color is null.
NOT NULL (MANDATORY)	Indicating whether the data item value is mandatory (not null) or optional. The "not null" option is required for primary keys.	Employee number is mandatory.
UNIQUE	Indicating whether stored values for this data item must be unique (unique compared to other values of the item within the same table or record type). The unique option is also required for identifiers.	Supplier number is unique.

supplied to the DBMS. Table 18–5 contains some typical specifications of integrity constraints in different data definition languages. The first three examples are taken for a CODASYL/DBTG model (see Chapter 14), while the fourth example is for a relational DBMS. The examples show how some of the integrity constraints discussed in Table 18–4 are implemented.

Data quality control does not end with the application of integrity constraints. When-

Table 18–5 **Examples of Integrity Constraints for Different Data Definition Languages**

Examples	Explanation
`ON-ORDER TYPE IS FIXED` `    CHECK IS GT 0.`	On-order is an integer number (the size is the default for an integer) that must be greater than zero.

`SALARY-TYPE IS DECIMAL (7)`
`    CHECK IS PROCEDURE EDIT-SALARY`
`    ON ERROR CALL SALARY-RESPONSE`
	Salary must be 7 or less decimal digits.
	
	When the value is changed, a procedure called EDIT-SALARY is called to perform edits.
	
	If the edit fails, the procedure SALARY-RESPONSE is executed.

`KEY ITEM-CODE.`
`    ITEM-CODE TYPE IS CHAR(5)`
`    CHECK IS NOT NULL.`
	Key statement implies ITEM-CODE must be unique and the NOT NULL indicates a value must always be supplied. ITEM-CODE must be 5 or less alphanumeric characters.

`CREATE TABLE STOCK`
`    (STKCODE CHAR(3) NOT NULL,`
`    ...`
`    NATCODE  CHAR(3),`
`        PRIMARY KEY (STKCODE),`
`        FOREIGN KEY NATIONCODE(NATCODE)`
`            REFERENCES NATION`
`                ON DELETE RESTRICT)`
	STKCODE must always be assigned a value of 3 or less alphanumeric characters. STKCODE must be unique because it is a primary key.
	
	NATCODE must be assigned a value of 3 or less alphanumeric characters. NATCODE must exist as the primary key of the table NATION.
	
	Do not allow the deletion of a row in NATION while there still exist rows in STOCK containing the corresponding value of NATCODE.

ever an error or unusual situation is detected by the DBMS, some form of response is required. Response rules need to be given to the DBMS along with the integrity constraints. The responses can take many different forms such as: abort the entire program, reject entire update transaction, display a message and continue processing, and let the DBMS attempt to correct the error (as shown in the second example in Table 18–5). The response may vary depending on the type of integrity constraint violated. If the DBMS does not allow the specification of response rules, then it must take a default action when an error is detected. For example, if alphabetic data are entered in a numeric field, most DBMSs will have a default response and message (e.g., non-numeric data entered in numeric field). In the case of application programs, an error code is passed to the program from the DBMS. The program would then use this error code to execute an error handling procedure. (For an example, see the program segment discussed in the section on recovery procedures.)

An Inventory Disaster

Warehouse Manager, an inventory control package released by NCR (now AT&T Global Information Systems), promised to manage the thousands of items in a typical firm's warehouse. The software was inadequately tested, however, and performed poorly in business environments. The results were disastrous for some firms. A wood-laminating company was unable to place a purchase order in the first five weeks after switching over to the new package. The backlog cost the firm $2000 per day. A supplier of heavy construction parts complained that the program corrupted files. A machine part that cost $114 was listed for sale at 54 cents. A parts-supply business found that response time for the new system varied from half a minute to several minutes. As a result, customers were forced to wait in long lines. The firm eventually lost its biggest customer because it could not meet the contractual requirement to fill 90 percent of any order within 48 hours.

Originally developed for computers running an operating system developed by Burroughs (now part of Unisys), the package was working successfully at 200 locations that used Burroughs equipment; however, the conversion to an NCR operating system clearly had some problems. NCR concedes the package was a disaster and stopped selling it seveal years ago.

There is always a risk associated with converting to a new computer system. This risk is magnified when the data maintained by the system are key to the profitability and survival of the firm. This is not a unique story and most software suppliers seem to have suffered at least one disaster.[7]

Concurrent Update Control

We have explored two of three DBMS functions that are dedicated to maintaining data quality: ensuring that update actions are performed by authorized persons and comply with stated integrity constraints or rules. Once an update action has met these criteria, the transaction will be applied to the database. The third function, concurrent update control, focuses on making sure the updated results are correctly recorded in the database.

When updating a database, most users implicitly assume that their actions do not interfere with any other users' actions. If the DBMS is a single-user system, then lack of interference is guaranteed. Most DBMS, however, are multi-user systems, where multiple users can be accessing a given database at the same time. When two or more transactions are allowed to update a database concurrently, the integrity of the database is threatened. For example, multiple agents selling airline tickets may sell the same seat twice. Similarly, inconsistent results

---

[7]Adapted from Geyelin, M. Doomsday device: how an NCR system for inventory turned into a virtual saboteur. *Wall Street Journal*, August 18, 1994; A1.

can be obtained by a retrieval transaction when retrievals are being made simultaneously with updates. This gives the appearance of loss of database integrity. We will first discuss the integrity problems caused by concurrent updates and then how to control them to ensure database quality.

Lost Updates: A Threat to Database Integrity

Uncontrolled concurrent updates can result in the "lost update" or "phantom record" problem. To illustrate the lost update problem, suppose two concurrent update transactions simultaneously want to update the same record in an inventory file. Both want to update the quantity on hand (QUANTITY) field. Assume the field QUANTITY has a current value of 40. One update transaction wants to add 80 units (a delivery) to QUANTITY, while the other transaction wants to subtract 20 units (a sale).

Suppose the transactions have concurrent access to the record. That is, each transaction is able to read the record from the database before a previous transaction has been committed. This sequence is depicted in Figure 18–5. Note that the first transaction, A, has not updated the database when the second transaction, B, reads the same record. Thus, both A and B read in a value of 40 for QUANTITY. Both make their calculations, then A writes the value of 120 to disk, followed by B promptly overwriting the 120 with 20. The result is that the delivery of 80 units, transaction A, is "lost" during the update process.

Inconsistent retrievals occur when a transaction calculates some aggregate function (e.g., sum) over a set of data while other transactions are updating the same data. The problem is the retrieval may read some data before they are changed and other data after they are changed, thereby yielding inconsistent results.

Figure 18–5   Lost updates when concurrent accessing is allowed

The Solution: Lockout

To prevent "lost updates" and inconsistent retrieval results, the DBMS must incorporate a resource locking mechanism. That is, any data retrieved by one user with the intent of updating must be locked out or denied access by other users until the update is completed. Consider the example used previously. When A accesses the record for update, the DBMS must refuse all further accesses to that record until transaction A is complete. As Figure 18–6 shows, B's first attempt to access the record is denied until transaction A is finished. As a result, database integrity is maintained. Unless the DBMS controls concurrent access, a multi-user database environment can create both data and retrieval integrity problems.

To administer lockout procedures, a DBMS requires two pieces of information:

1. whether a particular transaction will update the database;
2. where the transaction begins and ends (completed).

Usually, the data required by an update transaction are locked when the transaction begins and released when the transaction is completed (i.e., committed to the database) or aborted. Locking mechanisms can operate at different levels or granularity: database, file (or table), page, record (or row), or data item. At the most precise level, a DBMS can lock individual data items so that different update transactions can update different items in the same record concurrently. This approach increases processing overhead but provides the fewest resource conflicts. At the other end of the continuum, the DBMS can lock the entire database for each update. If there were many update transactions to process, this would be very unacceptable because of the long waiting times. Locking at the record level is the most common approach taken by commercial DBMSs.

In most situations, users are not concerned with locking because it is handled entirely by

Time	Time		Database record	
			Part #	*Quantity*
			P10	40
T1	User A receives paperwork for a delivery of 80 units of P10			
T2	User A reads P10	⟵	P10	40
T3	User B sells 20 units of P10			
T4	User B attempts to read P10	denied	P10	40
T5	User A processes the delivery (40 + 80 = 120)			
T6	User A updates the file	⟶	P10	120
T7	User B reads P10	⟵	P10	120
T8	User B processes the sale (120 − 20 = 100)			
T9	User B updates the file	⟶	P10	100

Figure 18–6   Valid update when concurrent accessing is not allowed.

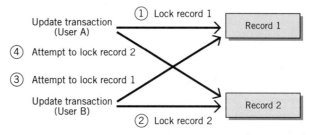

Figure 18–7   An example of deadlock

the DBMS. But in some DBMS, choices are provided to the user. These are primarily limited to procedural programming language (e.g., COBOL) interfaces.

Resource locking solves some data and retrieval integrity problems, but it may lead to another problem, referred to as **deadlock** or the **deadly embrace**. Deadlock is an impasse that occurs because two users lock certain resources, then request resources locked by the other user. Figure 18–7 illustrates a deadlock situation. Both transactions require records 1 and 2. Transaction A first accesses record 1 and locks it. Then transaction B accesses record 2 and locks it. Next, B's attempt to access record 1 is denied, so the application waits for the record to be released. Finally, A's attempt to access record 2 is denied, so the application waits for the record to be released. Thus, user A's update transaction is waiting for record 2 (locked by user B), and user B is waiting for record 1 (locked by user A). Unless the DBMS intervenes, both users will wait indefinitely.

There are two ways to resolve deadlock: prevention and resolution. **Deadlock prevention** requires users to lock in advance all records they will require. User B would have to lock both records 1 and 2 (in Figure 18–7) before processing the transaction. (If records are locked, B would have to wait.) Taking this action prevents deadlock, but since it is often difficult to predict record usage in advance, deadlock prevention is not often practical.

Deadlock resolution uses the DBMS to detect and break deadlocks. The DBMS usually keeps a resource usage matrix, which instantly reflects what users (e.g., update transactions) are using what resources (e.g., records). By scanning the matrix, the DBMS can detect deadlocks as they occur. The DBMS then resolves the deadlock by backing out one of the deadlocked transactions. For example, the DBMS might release user A's lock on record 1, thus, allowing user B to proceed. Any changes made by user A up to that time (e.g., updates to record 1) would be rolled back. User A's transaction would be restarted when required resources became available.

ENSURING CONFIDENTIALITY

Thus far, we have discussed how the first two goals of data integrity can be accomplished: data are available when needed (protecting existence); and data are accurate, complete, and current (maintaining quality). This section deals with the final goal, ensuring confidentiality or data security. Two DBMS functions, access control and encryption, are the primary means of ensuring the data are accessed only by those authorized to do so. We begin by discussing an overall model of data security.

General Model of Data Security

Figure 18–8 depicts the two functions for ensuring data confidentiality, access control, and encryption. Access control consists of two basic steps—identification and authorization. Once past access control, the user is permitted to access the database. Access control is applied only to the established avenues of entry to a database, however. Clever people may be able to circumvent the controls and gain unauthorized access. Thus, to counteract this possibility, it is often desirable to obscure or hide the meaning of stored data. This is done by encrypting data so that it is impossible to interpret their meaning. Encrypted data are stored in a transformed or coded format that can only be decrypted and read by those with the appropriate key.

Now, let's walk through Figure 18–8 in detail. First, a user must be identified and provide additional information required to authenticate this identification (e.g., a userid and password). User profile information (e.g., a password or a voice print) is used to verify or authenticate a user. Having authenticated the user, the authorization step is initiated by a user request (retrieve or update database). The previously stored user authorization rules (the data each user can access and the authorized actions on that data) are checked in order to determine if the user has the right or privilege to access the requested data. (The previously stored user privileges are created and maintained by an authorized person, database owner, or administrator.) User privileges are matched against the user request, and a decision is made to permit or deny the execution of the user's request. If access is permitted, the user's transaction is processed against the database. Data to be stored are encrypted before storage and data retrieved decrypted before being presented to the user.

Figure 18–8   General model of data security

It is Electronically Elementary, My Dear Watson

Stop! Don't write that check without first considering the personal information you are divulging to a possible stranger. Does your check contain your name, address, telephone number, Social Security or driver's license number? Consider what students at The University of Alabama at Birmingham discovered about their instructor, with just his name, as part of a class project on Privacy Issues in the United States.

First, they went to the offices of the Tax Assessor and Collector at the courthouse in the county where the instructor lived. These offices provided the students with the information the government had on the properties (in this case, a house and two cars) on which he paid taxes. In fact, the offices gave them photocopies and duplicates of the tax bills and other information (e.g., location of the house, amount of mortgage, the seller, the lien holder, and the valuation and description of the properties.) This information is in the public domain and is available to anybody in the United States. Included among the documents found at the courthouse was the professor's Social Security number, which, along with his name and address, provided enough information for the students to get his credit report.

The following is a partial list of information maintained by credit bureaus:

1. birth date;
2. family makeup;
3. current and previous addresses;
4. telephone numbers;
5. Social Security number;
6. employment and salary history;
7. credit transaction and balances;
8. mortgage rates;
9. bankruptcies;
10. tax liens.

Having obtained his license tag number from the courthouse, the students then called the Department of Motor Vehicles, who proceeded to give them his entire driving record. In addition, they went to the university library and looked up his employment record. Being a state employee, the instructor's salary, rank, position, and date of employment are public information. At this point the students stopped, but could have obtained further public domain information about his marital and criminal history.

The students gathered all the information in about a week. These aspiring Sherlock Holmeses used the following two books as a guideline:

Gunderson, T. L. *How to locate anyone anywhere without leaving home.* New York, NY: Dutton; 1989.

Culligan, J. J. *You, too, can find anybody: a reference manual.* Miami, FL: Hallmark; 1993.

You might think, "Gee, I'm safe because I do not own any property, and I'm not a state employee." Consider the following information extracted from the sales brochure of a nationwide electronic tracking company.

1. With name and address, a nationwide search for a Social Security number. Price $10, in two hours.

2. With name and Social Security number, employment and earnings history for 10 years. Price $175, in three to five days.

3. A person's credit history: $10, in one to two hours.

4. A person's criminal history: $100, in one week.

5. With a person's name and address, obtain names, phone numbers, and addresses of up to nine current neighbors: $10, in one to two hours.

Electronic tracking services are readily available at low cost. For example, the Internet Credit Bureau, Inc., offering its services via the World Wide Web (http://www.satelnet.org/credit/), charges $7.50 to identify the owner of a Social Security number.

How private is your life? Many people mistakenly believe that privacy is a fundamental right protected by the Constitution. As we move towards the computerization of governmental and organizational databases, personal information will become even more accessible. The Social Security Administration is currently debating whether to let outside organizations have access to its databases. All this has prompted many Americans to think they have lost all control over how their personal information is being collected and distributed. According to a recent Harris–Equifax Poll, 68 percent believe that computers represent a threat to their privacy, and 89 percent believe that computers have made it easier for others to improperly obtain personal and confidential information.[8]

Data Access Control

Data access control begins with some identification of the user or subject, an organizational entity that can access the database. Examples are individuals, departments, groups of people, transactions, terminals, and application programs. Subjects also may be combinations—for example, a particular person entering a certain transaction at a particular terminal. A user identification (often called userid) is the first piece of data the DBMS receives from the subject. It may be a name or number. The user identification enables the DBMS to locate the corresponding entry in the stored user profiles and authorization tables (see Figure 18–8).

Taking this information, the DBMS goes through the process of authentication. The system attempts to match additional information supplied by the intended user with the infor-

---

[8]This case was written by Dr. Sanjay Singh, Department of Management, The University of Alabama at Birmingham.

Table 18–6   Authenticating Mechanisms[9]

Class	Examples
1. Something a person **knows—remembered information**	Name, account number, password
2. Something the person **has—possessed objects**	Badge, plastic card, key
3. Something the person **is—personal characteristics**	Fingerprint, voiceprint, signature, hand size

mation previously stored in the user profile. The system may perform multiple matches to ensure the identity of the user (see Table 18–6 for the different types). If all tests are successful, the DBMS assumes the subject is an authenticated user.

Most systems in the past have used remembered information to control access. The problem with remembered information is that it does not positively identify the user. Passwords have been the most widely-used form of access control. If used correctly, they can be very effective; unfortunately, people leave them around where others can pick them up, allowing unauthorized people to gain access to databases.

To deal with this problem, organizations are moving toward using personal characteristics and combinations of authenticating mechanisms to protect sensitive data. Collectively, these mechanisms can provide even greater security. For example, access to a large consumer firm's very valuable marketing planning models database requires a smart card with fingerprints—a combination of personal information and a possessed object. The database can only be accessed through a few terminals in specific locations—an isolation strategy. Once the smart card test is passed, the DBMS requests entry of other remembered information—password and account number—before granting access.

Data access authorization is the process of permitting users, whose identity has been authenticated, to perform certain operations on certain data objects in a shared database. The authorization process is driven by rules incorporated into the DBMS. Authorization rules are readily shown in a table that includes subjects, objects, actions, and constraints for a given database. An example of such a table is shown in Table 18–7 for the database described in Chapter 10. Each row of the table indicates that a particular subject is authorized to take a certain action on a database object, perhaps subject to some constraint. For example, the last entry of the table indicates that Brier is authorized to delete supplier records with no restrictions.

We have already discussed subjects, but not objects, actions, and constraints. Objects are database entities protected by the DBMS. Examples are databases, views, files, records, and data items. In Table 18–7, the objects are all records. A view is another form of security. It restricts the user's access to a database. Any data not included in a view are unknown to the user. Although views promote security, several persons may share a view or unauthorized persons may gain access. Thus, a view is another object to be included in the authorization process. Typical actions that can be taken on objects are shown in Table 18–7: read, insert,

[9]Adapted from Everest, *Database management*, op cit.

Table 18–7 Sample Authorization Table

Subject/User	Action	Object	Constraint
Accounting department	Insert	Supplier record	None
Purchase department clerk	Insert	Supplier record	If quantity < 200
Purchase department supervisor	Insert	Delivery record	If quantity ≥ 200
Production department	Read	Delivery record	None
Todd	Modify	Item record	Type and color only
Order processing program	Modify	Sale record	None
Brier	Delete	Supplier record	None

modify, and delete. Constraints are particular rules that apply to a subject–action–object relationship. As Table 18–7 shows, Todd (subject) can only modify (action) the type and color fields in the item record (object).

Implementing Authorization Rules

Most contemporary DBMSs do not implement the complete authorization table shown in Table 18–7. Usually, they implement a simplified version. The most common form is authorization tables for subjects with limited applications of the constraints column. Let's take the granting of table privileges in SQL as an example. Table privileges are needed in order to authorize subjects to perform operations on both tables and views (see Table 18–8).

The GRANT and REVOKE SQL commands discussed in Chapter 9 are used to define and delete authorization rules. Some examples:

```
GRANT SELECT ON QSPL TO VIKKI
GRANT SELECT, UPDATE (SPLNAME) ON QSPL TO HUANG
GRANT ALL PRIVILEGES ON QITEM TO VIKKI
GRANT SELECT ON QITEM TO HUANG
```

Table 18–8 Authorization Commands

SQL Command	Result
SELECT	permitted to retrieve data
UPDATE	permitted to change data; can be column specific
DELETE	permitted to delete records or tables
INSERT	permitted to add records or tables

Table 18–9 Sample Authorization Table

User	Object (table)	Action	Constraint
Vikki	QSPL	SELECT	None
	QITEM	UPDATE	None
	QITEM	INSERT	None
	QITEM	DELETE	None
	QITEM	SELECT	None
Huang	QSPL	SELECT	None
	QSPL	UPDATE	SPLNAME only
	QITEM	SELECT	None

The GRANT commands have essentially created two authorization tables, one for user Huang and the other for user Vikki. These tables, shown in Table 18–9, illustrate how most current systems create authorization tables for subjects using a limited set of objects (e.g., tables) and constraints.

Because authorization tables contain highly sensitive data, they must be protected by stringent security rules and encryption. Normally, only selected persons in data administration have authority to access and modify them.

Encryption

Encryption techniques complement access control. As Figure 18–8 illustrates, access control applies only to established avenues of access to a database. There is always the possibility that people will circumvent these controls and gain unauthorized access to a database. To counteract this possibility, encryption can be used to obscure or hide the meaning of data. Encrypted data cannot be read by an intruder unless that person knows the method of encryption and the key. Considerable research has been devoted to developing encryption methods. Some are very simple, but are usually not very useful in a DBMS environment. Others provide a high level of protection because they are very difficult to decipher.

Encryption is any transformation applied to data that makes it difficult to extract meaning. To implement it, you need an encrypting technique to transform data to cipher text, and a decryption technique to reconstruct the original data from cipher text. To demonstrate encryption, examine the simple method shown in Table 18–10. We have used a substitution method to shift each letter to its immediate successor in the alphabet. (We assume that the "blank" appears immediately before the letter A and that it follows the letter Z.) It would be difficult for an authorized user to understand "M mbx." But if they examine a number of

Table 18–10   A Simple Encryption Method

Original data		Cipher text
Nancy	Encryption	M mbx
M mbx	Decryption	Nancy

words, they probably will break the code. DBMSs use far more sophisticated encryption techniques to protect sensitive data.

Data Encryption Standard (DES) and public key encryption are the most common techniques. The DES algorithm, which can be implemented in hardware or software, uses a variable 56-bit key supplied by the sender. The sender uses the algorithm to encode data in a series of complex operations. The receiver applies the same key, and the DES algorithm reverses the operations to decode the message. Using a very fast supercomputer, it is possible to try all variations of possible keys to decipher a message. Finding a secure method of distributing the secret key is another major shortcoming of DES. This problem is exacerbated by the frequent need to change keys in case there has been a security leak and the existing key is no longer secret.

Public key encryption attempts to overcome some of the problems with DES. A public-key system has private and public keys. A person's public key can be freely distributed because it is quite separate from her private key. To send and receive messages, communicators first need to create private and public keys and then exchange their public keys The sender encodes a message with the intended receiver's public key, and upon receiving the message, the receiver applies her private key (see Figure 18–9). The receiver's private key, the only one that can decode the message, must be kept secret to provide secure message exchanging. In a DBMS environment, encryption techniques can be applied to **transmitted data** sent over communication lines to and from terminals, or between computers; and to all or highly sensitive **stored data** in active databases or their backup versions. Some DBMS products include encryption routines that automatically encrypt sensitive data when they are stored or transmitted over communication channels. Other DBMS products provide exits that allow users to code their own encryption routines. Encrypted data may also take less storage space because they are often compressed.

Figure 18–9   Public key encryption

Clipper Versus PGP

The U.S. government's National Security Agency (NSA) gathers information for national security purposes by eavesdropping on overseas phone calls and cables. It has done everything in its power to make sure nobody had a code that it couldn't break. It kept tight reins on the keys used to encode text, prohibiting the export of secret codes under American munitions laws and ensuring that the encryption scheme used by business—the so-called Data Encryption Standard—was weak enough that NSA supercomputers could easily decipher messages.

As computers have become more powerful, so have encryption algorithms. Telephones that offer nearly airtight privacy are available, and in January 1994 American computer makers said they were ready to adopt a new encryption standard so robust that even the NSA couldn't crack it.

Thus the stage was set for a technology-policy battle—the Clipper Chip war. Lined up on one side are NSA, the CIA, the FBI, and the Clinton Administration. Opposing them are a coalition of computer firms, civil libertarians, conservative columnists, and a strange breed of cryptoanarchists who call themselves cypherpunks.

At the center is the Clipper Chip, which NSA developed and wants installed in every telephone, computer modem, and fax machine. The chip has a powerful encryption algorithm, but a phone equipped with the chip could, with proper authorization, be tapped by the government. Law enforcement agencies say they need this capability to keep tabs on drug runners, terrorists, and spies. The opposition sees it as a potential invasion of privacy.

The present conflict follows from the work of Whitfield Diffie who, as a student at MIT over 20 years ago, developed a public key encryption system. His innovation is extremely useful for companies wanting to do business on the information highway. It's not easy to verify credit cards on a computer or telephone network. Public key encryption, however, is the means of introducing an unforgeable digital signature.

Public key encryption also gives ordinary citizens and smart criminals a secure way to exchange messages that NSA cannot easily decipher. The problem was compounded for NSA when in 1991, cypherpunk programmer Phil Zimmermann combined public key encryption with some conventional algorithms to create PGP—pretty good privacy—and proceeded to place it on anonymous FTP sites as freeware.

It is probably unconstitutional for the U.S. government to outlaw PGP, but it is trying to make it difficult for it and any other alternative schemes to be adopted. If Clipper becomes the standard for telephone, fax, and computer communication, then other systems will be locked out of the market because only those using the same encryption technology can communicate. Zimmermann is now working on a version of PGP for voice communications that could compete directly with Clipper.[10]

---

[10]Adapted from Elmer-Dewitt, P. Who should keep the keys? *Time*. 11 March 1994: America Online.

SUMMARY

The management of organizational memories is driven by the joint goals of availability and integrity. Availability deals with making data available to whoever needs it, when and where they need it, and in a meaningful form. Maintaining integrity implies protecting existence, maintaining quality, and ensuring confidentiality. There are three strategies for maintaining data integrity: legal, administrative, and technical. A consistent database is one in which all data integrity constraints are satisfied. Manual systems cannot approach the degree of data integrity available in a well-designed computerized system. A DBMS is single-user if only one user at a time can use it, and is multi-user if many can use the system concurrently. DBMSs in most environments are multi-user. In a multi-user DBMS, stored data records and items are accessed by user programs or transactions. A transaction must be entirely completed or aborted before there is any effect on the database. Transactions are processed as logical units of work to ensure data integrity.

Isolation is a preventive strategy that involves administrative procedures to insulate the physical database from destruction. Database backup and recovery is a curative strategy that protects an existing database and re-creates or recovers the data whenever loss or destruction occurs. Possible causes of data loss or damage include: storage medium destruction, abnormal termination of an update transaction, and incorrect data discovered. A DBMS needs to provide backup, journaling, and recovery facilities to restore a database to a consistent state and restart the processing of transactions. A journal or log is a special database or file that stores information for backup and recovery. A before image is a copy of a database record before a transaction changes the record. An after image is a copy of a database record after a transaction has updated the record.

In order to recover from data loss or damage, it is necessary to store redundant, backup data. The recovery method is highly dependent on the backup strategy. The cost of keeping backup data is measured in terms of: interruption of database availability, storage of redundant data, and degradation of update efficiency. The four major recovery strategies are: switch to a duplicate database, backward recovery or rollback, forward recovery or roll forward, and reprocessing transactions. Database administration personnel often implement recovery strategies that are automatically carried out by the DBMS. The SQL statements COMMIT and ROLLBACK are used with a procedural programming language for implementing recovery procedures.

Maintaining quality implies keeping the data accurate, complete, and current. The first step is to ensure that anyone wanting to update a database has authorization. In SQL, access control is implemented through GRANT and REVOKE. Data validation cannot be performed without integrity constraints or rules. Data validation can be performed external to the DBMS by people or within the DBMS based on defined integrity constraints. Because maintaining data quality is of paramount importance, it is desirable that the DBMS handle data validation rather than the user. Whenever an error or unusual situation is detected by the DBMS, some form of response is required. Response rules need to be given to the DBMS along with the integrity constraints.

Concurrent update control focuses on making sure updated results are correctly recorded in a database. When two or more update transactions are allowed to update a database concurrently, the integrity of the database is threatened. To prevent loss of updates and inconsistent retrieval results, a DBMS must incorporate a resource locking mechanism. Deadlock is an impasse that occurs because two users lock certain resources, then request resources locked by the other user. Deadlock prevention requires users to lock all records they will require at the beginning of the transaction. Deadlock resolution uses the DBMS to detect and break deadlocks.

Two DBMS functions, access control and encryption, are the primary mechanisms for ensuring the data are accessed only by authorized persons. Access control consists of identification and authorization. Organizations are moving toward using personal characteristics and combinations of authenticating mechanisms to identify authorized users. Data access authorization is the process of permitting users, whose identity has been authenticated, to perform certain operations on certain data objects in a shared database. Encryption is any transformation applied to data that makes it difficult to extract meaning. Encrypted data cannot be read by an intruder unless that person knows the method of encryption and the key. DES and public key encryption are the most common techniques. Public key encryption attempts to overcome some of the problems with DES. In a DBMS environment, encryption techniques can be applied to transmitted data sent over communication lines to and from terminals, or between computers and stored data.

KEY TERMS AND CONCEPTS

Administrative strategies
After image
Authorization
Backup
Before image
COMMIT
Concurrent update control
Consistent database
Data access control
Data availability
Data Encryption Standard (DES)
Data quality
Data security
Database integrity
Deadlock prevention
Deadlock resolution
Deadly embrace
Decryption
Encryption
Ensuring confidentiality
GRANT

Integrity constraints
Isolation
Journal
Legal strategies
Lockout
Maintaining quality
Multi-user database
Multiprocessing
Multiprogramming
Protecting existence
Public key encryption
Recovery
Reprocessing
REVOKE
ROLLBACK
Rollback
Roll forward
Single-user database
Technical strategies
Transaction
Validation

REFERENCE AND ADDITIONAL READINGS

Clarke, R. A. Information technology and dataveillance. *Communications of the ACM.* 1988; 31(5): 498–512.

Culnan, Mary J. "How did they get my name?": An exploratory investigation of consumer attitudes toward secondary information use. *MIS Quarterly.* 1993; 17(3): 341–363.

EXERCISES

1. What are the three goals of maintaining organizational memory integrity?
2. What strategies are available for maintaining data integrity?
3. A large corporation needs to operate its computer systems continuously to remain viable. It currently has data centers in Miami and San Francisco. Do you have any advice for the CIO?
4. An investment company operates out of a single office in Boston. Its business is based on many years of high quality service, honesty, and reliability. The CEO is concerned that the firm has become too dependent on its computer system. If some disaster should occur and the firm's databases were lost, its reputation for reliability would disappear overnight—and so would many of its customers in this highly competitive business. What should the firm do?
5. What mechanisms should a DBMS provide to support backup and recovery of a database?
6. What is the difference between a "before image" and "after image"?
7. A large organization has asked you to advise on backup and recovery procedures for its weekly, batch payroll system. They want reliable recovery at the lowest cost. What would you recommend?
8. An on-line information service operates globally and prides itself on its uptime of 99.98 percent. What sort of backup and recovery scheme is this firm likely to use? Describe some of the levels of redundancy you would expect to find.
9. The information systems manager of a small manufacturing company is considering the backup strategy for a new production planning database. The database is used every evening to create a plan for the next day's production. As long as the production plan is prepared before 6 A.M. the next day, there is no impact upon plant efficiency. The database is currently 200 Mbytes and growing about 2 percent per year. What backup strategy would you recommend and why?
10. How do backward recovery and forward recovery differ?
11. What are the advantages and disadvantages of reprocessing transactions?
12. When would you use ROLLBACK in an application program?
13. When would you use COMMIT in an application program?
14. Give three examples of data integrity constraints.
15. What is the purpose of locking?

16. What is the likely effect on performance between locking at a row compared to locking at a page?

17. What is a deadly embrace? How can it be avoided?

18. What are three types of authenticating mechanisms?

19. What is encryption?

20. What are the disadvantages of the Data Encryption Standard (DES)?

21. What are the advantages of public key encryption?

22. A national stock exchange requires listed companies to transmit quarterly reports to its computer center electronically. Recently, a hacker intercepted some of the transmissions and made several hundred thousands of dollars because of advance knowledge of one firm's unexpectedly high quarterly profits. How could the stock exchange reduce the likelihood of this event?

Chapter 19

Data Administration

Bad administration, to be sure, can destroy good policy; but good administration can never save bad policy.

Adlai Stevenson, speech in Los Angeles, September 11, 1952

Learning Objectives

After completing this chapter you will:

- understand the importance and role of data administration in managing organizational resources;
- understand how system level data administration functions are used to successfully manage a database environment;
- understand how project level data administration activities support the development of a database system;
- understand what skills data administration requires and why it needs a balance of people, technical, and business skills to carry out its roles effectively;
- understand the key data administration skills;
- understand the complexity involved in managing a database environment and how computer-based tools can be used to support data administration activities;
- learn how the five major classes of computer-based tools—data dictionary, DBMS, performance monitoring, CASE, and groupware—are used by data administration staff;
- understand the management issues involved in initiating, staffing, and locating data administration organizationally.

The Expeditioner

> he Tahiti tourist resort had been an outstanding success for The Expeditioner. Located 40 minutes from Papeete, the capital city, on a stretch of tropical forest and golden sand, the resort had soon become the favorite meeting place for The Expeditioner's board. No one objected to the long flight to French Polynesia. The destination was well worth the journey, and The Expeditioner had historic ties to that part of the South Pacific. Early visitors to Tahiti, James Cook and William Bligh, had been famous customers of The Expeditioner in the eighteenth century. Before Paul Gauguin embarked on his journey to paint scenes of Tahiti, he had purchased supplies from L'Explorateur—now the French division of The Expeditioner.

Although The Expeditioner is very successful, there are always problems for the board to address. A number of board members are very concerned by the seeming lack of control over the various database systems that are vital to the firm's profitability. Recently there had been a number of incidents that had underscored the problem. Purchasing had made several poor decisions. For example, it had ordered too many parkas for the North American stores and had to discount them heavily to sell all the stock. The problem was traced to poor data standards and policies within Sales. Personnel and Marketing had been squabbling for some time over access to the personnel database. Personnel claimed ownership of the data and was reluctant to share data with Marketing, who wanted access to some of the data to support its new incentive program. A new database project for the Travel Division had been seriously delayed when it was discovered that the Travel Division's development team was planning to implement a system incompatible with The Expeditioner's existing hardware and software.

After the usual exchange of greetings and a presentation of the monthly financial report, Alice forthrightly raised the database problem. "We all know that we depend on information technology to manage The Expeditioner," she began as she glanced at her notes on her personal digital assistant. "The Information Systems department does a great job running the computers, building new systems, and providing us with excellent service, but," she stressed, "we seem to be focusing on managing the wrong things. We should be managing what really matters: the data we need to run the business. Data errors, internecine[1] fighting over data, and project delays are costly. Our present system for managing data is fragmented. We don't have anyone or any group who manages data centrally. It is critical that we develop an action plan for the organizational management of data." Pointing to Bob, she continued, "I have invited Bob to brief us on data administration and present his proposal for solving our data management problem. It's all yours, Bob."

INTRODUCTION

The Data Resource

In the information age, data are the lifeblood of every organization and need to be properly managed to retain their value to the organization. The importance of data as a key organizational resource has been emphasized throughout this book. Data administration is the management of organizational memories.

Information technology permits organizations to capture, organize, and maintain a greater variety of data. These data can be hard (e.g., financial or production figures) or soft (e.g., management reports, correspondence, voice conversations, and video). If these data are to be used in the organization, they must be managed just as diligently as accounting information. Data administration is the common term applied to the task of managing organizational memory. Although common, basic management principles apply to most kinds of organizational memories, the discussion in this chapter refers primarily to databases.

---

[1] She had certainly waited a long time to use this word, learned when studying for the university admission exam.

Why Manage Data?

Data are constantly generated in every act and utterance of every stakeholder—employee, shareholder, customer or supplier—in relation to the organization. Some of these data are formal and structured, for instance, invoices, grade sheets, or bank withdrawals. A large amount of relatively unstructured data is generated too, such as feedback from customers. Much of the unstructured data generated in organizations, while potentially useful, are never captured and recorded.

Organizations typically begin maintaining systematic records for data most likely to impinge on their performance. Often, different departments or individuals would like to maintain records for the same data. For instance, you may have experienced completing multiple copy forms—perhaps forms with half a dozen copies. Each copy was required by a different functional group or department. The same data may be used in different ways by each department, and so each department may adopt a different system of organizing the data. Over time, an organization accumulates a great deal of redundant data, which demands considerable, needless administrative overhead for its maintenance. Inconsistencies may begin to emerge between the various forms of the same data. A department may incorrectly enter some data, which could result in embarrassment at best or a serious financial loss for the organization at worst.

When data are fragmented across several departments or individuals, and especially when there is personnel turnover, data may not be accessible when most needed. This is nearly as serious a problem as not having any data. Yet another motivation is that effective data management can greatly simplify and assist in the identification of new information system application development opportunities. Also, poor data management can result in breaches of security. Valuable information may be revealed to competitors or antagonists.

In summary, the problems arising from the poor management of data are:

- the same data may be represented through multiple, inconsistent definitions;
- there may be inconsistencies among different representations;
- essential data may be missing from the database;
- data may be inaccurate or incomplete;
- some data may never be entered into the database and thus are effectively lost to the organization;
- there may be no way of knowing how to locate data when they are needed.

The overall goal of data administration is to prevent the occurrence of these problems by enabling users to access the data they need in the format most suitable for achieving their organizational goals; and by assuring the integrity of organizational databases.

MANAGEMENT OF THE DATABASE ENVIRONMENT

In many large organizations, there is a formal data administration function to manage corporate data. The relationship between these components is shown in Figure 19–1. Note that there are two levels of data administration—system and project—with the project level contained within the system level.

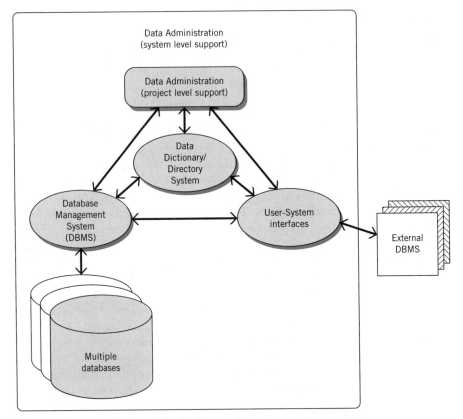

Figure 19-1   Management of the database environment

Database Management System (DBMS)

A DBMS is a general-purpose software system for organizing data. It is used to define, create, retrieve, manage, and protect data within the database. DBMSs have been covered in depth in previous chapters.

Database(s)

Each database contains a shared collection of logically related data used by one or more people. A DBMS can manage multiple databases covering different aspects of an organization's activities. When a database has multiple users, it may be designed to meet all their requirements, even though a specific user may need only a portion of the data contained within the database. For instance, a finished goods database may be accessed by production and finance, as well as marketing. It may contain costing information that is accessible by production and finance, but not by marketing. It may contain pricing information that is accessible to finance and marketing but not to production.

User Interface

The user interface consists of screen formats, menus, icons, and command languages that enable users to direct the system to manipulate data. Users may range from casual novices, who need to be insulated from the underlying complexity of the data, to expert application developers who manipulate the data using programming languages or other data manipulation tools.

Data Dictionary

A data dictionary is a reference repository containing *meta*data (i.e., "data about data") that is stored in the database. Among other things, the data dictionary contains a list of all the databases; their component parts and detailed descriptions such as field sizes, data types and data validation information for data entry purposes, authorized users and their access privileges, and ownership details.

A data dictionary is a map of the data in organizational memory. It permits the data administration staff and users to document the database, design new applications, and redesign the database if necessary. The data dictionary/directory system (DD/DS), itself a DBMS, is software for managing the data dictionary.

Early DBMSs did not include a data dictionary as part of the basic software—DD/DSs were add-ons developed by DBMS vendors and third party software developers. Given the importance of a data dictionary and the intense competition in the DBMS market, it is becoming increasingly common for DBMS vendors to provide an integrated DD/DS within their DBMS.

External Databases

For organizations to remain competitive in a rapidly changing marketplace, access to data from external sources is becoming increasingly critical. Research and development groups need access to the latest developments in their technical fields and need to track information such as patents filed, research reports, and new product releases. Marketing departments need access to data on market conditions and competitive situations as reported in various surveys and the media in general. Financial data regarding competitors and customers is important to senior executives. Monitoring political situations may be critical to many business decisions, especially in the international business arena. Such external data are often delivered to executives via an EIS.

Extensive external data are available electronically through commercial information services such as Dow Jones News Service (financial data), Reuters (news), and LEXIS–NEXIS (legal data), or from various FTP, Gopher, and WWW sites via the Internet (see Chapter 17). Tools are available to download external data into internal databases, from which they may be accessed through the same interface as for internal data.

DATA ADMINISTRATION

Data administration is responsible for the management of data-related activities. There are two levels of data administration activities: system and project. System level functions deal with management issues applicable to the entire database environment and all databases managed within that environment. System level functions include planning, development of data standards and policies, establishing data integrity procedures, resolving data conflict issues, and managing the DBMS and data dictionary.

At the project level, data administration supports the development and use of a specific database system. Data administration project level activities include defining user requirements, developing data models, training and consulting, establishing and monitoring data integrity, monitoring database usage, and controlling database changes. Both system and project level functions will be discussed in depth.

Data Administration Versus Database Administration

Organizational data may be managed at two different functional levels, which may be termed the system level and the project level. System level administration is broader in scope. Another pair of terms that has been used to capture this distinction is data administration and database administration. These terms, however, are confusing because of their similarity. We feel it is better to discuss data administration activities in terms of scope or level: systems and project. Also, in keeping with our managerial perspective, we will use data administration rather than database administration.

System level administration is concerned with establishing overall policies and procedures for the management and use of data in the organization. Formulating a data strategy and specifying an information architecture for the organization are also system level data administration functions. System level responsibilities may cover both electronic and non-electronic corporate data.

Project level data administration deals more with the specifics such as the optimization of specific databases for operational efficiency, establishing and implementing database access rights, creating new databases, and monitoring database use.

In general, the system level function takes a broader perspective of the role played by data in achieving business objectives, while the project level function is more concerned with the actual mechanics of database implementation and operation. We will use the term *data administration* to refer to both functional levels.

Data Administration Functions and Roles

A function is a related set of routine and non-recurring organizational activities that must be performed in order to achieve some organizational objective. Accounting, marketing, and manufacturing are examples of organizational functions. A function is fulfilled by one or more individuals, each of whom is assigned a role and performs some or all of the activities required of the function. In some organizations, the accounting function is performed by an entire accounting department, which may include several roles such as accounts manager, accountant, account clerk, and secretary. Each of these roles may be occupied by one or more individuals. For instance, there may be one manager (accounts), two accountants, several account clerks, and a secretary. In a small firm, the accounting function may be totally performed by a single accountant.

The functions of data administration may be accomplished through multiple roles or job titles such as database administrator, database developer, database consultant, and database analyst—people collectively referred to as the data administration staff. A single role could be responsible for both system and project levels of data administration, or responsibility may be distributed among several persons, depending on the size of the organization, the number of database applications, and the number of users.

In addition, data administration could be carried out entirely in a user department. For instance, a user could be the data steward responsible for managing all corporate data for some critical business-related entity or activity (e.g., a customer, a production facility, a supplier, a division, a project, or a product) regardless of the purpose for which the data are used. Data stewards coordinate planning of the data for which they are responsible. Tasks include data definition, quality control and improvement, and security and authorizing access. The data steward role is especially important today because of the growing emphasis on customer satisfaction and cross-functional teams. Data stewardship seeks to align data management with organizational strategy.

Database Levels

Databases may be maintained at several levels of use: personal, workgroup (e.g., project team or department), and organizational. The more users, the greater the complexity of both the database and its management.

Personal databases in the form of diaries, planners, and name and address books have existed for a long time. The availability of notebook computers and personal digital assistants (PDAs) has made it convenient to maintain electronic personal databases. Personal databases may not require a sophisticated DBMS—indeed, versatile software tools known as personal information managers (PIMs) are often better suited for the task of storing personal information. PIMs are able to store both structured and unstructured personal information such as calendars and appointments; names, addresses and contact information; to-do lists; and meeting notes and observations.

Workgroup databases cannot be as idiosyncratic because they are shared by many people. Managing them requires more planning and coordination to ensure that all users' addressed. Organizational databases are the most complex in terms of both structure and need for administration. All databases, regardless of scope or level, require administration.

Managing a personal database is relatively simple. Typically, the user of the database is also its developer and administrator. Issues such as access rights and security are settled quite easily, perhaps by the user locking the computer when away from the desk. Managing workgroup databases is more complex. Controls almost certainly will be needed to restrict access to certain data. On the other hand, some data will need to be available to many group members. Also, responsibility for backup and recovery must be established. Small workgroups may jointly perform both system and project level data administration activities. Meetings may be one way to coordinate system level data administration activities, and project level activities may be distributed among different workgroup members. Larger groups may have a designated data administrator, who is also a group member.

Managing organizational databases is typically a full-time job requiring special skills to work with complex database environments. In large corporations, several persons may handle data administration, each carrying out different data administration activities. System level data administration activities may be carried out by a committee led by a senior IS executive (who may be a full-time or part-time data administrator), while project level data administration activities may be delegated to individual data administration staff members.

System Level Data Administration Functions

System level data administration functions, which may be performed by one or more persons, are summarized in Table 19–1.

Table 19–1   System Level Data Administration Functions

Planning
Development of data standards and policies
Data integrity
Data conflict resolution
Managing the DBMS
Establishing and maintaining the Data Dictionary
Selection of hardware and software
Managing external databases
Internal marketing

Planning

Because data are a strategic corporate resource, planning is perhaps the most critical data administration function. A key planning activity is creating an organization's information architecture, which includes all the major data entities and the relationships between them. It indicates which business functions and applications access which entities. An information architecture also may address issues such as how data will be transmitted and where they will be stored. Since an information architecture is an organization's overall strategy for data and applications, it should dovetail with the organization's long-term plans and objectives.

Development of Data Standards and Policies

Whenever data are used by more than one person — for example, a workgroup or even an entire organization — there must be standards to govern this use. Data standards become especially critical in organizations using heterogeneous hardware and software environments. Why could this become a problem? For historical reasons, different departments may use different names and field sizes for the same data item. These differences can cause confusion and misunderstanding. For example, "sales date" may have different meanings for the legal department (e.g., the date the contract was signed) and the sales department (e.g., the date of the sales call). Furthermore, the legal department may store data in the form *yyyy-mm-dd* and the sales department as *dd-mm-yy*. Data administration's task is to develop and publish data standards so that field names are clearly defined and a field's size and format are consistent across the enterprise.

Furthermore, some data items may be more important to certain departments or divisions. For instance, customer data are often critical to the marketing department. It is useful in such cases to appoint a data steward from the appropriate functional area as custodian for these data items.

Policies need to be established regarding who can access and manipulate which data when and from where. For instance, should employees using their home computer be allowed to access corporate data? If such access is permitted, then data security and risk exposure must be considered and adequate data safeguards implemented.

Data Integrity

Data must be made available when needed but only to authorized users. The data management aspects of data integrity were discussed at length in Chapter 18.

Data Conflict Resolution

Data administration involves the custodianship of data "owned" or originating in various organizational departments or functions, and conflicts are bound to arise at some point. For instance, one department may be concerned about a loss of security when another department is allowed access to its data. In another instance, one group may feel that another is contaminating a commonly used data pool because of inadequate data validation practices. A department may want exclusive control over a particular database because of the department's high transaction volume. Incidents like these, and many others, require management intervention and settlement through a formal or informal process of discussion and negotiation in which all parties are assured of a fair hearing. Data administration facilitates negotiation and mediates dispute resolution.

Managing the DBMS

While project level data administration is concerned more directly with the DBMS, the performance and characteristics of the DBMS ultimately impinge on the effectiveness of the system level data administration function. It is, therefore, important to monitor some characteristics of the DBMS. Over a period, benchmark statistics for different projects or applications will need to be compiled. These statistics are especially useful for addressing user complaints regarding the performance of the DBMS, which may then lead to design changes, tuning of the DBMS, or additional hardware.

Database technology is rapidly advancing. For example, relational DBMSs are continually being extended and ODBMS technology promises greater versatility and flexibility for some applications (see Chapter 15). Keeping track of developments, evaluating their benefits, and deciding on converting to new database environments is a critical system level data administration function that can have strategic implications for the corporation.

Establishing and Maintaining the Data Dictionary

A data dictionary is a key data administration tool that provides details of data in the organizational database and how they are used (e.g., by various application programs). If modifications are planned for the database (e.g., deleting a column or changing the size of a column in a table), the data dictionary helps to determine which applications will be affected by the proposed changes.

In the early days of data administration, data dictionaries were manually maintained. The widespread need and demand for a data dictionary facility resulted in some independent vendors creating the necessary data dictionary software for a variety of commercial DBMSs. Some data dictionary systems are merely electronic versions of a manual data dictionary, in that they operate independently of the database itself. Any changes in the database are not automatically reflected in the data dictionary. Someone must remember to update the data dictionary. More sophisticated data dictionary systems are closely integrated with specific database products. They are updated automatically whenever the structure of the underlying database is changed.

The initial purchase price of an automatic data dictionary may be higher, but the additional cost may be worthwhile. Automatic data dictionaries have more safeguards against human error. Competition in the DBMS market has led to several database vendors providing integrated, automatic data dictionaries along with their DBMSs.

Selection of Hardware and Software

Evaluating and selecting the appropriate hardware and software for an organizational database is a critical responsibility with strategic organizational implications. This is not an easy task due to the dynamic nature of the database industry, the continually changing variety of available hardware and software products, and the rapid pace of change within many organizations. Today's excellent choice might become tomorrow's nightmare, if, for instance, the vendor of a key database component goes out of business or ceases product development.

Selection of a query language may be an important decision. Should the firm select SQL or a proprietary query language? SQL is an industry standard, and there is likely to be a large pool of skilled programmers. On the other hand, SQL may not be ideal for the intended application, and a proprietary query language may be more suitable for the organization's needs.

Extensive experience and knowledge of the database software business and technological progress in the field are essential to making effective database hardware and software decisions. The current and future needs of the organization need to be assessed in terms of capacity as well as features. Relevant questions include:

- How many users will simultaneously access the database?
- Will the database need to be geographically distributed? If so, what is the degree to which the database will be replicated, and what is the nature of database replication that is supported?
- What is the maximum size of the database?
- How many transactions per second can the DBMS handle?
- What kind of support for on-line transaction processing is available?
- What are the initial and ongoing costs of using the product?
- What is the extent of training required, who can provide it, and what are the associated costs?

DBMS selection should cover technical, operational, and financial considerations. An organization's selection criteria are often specified in a Request For Proposal (RFP). This document is sent to a short list of potential vendors, who are invited to respond with a software or hardware/software proposal outlining how their product or service meets each criterion in the RFP. Visits to current user sites are usually desirable to gain confirming evidence of a vendor's claims. The final decision should be based on the manner and degree to which each vendor's proposal satisfies these criteria.

Managing External Databases

Providing access to external databases has increased the level of complexity of data administration, which now has the additional responsibility of identifying information services that meet existing or potential managerial needs. Data administration must determine the quality of such data and the means by which they can be channeled into the organization's existing information delivery system. Costs of data may vary among vendors. Some may charge a flat monthly or annual fee, while others may have a usage charge. Data may arrive in a variety of formats, and data administration may need to make them adhere to corporate standards. Data from different vendors and sources may need to be integrated and presented in a unified format and on common screens, perhaps including them in an EIS.

Monitoring external data sources is critical because data quality may vary over time.

Data administration must determine whether user needs are continuing to be met and data quality is being maintained. If not, a subscription may be canceled and an alternative vendor sought. Security is another critical problem. When corporate databases are connected to external communication links there is a threat of hackers breaking into the system and gaining unauthorized access to confidential internal data. Also, corporate data may be contaminated by spurious data, or even by viruses entering the internal databases from external sources. Data administration must be cautious when incorporating external data into the database.

Training users to access external databases also can be a data administration responsibility. If using external databases is very cumbersome or time-consuming for users, the data administration staff may have to access external databases on behalf of users.

Cruisin' the Net

From a data administration perspective, the Internet (known variously as the *Information Highway*, *I-Way*, or *Infobahn*) presents both opportunities and challenges. Connecting the organization to the Internet opens the gates to a vast storehouse of data available through individuals, businesses, governments, and other kinds of organizations. Searching for the data one needs, unfortunately, is often like looking for the proverbial needle in a haystack. Today, several tools are becoming available to "cruise" the Internet. Nevertheless, the average business executive may not have the time to cruise even for vital data. One suggested solution is to create a position of Net Librarian, who will use powerful tools to search constantly for data of possible interest to the organization. The Net Librarian then makes these data available to the right people in the right form, but always being mindful of not overloading users with too much irrelevent data.[2]

Internal Marketing

Because IS applications can have a major impact on organizational performance, the IS function is becoming more proactive in initiating the development of new applications. Many users are not aware of what is possible with newly emergent technologies, and hence do not see opportunities to exploit these developments. Also, as custodian of organizational data, data administration needs to communicate its goals and responsibilities throughout the organization. People and departments need to be persuaded to share data that may be of value to other parts of the organization. There may be resistance to change when people are asked to switch to newly established data standards. In all these instances, data administration must be presented in a positive light to lessen resistance to change. Data administration needs to market internally its products and services to its customers.

---

[2]Adapted from Letter to the Editor. Cruisin' for a bruisin'. *InfoWorld,* July 18, 1994: 45.

Project Level Data Administration

At the project level, data administration focuses on the detailed needs of individual users and applications. Data administration supports the development and use of a specific database system.

Systems Development Life Cycle

Database development follows a fairly predictable sequence of steps or phases similar to the systems development life cycle for applications. This database development sequence can be called the database development life cycle (DDLC). The database and application development life cycles together constitute the systems development life cycle (SDLC) described in Table 19–2.

Application development involves the eight phases shown in Table 19–2. It commences with project planning which, among other things, involves determining project feasibility and allocating the necessary personnel and material resources for the project. This is followed by requirements definition, which involves considerable interaction with clients to clearly specify the system. These specifications become the basis for a conceptual application design which is then constructed, through program coding, and tested. Once the system is thoroughly tested, it is installed and user operations begin. Over time, changes may be needed to upgrade or repair the system, and this is called system maintenance.

Database development phases parallel application development. Data administration is responsible for the DDLC. Data is the focus of database development, rather than procedures or processes. Database construction is folded into the testing phase since database testing typically involves minimal effort. In systems with integrated data dictionaries, the process of constructing the data dictionary also creates the database shell (i.e., tables without data). While the sequence of phases in the cycle as presented is generally followed, there is often a number of iterations within and between steps. Data modeling is iterative, and the final database design evolves from many data modeling sessions. A previously unforeseen requirement may surface during the database design phase, and this may prompt a revision of the specifications completed in the earlier phase.

Table 19–2   Systems Development Life Cycle

Application Development Life Cycle (ADLC)	Database Development Life Cycle (DDLC)
Project planning	Project planning
Requirements definition	Requirements definition
Application design	Database design
Application construction	
Application testing	Database testing
Application implementation	Database implementation
Operations	Database usage
Maintenance	Database evolution

System development may proceed in three different ways:

1. The database may be developed independently of applications, following only the DDLC steps;

2. Applications may be developed for existing databases, following only the ADLC steps;

3. Application and database development may proceed in parallel, with both simultaneously stepping through the ADLC and DDLC.

Consider further each of these possibilities.

A database may be developed independently of applications. Database development may proceed independently of application development for a number of reasons. The database may be created for storing information that later may be used by an application, or for ad hoc querying using a built-in query language. In another case, an existing database may undergo changes to improve efficiency or integrity. For instance, if it is found that a new query cannot be efficiently handled by the current database model (i.e., processing takes an inordinate amount of time), redesigning the database may overcome the problem. In such situations, the developer goes through the appropriate stages of the DDLC.

Application development may proceed based on an existing database. In some instances, the required database may already be in place. For instance, a personnel database may already exist to serve a set of applications, such as payroll. This database could be used as the basis for a new personnel benefits application, which must go through all the phases of the ADLC.

A new system requires both application and database development. Frequently, a new systems will require creation of both a new database and applications. For instance, a computer manufacturer may start a new mail-order sales division and wish to monitor its performance. The vice-president in charge of the division may be interested in receiving daily sales reports by product and by customer, and a weekly moving sales trend analysis for the prior 10 weeks. This requires both the development of a new sales database as well as a new application for sales reporting. Here, the ADLC and DDLC are both instituted to manage development of the new system.

Another possibility is that a newly introduced DBMS may provide easy-to-use query facilities that are superior to existing applications. Here again, changing the database may trigger a corresponding change in applications.

Database Development Roles

Database development involves several roles, chiefly those of developer, end user, and data administrator. The roles and their responsibilities are outlined in Table 19–3.

The database developer shoulders the bulk of the responsibility for developing data models and implementing the database. This can be seen in Table 19–3, where most of the cells in the *database developer* column are labeled "Does." The database developer does project planning, requirements definition, database design, database testing, and database implementation, and in addition, is responsible for database evolution.

The user's role is to establish the goals of a specific database project, provide the database developers with access to all information needed for project development, and review and regularly scrutinize the developer's work.

The data administrator's prime responsibilities are implementing and controlling, but the

Table 19-3   Database Development Roles

Database Development Phase	Database Developer	Data Administrator	User
Project planning	Does	Consults	Provides information
Requirements definition	Does	Consults	Provides requirements
Database design	Does	Consults Does data integrity	Validates data models
Database testing	Does system and user testing	Consults Does data integrity	Does user testing
Database implementation	Does system related activities	Consults Does data integrity	Does user activities
Database usage	Consults	Does data integrity monitoring	Uses
Database evolution	Does	Does change control	Provides additional requirements

person also may be required to perform activities and consult. In some situations, the database developer is not part of the data administration staff, and may be located in a user department or be an analyst from an IS project team. In these cases, the data administrator advises the developer on organizational standards and policies as well as providing specific technical guidelines for successful construction of a database. When the database developer is part of the data administration staff, developer and data administration activities may be carried out by the same person, or by the person(s) occupying the data administration role. In all cases, the data administrator should understand the larger business context in which the database will be used and should be able to relate business needs to specific technical capabilities and requirements.

Database Development Life Cycle (DDLC)

Previously, we discussed the various roles involved in database development and how they may be assigned to different persons. In this section, we will assume that administration and development are carried out by the data administration staff, since this is the typical situation encountered in many organizations. The activities of developer and administrator shown in the first two columns of Table 19-3 are assumed to be performed by data administration staff.

Now, let's consider data administration project level support activities in detail (see Figure 19-2). These activities are discussed in terms of the DDLC phase they support.

Database Project Planning

Database project planning includes establishing project goals, determining project feasibility (financial, technical, and operational), creating an implementation plan and schedule,

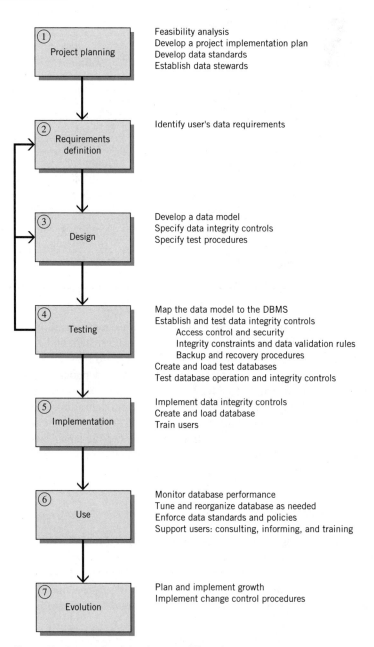

Figure 19-2 Database development life cycle

assigning project responsibilities (including data stewards), and establishing standards. All project stakeholders, including users, senior management, and developers are involved in planning. They are included for their knowledge as well as to gain their commitment to the project.

Requirements Definition

During requirements definition, users and developers establish what the users' needs are and develop a mutual understanding of what the new system will deliver. Data are defined and the resulting definitions stored in the data dictionary. Requirements definition generates documentation that should serve as an unambiguous reference for database development. While in theory the users are expected to "sign-off" on the specifications and accept the developed database as is, in practice, users' needs may actually change. Users may gain greater understanding of their requirements and business conditions may change. Consequently, the original specifications may require revision. In Figure 19–2, the arrows connecting phase 4 (database testing) and phase 3 (database design) to phase 2 (requirements definition) indicate that modeling and testing may identify revisions to the database specification and these amendments are then incorporated into the design.

Database Design

Conceptual and internal models of the database are developed during database design. Conceptual design, or data modeling, is discussed extensively in Section 2. Database design should also include specification of procedures for testing the database. Any additional controls for ensuring data integrity are also specified. The external model should be checked and validated by the user.

Database Testing

Database testing requires previously developed specifications and models to be tested using the intended DBMS. Users are often asked to provide operational data to support testing the database with realistic transactions. Testing should address a number of key questions:

Does the DBMS support all the operational and security requirements?

Is the system able to handle the expected number of transactions per second?

How long does it take to process a realistic mix of queries?

Testing assists in making early decisions regarding the suitability of both the database design and the selected DBMS.

It Never Hurts to Test

After a year's effort, IS staff at a mid-sized durable goods manufacturer had designed and created a database of six million invoices that ran to several hundred Mbytes on a Teradata relational database machine. A typical schema was made up of about fifty tables. When users began testing the database, the $2 million machine could handle only sixty queries a day! The database staff adopted a new technique called dimensional modeling to reorganize the database. The revised database design, with the same basic data loaded into only five tables, dramatically raised performance to 1000 queries daily.[3]

---

[3]Adapted from Why decision support fails, and how to fix it. *Datamation*. June 1, 1994: 40–45.

Another critical aspect of database testing is verifying data integrity controls. Testing may include checking backup and recovery procedures, access control, and data validation rules.

Database Implementation

Testing is complete when the users and developers are extremely confident the system meets specified needs. Data integrity controls are implemented, operational data are loaded (including historical data, if necessary), and database documentation is finalized. Users are then trained to operate the system.

Database Use

Users may need considerable support as they learn and adapt to the system. Database performance monitoring is critical to keeping users satisfied. Performance monitoring enables the data administrator to anticipate problems even before the users begin to notice and complain about them, and tune the system to meet users' needs. Performance monitoring during the initial stages of database implementation also helps to enforce data standards and policies.

Database Evolution

Since organizations cannot afford to stand still in today's dynamic business environment, business needs are bound to change over time, perhaps even after a few months. Data administration should be prepared to meet the challenge of change. Minor changes, such as changes in display formats, or performance improvements, may be continually requested. These have to be attended to on an ongoing basis. Other evolutionary changes may emerge from constant monitoring of database use by the data administration staff. Implementing these evolutionary changes involves repeating phases 3 to 6 of Figure 19–2. Significant business changes may merit a radical redesign of the database. Major redesign may require repeating all phases of the DDLC.

Data Administration Interfaces

Data administration is increasingly a key corporate function, and it requires the existence of established channels of communication with various organizational groups. The key data administration interfaces are with users, management, development staff, and computer operations. The central position of the data administration staff in Figure 19–3 reflects the liaison role that it plays in managing databases. Each of the groups has a different focus and different terminology and jargon. Data administration should be able to communicate effectively with all participants. For instance, operations staff will tend to focus on technical, day-to-day issues to which management is unlikely to pay much attention. These different focuses can, and frequently do, lead to conflicting views and expectations among the different groups. Good interpersonal skills are a must for data administration staff in order to deal with a vari-

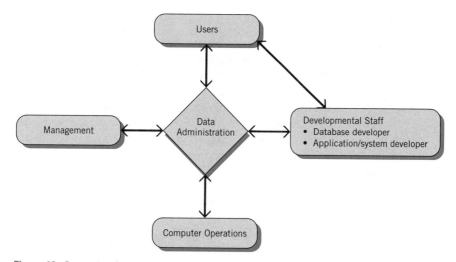

Figure 19–3   Major data administration interfaces

ety of conflict-laden situations. Data administration, therefore, needs a balance of people, technical, and business skills for effective execution of its tasks.

Data administration probably will communicate most frequently with computer operations and development staffs, somewhat less frequently with users, and least frequently with management. These differences, however, have little to do with the relative importance of communicating with each group. The interactions between the data administration staff and each of the four groups are discussed next.

Management

Management sets the overall business agenda for data administration, which must ensure that its actions directly contribute to the achievement of organizational goals. In particular, management establishes overall policy guidelines, approves data administration budgets, evaluates proposals, and champions major changes. For instance, if the data administration staff is interested in introducing new technology, management may request a formal report on the anticipated tangible and intangible benefits of the proposed expenditure.

Interactions between the data administration staff and management may focus on establishing and evolving the information architecture for the organization. In some instances, this may involve the introduction of a new technology that could fundamentally transform the organization. For example, consider the introduction of Lotus Notes (see Chapter 16) into a management consulting company on a enterprise-wide basis. The introduction of Notes was a strategic technology decision that transformed the company's information architecture because it allowed consultants around the world to exchange information and gain access to in-house expertise rapidly. This capability became a significant source of competitive advantage. Such technological change never would have occurred without management's approval and wholehearted support.

Users

On an ongoing basis, most users will be less concerned with architectural issues and will focus on their personal needs. Data administration must determine what data should be collected and stored, how they should be validated to ensure integrity, and in what form and frequency they should be made available. For instance, the Chief Financial Officer may use the existing EIS to access financial data from external data vendors.

Typically, the data administration staff is responsible for managing the database while the data supplier is responsible for ensuring accuracy. This may cause conflict, however, if there are multiple users from separate departments. If conflict does arise, data administration has to arbitrate.

Development Staff

Having received strategic directions from management, and having determined users' needs, data administration next works with the development staff—both applications and database developers—in order to fulfill the organization's goals for the new system. On an ongoing basis, this may consist of developing specifications for implementation. Data administration works on an advisory basis with systems development, providing inputs on the database aspects. For instance, data administration is responsible for establishing standards for program–database interfaces, and making developers aware of these standards. Developers may need to be told which commands may be used in their application programs and which databases they can access.

As a consultant, data administration works closely with database developers. In addition to new database projects, data administration periodically may interact with developers to make relatively minor changes to or optimize existing databases.

In many organizations, database development is part of data administration and has a very direct role in database design and implementation. In such instances, communication between data administration and database development is within the group. In other organizations, database development is not part of data administration and communication is between groups.

Being a change agent is another important role for data administration. As the Lotus Notes example illustrates, data administration needs to educate development personnel on the availability of new data technologies. Such technologies may transform the systems development process and perhaps even the composition of the development team. A new database technology may improve development productivity several times. For instance, a decision to move to a new database system with an advanced fourth generation language (4GL) in a previously COBOL-dominated IS organization may result in significant improvements in programmer productivity. It may also result in hiring new programmers or the retraining of current staff.

Computer Operations

The focus of computer operations is on the physical hardware, procedures, schedules and shifts, staff assignments, the physical security of data, and the execution of programs. Data administration responsibilities include establishing and monitoring procedures for operating the database. The data administration staff needs to establish and communicate database backup, recovery, and archiving procedures to computer operations. Also, the scheduling of new database and application installations need to be coordinated with computer operations personnel.

Computer operations provides data administration with operational statistics and exception reports. These data are used by data administration to ensure that corporate database objectives are being fulfilled.

Communication

The different parties with which data administration communicates often see things differently. This can lead to misunderstandings and result in systems that fail to meet the needs of users. Part of the problem arises from a difference in perspective and approaches to viewing database technology.

Management is interested in understanding how implementing database technology will contribute to strategic goals. In contrast, users are interested in how the proposed database and accompanying applications will affect their daily work. Developers are concerned with translating management and users' needs into conceptual models and converting these into physical data models and applications. Operations staff are concerned primarily with efficient daily management of database technology, computer hardware, and software.

Data models can serve as a common language for bridging the varying goals of users, developers, management, and operational staff. A data model can reduce the ambiguity inherent in verbal communications and thereby ensure that users' needs are more closely met and all parties are satisfied with the results. A data model provides a common meeting point and language for understanding the needs of each group.

As we have seen, data administration involves working closely with a variety of database stakeholders. As critical as it is to possess technical knowledge, it is equally important for data administration staff to possess excellent interpersonal skills. Data administration does not work in isolation. It must communicate successfully with all its constituents in order to be successful. The capacity to understand and correctly translate the needs of each stakeholder group is the key to competent data administration.[4]

Data Administration Tools

The database environment depicted in Figure 19–1 is very complex. Even in a small organization or work unit, there may be several thousand data items. These data items may

---

[4]For a more extensive discussion and guidance on improving your interpersonal skills in relation to IS development projects, see Bostrom (1989), Cause and Weinberg (1989), Weinberg (1986). There are many more books that discuss communication skills in a wider context and serve as useful references for self-development. Some of the most useful are: Doyle and Strauss (1976), and Kayser (1990). Full details are provided at the end of the chapter.

appear in hundreds of files, reports, and input transactions. It is impossible to manage this data environment without computer-based tools to support data administration activities.

Several computer-based tools have emerged to support various data administration functions. There are five major classes of tools: data dictionary, DBMS, performance monitoring, computer-aided software engineering (CASE), and groupware tools. Each of these tools is now examined and its role in supporting data administration considered. We focus on how these tools support the database development life cycle shown in Table 19–3. Note, however, that groupware is not shown in Table 19–4 because it is useful in all phases of the life cycle.

Data administration staff, users, and computer operations all require information about organizational databases. Ideally, such information should be stored in one central repository. This is the role of the data dictionary (or data dictionary/directory system), perhaps the main data administration tool. Thus, we start our discussion of tools with the data dictionary/directory system.

Table 19–4   Data Administration Tool Usage During the Database Development Life Cycle

Database Development Phase	Data Dictionary (DD)	Database Management System (DBMS)	Performance Monitoring	Case Tools
1. Project planning tools	Document Data map Design aid			Estimation
2. Requirements definition	Document Design aid			Document Design aid
3. Database design	Document Design aid Data map Schema generator			Document Design aid Data map
4. Database testing	Data map Design aid Schema generator	Define, create, test, data integrity	Impact analysis	Test data generator Design aid
5. Database implementation	Document Change control	Data integrity Implement Design	Monitor Tune	
6. Database usage	Document Data map Schema generator Change control	Provide tools for retrieval and update Enforce integrity controls and procedures	Monitor Tune	
7. Database evolution	Document Data map Change Control	Redefine	Impact analysis	

Data Dictionary/Directory System

The data dictionary/directory system (DD/DS) is a database application that manages the data dictionary. It is an essential tool for data administration staff and users. In this segment, we describe the DD/DS, and its general and specific uses in supporting various activities during the DDLC. Our focus is on the use of the data dictionary by data administration.

The data dictionary is the repository for organizational metadata, such as data definitions, relationships, user's privileges, and so forth. The DBMS manages organizational databases, and the DD/DS manages data about data. The DD/DS also uses the data dictionary to generate table definitions or schema required by the DBMS and application programs to access databases.

Users and data administration can utilize the DD/DS to ask questions about characteristics of data stored in organizational databases such as:

List the names of all tables for which the user Todd has delete privileges?
Report where the data item customernumber appears or is used

The report for the second query could include the names and tables, transactions, reports, display screens, user's names, and application programs.

In some systems, such as a relational DBMS, the catalog (see Chapter 9) performs some of the functions of a DD/DS although the catalog does not contain the same level of detail. The catalog essentially contains data about tables, columns, and owners of tables whereas the DD/DS can include data about applications, forms, transactions, and many other aspects of the system. Consequently, a DD/DS is of greater value to data administration.

Although there is no standard format for data stored in a data dictionary, several features are common across systems. For example, a data dictionary for a typical relational database environment would contain descriptions of:

- All data elements that are defined in all tables of all databases. The data dictionary stores specific data characteristics such as name, data type, display format, internal storage format, and validation rules and integrity constraints. It indicates where an element is used and by whom.
- All relationships among data elements, what elements are involved, and characteristics of relationships such as cardinality and degree.
- All defined databases, including who created each database, the date of creation, and where the database is located.
- All tables defined in all databases. The data dictionary is likely to store details of who created the table, the date of creation, primary key, and the number of columns.
- All indexes defined for each of the database tables. For each of the indexes the DBMS stores data such as the index name, the location, specific index characteristics, and the creation date.
- All users and their access authorizations for various databases.
- All programs that access the database, including screen formats, report formats, application programs, and SQL queries.

A data dictionary may be integrated or stand alone. An integrated data dictionary is included as part of the DBMS although some older DBMSs do not have one built in. In these cases, data administration has to use a third-party, stand alone data dictionary.

The data dictionary can serve useful purposes for both systems and project level data administration activities. The five major uses of a data dictionary are:

1. **Documentation support**:   recording, classifying, and reporting metadata.
2. **Data maps**:   a data map of available data for data administration staff and users. A data map allows users to discover what data exists, what it means, where it is stored, and how it is accessed.
3. **Design aid**:   documenting the relationships between data entities and performing impact analysis.
4. **Schema generation**:   automatic generation of data definition statements needed by software systems such as the DBMS and application programs.
5. **Change control**:   setting and enforcing standards; evaluating the impact of proposed changes and implementing amendments such as adding new data items.

To better understand the uses of a data dictionary, we can examine how it is used during each phase of the database development life cycle. The five general uses are mapped to each phase as illustrated in Table 19–4 and summarized below by phase.

1. **Project planning:**   As part of the planning phase, a high level data model may be created. The DD/DS is a design aid and data map to support planning. The outputs are documented in the data dictionary.
2. **Requirements definition:**   Considerable detail is captured during requirements definition. Database developers collect facts and opinions from users on current and future uses of data. Data items, reports, and transactions are defined and described. The captured data requirements are stored in the data dictionary. Thus, the DD/DS is used as a documentation tool and design aid during requirements definition.
3. & 4. **Database design and testing:**   As shown in Table 19–4, the data dictionary is used as a documentation tool, design aid, schema generator, and data map during these two phases. Database design results in a conceptual data model that can be implemented in a target DBMS. During testing, the data model is tested in terms of database operations and integrity controls. The DD/DS is used as a design aid and data map in developing data models. The DD/DS is also used to generate schemas for DBMS and applications programs, and to generate data to test database operations and controls. Finally, the conceptual data model and physical databases are documented in the data dictionary and used to generate user and system documentation.
5. **Database implementation:**   During database implementation, the DD/DS is used primarily for documentation support and change control. For example, users require data descriptions so they can practice writing queries during training. In terms of control, data administration uses the data dictionary to resolve inconsistencies when loading the database and enforcing standards during implementation.
6. **Database use:**   Database use involves the ongoing update and retrieval of data from a database. A data map created by the DD/DS helps users locate and understand stored data. The DD/DS also becomes a primary control tool when it is used to enforce integrity controls such as data validation.

7. **Database evolution:**   The data dictionary is useful for planning growth and change. Data administration utilizes performance monitoring software to document use and evaluate performance (see the section on these tools). This information, plus users' change requests, leads to potential enhancements to database systems. The DD/DS is a primary tool for planning and evaluating these enhancements. For example, it can be employed to perform an impact analysis of proposed changes, such as adding new relationships or data items.

DATABASE MANAGEMENT SYSTEM (DBMS)

The DBMS is the primary tool for maintaining database integrity and making data available to users. Availability means making data accessible to whoever needs it, when and where they need it, and in a meaningful form. Maintaining database integrity implies the implementation of control procedures to achieve the three goals discussed in Chapter 18: protecting existence, maintaining quality, and ensuring confidentiality. In terms of the DDLC life cycle (see Table 19–4), data administration uses, or helps others to use, the DBMS to create and test new databases, define data integrity controls, modify existing database definitions, and provide tools for users to retrieve and update databases. Since much of this book has been devoted to DBMS functions, we limit our discussion to reviewing its role as a data administration tool.

Performance Monitoring Tools

Performance monitoring tools are often integrated into the DBMS or DD/DS. We discuss them separately, however, because in many cases they can be purchased as individual products.

Monitoring the performance of DBMS and database operations by gathering usage statistics is essential to improving performance, enhancing availability, and database evolution. As shown in Table 19–4, monitoring tools are used to collect statistics and improve database performance during the implementation and use stages of the DDLC. Monitoring tools can also be used to collect data to evaluate design choices during testing.

Many database factors can be monitored and a variety of statistics gathered. Monitoring growth in the number of rows in each table can reveal trends that are helpful in projecting future needs for physical storage space. Database access patterns can be scrutinized to record data such as:

type of function requested: query, insert, update, or delete,

response time (elapsed time from query to response),

number of disk accesses,

identification of user,

identification of error conditions.

The observed patterns help to determine performance enhancements. For example, these statistics could be used to determine which tables or files should be indexed.

Since gathering statistics can result in some degradation of overall performance, it should be possible to turn the monitoring function on or off with regard to selected statistics.

Case Tools

A computer-aided software engineering (CASE) tool, as broadly defined, provides automated assistance for systems development, maintenance, and project management activities. Data administration may use project management tools to coordinate all phases within the DDLC. The dictionary provided by CASE systems can be used to supplement the DD/DS, especially where the database development effort is part of a systems development project.

One of the most important components of a CASE tool is an extensive dictionary that tracks all objects created by systems designers. Database and application developers can use the CASE dictionary to store descriptions of data elements, application processes, screens, reports, and other relevant information. Thus, during the first four phases of the life cycle (see Table 19–4), the CASE dictionary performs functions similar to a DD/DS. During stages 4 and 5, data from the CASE dictionary would be transferred, usually automatically, to the DD/DS.

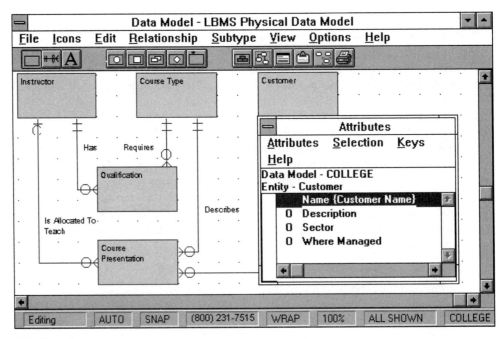

A CASE tool screen.

Groupware

Groupware, discussed in depth in Chapter 16, can be applied by data administration to support any of the DDLC phases shown in Table 19–4. Groupware supports communication between people and thus enhances access to organizational memory residing within humans. As we have pointed out, data administration interfaces with four major groups during the DDLC: management, users, developers, and computer operations. Groupware supports interactions with all of these groups, as the following scenario illustrates.

Pretend you are part of data administration; you are a database developer on the requirements definition phase of a project to develop a personnel database. Picture yourself in a design team meeting to identify the project's goals. Representatives of all the significant stakeholders and data administration staff assigned to the project are seated around a horseshoe-shaped table. Today's agenda demands that the group identifies the project's goals.

Now imagine an identical situation, except with personal computers added to your picture. A color monitor and keyboard are in front of each person, and there are two five-foot display screens at the head of the conference table. Computers are networked to exchange information. Software provides support for generating, organizing, and evaluating ideas and judgments. A technical facilitator runs the software and provides whatever instructions and orientation assistance are needed. A second facilitator, who is assisting the project team leader, helps the group systematically work through each step of this electronic meeting.

Now switch your attention back to the regular (computerless) meeting. You listen to the group's discussion switch from issue to issue. Nothing seems to get resolved. A couple of people dominate most of the discussion, monopolizing the floor, and attempting to influence the group's direction. New ideas, when raised, are often criticized as soon as they are offered.

Now, refocus your attention on the computer-supported meeting. Special software to accommodate group brainstorming is displayed on each computer screen. The bottom part of the screen has an area for you to enter your ideas for the project's objectives. The top section displays the question: *What are the objectives of the personnel database project?* Each person enters objectives ("all talk at once"). Later in the meeting, using other groupware tools, the team will rank the objectives by levels of importance.

Computer support for the meeting outlined above is an example of using groupware in the DDLC. Research and experience has shown that the benefits of groupware (e.g., reduced project time, faster implementation, improved quality, and greater use of team diversity,) discussed in Chapter 16 are applicable to IS projects such as database development. Although groupware could be used in all phases of DDLC, its potential impacts are the greatest in the requirements definition and database design stages (see Figure 19–2 and Table 19–4) because this is when the most frequent and intensive interactions between users and developers take place.

Data administration is a complex task involving a variety of technologies and the need to interact with and satisfy the needs of a diverse range of users. Managing such a complex environment demands the use of computer-based tools. New tools are making data administration more manageable and effective. Software tools, such as CASE and groupware, can improve data administration. The emergence of such tools also signals an increasing awareness of the importance of data administration and an understanding of what it entails.

Data Administration—A Career Opportunity

As companies realize data is a corporate resource, many are discovering the need for data administrators—people who organize and manage corporate data. Demand is primarily from large companies, particularly banks and service companies.

A data administrator at a major utility describes how he spends much of his time meeting with business managers to see how the business works, what information is required, and how it is used. Excellent analytic and communications skills are prerequisites for data administrators.

Data administration will become increasingly important as technology becomes more pervasive. As data access tools become more powerful, users will need data administrators to help them understand what data are available, where they are, and what they mean.[5]

ORGANIZING DATA ADMINISTRATION

Data administration is essential to ensuring the availability and integrity of shared databases. To ensure that this function is properly performed, its importance must first be recognized. Then the necessary steps must be taken to formally integrate data administration into the organization. These steps include: establishment of a data administration function, assigning data administration roles, and locating data administration in the formal organization. These steps are not necessarily carried out in sequence; indeed, there may be value in performing all three simultaneously. In most large organizations, all three steps have already been undertaken. Many smaller organizations, however, may have yet to embark on them. Even where all three steps have been completed, the second and third are continually monitored and reviewed because of rapid changes in current information technologies.

The mainframe-oriented centralized database architecture of the past is being supplanted by client/server computing based on a distributed architecture. Both computing power and databases are being spread throughout the organization rather than being controlled by a central IS group. In many instances, databases are becoming locally managed by individual workgroups or departments. This transformation creates a need for data administration to be performed where workgroup or departmental databases are located rather than centrally. Where users and databases are linked by local area networks, there is a need for both local and central data administration. Central data administration is responsible for coordinating the functioning of the separate local database administrators.

---

[5]Adapted from Radding, A. Dabbling in data. *Computerworld* November 7, 1994: 116.

Initiating Data Administration

Initially, the need for data administration is unlikely to be recognized by senior management. More likely, it is major data users, or someone in the IS function who first feels the need for data administration. Establishing data administration typically involves convincing management of the importance of data administration and the need for a formal organizational function with assigned roles. A survey of data needs and practices in the organization is one approach to justifying establishment of data administration.

Data administration typically possesses very little organizational power. The power that it has derives from the extent to which senior management recognizes its importance. Management support is crucial since the function affects the generators and users of data throughout the organization.

Implementing data administration requires funds for salaries, tools, office space, and training. Management may feel that data administration can be performed without allocating separate personnel, time, or additional tools. This may be true in a small organization, but larger corporations have too much at stake to permit allocation of insufficient resources. The sponsor of data administration should emphasize the importance of providing the necessary budget to support effective performance.

Selecting Data Administration Staff

If data administration is to be performed as an additional responsibility of existing IS or user staff, the nature and scope of duties must be detailed and clearly assigned to the nominated IS staff. If data administration requires full-time responsibility, either a data administrator is hired, or someone from within the organization is reassigned. An internal hire may be more familiar with organizational needs, but may not possess the necessary skills and thus require additional training. An external hire may come with the experience and skills to transform the organization, but will take time to learn how the organization operates.

Data administration could be undertaken by both IS department staff as well as by users, depending on the size of the organization, and the nature of the databases. Further, where data are distributed in various locations, connected via local or wide area networks, several persons may be assigned data administration roles and responsibilities. Depending on their managerial and technical skills, data administrators will need training for their new positions.

An effective data administrator should possess a variety of interpersonal, business, and technical skills. For system level support, there is a relatively greater emphasis on managerial and business skills. At the project level, a greater degree of technical ability is needed. In both cases, interpersonal and communication skills are essential.

Locating Data Administration in the Organization

Throughout this chapter we have spoken of data administration as a function or set of activities rather than as a department to emphasize that organizations can choose to locate the function in a variety of ways. The most common location for data administration is in the IS department. Where data administration is considered highly critical, there may be a separate data administration manager who reports to the CIO. The data administration staff is organized within this group (see Figure 19–4).

In some organizations, data administration may be included as part of a larger group, such as support services, which may include the information center and help desk staff (see Figure 19–5). The data administration staff also could be located in application development, computer operations, or some other group reporting to the CIO.

A matrix organization, a very different approach from the structures described previously, is another choice for the location of data administration (see Figure 19–6). In a matrix organization, data administration staff belongs to the data administration group in terms of the functions performed, but are also members of specific project teams. Staff members are responsible to the project leader for all project specific responsibilities and deliverables. At the same time, there is a data administration manager who coordinates the performance of data administration activities across all projects and monitors and supervises data administration staff on all projects. Data administration staff report to individual project leaders for the duration of a specific DDLC, while also being administratively supervised by the data administration manager.

A major benefit of a matrix organization is that data administration members are in close communication with other project personnel, and consequently the resulting database may be more closely integrated with the system under development and hence more effectively satisfy user needs. Furthermore, the data administration member may be able to draw on more resources when needed (from the manager, and perhaps from other projects) because of the additional relationship outside of the project. Not all organizations, however, prefer to use this structure. A data administration member has, in effect, two supervisors and this po-

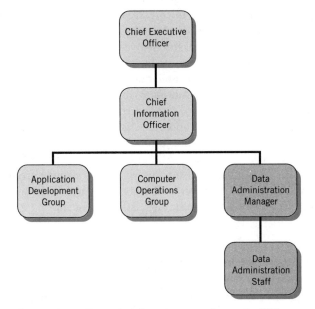

Figure 19–4   Data administration reporting to the CIO

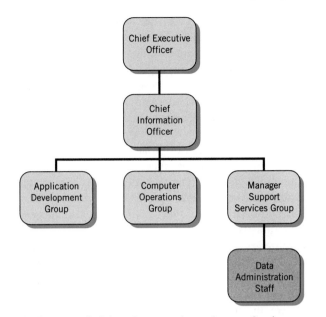

Figure 19–5   Data administration reporting to Support Services

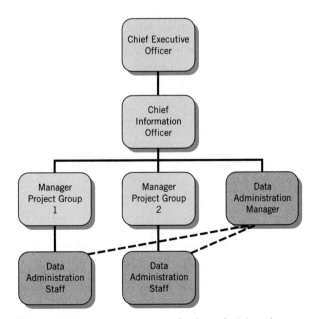

Figure 19–6   A matrix structure for data administration

tentially can result in conflicting situations and affect performance and productivity. Avoiding or resolving conflicts requires extensive communication and coordination among data administration staff, project managers, as well as the data administration manager. When properly managed, a matrix structure is useful in many organizational contexts.

In some instances, data administration is a staff function within the office of the CIO performed by an advisory committee drawn from within the IS function and user departments (Figure 19–7). This committee is concerned typically with system level data administration issues. Within the IS department, the advisory committee may serve to advise and coordinate the data administration activities of project database staff. If the database technology is new to the organization, the committee may undertake database architectural planning and data administration policy development. Once a DBMS is implemented, a more formal and operational organizational structure is typically adopted. In workgroups or user departments, a data administration staff advisory committee helps to manage local databases in distributed database environments.

In decentralized database environments, data administration responsibilities also may be distributed among various departments, divisions, or workgroups. Local data administration reports to its respective workgroup heads, while coordinating its relevant activities via a data administration manager located in the IS function (Figure 19–8). There are two different possibilities here. In one instance—perhaps in multiple, relatively independent divisions—local data administration is fully responsible for local data administration, and the staff manager is mainly a consultant who coordinates the development and enforcement of organizational standards, and provides expert advice to local staff when requested. In another instance—say, multiple offices within a single campus—local data administration may actually report to the staff data administration manager who plans all local data administration activity together with local staff. In this case, the involvement and local responsibility of the data administration manager is far greater. The latter instance is an example of a true matrix organization, while in the former, the extra-departmental relationship is purely consultative.

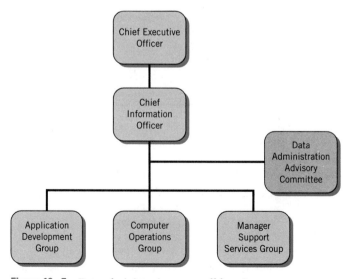

Figure 19–7   Data administration as a staff function

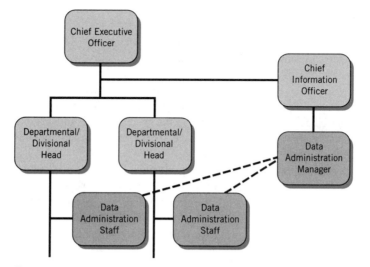

Figure 19–8 Decentralized data administration

The organizational designs described are encountered quite frequently, but are not the only ways to organize data administration. Each situation demands a different way to organize, and the particular needs of the organization need to be fully considered before adopting any particular structure. In most organizations, the nature, importance, and location of data administration changes over time, and is influenced by new technologies, organizational growth, and evolving patterns of database usage. It is important to remain alert to such changes and reorganize data administration when necessary to ensure that the organization's data requirements are constantly satisfied.

The DBMS Market

A recent Ovum report predicts the European and American DBMS market will grow from $4 billion in 1994 to $8.7 billion in 2000. Highest growth will be in the Unix and LAN-server markets due to the ongoing switch from mainframe hierarchical databases.

Key players in the Unix market are Oracle, Sybase and Informix. IBM dominates the hierarchical and relational mainframe markets with IMS and DB2; however, as the importance of this market diminishes, IBM needs to generate sales from its Unix and LAN-server products. Microsoft could dominate the PC market with Access and FoxPro. Its SQL server on Windows NT is aimed at the LAN-server market. But, unless NT makes inroads into the Unix market, Microsoft will not be competing in the largest sector of the market.[6]

---

[6]Adapted from a press release, 'DBMS market to be worth $8.7 billion by 2000,' by Ovum Ltd, London. Oct. 6, 1994.

SUMMARY

Data administration is the task of managing that part of organizational memory that involves electronically available data. Managing electronic organizational memory is important because key organizational decisions are based on information drawn from it, and it is necessary to ensure that reliable data are available when needed. Data administration is carried out at both the system level, which involves overall policies and alignment with organizational goals, as well as the project level, where the specific details of each database are handled. Key modules in data administration are the DBMS, the Data Dictionary/Directory System, user interfaces, and external databases.

Data administration is a function performed by those with assigned organizational roles. Data administration may be carried out by a variety of persons either within the IS department or in user departments. Also, this function may occur at the personal, workgroup, or organizational levels.

Data administration involves communication with management, users, developers, and computer operations staff. It needs the cooperation of all four groups to perform its functions effectively. Since each group may hold very different perspectives, which could lead to conflicts and misunderstandings, it is important for data administration staff to possess superior communication skills. Success at data administration requires a combination of interpersonal, technical, and business skills.

Data administration is complex, and its success partly depends on a range of computer-based tools. Available tools include DD/DS, DBMS, performance monitoring tools, CASE tools, and groupware.

A variety of options are available for organizing data administration, and a choice has to be made based on the prevailing organizational context.

KEY TERMS AND CONCEPTS

Application development life cycle (ADLC)
Change agent
Computer-aided software engineering (CASE)
Data administration
Data dictionary
Data dictionary/directory system (DD/DS)
Data integrity
Data steward
Database administrator
Database developer
Database development life cycle (DDLC)

Database management system (DBMS)
External database
Groupware
Matrix organization
Performance monitoring
Project level data administration
Request for proposal (RFP)
System level data administration
Systems development life cycle (SDLC)
User interface

REFERENCES AND ADDITIONAL READINGS

Bostrom, R. P. Successful application of communication techniques to improve the systems development process. *Information & Management.* 1989; 16: 279–295.

Cause, D. E.; Weinberg, G. M. *Exploring requirements: quality before design.* New York, NY: Dorset House; 1989.

Davenport, T. H.; Eccles, R. G.; Prusak, L. Information politics. *Sloan Management Review.* 1992; 34(1): 53–65.

Doyle, M.; Strauss, D. *How to make meetings work: the new interaction method.* New York, NY: Jove; 1976.

Goodhue, D. L.; Quillard, J. A.; Rockart, J. F. Managing the data resource: a contingency perspective. *MIS Quarterly.* 1988; 12(3): 373–391.

Goodhue, D. L.; Wybo, M. D.; Kirsch, L. J. The impact of data integration on the costs and benefits of information systems. *MIS Quarterly.* 1992; 16(3): 293–311.

Kayser, T. A. *Mining group gold.* El Segundo, CA: Serif; 1990.

Weinberg, G. M. *Becoming a technical leader: an organic problem solving approach.* New York, NY: Dorset House; 1986.

EXERCISES

1. Why do organizations need to manage data?
2. What problems can arise because of poor data administration?
3. What is the purpose of a data dictionary?
4. Do you think a data dictionary should be part of a DBMS or a separate package?
5. How does the management of external databases differ from internal databases?
6. What is the difference between system and project level data administration?
7. What is a data steward? What is the purpose of this role?
8. What is the difference between workgroups and organizational databases? What are the implications for data administration?
9. What is an information architecture?
10. Why do organizations need data standards? Give some examples of typical data items that may require standardization.
11. You have been asked to advise a firm on the capacity of its database system. Describe the procedures you would use to estimate the size of the database and the number of transactions per second it will have to handle.
12. Why would a company issue an RFP?
13. How do the roles of database developer and data administrator differ?
14. What do you think is the most critical task for the user during database development?
15. A medium-sized manufacturing company is about to establish a data administration group within the MIS department. What software tools would you recommend that group acquire?
16. What is a stakeholder? Why should they be involved in database project planning?
17. What support do CASE tools provide for the DDLC?
18. How can groupware support the DDLC?
19. A large international corporation has typically operated in a very decentralized manner with regional managers having considerable autonomy. How would you recommend the corporation establish its data administration function?

20. Describe the personality of a successful data administration manager. Compare your assessment to the personality appropriate for a database technical advisor.

21. Write a job advertisement for a data administrator for your university.

22. What types of organizations are likely to have data administration reporting directly to the CIO?

23. What do you think are the most critical phases of the DDLC? Justify your decision.

24. When might application development and database development proceed independently?

25. Why is database monitoring important? What data would you ask for in a database monitoring report?

Glossary

A

Access time. The amount of time it takes for information to be read from or written to a disk. The sum of search time plus seek time.

Acronym. A word formed by taking the first letters or sounds of each word in a phrase and capitalizing them. For example, RAM (pronounced as a word) is an acronym for random-access memory.

Address. A location in memory where data are stored and can be retrieved.

Administrative strategies. Organizational policies and procedures for maintaining data integrity.

After image. A copy of a record after a change has been made. It is used for forward recovery.

Aggregate entity. An entity created from several entities having similar attributes often distinguished by a prefix or suffix.

Aggregate function. A function, such as COUNT and SUM, that operates on multiple columns.

Aggregation. A special version of an association relationship that reflects strong ties between objects.

Alphanumeric. Data represented in both alphabetic (the letters A–Z) and numeric (the numbers 0–9) form.

ALTER TABLE. An SQL command to add a column to an existing table or change the status of a referential integrity constraint.

Alternate key. A candidate primary key that was not selected as the primary key.

Anomaly. An undesirable result following update, insertion, or deletion of a record.

ANSI. American National Standards Institute.

Application development life cycle (ADLC). The stages of developing and maintaining an application.

Application software. A computer program or set of programs intended to perform a specific function, such as accounting, payroll, word processing, spreadsheet calculating, or database management.

Archie. An Internet service for quickly and easily scanning the directories of anonymous FTP sites.

Architecture. A term used by computer designers to designate the structure of complex information-processing systems. It includes the kinds of instructions and data used, the memory organization and addressing, and the methods by which the system is implemented.

Archival file. A file kept as a permanent record.

Arithmetic expression. An expression consisting of only numbers and operators, for example, 7 + 6.

Artificial intelligence (AI). The branch of computer science that attempts to understand the nature of intelligence and produces new classes of intelligent machines. Areas of study include robotics, speech recognition, image recognition, natural-language processing, and expert systems.

ASCII. An acronym for American Standard Code for Information Interchange. A seven- or eight-bit code that specifies a unique set of binary digits that represent a character set.

Association. Links or connections between object occurrences.

Attribute. A fact about an entity that becomes a column in a table.

Authorization. Permission to take particular actions on a database (e.g., insert rows).

AVG. A SQL built-in function for determining the average of the values in a numeric column.

B

B-tree. A file in which the records are structured into an inverted tree based on a series of midpoints. For example, the root of the tree is the midpoint of a file, and more midpoints occur in each succeeding level.

Backing up. Copying program or data files in case the original is lost or destroyed.

Backup file. A copy of a file made for safekeeping in case the original is lost or damaged.

Bandwidth. The term used as a measure of the capacity of a communication channel, expressed in bits per second.

Base table. An autonomous, named table.

Before image. A copy of a record before a change has been made. It is used for backward recovery.

Benchmarking. The establishment of goals based on best industry practices.

Binary digit. The smallest unit of information capable of being represented in a computer or communication system.

Binary relationship. A relationship between exactly two entities.

Binary search. A search method in which a list of items is successively halved until the sought item is located.

Bit. Short for binary digit.

Bits per second. The number of bits of information that pass a given point in one second. A measure of the carrying capacity of a channel.

Bottom-up design. In software development, a technique that starts with the parts or most basic functional components and proceeds to build a whole or complete program.

Boyce-Codd normal form. A relation in third normal form in which every determinant is a candidate key.

Built-in function. An SQL function such as AVG, COUNT, MAX, MIN, or SUM.

Bulletin board. An Internet service for sharing information within a group of people with a common interest. Also called a discussion list or listserv.

Byte. A sequence of eight consecutive bits used in coding systems to represent one character of data or information.

C

C. A high-level programming language that is very popular because of its transportability between computer systems.

Candidate key. An attribute or group of attributes that is a potential primary key for a table.

Cardinality. The number of rows in a relational table.

Cartesian product. A relational operation on two tables, A and B, that produces all possible combinations of the concatenation of a row from A and a row from B.

Catalog. A database that contains details of databases.

CD-ROM. An acronym for compact disk–read-only memory. An optical disk on which data are encoded for retrieval by a laser.

Change agent. A person leading or guiding an organizational change.

Change information. Information that helps managers determine which actions might successfully close the gap between actual and desired performance.

Channel. A pathway for the transmission of data or information to and from a computer or communication system.

Child. A row on the many side of a 1:m relationship.

Class. In object-oriented programming, a generalized category that describes a group of objects that can exist within it. The class serves as the template from which specific objects are created.

Client. An end user or computer program that requests resources across a network.

Client/server computing. A combination of clients and servers that provides the framework for distributing files and databases across a network. In a database, client/server describes the situation where a client runs a database application (front end) that accesses information from a DBMS on a server (back end).

Clustering. Storing in the same area, or adjacent physical areas, records that are frequently accessed together.

COBOL. An acronym for COmmon Business Oriented Language. A high-level programming language that is used primarily for business-oriented applications.

CODASYL/DBTG. The task group that developed the network data model.

Code. (1) A set of symbols, such as the dots and dashes of the Morse code, that represents another set of symbols, such as the letters of the alphabet. (2) The set of rules that defines the way in which bits can be arranged to represent numbers and letters. Example: ASCII. (3) To write a computer program in a specific programming language.

Column. A vertical group of facts in a table. All values in a column have the same meaning.

Command. An instruction that tells a computer to perform an operation.

COMMIT. An SQL command to make a set of database changes permanent.

Communicability objective. The notion that a database model should facilitate effective and efficient communication between users and MIS personnel.

Communication. (1) A process by which information is exchanged between individuals through the use of a commonly agreed-on set of symbols. (2) From an engineering standpoint, the movement of electronic traffic from one point to another.

Communication server. A device that connects local-area networks (LANs) to wide-area (WANs) or telecommunication networks.

Communication system. A system that consists of senders (transmitters), physical channels, and receivers.

Communication software. Programs that enable a computer to connect to other computers and exchange information.

Compatibility. (1) The ability to connect different computer systems, devices, or software so they can work together. (2) The capability of different computer systems to process the same applications.

Compiler. A computer program (software) that reads a high-level program to (1) check it for spelling and grammar errors and (2) translate it into lower-level language instructions.

Complete database language. A language that can be used for defining a database, creating views, specifying queries, and modifying records.

Complete programming language. A general purpose programming language that can be used to write an entire application (e.g., COBOL).

Complex service. A non-standard service for an object.

Composite key. A key with more than one attribute or column.

Composition. A structure in which one object is composed of others. Also known as a whole/part structure.

Compression. Techniques for compacting data so that they require less storage space.

Computer address. (1) The address of a location within a computer's memory. (2) The Internet identification code of a computer (e.g., uga.cc.uga.edu).

Computer-aided design (CAD). The use of a computer system to aid the process of design.

Computer-aided software engineering (CASE). A set of tools to automate the tasks involved in designing and developing large-scale or complex software projects. Included are data dictionaries, diagram generators, prototyping tools, and consistency-checking tools.

Conceptual schema. An abstract view of a database.

Concurrent program execution. The execution of two or more programs at the same time. They actually take turns using the computer so rapidly that they give the illusion of operating concurrently.

Concurrent update control. An error arising when one transaction's changes are overwritten by another transaction's changes. Also known as the *lost update problem*.

Consistent database. A database in which all data integrity constraints are satisfied.

Control break reporting. A method of reporting a sorted file with new headers or footers each time the sort key changes.

Correlated subquery. A subquery that cannot be evaluated once and for all before the outer query is evaluated. The inner query depends on a variable that changes in the outer query.

COUNT. An SQL built-in function for determining the number of values in a column.

CREATE INDEX. An SQL command to create an index.

CREATE TABLE. An SQL command to create a table.

CREATE VIEW. An SQL command to create a view.

Culture. The set of shared beliefs, values, attitudes, and norms that influences the behavior and expectations of each person in a group.

Cursor. A pointer indicating the row to be processed when using embedded SQL.

Customer service life cycle. The various phases customers pass through as they acquire, use, and dispose of a product or service.

Cycle time. The time taken to complete an activity.

Cylinder. The imaginary surface composed of all the tracks that lie directly above and below one another on a multiple-platter disk pack.

D

Data. A general term meaning the facts, numbers, letters, and symbols processed by a computer or communication system to produce information.

Data access control. Procedures for controlling which individuals, departments, groups of people, transactions, terminals, or application programs can access data.

Data administration. The administration of an organization's data resources.

Data administrator. A person responsible for data administration.

Data communications. The transfer of data or information between computer-related devices.

Data communications manager. Software that manages communication between computers and devices.

Data definition language (DDL). A language for describing the structure of a database.

Data dictionary/directory system (DD/DS). (1) In systems design, a listing of all the data elements and data structures within a system. (2) In a database system, a file that contains descriptions of relationships among a collection of data.

Data Encryption Standard (DES). An encryption system developed by IBM and approved in 1976 by the U.S. National Bureau of Standards for governmental use.

Data independence. The ability of a database to exist independently of specific applications.

Data integrity. Techniques for protecting data from invalid alteration, destruction, or access and ensuring data are accurate and reliable.

Data management. The management of an organization's data resources.

Data manipulation language (DML). A language for describing the processing of a database.

Data model. A graphical description of the entities, attributes, identifiers, and relationships in a database.

Data model quality. An assessment of the degree to which a data model is well-formed and its fidelity of image.

Data processing. A general term that stands for all the logical, arithmetic, and input/output operations that can be performed on data by a computer.

Data quality. The accuracy, completeness, and currency of data.

Data security. Techniques for protecting a database against access or modification without authorization.

Data steward. A person responsible for managing all corporate data for some critical business-related unit or activity.

Data structure. An organizational scheme used to structure or organize data so that they can be stored, retrieved, and manipulated by a program. Examples include records, lists, and arrays.

Data type. A data format (e.g., integer) that can be defined for a column.

Data item. A field or attribute in DL/I and the network model.

Database. (1) A collection of different types of data organized according to a structure that minimizes redundancies and facilitates the manipulation of the data. (2) A collection of one or more files treated as a whole unit.

Database administration. (See data administration.)

Database administrator. (See data administrator.)

Database architecture. A general model for the storage of organizational data.

Database development life cycle (DDLC). The stages of developing and maintaining a database.

Database integrity. Techniques for protecting a database from invalid alteration, destruction, or access and ensuring data are accurate and reliable.

Database machine. A special purpose computer designed for processing databases.

Database management system (DBMS). Software that organizes, manipulates, and retrieves data stored in a database.

Database server. Software that services requests to a database across a network.

Database system. An information system that integrates a collection of data and makes it available to a wide variety of people in an organization.

Database transaction. A group of database modifications treated as a single unit.

Dataflow diagram. A graphical method for illustrating business processes.

DBMS/server. A server that runs a DBMS and processes actions on the database at the request of client programs.

Deadlock prevention. A technique for resolving or avoiding a deadly embrace.

Deadly embrace. A condition that can occur when two transactions are competing for the same resources. Both transactions are waiting to access data the other transaction has locked. Also known as deadlock.

Decision making. The process of identifying and selecting a course of action to solve a specific problem.

Decision quality. An assessment of the decision making process.

Decision support system (DSS). An interactive, user-friendly system for supporting decision-makers.

Decode. To modify information from a computer-readable form into a form that people can read or use.

Decryption. The decoding of an encrypted electronic transmission. (See also encryption.)

Degree. The number of columns in a relational table.

DELETE. The SQL command for deleting one or more rows.

Dependent entity. An entity that relies on another for its existence and identification. A dependent entity is indicated by a bar on its end of a relationship arc.

Determinant. One or more attributes that functionally determine another attribute or attributes. In the case where A -> B, A is the determinant.

Difference. A relational algebra operation on two union-compatible relations A and B, where the new relation contains all rows in A that are not in B.

Digitizing. The process of translating analog data into digital data.

Direct-access file. A type of file organization scheme designed for processing records in an order other than sequential. Also called a random-access file.

Discussion list. (See bulletin board.)

Disk. A circular platter on which a magnetic or reflective coating is applied. Used for long-term storage of data.

Disk array. The combination and synchronization of multiple disk drives into one self-contained unit. A disk array features faster data access and higher data throughput than an equivalent-sized single disk drive.

Disk cartridge. Removable disks that are sealed in a container similar to a videotape cartridge.

Disk drive. A device that houses the motor to spin the disk and the read/write head for accessing and storing information on the disk.

Disk manager. A part of the operating system responsible for physical I/O.

Disk pack. A removable stack of hard disks joined together by a common spindle.

DISTINCT. The keyword used in a SELECT statement to indicate that duplicate rows should be eliminated.

Distributed computing. A type of processing that uses a number of small computers distributed throughout an organization.

Distributed database. A capability in which different parts of a database reside on physically separate computers. The goal is to access information without regard to where the data might be stored.

Distributed query processing. Query processing when a database is distributed.

Distributed transaction processing. Transaction processing when a database is distributed.

Divide. A relational algebra operation that in its simplest form creates a new relation (the quotient) from binary (the dividend) and unary (the divisor) relations. The result of dividing A (the dividend) by B (the divisor) is C (the quotient) is such that for every value of x in C, the pair (x,y) appears in A for all values of y in B.

DL/I (Data Language I). IBM's language to define and process a hierarchical database.

Document. Any text or collection of characters (letters, numbers, spaces, punctuation marks, and other symbols); usually associated with word processing and desktop-publishing applications.

Documentation. (1) The books, manuals, or tutorials that accompany a computer-related product. (2) Written specifications that are a part of the process of developing software.

Domain. The set of all possible legal values of an attribute.

DROP INDEX. The SQL command to delete an index.

DROP TABLE. The SQL command to delete a table.

DROP VIEW. The SQL command to delete a view.

Dynamic model. A representation that describes what a system actually does for any particular event.

E

EBCDIC. An acronym for Extended Binary-Coded Decimal Interchange Code. An eight-bit code designed by IBM that assigns binary digits to specific symbols. Used primarily by IBM computers.

Electronic brainstorming. The use of computer and communications technology to help a group generate ideas.

Electronic conference. A meeting that is conducted over an electronic network using terminals or personal computers.

Electronic mail. An electronic technology that handles the sending and receiving of messages.

Embedded SQL. SQL statements enclosed within the structure of a general purpose programming language.

Empowerment. The act of delegating power and authority to subordinates to further organizational goals.

Encapsulation. The concept whereby data and processes contained within an object are not visible to and cannot be changed by other objects.

Encryption. The coding of an electronic transmission for purposes of security or privacy.

End user. A person who uses a product, as opposed to a person who develops or markets the product.

Entity. Something in the real world that is represented in a data model and about which data must be stored. An entity is the basic building block of a data model.

Entity integrity. Every instance of an entity defined in a relational database is uniquely identified.

Entity-relationship (E-R) model. A data model constructed following the principles of the E-R approach to data modeling.

Equijoin. A join containing both matching columns.

Erasable optical disk. An optical disk that uses lasers to read and write information to and from the disk, but also uses a magnetic material on the surface of the disk and a magnetic write head to achieve erasability.

Exclusive lock. A lock on a data resource that prevents any other transaction from reading or updating the resource.

Exhaustive class. A subclass or a set of subclasses in an inheritance structure that by covering all the relevant objects results in the superclass containing no objects.

EXISTS. The SQL implementation of the *existential quantifier*. EXISTS is used in a WHERE clause to test whether a table contains at least one row satisfying a specified condition. It returns the value *true* if and only if some row satisfies the condition, otherwise it returns *false*.

Expert system. A computer program that solves specialized problems at the level of a human expert.

External database. A database maintained by a party external to an organization.

External memory. Additional memory that is not contained within a system.

External schema. A user's view of a database.

F

Fault-tolerant computer. A computer that uses redundant hardware or software components to prevent failure from disrupting the operation of the system. The system can continue processing while the faulty component is replaced or repaired.

Field. The smallest unit of named data that has meaning in a record. A field usually describes an attribute of the record, such as a name or address.

Fifth normal form. A relation is in fifth normal form (5NF) if and only if every join dependency of the relation is a consequence of the candidate keys of the relation.

File. A collection of organized data stored as one complete unit for processing.

File manager. A single file, its indexes, and a program to handle basic tasks, such as entering, modifying, retrieving, and printing data from the file.

File server. Software that services requests to a file across a network.

File transfer protocol (FTP). A protocol that supports file transfers over the Internet.

First normal form. A relation is in first normal form (1NF) if and only if all columns contain atomic values only.

Flat file. A single file consisting of rows (records) and columns (fields) of data that resemble a two-dimensional spreadsheet.

Floppy disk. A flexible plastic disk coated with a magnetic recording material.

Foreign key. An attribute that is a primary key in the same table or another table. It is the method of recording relations in a relational database.

Fourth normal form. A relation is in fourth normal form (4NF) if it is in BCNF and all multivalued dependencies on the relation are functional dependencies.

Fourth-generation language. A term that encompasses (1) presentation languages, such as query languages and report generators; (2) specialty languages, such as spreadsheets and database languages; (3) application generators that define, input, modify or update, and report data to build applications; and (4) very high-level languages that are used to generate application code. Often abbreviated as 4GL.

Full-text retrieval software. Software that allows text to be indexed, edited, annotated, linked, and searched for in an electronic document.

Fully relational database. A relational database system that supports structures (domains and relations), integrity rules (primary and foreign keys), and a manipulation language (relational algebra).

Functional dependency. A relationship between attributes in which one attribute or group of attributes determines the value of another. It is shown as A -> B and read as "A determines B" or "B is functionally dependent on A."

G

Gap information. Information that reveals a gap between desired and actual performance (e.g., an exception report).

Generalization/specialization. A structure in which one object generally describes more specialized objects (e.g., transportation is a generalization of car).

Geographical information system (GIS). A system that digitizes maps and images of distributions of statistical data and displays them as graphics.

Gigabyte (Gbyte). A unit of measure that is the equivalent of 2^{30}, or 1,073,741,824 bytes.

Global change. Change occurring in many different countries simultaneously.

Goal setting information. Information that helps managers to set realistic targets for expected performance.

Gopher. A distributed document search and retrieval system.

GRANT. An SQL command for granting privileges to a user or users.

Granularity. The level of database resources that can be locked. Locking at the database level is large granularity. Locking a column or row is low granularity.

Graphical user interface (GUI). An interface that uses pictures and graphic symbols to represent commands, choices, or actions.

Graphics. The term encompassing several elements, including color, motion, and resolution, that together result in the ability of a computer to show line drawings, pictures, or animation on a display screen or printer. Differs from an image in that it can contain embedded information.

GROUP BY. The SQL phrase for rearranging a table into groups so that all rows in a group have the same value for a specified column.

Groupware. Application software that supports collaborative work and integrates applications such as electronic mail, conferencing, calendar and scheduling software; workflow software, which automates the routing of business processes and forms over a network; document management software to handle the creation and revision of shared documents on a network; and group support software to facilitate electronic meetings.

H

Hard disk. A disk made of a rigid base, such as aluminum, and coated with a magnetic-oxide layer.

Hash function. The function for computing a *hash address* from a *hash field*.

Hashing. A mathematical technique for assigning a unique number to each record in a file.

HAVING. The SQL keyword specifying the condition the groups returned by a GROUP BY clause must satisfy. HAVING is to groups what WHERE is to rows.

Hierarchical model. A method for storing data in a database that structures data into an inverted tree in which records contain (1) a single root or master key field that identifies the type, location, or

ordering of the records, and (2) a variable number of subordinate fields that defines the rest of the data within a record.

High fidelity image. A data model that faithfully describes the world it is meant to represent.

Homonym. One of a group of words pronounced or spelled the same way but having different meanings.

Host/terminal. A data processing architecture based on using terminals to access a host computer that stores and processes data.

Hybrid architecture. A relatively integrated mix of data processing and storage architectures that has developed over time.

Hybrid object relational model. A data model that combines features of the object and relational models.

Hypermedia. An extension of hypertext that includes graphics, video, sound, and music.

Hypertext. Electronic files in which an author can link information and create nonlinear paths through related material.

I

Identifier. An attribute or collection of attributes that uniquely distinguishes an entity.

Image scanner. A device that converts optically focused images, such as photographs or drawings, into digital images that can then be processed like any other digital data. A photoreceptor device is required to convert reflected light into digital images.

Images. Data in the form of pictures. Differs from a graphic in that they do not contain embedded information.

Imaging system. Information technology that converts paper documents to electronic images.

Impedance problem. The mismatch between set-at-a-time processing of a relational database and record-at-a-time processing of programming languages.

IMS. Information Management System. IBM's transaction processing system that includes a data communications monitor (IMS/DC) and an implementation of DL/I (IMS/DB).

IN. An SQL keyword preceding a set of values to be searched (e.g., FNAME IN ('Tom', 'Dick', 'Harry')).

Independent entity. An entity that is central to a data model and often prominent in the client's mind. It often has a single, arbitrary identifier.

Index. A list containing an entry for each record in a file organized in a certain way.

Index sequential. A file organization method that provides both sequential and direct-access capability.

Index set. A tree structure providing fast direct access to records in a B-tree.

Information. Data transformed into a form and content relevant for a particular situation.

Information delivery system. A system that provides information to those who need it.

Information engineering. A general approach using CASE tools to develop an enterprise-wide plan for systems development and maintenance.

Information hardness. A subjective measure of the accuracy and reliability of some information.

Information integration. The process of assembling data in many forms and from many sources to satisfy a user's needs.

Information organization. An

organization that relies on information to create profitable products and services.

Information processing. The work that information systems perform, consisting of responding to input, processing that input according to instructions, and providing output.

Information requirements. A specification of the information a user or group of users needs to solve problems.

Information revolution. (1) A term used to indicate the point at which modern society shifted from being an industrial society to being an information society. No agreed-on date. (2) The reshaping of economic, social, political, and technical structures resulting from the teaming of people and computers.

Information richness. The concept that information can be rich or lean depending on the information delivery medium.

Information satisficing. The practice of decision-makers collecting enough information to make a satisfactory decision.

Information service. A business specializing in the collection and distribution of information.

Information society. A society structured around the principles of information as a commodity and as a strategic resource.

Information superhighway. The concept that every home and business will be connected electronically over a vast network of links to a wide variety of sources of information and entertainment.

Information system. A system that takes input, processes it, and produces information as output.

Information technology. A collective term for computer-and-communication hardware and system-and-application software.

Inheritance. In object-oriented programming, the passing along of certain behavior and structure from a class to its descendants. Inheritance allows new objects to be created from old ones.

INSERT. The SQL command for adding one or more rows to a table.

Instance. A particular occurrence of an entity.

Integrity constraints. Rules and procedures for maintaining data integrity.

Inter-file clustering. Clustering is applied to records in several files.

Internal memory. Memory contained within a system.

Internal schema. A low-level description of a database. It specifies data types for fields and may indicate other physical details.

Internet. A worldwide network of computers and computer networks at private organizations, government institutions, and universities, over which people share files, send electronic messages, and have access to vast quantities of information.

Internet relay chat (IRC). An Internet service that supports real time conversations. Internet CB radio.

Intersect. A relational algebra operation performed on two-union compatible tables, A and B, that results in a new table containing the rows that are in both A and B.

Intersection entity. The byproduct on an m:m relationship. It stores data about an m:m relationship.

Intra-file clustering. Clustering is applied to records within a single file.

Inverted list. An alternative term for an index.

ISO. International Standards Organization.

Isolation. A preventive strategy that involves administrative procedures to insulate a physical database from destruction.

J

Join. A relational algebra operation on two tables, A and B, that produces a new table containing the concatenation of a row from A and a row from B where the rows in A and B satisfy a specified condition (e.g., column (a) of A = column (b) of B).

Journal. A file containing a record of database changes or transactions.

K

Key. A field in a file used to identify records for purposes of retrieval or sorting.

Kilobyte (Kbyte). A unit of measure equal to 2^{10} or 1024 bytes.

Knowledge. The capacity to request, structure, and use information.

Knowledge base. The collection of facts, data, beliefs, assumptions, and heuristic methods about a problem area.

Knowledge work. A term used for occupations in which the primary activities involve receiving, processing, and transmitting information. Often called information work.

L

Layer. A level of detail of an OO model.

Legacy system. A system developed using prior technology that must be maintained because it still provides useful information or processes important business transactions.

Legal strategies. Externally imposed laws, rules, and regulations for maintaining data integrity.

LIKE. The SQL keyword preceding a

description of characters to be searched for within a particular column (e.g., FNAME LIKE '%Fred%').

Linked list. A data storage structure that maintains relationships between records using pointers.

Local-area network (LAN). A communication channel along with interface circuitry that connects devices, such as computers or peripherals, within a limited geographical distance.

Locking. Allocating a particular database resource to a transaction or user.

Log. A file containing a record of database changes or transactions.

Logical record. A record that is defined according to its content or function.

Loop. A series of program instructions that is performed repeatedly until a specified condition is satisfied.

M

Magnetic disk. A direct access storage device that uses magnetization and demagnetization to store data on a magnetic surface.

Magnetic tape. A sequential access storage device that uses magnetization and demagnetization to store data on a magnetic surface.

Magneto – optical disk. A read – write optical disk.

Mainframe. A class of computer providing large storage capacity, high-speed processing, and complex data-handling capabilities.

Management information system (MIS). A system that gathers, condenses, and filters data until they become information, then makes them available on time, and in a useful form, for use in decision making at various levels of management within an organization.

Managerial work. A manager's typical behavior and activities when working.

Many-to-many recursive relationship. A relationship within a single entity in which one instance in the entity can be related to many instances in the same entity, and any instance receiving multiple relationships can itself be related to many instances in the same entity.

Many-to-many relationship. A relationship between two entities in which one instance in the first entity can be related to many instances in the second entity, and one instance in the second entity can be related to many instances in the first entity.

Mass storage. A high capacity storage device that is typically slower than magnetic disk, but less costly per megabyte.

Master file. A type of file that can be thought of as a relatively permanent collection of records.

Matrix organization. An organizational structure in which an employee reports to both a functional or divisional manager and to a project or group manager.

MAX. An SQL built-in function for determining the largest value in a column.

Megabyte (Mbyte). A unit of measure that is the equivalent of 2^{20} or 1,048,576 bytes.

Member. A record type that is at the many side of a 1:m relationship in the CODASYL/DBTG model.

Memory. The component of a computer system that stores programs and data while waiting to be processed by the CPU. Also called primary storage.

Message passing. The method by which objects can communicate.

Method. A set of instructions attached to an object. Also known as a service.

Micro. (1) In precise measurement, a prefix meaning one millionth. (2) In inexact measurement, a prefix meaning small. (3) Short for microcomputer.

Microcomputer. A computer system based on a single-chip microprocessor as the central processing unit.

Microsecond. A measure of time equivalent to one-millionth (1/1,000,000) of a second.

Millisecond. A measure of time equivalent to one-thousandth (1/1000) of a second.

MIN. An SQL built-in function for determining the smallest value in a column.

Minicomputer. A type of medium-sized computer introduced in the 1960s that provides lower-cost processing and storage capacities than the larger mainframe computers.

MIPS. An acronym for million instructions per second. Most often used as a unit of measure for comparing the processing speed of different computers.

Mirroring. The technique of writing identical copies of a record to each drive of a RAID unit.

MIS department. A department within an organization that helps people put information to work.

Mosaic. A World Wide Web (WWW) browser or client.

Multi-user database. A database that can be concurrently accessed by more than one person or transaction.

Multimedia. The combination of text with dynamic data types such as sound, animation, and video.

Multiple user dimensions (MUDs). Addictive role playing games played on the Internet mainly by teenagers and college students.

Multiprocessing. A computer system that uses two or more processors that share memory and input and output devices.

Multiprogramming. A computer system in which two or more programs are executed concurrently by one computer. In effect, the programs take turns running, usually giving the user the illusion of being the only user of the system.

Multitasking. A technique for concurrently executing tasks, or basic units of work performed by a program, on the same computer system. It is similar to multiprogramming, except the processor may be working on several portions of a program instead of several programs.

Multi-user. Systems that allow several users to share a computer's processor, memory, and mass storage simultaneously. Often characterized by systems with several terminals connected to a single central processor.

N

Nanosecond. A measure of time equivalent to one-billionth (1/1,000,000,000) of a second.

Natural join. A join from which one of the matching columns has been deleted.

Natural-language interface. An interface that allows the user to input simple English or other natural-language phrases in lieu of complex computer commands.

Network. An interconnected system of computers.

Network data model. A data model supporting network relationships.

Network model. A technique used in database systems to store data by combining records with a linked list of pointers.

Node. The term for a device, such as a terminal, computer, or disk drive, connected to a communication network.

Normal form. One or more rules for governing the structure of tables.

Normalization. The process of converting a table in low normal form to a higher normal form.

NOT. The SQL keyword to select the opposite of a condition (e.g., NOT EXISTS).

NOT EXISTS. The negative of EXISTS. It is used in a WHERE clause to test whether all rows in a table do not satisfy a specified condition. It returns the value *true* if there are no rows satisfying the condition, otherwise it returns *false*.

NREN (National Research and Education Network). A U.S. government project to create a national information highway.

Null. A value that may be unknown, not required, not applicable, undefined, or missing. It is *not* a blank or zero.

O

Object. A module that contains both data and instructions and can perform specific tasks. In software engineering, an object is an instance of a class or a logical grouping of objects.

Object class. A set of objects with a common structure.

Object code. Output from a compiler or an assembler that is linked with other code to produce executable machine-language code.

Object data language (ODL). A language for defining objects.

Object data model (ODM). A defined set of built-in types that is used to create and represent composite structures that mirror real world objects.

Object identifier. An attribute used to uniquely identify an object.

Object Management Group (OMG). An industry group with the goal of creating and promulgating standards for OO technology and object interaction.

Object model. In database systems, data and instructions are combined into objects—modules that perform specific tasks when they are sent an appropriate message.

Object-orientation (OO). An approach to systems development, design, and programming based on object concepts.

Object-oriented Database Management System (ODBMS). Software that organizes, manipulates, and retrieves data stored in an object-oriented database.

Object-oriented programing. A technique in which the programmer breaks the problem into modules called objects, which contain both data and instructions and can perform specific tasks. The programmer then organizes the program around the collection of objects. An example is Smalltalk.

One-to-many (1:m) recursive relationship. A relationship within a single entity in which one instance in the entity can be related to many instances in the same entity, and any instance receiving multiple relationships is itself related to only one instance.

One-to-many (1:m) relationship. A relationship between two entities in which one instance in the first entity can be related to many instances in the second entity, and an instance in the second entity can be related to at most one instance in the first entity.

One-to-one (1:1) recursive relationship. A relationship within a single entity in which one instance in the entity can be related to at most one instance in the same entity, and an instance receiving a relationship can itself be related to at most one instance in the same entity.

One-to-one (1:1) relationship. A relationship between two entities in which one instance in the first entity can be related to at most one instance in the second entity, and an instance in the second entity is related to at most one instance in the first entity.

OO model. A graphical representation of objects in an application.

OO programming language (OOPL). A language that supports the OO concepts.

Optical disk. Disks that record and retrieve data using laser beams of light instead of magnetic methods. There are three types of optical disks: read only, also called CD–ROM; write once, which can be recorded on once by the end user; and erasable, which combines optical and magnetic techniques to record on the surface of the disk.

ORDER BY. The SQL clause for identifying columns on which to sort rows.

Organizational change. The adoption of a new idea or behavior by an organization.

Organizational memory. An organization's record of the details necessary for transacting business and making decisions.

Owner. A record that is at the one

end of a 1:m relationship in CODASYL/DBTG database.

P

Page. A unit of disk storage.

Parent. A row on the one side of a 1:m relationship.

Parity. A bit, used for error checking, that is part of a binary code that indicates the number of 1's in the code.

Password. A unique, usually secret code used to identify users, which allows them to access a system. The system can be accessed by multiple users.

Performance monitoring. Collecting statistics on the performance of a system (e.g., number of transactions per minute).

Peripheral. A device that operates in conjunction with — but is not a part of — a computer, such as a printer, disk drive, or graphics tablet.

Persistent object. An object that exists between executions of a program.

Personal computer. A microcomputer usually targeted to the information processing needs of an individual, often called a microcomputer.

Physical file. The way in which the actual data in a database system are stored and accessed on a medium such as a disk.

Physical record. A record that is composed of one or more logical records.

Pointer. An address that specifies a storage location where data can be found.

Polymorphism. The capability to send a common message to objects of different types. Each object will respond with its own particular behavior.

Primary key. The candidate key selected as the unique identifier of a row in a table.

Product. A relational operation on two tables, A and B, that produces all possible combinations of the concatenation of a row from A and a row from B.

Project. A relational algebra operation that creates a new relation from some of the columns of an existing relation.

Project level database administration. Management and support of the development and use of a specific database system.

Protocol. A formal set of rules for specifying the format and relationships when exchanging information between communicating devices.

Prototyping. The process of building working models of a system's inputs, outputs, and files.

Public key encryption. An encryption system comprising public and private keys. The public key can be freely distributed because it is quite separate from the private key.

Q

Qualified name. The name of a column when it is prefixed by the name of the table in which it is found (e.g., STOCK.STKPRICE).

Query. A question or request for information.

Query by example (QBE). A fill-in-the-blanks approach to questioning a database. The user searches for information by filling out a query form on the display screen.

Query language. The capability to question a database or file of information without any knowledge of how or where the information is stored.

R

RAID. An acronym for a redundant array of inexpensive or independent drives. It uses a combination of mirroring and striping to give greater data protection.

RAM. An acronym for random-access memory. Its name comes from the method used to access information from the memory: random access. This means that it takes the same amount of time to access any one piece of information as it does another.

Random-access device. A device that can read and write information at any location on the device in the same amount of time, regardless of its physical location.

Random-access method. A method of accessing a file that allows a program to read or write any record in the file in the same amount of time without regard to its physical location.

Rapid application development. An approach to application development that stresses completion of a system in a short period.

Read-only optical disks. Optical disks that cannot be written on and so have the functional equivalency of read-only memory (ROM).

Record. A collection of related data treated as a unit (e.g., the payroll data about one person).

Recovery. The process of restoring a database to a consistent state.

Recursive relationship. A relationship within a single entity (e.g., a monarch is preceded by one other monarch).

Referential integrity constraint. The requirement that a foreign key cannot be defined unless its corresponding primary key exists.

Relation. A two-dimensional table in the formal terminology of relational databases.

Relational algebra. A set of high level operators that operates on relations.

Relational database. A database consisting of relations or tables.

Relational Database Management System (RDBMS). Software that organizes, manipulates, and retrieves data stored in a relational database.

Relational model. A technique used in database systems in which one or more flat files or tables create relationships among the tables on the basis of a common field in each of the tables.

Relationally complete. A relational database management system that supports SQL, but not domains or integrity rules.

Relationship. An association between entities or objects.

Relationship descriptor. A description of a relationship.

Remote job entry. The electronic submission of a program to be executed on a remote computer.

Replication. Maintaining copies of a database at several sites.

Request for proposal (RFP). A document sent to vendors seeking their response to a list of mandatory and optional capabilities and features.

Requirements planning. A broad term that includes planning for outputs, inputs, and file/storage and processing requirements. It also includes specifying any constraints and the costs and benefits associated with the system.

Restrict. A relational algebra operation that creates a new relation from some of the rows of an existing relation. This operation is sometimes called select, but

should not be confused with the SQL SELECT statement.

REVOKE. An SQL command for removing privileges from a user or users.

ROLLBACK. An SQL command to reverse a set of temporary database changes.

Rollback. The process of recovering a database by applying before images to return the database to a consistent earlier state.

Roll forward. The process of recovering a database by applying after images to bring the database to a consistent state.

ROM. An acronym for read-only memory. A permanent memory whose contents can neither be erased nor written over—thus, the name, read-only memory.

Root. The top record or node in a tree.

Row. All columns in a table pertaining to the same instance of an entity (e.g., all the facts about a share).

S

Scalar function. A function operating on a single value (e.g., DAYS).

Scanner. A device that examines a pattern and converts it into a digital representation suitable for computer processing. Patterns then can be manipulated into a form suitable for the application.

Scenario. A typical event or sequence of events in the problem domain and the related behavior of the information system.

Search time. The time required to rotate the needed record under the read/write head of a magnetic disk.

Second normal form. A relation is in second normal form (2NF) if and only if it is in 1NF and all non-key columns are dependent on the key.

Secondary index. In DL/I, an index on a data item other than the primary key.

Secondary storage. The component of a computer system in which programs and data are stored while not in use.

Sector. The smallest block of physical data that can be written to or read from a disk device.

Security. Precautions taken to ensure that data are protected from unauthorized use or modification.

Seek time. The time required to position the read/write head over the proper track on a magnetic disk.

Segment. In DL/I, a collection of fields that constitutes a node in a database record.

SELECT. The SQL command for retrieving rows from a database.

Sequence set. A single-index to the data in a file.

Sequential file. A file organization method that involves storing records in a predetermined sequence based on one or more key fields.

Server. A computer running software that fulfills requests from clients across a network.

Service. A set of instructions attached to an object. Also known as a method.

Set. A structure for representing a 1:m relationship in the CODASYL/DBTG model.

Set processing. The capability of a language to process multiple records at a time.

Shareable data. Data that can be readily accessed, not necessarily simultaneously, by more than one person.

Simple service. A standard service that nearly all objects need to be able to perform (e.g., create).

Social memory. A society's record of the details necessary for maintaining itself.

Social network. A relationship between a group of people.

Software. Programs that control the functions of a computer system.

Sparse index. An index that does not contain an entry for every record. Also called a non-dense index.

Special register. In SQL, a built-in value (e.g., CURRENT DATE).

SQL (Structured query language). A query language that manipulates data in a relational database.

Standard operating procedures. The rules and procedures for handling routine or common tasks.

Static model. A representation that shows what objects are capable of doing and remembering.

Storage device. A device (e.g., filing cabinet or hard disk) for storing data.

Storage medium. The material used for storing data (e.g., paper, magnetic film).

Storage structure. A formalized arrangement for storing data.

Strategy. A plan of action designed to cope with change, competition, and uncertainty.

Streaming tape. A form of magnetic tape that is specifically designed to store backup copies of disk files. Also called cartridge tape.

Striping. The technique of writing different parts of a record and parity data to different drives in a RAID unit.

Structured analysis. The examination of a complex problem by dividing it into simple functions.

Structured design. The process of designing the components of a computer program and their interrelationship in the best possible way.

Structured programming. The application of top-down design methods to programming.

Subclass. In a generalization/specialization hierarchy, an object that is a specialization of the generalization.

Subject. A cluster of objects. The subject layer reduces the overall complexity of an OO model.

Subordinate entity. An entity that stores data about an entity that varies among instances. It is used when an entity consists of mutually exclusive classes that have different descriptions.

Subquery. A query nested within another query.

Subroutine. A part of a program that can be executed repeatedly by a single statement.

SUM. An SQL built-in function for determining the sum of values in a numeric column.

Superclass. In a generalization/specialization hierarchy, the collection of objects that makes the generalization.

Supercomputers. The fastest computers made.

Synonym. A word that means the same as another word.

SYSCATALOG. In SQL, a catalog table containing a row for every base table or view in the database.

SYSCOLUMNS. In SQL, a catalog table containing a row for every column of every table in the database.

SYSINDEXES. In SQL, a catalog table containing a row for every index in the database.

System. (1) In general systems theory, a set or arrangement of parts acting together to perform a function. (2) In systems analysis, a network of interrelated procedures performed by people with the aid of tools or machines.

System level database administration. Management of issues applicable to the entire database environment and all databases managed within that environment.

System software. Programs or commands used to control the operation of the computer system.

Systems analysis. The process of understanding a user's needs and, from those needs, deriving the functional requirements of a system.

Systems development life cycle (SDLC). The stages of developing and maintaining a system.

T

Table. In relational database terminology, a table consists of rows and columns. Each row identifies a record and each column corresponds to a field. Also called a relation.

Talk. An Internet service supporting real-time conversations. The Internet version of the telephone.

Tape drive. A device that stores data recorded on magnetic tape.

Technical strategies. Computer-based procedures designed to maintain data integrity.

Telnet. The main Internet protocol for connecting to a remote machine.

Temporary name. A name given to a table or view that remains current only for the duration of a query.

Terabyte (Tbyte). A unit of measure equivalent to 2^{40}, or 1,099,511,627,776 bytes. Used to measure capacities of large-scale mass-storage devices.

Terminal. A device that is used in communication systems to enter or receive data.

Text database. A collection of words such as articles in the *Wall Street*

Journal or a series of legal abstracts. Text databases are stored either on-line or on CD-ROM and include the means to search through massive amounts of data to answer specific questions.

Third normal form. A relation is in third normal form (3NF) if and only if it is in second normal form and has no transitive dependencies.

Top-down approach. A technique used by systems analysts and software developers that refers to starting with the whole problem and developing more and more detail as the solution develops.

Track. A concentric circle on which data are stored on a disk.

Track density. The number of tracks per inch on a disk.

Transaction. An event about which data are recorded and processed, for example, a request for a seat on an airline flight.

Transaction file. A type of file in which records created during the input process are stored until needed for further processing.

Transaction processing. The processing of transactions.

Transitive dependency. The situation in a relation where if A determines B, and B determines C, then A determines C.

Transparent. A term used by computer designers to indicate a function of which the user is unaware. In effect, the user "sees right through it" and does not notice that it is there.

Tree structure. A collection of records or other data structures in which the child has at most one parent.

Tuple. A row in a two-dimensional database.

U

Union. A relational algebra operation on two union-

compatible relations A and B, where the new relation contains all rows that are in both A and B, with duplicate rows deleted.

Union compatible. The condition that two tables have the same number of columns and that values in corresponding columns are drawn from the same domain.

Unique key. A key that cannot have duplicate values.

UPDATE. The SQL command for updating one or more rows of a table.

Update. A term for the modification of records in a master file by replacing older information with more current information.

Use relationship. A communication relationship between objects.

Usenet news. A vast set of discussion lists which can be accessed through the Internet.

User friendly. A term describing how easy a system or program is to learn and use and how gently it tolerates errors or mistakes on the part of the user.

User interface. That portion of a program that handles the human interaction with the program.

Userid. A person's user identification code.

V

Validation. The process of ensuring data quality.

Veronica. An Internet service for searching Gopher sites by key words in a menu or document titles.

Video conference. A conference held by means of one- or two-way interactive television.

Videotex. A form of electronic publishing.

View. A table constructed dynamically from operations on base tables. Also called a virtual table.

Voice data. A record of speech or sound.

Voice mail. A technology in which spoken messages are digitized, stored in computers, and later retrieved by the recipient.

Volatile file. A file in which a high percentage of records accessed are changed or records are added or deleted.

VSAM (Virtual Storage Access Method). IBM's implementation of the B-tree concept.

W

Well-formed data model. A data model that clearly communicates information to the client. It obeys all the construction rules.

WHERE. The SQL keyword specifying the condition that the rows returned by a SELECT statement must satisfy.

Whole/part structure. An object structure in which one object is composed of others. Also known as a composition.

Wide area information servers (WAIS). An easy-to-use full-text Internet information retrieval service.

WIMP. Windows, icon, mouse, pointer.

Winchester disk. A high-speed, medium- to large-capacity, sealed magnetic-storage medium for computer systems.

Workflow. The manual or electronic flow of work between people.

Workgroup computing. Computer and communication technology that facilitates the process of people working together in groups that are electronically connected.

Workstation. A type of small computer targeted to the needs of high-performance specialized applications, such as computer-aided design, publishing, modeling, and visualization.

World Wide Web (WWW). A body of software, a set of protocols, and conventions based on hypertext and multimedia techniques that make the Internet easy for anyone to browse and add contributions.

Write-once read-many (WORM) optical disks. Blank disks that are recorded on by the user. To write data, a powerful beam of laser light burns tiny spots or pits into the coating that covers the surface of these disks. Once burned in, the spots are not erasable. Also called write-once, read-mostly, or WORM.

WYSIWYG. An acronym for what-you-see-is-what-you-get. The display of information in a form that very closely resembles what will eventually be printed. The term is often used in word processing, desktop publishing, and typesetting.

Photo Credits

Chapter 1　Page 9: Frank Pryon/Courtesy Apple Computers. Page 22: Courtesy Genasys II Inc.

Chapter 2　Page 37: Directorate General of Antiquities. Page 54: Courtesy Compro Supply Company.

Chapter 11　Page 279: Courtesy Seagate Technology. Page 292: Courtesy Conner Peripherals, Inc. Page 297: Courtesy Digital Equipment Corp. Page 300: Courtesy Eastman Kodak Company. Page 301: Courtesy Eastman Kodak Company.

Chapter 12　Page 309: Paul Shambloom/Cray. Page 310: Courtesy of International Business Machines Corporation. Page 311: Courtesy of International Business Machines Corporation. Page 313: Courtesy Digital Equipment Corp.

Chapter 16　Page 403: Courtesy Ventana Corp. Page 406: Courtesy Intel. Page 420: Courtesy Grolier. Page 426: Courtesy Eastman Kodak Company.

Chapter 17　Page 459: Courtesy CompuServe, Inc.

Chapter 19　Page 528: Courtesy of LBMS, Inc.

Index

A

Abstraction levels, object-oriented database management system modeling, 373
Accuracy, organizational memory attributes, 14
Active on-line catalog, fully relational database, 339
Activities, data modeling, quality improvement, 157–159
Adding features, object-oriented database management systems, 372
Address books, individual memory systems, 7
Addresses:
    data modeling recommendations, 164–166
    Internet, 437–439
Aggregate entity, data modeling, entity types, 161
Aggregate functions, standard Query Language (SQL), data manipulation, 217
Agricultural society, information and, 36
ALL, ONLY and, SQL playbook, 249–250
Alternate key, data structures, relational model, 331
ALTER TABLE, Standard Query Language (SQL), data definition, 207–208
American National Standards Institute (ANSI), 63, 198, 272–273
America Online, described, 455–456
AND, intersection, SQL playbook, 254–255
ANOTHER FULL TOSS, SQL playbook, 238
Archie server, Internet, 444–445
Architecture arithmetic, data storage/processing architecture, 316–318
Association relationships, object-oriented database management system modeling, 385
AT LEAST some, SQL playbook, 240, 250, 253
Attribute layer, object-oriented database management system modeling, 383–385
Attributes:
    data modeling components, 143–144
    data modeling recommendations, 164
    single-entity modeling, 61
Augmented human information processing system, 3
Authorization rules, data access control, confidentiality, 495–496
Averaging:
    with condition, SQL playbook, 256
    detailed averaging, SQL playbook, 261
    difference from average, SQL playbook, 260
    with GROUP BY, SQL playbook, 242
    with join, condition, and grouping, SQL playbook, 256
    more than the average with grouping, SQL playbook, 259
    with multiple grouping, SQL playbook, 259
    with multiple joins
        multiple groupings, and condition, SQL playbook, 260
        SQL playbook, 256–257
    simplest, SQL playbook, 260

B

Backup, data integrity, 476–479
Backward recovery (rollback), described, 480
Basic structures (relational model), 185–197
    one entity, 185–189
    relationship descriptors as identifiers, 191–196
    two entities, 189–191
Benchmarking, organizational change and, 41–42
BLOB, Standard Query Language (SQL), data definition, 207
Boyce-Codd normal form, data modeling, normalization, 172–173
Broadcast, groupwear products, 412
B-trees, data structures, 285–287
Built-in functions, single-entity modeling, database querying, 78

C

Calculating, single-entity modeling, database querying, 77
Candidate key, data structures, relational model, 330
Catalog, Standard Query Language (SQL), 226–227
CD-ROM, optical data storage devices, 298–299
Central site reliance, data storage/processing architecture, 322
Change:
    accommodation of, object-oriented database management systems, 372
    enablement, groupwear and, 408–409
    information for, organizational change and, 43–44
CHAR, Standard Query Language (SQL), data definition, 205–206

Character sorting, numeric sorting versus, single-entity modeling, database querying, 77

Chat and Talk, Internet, 442

Classes, object-oriented database management systems, 367–368
modeling, 377

Client-developer mind-frame gap, object-oriented database management system modeling, 373–374

Client/server architecture, data storage/processing architecture, 315–316

Client/server designs, data storage/processing architecture, 318–319

Clipper Chip, 498

Clustering, head movement reduction techniques, 280

CODASYL/DBTG:
data manipulation language, Hierarchical and network models, 359–361
network data model and, 355

Column definition, Standard Query Language (SQL), data definition, 201

Column name qualification, Standard Query Language (SQL), data manipulation, 211

Column ordering, database querying, 75

Communication, data administration, 523

Comparing to average:
with a join, SQL playbook, 258
with a product, SQL playbook, 259

Comparisons, SQL playbook, 243

Complete database language, Standard Query Language (SQL), 198

Complex counting, SQL playbook, 257

Composite key, Standard Query Language (SQL), data definition, 199

Comprehensive data sublanguage rule, fully relational database, 339

CompuServe, described, 456–457

Computer-aided design (CAD):
graphics, organizational memory components, 21, 23
information delivery systems, 52

Computer operations, data administration, 522–523

Concurrent update control, quality maintenance, 487–490

Conditions, summing with joins, conditions, and grouping, SQL playbook, 257–258

Confidentiality, 490–498
data access control, 493–496
encryption, 496–498
general model, 491–493

Consistency, data modeling recommendations, 164

Context, data modeling, quality improvement, 147–148

Contraction, data modeling recommendations, 162–163

Control break reporting, database querying, one-to-many relationship, 98–101

Conversation:
information delivery systems, 50
organizational memory components, 17–18

Copies, DIVISION with, SQL playbook, 246

Correlated subquery, Standard Query Language (SQL), data manipulation, 217

COUNT:
GROUP BY and, IN clause with, Standard Query Language (SQL) playbook, 242
SQL playbook, 245, 252

Counting pairs, SQL playbook, 261

CREATE INDEX, Standard Query Language (SQL), data definition, 210

CREATE TABLE, Standard Query Language (SQL), data definition, 201–203

CREATE VIEW, Standard Query Language (SQL), data definition, 208–210

Creativity, information and, 36

Customer service, organizational change and, information as means of change, 45–46

Cylinders, head movement reduction techniques, 279–280

D

Data:
object-oriented database management system modeling, 374
organizational memory and, 28–29

Data access control, confidentiality, 493–496

Data administration, 503–538. See also Data integrity
database administration contrasted, 508
database environment, 505–508
database levels and, 509–510
database management system (DBMS), 527–530
functions and roles, 509
interfaces, 520–523
organization, 530–535
overview of, 504–505
project level functions, 515–520
system level functions, 510–514
tools for, 523–527

Database:
defined, 59
single entity, 61–88. See also Single-entity modeling

Database access, data structures, 277

Database administration, data administration contrasted, 508

Database architectures, development of, 271–274
Database creation:
    many-to-many relationship, 111–113. *See also*
        Many-to-many relationship
    one-to-many relationship, 91–95
    single-entity modeling, 63–67. ≤i>See also Single-
        entity modeling
Database environment, data administration,
        505–508
Database integrity, hierarchical and network models,
        358–359
Database management system (DBMS), data
        administration, 527–530
Database querying. *See* Querying
Data control, organizational memory problems, 26
Data definition, Standard Query Language (SQL),
        199–211
Data definition language (DDL):
    database creation, 63
    defined, 60
    hierarchical and network models, 355–358
    Standard Query Language (SQL), 198
Data dictionary, data administration, 507
Data dictionary/directory system, data
        administration tools, 525–527
Data extraction, hierarchical and network models,
        361–362
Data integration, organizational memory problems, 28
Data integrity, 471–502. *See also* Data administration
    confidentiality, 490–498
        data access control, 493–496
        encryption, 496–498
        general model, 491–493
    data administration and, 511
    existence protection, 475–483
        backup and recovery, 476–482
        generally, 475
        recovery strategies, 479–481
    overview of, 471–474
    quality maintenance, 483–490
        concurrent update control, 487–490
        data validation, 484–486
        update authorization, 483
    single-user and multi-user systems, 474–475
Data item, DDL, hierarchical and network models,
        355
Data management, organizational memory and, 5
Data manipulation, Standard Query Language
        (SQL), 211–223
Data manipulation language (DML):
    CODASYL/DBTG, 359–361
    database creation, 63
    defined, 60
    Standard Query Language (SQL), 198

Data model, defined, 60
Data modeling, 142–184
    components of, 142–145
        attributes, 143–144
        entity, 143
        identifier, 145
        relationship, 144–145
    entity types, 159–161
        aggregate entity, 161
        dependent entity, 159
        independent entity, 159
        intersection entity, 160
        subordinate entity, 161
    importance of, 60
    normalization, 168–178
        Boyce-Codd normal form, 172–173
        fifth normal form, 174–178
        first normal form, 169
        fourth normal form, 173–174
        functional dependency, 169
        generally, 168–169
        second normal form, 169–170
        third normal form, 170–171
    overview of, 142
    quality improvement, 146–159
        detail and context, 147–148
        families, 150–152
        geography, 148–149
        historical data, 154–155
        leasing, 155–157
        libraries, 152–154
        plans and activities, 157–159
    recommendations, 162–168
    single entity, 61–88. *See also* Single-entity
        modeling
    varieties of, 179–180
Data storage devices, 290–302
    magnetic technology, 291–298
        fixed disk, 292–293
        floppy disk, 297
        generally, 291–292
        mass storage, 298
        RAID, 293–296
        removable magnetic disk, 296
        tape, 297
        tape cartridges, 297
    optical technology, 298–302
        CD-ROM, 298–299
        generally, 298
        magneto-optical disk, 301–302
        WORM, 300
    overview of, 290–291
Data storage/processing architecture, 307–326
    architecture arithmetic, 316–318

Data storage/processing architecture *(Continued)*
  client/server architecture, 315–316
  client/server designs, 318–319
  DBMS/server, 314–315
  distributed database, 319–320
  file/server, 314
  host/terminal, 311–312
  hybrid architecture, 320–324
  LAN-based architecture, 312–313
  overview of, 307–308
  personal database, 309–311
  remote job entry, 308
Data structures, 276–289
  B-trees, 285–287
  database access, 277
  disk accesses reduction techniques, 280–285
    indexing, 280–283
    multiple indexes, 283
    sparse indexes, 284–285
  disk manager, 277–278
  file manager, 278
  hashing, 287–288
  head movement reduction techniques, 279–280
  linked lists, 288–289
  overview of, 276–277
  relational model, 328–331
Data sublanguage rule, comprehensive, fully
    relational database, 339
Data types, Standard Query Language (SQL), data
    definition, 203
Data validation, quality maintenance, 484–486
DATE, Standard Query Language (SQL), data
    definition, 206
DBMS independence, data storage/processing
    architecture, hybrid architecture, 324
DBMS/server, data storage/processing architecture,
    314–315
Debriefing, single-entity modeling, database
    querying, 82
DECIMAL, Standard Query Language (SQL), data
    definition, 205
Decision making:
  organizational memory, 10–12
  organizational memory components, 24–25
Decision support system (DSS):
  information delivery systems, 52
  models, organizational memory components,
    23–24
Delays, in response, organizational memory
    problems, 27
Delete:
  one-to-many relationship, 91
  Standard Query Language (SQL), data
    manipulation, 222–223

DELETE, single-entity modeling, database querying,
    82
Delivery systems, information, 49–55
Dependent entity:
  data modeling, entity types, 159
  relationship descriptors as identifiers, basic
    structures, relational model, 193
Descriptors, as identifiers, relationship, basic
    structures, relational model, 191–196
Detail, data modeling, quality improvement,
    147–148
Developmental staff, data administration, 522
Diaries, individual memory systems, 6
Difference, relational model and, 335
Directories, Internet, 452–453
Discussion applications, groupwear products, 413
Discussion lists, Internet, 440–441
Disk accesses reduction techniques, 280–285
  indexing, 280–283
  multiple indexes, 283
  sparse indexes, 284–285
Disk manager, data structures, 277–278
DISTINCT (duplication elimination), single-entity
    modeling, database querying, 81
Distributed database, data storage/processing
    architecture, 319–320
Distributed query processing, data
    storage/processing architecture, hybrid
    architecture, 322
Distributed transaction processing, data
    storage/processing architecture, hybrid
    architecture, 322
Distribution independence, fully relational database,
    340
DIVIDE:
  with extra condition, SQL playbook, 250
  MINUS and, SQL playbook, 245–246
Divide:
  many-to-many relationship, database querying,
    117–121
  relational model and, 336–337
DIVIDES:
  IN clause with, SQL playbook, 249
  with matching condition, SQL playbook, 248
  restricted, SQL playbook, 248–249
  two, with intersection, Standard Query Language
    (SQL) playbook, 247–248
DIVIDING, SQL playbook, 239–240
DIVISION, with copies, SQL playbook, 246
Documents, organizational memory components,
    19–20
Domain, data structures, relational model, 328–329
Domain constraints, database integrity, hierarchical
    and network models, 358–359

Double divide:
  recovery from, SQL playbook, 245
  with restriction, SQL playbook, 250–251
  SQL playbook, 244
Dow Jones News/Retrieval, described, 458–459
DROP INDEX, Standard Query Language (SQL),
    data definition, 211
DROP TABLE, Standard Query Language (SQL),
    data definition, 208
DROP VIEW, Standard Query Language (SQL), data
    definition, 210
Dun & Bradstreet, information services, 460–464
Duplication elimination, single-entity modeling,
    database querying, 81
Dynamics, object-oriented database management
    system modeling, 374–375

E

Electronic mail:
  groupwear and, 406
  information delivery systems, 51
  Internet, 440
Embedded SQL, described, 227–231
Empowerment, organizational change and,
    information as means of change, 46–47
Encapsulation:
  object-oriented database management systems,
    367
  UniSQL/X commercial system, 393
Encryption, confidentiality, 496–498
Entity:
  data modeling components, 143
  single-entity modeling, 61
Entity-relationship model, data modeling, 179–180
Entity types, 159–161
  aggregate entity, 161
  dependent entity, 159
  independent entity, 159
  intersection entity, 160
  subordinate entity, 161
Error, object-oriented database management
    systems, 371–372
Exceptions, data modeling recommendations,
    167–168
Executive information system (EIS), information
    delivery systems, 54
Existence protection, 475–483
  backup and recovery, 476–482
  generally, 475
EXISTS, many-to-many relationship, database
    querying, 114–115
Expansion, data modeling recommendations,
    162–163

Expert system (ES), information delivery systems, 53
External databases, data administration, 507–508
External memory:
  individual memory systems, 6
  organizational memory components, 25
Extra condition, DIVIDE with, SQL playbook, 250

F

Face-to-face meetings, groupwear and, 405
Families, data modeling, quality improvement,
    150–152
Fidelity, data modeling recommendations, 168
Fifth normal form, data modeling, normalization,
    174–178
File manager, data structures, 278
File/server, data storage/processing architecture, 314
File Transfer Protocol (FTP), Internet, 441–442
First normal form, data modeling, normalization,
    169
Fixed disk, magnetic data storage devices, 292–293
FLOAT, Standard Query Language (SQL), data
    definition, 205
Floppy disk, magnetic data storage devices, 297
Forall (universal qualifier), many-to-many
    relationship, database querying, 117–121
Foreign key:
  data structures, relational model, 331
  one-to-many relationship, database creation, 93–94
Forward recovery (roll forward), described, 480
Fourth normal form, data modeling, normalization,
    173–174
Fragmentation independence, data
    storage/processing architecture, hybrid
    architecture, 322–323
Fully relational database, relational model, 337–341
Functional dependency, data modeling,
    normalization, 169

G

Gap information, organizational change and, 42–43
Generalization/specialization hierarchies, object-
    oriented database management systems, 368
Generalization/specialization structures, object-
    oriented database management system
    modeling, 377–380
Geographic information system (GIS):
  graphics, organizational memory components, 23
  information delivery systems, 52
Geography, data modeling, quality improvement,
    148–149
Get Next, IMS, hierarchical and network models, 353
Get Next Within Parent, IMS, hierarchical and
    network models, 353–354

Get Unique, IMS, hierarchical and network models, 353

Goal setting information, organizational change and, 40–42

Gopher, Internet, 445–448

GRANT, Standard Query Language (SQL), security, 223–225

GRAPHIC, Standard Query Language (SQL), data definition, 206–207

Graphics, organizational memory components, 21–23

GROUP BY:
  averaging with, SQL playbook, 242
  COUNT and, IN clause with, Standard Query Language (SQL) playbook, 242
  HAVING and, SELF-JOIN with, Standard Query Language (SQL) playbook, 242
  one-to-many relationship, control break reporting, 99–100
  SELF-JOIN and, SQL playbook, 241
  Standard Query Language (SQL), data manipulation, 217–218
  SUM and, IN clause with, Standard Query Language (SQL) playbook, 243

Grouping, summing with joins, conditions, and grouping, SQL playbook, 257–258

GroupSystems V, groupwear products, 415–416

Groupware, 402–417
  applications, 404–409
  defined, 401
  information delivery systems, 51
  overview of, 402–404
  products, 409–417

Guaranteed access rule, fully relational database, 339

H

Hardness, information characteristics, 37–39

Hardware, information delivery systems, 53

Hardware independence, data storage/processing architecture, hybrid architecture, 323

Hash address, 287

Hash field, 287

Hash function, 287

Hashing, data structures, 287–288

HAVING:
  GROUP BY and, SELF-JOIN with, Standard Query Language (SQL) playbook, 242
  one-to-many relationship, control break reporting, 100–101
  Standard Query Language (SQL), data manipulation, 217–218

Head movement reduction techniques, 279–280
  clustering, 280
  cylinders, 279–280

Hierarchical and network models, 344–364
  CODASYL/DBTG data manipulation language, 359–361
  database integrity, 358–359
  data extraction, 361–362
  DDL, 355–358
  described, 345–350
  IMS, 351–355
  network data model and CODASYL/DBTG, 355
  overview of, 345–346

Hierarchy. See Organizational memory hierarchy

High fidelity data model, quality, 146–147

Historical data, data modeling, quality improvement, 154–155

Homonyms, data modeling recommendations, 167

Host/terminal, data storage/processing architecture, 311–312

Human information processing system:
  augmented, 3
  external tools for, 2–3
  Newell-Simon model, 1–2

Hybrid architecture, data storage/processing architecture, 320–324

Hypertext, 418–425
  defined, 401
  documents, organizational memory components, 20
  hypercard, 422–424
  overview of, 418–421

I

Identifier:
  data modeling components, 145
  data modeling recommendations, 163
  single-entity modeling, 62

Image processing system (IPS), information delivery systems, 52

Images, organizational memory components, 20–21

Imaging, 425–431
  advantages of, 427–428
  character databases and, 430
  defined, 401
  disadvantages of, 428–429
  indexing, 429–430
  overview of, 425
  system components, 425–427

IMS, hierarchical and network models, 351–355

IN clause:
  with DIVIDES, SQL playbook, 249
  with GROUP BY and COUNT, SQL playbook, 242
  with GROUP BY and SUM, SQL playbook, 243
  SQL playbook, 240

Incorrect specifications, object-oriented database management systems, 372

Independent entity, data modeling, entity types, 159
Indexes, Standard Query Language (SQL), data definition, 199–200
Indexing:
  disk accesses reduction techniques, 280–283
  imaging and, 429–430
Index set, B-trees, data structures, 285, 287
Individual memory systems, organizational memory and, 6–9
Industrial revolution, information and, 36
Information, 35–58. *See* Data
  characteristics of, 37–40
  delivery systems, 49–55
    hardware, 53
    integration, 53–55
    software, 49–53
  historical perspective on, 36
  managerial work and, 47–49
  organizational change and, 40–47
    change information, 43–44
    gap information, 42–43
    goal setting information, 40–42
    information as means of change, 44–47
  overview of, 35–36
Information rule, fully relational database, 339
Information services, 455–465. See also Internet
  America Online, 455–456
  CompuServe, 456–457
  Dow Jones News/Retrieval, 458–459   Dun & Bradstreet, 460–464
  LEXIS-NEXIS, 459–460
  Prodigy, 460
  Télétel, 465
Information society, 36
Inheritance:
  object-oriented database management systems, 369–370
  UniSQL/X commercial system, 393
IN keyword, database querying, 73–74
Insert:
  one-to-many relationship, 91
  Standard Query Language (SQL), data manipulation, 220–221
Instance, single-entity modeling, 61–62
INTEGER, Standard Query Language (SQL), data definition, 203
Integration, information delivery systems, 53–55
Integrity independence, fully relational database, 340
Integrity rules, relational model, 331
Interface:
  data administration, 520–523
  organizational memory problems, 27
Internal marketing, data administration and, 514
Internal memory, individual memory systems, 6

Internet, 435–455. *See also* Information services
  addresses, 437–439
  Archie server, 444–445
  Chat and Talk, 442
  directories, 452–453
  discussion lists, 440–441
  electronic mail, 440
  File Transfer Protocol (FTP), 441–442
  Gopher, 445–448
  Internet Relay Chat, 442–443
  multiple user dimensions (MUD), 453
  National Research and Education Network (NREN), 454
  organizational memory and, 454–455
  overview of, 435–437
  physical connections, 437
  Project Gutenberg, 454
  Telnet, 443–444
  Usenet News, 449
  Wide Area Information Servers (WAIS), 448–449
  World Wide Web, 449–452
Internet Relay Chat, Internet, 442–443
Inter-record constraints, database integrity, hierarchical and network models, 359
Intersect, relational model and, 335
Intersection:
  DIVIDES with, SQL playbook, 247–248
  triple divide with, SQL playbook, 251–252
Intersection entity:
  data modeling, entity types, 160
  relationship descriptors as identifiers, basic structures, relational model, 193–194
Intersection/union, SQL playbook, 255
Intra-record constraints, database integrity, hierarchical and network models, 359

J

Join(s):
  database querying, one-to-many relationship, 95–98
  relational model and, 335–336
  Standard Query Language (SQL), data manipulation, 216
  summing with, SQL playbook, 257
  summing with joins, conditions and grouping, SQL playbook, 257–258

K

Keys, Standard Query Language (SQL), data definition, 199
Knowledge:
  organizational memory and, 28–29
  organizational memory components, 24

L

Labeling, of relationships, data modeling recommendations, 168
LAN-based architecture, data storage/processing architecture, 312–313
Leasing, data modeling, quality improvement, 155–157
LEXIS-NEXIS, described, 459–460
Libraries, data modeling, quality improvement, 152–154
LIKE (pattern matching), single-entity modeling, database querying, 80–81
Linked lists, data structures, 288–289
Local autonomy, data storage/processing architecture, hybrid architecture, 322
Logical data independence, fully relational database, 340
Logical error, object-oriented database management systems, 371–372
Lotus notes, groupwear products, 410

M

Magnetic data storage devices, 291–298
    fixed disk, 292–293
    floppy disk, 297
    generally, 291–292
    mass storage, 298
   RAID, 293–296
    removable magnetic disk, 296
    tape, 297
    tape cartridges, 297
Magneto-optical disk, optical data storage devices, 301–302
Maintenance, object-oriented database management systems, 371–373
Management information system (MIS), information delivery systems, 51–52
Management interfaces, data administration, 521
Managerial work, information and, 47–49
Managing organizational memory. *See* Organizational memory management
Manipulation, relational model, 331–337
Many-to-many relationship, 108–123
    basic structures, two entities, 190–191
    database creation, 111–113
    database querying, 113–123
        divide, 117–121
        three-table join, 113–116
    overview of, 108–110
    rationale for, 110
Marketing, organizational change and, information as means of change, 44–45
Mass storage, magnetic data storage devices, 298

Matching condition, DIVIDES with, SQL playbook, 248
Mathematical models, organizational memory components, 23–24
MAX, single-entity modeling, database querying, 78–79
Meetings, information delivery systems, 50, 51
Member of a set, DDL, hierarchical and network models, 356
Message connections, object-oriented database management system modeling, 386–389
Message passing, object-oriented database management systems, 368
Microcomputer approach:
    one-to-many relationship, database querying, 104
    single-entity modeling, database querying, 82
MIN, single-entity modeling, database querying, 78–79
MINUS:
    after grouping, SQL playbook, 254
    DIVIDE and, SQL playbook, 245–246
Mirroring, magnetic data storage devices, RAID, 293
Missing specifications, object-oriented database management systems, 372
Models, organizational memory components, 23–24
MUD (multiple user dimensions), Internet, 453
Multiple indexes, disk accesses reduction techniques, 283
Multiple inheritances, object-oriented database management system modeling, 380
Multiple user dimensions (MUD), Internet, 453
Multiple values, UniSQL/X commercial system, 393
Multi-user database systems, data integrity, 474–475

N

Names, data modeling recommendations, 164–166
National Center for Supercomputing Applications (NCSA), Internet, 452
National Research and Education Network (NREN), Internet, 454
National Security Agency (NSA), 498
Network independence, data storage/processing architecture, hybrid architecture, 324
Newell-Simon model, 1–2
Nonsubversion rule, fully relational database, 341
No relationships, basic structures:
    one entity, 185–187
    two entities, 189
Normalization, data modeling, 168–178
    Boyce-Codd normal form, 172–173
    fifth normal form, 174–178
    first normal form, 169
    fourth normal form, 173–174

functional dependency, 169
generally, 168–169
second normal form, 169–170
third normal form, 170–171
Notation, Standard Query Language (SQL), data definition, 200
NOT EXISTS:
many-to-many relationship, database querying, 114–116
NOT IN like, SQL playbook, 253
NOT IN, NOT EXISTS like, SQL playbook, 253
NOT IN keyword, database querying, 74–75
NREN (National Research and Education Network), Internet, 454
Nulls, Standard Query Language (SQL), 2233
Null values, systematic treatment of, fully relational database, 339
Numeric sorting, character sorting versus, single-entity modeling, database querying, 77

O

Object layer, object-oriented database management systems, modeling, 377
Object-oriented database management systems, 365–397
concepts, 367–370
future of, 394
historical development of, 366
maintenance, 371–373
modeling, 373–389
abstraction levels and, 373
attribute layer, 383–385
class and object layer, 377
client-developer mind-frame gap, 373–374
data and procedures, 374
message connections and use relationships, 386–389
scenarios, 375
service layer, 386
static modeling, 375–377
statics and dynamics, 374–375
structure layer, 377–382
subject layer, 382–383
ODBMS, 390–395
overview of, 365–366
persistent objects, 390
productivity and, 370–371
standards, 392
UniSQL/X commercial system, 392–393
Object types, object-oriented database management systems, 367–368
ODBMS. *See* Object-oriented database management systems

Office automation system, information delivery systems, 52
One-to-many relationship, 89–107
basic structures, two entities, 189–190
database creation, 91–95
database querying, 95–104
control break reporting, 98–101
join, 95–98
microcomputer approach, 104
subqueries, 101–102
views (virtual tables), 102–104
rationale for, 91
recursive relationships, 126–128. *See also* Recursive relationships
relations, 89–91
One-to-one relationship, 125–126
basic structures, two entities, 189
mapping of, 125–126
modeling of, 125
querying of, 128
On-line catalog, active, fully relational database, 339
ONLY, ALL and, SQL playbook, 249–250
Only one, SQL playbook, 252–253
OO concepts. *See* Object-oriented database management systems
Operating system independence, data storage/processing architecture, hybrid architecture, 323
Optical data storage devices, 298–302
CD-ROM, 298–299
generally, 298
magneto-optical disk, 301–302
WORM, 300
OR, union, SQL playbook, 255
Oral reports, information delivery systems, 50
Order, data modeling recommendations, 163–164
Organizational change, information and, 40–47
Organizational culture, organizational memory components, 17
Organizational memory, 3, 5–34
attributes of, 12–15
challenge facing, 30–31
components of, 15–25
decisions, 24–25
documents, 19–20
external memory, 25
generally, 15–16
graphics, 21–23
images, 20–21
knowledge, 24
models, 23–24
people, 16–18
specialized memory, 25

Organizational memory *(Continued)*
    tables, 18–19
    voice, 23
  data, 28–29
  decision making, 10–12
  forms of, 3–4
  individual memory systems and, 6–9
  Internet and, 454–455
  overview of, 5, 9–10
  problems with, 26–28
    data control, 26
    data integration problems, 28
    delays in response, 27
    interface problems, 27
    reality and, 27–28
    redundancy, 26
  transaction processing, 10
Organizational memory hierarchy, databases, 59–60
Organizational memory management, 469. See also
    Data administration; Data integrity
Organizational memory technologies, overview of,
    399–400
Owner of a set, DDL, hierarchical and network
    models, 356

P

Pairing, SQL playbook, 247
Pairs, counting of, SQL playbook, 261
Pattern matching, single-entity modeling, database
    querying, 80–81
People, organizational memory components, 16–18
Personal database, data storage/processing
    architecture, 309–311
Physical data independence, fully relational database,
    340
Planning, decision making, organizational memory,
    10–12
Planning information, organizational change and,
    40–41
Plans, data modeling, quality improvement, 157–159
Polymorphism, UniSQL/X commercial system, 393
Position, data modeling recommendations, 163–164
Primary key:
    database querying, 73
    data structures, relational model, 329–330
Primary key definition, Standard Query Language
    (SQL), data definition, 201
Primitive set, relational model, 337
Problem identification, organizational change and,
    42
Procedures, object-oriented database management
    system modeling, 374
Prodigy, described, 460

Product:
    relational model and, 333–334
    Standard Query Language (SQL), data
        manipulation, 212–215
Productivity, object-oriented database management
    systems, 370–371
Project:
    database querying, 69–70
    relational model and, 333
    restrict combined with, database querying, 72
Project Gutenberg, Internet, 454
Project level functions, data administration, 515–520

Q

Quality improvement:
    data modeling, 146–147, 147–159
        detail and context, 147–148
        families, 150–152
        geography, 148–149
        historical data, 154–155
        leasing, 155–157
        libraries, 152–154
        plans and activities, 157–159
    groupwear and, 408
Quality maintenance, 483–490
    concurrent update control, 487–490
    data validation, 484–486
    update authorization, 483
Query, defined, 68
Querying:
    importance of, 60
    many-to-many relationship, 113–123
    one-to-many relationship, 95–104. See also One-
        to-many relationship
    one-to-one relationship, 128
    recursive relationships, one-to-many, 128–132
    single-entity modeling, 68–84. See also Single-
        entity modeling
    single table database, 68–84

R

RAID, magnetic data storage devices, 293–296
Rationally complete operator, 331
Reality, organizational memory problems, 27–28
Record, DDL, hierarchical and network models,
    355–356
Recovery:
    described, 476–479
    procedure use in, 482–483
    strategies for, 479–481
Recursive relationships (many-to-many):
    basic structures, one entity, 188–189
    mapping of, 136–137

modeling of, 135–136
  querying of, 137–139
Recursive relationships (one-to-many):
  basic structures, one entity, 187–188
  mapping of, 126–128
  querying of, 128–132
Recursive relationships (one-to-one):
  basic structures, one entity, 185–187
  mapping of, 133
  modeling of, 132–133
  querying of, 133–134
Redundancy, organizational memory problems, 26
Reference, groupwear products, 412–413
Referential constraint definition, Standard Query
    Language (SQL), data definition, 202
Referential integrity constraint, one-to-many
    relationship, database creation, 94
Referential integrity rules, relational model, 331
Relational algebra, 331
  querying, 68
Relational database, data structures, relational model,
    329
Relational model, 59, 327–343
  basic structures, 185–197
    one entity, 185–189
    relationship descriptors as identifiers, 191–196
    two entities, 189–191
  data structures, 328–331
  fully relational database, 337–341
  hierarchical model contrasted, 346
  integrity rules, 331
  manipulation, 331–337
  overview of, 327–328
  primitive set, 337
Relations:
  data structures, relational model, 329
  one-to-many relationship, 89–91
Relationship, data modeling components, 144–145
Relationship descriptors, as identifiers, basic
    structures, relational model, 191–196
Relationship labeling, data modeling
    recommendations, 168
Relevancy, organizational memory attributes, 15
Remote job entry, data storage/processing
    architecture, 308
Removable magnetic disk, magnetic data storage
    devices, 296
Replication, groupwear products, 414
Replication independence, data storage/processing
    architecture, hybrid architecture, 323
Restrict:
  database querying, 70–71
  project combined with, database querying, 72
  relational model and, 332

Reuse, object-oriented database management
    systems, 370
Richness, information characteristics, 39–40
Rollback (backward recovery), described, 480
Roll forward (forward recovery), described, 480
Row insertion, single-entity modeling, database
    creation, 65–67
Row ordering, database querying, 75–76

S

Sabotage, data integrity, 475
Scalar functions, Standard Query Language (SQL),
    data manipulation, 218–220
Scenarios, object-oriented database management
    system modeling, 375
Scorekeeping information, organizational change
    and, 42–43
Secondary indexes, IMS, hierarchical and network
    models, 354
Second normal form, data modeling, normalization,
    169–170
Security:
  organizational memory attributes, 14
  Standard Query Language (SQL), 223–225
Select, Standard Query Language (SQL), data
    manipulation, 212
SELF-JOIN:
  with conditions, SQL playbook, 243
  GROUP BY and, SQL playbook, 241
  with GROUP BY and HAVING, SQL playbook,
    242
  SQL playbook, 240
  SUBTRACT FROM ALL and, SQL playbook, 241
  with two matching conditions, SQL playbook, 241
Sequence set, B-trees, data structures, 285
Service layer, object-oriented database management
    system modeling, 386
Sets, DDL, hierarchical and network models, 356
Shareability, organizational memory attributes, 13
Simple subquery, Standard Query Language (SQL),
    data manipulation, 217
Single-entity modeling, 61–88
  database creation, 63–67
    generally, 63–64
    row insertion, 65–67
    table defining, 64–65
  database modeling, 62–63
  database querying, 68–84
    built-in functions, 78
    calculating, 77
    column ordering, 75
    debriefing, 82
    DELETE, 82

Single-entity modeling *(Continued)*
    DISTINCT (duplication elimination), 81
    IN keyword, 73–74
    LIKE (pattern matching), 80–81
    microcomputer database software, 82
    NOT IN keyword, 74–75
    numeric versus character sorting, 77
    primary key, 73
    project, 69–70
    project/restrict combined, 72
    restrict, 70–71
    row ordering, 75–76
    subqueries, 79
    SUM, MIN, MAX, 78–79
    table display, 68–69
    WHERE clause, 72
  overview of, 61–62
Single-instance entities, data modeling
    recommendations, 166
Single-user database systems, data integrity, 474–475
SKINNING A CAT, SQL playbook, 236–238
SLOW FULL TOSS, SQL playbook, 236
SMALLINT, Standard Query Language (SQL), data
    definition, 203
Social memory, information and, 36
Social networks, organizational memory
    components, 17
Software, information delivery systems, 49–53
Sparse indexes, disk accesses reduction techniques,
    284–285
Specialized memory, organizational memory
    components, 25
Special registers, Standard Query Language (SQL),
    data definition, 207
Standard operating procedure, organizational
    memory components, 18
Standard Query Language (SQL), 198–234
  catalog, 226–227
  database creation, 63
  data definition, 199–211
    alter table, 207–208
    create index, 210
    CREATE TABLE, 201–203
    create view, 208–210
    data types, 203–207
    drop index, 211
    drop table, 208
    drop view, 210
    generally, 199
    indexes, 199–200
    keys, 199
    notation, 200
  data manipulation, 211–223
    aggregate functions, 217

    column name qualification, 211
    delete, 222–223
    GROUP BY and HAVING, 217–218
    insert, 220–221
    joins, 216
    product, 212–215
    scalar functions, 218–220
    select, 212
    subqueries, 217
    temporary names, 211–212
    update, 221–222
  embedded SQL, 227–231
  nulls, 2233
 overview of, 198
  security, 223–225
  synonyms, 226
Standard Query Language (SQL) playbook, 235–269
  ALL and ONLY, 249–250
  ANOTHER FULL TOSS, 238
  averaging
    with condition, 256
    detailed averaging, 261
    difference from average, 260
    with join, condition, and grouping, 256
    more than the average with grouping, 259
    with multiple grouping, 259
    with multiple joins, 256–257
      multiple groupings, and condition, 260
    simplest, 260
  Booleans, 261–262
  IN clause, 240
    with GROUP BY and COUNT, 242
    with GROUP BY and SUM, 243
  comparing to average
    with a join, 258
    with a product, 259
  comparison making, 243
  complex counting, 257
  COUNT, 245
 count, 252
  counting pairs, 261
  DIVIDE, with extra condition, 250
  DIVIDES
    IN clause with, 249
    with matching condition, 248
    restricted, 248–249
    two, with intersection, 247–248
  DIVIDING, 239–240
  DIVISION, with copies, 246
  double divide, 244
    recovery from, 245
    with restriction, 250–251
  GROUP BY, averaging with, 242
  intersection (and), 254–255

intersection/union, 255
AT LEAST some, 250
AT LEAST SOME NUMBER, 240, 253
MINUS, after grouping, 254
MINUS and DIVIDE, 245–246
NOT IN like NOT EXISTS, 253
only one, 252–253
overview of, 235
pairing, 247
SELF-JOIN, 240
    with conditions, 243
    GROUP BY and, 241
    with GROUP BY and HAVING, 242
    SUBTRACT FROM ALL and, 241
    with two matching conditions, 241
SKINNING A CAT, 236–238
SLOW FULL TOSS, 236
something to all, 254
SUBTRACTING FROM ALL, 238–239
summing
    advanced, 258
    with joins, conditions, and grouping, 257–258
    with joins and conditions, 257
three-join table, 253
triple divide, with intersection, 251–252
union (or), 255
Standards, object-oriented database management
    systems, 392
Static modeling, object-oriented database
    management system modeling, 375–377
Statics, object-oriented database management system
    modeling, 374–375
Striping, magnetic data storage devices, RAID, 293
Structure layer, object-oriented database
    management system modeling, 377–382
Subject layer, object-oriented database management
    system modeling, 382–383
Subordinate entity, data modeling, entity types, 161
Subqueries:
    one-to-many relationship, database querying,
        101–102
    single-entity modeling, database querying, 79
    Standard Query Language (SQL), data
        manipulation, 217
SUBTRACTING FROM ALL:
    SELF-JOIN and, SQL playbook, 241
    SQL playbook, 238–239
SUM:
    GROUP BY and, IN clause with, Standard Query
        Language (SQL) playbook, 243
    single-entity modeling, database querying,
        78–79
Summing:
    advanced, SQL playbook, 258

with joins, conditions, and grouping, SQL
    playbook, 257–258
joins with, SQL playbook, 257
Synonyms:
    data modeling recommendations, 167
    Standard Query Language (SQL), 226
Syntactical error, object-oriented database
    management systems, 371–372
Systematic treatment, of null values, fully relational
    database, 339
System level functions, data administration, 510–514

T

Table defining, single-entity modeling, database
    creation, 64–65
Tables, organizational memory components, 18–19
Tape, magnetic data storage devices, 297
Tape cartridges, magnetic data storage devices, 297
Team room, groupwear and, 406
Telnet, Internet, 443–444
Temporary names, Standard Query Language (SQL),
    data manipulation, 211–212
Third normal form, data modeling, normalization,
    170–171
Three-join table, SQL playbook, 253
Three-table join, many-to-many relationship,
    database querying, 113–116
TIME, Standard Query Language (SQL), data
    definition, 206
Timeliness, organizational memory attributes, 15
To-do lists, individual memory systems, 7
Tracking, groupwear products, 410–411
Transaction processing, organizational memory, 10
Transparency, data storage/processing architecture,
    hybrid architecture, 321
Transportability, organizational memory attributes,
    14
Tree structure, relationship descriptors as identifiers,
    basic structures, relational model, 194–196
Triple divide, with intersection, SQL playbook,
    251–252

U

Union, relational model and, 334
Unique definition, Standard Query Language (SQL),
    data definition, 202–203
UniSQL/X commercial system, described, 392–393
Universal qualifier (forall), many-to-many
    relationship, database querying, 117–121
Update:
    one-to-many relationship, 91
    Standard Query Language (SQL), data
        manipulation, 221–222

Update authorization, quality maintenance, 483
Usenet News, Internet, 449
User-defined data types, UniSQL/X commercial system, 393
Use relationships, object-oriented database management system modeling, 386–389
User interface, data administration, 507, 522

V

VARCHAR, Standard Query Language (SQL), data definition, 205–206
VARGRAPHIC, Standard Query Language (SQL), data definition, 206–207
Veronica, Internet, 446–448
Video conferencing, groupwear and, 406
Views (virtual tables), one-to-many relationship, database querying, 102–104
View updating rule, fully relational database, 340
Virtual tables (views), one-to-many relationship, database querying, 102–104

Voice, organizational memory components, 23
Voice mail, information delivery systems, 50

W

WAIS (Wide Area Information Servers), Internet, 448–449
Well-formed data model, quality, 146
WHERE clause, database querying, 72
WHERE clause of groups (HAVING), one-to-many relationship, control break reporting, 100–101
Whole/part structures, object-oriented database management system modeling, 380–382
Wide Area Information Servers (WAIS), Internet, 448–449
Workflow, groupwear products, 413–414
Work selection, data modeling recommendations, 166
World Wide Web, Internet, 449–452
WORM, optical data storage devices, 300
Written reports, information delivery systems, 51